Nature-Inspired Informatics for Intelligent Applications and Knowledge Discovery:
Implications in Business, Science, and Engineering

Raymond Chiong
Swinburne University of Technology, Malaysia

INFORMATION SCIENCE REFERENCE

Hershey · New York

Director of Editorial Content: Kristin Klinger
Senior Managing Editor: Jamie Snavely
Managing Editor: Jeff Ash
Assistant Managing Editor: Carole Coulson
Typesetter: Jeffrey Ash, Michael Brehm, Carole Coulson, Elizabeth Duke-Wilson, Jennifer Johnson, Chris Hrobak, Jamie Snavely, Sean Woznicki
Cover Design: Lisa Tosheff
Printed at: Yurchak Printing Inc.

Published in the United States of America by
        Information Science Reference (an imprint of IGI Global)
        701 E. Chocolate Avenue,
        Hershey PA 17033
        Tel: 717-533-8845
        Fax: 717-533-8661
        E-mail: cust@igi-global.com
        Web site: http://www.igi-global.com/reference

and in the United Kingdom by
        Information Science Reference (an imprint of IGI Global)
        3 Henrietta Street
        Covent Garden
        London WC2E 8LU
        Tel: 44 20 7240 0856
        Fax: 44 20 7379 0609
        Web site: http://www.eurospanbookstore.com

Library of Congress Cataloging-in-Publication Data

Nature-inspired informatics for intelligent applications and knowledge

discovery : implications in business, science, and engineering / Raymond

Chiong, editor.

      p. cm.

  Includes bibliographical references and index.

  Summary: "This book provides the latest findings in nature-inspired

algorithms and their applications for breakthroughs in a wide range of

disciplinary fields"--Provided by publisher.

  ISBN 978-1-60566-705-8 (hardcover) -- ISBN 978-1-60566-706-5 (ebook) 1.

Evolutionary programming (Computer science) 2. Algorithms. I. Chiong,

Raymond, 1979-

  QA76.618.N38 2009

  005.1--dc22

                        2009010453

British Cataloguing in Publication Data
A Cataloguing in Publication record for this book is available from the British Library.

All work contributed to this book is new, previously-unpublished material. The views expressed in this book are those of the authors, but not necessarily of the publisher.

Table of Contents

Section 3
Nature-Inspired Solutions in Science

Section 4
Nature-Inspired Solutions in Computing & Engineering

Detailed Table of Contents

Section 1
Introduction

> *Raymond Chiong, Swinburne University of Technology (Sarawak Campus), Malaysia*
> *Ferrante Neri, University of Jyväskylä, Finland*
> *Robert I. McKay, Seoul National University, Korea*

Nature has always been a source of inspiration. Over the last few decades, it has stimulated many successful techniques, algorithms and computational applications for dealing with large, complex and dynamic real world problems. In this chapter, the authors discuss why nature-inspired solutions have become increasingly important and favourable for tackling the conventionally-hard problems. They also present the concepts and background of some selected examples from the domain of natural computing, and describe their key applications in business, science and engineering. Finally, the future trends are highlighted to provide a vision for the potential growth of this field.

Section 2
Nature-Inspired Solutions in Business

> *Muneer Buckley, University of Adelaide, Australia*
> *Zbigniew Michalewicz, University of Adelaide, Australia; Institute of Computer Science,*
> *   Polish Academy of Sciences & Polish-Japanese Institute of Information Technology, Poland*
> *Ralf Zurbruegg, University of Adelaide, Australia*

There is a great need for accurate predictions of foreign exchange rates. Many industries participate in foreign exchange scenarios with little idea where the exchange rate is moving, and what the optimum decision to make at any given time is. Although current economic models do exist for this purpose, improvements could be made in both their flexibility and adaptability. This provides much room for models that do not suffer from such constraints. This chapter proposes the use of a genetic program (GP) to predict future foreign exchange rates. The GP is an extension of the DyFor GP tailored for forecasting in dynamic environments. The GP is tested on the Australian / US (AUD/USD) exchange rate and compared against a basic economic model. The results show that the system has potential in forecasting long term values, and may do so better than established models. Further improvements are also suggested.

Chapter 3

Markus Kress, University of Karlsruhe, Germany
Sanaz Mostaghim, University of Karlsruhe, Germany
Detlef Seese, University of Karlsruhe, Germany

In this chapter, the authors study a new variant of Particle Swarm Optimization (PSO) to efficiently execute business processes. The main challenge of this application for the PSO is that the function evaluations typically take a high computation time. They propose the Gap Search (GS) method in combination with the PSO to perform a better exploration in the search space and study its influence on the results of our application. They replace the random initialization of the solutions for the initial population as well as for the diversity preservation method with the GS method. The experimental results show that the GS method significantly improves the quality of the solutions and obtains better results for the application as compared to the results of a standard PSO and Genetic Algorithms. Moreover, the combination of the methods the authors used show promising results as tools to be applied for improvement of Business Process Optimization.

Section 3
Nature-Inspired Solutions in Science

Chapter 4

Eugene Ch'ng, University of Wolverhampton, UK

The complexity of nature can only be solved by nature's intrinsic problem-solving approach. Therefore, the computational modelling of nature requires careful observations of its underlying principles in order that these laws can be abstracted into formulas suitable for the algorithmic configuration. This chapter proposes a novel modelling approach for biodiversity informatics research. The approach is based on the emergence phenomenon for predicting vegetation distribution patterns in a multi-variable ecosystem where Artificial Life-based vegetation grow, compete, adapt, reproduce and conquer plots of landscape in order to survive their generation. The feasibility of the modelling approach presented in this chapter may provide a firm foundation not only for predicting vegetation distribution in a wide variety of landscapes, but could also be extended for studying biodiversity and the loss of animal species for sustainable management of resources.

Óscar Ibáñez, European Centre for Soft Computing, Spain
Oscar Cordón, European Centre for Soft Computing, Spain
Sergio Damas, European Centre for Soft Computing, Spain
José Santamaría, University of Jaen, Spain

Craniofacial superimposition is a forensic process that aims to identify a missing person by overlaying a photograph and a model of the skull. This process is usually carried out manually by forensic anthropologists, thus being very time consuming and presenting several difficulties when trying to find a good fit between the 3D model of the skull and the 2D photo of the face. This contribution aims to provide both a detailed description of the problem and the proposal of two different designs of a multimodal (clearing) genetic algorithm to tackle it. The new proposals will be tested on superimpositions for different real-world identification cases from the Physical Anthropology lab at the University of Granada in Spain, including positive and negative cases, taking the manual and the basic genetic algorithm solutions as baselines for their quality.

Rajasvaran Logeswaran, Multimedia University, Malaysia

Automatic detection of tumors in the bile ducts of the liver is very difficult as often, in the defacto non-invasive diagnostic images using magnetic resonance cholangiopancreatography (MRCP), tumors are not clearly visible. Specialists use their experience in anatomy to diagnose a tumor by absence of expected structures in the images. Naturally, undertaking such diagnosis is very difficult for an automated system. This chapter proposes an algorithm that is based on a combination of the manual diagnosis principles along with nature-inspired image processing techniques and artificial neural networks (ANN) to assist in the preliminary diagnosis of tumors affecting the bile ducts in the liver. The results obtained show over 88% success rate of the system developed using an ANN with the multi-layer perceptron (MLP) architecture, in performing the difficult automated preliminary detection of the tumors, even in the robust clinical test images with other biliary diseases present.

Casey S. Greene, Dartmouth College, USA
Jason H. Moore, Dartmouth College, USA

In human genetics the availability of chip-based technology facilitates the measurement of thousands of DNA sequence variations from across the human genome. The informatics challenge is to identify combinations of interacting DNA sequence variations that predict common diseases. The authors review three nature-inspired methods that have been developed and evaluated in this domain. The two approaches this chapter focuses on in detail are genetic programming (GP) and a complex-system inspired GP-like computational evolution system (CES). The authors also discuss a third nature-inspired approach known as ant colony optimization (ACO). The GP and ACO techniques are designed to select relevant attributes, while the CES addresses both the selection of relevant attributes and the modeling of disease risk. Specifically, they examine these methods in the context of epistasis or gene-gene interactions. For the work discussed here we focus solely on the situation where there is an epistatic effect but no detectable main effect. In this domain, early studies show that nature-inspired algorithms perform no better than a simple random search when classification accuracy is used as the fitness function. Thus, the challenge for applying these search algorithms to this problem is that when using classification accuracy there are no building blocks. The goal then is to use outside knowledge or pre-processing of the dataset to provide these building blocks in a manner that enables the population, in a nature-inspired framework, to discover an optimal model. The authors examine one pre-processing strategy for revealing building blocks in this domain and three different methods to exploit these building blocks as part of a knowledge-aware nature-inspired strategy. They also discuss potential sources of building blocks and modifications to the described methods which may improve our ability to solve complex problems in human genetics. Here it is argued that both the methods using expert knowledge and the sources of expert knowledge drawn upon will be critical to improving our ability to detect and characterize epistatic interactions in these large scale biomedical studies.

Section 4
Nature-Inspired Solutions in Computing & Engineering

Chapter 8

Ralf Salomon, University of Rostock, Germany
Stefan Goldmann, University of Rostock, Germany

Smart-appliance ensembles consist of intelligent devices that interact with each other and that are supposed to support their users in an autonomous, non-invasive way. Since both the number and the composition of the participating devices may spontaneously change at *any* time without *any* notice, traditional approaches, such as rule-based systems and evolutionary algorithms, are not appropriate mechanisms for their self-organization. Therefore, this chapter describes a new evolutionary framework, called appliances-go-evolution platform (AGE-P) that accounts for the inherent system dynamics by distributing all data structures and all operations across all participating devices. This chapter illustrates the behavior of this framework by presenting several results obtained from simulations as well as real-world case studies.

Chapter 9

Erwan Le Martelot, University College London, UK
Peter J Bentley, University College London, UK

Natural systems provide unique examples of computation in a form very different from contemporary computer architectures. Biology also demonstrates capabilities such as adaptation, self-repair, and self-organisation that are becoming increasingly desirable for our technology. To address these issues a computer model and architecture with natural characteristics is presented. Systemic computation is

Turing Complete; it is designed to support biological algorithms such as neural networks, evolutionary algorithms and models of development, and shares the desirable capabilities of biology not found in conventional architectures. In this chapter the authors describe the first platform implementing such computation, including programming language, compiler and virtual machine. They first demonstrate that systemic computing is crash-proof and can recover from severe damage. The authors then illustrate various benefits of systemic computing through several implementations of bio-inspired algorithms: a self-adaptive genetic algorithm, a bio-inspired model of artificial neural networks, and finally we create an "artificial organism" - a program with metabolism that eats data, expels waste, clusters cells based on data inputs and emits danger signals for a potential artificial immune system. Research on systemic computation is still ongoing, but the research presented in this chapter shows that computers that process information according to this bio-inspired paradigm have many of the features of natural systems that we desire.

Chapter 10

Inspired by observing bacterial growth in agar and by the transfer of information through simple agar simulations, the cognitive simulation of Noble Ape (originally developed in 1996) has defined itself as both a philosophical simulation tool and a processor metric. The Noble Ape cognitive simulation was originally developed based on diverse philosophical texts and in methodological objection to the neural network paradigm of artificial intelligence. This chapter explores the movement from biological observation to agar simulation through information transfer into a coherent cognitive simulation. The cognitive simulation had to be tuned to produce meaningful results. The cognitive simulation was adopted as processor metrics for tuning performance. This "brain cycles per second" metric was first used by Apple in 2003 and then Intel in 2005. Through this development, both the legacy of primitive agar information-transfer and the use of this as a cognitive simulation method raised novel computational and philosophical issues.

Chapter 11

Robust Automatic Speaker Verification has become increasingly desirable in recent years with the growing trend toward remote security verification procedures for telephone banking, bio-metric security measures and similar applications. While many approaches have been applied to this problem, Genetic Programming offers inherent feature selection and solutions that can be meaningfully analyzed, making it well suited for this task. This chapter introduces a Genetic Programming system to evolve programs capable of speaker verification and evaluates its performance with the publicly available TIMIT corpora. Also presented are the effects of a simulated telephone network on classification results which highlight the principal advantage, namely robustness to both additive and convolutive noise.

      Sergio Ivvan Valdez Peña, Centre for Research in Mathematics, Mexico
      Arturo Hernández Aguirre, Centre for Research in Mathematics, Mexico
      Salvador Botello Rionda, Centre for Research in Mathematics, Mexico
      Cyntia Araiza Delgado, Centre for Research in Mathematics, Mexico

The authors introduce new approaches for the combinational circuit design based on Estimation of Distribution Algorithms. In this paradigm, the structure and data dependencies embedded in the data (population of candidate circuits) are modeled by a conditional probability distribution function. The new population is simulated from the probability model thus inheriting the dependencies. The authors explain the procedure to build an approximation of the probability distribution through two approaches: polytrees and Bayesian networks. A set of circuit design experiments is performed and a comparison with evolutionary approaches is reported.

      Moussa Diaf, Université Mouloud Mammeri, Algérie
      Kamal Hammouche, Université Mouloud Mammeri, Algérie
      Patrick Siarry, Université Paris 12 Val de Marne, France

Biological studies highlighting the collective behavior of ants in fulfilling various tasks by using their complex indirect communication process have constituted the starting point for many physical systems and various ant colony algorithms. Each ant colony is considered as a superorganism which operates as a unified entity made up of simple agents. These agents (ants) interact locally with one another and with their environment, particularly in finding the shortest path from the nest to food sources without any centralized control dictating the behavior of individual agents. It is this coordination mechanism that has inspired researchers to develop plenty of metaheuristic algorithms in order to find good solutions for NP-hard combinatorial optimization problems. In this chapter, the authors give a biological description of these fascinating insects and their complex indirect communication process. From this rich source of inspiration for researchers, the authors show how, through the real ant, artificial ant is modeled and applied in combinatorial optimization, data clustering, collective robotics, and image processing.

      Sergio Nesmachnow, Universidad de la República, Uruguay
      Héctor Cancela, Universidad de la República, Uruguay
      Enrique Alba, Universidad de Málaga, Spain

The speedy pace of change in telecommunications and its ubiquitous presence have drastically altered the way people interact, impacting production, government, and social life. The infrastructure for providing telecommunication services must be continuously renewed, as innovative technologies emerge and drive changes by offering to bring new services to the end users. In this context, the problem of efficiently designing the underlying networks in order to satisfy different requirements while at the same time keeping the capital and operative expenditures bounded is of ever growing importance and actuality. Network design problems have many variations, depending on the characteristics of the technologies to be employed, as well as on the simplifying hypothesis that can be applied on each particular context, and on the planning horizon. Nevertheless, in most cases they are extremely complex problems, for which exact solutions cannot be found in practice. Nature-inspired optimization techniques (belonging to the metaheuristic computational methods) are important tools in these cases, as they are able to achieve good quality solutions in reasonable computational times. The objective of this chapter is to present a systematic review of nature-inspired techniques employed to solve optimization problems related to telecommunication network design. The review is aimed at providing an insight of different approaches in the area, in particular covering four main classes of applications: minimum spanning trees, reliable networks, local access network design and backbone location, and cellular and wireless network design. A large proportion of the papers deal with single objective models, but there is also a growing number of works that study multi-objective problems, which search for solutions that perform well in a number of different criteria. While genetic algorithms and other evolutionary algorithms appear most frequently, there is also significant research on other methods, such as ant colony optimization, particle swarm optimization, and other nature-inspired techniques.

Preface

The world has become increasingly more complex and connected in recent times, resulting in many real world problems to be large and difficult to solve. As such, we need to take a fresh look at how we could solve problems more effectively and efficiently in the context of this new world.

Nature-Inspired Informatics is the study of using computational techniques and tools inspired in part by nature and natural systems for the collection and organisation of information, which will in turn produce knowledge. It is a new area within the field of natural computing, and its aim is to develop innovative approaches and intelligent applications for representation and processing of information from real-world problems in various disciplines. Nature-inspired techniques take a different approach to problem solving than do conventional methods. Conventional methods normally use an algorithmic approach, that is, a set of instructions is followed in order to solve a particular problem. However, to develop a specific algorithm for a problem, the problem must first be successfully solved. This limits the problem-solving capability of conventional methods to only problems that we already understand and know how to solve. It would be much better and more useful if we could find approaches to solve problems that we do not exactly know how to solve!

Nature, broadly speaking, refers to the natural world, the physical universe. This includes the phenomena of the physical world as well as all life forms in general. Nature has already solved many extraordinarily complex problems. Novel computational models and systems inspired by nature can lead us to unexpected and elegant solutions to real-world problems. Such systems are often imbued with the use of concepts, principles and mechanisms based on natural patterns, behaviours and living organisms. For example, we have bio-inspired computing, a major subset of natural computing, that makes use of biology as inspiration for the development of problem-solving techniques such as evolutionary algorithms, neural networks, artificial immune systems, swarm intelligence algorithms, and so forth. On the other hand, we also have computer systems to simulate or emulate nature, systems aimed at mimicking various natural phenomena in order to increase our understanding of nature and our insights about computer modelling. These include, for example, models of climate or of biological evolution.

We can note that there is yet another branch in the field of natural computing – the study of using "unusual" natural materials to perform computations. This field includes, for example molecular, membrane and quantum computing, but is not a subject of this volume.

OBJECTIVE OF THE BOOK

As one of the very first books where the term "Nature-Inspired Informatics" is used, this special volume has assembled some of the most intriguing applications and additions to the methodology of natural computing. Its main objective is to provide a central source of reference on nature-inspired informatics and their applications in business, science, and engineering. It contains open-solicited and invited chapters written by leading researchers, academics, and practitioners in the field. All contributions were peer reviewed by at least three reviewers.

TARGET AUDIENCE

This book covers the state of the art plus latest research discoveries and applications of nature-inspired computation, thus making it a valuable reference for a large community of audiences. It will be an important reference to researchers and academics working in natural computing and its related fields, such as artificial intelligence, multi-agent systems, machine learning, pattern recognition, optimisation, knowledge-based systems, and so forth. It will also be useful to business professionals, engineers, and senior undergraduate as well as postgraduate students.

ORGANISATION OF THE BOOK

This book comprises 14 chapters, which can be categorised into the following 4 sections:

Section 1: Introduction
Section 2: Nature-Inspired Solutions in Business
Section 3: Nature-Inspired Solutions in Science
Section 4: Nature-Inspired Solutions in Computing & Engineering

Section: 1 Introduction

The first section is composed solely of one chapter. In this chapter, Chiong et al. discuss why nature has been such an appealing choice for solving the conventionally hard problems, and why nature-inspired solutions have become increasingly important and favourable nowadays. They also briefly present some popular nature-inspired techniques, from evolutionary algorithms to memetic algorithms, swarm intelligence algorithms and artificial neural networks, and clarify the significance as well as the successful use of these techniques in the fields of business, science and engineering. The chapter sets the scene for the book, and ends by providing a vision of the future trends.

Section 2: Nature-Inspired Solutions in Business

The second section deals with nature-inspired solutions in business. It consists of Chapter 2 and Chapter 3, with the first presenting an application of genetic programming, a subclass of evolutionary algorithms, to forecasting foreign exchange rates, and the second on intelligent business process execution using particle swarm optimisation.

In Chapter 2, Buckley et al. propose the use of genetic programming for creating a more robust forward rate prediction system. While a number of economic models used for forecasting forward rates exist, majority of them do not adequately model the nonlinear nature of the market, and more importantly, do not dynamically adapt to changing market conditions. The system presented by Buckley et al. is an extension of the DyFor model tailored for forecasting in dynamic environments. They test their system on the Australian/American (AUD/USD) exchange rate and compare it against a basic economic model. The experimental results show that their system has potential in forecasting long term values, and may do so better than the established models. This work is important as there is a great need in many industries for accurate future foreign exchange rate prediction.

Chapter 3 by Kress et al. presents a study on a new variant of particle swarm optimisation to efficiently execute business processes. They propose a combination of the Gap Search method with the particle swarm algorithm for better exploration. In doing so, they replace the random initialisation of the solutions for the initial population as well as for the diversity preservation method in particle swarm algorithm with the Gap Search mechanism. They use a case study to demonstrate the usefulness of their proposed approach in business process execution, and compare its performance with the standard particle swarm algorithm and genetic algorithm. The experimental results show that the Gap Search method is able to significantly improve the quality of the solutions and achieve better results in their application. This indicates that the hybrid approach introduced in this chapter could be a promising tool for business process optimisation.

Section 3: Nature-Inspired Solutions in Science

The third section contains four chapters, Chapters 4 to 7, and each addresses a unique domain of its own, giving us a diverse view of nature-inspired solutions in science.

The section starts with Chapter 4 where Ch'ng proposes a novel artificial life-based vegetation modelling approach for biodiversity research. The approach is based on the emergence phenomenon for predicting vegetation distribution patterns in a multi-variable ecosystem, where artificial life based vegetation plants grow, compete, adapt, reproduce and conquer plots of landscape in order to survive their generation. The core of this approach lies in the simulation of natural selection – the distribution of autonomous agents on a landscape coupled with selection pressures in the environment. Rather than centralising decisions based on a global principle, the method imparts life and autonomy into individual vegetation with simple rules built into individual plant entities. Experimental studies presented show that the proposed approach is indeed the solution for overcoming barriers in the predictive modelling of vegetation distribution patterns. The modelling approach presented in this chapter is of significant importance as it may provide a firm foundation not only for predicting vegetation distribution in a wide variety of landscapes, but could also be extended for studying biodiversity and the loss of animal species for sustainable management of resources.

Subsequently, Chapter 5 by Ibáñez1 et al. presents a multimodal genetic algorithm for craniofacial superimposition. Craniofacial superimposition is a forensic process that aims at identifying a missing person by overlaying a photograph and a model of the skull. This process is usually carried out manually by forensic anthropologists, thus being very time consuming and presenting several difficulties when trying to find a good fit between the 3D model of the skull and the 2D photo of the face. As such, effective software tools for the automation of their work are a real need. In their attempt to address some limitations and improve the performance of the classical genetic algorithm approach they previously developed, in this chapter Ibáñez1 et al. introduce two different designs of a multimodal (clearing) genetic algorithm. They test it on superimpositions for different identification cases from the Physical Anthropology Lab at the University of Granada in Spain, with both positive and negative cases included, taking the manual and the basic genetic algorithm solutions as baselines for its quality. The experimental results show that the proposed method is fast and fully automated, and therefore very useful for the forensic anthropologists. As part of a project that aims to design a complete, automatic, soft computing-based procedure to aid the forensic anthropologist in the identification task of photographic supra-projection, the significance of this work is beyond doubt.

Chapter 6 by Logeswaran deals with the use of artificial neural networks in medicine. Although artificial neural networks have been applied extensively for various medical applications in the past two decades, there are still many more diagnostic systems for diseases and organs that would be able to gain from this technique. In this chapter, a system based on a combination of the manual diagnosis principles along with image processing techniques and artificial neural networks is proposed to assist in the preliminary diagnosis of tumors affecting the bile ducts in the liver. It presents a multi-stage detection scheme that mimics the radiologist's diagnosis strategy, and the scheme is augmented with the artificial neural networks to improve the system performance in tackling automatic preliminary detection of a difficult and much less researched set of tumors affecting the bile ducts, using the defacto diagnostic imaging technology for the liver and pancreato-biliary system. The experimental results obtained show over 88% success rate of the system in performing the difficult automated preliminary detection of the tumors, even in the robust clinical test images with other biliary diseases present.

The last chapter in this section, Chapter 7 by Greene and Moore, focuses on the use of nature-inspired algorithms in human genetics. Three nature-inspired methods, namely the genetic programming, a computational evolution system, and the ant colony optimisation, have been reviewed and examined in the context of epistasis or gene-gene interactions. While the genetic programming and ant colony optimisation techniques are designed to select relevant attributes, the computational evolution system addresses both the selection of relevant attributes and the modelling of disease risk. In earlier studies, it has been shown that nature-inspired methods perform no better than a simple random search when classification accuracy is used as the fitness function in this domain. This chapter demonstrates how domain-specific knowledge can be used along with nature-inspired algorithms to discover an optimal model for solving complex problems in human genetics.

Section 4: Nature-Inspired Solutions in Computing & Engineering

The last section presents seven chapters, Chapter 8 to 14, dealing with various kinds of computing and engineering problems. The first five chapters are application chapters, while the last two are review chapters.

In Chapter 8, Salomon and Goldmann start off with a new evolutionary framework, called appliances-go-evolution platform (AGE-P), for the self-organisation of smart-appliance ensembles. Smart-appliance ensembles refer to devices such as laptops, personal digital assistants, cellular phones, beamers, window blinds, light bulbs, etc that are present in everyday life and are equipped with some communication interface or computational resources. In this chapter, the behaviour of AGE-P is illustrated via several simulations as well as some real world case studies. The unique feature of this evolutionary framework is that it does not maintain assembled genomes in the traditional sense. Rather, AGE-P physically distributes all gene values across all devices, and evaluates only the resulting sensor modalities. Moreover, the application of the variation operators is done by the actuators rather than a central processing instance, hence the distributed evolution. The presented results from simulation and real world experiments indicate that AGE-P is indeed suitable for self-organising smart-appliance ensembles. In addition to the required basic adaptation capabilities, the AGE-P framework scales well too. It has no problem to cope with the inherent system dynamics of the ensembles, such as failing lights and changing user demands.

Chapter 9 by Martelot and Bentley describes a platform for the newly introduced systemic computation model. Systemic computation is designed to support biological algorithms such as neural networks, evolutionary algorithms and models of development, and shares the desirable capabilities of biology not found in conventional architectures. The platform for systemic computation presented in this chapter comes with several concrete applications. First, the authors demonstrate that systemic computing is crash-proof, and it can recover from severe damage. They then illustrate various benefits of systemic computing through several implementations of bio-inspired algorithms: a self-adaptive genetic algorithm, a bio-inspired model of artificial neural networks, and an "artificial organism" - a program with metabolism that eats data, expels waste, clusters cells based on data inputs and emits danger signals for a potential artificial immune system. While the research on systemic computation is still ongoing, the work presented here shows that computers that process information according to the bio-inspired paradigm have many of the features of natural systems that we desire.

Chapter 10 by Barbalet presents the Noble Ape's Cognitive Simulation, a unique artificial life simulator originally developed in 1996. Inspired by observing bacterial growth in agar and by the transfer of information through simple agar simulations, the cognitive simulation of Noble Ape has defined itself as both a philosophical simulation tool and a processor metric. It was adopted as processor metrics for tuning performance first by Apple in 2003 and then by Intel in 2005. In this chapter, the movement from biological observation to agar simulation through information transfer into a coherent cognitive simulation is explored. The chapter is significant in its contribution to simulation related to information transfer, tuning and cognitive simulation. It shows not only the particular use of the Noble Ape Simulation, but also the potential for this method to be used in other applications. Through this development, both the legacy of primitive agar information-transfer and the use of this as a cognitive simulation method raised novel computational and philosophical issues.

In Chapter 11, Day and Nandi demonstrate the competitiveness of genetic programming in solving the automatic speaker verification problem. Robust automatic speaker verification has become increasingly desirable in recent years with the growing trend towards remote security verification procedures for telephone banking, bio-metric security measures and similar applications. While many approaches have been applied to this problem, genetic programming offers inherent feature selection and solutions that can be meaningfully analysed, making it well suited for the task. In this chapter, a system based on genetic programming is introduced to evolve programs capable of speaker verification, and the authors evaluate the performance of their system using the publicly available TIMIT corpora. The experimental results show that the generated programs can be evolved to be resilient to noisy transmission paths. Also presented are the effects of a simulated telephone network on classification results which further highlight the robustness of the system to both additive and convolutive noise.

In Chapter 12, Peña et al. introduce two new approaches for the combinational circuit design based on estimation of distribution algorithms (EDAs). In their attempt to overcome the scalability problem evolutionary algorithms have on this problem, they propose polytree EDA and Bayesian EDA. In these approaches, the structure and data dependencies embedded in the data (population of candidate circuits) are modelled by a conditional probability distribution function. The new population is simulated from the probability model, thus inheriting the dependencies. In this chapter, the procedure for building an approximation of the probability distribution through polytrees and Bayesian networks are explained. A set of circuit design experiments is then performed and the polytree EDA and Bayesian EDA are compared with other evolutionary approaches, such as genetic algorithms, particle swarm algorithms and ant systems. The results show that the proposed EDAs are very competitive, and in most cases are better than the evolutionary approaches.

Chapter 13 by Diaf et al. reviews the ant-based algorithms and their applications to various areas, including combinatorial optimisation, data clustering, collective robotics and image processing. In this chapter, the authors first present a biological description of the real ants, and then show how the anatomy and the behaviour of real ants have inspired various types of ant-based algorithms, commonly known as ant colony optimisation algorithms nowadays. Its uniqueness lies in the biological part of the real ants, as very few other related papers have attempted to draw parallel between the real ants with the artificial ones. In terms of applications, the authors have illustrated the use of ant system and ant colony system in combinatorial optimisation based on the widely studied travelling salesman problem. Following which, variants of ant-based algorithms inspired by the way real ants naturally cluster eggs or dead bodies of other ants are described in the context of data clustering. Next, existing works that have applied the collective intelligence of ants in building collective robots are described. Finally, an application of ant colony optimisation in image segmentation is proposed.

Chapter 14, the last chapter of this volume, by Nesmachnow et al. is a comprehensive survey chapter where they systematically review the use of nature-inspired techniques in solving optimisation problems related to telecommunication network design. The review is aimed at providing an insight of different approaches employed in the area. In particular, it covers four main classes of applications in telecommunication network design: minimum spanning trees, reliable networks, local access network design and backbone location, as well as cellular and wireless network design. While genetic algorithms and other evolutionary algorithms have been used most frequently in this domain, other methods such as ant colony optimisation and particle swarm optimisation are also gaining much popularity in recent years. The long list of works presented in this chapter reveals the high impact of using nature-inspired techniques for solving network design problems.

Raymond Chiong
January, 2009

Acknowledgment

I would like to thank all the authors for their excellent contributions to this book. I also wish to acknowledge the support of the editorial advisory board and the help of all who involved in the collection and review process of this book. Without them, this book project could not have been satisfactorily completed. Special thanks go to all those who provided constructive and comprehensive review comments, as well as those who willingly helped in some last-minute urgent reviews.

A further special note of thanks goes to the staff members at IGI Global. Their editorial assistance and professional support, from the inception of the initial idea to final publication, have been invaluable. In particular, I would like to thank Kristin Klinger, Heather Probst and Tyler Heath who continuously prodded me with e-mail to keep the project on schedule, and Mehdi Khosrow-pour whose invitation motivated me to take on this project.

Finally, I hope the readers would enjoy reading this book as much as I have enjoyed putting it together.

Raymond Chiong
January, 2009

Section 1
Introduction

Chapter 1
Nature that Breeds Solutions

Raymond Chiong
Swinburne University of Technology (Sarawak Campus), Malaysia

Ferrante Neri
University of Jyväskylä, Finland

Robert I. McKay
Seoul National University, Korea

ABSTRACT

Nature has always been a source of inspiration. Over the last few decades, it has stimulated many successful techniques, algorithms and computational applications for dealing with large, complex and dynamic real world problems. In this chapter, the authors discuss why nature-inspired solutions have become increasingly important and favourable for tackling the conventionally-hard problems. They also present the concepts and background of some selected examples from the domain of natural computing, and describe their key applications in business, science and engineering. Finally, the future trends are highlighted to provide a vision for the potential growth of this field.

INTRODUCTION

For at least half a century now, the field of natural computing has grown in popularity. This popularity is largely driven by the successful use of nature-inspired approaches, such as evolutionary algorithms, artificial neural networks, swarm intelligence algorithms, artificial immune systems and many others, in solving various problems. These techniques have proven their important role on many practical implementations, and tend to improve computational efficiency at the cost of its quality – a

trade-off that is necessary due to the exponential growth of the problem space for many real world applications today, where there is no known feasible exact method to find solutions.

Before the emergence of these techniques, computer scientists and engineers often devised their solutions by relying on the input from human intelligence. Following the conventional artificial intelligence methods, they have to first design the 'intelligence' based on their thoughts and judgements, and thereafter get the computer to automate their thinking process in a logical way to solve problems. The major drawback with this kind of conventional method is the usual linearity of human thinking pro-

DOI: 10.4018/978-1-60566-705-8.ch001

cesses, so that solutions conceived via this logic are frequently hindered by preconceptions about how problems should be tackled. These days, not only computer scientists and engineers, but also business analysts, can develop solutions to their hardest problems without scratching and cracking their heads, by seeking inspiration from nature, i.e. imitating the way nature works. Evolutionary computing, for example, uses principles of natural evolution as a paradigm for problem-solving. The field of neural computing uses the human brain to learn something useful, by looking at the brain organisation and the way the neurones are linked. Swarm computing, on the other hand, observes phenomena in the natural world in the form of ant colonies, flocks of birds, etc.

In this chapter, our aim is to discuss why nature has been such an appealing choice for dealing with conventionally hard-to-solve problems. We also briefly present some popular nature-inspired techniques, and clarify the significance as well as the successful use of these techniques in the fields of business, science and engineering. It is necessary to note that this chapter is intended for general readers who have little knowledge of natural computing, and we hope it will serve as a stepping stone for those who are interested to build on the many existing ideas introduced here. The chapter ends by looking into what the future holds for the field.

WHY NATURE?

Recently, an eminent colleague, on hearing that one of us worked in evolutionary computing, responded jokingly 'Have you heard of sand computing?', making the argument that a heap of sand, through its chaotic dynamic behaviour solves a problem far beyond the scope of computing systems – but implicitly also making the point that this complex behaviour might not be very useful. Why should we expect that nature can inspire useful systems?

In the case of biologically-inspired systems, there is an obvious argument. Terrestrial biological systems have been evolving for at least 3.5 billion years (Schopf *et al.*, 2002), and potentially far longer under the panspermia hypothesis (Thomson, 1871; Crick & Orgel, 1973). In doing so, they have not only solved specific problems, but also evolved more general problem-solving capabilities. Thus the genetic code has itself been optimised as a representation language for specifying proteins (Freeland, Wu & Keulmann, 2003), the organisation of genes into chromosomes is subject to on-going evolution to permit faster and more effective response to selective pressures (Batada & Hurst, 2007) and even sexual reproduction itself probably arose as an evolutionary response to co-evolutionary pressures from parasites (Hamilton, Axelrod & Tanese, 1990).

So why is this different from 'sand computing'? Why should we assume that the optimisation and learning problems that biological systems solve bear any relationship to those we wish to solve? Why should we assume that the techniques would be useful for our business, scientific and engineering problems?

In many cases, we can give a direct and convincing answer: our problem is so directly analogous to that which the biological system had to solve, that the solution technique inevitably transfers. Finding efficient paths in complex landscapes using only local information is precisely the problem ants have to solve in exploiting scattered food resources. It is hardly surprising that they have evolved good solutions to the problem, nor that those solutions, when abstracted as algorithms, perform similarly well on similar problems of importance to us.

In other cases, however, the analogy is less clear. Why should we expect neural networks, abstracted from the neural control mechanisms of animals, to work well not only for control problems, but also for completely unrelated optimisation problems? Why should evolutionary algorithms extend so well to multi-objective optimisation, when the mechanisms for spreading along the pareto front often have little to do with biological mechanisms?

Waxing metaphysical, we might consider the role of Ockham's razor: both biological systems and we are can successfully tackle only problems which are solvable by some form of Ockham's razor bias. For any particular problem domain, with its particular bias requirement, that we might be interested in, it is likely that some problem with a similar bias requirement has previously arisen in a biological system, and hence biological systems have been under evolutionary pressure to find suitable solution algorithms. In many cases, they have succeeded.

Even further into the metaphysical, we might wonder why the World is learnable at all. After all, much of machine learning theory (especially the celebrated No Free Lunch Theorem (Wolpert & Macready, 1997)) suggests that learnability is a rare condition: that a random World would not be likely to be learnable. One might speculate that such a non-learnable World would not survive: that is, that there is competition at the very basis of nature, that too-random physics leads to universes that lose out in the competition for actualisation (see Schmidhuber (2002) for related theories). Maybe sand computing will turn out to be useful after all!

From a practical perspective, none of this matters. The evidence is clear. Biological metaphors have given rise to a large number of effective algorithms, as this volume, and the immense literature it cites, clearly demonstrates. For the past forty years or so, biological systems have been yielding effective insights into efficient algorithms for specific problems. Some practitioners have emphasised the engineering aspects, taking a simple biological analogy and re-engineering it for specific problems; at the other extreme, some have built detailed analogues of biological systems, investigating which aspects were important for practical application.

In some cases, this has led to parallel development of whole fields. Thus estimation of distribution algorithms, primarily driven by statistical insights, have developed in parallel with heavily biologically-inspired ant colony optimisation algorithms. The resulting systems have often been remarkably similar, readily describable in the language of either.

It seems clear that this intertwined development is fated to continue. The bottom line is, biological systems are still many orders of magnitudes more effective for tough problems than are the current systems they have inspired. There is still far more to learn about how they work, to drive future algorithm research and development. No existing artificial neural network can perform with anything like the virtuosity of vertebrate neural systems; no current evolutionary algorithm can evolve the sophistication of even a virus. This is not simply a matter of scale; scaling of these artificial systems ceases to yield substantial benefits even at the scales we can implement in computers; it's clear that scaled-up systems would not behave in similar ways to the biological systems – that is, that some aspects of the biological systems we have not yet modelled are crucial to their algorithmic behaviour. The key problem is to determine which. Doubtless, some of the important aspects are already known to biologists, and we have simply failed so far to grasp their importance; others will require new insights into the actual operation of biological systems.

Potentially, also, we will see some reverse traffic. So far, the inspiration has largely passed one way: from biology to algorithms. The field of artificial life gives some hint of traffic the other way, especially through agent-based simulations validating hypotheses about aspects of the interactions of population dynamics and evolution (Krivenko & Burtsev, 2007). However, the fields of optimisation and machine learning, in particular, have well-developed mathematical theories. So far, we have seen very little application of these theories in biological systems; when we do, there is enormous potential for better understanding of the constraints on biological systems. Equally important, the resulting questions should lead to better understanding of what aspects of biological systems are actually essential to their effectiveness, and hence to further ideas for nature-inspired algorithmic systems.

Apart from what we have discussed, it is important to note that there are several other bio-inspired paradigms which we have not mentioned. These bio-inspired paradigms emerged more recently, among them artificial immune systems, membrane computing, amorphous computing and molecular computing (Kari & Rozenberg, 2008). Artificial immune systems are inspired by the biological immune system, membrane computing by the compartmentalised organisation of the living cells, amorphous computing by morphogenesis, and molecular computing by encoded biomolecules such as DNA[1] strands. Besides these bio-inspired paradigms, there is also another paradigm that uses an alternative "hardware" for performing computations based on the laws of quantum physics, known as quantum computing (Kaye, Laflamme & Mosca, 2007).

SELECTED EXAMPLES OF NATURE-INSPIRED SOLUTIONS

In the following sections, some popular nature-inspired techniques will be introduced and we will attempt to clarify the concepts and significance of such techniques by providing a few examples of the successful use of these techniques in the fields of business, science and engineering. We hope that an understanding of these techniques will aid in the development of new heuristic methods.

Evolutionary Algorithms

During the 20th century, the scientific community started considering the possibility of transferring by means of a metaphor, some physical phenomena into computer science. The diffusion and common acceptance of evolutionary theories proposed by Darwin suggested to computer scientists a straight-forward but ingenious intuition: if the evolution of species tends to a general improvement over the time and a progressive adaptation to the surrounding environment, an evolution of an artificial species can be simulated in a computer with the aim of solving an optimisation problem.

The idea of applying evolutionary principles to computer science was stated for the first time during the forties. In 1948 Turing proposed "genetical or evolutionary search" and during the 1950s Bremermann executed experiments on "optimisation through evolutionary and recombination" methods. During the sixties three different implementations of this basic idea were developed in parallel. In Fogel, Owens & Walsh (1965) and Fogel, Owens & Walsh (1966), *evolutionary programming* was introduced. In Holland (1973), Holland (1992a) and Holland (1992b), a novel optimisation method called *genetic algorithm* was defined. During the same period, a similar optimisation algorithm, the *evolution strategy*, was designed (Rechenberg, 1973; Schwefel, 1981). From the early 1990s the scientific community realised that these techniques can be seen as different manifestations of a unique algorithmic philosophy now known as evolutionary computing (see Bäck, 1996; Bäck, Fogel & Michalewicz, 2000a; Bäck, Fogel & Michalewicz, 2000b), and the general set of algorithms based on this philosophy are known as evolutionary algorithms. Two important evolutionary algorithms have been subsequently defined during the nineties: *genetic programming* introduced in Koza (1992) and Koza (1994) and *differential evolution*, proposed in Storn & Price (1995). Today, most systems combine ideas from two or more of these systems – for example, a typical system might combine tournament selection, tracing its origins back to evolutionary programming, with mutation operators and floating point representation derived from evolution strategies, and crossover operators and generational structures more traditionally associated with genetic algorithms.

In general, an evolutionary algorithm can be schematised as a population based metaheuristic which is characterised by an initial creation of a set of solutions and a generation cycle; the population of solutions is presumed to evolve over the generation cycles. The individuals of the population are encoded into a genotype, which represents a candidate solution for the optimisation problem of interest. To each candidate solution a fitness value can be associated by means of the quality function which we desire to maximise or minimise. During the generation cycle, the solutions undergo parent selection – that is, a process which selects those individuals which should recombine and generate offspring. Recombination is an operator which processes two or more solutions to generate a set of offspring solutions. The newly generated solutions might undergo a mutation process in order to enhance the exploratory capability of the search algorithm. When the population of offspring is generated, a survivor selection scheme selects the solutions belonging to the population at the subsequent generation cycle. A pseudo-code showing the working principle of a general evolutionary algorithm is given in Figure 1.

Figure 1. General pseudo-code of an evolutionary algorithm

```
Generate initial population;
Evaluate each candidate solution;
while termination conditions
        select parents;
        recombine the parents;
        mutate the resulting offspring;
        evaluate offspring;
        select survivors for the next generation;
end-while
```

Evolutionary Programming

In evolutionary programming, each individual is a real-valued vector composed of its candidate solution representation $\bar{x}$ and a set of self-adaptive parameters $\bar{\sigma}$:

$$(\bar{x}, \bar{\sigma}) = (w_1, ..., x_i ..., \sigma_1, ..., \sigma_i, ..., \sigma_n)$$

During the generation cycle, each individual generates an offspring. For the generic i^{th} design variable (or gene), the update is performed in the following way:

$$\sigma'_i = \sigma_i (1 + \alpha . N(0,1))$$

$$x'_i = x_i + \sigma'_i . N(0,1)$$

where the index $'$ indicates the newly generated gene, $N(0,1)$ is a zero-mean normal distribution characterised by a standard deviation equal to 1 and α is a constant value traditionally set equal to 0.2. When all the offspring solutions are generated, a population composed of parents and offspring undergoes a survivor selection. The fitness value of each individual of this extended population is compared with the fitness values of a set of other randomly selected solutions. When all the comparisons have been performed, the solutions which won a higher number of comparisons are selected for the subsequent generation.

The literature provides a plethora of variants and application examples for evolutionary programming. It is worth mentioning that a prominent area where evolutionary programming has been heavily used is neural network training. A famous example of this can be found in its employment for the generation of an artificial checkers player (Chellapilla & Fogel, 1999; Chellapilla & Fogel, 2001). In addition, evolutionary programming has also been widely applied in areas from power generation (Lai & Ma, 1997; Shi & Xu, 2001) to protein-protein interaction (Duncan & Olson,

1996) and medical image understanding (Fogel *et al.*, 1998). In business, it has been used for portfolio selection (Lim, Wuncsh & Ho, 2000) and business risk identification (Yu, Lai & Wang, 2008).

Genetic Algorithms

In their original implementation, genetic algorithms handle individuals encoded as binary strings. There is a variety of suggested encodings to obtain the binary strings; the best known being direct binary conversion and the Gray code representation (Eiben & Smith, 2003). However, in many modern implementations, integer and real-valued genetic algorithms have been proposed.

High importance is attached to the parent selection, which is the core of the genetic algorithm selection method. There are many studies and proposals in the literature for selecting the solutions undergoing recombination. The most popular are proportionate selection, which assigns a fitness-based selection probability to the potential parents; ranking selection, which sorts the solutions according to their fitness values and assigns a selection probability based on their position in this sorted list; and *k-tournament* selection, which fills a parent list through a set of random *k*-fold comparisons.

The recombination in the standard genetic algorithms occurs by means of a crossover – the offspring solutions contain a section of each binary parent. As with selection, many variants have been proposed, e.g. the crossover can be single-point in which each offspring is generated by merging two sections of the genotype of each parent, or multi-point where each parent is divided in several subsections which are subsequently recombined to generate the offspring. There are also more complex recombination schemes, e.g. mask crossover or partially mapped crossover (see Eiben & Smith (2003) for more details).

In genetic algorithms, the newly generated solutions undergo mutation: with a low probability a small perturbation is performed, e.g. in binary

representation a bit is flipped from 0 to 1 and vice versa. The meaning of this operation is that an extra change is given to the evolution with the hope that the mutated individual will detect a new promising area of the decision space. Finally, the survivor selection in genetic algorithms follows the so called generational strategy i.e. the newly generated offspring completely replace the parent population.

Genetic algorithms have been intensively applied to many fields. In order to give just some example of their strengths in optimisation, we can mention two books (Karr & Freeman, 1998) and (Dawid, 1999), entirely devoted to applications of genetic algorithms to industrial problems and economic models, respectively. Genetic algorithms are also valued for their creative rather than optimal properties, as seen in their application to evolving art and music (Romero & Machado, 2008). We can illustrate the wide range of genetic algorithms with just a few examples. They have been used for rental car distribution (Michalewicz & Smith, 2007), in which genetic algorithms combine with other methods to generate near-optimal economic distribution for the distribution of rental cars. Kaitani *et al.*, (1999) use them for control of a prosthetic hand, dramatically reducing the effort required by a new user to accustom him/herself to the prosthetic. Biles (2001) uses them for real-time performance of jazz improvisations, while they are also at the core of GARP, the leading system for animal species distribution modelling (Stockwell & Peters, 1999).

Evolution Strategies

Evolution strategies are evolutionary algorithms designed for solving real-valued problems. The representation in evolution strategies is similar to that shown for evolutionary programming, since a solution is composed of the candidate solution genotype and a set of real-valued self-adaptive parameters. In many evolution strategy variants, a set of self-adaptive parameters of a second kind can be added to the solution encoding.

At each generation cycle, parent selection relies on pseudo-randomly selecting some solutions to undergo recombination and mutation. In evolution strategies a big emphasis is placed on mutation while recombination plays a minor role. The general mutation rule is defined, for the generic i^{th} design variable, by:

$$x'_i = x_i + \sigma'_i . N(0,1)$$

where $N(0, 1)$ has the same meaning described for the evolutionary programming. The update of σ_i can be performed by means of several rules proposed in literature. The most famous are the 1/5 success rule (Rechenberg, 1973), uncorrelated mutation with one step size, uncorrelated mutation with n step sizes and correlated mutation, for details see Eiben & Smith (2003). The general idea is that the solutions are mutated within their neighborhood based on a certain probabilistic criterion with the aim of generating new promising solutions.

The recombination can be discrete or intermediary: discrete recombination generates an offspring solution by pseudo-randomly choosing the genes from two parent solutions, while intermediary recombination generates an offspring whose genes are obtained by calculating a randomly weighted average of the corresponding genes of two parents.

The parent selection can be performed, either in the genetic algorithm fashion by replacing the whole parent population with the offspring population or by merging parent and offspring populations and selecting the wanted number of individuals on the basis of their fitness values. These strategies are usually known as comma and plus strategy respectively.

As with genetic algorithms, evolution strategies have been extensively applied to a broad spectrum of problems in science, engineering, and economics. A famous application in mechanical engineering is given in Klockgether & Schwefel (1970). More modern examples of evolution strategies' applications include: the design of a tracking filter (Herrero *et al.*, 2003), the development of self-adaptive business applications (Bäck, 2002), and various engineering problems (Thierauf & Cai, 1999). In science, evolution strategies have recently been used for automatic segmentation of skin lesion images for early detection of skin cancer (Yuan, Situ & Zouridakis, 2008), for the reconstruction of multiple neuromagnetic sources (Eichardt *et al.*, 2008), and for improving enzymatic performance (Hibbert & Dalby, 2005), among others.

Genetic Programming

Genetic programming is an evolutionary algorithm which aims to find an expression able to solve a specific task. In genetic programming, the representation of a solution is performed by encoding the candidate solution into a structure known as a parse tree. This tree can represent a mathematical formula, a logical expression or a computer procedure and contains in its internal nodes mathematical operators and logical programming structures and in the external nodes (leaves) the constant and variables taking part in the procedure.

Genetic programming can be seen as just a specific implementation of an evolutionary algorithm with a special structure for the individual representation. However the variable complexity of individuals and the complexity of the search space means that, both theoretically and practically, it behaves very differently from other evolutionary algorithms.

As with the other evolutionary algorithms, the individual of the population (trees in this case) are selected for recombination and mutation. The parent selection is traditionally carried out by means of a (fitness based) proportionate selection similar to genetic algorithm, though tournament selection is probably more common today. In some systems, a specific genetic programming parent selection called over-selection is used. This over-selection at first ranks the population by fitness values and then divide it into two groups, the first one containing the top individuals and the second containing the others. The parent selection is then performed by giving a higher chance to the top group. The group sizes are empirically chosen on the basis of the total population size by means of the so called rule of thumb, see Langdon & Poli (2001).

The most common recombination mechanism in genetic programming consists in swapping a subtree from two parents in order to generate two offspring solutions. Mutation consists of removing a sub-tree and substituting it with a pseudo-randomly generated tree. The issue of the mutation in genetic programming has been discussed over the years; in the first implementations, no mutation was advised (Koza, 1992) but subsequent further studies showed that a low mutation probability can be efficient in the genetic programming evolution, see Luke & Spector (1997) and Banzhaf *et al.* (1998). Both crossover and mutation have been the subject of intensive study, and many alternatives have been proposed and validated.

The survivor selection is traditionally generational, similarly to a genetic algorithm. However, in many new implementations different survivor selection schemes are employed.

Since genetic programming aims at generating an efficient solution expression, it is a useful tool for a wide range of applications, not amenable to most other techniques. Some example applications include machine vision (Chien, Lin & Yang, 2004), games (Ferrer & Martin, 1995; Chen & Yeh, 1996), and virtual reality (Das *et al.*, 1994). Genetic programming is also the primary subject of the annual human-competitive competition, which requires systems to generate solutions which, if they were generated by a human, would be regarded as exhibiting a high level of intelligence and creativity. These include evolving high-quality quantum circuits (Barnum, Bernstein & Spector, 2000), radio antennas (Lohn, Hornby & Linden, 2005) and optic fibres (Manos, Large & Poladian, 2007).

There are numerous applications of genetic programming in solving business and industrial problems too. For example, it has been applied for drug discovery in the pharmaceutical industry (Langdon & Buxton, 2003), organisation design optimisation (KHosraviani, Levitt & Koza, 2004), intelligent business logic engineering (Wilson & Heywood, 2007), bankruptcy prediction (Etemadi, Rostamy & Dehkordi, 2008), and business process mining (Turner, Tiwari & Mehnen, 2008), etc. In medicine, it has been applied in cancer research (Worzel *et al.*, 2009), epileptic seizure prediction (Hiram, Erik & Javier, 2005), burn diagnosing (de Vega *et al.*, 2000), and so on.

Differential Evolution

Differential evolution is a population based optimisation heuristic employing a classical evolutionary logic, apparently very efficient for solving real-valued problems and often able to handle non-linearities and multimodalities (Storn & Price, 1997). Despite its simplicity, differential evolution (also thanks to the few parameters to be tuned) is often a reliable approach, exhibiting very good performance for a wide range of optimisation problems and can thus be employed for various real-world applications. The main advantages of differential evolution, such as a simple and straightforward logic, compact structure, ease of use, high convergence characteristics, and robustness, make it a high-class technique for real-valued parameter optimisation.

Several variants have been proposed in literature but the general algorithmic structure is described in the following. An initial pseudo-random sampling of individuals is executed with a uniform distribution function within the decision space.

At each generation, for each individual x of the population, three individuals x_r, x_s and x_t are pseudo-randomly extracted from the population. According to the logic of differential evolution, a provisional offspring x'_{off} is generated by mutation as:

$$x'_{off} = x_t + F(x_r - x_s)$$

where F [0,1+] is a scale factor which controls the length of the exploration vector $(x_r - x_s)$ and thus determines how far from point x the offspring should be generated. The mutation scheme shown in the equation above is also known as DE/rand/1. Other variants of the mutation rule have been subsequently proposed in the literature, e.g. see Qin & Suganthan (2005).

When mutation occurs, to increase exploration, each gene of the new individual x'_{off} is switched with the corresponding gene of x with a uniform probability CR [0,1] and the final offspring x_{off} is generated:

$$x_{off,j} = \begin{cases} x_j & if\ rand(0,1) < CR \\ x'off,j & otherwise \end{cases}$$

where $rand(0,1)$ is a random number between 0 and 1; j is the index of the gene under examination.

The resulting offspring x_{off} is evaluated and, according to a one-to-one spawning logic, it replaces x_i if and only if $f(x_{off}) < f(x_i)$; otherwise no replacement occurs.

Due to its structure, differential evolution seems to be very promising for continuous problems and still applicable, albeit with a lower performance, for discrete problems (Price, Storn & Lampinen, 2005). Several interesting applications have been proposed, e.g. in Joshi & Sanderson (1999) a differential evolution application to the multisensor fusion problem is given; in Chang & Chang (2000) a differential evolution application to power electronics is presented; in Liu & Lampinen (2005) a differential evolution variant is employed for training a radial based function; in Storn (2005) a filter design is carried out by differential evolution; in Tirronen *et al.* (2008) a differential evolution based algorithm designed a digital filter for paper industry applications.

MEMETIC ALGORITHMS

According to their original definition (Moscato & Norman, 1989), memetic algorithms are population based metaheuristics which contain one or more local search components integrated within the generation loop of an evolutionary framework. The metaphor descends from the philosophical concept of meme, introduced in Dawkins (1976), which is the elementary abstract entity of the cultural transmission in a social environment. The meme is a thought, an idea, a theory, a gesture, a fashion, a habit, etc which can be transmitted from an individual to another one, enriched and propagated within a society.

Memetic algorithms are thus systems which deal with a population of solutions which genotypically, by means of the evolutionary operators, and culturally, by means of the local search strategy, evolve in order to solve a global optimisation problem. The main rationale behind such kind of hybrid approaches is the conviction that the combination of several competitive/cooperative algorithmic components is more efficient than the application of single component at once.

In order to comprehend their significance, memetic algorithms should be put into relationship to the diffusion of the No Free Lunch Theorem (Wolpert & Macready, 1997). The No Free Lunch Theorem states that the average performance of all the optimisation methods over all possible problems is the same; its most immediate consequence is that for each optimisation problem a specific algorithm must be designed. A memetic algorithm, unlike for example a genetic algorithm, is not just a specific algorithm with fairly fixed features but a broad and general class of algorithms leaving to the algorithmic designer the burden of choosing among a nearly infinite variety of components and combinations.

A first important classification of the structures of memetic algorithms is given in Lozano *et al.* (2004): the local search can either be implemented within the variation operators (e.g. crossover or mutation) for controlling the offspring generation or as a life-time learning i.e. on already generated solutions in order to improve upon their initial fitness values.

Several further questions arise during the design of memetic algorithms: how often the local search should be performed, how many and which individuals should be selected for undergoing local search, the budget of the local search with respect to the global one, etc. Unfortunately a universally efficient recipe cannot be given, since the efficiency of the algorithmic components and their coordination heavily depends on the problem under analysis. In addition, the empirical suggestions, on design issues, presented in the literature are often contradictory. However, some generally valid indications, for the design of a memetic algorithm, can be extracted:

1. To use multiple local search components (Krasnogor, 2002; Krasnogor *et al.*, 2002);

2. To choose local search algorithms which employ a variety of search logics (Krasnogor, 2004);

3. To properly balance the global and local search (Ishibuchi, Yoshida & Murata, 2003; Ong & Keane, 2004);

4. To pay attention to the variation in the population diversity in order to coordinate the algorithmic components (Caponio *et al.*, 2007; Neri *et al.* 2007).

Since the coordination of the various components plays a crucial role in the success of the algorithm, several adaptive and self-adaptive systems have been presented in the literature with the purpose of obtaining robust algorithms which do not need a human decision in the component coordination. A classification of adaptation in memetic algorithms is presented in Ong *et al.* (2006).

However, memetic algorithms can be very powerful tools for various hard-to-solve real world problems and can significantly outperform classical optimisation methods and traditional metaheuristics (e.g. genetic algorithms, evolution strategies, particle swarm optimisation, etc), under the condition that a proper domain specific algorithmic design is carried out. Many applications to engineering have been proposed in the literature. For example, in Caponio *et al.* (2007) and Caponio, Neri & Tirronen (2008) memetic algorithms are used for designing the optimal control system for electric motors. In Burke & Smith (2000) and Liu, Wang & Jin (2007), the authors show that memetic approaches can outperform traditional metaheuristics for combinatorial problems with reference to industrial scheduling. In Ong & Keane (2004), the applicability of sophisticated memetic algorithms is presented for an aerodynamic design problem. In Tirronen & Neri (2008) and Caponio, Neri & Tirronen (2008), the deployment of memetic algorithms for image processing of a paper industry application is proposed. In Areibi & Yang (2004) and Tang & Yao (2007), the applicability of memetic algorithms to the design of electronic circuits is shown.

The memetic algorithms have also been successfully applied to various biological and medical problems. For example, the molecular prediction and the gene expression problems by memetic algorithms are intensively studied in the literature, e.g. see Krasnogor *et al.* (2002), Smith (2004), and Merz (2003). Finally, memetic algorithms are also used for designing optimal therapies. A tailored memetic approach is proposed for cancer in Tse *et al.* (2007) and for human immunodeficiency virus in Neri *et al.* (2007) and Neri, Toivanen & Mäkinen (2007).

ARTIFICIAL NEURAL NETWORKS

An artificial neural network is a computational method modelled after the way biological nervous systems process information. Just as there are many neurones in the brain, artificial neural networks consist of a large number of highly interconnected artificial neurones that work in unison to solve specific problems. These neurones are the core information processing units of the artificial neural networks, and each of them is defined by relatively simple input-output relations (Hopfield, 1982).

In general, all the neurones have a number of inputs, but only one output. Each input is associated with a weight. When a neurone receives inputs (signals), each input is combined with the weight for that input in some way to give a contribution to the internal activation of the neurone. All these contributions are later combined to give the total internal activation. Therefore, if there are enough inputs received at the same time, the neurone gets activated. Once activated, it will give an output that may activate its neighbouring neurones.

Like humans, neural network models learn by example. Learning in artificial neural networks involves adjustments to the synaptic connections that exist between the neurones. As such, the behaviour of a particular network depends on how strong the connections between the neurones are. While various neural network models have been proposed in past decades, these models can all be seen as extensions of the McCulloch-Pitts model (McCulloch & Pitts, 1943). For example, Multi-layer Perceptrons (MLP) employ, instead of one single neurone, a collection of inter-connected neurones arranged in multiple layers; the Radial Basis Function (RBF) network, similar in architecture to MLP, uses a different activation in its neurone; etc.

In terms of learning, artificial neural network applications can be broadly categorised into three main types as depicted in Figure 2: namely supervised learning, unsupervised learning and reinforcement learning. In supervised learning (e.g. MLP, RBF, etc) the artificial neural network is given a large set of input-output pair to train on. The goal of the artificial neural network is then to learn a mapping which transforms the inputs to the outputs. This mapping is usually subjected to minimisation of a given error measure.

Figure 2. Three general learning methods for artificial neural networks

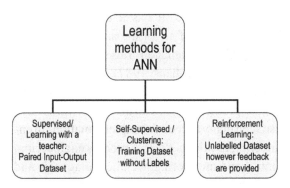

For unsupervised learning (e.g. Self Organising Map, *k*-Nearest Neighbours, etc), the artificial neural network is also given a training dataset. Unlike supervised learning, this dataset has no label, and the artificial neural network's task is then to learn the statistical distribution of the dataset and store a simplified model of the dataset. Normally, the accuracy of the model is subjected to the prescribed architecture of the artificial neural network.

Reinforcement learning takes a slightly different approach. It relates to maximising a numerical reward function through a kind of trial-and-error search. While the dataset is not labelled, the artificial neural network is rewarded each time it makes a correction decision and penalised each time a wrong move is called.

Artificial neural networks are well suited to data processing, classification, pattern recognition, and function approximation problems (see de Castro, 2007 for an overview), and as such are found in a broad variety of real world applications. In fact, they have already been successfully applied in many industries and used for all kinds of business problems, such as sales forecasting, industrial process control, customer research, data validation, risk management and target marketing. One example of a marketing application can be found in the Airline Marketing Tactician, a computer system integrated with a feedforward neural network. This system is used to assist the marketing control of airline seat allocations, as well as monitor and recommend booking advice for each departure. It has a direct impact on the profitability of an airline and can provide a technological advantage for users of the system (Hutchison & Stephens, 1987).

Besides the applicability in business and industrial problems, artificial neural networks have also seen many successful implementations in engineering problems, such as process engineering, control and monitoring, technical diagnosis and nondestructive testing, power systems, robotics, transportation, telecommunications, remote sensing, etc. For more details, see Soulié & Gallinari (1998). In Flood (2001), a review of artificial neural networks in civil engineering is presented. Apart from these, several prototypical applications of neural network technology to engineering problems are described in Garrett *et al.* (1993). These include an adaptive controller for building thermal mass storage; an adaptive controller for a combine harvester; an interpretation system for non-destructive evaluation of masonry walls; a machining feature recognition system for use in process planning; an image classification system for classifying land coverage from satellite or high-altitude images; and a system for designing the pumping strategy for contaminated groundwater remediation.

In recent years, artificial neural networks are being used increasingly in the field of medicine. Extensive application of artificial neural networks to biomedical systems can be easily scouted. It seems that they are doing particularly well on problems with a high degree of complexity for which there is no algorithmic solution, or where the solution is too complex for traditional techniques to determine. Medical areas that have found success stories with this computational method include drug development, patient diagnosis, and image analysis. More specifically, we see functional recovery of stroke survivors in Oczkowski & Barreca (1997), control of arm movements application in Lan, Feng & Crago (1994), mammography in Wu

et al. (1993), and temporal gene expression data in Krishna, Narayanan & Keedwell (2005), etc.

ANT COLONY OPTIMISATION

Ant colony optimisation is a population-based metaheuristic inspired by the foraging behaviour of ant colonies. Originally developed by Dorigo (1992) as Ant System (AS), its aim was to find the optimal path in a graph. Different variants of the AS were subsequently proposed, e.g. the Ant Colony System (ACS) by Dorigo & Gambardella (1997) and MAX-MIN Ant System (MMAS) by Stützle & Hoos (2000), and used to solve various combinatorial optimisation problems with discrete search spaces. For a good overview of ant colony optimisation, see Blum (2005).

To apply ant colony optimisation algorithms, a problem first needs to be transformed into the context of finding the best path on a weighted graph. Each solution is then represented by an (artificial) ant moving on the graph. At the beginning, ants move around randomly, resulting in solutions being constructed stochastically. Upon finding food they return to their colony while laying down pheromone on the path; other ants that find such path are likely to follow the trail and reinforce it if they eventually find the food source too. The pheromone that is laid soon starts to evaporate, hence reducing the attractiveness of the path. The longer it takes for an ant to travel down the path and back again, the longer the pheromone gets evaporated. This means that if a path is short, it gets marched over quicker, and therefore the density of its pheromone would remain high as it is laid on the path as fast as it can evaporate. Thus, when one ant finds a good (i.e., short) path from the colony to a food source, other ants are more likely to follow that path, and positive feedback eventually leads all the ants following a single path.

The pheromone model, technically speaking, is a set of parameters associated with graph components (either nodes or edges) whose values are modified at runtime by the ants. It is considered one of the most distinctive features in ant colony optimisation algorithms. An essential part of the model is the concept of evaporation. Evaporation is vital for ant colony optimisation algorithms to avoid getting stuck in local optima, as otherwise the paths that are chosen by the first ants will be more attractive than those that follow. In such a case, the exploration of the search space would be limited.

Ant colony optimisation, in recent years, has found application in wide range of different problems. Initially, NP-hard combinatorial optimisation problems were its main focus and continue to be the largest body of ant colony optimisation research to this day. The interested reader is referred to Dorigo & Stützle (2004) for a complete overview of these applications.

Ant colony optimisation was also applied successfully to routing in telecommunication networks. AntNet (Di Caro & Dorigo, 1998) is an example of a particularly successful application of it in this research area.

Currently, research in ant colony optimisation is concentrated both on theoretical development as well as the application of those theories to new as well as existing problems. The development of theoretical foundations was first initiated by Gutjahr (2000) by proving the convergence in probability of an ant colony optimisation algorithm. An overview of theoretical results available for ant colony optimisation is provided in Dorigo & Blum (2005).

As per its applications, contemporary research is focused on the solution of dynamic, multi-objective, stochastic, continuous and mixed-variable optimisation problems along with the creation of parallel implementations in order to fully utilise the power offered by parallel hardware. Apart from its success in routing problems, there are also many success stories in other domains, e.g., in business (Marinakis, Marinaki & Zopounidis, 2008; Tenneti & Allada, 2008), in medicine (Rob-

bins *et al.*, 2007; Marinakis & Dounias, 2008), in bioinformatics problems (Basiri, Ghasem-Aghaee & Aghdam, 2008; Shyu & Tsai, 2008; Lopes & Perretto, 2008), and so on. Very recently, the multiple-objective ant colony optimisation algorithms are a fast growing area of research (see Angus & Woodward, 2009).

PARTICLE SWARM OPTIMISATION

Particle swarm optimisation is a population-based optimisation metaheuristic introduced by Kennedy & Eberhart (1995), and then developed in various variants for test problems and applications. The main metaphor employed in particle swarm optimisation is that a group of particles makes use of their "personal" and "social" experience in order to explore a decision space and detect solutions with a high performance. More specifically, a population of candidate solutions is pseudo-randomly sampled within the decision space. Subsequently, the fitness value of each candidate solution is computed and the solutions are ranked on the basis of their performance. The solution associated to the best fitness value overall detected is named global best x_{gb}. At the first generation, each solution x_i is identified with the corresponding local best solution x_{i-lb}, i.e. the most successful value taken in the history of each solution. At each generation, each solution x_i is perturbed by means of the following rule:

$$x_i = x_i + v_i$$

where the velocity vector v_i is a perturbation vector generated in the following way:

$$v_i = v_i + \text{rand}(0, 1)(x_{i-lb} - x_i) + \text{rand}(0, 1)(x_{gb} - x_i)$$

in which *rand (0, 1)* is a pseudo-random number generated by means of a uniform distribution within the interval (0, 1), i.e. 0 excluded and 1 included. The fitness value of the newly generated x_i is calculated and if it outperforms the previous local best value the value of x_{i-lb} is updated. Similarly, if the newly generated solution outperforms the global best solution, a replacement occurs. At the end of the optimisation process, the final global best detected is the estimate of the global optimum returned by the particle swarm algorithm. It is important to remark that in particle swarm optimisation, there is a population of particles which has the role of exploring the decision space and a population of local best solutions (the global best is the local best with the highest performance) to keep track of the successful movements.

In order to better understand the metaphor and thus the algorithmic philosophy behind particle swarm optimisation, the population can be seen as a group of individuals which search for the global optimum by combining the exploration along two components: the former is the memory and thus a learning due to successful and unsuccessful moves (personal experience) while the latter is a partial imitation of the successful move of the most promising individual (social experience). In other words, as shown in the formula above, the perturbation is obtained by the vectorial sum of a move in the direction of the best overall solution and a move in the direction of the best success achieved by a single particle. These directions in modern particle swarm optimisation algorithms are weighted by means of random scale factors, since the choice has to turn out to be beneficial in terms of diversity maintenance and prevention of premature convergence.

Particle swarm optimisation has been widely applied in many disciplines, including medicine, engineering and economics. For a glimpse of various modifications that have been presented with the aim of enhancing the robustness of the optimiser and for performance-specific application domains, see Parsopoulos & Vrahatis (2002) and

Poli, Kennedy & Blackwell (2007). An example of the use of particle swarm optimisation in the medical domain can be found in the work of Salerno (1997), where he used the technique to train a recurrent neural model. In engineering, we see that Yoshida *et al.* (2000) used a variant of particle swarm optimisation for reactive power and voltage control. Besides that, Krohling, Knidel & Shi (2002) solved the numerical equations of hydraulic problems with particle swarm optimisation; Kadrovach & Lamont (2002) proposed a particle swarm model for swarm-based networked sensor systems; Omran, Salman & Engelbrecht (2002) used particle swarm optimisation for image classification and Coello Coello, Luna & Aguirre (2003) used particle swarm optimisation to design combinatorial logic circuits. Hu, Eberhart & Shi (2003) also proposed a modified particle swarm algorithm tailored for constrained optimisation to solve some engineering problems. In Robinson & Rahmat-Samii (2004), an exhaustive set of applicative examples of particle swarm optimisation applications in electromagnetism is given. In Chatterjee *et al.* (2005), a particle swarm optimisation application to neural network training with reference to robotics has been proposed. In Liao, Tseng & Luarn (2007) and Pan, Tasgetiren & Liang (2008), particle swarm optimisation applications to discrete problems with application to scheduling are given. In finance and economics, we see the applications of particle swarm optimisation in financial risk early warning (Huang *et al.*, 2006), investment decision-making (Nenortaite & Simutis, 2005), investment portfolio selection (Chen *et al.*, 2006; Xu & Chen, 2006), electricity market (Yuan *et al.*, 2005), among others.

FUTURE TRENDS

In recent years, especially after the publication of the No Free Lunch Theorem, engineers, scientists and practitioners had to radically change their view about optimisation and natural computing. More specifically, since a theoretical result proved that the performance of each algorithm over all possible problems is the same, it was clear there was no longer value in discussing which algorithm is universally better or worse. Thus, instead of trying to propose universally applicable algorithms, algorithmic designers started to propose algorithms which were tailored to specific problems. This would suggest that in the future, evolutionary computing will further focus on domain specific applications.

On the other hand, the necessity of designing robust algorithms will lead to the definition of algorithms which do not offer a high performance on specific applications but are suitable for classes of problems which have a high relevance in applied science and engineering. Thus, in the future we expect to see the definition of sub-fields of computational intelligence such as the design of algorithms devoted to large scale optimisation problems, noisy fitness problems, dynamic problems, computationally expensive problems, etc.

A second response to the No Free Lunch Theorem is to incorporate problem-specific human knowledge and expertise into the system. At first, the primary emphasis was on problem-specific representations and operators. While this problem-specific work continues, today's research also encompasses general methods permitting users to encode their problem-specific knowledge in formalisms such as grammars or logic.

Another approach seeks ways to decompose a problem – fully or partially automatically – into simpler problems, more amenable to solution by previously-described techniques. Many variants of co-evolutionary and ensemble methods fall into this class.

Yet another approach tackles the 'meta' problem: given a family of problems, is it possible, by observing problem-solving behaviour on simpler members of the family, for a system to optimise itself to solve more complex members of the same family? Such 'hyper-heuristics' are the subject of increasing interest at present.

In apparent contradiction with the No Free Lunch Theorem, computer scientists will also try to define novel algorithmic solutions which are able to solve relatively broad classes of problems. One of the most successful attempts to reach this aim is the implementation of memetic algorithms, which offer a high performance by combining diverse algorithms within the same framework. This approach can be seen, at the same time, as a domain specific approach, since the success of a memetic algorithm strictly depends on the choice of the algorithms employed and their coordination; and as a robust approach since various algorithms can have a better chance than one to achieve at least some partial enhancements. The effort of algorithmic designers will be on the design of adaptive systems which can improve both, high performance in specific cases and good robustness features, thus attempting to push towards "the outer limit" of the NFL. The final aim would be the implantation of "fully intelligent algorithms" which can automatically detect the suitable algorithmic components or might be even able to design the algorithms during the run time on basis of the fitness landscape response without any human decision. Although some interesting work has been already done, completely avoiding human decision within the algorithmic design phase is still very far from achievable.

Modern algorithms could spend some of the initial budget to analyse features of the problems in order to automatically set some parameters and adjust some algorithmic components. However, the computational effort to perform the initial analysis and to allow the machine to "understand" the problem should be taken into account. More specifically, if a proper analysis requires a high computational effort, this approach might have limited success. Nevertheless, such a double stage analyser/optimiser can provide a new direction for natural computing in general and evolutionary computing in particular. However we still need appropriate and efficient algorithmic structures, as well as increased computational power (hardware) before this result can be achieved.

ACKNOWLEDGMENT

We gratefully acknowledge feedback and comments on some sections of this chapter by M. Clerc, O. Cordón and L. Seldon.

REFERENCES

Angus, D., & Woodward, C. (2009). Multiple objective ant colony optimisation. *Swarm Intelligence*, *3*(1), 69–85. doi:10.1007/s11721-008-0022-4

Areibi, S., & Yang, Z. (2004). Effective memetic algorithms for VLSI design = genetic algorithms + local search + multi-level clustering. *Evolutionary Computation . Special Issue on Memetic Algorithms*, *12*(3), 327–353.

Bäck, T. (1996). *Evolutionary algorithms in theory and practice*. Oxford University Press.

Bäck, T. (2002). Adaptive business intelligence based on evolution strategies: Some application examples of self-adaptive software. *Information Sciences—Applications . International Journal (Toronto, Ont.)*, *148*(1-4), 113–121.

Bäck, T., Fogel, D. B., & Michalewicz, Z. (2000a). *Basic algorithms and operators*. Institute of Physics Publishing.*Evolutionary Computation*, 1.

Bäck, T., Fogel, D. B., & Michalewicz, Z. (2000b). *Advanced algorithms and operators*. Institute of Physics Publishing.*Evolutionary Computation*, 2.

Banzhaf, W., Nordin, P., Keller, R. E., & Francone, F. D. (1998). *Genetic programming – An introduction on the automatic evolution of computer programs and its application*. Morgan Kaufmann.

Barnum, H., Bernstein, H. J., & Spector, L. (2000). Quantum circuits for OR and AND of ORs. *Journal of Physics. A, Mathematical and General*, *33*(45), 8047–8057. doi:10.1088/0305-4470/33/45/304

Basiri, M. E., Ghasem-Aghaee, N., & Aghdam, M. H. (2008). Using ant colony optimization-based selected features for predicting post-synaptic activity in proteins. In E. Marchiori & J. H. Moore (Eds.), *Evolutionary Computation, Machine Learning and Data Mining in Bioinformatics* (LNCS 4973, pp. 12-23). Berlin: Springer Verlag.

Batada, N. N., & Hurst, L. D. (2007). Evolution of chromosome organization driven by selection for reduced gene expression noise. *Nature Genetics*, *39*, 945–949. doi:10.1038/ng2071

Biles, J. A. (2001). GenJam: Evolution of a jazz improviser. In P. J. Bentley & D. W. Corne (Eds.), *Creative evolutionary systems* (pp. 165-187). San Francisco: Morgan Kaufmann.

Blum, C. (2005). Ant colony optimization: Introduction and recent trends. *Physics of Life Reviews*, *2*, 343–373. doi:10.1016/j.plrev.2005.10.001

Burke, E. K., & Smith, A. J. (2000). Hybrid evolutionary techniques for the maintenance scheduling problem. *IEEE Transactions on Power Systems*, *15*(1), 122–128. doi:10.1109/59.852110

Caponio, A., Cascella, G. L., Neri, F., Salvatore, N., & Sumner, M. (2007). A fast adaptive memetic algorithm for online and off-line control design of PMSM drives. *IEEE Transactions on System, Man and Cybernetics, Part B . Special Issue on Memetic Algorithms*, *37*(1), 28–41.

Caponio, A., Neri, F., & Tirronen, V. (2008). (to appear). Super-fit control adaptation in memetic differential evolution frameworks. *Soft Computing – A Fusion of Foundations . Methodologies and Applications*.

Chang, T. T., & Chang, H. C. (2000). An efficient approach for reducing harmonic voltage distortion in distribution systems with active power line conditioners. *IEEE Transactions on Power Delivery*, *15*(3), 990–995. doi:10.1109/61.871364

Chatterjee, A., Pulasinghe, K., Watanabe, K., & Izumi, K. (2005). A particle-swarm-optimized fuzzy-neural network for voice-controlled robot systems. *IEEE Transactions on Industrial Electronics*, *52*(6), 1478–1489. doi:10.1109/TIE.2005.858737

Chellapilla, K., & Fogel, D. (1999). Evolving neural networks to play checkers without relying on Expert Knowledge. *IEEE Transactions on Neural Networks*, *10*(6), 1382–1391. doi:10.1109/72.809083

Chellapilla, K., & Fogel, D. (2001). Evolving expert checkers playing program without using human expertise. *IEEE Transactions on Evolutionary Computation*, *5*(4), 422–428. doi:10.1109/4235.942536

Chen, S. H., & Yeh, C. H. (1996). Genetic programming in the coordination game with a chaotic best-response function. In L. J. Fogel, P. J. Angeline & T. Bäck (Eds.), *Evolutionary programming V: Proceedings of the 5th Annual Conference on Evolutionary Programming* (pp. 277-286). Cambridge, MA: The MIT Press.

Chen, W., Zhang, R. T., Cai, Y. M., & Xu, F. S. (2006). Particle swarm optimization for constrained portfolio selection problems. In *Proceedings of the International Conference on Machine Learning and Cybernetics* (pp. 2425-2429). Piscataway, NJ: IEEE Press.

Chien, B., Lin, J. Y., & Yang, W. (2004). Learning effective classifiers with z-value measure based on genetic programming. *Pattern Recognition*, *37*(10), 1957–1972. doi:10.1016/j.patcog.2004.03.016

Coello Coello, C. A., Luna, E. H., & Aguirre, A. H. (2003). Use of Particle Swarm Optimization to Design Combinational Logic Circuits. In A. M. Tyrrell, P. C. Haddow & J. Torresen (Eds.), *Evolvable Systems: From biology to hardware* (LNCS 2606, pp. 123-130). Berlin: Springer Verlag.

Crick, F. H., & Orgel, L. E. (1973). Directed Panspermia. *Icarus*, *19*, 341–346. doi:10.1016/0019-1035(73)90110-3

Das, S., Franguiadakis, T., Papka, M. E., Defanti, T. A., & Sandin, D. J. (1994). A genetic programming application in virtual reality. In *Proceedings of the 1st IEEE Conference on Evolutionary Computation* (pp. 480-484). Piscataway, NJ: IEEE Press.

Dawid, H. (1999). *Adaptive learning by genetic algorithms: Analytical results and applications to economic models*. Springer Verlag.

Dawkins, R. (1976). *The selfish game*. Oxford University Press.

de Castro, L. N. (2007). Fundamentals of natural computing: An overview. *Physics of Life Reviews*, *4*(1), 1–36. doi:10.1016/j.plrev.2006.10.002

de Vega, F. F., Roa, L. M., Tomassini, M., & Sanchez, J. M. (2000). Medical knowledge representation by means of multipopulation genetic programming: An application to burn diagnosing. In *Proceedings of the 22nd Annual International Conference of the IEEE Engineering in Medicine and Biology Society* (pp. 619-622), Chicago, IL, USA.

Dorigo, M. (1992). *Optimization, learning and natural algorithms*. Doctoral thesis, Politecnico di Milano, Italy.

Dorigo, M., & Gambardella, L. M. (1997). A cooperative learning approach to the traveling salesman problem. *IEEE Transactions on Evolutionary Computation*, *1*(1), 53–66. doi:10.1109/4235.585892

Duncan, B. S., & Olson, A. J. (1996). Applications of evolutionary programming for the prediction of protein-protein iInteractions. In L. J. Fogel, P. J. Angeline & T. Bäck (Eds.), *Evolutionary programming V: Proceedings of the 5th Annual Conference on Evolutionary Programming* (pp. 411-417). Cambridge, MA: The MIT Press.

Eiben, A. E., & Smith, J. E. (2003). *Introduction to evolutionary computation*. Springer Verlag.

Eichardt, R., Haueisen, J., Knosche, T. R., & Schukat-Talamazzini, E. G. (2008). Reconstruction of multiple neuromagnetic sources using augmented evolution strategies – A comparative study. *IEEE Transactions on Bio-Medical Engineering, 55*(2), 703–712. doi:10.1109/TBME.2007.912656

Etemadi, H., Rostamy, A. A. A., & Dehkordi, H. F. (2009). A genetic programming model for bankruptcy prediction: Empirical evidence from Iran. *Expert Systems with Applications, 36*(2), 3199–3207. doi:10.1016/j.eswa.2008.01.012

Ferrer, G. J., & Martin, W. N. (1995). Using genetic programming to evolve board evaluation functions. In *Proceedings of the IEEE International Conference on Evolutionary Computation* (pp. 747-752). Piscataway, NJ: IEEE Press.

Firpi, H., Goodman, E., & Echauz, J. (2005). On prediction of epileptic seizures by computing multiple genetic programming artificial features. In M. Keijzer *et al.* (Eds.), *Proceedings of the 8th European Conference on Genetic Programming* (LNCS 3447, pp. 321-330). Berlin: Springer Verlag.

Flood, I. (2001). Neural networks in civil engineering: A review. In B. H. V. Topping (Ed.), *Civil and structural engineering computing: 2001* (pp. 185-209). Saxe-Coburg Publications.

Fogel, D. B., Wasson, E. C., Boughton, E. M., & Porto, V. W. (1998). Evolving artificial neural networks for screening features from mammograms. *Artificial Intelligence in Medicine, 14*(3), 317–326. doi:10.1016/S0933-3657(98)00040-2

Fogel, L. J., Owens, A. J., & Walsh, M. J. (1965). Artificial intelligence through a smulation of the evolution. In A. M. Maxfield & L. J. Fogel (Eds.), *Biophysics and cybernetics systems* (pp. 131-156). Washington, DC: Spartan Book Co.

Fogel, L. J., Owens, A. J., & Walsh, M. J. (1996). *Artificial intelligence through simulated evolution.* John Wiley & Sons, Inc.

Freeland, S. J., Wu, T., & Keulmann, N. (2003). The case for an error minimizing genetic code. *Origins of Life and Evolution of the Biosphere, 33*(4/5), 457–477. doi:10.1023/A:1025771327614

Garrett, J. H., Case, M. P., Hall, J. W., Yerramareddy, S., Herman, A., & Sun, R. F. (1993). Engineering applications of neural networks. *Journal of Intelligent Manufacturing, 4*(1), 1–21. doi:10.1007/BF00124977

Hamilton, W. D., Axelrod, R., & Tanese, R. (1990). Sexual reproduction as an adaptation to resist parasites (A review). *Proceedings of the National Academy of Sciences of the United States of America, 87*(9), 3566–3573. doi:10.1073/pnas.87.9.3566

Herrero, J. G., Portas, J. A. B., de Jesús, A. B., López, J. M. M., de Miguel Vela, G., & Corredera, J. R. C. (2003). Application of evolution strategies to the design of tracking filters with a large number of specifications. *EURASIP Journal on Applied Signal Processing*, (8), 766–779. doi:10.1155/S1110865703302057

Hibbert, E. G., & Dalby, P. A. (2005). Directed evolution strategies for improved enzymatic performance. *Microbial Cell Factories, 4*, 29. doi:10.1186/1475-2859-4-29

Holland, J. H. (1973). Genetic algorithms and the optimal allocation of the trials. *SIAM Journal on Computing, 2*, 88–105. doi:10.1137/0202009

Holland, J. H. (1992a). *Adaptation in natural and artificial systems: An introductory analysis with applications to biology, control, and artificial intelligence*. The MIT Press. Holland, J. H. (1992b). Genetic algorithms. *Scientific American, 278*, 66–72.

Hopfield, J. J. (1982). Neural networks and physical systems with emergent collective computational abilities. *Proceedings of the National Academy of Sciences of the United States of America, 79*(8), 2554–2558. doi:10.1073/pnas.79.8.2554

Hu, X., Eberhart, R. C., & Shi, Y. (2003). Engineering optimization with particle swarm. In *Proceedings of the IEEE Swarm Intelligence Symposium* (pp. 53-57). Piscataway, NJ: IEEE Press.

Huang, F. Y., Li, R. J., Liu, H. X., & Li, R. (2006). A modified particle swarm algorithm combined with fuzzy neural network with application to financial risk early warning. In *Proceedings of the IEEE Asia-Pacific Conference on Services Computing* (pp. 168-173). Washington, DC: IEEE Computer Society.

Hutchison, W. R., & Stephens, K. R. (1987). The airline marketing tactician (AMT): A commercial application of adaptive networking. In *Proceedings of the 1st IEEE International Conference on Neural Networks* (pp. 753-756). Piscataway, NJ: IEEE Press.

Ishibuchi, H., Yoshida, T., & Murata, T. (2003). Balance between genetic search and local search in memetic algorithms for multi-objective permutation flow shop scheduling. *IEEE Transactions on Evolutionary Computation, 7*(2), 204–223. doi:10.1109/TEVC.2003.810752

Joshi, R., & Sanderson, A. C. (1999). Minimal representation multisensor fusion using differential evolution. *IEEE Transactions on Systems, Man and Cybernetics . Part A, 29*(1), 63–76.

Kadrovach, B. A., & Lamont, G. (2002). A particle swarm model for swarm-based networked sensor systems. In *Proceedings of the ACM Symposium on Applied Computing* (pp. 918-924). New York: ACM Press.

Kajitani, I., Murakawa, M., Nishikawa, D., Yokoi, H., Kajihara, N., Iwata, M., et al. (1999). An evolvable hardware chip for prosthetic hand controller. In *Proceedings of the 7th International Conference on Microelectronics for Neural, Fuzzy and Bio-inspired Systems* (pp. 179-186). Washington, DC: IEEE Computer Society.

Kari, L., & Rozenberg, G. (2008). The many facets of natural computing. *Communications of the ACM, 51*(10), 72–83. doi:10.1145/1400181.1400200

Karr, C. L., & Freeman, L. M. (1998). *Industrial applications of genetic algorithms*. CRC Press.

Kaye, P., Laflamme, R., & Mosca, M. (2007). *An introduction to quantum computing*. Oxford University Press.

Kennedy, J., & Eberhart, R. C. (1995). Particle swarm optimization. In *Proceedings of IEEE International Conference on Neural Networks* (pp. 1942-1948). Piscataway, NJ: IEEE Press.

KHosraviani. B., Levitt, R. E., & Koza, J. R. (2004). *Organization design optimization using genetic programming*. Late Breaking Papers at the 2004 Genetic and Evolutionary Computation, Seattle, Washington, USA.

Klockgether, J., & Schwefel, H. P. (1970). Two-phase nozzle and hollow core jet experiments. In D. G. Elliott (Ed.), *Proceedings of the 11th Symposium on Engineering Aspects of Magnetohydrodynamics* (pp. 141-148). Pasadena, CA: California Institute of Technology.

Koza, J. R. (1992). *Genetic programming: On the programming of computers by means of natural selection*. The MIT Press.

Koza, J. R. (1994). *Genetic programming II*. The MIT Press.

Krasnogor, N. (2002). *Studies in the theory and design space of memetic algorithms*. Doctoral thesis, University of West England, UK.

Krasnogor, N. (2004). Towards robust memetic algorithms. In W. E. Hart, N. Krasnogor & J. E. Smith (Eds.), *Recent advances in memetic algorithms* (pp. 185-207). Studies in Fuzziness and Soft Computing 166, Berlin: Springer Verlag.

Krasnogor, N., Blackburne, B., Burke, E., & Hirst, J. (2002). Multimeme algorithms for protein structure prediction. In J. J. M. Guervós *et al.* (Eds.), *Parallel problem solving from nature – PPSN VII LNCS 2439* (pp. 769-778). Berlin: Springer Verlag.

Krishna, A., Narayanan, A., & Keedwell, E. C. (2005). Neural networks and temporal gene expression data. In F. Rothlauf et al. (Eds.), *Applications on evolutionary computing,* (LNCS 3449, pp. 64-73). Berlin: Springer Verlag.

Krivenko, S., & Burtsev, M. (2007). Simulation of the evolution of aging: Effects of aggression and kin-recognition. In F. A. e Costa et al. (Eds.), *Advances in artificial life*. (LNCS 4648, pp. 84-92) Berlin: Springer Verlag.

Krohling, R. A., Knidel, H., & Shi, Y. (2002). Solving numerical equations of hydraulic problems using particle swarm optimization.In *Proceedings of the IEEE Congress on Evolutionary Computation* (pp. 1688-1690). Washington, DC: IEEE Computer Society.

Lai, L. L., & Ma, J. T. (1997). Application of evolutionary programming to reactive power planning – Comparison with nonlinear programming approach. *IEEE Transactions on Power Systems, 12*(1), 198–206. doi:10.1109/59.574940

Lan, N., Feng, H. Q., & Crago, P. E. (1994). Neural network generation of muscle stimulation patterns for control of arm movements. *IEEE Transactions on Rehabilitation Engineering, 2*(4), 213–224. doi:10.1109/86.340877

Langdon, W. B., & Buxton, B. F. (2003). *The application of genetic programming for drug discovery in the pharmaceutical industry*. (Final Report of EPSRC project GR/S03546/01 with GlaxoSmith-Kline). UK: University College London.

Langdon, W. B., & Poli, R. (2001). *Foundations of genetic programming*. Springer Verlag.

Liao, C. J., Tseng, C. T., & Luarn, P. (2007). A discrete version of particle swarm optimization for flowshop scheduling problems. *Computers & Operations Research, 34*(10), 3099–3111. doi:10.1016/j.cor.2005.11.017

Lim, M. H., Wuncsh, D., & Ho, K. W. (2000). An evolutionary programming methodology for portfolio selection. In *Proceedings of the IEEE/IAFE/INFORMS Conference on Computational Intelligence for Financial Engineering* (pp. 42-46), New York, USA.

Liu, B., Wang, L., & Jin, J. H. (2007). An effective PSO-based memetic algorithm for flow shop scheduling. *IEEE Transactions on Systems, Man and Cybernetics . Part B, 37*(1), 18–27.

Liu, J., & Lampinen, J. (2005). A fuzzy adaptive differential evolution algorithm. *Soft Computing – A Fusion of Foundations . Methodologies and Applications, 9,* 448–462.

Lohn, J. D., Hornby, G. S., & Linden, D. S. (2005). Evolution, re-evolution, and prototype of an X-band antenna for NASA's space technology 5 mission. In J. M. Moreno, J. Madrenas & J. Cosp (Eds.), *Evolvable systems: From biology to hardware*. (LNCS 3637, pp. 205-214). Berlin: Springer Verlag.

Lopes, H. S., & Perretto, M. (2008). An ant colony system for large-scale phylogenetic tree reconstruction. *Journal of Intelligent and Fuzzy Systems, 18*(6), 575–583.

Lozano, M., Herrera, F., Krasnogor, N., & Molina, D. (2004). Real-coded memetic algorithms with crossover hill Climbing. *Evolutionary Computation. Special Issue on Memetic Algorithms*, *12*(3), 273–302.

Luke, S., & Spector, L. (1997). A comparison of crossover and mutation in genetic programming. In J. R. Koza et al. (Eds.), *Genetic programming 1997: Proceedings of the 2nd Annual Conference* (pp. 240-248). San Francisco: Morgan Kaufmann.

Manos, S., Large, M. C. J., & Poladian, L. (2007). Evolutionary design of single-mode microstructured polymer optical fibres using an artificial embryogeny representation. In *Proceedings of the Genetic and Evolutionary Computation Conference* (pp. 2549-2556). New York: ACM Press.

Marinakis, Y., & Dounias, G. (2008). Nature inspired intelligence in medicine: Ant colony optimization for Pap-smear diagnosis. *International Journal of Artificial Intelligence Tools*, *17*(2), 279–301. doi:10.1142/S0218213008003893

Marinakis, Y., Marinaki, M., & Zopounidis, C. (2008). Application of ant colony optimization to credit risk assessment. *New Mathematics and Natural Computation*, *4*(1), 107–122. doi:10.1142/S1793005708000957

McCulloch, W., & Pitts, W. (1943). A logical calculus of the ideas immanent in nervous activity. *Bulletin of Mathematical Biology*, *5*(4), 115–133.

Merz, P. (2003). Analysis of gene expression profiles: An application of memetic algorithms to the minimum sum-of-squares clustering problem. *Bio Systems*, *72*(1-2), 99–109. doi:10.1016/S0303-2647(03)00137-0

Michalewicz, Z., & Schmidt, M. (2007). Parameter control in practice. In F. G. Lobo, C. F. Lima & Z. Michalewicz (Eds.), Parameter setting in evolutionary algorithms). *Studies in Computational Intelligence 54,* 277-294. Berlin: Springer Verlag.

Moscato, P., & Norman, M. (1989). *A competitive-cooperative approach to complex combinatorial search.* (Technical Report C3P-790). Pasadena, CA: California Institute of Technology.

Nenortaite, J., & Simutis, R. (2005). Adapting particle swarm optimization to stock markets. In *Proceedings of the 5th International Conference on Intelligent Systems Design and Applications* (pp. 520-525). Washington, DC: IEEE Computer Society.

Neri, F., Toivanen, J., Cascella, G. L., & Ong, Y. S. (2007). An adaptive multimeme algorithm for designing HIV multidrug therapies. *IEEE/ACM Transactions on Computational Biology and Bioinformatics*, *4*(2), 264–278. doi:10.1109/TCBB.2007.070202

Neri, F., Toivanen, J., & Mäkinen, R. A. E. (2007). An adaptive evolutionary algorithm with intelligent mutation local searchers for designing multidrug therapies for HIV. *Applied Intelligence*, *27*(3), 219–235. doi:10.1007/s10489-007-0069-8

Oczkowski, W. J., & Barreca, S. (1997). Neural network modeling accurately predicts the functional outcome of stroke survivors with moderate disabilities. *Archives of Physical Medicine and Rehabilitation*, *78*(4), 340–345. doi:10.1016/S0003-9993(97)90222-7

Omran, M., Salman, A., & Engelbrecht, A. (2002). Image classification using particle swarm optimization. In *Proceedings of the 4th Asia-Pacific Conference on Simulated Evolution and Learning* (pp. 370-374). Singapore: Nanyang Technical University Press.

Ong, Y. S., & Keane, A. J. (2004). Meta-Lamarkian learning in memetic algorithms. *IEEE Transactions on Evolutionary Computation, 8*(2), 99–110. doi:10.1109/TEVC.2003.819944

Ong, Y. S., Lim, M. H., Zhu, N., & Wong, K. W. (2006). Classification of adaptive memetic algorithms: A comparative study. *IEEE Transactions on Systems, Man and Cybernetics . Part B, 36*(1), 141–152.

Pan, Q. K., Tasgetiren, M. F., & Liang, Y. C. (2008). A discrete particle swarm optimization algorithm for the no-wait flowshop scheduling problem. *Computers & Operations Research, 35*(9), 2807–2839. doi:10.1016/j.cor.2006.12.030

Parsopoulos, K., & Vrahatis, M. (2002). Recent approaches to global optimization problems through particle swarm optimization. *Natural Computing, 1*(2/3), 235–306. doi:10.1023/A:1016568309421

Poli, R., Kennedy, J., & Blackwell, T. (2007). Particle swarm optimization: An overview. *Swarm Intelligence, 1*(1), 33–57. doi:10.1007/s11721-007-0002-0

Price, K. V., Storn, R., & Lampinen, J. (2005). *Differential evolution: A practical approach to global optimization.* Springer Verlag.

Qin, A. K., & Suganathan, P. N. (2005). Self-adaptive differential evolution algorithm for numerical optimization. In *Proceedings of the IEEE Congress on Evolutionary Computation* (pp. 1785-1791). Piscataway, NJ: IEEE Press.

Rechenberg, I. (1973). *Evolutionstrategie: Optimierung Technisher Systeme nach prinzipien des Biologischen Evolution.* Fromman-Hozlboog Verlag.

Robbins, K. R., Zhang, W., Bertrand, J. K., & Rekaya, R. (2007). The ant colony algorithm for feature selection in high-dimension gene expression data for disease classification. *Mathematical Medicine and Biology: A Journal of the IMA, 24*(4), 413-426.

Robinson, J., & Rahmat-Samii, Y. (2004). Particle swarm optimization in electromagnetics. *IEEE Transactions on Antennas and Propagation, 52*(2), 397–407. doi:10.1109/TAP.2004.823969

Romero, J., & Machado, P. (Eds.). (2008). *The art of artificial evolution: A handbook on evolutionary art and music.* Natural Computing Series, Springer Verlag. Salerno, J. (1997). Using the particle swarm optimization technique to train a recurrent neural model. In *Proceedings of the 9th IEEE International Conference on Tools with Artificial Intelligence* (pp. 45-49). Washington, DC: IEEE Computer Society.

Schmidhuber, J. (2002). The speed prior: A new simplicity measure yielding near-optimal computable predictions. In J. Kivinen & R. H. Sloan (Eds.), *Proceedings of the 15th Annual Conference on Computational Learning Theory* (LNAI 2375, pp. 123-127). Berlin: Springer Verlag.

Schopf, J. W., Kudryavtsev, A. B., Agresti, D. G., Wdowiak, T. J., & Czaja, A. D. (2002). Laser-Raman imagery of Earth's earliest fossils. *Nature, 416*, 73–76. doi:10.1038/416073a

Schwefel, H. (1981). *Numerical optimization of computer models.* John Wiley & Sons, Inc.

Shi, L., & Xu, G. (2001). Self-adaptive evolutionary programming and its application to multi-objective optimal operation of power systems. *Electric Power Systems Research, 57*(3), 181–187. doi:10.1016/S0378-7796(01)00086-4

Shyu, S. J., & Tsai, C. Y. (2009). Finding the longest common subsequence for multiple biological sequences by ant colony optimization. *Computers & Operations Research, 36*(1), 73–91. doi:10.1016/j. cor.2007.07.006

Smith, J. (2004). The co-evolution of memetic algorithms for protein structure prediction. In W. E. Hart, N. Krasnogor & J. Smith (Eds.), *Recent advances in memetic algorithms* (pp. 105-128). Studies in Fuzziness and Soft Computing 166, Berlin: Springer-Verlag.

Soulié, F. F., & Gallinari, P. (Eds.). (1998). *Industrial applications of neural networks*. World Scientific.

Stockwell, D. R. B., & Peters, D. P. (1999). The GARP modelling system: Problems and solutions to automated spatial prediction. *International Journal of Geographic Information Systems, 13*(2), 143–158. doi:10.1080/136588199241391

Storn, R. (2005). Designing nonstandard filters with differential evolution. *IEEE Signal Processing Magazine, 22*(1), 103–106. doi:10.1109/MSP.2005.1407721

Storn, R., & Price, K. (1995). *Differential evolution – A simple and efficient adaptive scheme for global optimization over continuous spaces*. (Technical Report TR-095-012). Berkeley, CA: International Computer Science Institute.

Storn, R., & Price, K. (1997). Differential evolution of simple and efficient heuristic for global optimization over continuous spaces. *Journal of Global Optimization, 11*, 341–359. doi:10.1023/A:1008202821328

Stützle, T., & Hoos, H. H. (2000). MAX – MIN ant system. *Future Generation Computer Systems, 16*(8), 889–914. doi:10.1016/S0167-739X(00)00043-1

Tang, M., & Yao, X. (2007). A memetic algorithm for VLSI floor planning. *IEEE Transactions on Systems, Man and Cybernetics . Part B, 37*(1), 62–69.

Tenneti, B., & Allada, V. (2008). Robust supplier set selection for changing product architectures. *International Journal of Computer Applications in Technology, 31*(3/4), 197–214. doi:10.1504/IJCAT.2008.018157

Thierauf, G., & Cai, J. (2000). Evolution strategies - Parallelisation and application in engineering optimization. In B. H. V. Topping (Ed.), *Parallel and distributed processing for computational mechanics: Systems and tools* (pp. 329-349). Edinburgh, UK: Civil-Comp Press.

Thomson (Lord Kelvin), W. (1871). Inaugural address to the British Association Edinburgh. *Nature, 4*, 262.

Tirronen, V., Neri, F., Kärkkäinen, T., Majava, K., & Rossi, T. (2008). An enhanced memetic differential evolution in filter design for defect detection in paper production. *Evolutionary Computation, 16*(4), 529–555. doi:10.1162/evco.2008.16.4.529

Tse, S.-M., Liang, Y., Leung, K.-S., Lee, K.-H., & Mok, T.-K. (2007). A memetic algorithm for multiple-drug cancer chemotherapy schedule optimization. *IEEE Transactions on Systems, Man, and Cybernetics . Part B, 37*(1), 84–91.

Turner, C. J., Tiwari, A., & Mehnen, J. (2008). A genetic programming approach to business process mining. In *Proceedings of the Genetic and Evolutionary Computation Conference* (pp. 1307-1314). New York: ACM Press.

Wilson, G., & Heywood, M. I. (2007). Foundations for an intelligent business logic engine using genetic programming and ruleML-based services. *International Journal of Business Process Integration and Management, 2*(4), 282–291. doi:10.1504/IJBPIM.2007.017753

Wolpert, D., & Macready, W. (1997). No free lunch theorems for optimization. *IEEE Transactions on Evolutionary Computation, 1*(1), 67–82. doi:10.1109/4235.585893

Worzel, W. P., Yu, J., Almal, A. A., & Chinnaiyan, A. M. (2009). Applications of genetic programming in cancer research. *The International Journal of Biochemistry & Cell Biology, 41*(2), 405–413. doi:10.1016/j.biocel.2008.09.025

Wu, Y., Giger, M. L., Doi, K., Vyborny, C. J., Schmidt, R. A., & Metz, C. E. (1993). Artificial neural networks in mammography: Application to decision making in the diagnosis of breast cancer. *Radiology, 187*, 81–87.

Xu, F. S., & Chen, W. (2006). Stochastic portfolio selection based on velocity limited particle swarm optimization. In *Proceedings of the 6th World Congress on Intelligent Control and Automation* (pp. 3599-3603), Dalian, China.

Yoshida, H., Kawata, K., Fukuyama, Y., Takayama, S., & Nakanishi, Y. (2000). A particle swarm optimization for reactive power and voltage control considering voltage security assessment. *IEEE Transactions on Power Systems, 15*(4), 1232–1239. doi:10.1109/59.898095

Yu, L., Lai, K. K., & Wang, S. Y. (2008). An evolutionary programming based knowledge ensemble model for business risk identification. In Bhanu Prasad (Ed.), *Soft computing applications in business* (pp. 57-72). Studies in Fuzziness and Soft Computing 230, Berlin: Springer Verlag.

Yuan, X. H., Yuan, Y. B., Wang, C., & Zhang, X. P. (2005). An improved PSO approach for profit-based unit commitment in electricity market. In *Proceedings of the IEEE/PES Transmission and Distribution Conference and Exhibition: Asia and Pacific* (pp. 1-4), Dalian, China.

Yuan, X. J., Situ, N., & Zouridakis, G. (2008). Automatic segmentation of skin lesion images using evolution strategies. *Biomedical Signal Processing and Control, 3*(3), 220–228. doi:10.1016/j.bspc.2008.02.003

ENDNOTE

[1]   deoxyribonucleic acid

Section 2
Nature-Inspired Solutions in Business

Chapter 2
An Application of Genetic Programming to Forecasting Foreign Exchange Rates

Muneer Buckley
University of Adelaide, Australia

Zbigniew Michalewicz
University of Adelaide, Australia
Institute of Computer Science, Polish Academy of Sciences & Polish-Japanese Institute of Information Technology, Poland

Ralf Zurbruegg
University of Adelaide, Australia

ABSTRACT

There is a great need for accurate predictions of foreign exchange rates. Many industries participate in foreign exchange scenarios with little idea where the exchange rate is moving, and what the optimum decision to make at any given time is. Although current economic models do exist for this purpose, improvements could be made in both their flexibility and adaptability. This provides much room for models that do not suffer from such constraints. This chapter proposes the use of a genetic program (GP) to predict future foreign exchange rates. The GP is an extension of the DyFor GP tailored for forecasting in dynamic environments. The GP is tested on the Australian / US (AUD/USD) exchange rate and compared against a basic economic model. The results show that the system has potential in forecasting long term values, and may do so better than established models. Further improvements are also suggested.

DOI: 10.4018/978-1-60566-705-8.ch002

INTRODUCTION

There is a great need in many industries for accurate future foreign exchange rate prediction. The uses of such a system are varied, from assisting international corporations dealing with international contracts to assisting currency speculators in determining the most profitable trading decisions. The process of predicting future foreign exchange rates is known as forward rate prediction. Forward rate prediction is an interesting problem that has seen research in many disciplines, including economics, mathematics and computer science (Álvarez-Díaz & Álvarez, 2005; Brabazon & O'Neill, 2004; Neely & Weller, 2003).

There are a number of economic models used to forecast forward rates, the majority of which do not adequately model the nonlinear nature of the market, and more importantly, do not dynamically adapt to changing market conditions. This has led to a large number of studies completed to determine the aptitude of computing based heuristic models, such as neural networks (NNs) and evolutionary algorithms (EAs), among others (Andreou, Georgopoulos, & Likothanasssis, 2002; Jan & Dirk, 1999).

The purpose of this chapter is to further explore the potential of genetic programming (GP), a subclass of EAs, at providing a more robust and adaptive alternative for predicting forward rates.

EAs are based on natural processes such as continuous evolution of a population using the Darwinian principle of survival of the fittest and genetic operators such as recombination (crossover) and mutation. EAs are adept solvers for a wide spectrum of problems, and are capable of overcoming problems such as escaping from local optima, searching through large and complex search spaces and adapting quickly to changing environmental conditions (Koza, 1993). GP is a sub-field of EAs that represents individuals as program trees. It is most adequate in environments where the space of potential solutions is a program or function (Koza, 1993). This makes

GP a good candidate for creating a robust forward rate prediction system.

In this chapter a system that uses GP for predicting forward rates is proposed and an implementation is developed and analysed. The goals of the chapter are:

- To assess the feasibility of defeating the Unbiased Interest rate Parity (UIP) by utilising limited information.
- To examine the effects of additional operators added to the system.
- To record the knowledge of the market derived by the GP system for use in other systems.

This chapter is organised in the following manner: The background section provides a brief overview of the fields of foreign exchange markets and forward rates and an introduction to EAs and GP. Next, we review some related work to both fields, followed by a detailed explanation of the objectives of the chapter. This is followed by a detailed description of the model used in this chapter and the methodology taken. The results section details the findings of the model along with its limitations. The chapter then concludes with a number of possible extensions as well as future work foreseen for this model is detailed.

BACKGROUND

This section serves as a basic introduction to forward rates and EAs, as an understanding of these is necessary for the reading of this chapter.

A forward rate is a part of a financial tool used to lower the risk associated with foreign exchange transactions. It is used in a forward contract between two parties in which they specify a date at which to exchange a specified amount of one currency into another using a specified rate, regardless of the actual exchange rate at that time. The rate that they agree to exchange at is the forward rate.

The forward rate of a currency pair is calculated using the UIP equation:

$$F_{(t,T)} = S_t \frac{(1+r_t)^T}{(1+p_t)^T} \quad (1)$$

where t is the current period, T is the period to be forecast (for example 1 week, 1 month, etc), F is the forward rate at time t for the period T, S is spot rate at time t and r and p are the domestic and foreign interest rates at time t respectively.

Equation 1 is considered according to economic rationale to be the best unbiased predictor of the future foreign exchange rate. The basis underlying this is that the future spot rate is determined primarily by the relationship between the interest rates of domestic and foreign countries. Any deviation away from this was put down to incalculable factors such as investors' expectations or deviations from the expected risk premiums (McCallum, 1994).

This is meant to explain the difference between exchange rates internationally. Without a changing spot rate, when there was a difference between interest rates, people would invest in those countries and currencies with higher interest rates to take advantage of the higher risk free interest rate. Therefore, over time, the exchange rate between the two countries changes to balance out the differences between the different interest rates. This is known as the "purchasing power parity theorem" (Anthony, 1989, p. 213).

Interest rates can be found for several time horizons, including one week, one month, three months and one year among others. When taken individually, they indicate the market rate for that term, but when viewed together, they provide valuable information as to the general direction the market believes interest rates and the economy in general are moving. This picture that emerges is known as the term structure and this information is useful to systems that are able to utilise it (Clarida & Taylor, 1997).

This chapter uses the GP approach, utilising methods similar to those found in Koza (1993), Neely & Weller (2003), and Wagner, Michalewicz, Khouja, & McGregor (2007). GPs are modern heuristic methods developed by Koza in 1992 as an extension of John Holland's original genetic algorithm (Koza, 1993). Koza describes the GP procedure as:

In Genetic Programming, populations of hundreds or thousands of computer programs are genetically bred. This breeding is done using the Darwinian principle of survival and reproduction of the fittest along with a genetic recombination (crossover) operation appropriate for mating computer programs. (Koza, 1993, p. 73)

As mentioned above, a genetic program defines individuals as computer programs that are described using terminal (leaf) and internal (branch) nodes that are defined in strict tree structures. GPs function best in environments where the space of potential solutions can be represented as a program tree or function (Koza, 1993). An example of a typical GP structure can be found in Figure 1. This tree evaluates to the equation *((Spot/(Foreign+Domestic))*log(Spot))*. As can be seen, evaluation order is determined by the structure of the tree.

Figure 1. An example GP individual

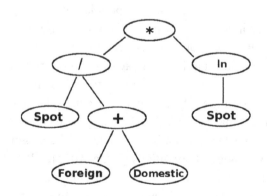

Figure 2. An example of GP crossover using identical parents. Figure from http://www.geneticprogramming.com

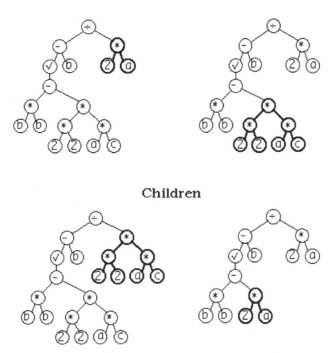

Children

Genetic programs are a subclass of the broader field of EAs. This field is characterised by its use of Darwin's principle of evolution through survival of the fittest. In it, a population of candidate solutions, or individuals, is created, assessed and assigned a "fitness". These individuals are then selected to participate in the breeding of the next generation, where each individual's probability of selection is biased by its fitness. Each new generation is then constructed using crossover and mutation operators. This process repeats for some period of time and the end result are solutions that are optimal or near optimal for the problem being solved.

The GP crossover operator differs significantly from that used in other EA's. The operator is similar in that random locations are chosen from each of the parents participating in the crossover, which the operator uses to swap the subtrees located at each of the selected locations. The GP crossover operator differs in that it can be used with two identical parents to produce a completely new offspring. An example of such a crossover can be found in Figure 2. The GP mutation operator will be discussed at greater length in the following sections.

In general modern heuristic methods have been found to be capable of overcoming many of the problems inherent in comparable economic models such as little to no adaptation and the assumption of a linear underlying process. They are also capable of being used in a wide variety of environments and are able to overcome local optima and find optimal or near optimal solutions in extremely large search spaces (Michalewicz & Fogel, 2004).

However, they are used to construct a model based on past data that they assume to be representative of the current environment, but this does not imply that the resulting model is adequate outside of the environment it is developed in.

RELATED WORK

This section details research completed in this area in both economics and computer science.

Modern economic methods of forecasting foreign exchange rates. Economists have progressed beyond using the UIP equation (Equation 1) as the sole method of forecasting foreign exchange rates and have developed more sophisticated models that use additional information, such as the term structure of interest rates and forward rates, to forecast to a higher degree of accuracy than the UIP equation (Brabazon & O'Neill, 2004; Clarida, Sarno, Taylor, & Valente, 2003; Clarida & Taylor, 1997).

A successful attempt to derive more useful information from the term structure of forward rates was outlined in Clarida & Taylor (1997) and developed further in Clarida et al. (2003). The system utilised in Clarida & Taylor (1997) is a vector error correction model (VECM). This is an extension of the more general vector auto-regression (VAR).

The VAR model is itself an extension of the basic auto-regression (AR) model. AR models define the change in a variable as a linear function of only their past values. A p-th order AR is one in which the last p values are used in the regression and is of the form:

$$y_t = c + \phi_1 y_{t-1} + \phi_2 y_{t-2} + \phi_3 y_{t-3} + \cdots + \phi_p y_{t-p} + e_t$$

A VAR extends the AR model to use vectors for the variables, with each item in each vector being the value of a specific time series, allowing the system to optimise for several time series simultaneously.

In Clarida et al. (2003), they developed the system further to use a Markov switching model. This model works by first passing over the historical data and determining the number and location of changes of trends in the data. It then determines the appropriate weights to use in the VECM to best approximate that trend. The system then linearly switches between the weights according to which model the current data best fits.

Applications of modern heuristic methods to calculating forward rates. A heuristic method is one which involves undertaking a search to find one or more solutions to the problem. Due to their ability to search through large and complex spaces, modern heuristic methods have been extensively researched in their ability to forecast foreign exchange rates.

In Andreou et al. (2002), they develop a neural network evolved by a genetic algorithm to forecast foreign exchange rates. They compare their model against auto-regressive and moving average models as well as naïve measures such as the current value. They found that their model was able to significantly generate more accurate forecasts than all of the competing models. They also found little difference in the behaviour of the model across different currencies due to its ability to adapt to the new environments (Andreou et al., 2002).

Álvarez-Díaz & Álvarez (2005) develop a model that utilises both a neural network and GP to forecast exchange rates. They then use a genetic fusion procedure to combine the two forecasts to generate forecasts of greater accuracy (Álvarez-Díaz & Álvarez, 2005). This hybrid model is not compared against any economic models. Instead the results are used to determine the statistical significance of the results as compared to a naïve predictor. The authors note that in some cases increasing the complexity of the system by using the genetic fusion process does not generate more accurate forecasts. The results do provide statistical evidence against the assumption that exchange rates follow a random walk process, and therefore the potential exists for accurate forecasts (Álvarez-Díaz & Álvarez, 2005).

The work completed by Neely and Weller (2003) shares some similarities to the objectives of this report. They attempted to construct trading rules for trading in the intra-day foreign exchange market using a relatively standard GP.

Their system was capable of consistently attaining positive returns, but there was very little emphasis on their models performance when compared to an econometric model that would be used for the same purposes.

The authors compare the model against a linear forecasting model, which is a simple autoregressive model. The authors find that when transaction costs are factored in, neither the GP nor the linear forecasting model achieves significant out-of-sample returns. However, they do find that the GP model discovers stable predictable components in the intra-day market, though these findings are not able to produce positive returns after taking into account transactions costs. Their findings are thus consistent with the efficient markets hypothesis (Neely & Weller, 2003).

The addition of higher order trigonometric functions to GP was discussed in (Schwaerzel & Bylander (2006). The authors compare the predictive accuracy of a standard GP, a GP with access to trigonometric functions which included sin, cos, tan, log and exp, and a basic ARMA (Auto-Regressive Moving Average) financial model. Their results indicate that the more complex functions do increase the accuracy of the model, though statistical significance measures are not given.

The dynamic forecasting (DyFor) GP system developed by Wagner et al. (2007) has many novel features which allowed it to forecast the US GDP and inflation with greater accuracy than a number of financial models. Primary among these features is the concept of a dynamic, adaptive time window. The DyFor model attempts to overcome the limitation inherent in many previous GP systems that assume a relatively static environment, through dynamically adapting to changes in the environment. The dynamic time window allows the system to determine when the underlying data generation process of the series being analysed is changing, and therefore can adapt itself to the changing conditions. This is an important ability

that the econometric community has attempted to attain through systems such as the Markov regime switching system. However, a strong limitation of the Markov switching system is that it must be given the number of data generating "regimes" which it then uses when running over the data. This introduces a large possibility of human error in determining the number of regimes the series is generated by. Further, the model is linearly switched between regimes. The DyFor system has no such limitation. The system utilises two time windows of different sizes to train two separate populations for some number of generations over separate data sets, and a separate verification period to verify the solutions developed. This process is referred to as a dynamic generation. If the smaller of the two time windows performs better, then the windows are re-evaluated to be smaller, otherwise they are re-evaluated to be larger. A number of successive window shrinkings likely occurs when the underlying data generation process has changed. This process is defined by Wagner et al. as:

The DyFor GP uses predictive accuracy to adapt the size of its analysis window automatically. When the underlying process is stable (i.e., the analysis window is contained inside a single segment), the windowsize (sic) is likely to expand. When the underlying process shifts (i.e., the analysis window spans more than one segment), the windowsize (sic) is likely to contract. (Wagner et al., 2007, p. 438)

The reason such a system is useful is that, contrary to popular thought, having access to longer periods of data does not necessarily signify that the resulting model will achieve more accurate forecasts than a model based upon less data.

An example of the dynamic time window can be found in Figure 3. This example shows the two window sizes (win1 and win2) expanding as they move over a contiguous segment of data, then shrinking as they begin to pass over into a new segment of data, after which they begin to grow once more.

Using such a process the system dynamically learns the number of regimes in the history of the data. The system automatically uses this information to create dynamically sized data windows to train the populations, ensuring that the system is trained on data from the most current regime. The system then adds another feature to take advantage of the knowledge that the underlying regime is changing. If the system passes through α (where α is a predetermined integer) or more consecutive stages of growth, the system saves several of the top individuals in the better population into a third population comprised of other individuals selected in this manner, since it assumes that the populations are being trained on a trend. In doing so it creates a population of individuals that are adapted to different environments.

When the system passes through α stages of window shortening, it assumes that the regime is changing, and begins to introduce a random amount of the saved individuals, in the hope that one of the individuals was developed in a similar regime and will thus perform well in this regime as well. This allows the system to gain an advantage in more quickly adapting to the new environment. This process provides the benefits of the Markov switching econometric model, but is more flexible in that it dynamically determines the number of regimes and dynamically adapts the population to thrive in this new environment.

The DyFor GP model also proposes a novel technique that attempts to overcome the problem of individual size inherent in GP. Most GP models limit the maximum size of individuals to prevent them from bloating to very large sizes (Chidambaran, 2003). In doing so however, they are making the assumption that the problem can be solved with a solution of less than the maximum size, which may not be correct. The DyFor GP model does not impose a maximum size for an individual, but instead imposes a maximum node count for the population. This ensures that the

evaluation never becomes too slow, but allows for large individuals, albeit a small number of them (Wagner et al., 2007).

Wagner et al. realise that by removing the maximum size for an individual, the population will tend towards a small number of very large individuals (Wagner et al., 2007). They overcome this problem by generating new populations after each dynamic generation.

The new populations are generated as a combination of:

- Random subtrees from the previous population
- New randomly constructed individuals
- If the process is undergoing a regime change, random subtrees from the saved best population

In this way, diversity and efficiency are maintained in a novel manner.

Utilising these methods, the DyFor GP is able to predict to some degree of accuracy the long term movements in the U.S. gross domestic product (GDP). The benefit of the DyFor GP over economic models is difficult to determine since it is compared against a linear regression model, one of the simpler economic prediction systems. The results show, however, that the DyFor GP significantly outperforms the linear regression model and the standard GP at forecasting economic time series'.

OBJECTIVE

The primary objective of the chapter is to attempt to surpass the predictive ability of the Unbiased Interest rate Parity (UIP) equation (Equation (1)) using only the information contained in the equation itself, which is the spot rate, s_t, and the foreign and domestic interest rates, f_t & d_t respectively, at time t. This is considered to be infeasible according to economic rationale since the UIP equation

Figure 3. An example of the dynamic time window extension to GP developed by Wagner et al.; Figure taken from Wagner et al. (2007)

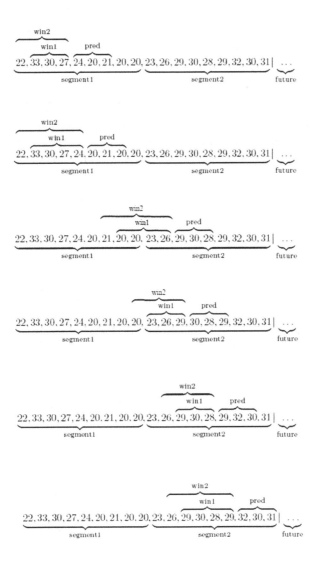

is theoretically the best unbiased indicator under the efficient markets hypothesis. It is not asinine to question why this is considered unachievable, given that the GP population is being seeded with the UIP equation. It could be that the equation is an inaccurate predictor of the future spot rate, but the best that can be achieved with the data provided. Possibly, therefore, any attempts to

defeat it using the same data set are very unlikely to succeed since they are basing themselves on a poor predictor and data to begin with. It is anticipated that through this systems increased flexibility and adaptability, it will be capable of defeating the UIP using same data.

As such, the objective of this chapter is an investigation into the general application of the

DyFor GP methodology developed in Wagner et al. (2007) to a new problem domain, that of foreign exchange rate forecasting.

Secondary to this is an examination of the impact of different sets of operators used in the DyFor GP in the task of forecasting. Some of these operators are unique, while the majority have been applied elsewhere. For the more sophisticated operators, the results will be analysed against the findings of past research that utilised the same operators. The novel operators will be discussed at greater length in the following section.

Another objective that is complementary to the primary objectives that will be explored is that the system has the potential to discover economically useful information during each stage of the experiments. For example, the system can find while in the process of its run that the UIP equation can be consistently defeated during certain recurring times (trends) through an equation it discovers. Such discoveries are important from an economic perspective since they highlight unknown relationships among the variables in the system, and may be a source of further research in the future.

APPROACH

The system will be run using the operators found in Table 1 and variables found in Table 2 for the

initial phase of the objective. The roles of each of these operators are straightforward. These operators comprise the typical set used in most GP implementations (Koza, 1993; Wang, 2000; Whitley, Richards, Beveridge, & da Motta Salles Barreto, 2006). The parameter γ is the future period the system is attempting to forecast, which can be 1, 4 or 12 weeks. The table also contains some additional operators that will be added to the system on separate runs to determine whether the addition of higher order trigonometric functions allows the system to create more accurate forecasts, which was the found in Schwaerzel & Bylander (2006). These operators can be found in Table 1 under the category 1+.

The system will be extended to have access to the additional operators in the assumption that doing so will allow the GP to derive more precise forecasting equations, but with the caveat that increasing operators in the system also decreases the systems predictive capabilities, as discussed below. These additional parameters therefore will only increase the predictive power of the system if they provide an integral role that was unfulfilled. If not, it is likely that their addition will decrease the systems forecasting capability.

The system will then be extended with the addition of a number of new operators given in Table 3 that extends the list already used for the previous experiments. These new operators are

Table 1. List of operators for the initial phase and extension

Category	Name	# Operands	Description
1	Add	2	Basic addition operator
1	Subtract	2	Basic subtraction operator
1	Multiply	2	Basic multiplication operator
1	Divide	2	Basic division operator
1	Exponential	1	Exponential operator that returns e^x
1	Logarithm	1	Natural logarithm operator $\ln(x)$
1+	Cos	1	Returns the cosine value of the input
1+	Sin	1	Returns the sine value of the input

responsible for giving the system access to past data values and data aggregations. The data aggregation operators pass over a specified number of previous data values and return either the average, maximum or minimum of the data analysed. There is also an operator for returning a lagged data value for use.

The final two variables used are novel variables created to attempt to emulate the success of Clarida et al. through attempting to provide the system with information regarding the term structure of the interest rates used. The variables return the value of the function generated by interpolating the different interest rates using the Newton divided difference interpolation method. An example of this interpolation process can be found in Figure

4. This method generates a function or curve that passes through each of the data points given. The operator takes one input, which it uses as the x value to the NDD function generated. It then returns the y value from the function output, which is the interpolated value of the interest rate for the given week (input).

The addition of more operators however increases the risk of providing the system with redundant data which it must first identify as such and remove before it can forecast successfully. Koza (1993) found that the introduction of redundant nodes decreases the probability of finding the optimum solution, finding that the addition of extraneous variables into his experiments approximately linearly decreased the systems

Table 2. List of variables for the initial phase and extension. The γ variable is the forecast period, and can have the value of 1, 4 or 12 weeks.

Category	Name	Description
1	Spot	The current spot rate
1	Foreign	The current γ week foreign interest rate
1	Domestic	The current γ week domestic interest rate
1	Random	A random number from (0,5]
1	Parity	Returns the value of the UIP model using the current domestic and foreign interest rates and spot rate

Table 3. List of operators for the secondary phase

Category	Name	# Operands	Description
2	Average	1	Returns the average of the last x spot values, where x is the input to the operator
2	Maximum	1	Returns the maximum of the last x spot values, where x is the input to the operator
2	Minimum	1	Returns the minimum of the last x spot values, where x is the input to the operator
2	Lag	1	Returns the spot value x periods previous, where x is the input to the operator
2	Foreign NDD	1	Returns the evaluation $f(x)$ using the function approximation generated by the NDD method of the foreign interest rates, where x is the parameter to the function generated by the NDD approximation
2	Domestic NDD	1	Returns the evaluation $f(x)$ using the function approximation generated by the NDD method of the domestic interest rates, where x is the parameter to the function generated by the NDD approximation

potential to succeed from 100% with 0 extraneous variables to less than 40% with 32 extraneous variables (Koza, 1993, p. 585).

The study undertaken in Koza (1993) also found that the addition of extraneous functions also decreased the systems ability to succeed, from 100% with 0 extraneous functions to less than 50% for any amount of extraneous functions over 7.

As the system will have access to over 11 functions at some point, there is the potential for

the system to become lost if the functions are in fact redundant. It is important to note however that in his experiments Koza ran the system for 50 generations, and the systems were still improving when the generation limit was reached. Since the system proposed in this chapter is run for at least 500 generations per step, the system may be able to derive the correct configuration of functions and variables and exclude the extraneous functions in the additional time given.

If the system is successful in consistently

Figure 4. An example interpolation with increasing data points using the Newton divided difference interpolation method

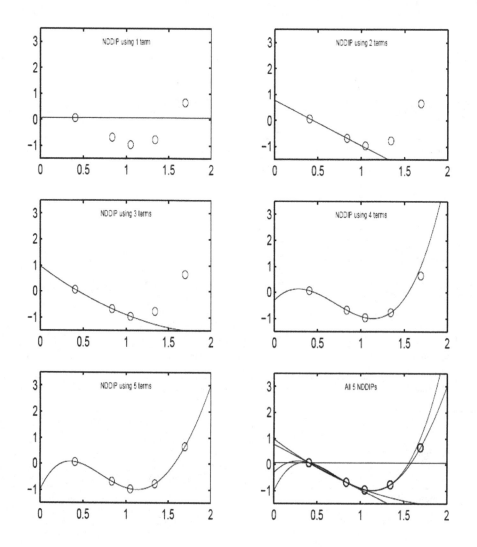

achieving more accurate forecasts, then this is further evidence that the UIP relationship is not the most efficient method of predicting forward rates using a restricted data set. The system is however expected to be able to defeat the UIP since there are many economic models that are capable of doing so, such as the models developed by Clarida et al. (2003) and Clarida & Taylor (1997).

The system assigns each fitness by running each individual over the spot and interest rate data in the specified time window and basing the fitness on a measure given from these predictions. This fitness is then used to determine the individual's likelihood of being selected to take part in the next generation. For this reason, the measure used is of vital importance in determining the overall ability of the system. From previous studies, it can be seen that there are two main measures that have been implemented to determine an individual's fitness for the task of forecasting. These are the mean error and the variance of the error.

The fitness assigned when utilizing the mean error measure is given by the equation:

$$f(i) = \overline{e} = E(|\,pred(i,t) - spot(t+\gamma)\,|) \qquad (2)$$

where $\overline{e}$ denotes the average of the errors, E denotes the expected value or average, $pred(i, t)$ is the prediction of individual i for time t and $spot(t+\gamma)$ is the actual spot rate at time $t+\gamma$, where γ is the forecast period. This is the most commonly used measure due to its simplicity. Although many studies rely solely on mean error to determine predictive ability, studies have shown that in some circumstances, models that rely solely on the mean to derive an individuals fitness perform worse than when used with other measures such as the variance (Wagner et al., 2007).

The variance of a set of data is a measure of its dispersion around its mean and is calculated as:

$$f(i) = Var(pred) = E((pred(i,t) - \overline{e})^2) \qquad (3)$$

where $\overline{e}$ is the average error calculated in equation (2), and the other terms have the same meaning as those defined in the same equation.

Studies completed in Wagner et al. (2007) found that in some circumstances, the variance alone provided a better overall result than the mean alone or the two measures combined. In order to out-predict economic models, the model developed should perform better in both mean error and variance. The methodology adopted in this chapter is to assign a dynamic weight to both measures and allow both to contribute to an individual's fitness as such:

$$f(i) = k * Var(pred) + (1 - k) * \overline{e} \qquad (4)$$

where k is between [0,1]. The system modifies the variable k every dynamic generation according to which measure is the more accurate in the best equation generated. If the best equation has a lower variance than mean error, k is decreased by a small amount (0.05). The opposite occurs if the mean is the lower error measurement. The rationale behind this is that if the best equations generated are those that focus on one of the measurements, then the system should focus on the other measurement to ensure that solutions are optimised for both mean error and variance.

Initialisation. The method of initialising the initial populations is of paramount importance to the final result of the system (Koza, 1993). As such, the initialisation method that was found to be the most effective was the ramped half-and-half method proposed by Koza (1993). The method requires the specification of a maximum depth, which in this case was set to 7. The method then generates an equal number of individuals for the depth range [2, 7]. Therefore 2000/6 = 333 individuals are created with depth 2, the same amount for depth 3, and so on until depth 7 (this is for one population, there are two populations constructed, for the different time windows). The individuals are generated using one of two methods with equal probability: "full" and "grow". Both methods are implemented by randomly selecting a root input node, then recursively randomly selecting input nodes to serve as child nodes until there are no more unfilled branches in the tree.

The full method restricts the set of input nodes to only include internal nodes for all depths up until the maximum depth. Once the maximum depth has been reached, it then restricts the set of selectable input nodes to only include terminal nodes. This ensures that all of the trees generated using this method have every branch ending at the maximum depth. The grow method involves selecting nodes from the set of all nodes, with the exception that when the maximum depth has been reached the selectable set is restricted to only include terminal nodes. This allows for the construction of variable sized and spaced trees where the maximum depth of any branch is set to the maximum depth, though the resulting trees could be any depth up to the maximum depth. The populations also have the option of being "seeded" with an individual that is equivalent to the UIP equation which will be discussed in more depth later.

Operators. The model has been tested with several varieties of operators, the best of which have been included in the system.

In traditional genetic algorithms, mutation plays the important role of modifying individuals to prevent the extinction of genes in the population, and to reintroduce genes that have become extinct. That role is still vital in GP. However, the crossover operator in GP differs so greatly from traditional GA crossover operations that many studies believe that it has the same effect as mutation (Badran & Rockett, 2007; Koza, 1993; Piszcz & Soule, 2006).

Mutation has been a topic of varying importance in GP literature ever since Koza (1993) stated that:

... to the extent that mutation serves the potentially important role of restoring lost diversity in a population for the conventional genetic algorithm,

it is simply not needed in genetic programming. (Koza, 1993, p. 106)

Later works such as Badran & Rockett (2007) and Piszcz & Soule (2006) show that the effectiveness of mutation in GP varies greatly depending upon the context of the problem being solved. Depending upon the mutation operator used, studies have shown that mutation in GP can provide the same results as crossover (Piszcz & Soule, 2006).

For the GP system used in this chapter, three types of mutation are used with the same probability. A summary of them can be found in Table 4 and an example of each mutation can be found in Figure 5.

For the purposes of this chapter, the crossover used is identical to that proposed by Koza (1993). This operator differs from classical GA crossover in that it can even be used with 2 identical individuals to produce entirely new offspring, as discussed previously.

The selection method chosen for this chapter uses the standard tournament selection. Tournament selection involves selecting a number of random individuals from the population and pitting them in a "tournament" against each other. The individual with the highest fitness proceeds to be selected.

The number of individuals selected is user defined and performance varies greatly depending on choice of this number, because if the number is too small, there will not be enough selective pressure to improve the population, and if the number is too large, the opposite occurs (Blickle & Thiele, 1996). A study completed in Blickle & Thiele (1996) found that for GP models with large populations, a tournament size of 7 was found to perform best. Two selection mechanisms were tested: two-tournament and seven-tournament. Other values were not tested due to time constraints and lack of support for other values in the literature. The findings were in support of those found in Blickle & Thiele (1996). Therefore seven-

Table 4. Summary of mutation operations used in the GP system

Name	Description
Terminal	Swaps the selected node with a terminal node and removes any children it previously had
Swap Same	Swaps the selected node with a node of the same type (a node with the same number of operands) leaving any children unchanged
Grow	Destroys the sub-tree located at the selected node and grows a new sub-tree of random size

tournament selection was used in this system.

Many GP implementations have suggested the use of a GP repair function that can be used to remove useless parts of an individual, such as a subtree that always evaluates to zero and repair infeasible individuals such that they become feasible. However, as mentioned in Wagner et al. (2007), allowing for such trees allows the system to preserve important parts of previous individuals that can be used in later generations. These subtrees are referred to as "introns". This provides a secondary, implicit, means of retaining useful individuals many generations later (Wagner et al., 2007). The repair function is also responsible for repairing infeasible individuals. This function is unnecessary for this chapter as the system uses strong typing to prevent infeasible individuals from being constructed.

Another aspect that many GP models consider important is the use of a parsimony measure that prevents population bloat (Badran & Rockett, 2007). However if a maximum individual size is implemented it may prevent the optimal solution from being found as it may be larger than the maximum size. The issue of bloat is dealt with in the manner described in Wagner et al. (2007), where a new population is constructed every dynamic generation from randomly generated individuals and subtrees of members of the previous generation to maintain diversity and population size. This ef-

Figure 5. Examples of the 3 mutation methods used in the chapter

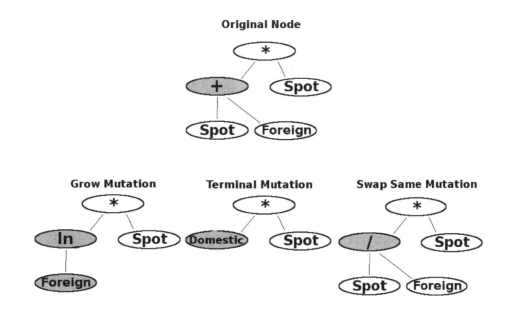

fectively prevents excessive bloat while allowing for individuals of extremely large size.

The inclusion of a penalty function to penalise large individuals is counterproductive to the DyFor model since it allows for individuals of unbounded size, which in this case is desirable for this research. For this reason it is not included.

The probabilities of the operators for all of the runs conducted can be found in Table 5. These probabilities were arrived at after extensive testing. The system was found to continuously improve when run for beyond 1000 generations, though in all cases, the improvement was most significant only until 500 generations. The remaining parameters were chosen due to their consistent improvements to the system when compared against alternative probabilities. They allowed for the most effective trade-off between exploration of new search areas and continuous improvement in promising areas discovered. All runs were conducted on a single 1.6Ghz dual core system with 2GB of RAM.

EXPERIMENTS AND RESULTS

A large number of experiments were conducted to assess to the performance of the system using different mechanisms and approaches. These included analysing the performance of the system using a traditional GP approach and an implementation of the DyFor GP. Analysis was also conducted on the use of different mutation and selection operators. The systems that performed best were run using several sets of operator and operand nodes to determine the impact that the different nodes would have on the results. Finally, the systems were run both seeded and unseeded. The seeded experiments add an individual to each new population that represents the UIP equation found in Equation (1). This was done to allow the system to have access to not only the results generated by the UIP equation, but also to the structure and variable relationships used by the

UIP equation. All results provided are the average of 5 runs of each of the systems.

Data. All of the systems were run using the weekly AUD/USD foreign exchange rate from 1/1/2003 to 1/5/2006. The system also used one week, four week and twelve week Australian and US interbank interest rates for the same period. All data was collected using the DataStream database. The systems were set to generate one forecast per week from 1/1/2005 to 1/1/2006.

Error measurement. This chapter uses four standard economic measurements to determine the accuracy of the systems. They are the root mean squared error (RMSE), the mean absolute error (MAE), the mean absolute percentage error (MAPE) and Thiel inequality coefficient (Thiel). They have been chosen due to their standard use in economic forecast studies.

The root mean squared error (RMSE) is calculated as:

$$RMSE = \sqrt{\sum_{t=n}^{N}(\hat{y}_t - y_t)^2 \Big/ (N-n)} \qquad (5)$$

the root mean square error provides a raw measurement of the difference between the forecast value and the actual exchange rate. The mean absolute error (MAE) is calculated as:

$$MAE = \sum_{t=n}^{N}|\hat{y}_t - y_t|/(N-n) \qquad (6)$$

the mean absolute error provides the same information as the RMSE except that it uses the absolute value of the difference rather than the square of the difference, which is useful in determining the magnitude of the raw error. The mean absolute percentage error (MAPE) is calculated as:

$$MAPE = 100 * \sum_{t=n}^{N}\frac{(\hat{y}_t - y_t)}{y_t} \Big/ (N-n) \qquad (7)$$

Table 5. Operator probabilities and values for the system

Parameter	Value
Number of generations	500
Elitism	1%
Crossover	90%
Mutation	5%
Terminal Mutation	1.66%
Swap Same Mutation	1.66%
Grow Mutation	1.66%

the MAPE provides a standardised measure of the average percentage difference between the forecast and actual exchange rates. Finally the Theil inequality coefficient is calculated as:

$$Theil = \frac{\sqrt{\sum_{t=n}^{N}(\hat{y}_t - y_t)^2 / (N-n)}}{\sqrt{\sum_{t=n}^{N}\hat{y}_t^2 / (N-n)} + \sqrt{\sum_{t=n}^{N}y_t^2 / (N-n)}} \quad (8)$$

the Theil inequality returns a standardised measure that is a combination of the mean error and variance of the errors. This is the most pertinent measure for this research as the system constructs individuals that are optimised for both the mean error and variance.

For all equations, $\hat{y}_t$ is the forecast value, y_t is the actual value and n and N are the start and end indices of predictions accordingly. Lower values indicate better results for all of the results.

Original GP implementation. The DyFor GP implemented is benchmarked against an original GP implementation along with the UIP benchmark. This GP has a fixed population size, and a maximum size for individuals, but more importantly, it lacks the novel "adaptive time window" system used by the DyFor GP.

Instead, the original GP is run using the standard out of sample method. The data set is divided into 2 sets, the set used to generate the forecasts over and a separate set for use in constructing the model.

This latter set is again divided into two sets: a set for training the GP and a separate set for verifying the individuals constructed. This is done to ensure that the GP is not overtrained on the data. The system does this for each forecast step.

Results of Objectives. The experiments for this section were initially conducted with the variables in Table 2 and the category 1 operators found in Table 1. The system was then run again with the full set of operators found in Table 1. Once these results had been accumulated, the systems were run once more, but this time seeding every dynamic generation with an individual that was a reconstruction of the UIP equation given in Equation (1). This was done to determine whether the UIP would maintain its place in the population due to elitism, or would disappear as the generations progressed. The results can be found in Table 6 which contains the 1, 4 and 12 week forecast results. For both tables, any GP results lower than the UIP results are provided with a symbol representing their statistical difference from the equivalent UIP results. The meanings of the symbols can be found in the table captions.

In the table, OGP1 and DyFor GP1 stand for the original GP and DyFor GP respectively using the category 1 operators defined in Table 1 and variables defined in Table 2, DyFor GP1+ indicates the DyFor GP run using the full set of inputs defined in Table 1; US signifies that the populations were not seeded upon creation, and S signifies the opposite, with populations being seeded with an individual representing the UIP equation. The best result for each measure is highlighted in bold for reader convenience.

The original GP generates results comparable to the UIP for the 1 week forecast while the DyFor GP performance is significantly worse. In the 4 week forecast all of the systems are roughly equivalent, though for the 12 week forecast the DyFor GP significantly outperforms the UIP while the performance of the original GP degrades significantly. These results were found to be significant at the 5% level, though not at the 1% level.

Interestingly, the addition of the higher order trigonometric functions does not appear to have made any difference to the forecasting accuracy of the system. The higher order functions did however require much longer times to evaluate. On average the runs with access to the higher order trigonometric functions took 16 hours to complete, double the average of runs without them, which averaged at just over 8 hours.

Also, the addition of the seeded individual did not appear to make any lasting impression on the forecasting ability of the systems. This implies that at no point in time was the UIP equation the most accurate forecaster within the system. Further, within a few generations the UIP individual disappeared from the population, being quickly overtaken by individuals better adapted to current conditions.

The system was then run with the enlarged function set as determined previously. The results of the runs can be found in Table 7 which contains the 1, 4 and 12 week forecast results. The table follows the same naming scheme outlined in the first set of results. The higher order trigonometric functions were excluded from these runs due to their long evaluation times and negligible impact on forecasting accuracy as found in the previous results. The results show that despite the expectations otherwise, the additional information did not assist the GP in consistently generating significantly more accurate forecasts.

Once again for the 1 week forecasts, the DyFor

GP performed very poorly, achieving a MAPE of almost double the UIP, regardless of whether the populations were seeded or unseeded. The original GP performed well again for the 1 week forecasts, almost reaching the accuracy of the UIP. When compared against the same system run for the initial objective, the results are almost identical, confirming that the addition of the new inputs had no real impact on the system. Once more, the results of the original GP that was seeded are marginally better than its unseeded counterpart, though this difference was found to be insignificant at even the 10% level.

For the 4 week forecasts, the results are once again similar to those found in the previous results, with one version of each of the original and DyFor GP achieving results similar to the UIP, though for this objective the alternative versions of each GP performed significantly worse. Also unexpected is that the worse performing system is the unseeded in the case of the original GP and seeded in the case of the DyFor GP. This can be put down to the limited number of runs performed, and the author would expect more consistent results if more runs were performed. This is also another indicator that the seeding of the populations did not affect the systems to any significant degree.

The 12 week forecasts once more tell the same story, with the DyFor GP able to generate a lower Theil inequality than both the UIP and Original GP, and the original GP generating forecasts significantly worse than its competition. Once again, there is very little difference between the results achieved for this objective and those found in the first results. However, in this case the results that were lower than those for the UIP were only significant at the 10% level.

The secondary objective of this chapter, that of deriving information that could be utilised outside the system, was realised by saving key individuals from each run of the system along with additional information to assist in determining the strengths of the individuals.

Two sets of individuals are saved. The first

Table 6. Results using first set of operators and operands. For these results, a superscript of β implies results are significantly different from UIP at the 5% level, γ implies at the 10% level and δ implies no statistical difference.

		1W RMSE	1W MAE	1W MAPE	1W Thiels
OGP1	US	0.00958	0.00736	0.96787	0.00806
	S	0.00942	0.00728	0.95786	0.00792
DyFor GP1	US	0.01411	0.01179	1.5529	0.01187
	S	0.01476	0.01245	1.63621	0.01241
DyFor GP1+	S	0.01501	0.01161	1.52924	0.01259
UIP		**0.00856**	**0.00681**	**0.89594**	**0.00721**
		4W RMSE	**4W MAE**	**4W MAPE**	**4W Thiels**
OGP1	US	0.01417	**0.01171**$^\delta$	**1.53822**$^\delta$	0.01193
	S	0.01453	0.01189	1.56262	0.01222
DyFor GP1	US	0.01552	0.01321	1.73926	0.01309
	S	0.0171	0.01443	1.90206	0.0144
DyFor GP1+	S	0.01689	0.01451	1.90875	0.01423
UIP		**0.01399**	0.01213	1.59648	**0.01179**
		12W RMSE	**12W MAE**	**12W MAPE**	**12W Thiels**
OGP1	US	0.03164	0.02428	3.20753	0.02711
	S	0.02986	0.02239	2.95892	0.02556
DyFor GP1	US	**0.01703**$^\beta$	**0.01434**$^\beta$	**1.90957**$^\beta$	**0.01445**$^\beta$
	S	0.02129	0.01731	2.30635	0.01797
DyFor GP1+	S	0.01955	0.01629	2.16066	0.01663
UIP		0.01896	0.01506	2.00932	0.01606

set is the "best" population that was created and maintained over the run. The individuals are also saved with the dates that they forecast most accurately over. This is done by saving the current data index whenever a new individual is added to the best population. The second set saved is the set of individuals that generated the forecasts used by the system. Once all dynamic generations have completed for a given forecast, a single individual is selected to generate the forecast for that period. This individual is then saved, along with the date that it was selected to forecast for.

It was hoped that further analysis of the evolved equations would lead to a greater under-standing of market movements or perhaps new discoveries being made. However the ability of users or other systems to make use of these equations is limited as many of them are thousands of nodes in length, which make them unintelligible. Any useful information in them is possibly lost due to their complexity. The individuals would need to pass through a post-processing function to extract any relevant information from them.

Limitations. There are a number of limitations to the potential effectiveness of the system. Several of these are addressed below.

The system has been run using static operator probabilities, which may have a negative impact upon the performance of the system. The decision

Table 7. Results using the extended set of operators and operands. For these results, a superscript of β implies results are significantly different from UIP at the 5% level, γ implies at the 10% level and δ implies no statistical difference.

		1W RMSE	1W MAE	1W MAPE	1W Thiels
OGP2	US	0.01094	0.00879	1.15546	0.00918
	S	0.00914	0.00724	0.95266	0.00769
DyFor GP2	US	0.01548	0.01353	1.77596	0.01301
	S	0.01451	0.01241	1.63331	0.01219
UIP		**0.00856**	**0.00681**	**0.89594**	**0.00721**
		4W RMSE	**4W MAE**	**4W MAPE**	**4W Thiels**
OGP2	US	0.02532	0.01735	2.26002	0.02145
	S	0.01811	0.01331	1.74606	0.0152
DyFor GP2	US	0.01651	0.01453	1.90846	0.0139
	S	0.03192	0.01664	2.18434	0.02671
UIP		**0.01399**	**0.01213**	**1.59648**	**0.01179**
		12W RMSE	**12W MAE**	**12W MAPE**	**12W Thiels**
OGP2	US	0.04577	0.04488	5.96549	0.03717
	S	0.0292	0.02156	2.83955	0.02507
DyFor GP2	US	0.02024	0.01712	2.27857	0.01713
	S	0.01878$^\gamma$	0.01512	2.01667	0.01598$^\gamma$
UIP		0.01896	**0.01506**	**2.00932**	0.01606

to use static operator probabilities was based on early experimentation results that found no increase in forecast accuracy when using dynamic mutation and crossover probabilities. However, later versions of the system were increasingly more complex than earlier models, and the dynamic probabilities may have more of an impact under the DyFor GP model than they did under a traditional GP.

Dynamic operator probabilities have been shown to be extremely beneficial to constrained or multi-objective systems (Badran & Rockett), and thus if this system is to be extended to become multi-objective, dynamic probabilities may become more beneficial.

The system only generates 52 forecasts, which span one year of foreign exchange. This is an insignificant amount to extract any substantial

conclusions from. The problem arises from the time required for the system to complete a single forecast, which ranges from ten to twenty minutes to complete. These large runtimes are due to the computationally intensive nature of the algorithm, which requires the evaluation of the equivalent of 2,000 individuals for 1,000 generations for each forecast. When this is compared against the runs performed by Koza in his initial GP implementations, which ran for 50 generations with up to 2,000 individuals, this system performs over 20 times that amount for each forecast, which is equivalent to 1,000 traditional GP runs for one complete run of the system for one forecast step, and thus 3,000 for each complete run (Koza, 1993). Further research would require access to a more powerful system to generate forecasts for larger timeframes.

Further, financial papers generally provide results for the performance of their model using several foreign exchange rates. This is due to each currency pair exhibiting its own unique behaviour, and a system that performs well across one or two currency pairs may not perform very well across others, as found in Álvarez-Díaz & Álvarez (2005).

Although it would have been beneficial to analyse the performance of this system against several foreign exchange rates, time and computational limitations have also prevented this. If further work was to be conducted on this system, then it would need to be run across several foreign exchange rates before any substantial claims can be made regarding its performance.

CONCLUSION AND FUTURE RESEARCH

The objective of this project was to assess the feasibility of using GP systems to forecast foreign exchange rates, to apply the DyFor GP to a new problem domain to determine its versatility and to assess the impact of functions of differing levels of complexity to GP performance. The results indicate that there is the potential for the UIP to be defeated using only the data that it has access to. This should be an avenue for further research in the future. The DyFor model also appears to retain its forecasting ability to a greater degree than the other models when longer forecasts are generated. It therefore warrants further experimentation using longer forecast periods.

The results also indicate that increasing the information available to the system through increasing the number of operators used by the system does not necessarily give the system any additional benefit and may be detrimental to its predictive accuracy due to the inclusion of superfluous functions. These results confirm the findings of Koza (1993) and imply that the extended set of functions do not provide any additional

benefit to the system. Therefore having access to past and aggregate data may not be necessary for a GP foreign exchange forecasting system.

The results in Table 7 also show the importance of using a fitness function that takes into account both the mean and the variance. The UIP results in Table 6 were lower than the DyFor for the MAE and MAPE, measures that do not take into account the variance. The Theil inequality is a measure that combines mean error and variance, and as the systems fitness measure is based on both mean and variance, it assists the DyFor GP in defeating the UIP in the Theil inequality.

Further, the results show that although seeding the populations with an individual representing the UIP equation does not provide the system with a large forecasting accuracy boost, it does in general increase the predictive accuracy, especially in the second phases of the experiments, though there are some cases where the opposite occurs. This implies that although the UIP is never the most accurate forecaster, it does provide some benefit to the system, most likely through some of its subtrees.

Extensions. The system as it currently stands could potentially improve its forecasting ability significantly if several extensions were made to it. These include simple extensions such as performing pre-processing on the data before the system uses it, to more complex extensions such as extending the system to be able to optimise several objectives simultaneously.

An immediate extension that should be followed is for the timeframe to be extended to allow for several years of results. This is because unlike the original GP or the UIP model, the forecasting ability of the DyFor GP is relatively consistent across the forecast periods, with its predictive accuracy diminishing far less than the other systems juxtaposed against. This implies that the DyFor GP should be able to forecast longer periods with even greater accuracy than the UIP. The authors are currently undertaking experiments into generating forecasts over 10 year periods. Initial results show the system greatly outperforms the UIP over longer timeframes, though they are only preliminary results.

Another extension of great potential benefit would be to allow the system to optimise several possibly conflicting objectives simultaneously, as this system has many objectives that it is attempting to achieve simultaneously. The explicit objectives are to minimise the mean error and variance while an implicit objective is for individuals to be no larger than they need to be, though this is not implemented in any way due to its potential conflict with the explicit objectives. Without the multi-objective extension, individual size problems are generally dealt with using parsimony measures that reduce the fitness of individuals the larger their size becomes. Much work has been completed in GP papers discussing the importance of parsimony measures to prevent bloat in individuals (Badran & Rockett, 2007). This objective is conflicting with other objectives such as minimising the mean because it prevents the construction of truly complex solutions to problems, since the larger individuals become the greater the impact it has on their fitness. Measures can be implemented to limit this such as using the logarithm of the size of an individual when determining its effect on its fitness. However, if a multi-objective system is developed then it allows for the discovery of several pareto fronts of individuals that hopefully span the full spectrum of possible variations. In doing so, the system is capable of addressing the issue of individual size without resorting to parsimony measures that limit the system.

Another extension that is typical in many papers that attempt to predict foreign exchange rates is to apply some form of preprocessing on the data before use (Álvarez-Díaz & Álvarez, 2005; Andreou et al., 2002; Neely & Weller, 2003). The objective in doing so is to try and modify the data such that it conveys the information more effectively into the system. In Neely & Weller (2003) the authors used the normalised value of the foreign exchange rate, which was the spot rate divided by the two

week moving average. There is a danger in doing so, however. Álvarez-Díaz & Álvarez (2005) recognise that by modifying the raw data, they are adding further noise into the system. This may lead to the system forecasting even less accurately than previously. Therefore careful thought and experimentation must be undertaken to determine the value of this extension.

There are also several problems inherent in this and most other GP implementations, one of which is selection of nodes from within the trees during mutation and crossover. Due to the nature of trees, it is very difficult to select nodes closer to the origin in the tree. This becomes significantly more difficult depending on the branching factor of the tree, or the number of children nodes each parent has. For the case of the binary tree, over 50% of the nodes in the tree are terminal or leaf nodes, over 75% of the nodes in the tree have a depth of 1 or less, over 87.5% have a depth of 2 or less, and so on. It becomes less probable that a subtree of significant complexity will be extracted from the individual, which is desirable in many cases. The solution to this problem is known as depth fair node selection. It assigns a probability of selection to each depth, and then a fraction of that probability to each node at each depth. In this situation, the root node would have the same probability of selection as all of the leaf nodes combined. This extension makes the extraction of complex subtrees much more probable. However, this also leads to bloat occurring much faster than it occurs currently and thus needs to be investigated before being added.

Another problem affecting this research is overly complex individuals. In Wong & Zhang (2006), they develop a methodology for algebraically simplifying individuals in a GP population during the evolution process. This would be very beneficial to the system used due to the unbounded size on individuals. It would require careful use, however, as at times the bloat in individuals is beneficial as the redundant aspects of each individual may carry vital introns for later generations.

ACKNOWLEDGMENT

This work was supported by grant N516 384734 from the Polish Ministry of Science and Higher Education (MNiSW) and by the ARC Discovery Grant DP0985723.

REFERENCES

Álvarez-Díaz, M., & Álvarez, A. (2005). Genetic multi-model composite forecast for non-linear prediction of exchange rates. *Empirical Economics*, *30*(3), 643–663. doi:10.1007/s00181-005-0249-5

Andreou, A. S., Georgopoulos, E. F., & Likothanasssis, S. D. (2002). Exchange-rates forecasting: a hybrid algorithm based on genetically optimized adaptive neural networks. *Computational Economics*, *20*(3), 191–210. doi:10.1023/A:1020989601082

Anthony, S. (1989). *Foreign Exchange in Practice*. The Law Book Company Limited.

Badran, K. M. S., & Rockett, P. I. (2007). The roles of diversity preservation and mutation in preventing population collapse in multiobjective genetic programming. *GECCO '07: Proceedings of the 9th Annual Conference on Genetic and Evolutionary Computation*, (pp. 1551-1558).

Blickle, T., & Thiele, L. (1996). A comparison of selection schemes used in evolutionary algorithms. *Evolutionary Computation*, *4*(4), 361–394. doi:10.1162/evco.1996.4.4.361

Brabazon, A., & O'Neill, M. (2004). Evolving trading rules for spot foreign-exchange markets using grammatical evolution. *Computational Management Science*, *1*(3-4), 311–327. doi:10.1007/s10287-004-0018-5

Chidambaran, N. K. (2003). New simulation methodology for risk analysis: genetic programming with monte carlo simulation for option pricing. *WSC '03: Proceedings of the 35th Conference on Winter Simulation*, (pp. 285-292).

Clarida, R. H., Sarno, L., Taylor, M. P., & Valente, G. (2003). The out-of-sample success of term structure models as exchange rate predictors: a step beyond. *Journal of International Economics*, *60*(1), 61–83. doi:10.1016/S0022-1996(02)00059-4

Clarida, R. H., & Taylor, M. P. (1997). The term structure of forward exchange premiums and the forecastability of spot exchange rates: correcting the errors. *The Review of Economics and Statistics*, *79*(3), 353–361. doi:10.1162/003465397556827

Jan, B., & Dirk, O. (1999). *SEMIFAR Forecasts, with Applications to Foreign Exchange Rates*. Center of Finance and Econometrics, University of Konstanz.

Koza, J. R. (1993). *Genetic Programming: On the Programming of Computers by Means of Natural Selection*. MIT Press.

McCallum, B. T. (1994). A reconsideration of the uncovered interest parity relationship. *Journal of Monetary Economics*, *33*(1), 105–132. doi:10.1016/0304-3932(94)90016-7

Michalewicz, Z., & Fogel, D. B. (2004). *How to Solve It: Modern Heuristics*. Springer.

Neely, C. J., & Weller, P. A. (2003). Intraday technical trading in the foreign exchange market. *Journal of International Money and Finance*, *22*(2), 223–237. doi:10.1016/S0261-5606(02)00101-8

Piszcz, A., & Soule, T. (2006). A survey of mutation techniques in genetic programming. *GECCO '06: Proceedings of the 8th Annual Conference on Genetic and Evolutionary Computation*, (pp. 951-952).

Schwaerzel, R., & Bylander, T. (2006). Predicting currency exchange rates by genetic programming with trigonometric functions and high-order statistics. *GECCO '06: Proceedings of the 8th Annual Conference on Genetic and Evolutionary Computation*, (pp. 955-956).

Wagner, N., Michalewicz, Z., Khouja, M., & McGregor, R. R. (2007). Time series forecasting for dynamic environments: the DyFor genetic program model. *IEEE Transactions on Evolutionary Computation, 11*(4), 433–452. doi:10.1109/TEVC.2006.882430

Wang, J. (2000). Trading and hedging in S&P 500 spot and futures markets using genetic programming. *Journal of Futures Markets, 20*(10), 911–942. doi:10.1002/1096-9934(200011)20:10<911::AID-FUT3>3.0.CO;2-K

Whitley, D., Richards, M., Beveridge, R., & da Motta Salles Barreto, A. (2006). Alternative evolutionary algorithms for evolving programs: evolution strategies and steady state GP. *GECCO '06: Proceedings of the 8th Annual Conference on Genetic and Evolutionary Computation*, (pp. 919-926).

Wong, P., & Zhang, M. (2006). Algebraic simplification of GP programs during evolution. *GECCO '06: Proceedings of the 8th Annual Conference on Genetic and Evolutionary Computation*, (pp. 927-934).

Chapter 3
Intelligent Business Process Execution using Particle Swarm Optimization

Markus Kress
University of Karlsruhe, Germany

Sanaz Mostaghim
University of Karlsruhe, Germany

Detlef Seese
University of Karlsruhe, Germany

ABSTRACT

In this chapter, the authors study a new variant of Particle Swarm Optimization (PSO) to efficiently execute business processes. The main challenge of this application for the PSO is that the function evaluations typically take a high computation time. They propose the Gap Search (GS) method in combination with the PSO to perform a better exploration in the search space and study its influence on the results of our application. They replace the random initialization of the solutions for the initial population as well as for the diversity preservation method with the GS method. The experimental results show that the GS method significantly improves the quality of the solutions and obtains better results for the application as compared to the results of a standard PSO and Genetic Algorithms. Moreover, the combination of the methods the authors used show promising results as tools to be applied for improvement of Business Process Optimization.

INTRODUCTION

The success of a business enterprise highly depends on its business processes as they are the basis of the economic collaboration within an enterprise and between enterprises. Many companies are facing a large variety of issues such as faster time-to-market, shorter product life cycles, and increasing competition due to the globalization. One of the methods

DOI: 10.4018/978-1-60566-705-8.ch003

to take up these challenges is to optimize the running business processes, among others. Business process management (BPM) methods must provide the required flexibility. In order to make use of standard BPM tools for the execution of business processes, the process models must be completely defined in the sense that every aspect and all the exceptions must be known and modelled in advance.

The so called Executable Product Model (EPM) approach proposed by Kress et al. (2007) combines a compact model with an intelligent control flow mechanism. The approach belongs to the product model based approaches such as those studied by Küster et al. (2007), Müller et al. (2007), and van der Aalst et al. (2001). The EPM is based on the product data model, which is extended in order to make it directly executable without having to derive a business process first.

The EPM provides a compact representation of the set of possible execution paths of a business process by defining information dependencies. It has been shown in Kress & Seese (2007a) and Kress & Seese (2007b) that multi-agent methods can be used to execute an EPM.

Intelligent agents take advantage of the flexibility provided by the EPM and select their actions based on relational reinforcement learning using a probabilistic policy. The agents individually learn how the EPM is efficiently executed based on the current situation and the objectives under consideration (e.g. the minimization of the cycle time). The probabilities of policies in such a model must be known or estimated using an adequate heuristic. Genetic Algorithms (GAs) have been successfully used to find the probability values (Kress & Seese, 2007a; Kress & Seese, 2007b). However, the main drawback of using GAs is that they require a high computation time to find the optimal values. Executing the business processes on a simulation model typically takes a high computation time and when combined with GAs the computation time drastically increases.

In this chapter, we study Particle Swarm Optimization (PSO) proposed by Kennedy & Eberhart (1995) to find the probability values of the policies for executing the business process using EPM. PSO is known to be successful in solving many real-world applications (Engelbrecht, 2006). Here, we study a new PSO using a Gap Search (GS) method. Inspired from the Binary Search (BS) introduced by Hughes (2003), GS is proposed to explore the large gaps which exist in the search space. We intentionally combine GS and PSO as the function evaluations in our application take a high computation time and the GS method is known to be reasonably quick in exploring the search space. Note that dealing with expensive function evaluations can also be done in several other ways such as Parallelization or meta-modelling (Alba & Tomassini, 2002; Cantu-Paz, 2000; Jones et al., 1998). Here, we select the GS mechanism as it is and show that it can easily be integrated into our approach.

An approach very similar to GS is a subdivision method, proposed by Schütze et al. (2003), where the search space is divided into different boxes. Through several iterations, the non-optimal boxes are removed and the good boxes are again divided into smaller boxes. This method requires a very high computation time for relatively low dimensional search spaces. The advantage of GS is that it has a very simple structure and can easily be implemented. We combine GS in several parts of PSO such as initialization, diversity, and feasibility preservation methods and study their influences on the results of the PSO.

The rest of the chapter is structured as follows. In the next section, we briefly present PSO and GS methods. We then explain the hybrid approach in Section 3. Section 4 describes the intelligent business execution model and the main application of this chapter. Sections 5 and 6 are dedicated to the experiments and conclusions, respectively.

PARTICLE SWARM OPTIMIZATION (PSO)

PSO was originally introduced by Kennedy & Eberhart (1995), motivated from the simulation of social behaviour in herds and schools of animals. A PSO contains a population of particles which explores the search space by moving with particular velocities towards the optimum. The velocity of each particle is influenced by a social impact coming from the population and the individual experience of the particle. PSO can be used to solve optimization problems. A solution *x* is a vector of *n* parameters which are bounded by a set of boundary conditions such as $\forall\ i \in \{0, ..., n\}: x_i^{(L)} \leq x_i \leq x_i^{(H)}$. These bounds define the feasible search (parameter) space *S*.

In PSO, a set of *N* particles is considered as the population P_t at the generation *t*. Each particle *i* has a position $x_i = \{x_1^i, x_2^i, ..., x_n^i\}$ and a velocity $v_i = \{v_1^i, v_2^i, ..., v_n^i\}$ in the parameter space *S*. In generation *t + 1*, the velocity and the position of each particle *i* is updated as follows:

$$v_{j,t+1}^i = wv_{j,t}^i + c_1 R_1(p_{j,t}^i - x_{j,t}^i) + c_2 R_2(p_{j,t}^{i,g} - x_{j,t}^i)$$

(1)

$$x_{j,t+1}^i = x_{j,t}^i + v_{j,t+1}^i$$

(2)

where *j = 1, ..., n*, *w* is called the inertia weight, c_1 and c_2 are two positive constants, and R_1 and R_2 are two random values selected in [0, 1].

In Equation (2), $p_{j,t}^{i,g}$ is the position of the global best particle. The global best particle is the particle with the best function value. $p_{j,t}^i$ is the best position particle *i* could find so far. Indeed, it is like a memory for the particle *i* and is updated in each generation. The inertia weight *w* is employed to control the impact of the previous history of velocities on the current velocity.

Topologies

In PSO, the velocity vector drives the optimization process and reflects the socially exchanged information. Particles tend to be influenced by the success of anyone they are connected to, and by the member of their neighbourhood that has had the greatest success so far. These neighbours are not necessarily particles which are close to each other in parameter space, but instead are particles that are close to each other in a topological space that defines the social structure of the population (Kennedy & Eberhart, 2001). There exist several neighbourhood topologies:

- **Individual best:** In this topology, particles are isolated, which means that there exists no connection between them. Each particle compares its current position only to its own best position found so far (pbest).
- **Global best:** This topology is the opposite of the individual best. In the global best (gbest) topology all members of the swarm are connected to one another. Each particle uses its history of experiences in terms of its own best solution so far (pbest) but, in addition, the particle uses the position of the best particle from the entire swarm (gbest). This structure is equivalent to a fully connected social network, i.e., a star topology such as the one shown in Figure 1 (a).
- **Local best:** In this topology, each individual is affected by the best performance of its immediate neighbours in the topological population. Particles are influenced by the best position within their neighbourhood (lbest), as well as their own past experience (pbest). The number of neighbours is parameterized. With two neighbours, this topology is equivalent to a ring such as the one shown in Figure 1 (b).
- **Wheels:** In this topology, one individual is connected to all others and they are

Figure 1. Different neighbourhood topologies are depicted. (a), (b), and (c) illustrate the star topology known as global best, the ring topology known as local best, and the wheel topology, respectively.

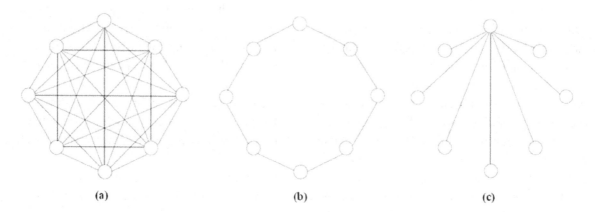

(a)   (b)   (c)

connected to only that one (Figure 1 (c)). Individuals are isolated from one another, as all information has to be communicated through the focal individual. The focal individual compares performances of all individuals in the population and adjusts its trajectory towards the best of them. That performance is eventually communicated to the rest of the population.

The gbest populations tend to converge more rapidly than lbest populations, but are also more susceptible to suffer from premature convergence (i.e., to converge to local optima).

Diversity Preserving Methods

In PSO, diversity preserving methods are employed to avoid the convergence to a local optimum. There are several approaches to prevent the premature stagnation of the basic PSO, most of which introduce randomness into the swarm:

- **Quality-based:** When particles do not improve their qualities over time, their positions are reinitialized (Kennedy & Eberhart, 1995).
- **Randomly:** After a fixed interval, a particle is randomly reinitialized (Xie et al.,

2002). This has also been known as craziness (Kennedy & Eberhart, 1995) or turbulence factor (Fieldsend & Singh, 2002), where after each iteration, some particles are randomly reinitialized.

- **Self-organized criticality:** Lovberg & Krink (2002) proposed a parameter called criticality which is defined for each particle (for the physical origin of this concept see the paper from Bak (1996)). If two particles get closer to each other than a threshold their criticality values are increased. If the criticality value of a particle is larger than a certain value, that particle is a good candidate for re-initialization. The re-initialization means replacing the particle in a randomly selected position in the parameter space.

All of the above methods increase the diversity of the swarm. However, the randomness in the re-initialization leads to the following issues.

a. It is possible that the particles revisit some parts of the search space through the re-initialization.
b. Such randomness is meant to explore the unexplored regions in the parameter space. The above methods do not consider this

Figure 2.

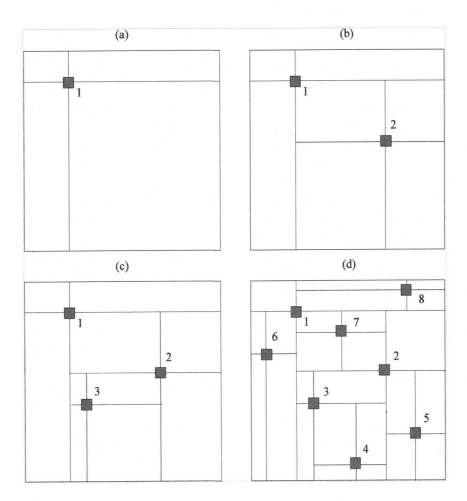

aspect. In fact, it is desired to make sure that the swarm visits most of the search space and that there is no gap which has not been explored.

Considering these aspects, we propose to use the GS method as an alternative to the existing diversity preserving methods, in the next section.

GAP SEARCH (GS)

The GS method is used to search the most unexplored regions of a search space, similar to the BS proposed by Hughes (2003). The BS is based on the iterative division of the search space into regions and exploring the large gaps. It has a similar but simpler mechanism than the Voronoi optimization. The proposed GS method starts with selecting a random point in the search space. Then, the largest gap in the search space is found by computing the distances between the first point and the boundaries of the search space. The difference between GS and BS is that in BS the promising areas in the search space are successively refined through a binary search whereas in GS the largest gaps are sampled.

Figure 2 shows an example for a two dimensional space. In (a) one solution is randomly selected in the search space. The second solution is randomly selected in the largest gap (Figure 2 (b)). This is an iterative method and can be performed to define any desirable number of solutions in the search space. These solutions are usually stored in a list.

In our experiments, we store only the points generated by the GS method in an archive. Alternatively one could also store all of the visited points of the search space. One disadvantage of GS could be that inserting a new point into a large list of solutions requires a relatively high computation time particularly for high (> 20) dimensions. Here, we consider very expensive fitness evaluations and as a consequence that our lists are small enough to ignore this computation time. In the following, we propose to use GS mechanism for the initialization of particles, the diversity, and feasibility preservation in a PSO. Before the description of the algorithm is given we will discuss how to initiate the population and how to preserve diversity and feasibility.

Initiate Population

The standard way of generating an initial population in PSO is to randomly find feasible positions of the particles. The goal is to ensure that the initial population is a uniform representation of the search space. In PSO, the initial population has a great impact on the exploration mechanism. We propose the GS method to produce the initial solutions. Using the GS method instead of the random generator has a particular advantage as GS tries to cover the entire search space. Of course, this depends on the number of initial particles and a very small initial population can never cover the entire search space. However, due to the storage of all of the found positions for the particles through the iterations, a good coverage of the search space can be preserved. Furthermore when using a random initial population, it has been shown that in high dimensional spaces, the probability that a particle is placed very close to the boundary is very high (Helwig & Wanka, 2007). Therefore, it is very probable that particles leave the feasible search space. Here, we want to avoid

this effect by intentionally initializing solutions in non-explored regions in the search space.

Diversity Preservation Mechanism

As we already discussed, in order to prevent premature stagnation and convergence to a local optimum, some particles of the population are randomly re-initialized in the search space. We propose to use GS instead of a random initialization. We select a relatively small percentage of the particles randomly and replace those particles by using the GS. In this way these particles are sent to the large gaps (most unexplored regions) in the space. Hence, we ensure that the particles never visit the same part of the search space twice. We employ the GS like the turbulence factor proposed by Fieldsend & Singh (2002): select one particle with a predefined probability at random and replace it in the search space by using the GS. The other issue in re-initializing the particles is to set an appropriate value for the velocity. In the literature, for example in Lovberg & Krink (2002) and Venter & Sobieszczanski-Sobieski (2003), the velocities of the reinitialized particles are set either to zero, to a random value or are kept as before.

Feasibility Preservation Mechanism

Another issue in PSO is the boundary handling method or the so called feasibility preserving mechanism (Mostaghim et al., 2006). During the iterations, it is possible that particles leave the feasible region of the search space. Those particles must be identified and sent back to the feasible space (usually the feasible space is defined by the constraints; here we consider the area surrounded by the boundaries of the search space). Typically if a particle leaves the feasible region, it is replaced either on the boundary or on a random position. The velocity of the particle is unchanged, set to zero or randomly selected. Indeed the most straight forward mechanism is to set the infeasible particles on the boundaries. This has an advantage when

Table 1. Information elements of the credit application

Information Element	Explanation
application data	application data of the customer
financial situation check	result of the financial situation check of the customer
customer history check	result of the check of past financial transactions of the customer
contract conditions	calculated contract conditions based on the checks and on the application data
contract approved	indicates whether the contract for the credit was approved or not
final decision	indicates whether the credit was granted or denied

the global optimum is close to the boundary. In this chapter we also analyze the performance of employing GS for replacing the infeasible particles in the search space.

The PSO Algorithm

Table 1 illustrates a PSO algorithm. The inputs to this algorithm are the feasible region S (the boundaries of the search space), N number of particles, and a maximum number of iterations T_{max}. The algorithm starts with the initialization of the particles at the generation $t = 0$. In the beginning the personal best memory of a particle is set to the position of the particle. In step 2 particles are evaluated. The global best and personal best particles are found. The function $\mathbf{Update}(\mathbf{P}_t, p_t^g)$ is used to update the population based on the global best particle. In this step, after updating the particles, we examine if the particle is still in the feasible space. If not, a feasibility preserving method has to be applied to the infeasible particle (see Section 3.3). Also, the diversity of the particles in the population is preserved at this step using one of the methods as described in Section 3.2. The output of this algorithm is the global best particle after a stopping criterion is met. A typical stopping criterion is to select a fixed amount of iterations such as T_{max}.

Algorithm 1. PSO algorithm
Input: $\boldsymbol{S, N, T_{max}}$

Output: $\boldsymbol{p^g1}$.
Initialization: Initialize a set of $\boldsymbol{N}$ particles in $\boldsymbol{S}$ as the population $\mathbf{P}_t$
    a. Set $\boldsymbol{t = 0}$
    b. Set $\boldsymbol{p^i}_t = \boldsymbol{x^i}_t2$.
Evaluation: Evaluate the population
    a. Find the global best particle: $\boldsymbol{p_t^g}$
    b. Update the personal best particles
  3. Update the population: $\mathbf{P}_{t+1}$ = $\mathbf{Update}(\mathbf{P}_t, \boldsymbol{p_t^g})$
    a. Preserve Feasibility
    b. Preserve Diversity
  4. Termination: Unless $\boldsymbol{t} = \boldsymbol{T_{max}}$
    a. t = t+1
    b. goto Step 2

INTELLIGENT BUSINESS PROCESS MANAGEMENT

In a fast changing environment, business processes must be continuously adapted and improved to assure sustainable performance. The development of flexible solutions is one of the possible methods for preparing the enterprises to cope with the dynamic change. In order to increase the flexibility of the execution of business processes, the executable product model (EPM) approach

Figure 3. Visualization of EPM elements

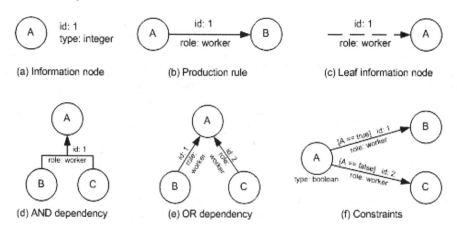

(a) Information node (b) Production rule (c) Leaf information node

(d) AND dependency (e) OR dependency (f) Constraints

has been introduced by Kress et al. (2007). The business processes are executed based on a special model called executable product model instead of a regular process model. The EPM defines information dependencies instead of activity sequences. Based on this EPM, the actual activity order of the business process is determined during runtime considering the current system state and the objectives. For this complex task, intelligent agents are applied in order to efficiently execute the business processes. Multi-agent systems (MAS) are capable of solving complex tasks in distributed environments and have been applied successfully in practice (e.g. in the production industry studied by Bussmann & Schild (2000)). In combination with the self-adaptation paradigm they are a powerful tool. Self-adaptation is the ability of a software system to adapt to dynamic and changing operating conditions autonomously (Weyns & Hovoet, 2007).

The Executable Product Model

The EPM is a graph consisting of information nodes and dependencies between them. In an EPM, the information nodes correspond to abstract information like application data, business objects, documents, decisions which are part of the business process. An information node has a type, descriptive name, a unique ID and is visualized as a circle as depicted in Figure 3 (a). The root node of a product model corresponds to the final decision (the outcome or result) of the related business process.

The dependencies between the information nodes determine which information must be available before the next information can be generated, e.g. a decision can be made only when the application form has been filled out correctly. These dependencies reflect the production or execution order of the information elements. These arcs represent production rules describing which activity has to be performed to create a new value stored in the information node the corresponding arc is pointing at. Figure 3 (a) and (b) show an example of an information node and a production rule respectively.

The information nodes that the production rule depends on are called origin nodes; the created node is the destination node of the production rule. Each information node is the destination node of at least one production rule (or several in the case of variants; in this case the indegree of this node is > 0). As leaf nodes do not depend on any other node, they have special production rules that can be executed at any time (visualized in Figure 3 (c)).

Two kinds of dependencies can be specified,

Figure 4. EPM of a simplified credit application

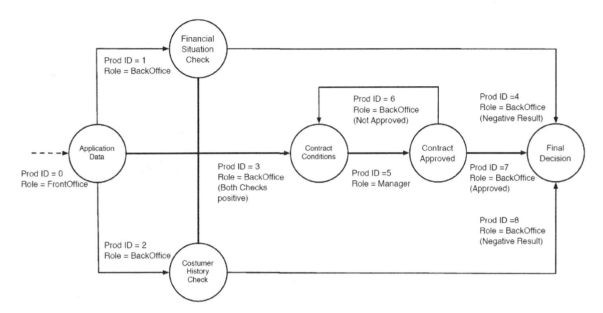

AND and OR dependencies. Figure 3 (d) shows an example of an AND dependency. In such a dependency all origin nodes of the related production rule must have been created before the production rule can become executable. A production rule with an OR dependency is depicted in Figure 3 (e). Here, A can be created using production rule 1 or 2 (variant). Both production rules depend on only one origin node (B and C respectively) and can be executed independently of each other. A constraint can be attached to each production rule as depicted in Figure 3 (f). Constraints determine the circumstances a production rule can be executed.

Example: As an example we use a simplified business process of a credit application. All possible information that is generated during the execution of the credit application process is listed in Table 1. For creating the EPM, the information nodes must be included in the model and the dependencies between them must be specified. The resulting EPM is depicted in Figure 4.

The business process can be explained as follows: At the beginning, the credit application must be submitted (production rule with ID 0).

Afterwards, two different checks of the customer can be carried out (ID 1 + 2). A negative result leads to a refusal of the credit application. The rejection correspondence is sent to the customer (ID 4 or 8). If both checks have a positive outcome, the contract conditions are calculated (ID 3). Based on the four eyes principle, the conditions are approved by another person (ID 5). A recalculation is necessary if the contract is rejected. (ID 6). If the contract is approved, the customer is informed about the approval of its credit application and the contract conditions.

As in standard BPM tools, a workflow engine is necessary for the dynamic execution of the model. In the EPM approach the workflow engine is composed by intelligent agents. The intelligence of the agents stems from machine learning algorithms that are applied for managing the control flow.

The Intelligent Control Flow Mechanism

An intelligent control flow mechanism for learning optimal execution decisions is to employ relational

Figure 5. The hybrid machine learning approach based on relational reinforcement learning and particle swarm optimization. The PSO is depicted based on a policy containing two rules. In general, the dimension of the positions of the particles corresponds to the number of policy rules.

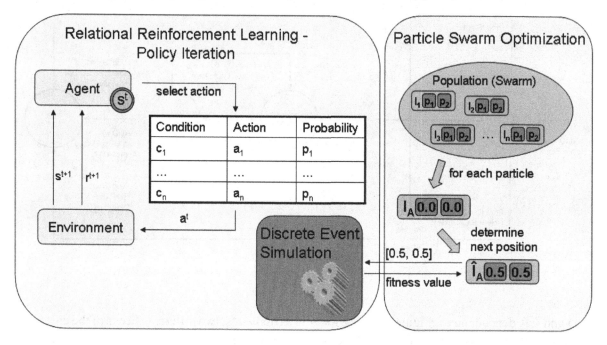

reinforcement learning (RRL) using probabilistic policies (Dzeroski et al., 2001; Itoh & Nakamura, 2004). The hybrid machine learning approach that we apply is depicted in Figure 5.

The probabilistic policy contains a definite set of predefined rules. Each rule has a condition and action part. Furthermore, one probability is assigned to each rule. In order to select an action based on this policy, the condition part of each rule is consecutively evaluated until one evaluates to true. If the condition is fulfilled, the corresponding action is executed based on the assigned probability. If the action is not executed, the next rule in the policy is tested. The probabilities of the policy must be determined for each scenario using an appropriate heuristic in an offline learning phase. This means that for each probability vector, a simulation is carried out. In general all agents use the same policy and probabilities in the simulation. Reinforcement learning (RL) requires a feedback mechanism, so the agents are

capable of learning optimal actions. In standard RL, agents receive a reward from the environment. In our case, the agents do not get a reward directly. Instead, the simulation runs are evaluated based on a fitness function which is composed of key performance indicators (KPI) of interest such as cycle times, throughput, or costs. The fitness function together with the policy rules must be carefully defined in order to achieve the desired behaviour of the agents. As heuristic, we apply PSO and GS in order to find the probabilities for the policies.

EXPERIMENTS

In this section, we examine the influence of the GS mechanism (Section 3) and PSO on an application in business process execution and compare the results with the results of a standard PSO proposed by Bratton & Kennedy (2007) and a GA approach.

Table 2. The pre-defined policy

No	Condition	Action	P
1	Not workloads_available, not workloads_requested	request_workload	P1
2	workloads_available, workloads_outdated, not workloads_requested	request_workload	P2
3	not failure_rates_available, not failure_rates_requested	request_failure_rate	P3
4	failure_rates_available, failure_rates_outdated, not failure_rates_requested	request_failure_rate	P4
5	number_of_activated_variants(No), No=0, minimum_weighted_duration(Variant, Duration)	activate(Variant)	P5
6	activated_variant(VariantA), weighted_variant_duration(VariantA, DurationA), minimum_weighted_duration(VariantB, DurationB), DurationA=<DurationB	proceed(VariantA)	P6
7	activated_variant(VariantA), weighted_variant_duration(VariantA, DurationA), minimum_weighted_duration(VariantB, DurationB), not VariantA=VariantB, DurationA>DurationB	switch(VariantA, VariantB)	P7

Case study: For the application, we use an EPM consisting of a simple parallel structure with two different variants (execution paths). Each path contains two production rules. The use of a simple structure facilitates the analysis and the understanding about the behaviour of the agents.

The fitness function: The following fitness function is used:

$$f = maxD - meanCT - 10 * meanN + 10 * meanT \qquad (3)$$

where **maxD** is the maximum duration of the simulation[1], **meanCT** is the average cycle time, **meanN** is the average number of IBOs in execution, and **meanT** is the average throughput. The factors **10** were selected as they led to the best results.

There is also the possibility that an agent decides not to finish the product model which increases the number of product model instances in execution. This KPI is used in the fitness function as penalty (as *meanN* in Equation (3)). Here, computing *f* is very time consuming as each time a simulation is carried out.

The policy: The parameters of the policy are listed as **p1** to **p7** in Table 2[2]. As the agents select their actions for controlling the execution flow on

the basis of the policy, the probabilities must be determined, so that the performed actions lead to an optimization of the three KPIs: cycle time, number of IBOs, and throughput (see Equation (3)). The manually created policy used in the conducted experiments is given in Table 2. The rules can be explained as follows:

- Rule (1): Requests work load information if it is not available and has not been requested yet.
- Rule (2): Assures that work load information is kept up-to-date.
- Rules (3) and (4): Both rules pertain to error-proneness information. The behaviour is analogous to rule (1) and (2).
- Rule (5): Activates the variant with the shortest estimated execution duration. If work load information or error proneness information is available, it is used in the calculation of the estimated duration. An activated variant results in the execution of one or more production rules.
- Rule (6): Assures that if the activated variant still has the one with the smallest estimated duration, its processing is continued.
- Rule (7): Switches the variants, if there is a shorter one than the activated one.

Parameter Settings: The PSO method is run with 20 particles for 30 iterations and 20 different initial seeds and two different topologies (star and ring). As we have seven policy rules, the dimension of the positions is seven as well. The term standard PSO refers to use the star topology. We indicate the ring topology in the following by the notation "ring". The inertia weight w, c_1 and c_2 values are selected as 0.4, 1.0 and 1.0. The selection of these parameters is based on the best combination obtained through several tests on the application in preliminary experiments.

The GA method is a real-vector GA using a Gaussian mutation. The mutation operator is applied to 15 percent of the genes of every individual selected through a binary tournament selection. As for the population size for the GA algorithm, we selected the same size as for the PSO.

In the following Random refers to the use of a Random generator for finding new positions.

Influence of Topologies

We compare the results obtained from standard PSO with different topologies with the results of the GA.

Figure 6 shows the results over generations. It can be observed that the ring topology, as expected before, converges slower than the PSO with star topology (indicated as standard in the figure). The GA obtains the best results at the end, but has the slowest convergence. Note that the quick convergence is of great importance in our application as the simulations and therefore the fitness evaluations are very time-intensive.

Influence of Initial Population:

These experiments are dedicated to examine the influence of the GS method in producing the initial population. In order to achieve this, we produce 250 different initial particles using GS and Random

Figure 6. The results of PSO with star and ring topologies (denoted as Standard and Standard-Ring) and the results of GA.

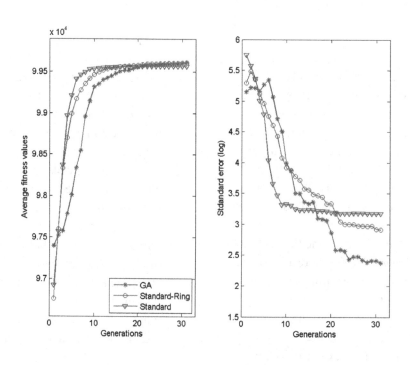

methods. Table 3 shows the minimum, average and maximum values of the fitness values of the produced initial populations on the business application. We observe that the GS is able to find better fitness values in average and minimum cases and with lower standard deviation.

We further analyze the influence of the initial populations on the results of the standard PSO and other methods. By these experiments, we also examine the influence of the initial velocities. Figure 7 shows the results of a standard PSO with different initial populations. The initial population is selected at random (R) or using the GS method (GS) and the initial velocities are set to zero (de-

noted as -0) or a random value (denoted as -R). It can be observed that the PSO with the population produced by GS and initial random velocities can perform better compared to the other cases and this effect is consistent over the iterations. Also the standard error obtained by GS-R is the lowest among the others. These experiments illustrate that if we select a different initial population we obtain different results meaning that the results depend on the initial population. We select the best from here, namely the GS-R, for further examinations.

Table 3. Fitness values of the initial population produced by GS and Random methods over 250 different runs.

Method	Minimum	Average	Maximum	Std. Deviation
BS	94200	97044	99253	1111.7
Random	93471	96936	99386	1136.1

Figure 7. A simple PSO with different initial populations and initial velocities.

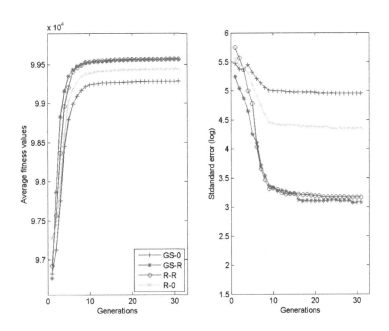

Influence of Diversity Preserving Methods

These experiments are carried out to observe the influence of employing GS to PSO in order to preserve the diversity in the population and avoid the local optimum. From the descriptions in Section 3.2, our expectation is that the GS method improves the performance of the PSO compared to the standard PSO and the GA algorithm. In these experiments we reinitialize the positions and the velocities of 10 percent of the population after each iteration using the GS method. The velocities of those particles are either kept unchanged (denoted as -K), set to zero (denoted as -0) or selected randomly (denoted as -R). In Figure 8, we observe that all the variations of PSO can outperform the GA algorithm for the first 15 iterations. As expected, the GS method improves the performance of the standard PSO.

Influence of Feasibility Preserving Methods

We examine a spectrum of different feasibility preserving methods for those particles leaving the feasible search space. Those particles are replaced on the boundary of the search space (denoted as border-) or reinitialized using the Gap Search (denoted as GS-). Their velocities are either kept unchanged (denoted as -K), selected at random (-R) or set to zero (-0). The results shown in Figure 9 indicate that setting the particles on the boundary and selecting a random velocity leads to better results than reinitializing the particles using the GS method. Also the standard error shown in Figure 9 illustrates that the border-R method is the best choice in our experiments. In fact, this is a reasonable strategy to replace the solutions which tend to go out of the search space on the borders and just give them a new velocity vector. If we assign them their old velocity vector, they tend to go out of the search space again.

Figure 8. A standard PSO and a PSO using the Gap Search method for diversity preserving.

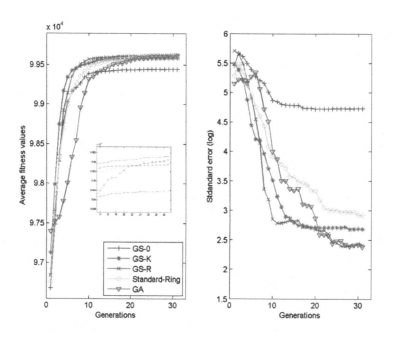

Figure 9. Different PSO method using different feasibility preserving methods (boundary handling methods).

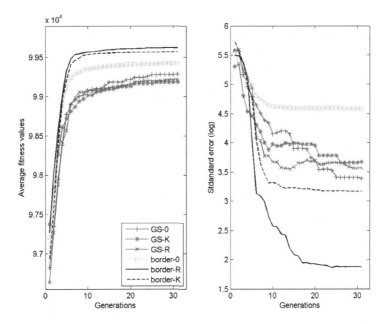

Final Experiments

Using all the above experiments, we select the best combination of the PSO and GS methods as follows: (a) Initialize the population of PSO using the GS method and set the initial velocities to random. (b) Employ a GS method to 10 percent of the particles for diversity preservation. (c) Use a simple feasibility preservation method such as the one denoted as border-R (described above). We compare this combination of GS and PSO with the GA algorithm and a standard PSO. Figure 10 shows the results as follows: Figure 10 left shows that the GS-PSO converges very fast to the optimal solution, where GA is relatively slow. At the end both methods find the optimal solution. The standard PSOs with star and ring topology perform much better than the GA but are outperformed by the GS-PSO. Also the standard PSO has a very large standard error compared to the others. The BS-PSO has the lowest standard error.

The standard PSO proposed by Bratton &

Kennedy (2007) suggests a population size of 50. However, due to the very timely intensive simulations, we selected a smaller population (20) in the above experiments. For comparison purposes, we further analyze the performance of the proposed GS-PSO containing 50 particles (denoted as GS-PSO50) with the standard PSO (with the two topologies). Figure 11 shows the results. We can observe that during the early generations, the GS-PSO performs like the Standard PSO (indicating the star topology) and both perform better than the Standard PSO with ring topology. This result is expected as the ring topology has a slow convergence (Kennedy and Eberhart, 2001). The GS-PSO outperforms both the standard variants at the end of the generations. Furthermore, the GS-PSO obtains much better average fitness value of the initial population than the other methods. This is due to the initialization of particles using the GS method. Overall, GS-PSO is able to converge very fast to a good solution and this is a desirable behaviour for our application with very

Figure 10. Average fitness values standard PSO variants, GS-PSO and GA.

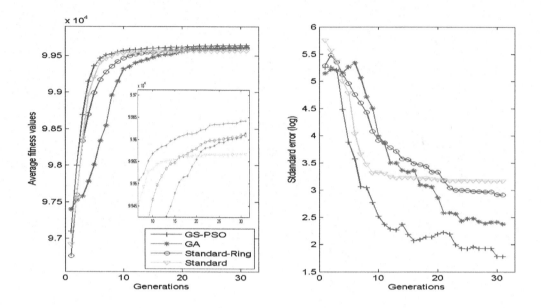

Figure 11. Average fitness values of GS-PSO, Standard PSO variants with 50 particles denoted as GS-PSO50, Standard50 and Standard-Ring50.

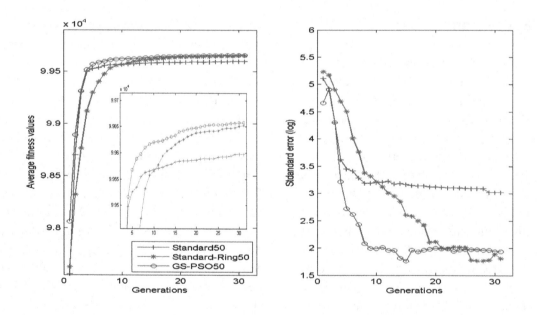

time consuming fitness evaluations.

SUMMARY AND FUTURE WORK

The combination of GS with PSO has been introduced in this chapter. The GS method is a very effective exploration technique which explores the large gaps in the search space and thereby covers the entire search space. GS can replace the random exploration in PSO, such as the random initialization and the diversity preservation. This combination is particularly useful for applications with expensive fitness evaluations, such as our application in executing the business processes. Using the hybrid learning approach, the agents were capable of learning the adequate behaviour. The agents requested work load information and selected the variant with the better estimated variant duration.

After a relatively large number of experiments, we introduce the best combination of PSO and GS for our application and compare the results with a standard PSO and GA. We observe that the new approach is able to find very good solutions after a few iterations compared to the other methods.

In future, we will study our application by changing the single-objective problem to a multi-objective one and further analyze the combination of PSO and GS for multi-objective problems using multi-objective PSO algorithms. Also as we deal with time-intensive function evaluations, we plan to investigate meta-modelling methods on this application.

REFERENCES

Alba, E., & Tomassini, M. (2002). Parallelism and evolutionary algorithms. *IEEE Transactions on Evolutionary Computation, 6*(5), 443–461. doi:10.1109/TEVC.2002.800880

Bak, P. (1996). *How Nature Works: The Science of Self-Organized Criticality*. New York, NY: Springer-Verlag.

Bratton, D., & Kennedy, J. (2007). Defining a standard for particle swarm optimization. *Proceedings of the IEEE Swarm Intelligence Symposium* (pp. 120-127). Honolulu, HI, USA.

Bussmann, S., & Schild, K. (2000). Self-organizing manufacturing control: An industrial application of agent technology. *Proceedings of the 4th International Conference on Multi-Agent Systems* (pp. 87-94). Boston, MA, USA.

Cantu-Paz, E. (2000). *Efficient and Accurate Parallel Genetic Algorithms*. Kluwer.

Dzeroski, S., de Raedt, L., & Driessens, K. (2001). Relational reinforcement learning. *Machine Learning, 43*, 7–52. doi:10.1023/A:1007694015589

Engelbrecht, A. (2006). *Fundamentals of Computationial Swarm Intelligence*. John Wiley.

Fieldsend, J. E., & Singh, S. (2002). A multi-objective algorithm based upon particle swarm optimisation, an efficient data structure and turbulence. *Proceedings of the Workshop on Computational Intelligence* (pp. 34-44). Birmingham, UK.

Helwig, S., & Wanka, R. (2007). Particle swarm optimization in high-dimensional bounded search spaces. *Proceedings of the IEEE Swarm Intelligence Symposium* (pp. 198-205). Honolulu, HI, USA.

Hughes, E. J. (2003). Multi-objective binary search optimisation. In C. M. Fonseca (Eds.), *Evolutionary Multi-Criterion Optimization* (pp. 72-87). LNCS 2632, Berlin, Germany: Springer-Verlag.

Itoh, H., & Nakamura, K. (2004). Towards Learning to learn and plan by relational reinforcement learning. *Proceedings of the Workshop on Relational Reinforcement Learning* (pp. 34-39). Banff, Alberta, Canada.

Jones, D., Schonlau, M., & Welch, W. (1998). Efficient global optimization of expensive black-box functions. *Journal of Global Optimization, 13*, 455–492. doi:10.1023/A:1008306431147

Kennedy, J., & Eberhart, R. C. (1995). Particle swarm optimization. *Proceedings of the IEEE International Conference on Neural Networks* (pp. 1942-1948). Perth, Australia.

Kennedy, J., & Eberhart, R. C. (2001). *Swarm Intelligence*. Morgan Kaufmann.

Kress, M., Melcher, J., & Seese, D. (2007). Introducing executable product models for the service industry. *Proceedings of the 40th Annual Hawaii International Conference on System Sciences* (p. 46). Waikoloa, HI, USA.

Kress, M., & Seese, D. (2007a). Executable product models - the intelligent way. *Proceedings of the IEEE International Conference on Systems, Man, and Cybernetics* (pp. 1987-1992). Montreal, Quebec, Canada.

Kress, M., & Seese, D. (2007b). Flexibility enhancements in BPM by applying executable product models and intelligent agents. *Proceedings of the 1st International Working Conference on Business Process and Services Computing* (pp. 93-104). Leipzig, Germany.

Küster, J., Ryndina, K., & Gall, H. (2007). Generation of business process models for object life cycle compliance. In G. Alonso, P. Dadam & M. Rosemann (Eds.), *Business Process Management* (pp. 165-181). LNCS 4714, Berlin, Germany: Springer-Verlag.

Lovberg, M., & Krink, T. (2002). Extending particle swarm optimisers with self-organized criticality. *Proceedings of the IEEE Congress on Evolutionary Computation* (pp. 1588-1593). Honolulu, HI, USA.

Mostaghim, S., Halter, W., & Wille, A. (2006). Linear multi-objective particle swarm optimization. In A. Abraham, C. Grosan & V. Ramos (Eds.), *Stigmergy optimization* (pp. 209-237). SCI 31, Berlin, Germany: Springer-Verlag.

Müller, D., Reichert, M., & Herbst, J. (2007). Data-driven modeling and coordination of large process structures. In R. Meersman & Z. Tari (Eds.), *On the Move to Meaningful Internet Systems 2007: CoopIS, DOA, ODBASE, GADA, and IS* (pp. 131-149). LNCS 4803, Berlin, Germany: Springer-Verlag.

Schütze, O., Mostaghim, S., Dellnitz, M., & Teich, J. (2003). Covering pareto sets by multi-level evolutionary subdivision techniques. In C. M. Fonseca (Ed.), *Evolutionary Multi-Criterion Optimization* (pp. 118-132). LNCS 2632, Berlin, Germany: Springer-Verlag.

van der Aalst, W. M. P., Reijers, H. A., & Limam, S. (2001). Product-driven workflow design. *Proceedings of the 6th International Conference on Computer Supported Cooperative Work in Design* (pp. 397-402). London, Ontario, Canada.

Venter, G., & Sobieszczanski-Sobieski, J. (2003). Particle swarm optimization. *AIAA Journal, 41*(8), 1583–1589. doi:10.2514/2.2111

Weyns, D., & Hovoet, T. (2007) An architectural strategy for self-adapting systems. *Proceedings of the International Workshop on Software Engineering for Adaptive and Self-Managing Systems* (p. 3). Minneapolis, MN, USA.

Xie, X. F., Zhang, W. J., & Yang, Z. L. (2002). Adaptive particle swarm optimization on individual level. *Proceedings of the 6th International Conference on Signal Processing* (pp. 1215-1218). Beijing, China.

ENDNOTES

[1] This constant ensures that the fitness values are non-negative which is a requirement of the GA implementation.

[2] The policy rules are written in PROLOG. The simulation uses the SWI-Prolog engine (www.swi-prolog.org) for setting the current system state of an agent and for evaluating whether a condition is fulfilled. The action parts of the rules are mapped to the corresponding agent actions.

Section 3
Nature–Inspired Solutions in Science

Chapter 4
An Artificial Life–Based Vegetation Modelling Approach for Biodiversity Research

Eugene Ch'ng
The University of Wolverhampton, UK

ABSTRACT

The complexity of nature can only be solved by nature's intrinsic problem-solving approach. Therefore, the computational modelling of nature requires careful observations of its underlying principles in order that these laws can be abstracted into formulas suitable for the algorithmic configuration. This chapter proposes a novel modelling approach for biodiversity informatics research. The approach is based on the emergence phenomenon for predicting vegetation distribution patterns in a multi-variable ecosystem where Artificial Life-based vegetation grow, compete, adapt, reproduce and conquer plots of landscape in order to survive their generation. The feasibility of the modelling approach presented in this chapter may provide a firm foundation not only for predicting vegetation distribution in a wide variety of landscapes, but could also be extended for studying biodiversity and the loss of animal species for sustainable management of resources.

INTRODUCTION

Vegetation modelling is an important topic in the sciences in at least two streams of applications. The former applies the modelling and simulation of vegetation for predicting the impacts of climate change on forestry, studies of forest succession for resource and habitat management, and animal habitat modelling while the latter attempts to recon- struct past landscapes for geological studies or for interpretive and mitigation strategies in landscape archaeology. The modelling techniques proposed in this chapter apply to both. A third stream while use- ful, are limited in its applicability to larger problems at hand. This stream relates to the modelling of the architecture or structure of plants and has been in development since the 1970s, e.g. Honda (1971) and Mech and Prusinkiewicz (1996).

A survey of literature in the two streams of research boundaries has shown differing but quite

DOI: 10.4018/978-1-60566-705-8.ch004

similar problems. These limitations relate to fine-scale predictions, biotic interactions, biological life-cycle, evolutionary change, species dispersal, discrete space, temporal activity, and three-dimensional analysis. Perhaps the core of the problem is that these models are top-down and centralised, in contrast to the bottom-up and decentralised approach associated with natural systems. Furthermore, application of the model in similar scenarios often yielded inconsistencies. For example, various comparisons of methods for predictive modelling of vegetation revealed that results vary depending on specific situations and that there were inconsistencies in the predictions (Cairns, 2001; Miller & Franklin, 2002; Moisen & Frescino, 2002; Muñoz & Felicísimo, 2004). A survey of the modelling approach of prominent works in the second stream showed that the algorithms used were similarly top-down (Spikins, 1999; 2000). It is difficult to find predictive methods that mimic nature. Prominent agent-based models of plants (Benes & Cordoba, 2003; Deussen, et al., 1998; Lane & Prusinkiewicz, 2002; Lange, et al., 1998) have also been studied to determine their limitations in order that novel modelling strategies may be defined.

While nature has afforded humankind abundant resources and have inspired creative principles in the sciences, it is time that the sciences assist nature with the principles nature has inspired. Artificial Life (Langton, 1990), an experimental science for the study of synthetic systems that exhibit behaviours characteristic of natural living systems may be the contributing informatics. Concepts central to Artificial Life are mainly nature-inspired. Artificial Life has not only been used for studying carbon based life forms but in the discipline's formative years as a new science has seen a tremendous increase in the applications of its principles for solving real world problems. It is observed that the increase is due to the fact that nature-inspired principles simply work in real world situations. The reason for the functional cause does not entirely credit the ability of the

human species as a more intelligent being capable of creating new approaches for solving problems in their domains, but in their ability to learn from nature by emulating nature's way of problem solving. After all, problem solving is intrinsic in nature. Already researchers have employed self-organisation, a principle in natural systems, for solving problems. In Swarm Smarts (Bonabeau and Theraulaz, 2000) software agents mimicking models of ants and social insects were used to solve complex problems such as the rerouting of traffic in a busy telecommunications network, bees were used for devising a technique for scheduling paint booths in a truck factory, and collaboration in ants were used for robot-task collaboration (Kube and Zhang, 1993). The flocking and schooling behaviour of fish and animals were not only used for the entertainment industry (games and movies that require swarm behaviours uses flocking and schooling algorithms) (Woodcock, 2000), but were also used for assistance in tasks that require coordinated movements (Ng, Leng, & Low, 2004; Schaefer, Mackulak, Cochran, & Cherilla, 1998). Decentralised multiple coordinated microbots for sharing information, cooperatively analyse large portions of a planet's surface or subsurface, and provide context for scientific measurements are also in development (Dubowsky, et al., 2005).

Nature-inspired informatics have been used for problem solving in many areas, perhaps it could also assist in solving nature's problem. The aim of this chapter is to investigate the nature-inspired algorithms in which vegetation can be modelled for synthesising their natural counterpart. The research attempts to depart from traditional modelling approach by leveraging the concept of emergence in the study. The main structure of the paper covers the current research in vegetation modelling and its associated problems. The methodology covers the principles in the design of Artificial Life where agent-based plants compete and interact with its environment. The core of the methodology defines the principles underlying the approach in Artificial Life-based vegetation modelling. The experiments section demonstrates the evidence of correlations between the artificial and the natural with some interesting phenomenon in the formation of plant communities in the landscape. Finally, the chapter conclude with the results and future work.

The objective of the chapter is to demonstrate that nature-inspired informatics, in particular, Artificial Life-based models of vegetation could potentially be useful for predicting the distribution of vegetation in both local and large spatial-temporal landscapes. The modelling technique presented in this chapter has been applied on a submerged ancient landscape under the North Sea (Ch'ng, 2007b; Ch'ng & Stone, 2006a, 2006b) (Mesolithic period 12,000 – 7,500bp, Shotton River) and the project has been featured in various international media, e.g. Spinney (2008).

BACKGROUND

The field of vegetation modelling has an increasingly important role in science and engineering. Its application areas are extensive and the potential usefulness of a model could solve difficult issues related to resource conservation planning, habitat and biodiversity management, and to assist in mitigation strategies, particularly in studies related to climate change. Two main streams of studies in vegetation modelling are related to attempts at predicting the distribution of vegetation across a landscape based on the relationship between the spatial distribution of vegetation and environmental variables. The first stream of research attempts to predict the projection of vegetation distribution into the future while the second stream endeavours to model effects of environmental change on vegetation distribution in the ancient past. A third stream examines the modelling of the architecture or structure of plants and its interactions with the environment on a local scale. This section reviews these researches in order that a strategic solution for modelling issues may be formulated. The

following paragraphs first examine the consistencies of statistical and probabilistic predictive modelling methods and the associated issues with Geographical Information Systems (GIS) in the first two streams. Secondly, the section covers issues related to fine-scale predictions, biotic interactions, evolutionary change, and species dispersals of predictive modelling techniques before examining bottom-up approaches in vegetation modelling.

Predictive modelling of vegetation patterns is defined as the predicting of geographic distribution of the vegetation composition across a landscape from mapped environmental variables (Miller & Franklin, 2002). Predictive system for spatial distribution of plants and animals such as BIOCLIM was developed in the 1980s (Busby, 1991; Nix, 1986) and has subsequently been customised to improve its limitations (Doran & Olsen, 2001). BIOCLIM has been subjected to criticisms as its use of all 35 parameters may lead to over-fitting of the model, which in turn may result in misinterpretations of species' potential ranges, and to the loss of biological reality (Beaumont, Hughes, & Poulsen, 2005). In recent years, the application of vegetation predictive modelling using GIS and statistical techniques has rapidly pervaded studies in ecology. These models are mainly static and probabilistic in nature since they statistically relate the geographical distribution of species or communities to their present environment (Guisan & Zimmermann, 2000). These techniques strategically position a plant type onto a pixel on the map under a given set of environmental conditions. Among the five more popular prediction models were Generalised Linear Models (GLMs), Generalised Additive Models (GAMs), Classification and Regression Trees (CART), Multivariate Adaptive Regression Splines (MARS), and Artificial Neural Networks (ANNs). There have been studies comparing these models but variations and inconsistencies were found. For example, Cairns (2001) compared Classification Trees, GLM and ANN and found that the accuracy of each method varies depending upon the specific situations. In Cairn's investigation, the ANN procedure produces the most accurate predictions while the Classification Tree predictions were the least accurate. This shows that there may not be a single best predictive method. Taverna, Urban and McDonald (2004) compared the predictive accuracy of CART and GLM and found that the CART models produced the more accurate predictions. In another study (Muñoz & Felicísimo, 2004), it was found that CART which may produce better numerical predictions on new data, generates complex models that can lead to no or spurious model interpretations, and is occasionally of no use for cartographic purposes. The same study found that MARS performed better and is more consistent. Miller and Franklin (2002) found that Classification Tree models had higher classification accuracy on the training data than GLMs, but accuracy of the Classification Tree models degraded more drastically when they were assessed using the test data. Moisen and Frescino (2002) compare GAMs to four alternative modelling techniques and found that MARS and ANN worked best when applied to simulated data, but less so when applied to real data and that GAMs and MARS were marginally best overall for modelling forest characteristics.

In the second stream, Spikins's models of past vegetation (Spikins, 1999, 2000) using GIS to combine a series of base maps for the predictions. The method uses a program designed within the GIS for determining the most probable dominant tree type in the landscape based on soil, climate preferences of each tree type along with information on the climate and presence of tree types for each phase. The simulation runs through two nested program 'loops' – the outer cycles through each date or period for which the model was being run, the inner circle through the mapping of each different possible woodland types allocating a dominant type for each unit. In Spikins (2000), Spikins hinted on the use of a rule-based algorithm for selecting the most likely probable dominant

woodland type for each area of layered information (Soils, topography, etc). The models in these two streams demonstrated the use of a top-down approach in the positioning of vegetation.

GIS has become an important element in such studies. In fact, GIS is indispensable in these studies. GIS however, has its limitations. One of its great limitations is the record of data in 3D space. Cross (2003) noted that in physical space, two items could occupy the same 2D location but could be several metres apart in vertical location. Since GIS references a physical item in 2D data, it has limitations with regard to 3D information, that is, what lies above or below a plane.

Ebert and Singer (2004) identified three main areas in which GIS can be considered lacking. The three limitations are cognitive representations, temporal analysis and three-dimensional analysis. These aspects are particularly important to the modelling and visualisation required for determining vegetation formations on different levels of the terrain. The lack in temporal analysis becomes evident when vegetation life cycle has to be accounted for. Furthermore, the migration of species and the competition between species requires time as an element. On the limitations of visualisation, the representations of objects as point, line or polygon may be useful in some instances, but more often, cognitive ideas becomes difficult. Additionally, the lack in 3D capabilities hinders the analysis of 3D topography.

Another drawback is the accuracy of the represented model. Fyfe (2005) noted that since GIS requires a simplification of the landscape, and the spatial scale (pixel size) applied within the analysis will determine the likely precision of the models when vegetation communities are applied, the accuracy is compromised. This is due to the fact that the pixel size of the elevation models are determined by the minimum available patch size within the simulations.

A number of critiques have recently questioned the validity of modelling strategies for predicting the potential impacts of climate change on the natural distribution of species. A research review by Pearson and Dawson (2003) showed that many factors other than climate determine species distributions and the dynamics of distribution changes. While predictive modelling strategies have often focused on the identification of a species' bioclimatic envelope, other factors such as biotic interactions, evolutionary change and species dispersals are not taken into account and therefore making predictions erroneous and misleading. Three experiments of different species consisting of aerial, terrestrial and marine organisms (Connell, 1961; A. J. Davis, Jenkinson, Lawton, Shorrocks, & Wood, 1998; Silander & Antonovics, 1982) suggest that biotic interactions are important elements of population dynamics, and must be included in predictions of biotic responses to climate change. While arguments exists that applying bioclimatic models at macro-scales where climatic influences on species distributions are shown to be dominant can minimise the impact of biotic interactions, prediction methods for micro-scale and various level of biological organisation is necessary when such interactions is an important determinant. According to Cairns (2001), "Species interactions such as through competition, predation, or symbiosis, make fine scale predictions more difficult to make than similar predictions at more aggregate levels (e.g., communities, functional groups, or ecosystems)." Evolutionary change of species is also an important factor. Some studies related to insects and plants (M. B. Davis & Shaw, 2001; Thomas, et al., 2001; Woodward, 1990) suggest that rapid evolutionary change occurs even in a short span of time, as opposed to the long time scales generally expected for genetic adaptation of a species. It should be noted that not all species will show adaptive responses to climate change (Etterson & Shaw, 2001). At present, adaptive changes have not been accounted for in predictive modelling. Species dispersals is another factor that bioclimate envelope models disregard, presenting a limitation to such models. Migration limitations such as landscape barriers,

deforestation, and man-made habitats can obstruct species movement. This however, is dependent on the species' migration ability. Highly mobile and dispersive species will be able to migrate at a sufficient rate to keep pace with the changing climate, while poor dispersers will only occupy current distribution areas that remain suitable, this is shown in a study of a bird species' geographic distributions based on the effects of climate change (Peterson, et al., 2001).

At this point, it is important to note that in order to predict vegetation distribution in both the global and local scale, it is necessary to depart from the traditional methods where vegetation are mapped to a discrete location based on a top-down rule. Therefore, the simulation of vegetation life-cycle is necessary. A bottom-up approach for simulating plant growth and distribution would be to model each plant as an individual entity with inbuilt rules encompassing reproduction, growth, competition, interaction, variation, and adaptation. Continuous space may be another requirement. For example, in the physical world, space is not partitioned into discrete blocks of squares for a plant or groups of plants to occupy as in a digital map where groups of vegetation types are mapped to each pixel representing n meters of space. An Artificial Life approach that includes biotic interactions, evolutionary change, and species dispersal requires a continuous space with temporal and three-dimensional processes in the model. The concept of a bottom-up approach for vegetation modelling will be elaborated in the methodological section.

The subsequent paragraphs survey the third stream in related research where the bottom-up approach is used. Literature in vegetation modelling that can be posited within the Artificial Life context is scarce. A survey revealed only a handful of articles of which only several are useful for simulation in large landscapes.

A study in the early stages of research initially found that there are at least three methods for modelling vegetation. One low-level method is to model the plant from the interacting cells forming its structures; another is to model the intermediate plant's vascular structure and its growth and interaction within a localised position, implementing each structure as an agent. The third approach is to model the plant as a reactive agent - a complete unit that responds to ecological factors so that collectively these agents could determine the local and global patterns they form on landscapes. To date, two approaches have been attempted. L-System or particle-based structural models are very popular and are frequently used to model the structure of trees, flowers, and roots of plants in computer graphics. Agent-based plant models are few, but seemed to be more suited to a wide scale of landscape conditions.

Structural growth and branching patterns of plants are well researched. The first computer model of tree structure was introduced by Honda (1971). Other early models of plants are based on fractals (Aono & Kunii, 1984; Mandelbrot, 1982; Oppenheimer, 1986). Within the fractals domain, a very realistic branching pattern approach is Oppenheimer's model (Oppenheimer, 1986). Oppenheimer presents a fractal computer model of branching objects, which generates very realistic pictures of simple orderly plants, complex gnarled trees, leaves, and vein systems. Work in modelling the branching patterns of plants later developed through formal specification resulting in the Lindenmayer systems (L-Systems). L-Systems introduced in Lindenmayer (1971a, 1971b) is a set of formal grammar (rules and symbols) that generates complex sentences from primitive components. It was first used for modelling plant structures in computer graphics (Smith, 1984). L-System was subsequently improved (Prusinkiewicz & Lindenmayer, 1990). Since then, L-systems has been widely used for describing the growth and developments of spatial structures of plants (e.g. Prusinkiewicz, Hammel, Hanan, & Mech, 1996; Prusinkiewicz, Hammel, Mech, & Hanan, 1995; Prusinkiewicz, Hanan, & Mech, 1999; Prusinkiewicz & Remphrey, 2005;

Runions, et al., 2005). Methods other than the early fractals and the popular L-Systems have also been developed (Fisher, 1977; Honda, Tomlinson & Fisher, 1981; Room, Maillette, & Hanan, 1994; Sakaguchi & Ohya, 1999; Weber & Penn, 1995), which contributed towards synthesising images of plants using computer graphics. Computer graphics models of plants, although realistic did not take into account the effects of environmental factors on plant developments. Therefore its uses were limited only to beautiful illustrations in computer graphics.

Useful models of plants on the other hand, require interaction with their environment. Attempts to simulate interaction between plants and their environments have resulted in the extension of L-System. Open L-Systems (Mech & Prusinkiewicz, 1996) was developed to allow interaction between plants and its environment. In the Open L-System, a bi-directional information exchange between plants and their environment is possible. Competition is threefold – branches are limited by collisions, roots compete for water in the soil, and the competition within and between trees for sunlight.

Particle systems for modelling plant structures was used for the first time by Reeves and Blau (1985). Arvo and Kirk (1988) and later Greene (1989, 1991) simulated climbing plants using the same method. Particles were also used for modelling climbing plants as systems of oriented particles that are able to sense their environment (Benes & Millan, 2002), but mainly with stationary objects. Algorithms for radiant energy transfers (lighting simulation) affecting plant growth has also been studied (Soler, Sillion, Blaise, & Dereffye, 2003). Others like Hanan *et al.* (Hanan, Prusinkiewicz, Zalucki, & Skirvin, 2002), modelled insect movement and the damage and development of 3D structures of a plant.

It is known that models based on the structures of plant growth require extensive computation. This is the reason why most structural plant models are static renderings or sequences of it.

For vegetation modelling in large landscapes, techniques using high-level models such as agents are necessary.

Collaborative agents (e.g. Nwana & Ndumu, 1998) emphasise autonomy and cooperation with other agents in order to perform tasks for their owners in open and time-constrained multi-agent environments. In a competitive environment however, collaborative agents can become non-collaborative and even intimidating when species compete for resources in order to survive and leave progenies. A competitive vegetation landscape is one such example. From a global viewpoint, vegetation agents collaborate by competition so that the task of distributing vegetation across a landscape is accomplished. But from a local perspective, they compete against each other for survival in an uncooperative way. This section surveys related agent-based plant models.

Modelling and realistic rendering of scenes with thousands of plants has been attempted. Deussen *et al.* (1998) introduces a pipe-line of tools for modelling and rendering of plants on terrain. The pipe-line is composed of two levels of simulation – modelling and rendering. The modelling aspect of plant distribution can either be determined by hand (using a set of grey-level images for defining the spatial distributions of plant densities), by ecosystem simulation, or by a combination of both techniques. Ecosystem simulation uses the Open L-System where each plant (represented as circles) is connected to another in a branching pattern characteristic of L-System. The simulation of competition is simple – if two circles intersects, the smaller plant dies. Plants reaching a set size limit are considered old and are eliminated. The model also manipulates the plant population and distribution using a simplified self-thinning (Ricklefs, 1990) algorithm based on a model of Firbank and Watkinson (1985) for simulating the phenomenon in plant population dynamics. Deussen *et al.*'s method is partially agent-based with L-System as a framework connecting each plant. Since the population and

distribution of plants are largely manipulated, the basic autonomy of plant species is dissimilar to that observed in natural systems, which by nature is bottom-up. Furthermore, there was no evidence of the inclusion of ecosystem factors in the plant distribution model.

Lane and Prusinkiewicz (2002) introduces a local-to-global and a global-to-local approach for generating spatial distribution of plant species. In the former approach, plants grow and interact in a way that leads to a certain plant distribution. This is a bottom-up approach. The second approach is top-down: plant distributions are specified by using gray-scale images before the system generates the corresponding images. The former approach is evaluated as it has the natural principles of growth. The local-to-global approach is an extension of Deussen *et al.*'s work (Deussen, et al., 1998) mentioned previously. While Deussen *et al.*'s approach uses self-thinning, Lane and Prusinkiewicz extended the previous L-System with a succession model. In the self-thinning method, the parameter *c* is used for interaction between plants, which sets *c=1* if the plant is not dominated and to *0* if the plant is dominated. The succession model is a closer approach to plant interaction in the real world. In the algorithm, new plants are added in every time step with local propagation – sowing new plants near plants of the same species. Shade competition replaces the two state domination parameter by introducing a probability of *1-shaded[sp]*, where *sp* is a plant identifier, and *shaded[sp]* is the shade tolerance of the plant, measured of how likely it is to survive in shadow. Senescence of plants is modelled by introducing a survival probability measure *oldage[sp]*. In the system, a plant that does not survive dies and is removed from the community. Both the self-thinning and succession model does not involve environmental factors.

Benes and Cordoba (2003) presented an ecosystem for the cultivation of virtual plants via procedural agents. The agent (a virtual farmer) can seed new plants, pull out weeds, water plants, and communicate by message passing to distribute their tasks. In Benes and Cordoba's work, an ecosystem is defined as "a set of individual plants in different stages of development" and "is a virtual environment represented as a 2D continuous area inhabited by virtual plants". Plant models are limited to English daisy, wheat, grasses, yellow tulip, and different procedurally generated trees obtained by the Strands model (Holton, 1994). Plants in the ecosystem are influenced by other plants, external resources, and procedural agents. The seeding of the terrain can either be random or interactive via some drawing program using colours as corresponding plant species. Seeded plants grow, compete, reproduce, and die. The article however, did not describe how the plants are influenced by competition and external sources.

The Nerve Garden, a real-time agent-based model (Damer, Marcelo, & Revi, 1998), whilst claiming to exhibit properties of growth, decay, and energy transfer reminiscent of a simple ecosystem, presents a somewhat primitive solution from an Artificial Life perspective since it does not support plant growth or interaction between plants and the environment according to a review (Luck & Aylett, 2000). Damer's project uses Virtual Reality Modelling Language (VRML), a web-based visualisation language that, except for collision detection, does not support interaction between objects. As such, it is impossible to simulate competition, much less the properties of an ecosystem.

A model that is closer to our approach is Lange *et al*'s TRAGIC++ (Lange, et al., 1998). Lange *et al*'s model uses a growth simulator within an abiotic environment. Each plant interacts with only two input fluxes – energy and a growth-limiting nutrient. The actual growth of each tree is derived from local competition for energy and nutrients. Evolutionary effects are included by random mutations of parameters related to height growth strategies of individual trees.

From the evaluation of previous work, certain fundamental principles required to properly syn-

thesise behaviours of plant species were found to be either partial or lacking. It is discovered that no single system mentioned above collectively tackle these issues for plant synthesis and predictive modelling. This article, then, seeks to address the issues for vegetation modelling that are partial and lacking in the following areas:

1. Generic vegetation model – capable of including all vegetation types
2. Individual plant life cycle – from seeds to senescence
3. Generic plant life cycle – growth, survival, competition, and reproduction (species dispersal)
4. Vegetation forms (trees, shrubs, herbs, grass, and etc)
5. Seasonal differences (evergreen, deciduous)
6. Competition based on vegetation types - canopy, density of leaves, height, and vegetation types
7. Competition for space, sunlight, and nutrient accessibility
8. Adaptability to ecological factors and resources – sunlight, temperature, carbon dioxide, altitude, soil, hydrology, and etc)
9. Ground conditions – soil acidity, soil depth, soil textures, ground slopes, and etc
10. Extensibility for evolutionary change

The article also attempts to resolve issues related to the modelling environment:

1. Inclusion of temporal processes
2. Continuous three-dimensional landscape for replacing discrete pixel-based maps
3. A system capable of simulating both small and large scale terrains
4. Observable growth and distribution of species
5. Foundation for inclusion of other species for research in managing resources and biodiversity

METHODOLOGY: NATURED-INSPIRED MODELLING

In this section, we examine the issues associated with the top-down approach and provide a nature-inspired solution for vegetation modelling.

The Top-Down Approach

A top-down approach relates to systems having central governance. A central governance or control involves the planning and influencing of a system via a global principle or sets of principles which when exercised, forms an orderly society of dependent system units. The units are dependent in that they do not possess any rights or freedom. Such units are non-autonomous and not self-regulating. As a consequence, the system as a whole is predictable. Each unit is directly slave to the global principles set forth by the governance. Such systems may also manifest a hierarchical control where a unit is indirectly associated with the global principles via a higher unit in the network. The centralised approach may be useful in man-made systems, but is a barrier, if not an impossibility in organic systems especially when nature is essentially self-organising from a bottom-up perspective. This is particularly true in studies in pattern formation in all levels of biological systems (Camazine, et al., 2001). Here we explore how nature works via examples. It will then become apparent that central governance is not a principle in natural systems.

Social insects such as bees and especially ants in Gordon's study (Gordon, 1999) are very good examples of models of decentralisation. As an individual unit, an insect accomplishes very little due to its simple state, but as a colony the simple rules built into the genes of each insect collectively achieve an intelligence and personality that displays nature's best example of self-organisation. In the ant colony, the queen is not an authoritarian figure and does not decide the tasks of each worker ant due to the fact that the queen's quarter is separated by several metres of intricate tunnels and chambers and thousands of ants, rendering her physically impossible to direct each worker ant's decision within the colony. But it is interesting to note that in dangerous circumstances, the rule of keeping the queen safe in the gene pool of the ants make them remove the queen to the escape hatch in an organised behaviour issuing from collective decision making. Self-organising behaviour is also seen in the separation of food, garbage and deceased ants in the colony. In a collective decision the garbage dump and cemetery are situated apart by the ants in Gordon's observation, with the cemetery situated at exactly the point that is furthest from the colony, solving spatial mathematical problems without a central command of intelligence.

The slime mould (Keller & Segel, 1970; Morse, 1949; Nakagaki, 2000; Segel, 2001) are thousands of distinct single-celled units moving as separate individuals from their comrades, oscillating between being a single celled creature and a swarm. Under suitable conditions, the single-celled organisms combined into a single, larger organism scavenging for food on the ground. In less hospitable conditions, the slime mould lives as a single organism. While being fairly simple as a single celled organism, the slime mould collectively displays an intriguing example of coordinated swarm behaviour via the individual release of a common substance called acrasin (or cyclic AMP). In a study (Nakagaki, 2000), the slime mould was found to be capable of finding the shortest possible route through a maze. In normal circumstances, the slime mould spreads out its network of tube-like legs, or pseudopodia to fill all available space. But when two pieces of food were placed at separate exit points in the maze, the organism squeezed its entire body between the two nutrients, adopting the shortest possible route, thus solving the maze. The aggregate slime mould changes its shape and maximises its foraging efficiency to increase its chances of survival. The slime mould aggregation is recognised as a classic case study of bottom-up behaviour.

The flocking (Reynolds, 1987) and schooling (Huth & Wissel, 1992; Niwa, 1994) behaviour of animals, birds and fish have been studied extensively in the past. It was discovered that there is no 'leader' bird or fish but simple rules built into the individuals form a collective behaviour. In schooling fishes, the rules of schooling are a consequence of the tendency of each fish to avoid others that are too close. They align their bodies to those at intermediate distances, and move towards others that are far away. Flocking and schooling can be synthesised via three simple rules in the computer: separation, alignment and cohesion.

Pattern formation in natural systems has also been formally studied. Camazine *et al.* (2001) noted that "patterns are a particular, organized arrangement of objects in space and time." Examples of self-organising biological patterns are found not only in static patterns, such as the complex architecture of a termite mound, lichen growth, and pigmentation patterns on shells, fish and mammals, but also dynamic patterns formed by a school of fish, a raiding column of army ants, and the synchronous flashing of fireflies. In Camazine *et al.*'s study, non-visual patterns generated from a bottom-up approach can also be observed from the sub-cellular level (DNA) up to the population dynamics of biological systems. The main observation was that patterns are formed in nature based on the interaction of entities with either a simple rule or a set of simple rules. The environment too, plays an important role in providing an initial condition and positive feedback for the shaping of the patterns. As such, the shaping of each complex entity's environment issues in variations of similar patterns. Similarly, the natural distribution of vegetation communities on landscapes does not depend on central governance or from some blueprints, templates, or principles set forth from a global level. It is the local interaction of many species of plants with individually different rules and the extra-

local ecological factors that they depend on that determines the formation of landscapes.

Because of the linearity and predictability of a top-down approach, it is particularly difficult when emergent phenomenon resulting from biotic interaction, species adaptive change and distribution are elements that needs to be considered in the model.

Artificial Life and the Bottom-Up Approach

Artificial Life is concerned with generating life-like behaviours within computers. Since the study focuses on the behaviours of life, it involves identifying the intrinsic mechanisms that generate such behaviours. These mechanisms are often very simple rules within the individuals of a collection of interacting organisms out of which complex behaviour emerges. Or on a higher level, the mechanism itself may be the simple behaviours of an organism. Together as cooperative entities, these organisms worked together as a larger 'organism' for the survival of the colony, yet from very basic pre-programmed rules. The phenomena or intelligence that emerges as a result of the simple interaction between individual entities is called *emergence* (Holland, 1998; Johnson, 2002), a central concept supporting studies in Artificial Life.

Systems that exhibit emergent behaviours are commonly expressed in the sentence "the whole is greater than the sum of its parts" (Kauffman, 1996). The term *emergence* was first used by an English philosopher G.H. Lewes (Lewes, 1875) over a hundred years ago and has been subsequently studied in philosophy (Goldstein, 1999; McLaughlin, 1992; Mill, 1843; Nagel, 1961). At the time, simulation models for studying emergent behaviour was limited until the advent of computers and the initiation of the theory of complexity (Holland, 1995; Lewin, 1993; Waldrop, 1993) coupled with experiments on Cellular Automata (CA) (Gutowitz, 1991; Kauffman, 1996; Langton, 1986; Toffoli & Margolus, 1987; von Neumann &

Burks, 1966). Studies in CA showed that simple rules in computer agents could give rise to complex behaviours. A particular CA 'Life rule' (Resnick & Silverman, 1996) invented by John Conway in the 1970s called the Game of Life demonstrated the idea of emergence where simple interactions between entities resulted in objects and patterns that are surprising and counter-intuitive. Referring to the definition of the term 'emergence', John Holland (Holland, 1998), a pioneer in complex systems and nonlinear science advised that "It is unlikely that a topic as complicated as emergence will submit meekly to a concise definition, and I have no such definition to offer", however, he adds that "The hallmark of emergence is this sense of much coming from little... where the behaviour of the whole is much more complex than the behaviour of the parts." Another definition (Mihata, 1997) states that emergence is "...the process by which patterns or global-level structures arise from interactive local-level processes. This "structure" or "pattern" cannot be understood or predicted from the behaviour or properties of the component units alone." In a more elaborate sentence given by Stacey (1996), "Emergence is the production of global patterns of behaviour by agents in a complex system interacting according to their own local rules of behaviour, without intending the global patterns of behaviour that come about. In emergence, global patterns cannot be predicted from the local rules of behaviour that produce them. To put it another way, global patterns cannot be reduced to individual behaviour."

The success of Artificial Life in problem solving is identified by the possibility of emulating nature's properties of *decentralisation, self-organisation, self-assembly, self-producing,* and *self-reproduction,* all of which are key concepts in the field. A decentralised system (Resnick, 1994) relies on lateral relationships for decision making instead of on the hierarchical structure of command or force. *Self-organisation* (Kauffman, 1993, 1996) refers to systems that manage themselves and increase in productivity automatically without guidance from an external source. In systems

with characteristics of *self-assembly,* patterns are seen to form from simple disordered components. *Self-producing* or *autopoiesis* (Mingers, 1995) connotes the idea that certain types of system continuously produce their constituents, their own components, which then participate in these same production processes. An autopoietic system has a circular organisation, which closes on itself, its outputs becoming its own inputs. Such systems possess a degree of autonomy from their environment since their own operations ensure, within limits, their future continuation. In *Self-replication* (Langton, 1986; Sipper, 1998; Sipper & Reggia, 2001), entities make copies of themselves. Such concepts are difficult, if not impossible to model from a top-down perspective.

Resnick (1994) states that orderly patterns can arise from simple, local interactions and that many things are "organised without an organisation, coordinated without a coordinator". In the same way, Farmer and Packard (1986) noted that in self-organising systems, patterns emerge out of lower-level randomness. Furthermore, Charles Darwin (Darwin, 1859) asserted that order and complexity arises from decentralised processes of variation and selection. One of the founders of Artificial Life stated that in order to model complex systems like life, the most promising approach is to dispense "with the notion of a centralised global controller" and to focus "on mechanisms for the distributed control of behaviour" (Langton, 1989).

The characteristics inherent in many decentralised systems are nonlinear, and the nonlinearity, as characterised by natural systems is what makes the outcome more than the sum of their parts – forming dynamic patterns, collective intelligence and unpredictable behaviours from the lateral interactions between similar entities. This is the difference between the bottom-up methods and the top-down approach in many traditional modelling techniques. By employing the bottom-up approach observed in nature, not only can we discover how certain systems work, but many complex problems previously impenetrable with top-down methods

Figure 1. Bottom-up approaches in vegetation modelling

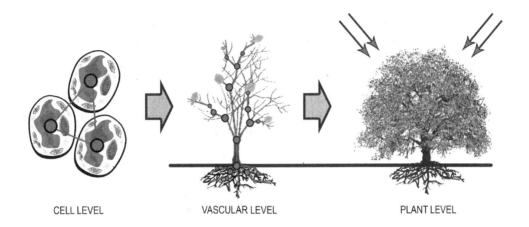

CELL LEVEL   VASCULAR LEVEL   PLANT LEVEL

can now be readily solved. The next section explores ways in which vegetation can be modelled based on the nature-inspired concepts covered in the preceding paragraphs.

Strategies for Vegetation Modelling

Since Von Neumann's work on the Theory of Self-Reproducing Automata (von Neumann & Burks, 1966), years of laborious investigations by a handful of individuals have revolutionised the way we think about the world and its systems. The paradigm shift from recognising physical systems as constrained by centrality to one that works via the interaction of distributed components has initiated new terrains for research.

According to the bottom-up approach, vegetation modelling could begin from the cellular level (Figure 1a), with interacting cells forming the smaller components of a tree, and the smaller components forming the vascular systems which structure eventually complete the tree. Another way is to model the vascular structure of a tree (Figure 1b) with its root and shoot system interacting with itself, the environment, and other plants to form a tree that is limited by its pattern architecture. Each of these approaches may be useful for certain studies, however, considering the limitations of computing resources for managing large collections of plant interactions, modelling vegetation

as complete entities (Figure 1c) that respond to ecological factors, availability of resources, and threats from competition and the environment may be a more feasible approach.

Learning from examples in living systems, we could perceive landscapes as large organisms composed of many decentralised entities (community, population, biocenosis) which collectively form and replenish the larger system (ecosystems, biospheres) by forming forest patterns, and relying on the availability of resources and the suitability of the ecology on the ecosystem. In accordance with the concept of emergence, the local interaction of these vegetation communities in addition to ecological variables should appropriately synthesise the formation of vegetation communities on the realised niche of each species' ecology.

How can the rules be modelled from vegetation as a complete entity? Observations and studies of vegetation biology and plant ecology have shown that their life cycle, preferences, and tolerance to environmental benefits and threats can be described by states and rules with structural characteristics similar to those of computer algorithms. Any matter that can be digitised – translated into numbers can be synthesised computationally. Furthermore, a mapping of real world parameters to variables within the program should appropriately simulate their behaviour. In addition, vegetation reaction to environmental factors such as temperature variation, and competition for sunlight, nutrients, space and so on are nothing more than simple rules of preferential tolerance that can be described in a computer program based on variable states in variable conditions. With a small amount of "fine tuning" of the properties of vegetation, individual plants can be modelled to a level of accuracy sufficient for solving problems in biodiversity research.

Modelling the Constitution of Vegetation

Nature is complex and presents a fundamental limitation to modelling. While it is impossible to model every aspect of a natural system, attempts should be made to include important determinants. The strategy is to model sufficiently to achieve the stated objective.

What should be modelled? In 1858, Darwin (1858) and Wallace (1858) combined results of their studies to suggest a hypothesis for evolution. Darwin called this natural selection in the *Origin of Species* based on four observations: reproduction, competition, variation, and adaptation. Out of the four observations, the first, second and fourth can be taken into account in the modelling. Variation is not modelled within each plant species as we are not observing evolutionary change in a single species but in the evolution of the landscape. This means that there are variations from different species of plants but not from the same species. Variations across the population of species means that some plant types are better equipped to compete, and cope with selection pressures, survive and reproduce. Environmental resources as selection pressures should be modelled so that survivability and competition is taken into account. It was decided that photosynthesis and energy transfers are presently not necessary as there is only interest in how plants react to biotic and abiotic interactions within the model.

In the model, the lifecycle of vegetation is reduced to four high-level stages – Seed – Ger-

mination – Growth – Reproduction. In the seed[1] state and the first instance of germination, the plant passes through the survival phase where environmental factors act as selection pressures in an attempt to terminate the plant life by having the plant react to ecological signals. The growth and reproduction of the plant is in the phase where competition occurs and is characterised not only by ecological factors, but also by the competition for resources such as space, nutrients, and sunlight. This cycle is common to all species of plants introduced into the model except for the span of time they occupy to complete each cycle as can be observed in annuals, biennials, and perennials. During a plant's reproductive stage, pollination and fertilisation are deemed to have occurred and seeds are dispersed at proximity or at a distance based on plant sizes and the types of dispersal agents used.

Plants are environmentally-sensitive and are modelled as cybernetic systems, sensing and receiving information from the environment. Plants at proximity communicate information such as their canopy, height, and size for competition of sunlight, space, and nutrients. As such, their well being is directly affected by the environment and the vegetation at proximity.

Plant names are specified according to the Binomial System of Classification. However for practicality of synthesising vegetation lifecycle, taxonomic categories between the levels of genus and kingdom employed by botanists are not used. Instead, plants are grouped according to their lifecycles, visible size and shape of growth. In the model, *Pinus* would be grouped under evergreen whereas *Corylus Avellana* (Hazel) is under deciduous. Ferns are placed under the perennials category. The grouping of plants under the evergreen and deciduous tree type implies that they live from year to year. Annuals are plants that complete their lifecycles in one growing season. Biennials need two growing seasons to complete its lifecycle (vegetative growth – dormancy/inactive – flower – reproduction – death in second season). Perennials live for more than three years are categorised under herbaceous. The reason for the separation of tree types from herbaceous plants is for synthesising competition and will be covered in later sections. 'Grass' as a sub-level of 'Vegetation' may be added for more intense competition. The Organism is a top-level abstract class in the object-oriented system available for extension of other living organisms such as animals, birds, fish and insects in future work. As we are attempting to model vegetation lifecycle, this hierarchy is sufficient.

The genotype of vegetation are described using the Extensible Markup Language (XML) structure, containing properties for growth, reproduction, interspecies variation, adaptation, and seed germination which will be initialised with the plant entity. The structure of the XML is designed to provide a generic form for the inclusion of all types of plants. Each category of descriptors stores information regarding the plant's maximum age, plant types, adaptation to environmental factors, reproductive functions and seed dispersal methods, and the conditions for their seeds to germinate. An example XML is shown below.

```xml
<Plant>
<Growth>
<MaximumAge>50</MaximumAge>
<Type LeafType="Deciduous">Tree</Type>
<BestSoil>Clay</BestSoil>
<AcceptableSoil>Compost</AcceptableSoil>
<MaxHeight>30</MaxHeight>
<Canopy>23</Canopy>
<LeafDensity>0.7</LeafDensity>
</Growth>
<Tolerance hardiness="0.3">
<Sunlight Upper="0.98" Lower="0.4">0.5</Sunlight>
<Temperature Upper="36" Lower="-6">20</Temperature>
<Moisture Upper="0.6" Lower="0.35">0.5</Moisture>
<Nutrient Upper="0.7" Lower="0.2">0.55</Nutrient>
<Elevation Upper="760" Lower="-5">312</Elevation>
<Space Upper="0.45" Lower="0.01">0.25</Space>
<CO2 Upper="0.6" Lower="0.4">0.5</CO2>
<SoilPh Upper="8" Lower="1.5">4</SoilPh>
<SoilDepth Upper="1" Lower="0.2">0.4</SoilDepth>
<Ground Upper="0.5" Lower="0">0.3</Ground>
</Tolerance>
<Reproduction>
<Type>Sexual</Type>
<DispersalType>Discharge</DispersalType>
<SexualMaturityAge>8</SexualMaturityAge>
<SeedCount>60</SeedCount>
<AverageGerminationPercentage>20</AverageGerminationPercentage>
<PollenReleaseDateStart>July</PollenReleaseDateStart>
<PollenReleaseDateEnd>August</PollenReleaseDateEnd>
<SeedingMonth>September</SeedingMonth>
</Reproduction>
<Germination>
<DaysStart>30</DaysStart>
<DaysEnd>180</DaysEnd>
<MonthStart>March</MonthStart>
<MonthEnd>August</MonthEnd>
<Season>Autumn</Season>
<TemperatureLower>15</TemperatureLower>
<TemperatureUpper>28</TemperatureUpper>
<MoistureLower>0.32</MoistureLower>
<MoistureUpper>0.58</MoistureUpper>
<Soil>Clay</Soil>
</Germination>
<KnownDisease />
</Plant>
```

Figure 2. An example of how vegetation preferences are modelled. The illustration showed plant adaptability towards hydrology and soil moisture content (© 2007, Eugene Ch'ng. Used with Permission)

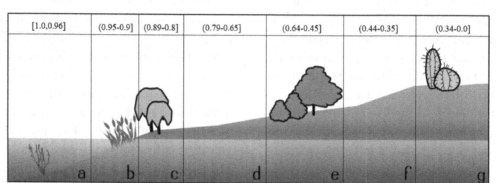

Modelling the Preference of Vegetation

Different species of vegetation possess different preferences towards the environment. Preferences can also be defined as tolerance or adaptability. These preferences are defined within the virtual plant's genotype constructs. Preferences that are well defined in botany are described with standard values whereas those which are not are measured between *[0,1]*. For example, temperature preferences of each species of plants are well defined. Tolerance to sunlight however, is often vague, with descriptions such as "full sun", "partial shade", "shady areas", and etc. Hydrological preferences are similarly, often described with a relative comparison between the ecology of interspecies preferences from studies of population concentrations. Grime, Hodgson and Hunt's *Comparative Plant Ecology* (Grime, Hodgson, & Hunt, 1988) is one example. Plant preferences use a relative measure based on Ch'ng's method (Ch'ng, 2007a). Figure 2 illustrates a scenario for modelling hydrological preferences.

In band *a*, the tolerance of aquatic plants is between 1.0 and 0.96~. Band *b* and *c* shows the tolerance of plants that live near water sources. These may be Cattails, Papyrus, Willows, and etc. Band *d*, *e*, and *f* are land based plants with plants in band *e* having a moderate preference. Plants preferring dry conditions are in band *g*.

Simple Rules in Vegetation

This section describes the rules for modelling vegetation. In the model, the growth of a plant is proportional to its age given that the conditions are favourable, although environmental factors and competition for resources from other plants may retard its size. The growth mechanism persists according to senescence, after which a plant expires. The age of the plant is incremented only after the seed is germinated.

Plant Reproduction

The reproduction in plants occurs when environmental signals and seasonal changes take place (e.g. spring in contrast to winter). Depending on the variation of reproduction in plants, at the appropriate time pollination and fertilisation are deemed to have occurred and seeds are dispersed onto the landscape. Based on the size of the plant, the majority of seeds are dispersed in a radial fashion within a dispersal distance from the parent plant. Dispersal agents (Abrahamson, 1989) such as ants, and vertebrates are simulated by dispersing a percentage of the seeds further across the landscape. Landscape barriers are not accounted for in the model. Values in the 'SeedCount' tag of the XML are parsed and utilised by each virtual plant. For example, the XML tag in Section 3.4 suggests a maximum of 60 seeds produced for each reproductive season for the associated plant (different plants have different seed count). This is an actual value used in the simulation. In the natural world, seeds are agents for future growth. Trees produce numerous seeds in order to counter the mortality rate. For example, a study (Howe, 1990) observed that the mortality of seeds and seedling of the Virola surinamensis (*Myristicaceae*) dropped under the parent crown exceeds 99%. In the study, 46% of the seeds drop under the parent tree while 54% are carried away. Only seeds regurgitated by birds away from parents have any chance of survival for 15 months in the understory (0.3-0.5%). In Darwinian thinking, it appears that seed mortality is so high because 'plants need only to leave one surviving offspring in a lifetime' (M. J. Crawley, 1992). It is important to note that different tree types in different environments have different seed and seedling mortality rates and it would be difficult at present to account for these complexities, but future models will look into these topics. As predator factors contributing to seed and seedling mortality are not in the model, the suggested value approximates the survival rate. Environmental and competition factors within the model then act as natural selection to decide the mortality of the seedlings. Two different methods are used for determining the number of seeds. The seeds that are produced by a tree or a shrub are dependent on their age of sexual maturity and the maximum age. This means that the more the plants grow, the more the seeds are produced. For all other types of vegetation, mostly herbaceous plants, the number of seeds is based on the fitness-seed ratio. The fitness-seed ratio is,

$$s_{herb} = s_{max} f \qquad (1)$$

where the total number of seeds produced is s_{herb}, s_{max} is the maximum number of seeds the plant is able to produce, and f is the fitness of the plant calculated using the fitness measure (see section 3.6.7):

The growth-seed ratio is modelled using the equation below.

$$s_{tree} = \left(1 + e^{s\left(g - \frac{x}{m} \right)} \right)^{-1} \qquad (2)$$

where s_{tree} is the total number of seeds produced for tree or shrub types, a is the current age, m is the maximum age, and x is the age of sexual maturity.

Seed Germination

The seeds of most plants require a period of dormancy before they will germinate (Murdoch & Ellis, 1992). In certain plants, dormancy usually cannot be broken except by exposure to cold or to light via a chemical inhibitor. In the model, seeds are assigned a seed age in days separate from the plant age where the dormancy period is tested. The *DaysStart* and *DaysEnd* assigned to the seed (as described in the XML genotype) is a probable period where the germination will occur. The ending of the dormancy at any probable time within the period is simulated with a 0.2 probability of occurrence. The value is an outcome of multiple tests, increasing the probability will produce similar results but will use more computational resources. The ideal conditions for seed germination such as the dormancy period, seasons and month, temperature preferences, moisture and soil types for this study can be obtained from Thompson and Morgan (2004).

Conditions for seed to germinate uses the environmental germination rule $L < E < U$ based on the plant genotype where E is the current environmental condition (the temperature), and L and U is the range of condition for the seed to germinate.

Plant Adaptation

Adaptation in vegetation denotes avoidance and tolerance to environmental hazards (M. J. E. Crawley, 1986). Plants evolve survival tactics by developing resistant bark, regeneration strategies from surviving stems, and avoidance by the possession of underground organs such as the lignotubers of Eucalyptus species. They reduce the rate at which they lose water through *evapotranspiration* (Slatyer, 1967). At sites prone to water logging, herbaceous vascular plants develops biochemical features which allow prolonged fermentation in the roots (Fitter & Haw, 1981). Others can even germinate underwater and their seedlings can survive considerable periods of submersion (Clark & Benforado, 1981). Plants living in permanent shade maximise their photosynthesis gain from the low levels of energy they receive, by means of reduced respiration rate, increased unit leaf rate, increased chlorophyll per unit leaf weight, increased leaf area per unit weight invested in shoot biomass (Bjorkman, 1968; Solbrig, 1981). Plants that adapt to low nutrient availability possesses small, leathery, long-lived leaves, and a high root: shoot ratios (Chapin, 1980; Vitousek, 1982). Other physiological traits that characterises plants at sites with low nutrients include slow growth rates, efficient nutrient utilisation, efficient mechanisms of internal nutrient recycling to ensure minimal losses through leaf fall, exudation or leaching (Clarkson & Hanson, 1980). Plants found to adapt to extremes of cold temperatures often possesses small, long-lived leaves and in extremes of hot temperatures, plants show small, dissected leaves which increase the rate of convective heat loss and physiological tolerance of very high tissue temperatures (M. J. E. Crawley, 1986). Ch'ng's adaptability measure (Ch'ng, 2007a) was used for measuring each environmental condition against the plants' preferences described in the genotype. Favourable conditions that suit the plant's preference will maintain its fitness whereas harsh condi-

tions may decrease it collectively over time to the eventual termination of the plant life.

Competition: Availability of Sunlight

The algorithms in this section define the rules for plant competition. The adaptability measure is used for calculating their tolerance to biotic interactions and selection pressures. Biotic interaction encompasses competition for space, sunlight, and nutrients.

The amount of light that may be received by a plant is determined by its height in relation to others. In larger plants (e.g., Trees, Shrubs), the density and radius of the canopy determine the shade they cast on smaller plants (e.g., Herbs) or the undergrowth. Figure 3 is an illustration of how competition for effective sunlight in a local setting occurs in the simulation. The vegetation in group A grow in a sparse setting and the effective sunlight is not annulled by any shade, therefore, no competition occurs. In group B, the shrubs growing under large trees in a forest setting receives limited sunlight due to shade. In a dense forest, there is a possibility that the canopy of trees completely filters the sunlight from reaching the undergrowth. Group C shows a collection of plants that are not fully covered. These receive some sunlight through the canopy.

The effective shade cast by an opponent U_i is,

$$U_i = c_i^{-1}\left[d_i\left|\sqrt{(x_i - x_s)^2 + (y_i - y_s)^2} - (r_i + r_s)\right|\right] \quad (3)$$

where i is the individual opponent with location, x_i and y_i, the canopy of each plant stated in the XML c_i, and leaf density d_i. The location of the source plant is at x_s, y_s with radius r_s.

The effective shade collectively of all opponents H is,

Figure 3. Logical scenarios depicting plant competition for sunlight

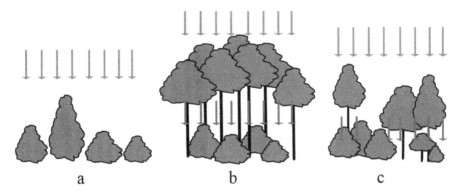

$$H = \begin{cases} 1 & if \ \sum_{i=1}^{n} U_i > 1 \\ \sum_{i=1}^{n} U_i & if \ 0 \le \sum_{i=1}^{n} U_i \le 1 \\ 0 & otherwise \end{cases} \quad (4)$$

where *n* is the number of plants in competition, *i* is an opponent. The effective sunlight *S* received by a plant under the shade of larger plants is,

$$S = L - (1 - H) \quad (5)$$

where *L=[0,1]* is the global sunlight before deducting from the effective shade *H*.

In shaded areas under large clusters of trees, the temperature may decrease slightly. This local temperature variation is simulated using the effective shade as defined below,

$$T_{shade} = H(-T_{max}) \quad (6)$$

where *H* is the effective shade collectively cast by opponent plants, T_{max} is the maximum decrease in temperature, and T_{shade} is the total decrease in temperature that is added to the effective temperature T_{eff} defined in section 3.6.8.

Competition: Availability of Space

Competition for space amongst plants is dependent on the size and form of the plant (tree, bushes, and undergrowth) and their inter-distances. The rules are defined so that a plant's establishment in age and its size are advantageous over smaller plants. The adaptation rules of a plant also differentiate trees from shrubs and herbs in that the latter will be more tolerant to crowded situations. Figure 4 demonstrates how competition for space occurs in the virtual environment in three different scenarios. 4a is a shrub type collection inclusive of herbaceous plants, 4b is tree type and 4c is a hybrid grouping of shrub and tree types. In 4a, shrub 1 is taller and therefore has no competitor; the use of space for shrub 3 is competed by shrub 1, 4, and 5; shrubs 4 and 5 compete for space with one another and with shrub 3. In 4b, tree 1 being larger, has no competitor. Tree 2's usage of space is competed by tree 1. Trees 3, 4, and 5 compete for space. In a hybrid setting in 4c, trees 1, 6, 7 and shrub 5 compete; shrub 4 competes with both 3 and 5. There is no competition between shrubs 2, 3, 4 with tree 1.

The logic in Figure 4 can be reduced to the rules that there is competition only if the opponent plant is larger and is a bush type or if it is equal or smaller in size with different intensity of the use of space for larger and smaller competitors. The intensity of the competition between different

Figure 4. Logical scenarios depicting the availability of space

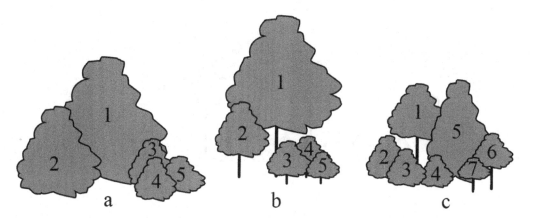

plants is dependent on their sizes. Two formulas are used for determining the use of space for larger opponents, or opponents smaller or equal in size. Figure 5 illustrates the concept where the curve on the left represents a plant smaller or equal in size to the agent plant (the dot) and the right curve represents a plant larger in size.

The space S_i occupied by larger opponents is defined with,

$$S_i = L\left[e^{\frac{x_i - ws}{I}} + 1 \right] \qquad (7)$$

where $L=[0.25, 0.3]$ is the space used if the source plant is at size s, x_i is the size of the opponent. For size $s \le 10$ *metres*, $I=5$, $w=3$. For size $10 > s < 25$ metres, $I=5$, $w=2$. For size $s > 25$ *metres*, $I=10$, $w=2$. I and w adjusts the function so that the space occupied by the large and smaller opponent joins at the point (Figure 5, Size of Plant).

The space S_i occupied by smaller opponents is defined with,

$$S_i = L e^{\frac{x_i - s}{I}} \qquad (8)$$

where $L=[0.25, 0.3]$ is the intensity of the use of space, x_i is size of the opponent, s is the size of

the source plant. For size $s \le 10$ metres, $I=1$. For size $10 > s < 25$ metres, $I=5$. For size $s < 25$ metres, $I=10$. I and w adjusts the function so that the space occupied by the large and smaller opponent continues at the dot (Figure 5, labelled 'Size of Plant').

The space occupied by all opponents is,

$$C = \begin{cases} 1 & if \ \sum_{i=1}^{n} S_i > 1 \\ \sum_{i=1}^{n} S_i & if \ 0 \le \sum_{i=1}^{n} S_i \le 1 \\ 0 & otherwise \end{cases} \qquad (9)$$

where C is the totality of the space occupied by opponent plants, n is the number of plants in competition, i is an opponent, and S_i is the space occupied by the opponent.

Competition: Availability of Nutrients

Nutrients exist in the soil and the decay of organic matter adds to the nutrients accessible to nearby plants. The availability of vegetation in a region adds to the accessibility of a higher source of nutrients from decaying matter. Figure 6 illustrates the availability of nutrients shown as white intensity among vegetation – whites are

Figure 5. Intensity of competition between opponents that are larger, smaller, or equal in size

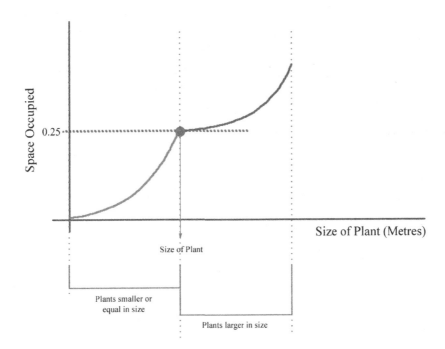

nutrient rich soils. The intensity increases around a higher number of clusters. The global nutrient intensity (at dark grey background value) is variable between seasons.

The nutrients produced by an individual plant is accessed only if

$$\sqrt{(x_i - x)^2 + (y_i - y)^2} - (r_i + r) \le 2r \, ,$$

where i is the plant at proximity with location, x_i and y_i. The location of the source plant is at x, y with radius r.

The level of nutrients from the decaying components of a living plant is,

$$N_i^{living} = c_i^{-1} \left(2d_i r_i \right) \qquad (10)$$

where c_i is the canopy of individual plant with leaf density d_i and radius r_i. The canopy and leaf density are specified in the XML.

After a plant dies, decay of plant matter begins and the plant continues to contribute to the local nutrient until the decay is completed. If a nearby plant has expired and is decaying, the nutrient generated by that plant is,

$$N_i^{decay} = 1^{-1} \left[e^{g\left(-s_i + td\right)} \right] \qquad (11)$$

where g is the gradient with the best range *[0.1, 0.5]*, s_i is the size of the plant at the time of death. t is the time-step from the virtual environment, and d is the rate of decay.

The equation below is the effective nutrients received by the source plant,

$$N^{eff} = \begin{cases} 1 & if \, N^{global} + \sum_{i=1}^{n} N_i^{living} + N_i^{decay} > 1 \\ N^{global} + \sum_{i=1}^{n} N_i^{living} + N_i^{decay} & if \, 0 \le N^{global} + \sum_{i=1}^{n} N_i^{living} + N_i^{decay} \le 1 \\ 0 & otherwise \end{cases}$$

$$(12)$$

Figure 6. Availability of nutrients near vegetation shown as higher intensity (white patches)

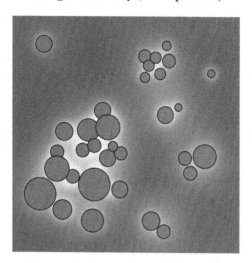

where n is the number of living and decaying plants at proximity. i, an individual plant, can be either dead N_i^{decay}, or living, N_i^{living}. N^{global} refers to the global nutrient level, which is set in the experiments later, to the inverse of the level of sunlight in Figure 7.

Fitness Measure

The fitness measure presented here determines the fitness of an individual plant measured through the adaptability measure. The fitness measure defined below operates and controls the sensitivity of individual plant species towards the environment.

$$f_i = C_i M_i S_i T_i g_i^{pH} g_i^{depth} g_i^{cond} \left[E_i w_1 + N_i w_2 + O_i w_3 \right]$$
(13)

where f_i is the fitness measure for a species where $f_i \in [0, 1]$ is the result of the adaptability measure (Ch'ng, 2007a) which measures each environmental factor: C_i is the tolerance based on competition for space, M_i is based on the soil moisture content, S_i for sunlight, and T_i for temperature. g_i^{pH} is based on the soil pH level,

g_i^{depth} for soil depth, and g_i^{cond} for ground condition. Factors considered more crucial of which plants are more sensitive to are listed before the brackets. Factors considered non-threatening are weighted. w_1 to w_3 are weights for controlling the sensitivity of each plant towards the factor where $\sum_{n}^{n} w_n = 1$, $n = 3$. E_i is the tolerance based on the location of a plant at its altitude, N_i for nutrient, and O_i is based on the levels of carbon dioxide in the atmosphere.

Global Model of the Environment

A typical yearly cycle of environmental signals for temperature, sunlight, humidity and level of carbon dioxide can be seen in Figure 7 with very minor variations throughout the months. These signals are sensed by the plant agents for tolerance computation using the adaptability measure. Except for temperature which reflects real world parameters, and elevation which is dependent on the coordinates of the plants, sunlight, moisture and other factors are measured with the value in the range *[0, 1]* with full sun and water logging/flooding at value 1.0.

Temperatures in the model decrease according to altitudinal limits, with a default of 0.6°C fall in temperature for each 100m above sea level. The temperature-altitudinal ratio is,

$$T_{eff} = \frac{-0.6E}{100} + T_{global}$$
(14)

Where T_{eff} is the effective temperature, E is the current altitude where a plant is at, and T_{global} is the seasonal global temperature defined in Figure 7.

Hydrology is measured in the range *[0,1]*. The distribution and increase of water is a continuous gradient to below the water surface so that marine vegetation and plants tolerant to water-logging can be simulated. The equation for hydrology in this

Figure 7. Graphs showed in sequence the trends for sunlight, humidity, level of carbon dioxide and temperatures in the experiments (© 2007, Eugene Ch'ng. Used with Permission)

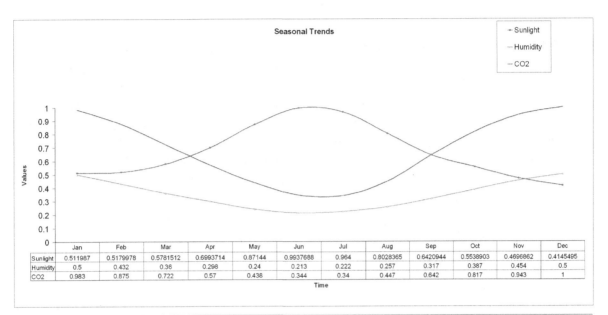

	Jan	Feb	Mar	Apr	May	Jun	Jul	Aug	Sep	Oct	Nov	Dec
Sunlight	0.511987	0.5179978	0.5781512	0.6993714	0.87144	0.9937688	0.964	0.8028365	0.6420944	0.5538903	0.4696862	0.4145495
Humidity	0.5	0.432	0.36	0.298	0.24	0.213	0.222	0.257	0.317	0.387	0.454	0.5
CO2	0.983	0.875	0.722	0.57	0.438	0.344	0.34	0.447	0.642	0.817	0.943	1

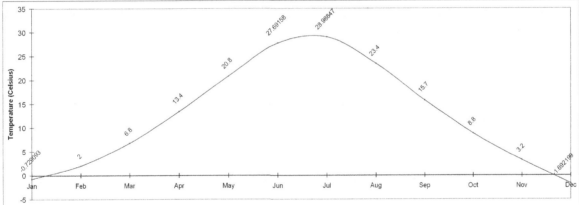

particular virtual environment is defined with,

$$W_{eff} = L \frac{1}{e^{\left(E-W_{surface}\right)g^{-1}}} \qquad (15)$$

where W_{eff} is the effective moisture level, L is the moisture level below the water surface ($L=0.5$), E is the current altitude where a plant is at, $W_{surface}$ is the height of the water surface, g is the gradient.

Local Model of the Environment

The local environment in which a plant draws its resources from is derived from two main sources. The first is defined by the number of adjacent plants in the surroundings which affects the effective sunlight, shade temperature, space, and nutrient availability in a local area. The second condition uses base maps (Grayscale height maps, Figure 16) to define soil acidity, soil depth, ground textures or slope. The darker areas in soil acidity base map have lesser concentration. Lighter areas in the soil depth base map are shallower grounds and lighter areas in the ground texture have courser soils.

Vegetation Synthesis: Simulations

In the simulation scenarios, the virtual plants were placed in segments of landscapes to demonstrate the effects of the preferences and rules defined in the previous sections. The simulationns first study the effects of plant interaction on foundation species and controlled scenarios. This is followed by further studies on real world plants.

Competition for Space

Figure 8 shows a scenario with three settings (*a*, *b*, *c*) containing three foundation species with different age and sizes. Figure 8a is a scenario with crowd tolerant plants, 8c contains crowd intolerant plants, and the plants in 8b possess a level of crowd tolerance intermediate between *a* and *c*. Table 1 lists the tolerance of each species in the 'space' genotype of their constitution.

In Figure 8a, plant 2 have two competitors while plant 1 and 3 both compete with plant 2. Since plants in this setting are highly tolerant to crowded situations, their fitness levels are all full (1.0). The scenario in Figure 8b is a similar setting containing plants with intermediate tolerance to crowded space. In this setting, plants 1 and 3 have full fitness level. The fitness of plant 2 however, is slightly lower at 0.902. The setting in Figure 8c contains plants intolerant to crowd. Plant 1 and 3 both compete with plant 2 each having a fitness of 0.84. Plant 2 having two competitors yielded a fitness of 0.0 (dead).

Figure 9 is a larger scenario with three different settings containing plants adaptable to crowd (a), plants possessing an intermediate adaptability to crowd (b), and plants intolerant to crowd (c). The species possess the same genotype as those in the previous experiments (Table 1). In *a*, plants having more than five competitors showed a fitness of 0.0 (dead). Plants having four competitors yielded a fitness of 0.332 and plants having less than three competitors showed full fitness level. In setting *b*, due to the intermediate crowd adaptability of the plants, their fitness is relatively low in comparison to *a*. In this case, plants having three competitors yielded a fitness of 0.075 whereas plants having two competitors yielded a fitness of 0.902. The plants in setting *c* have all died due to their lack of adaptability to crowding. Figure 10 is the same scenario with large clusters of different vegetation types competing for space.

Their genetic preferences of each species for space are shown in Table 2.

The scenarios above have demonstrated the main concept of the Artificial Life model developed earlier. In the scenarios, each plant senses its environment for competitors. The shapes and sizes of each plant directly affect the plants it is competing with and their genetic makeup influences their overall fitness over time. The fitness of these plants uses the fitness function measured through

Figure 8. Fitness studies of competition between the same species with different age and sizes

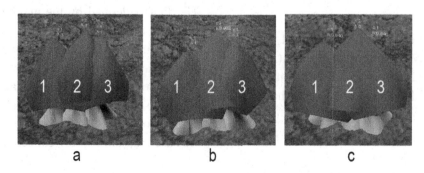

a b c

Figure 9. Fitness studies of competition between the species with the same age and sizes

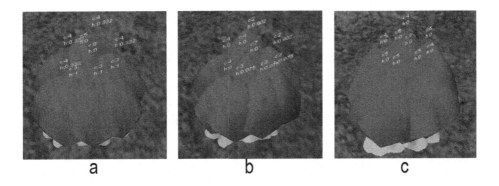

Table 1. Genetic makeup of plant adaptability to crowd

Plant Types	Lower	Preferred	Upper
Crowd Tolerant	0.0	0.55	0.98
Intermediate	0.0	0.3	0.68
Crowd Intolerant	0.0	0.15	0.32

Ch'ng's adaptability measure covered in 3.6.3. The figures shown above (Figure 8-10) are snapshots at particular time intervals for demonstrating the concept. It is important to note that the fitness of each plant changes at different stages of growth and snapshots taken a few simulation steps later may reflect different levels of fitness. The benefits of the addition of temporal processes bring the biotic interaction to a more realistic level.

Competition for Sunlight

Plants compete for sunlight if their canopy distances overlap. Taller plants with larger canopies have more advantage over sunlight whereas smaller plants in the undergrowth receive less sunlight. Plants growing under large trees could seriously impede their growth if they have low adaptability to shade. Figure 11 is a scenario where groups of plant representations of trees, shrubs, and herbs clustered together in a sparse setting. The competition indicator (c:0) of the taller trees showed no competitors. The level of sunlight at

0.6 units also matches their preference and the measure of the two factors yielded a full fitness level for the trees. Smaller trees however, are at a disadvantage. Two smaller trees at the centre foreground with the same age and preferences showed different fitness levels. The small tree at the left (1) without any competitor has full fitness. The tree to the right (2) having three competitors has a fitness of less than 0.01. The shrubs shown in the figure possesses different adaptability to sunlight in their genes. Shrubs that are not under the canopy have a fitness level of 0.829 (e.g., 3) while shrubs having a single competitor (4) yielded different fitness levels depending on the type, height, and size of their competitors. Herbs in this scenario have a lower tolerance to strong sunlight; this also means that they are shade tolerant. In this scenario, the herbs have a fitness of less than 0.01 due to strong sunlight (0.6 units). However, when the level of sunlight has decreased to 0.4 units, herbs without competition have a fitness level of 0.894 (Figure 12). If the canopy of trees shades the undergrowth (1 and 2 of Figure 12),

Figure 10. Fitness studies of competition between different species of plants

Table 2. Genetic preferences of different vegetation types to crowded settings

Plant Types	Lower	Preferred	Upper
Crowd Tolerant	0.0	0.15	0.32
Intermediate	0.0	0.3	0.68
Crowd Intolerant	0.0	0.55	0.98

the effective sunlight is decreased to a level ideal for the herbs (yielding a fitness of 1.0). A shrub (3 of Figure 12) also found the level of sunlight ideal for its growth. The genetic makeup of these vegetation types are shown in Table 3.

Behaviours on Soil Moisture

In the physical world, some species are distributed near sources of water whereas others appear in dry terrains. These differences in habitat are based on their adaptability to hydrological conditions.

In this experiment, plants are initially scattered randomly across the terrain (Figure 13a). After a few simulation steps, plants unable to adapt to their local condition die, leaving adaptable species on different patches of the terrain (b). It can be observed that the boundary of blue plants is limited to the island where the soil moisture content is highest. The population of the blue species is small due to the limited realised niche. Green plants are sparse having boundaries near the river banks of the terrain. This is due to its adaptability to intermediately dry conditions.

In the scenario, the yellow species possess the most adaptable genetic constitution, making it the fittest species able to adapt to both wet and dry conditions. The habitat of the yellow species spans the entire landscape. In the long run, the yellow species will outnumber the other species and drive them off the terrain. The genetic make of these species are shown in Table 4. The inset shows an outcome of a stricter rule for tolerance with species hardiness in the adaptability measure set to $b=0.3$ as compared to $b=0.5$ used in the simulation in Figure 13a and Figure 13b. A stricter rule of measure in each plant sets a clearer ecotone for the species.

Behaviours on Temperature Extremes

Different types of vegetation thrive in different climates and altitudes. The experiment in this section simulates temperature extremes in a strip of landscape 288.5m in elevation (Figure 14). Temperature and altitudinal ratio in the environment is set to decrease by -7°C over 100 metres in elevation instead of the normal -0.6°C. Summer temperatures at sea level can be as high as 28°C and during winter can be as low as -0.5°C. At the high altitude regions, summer temperatures averages 8°C and winter at the highest point can be as low as -20°C. Three species of plants adaptable to extremes of cold and hot temperatures were randomly distributed across the terrain. The landscape is divided into five divisions of approximately 48m each beginning from the sea level for measuring the population of each species. Figure 14 are selected screenshots and graphs of altitude divisions showing the population of each species in the terrain over time from year 3 (T3) to year 34 (T34). The black dots (temperate climate

Table 3. Genetic makeup of plant adaptability to sunlight and shade

Plant Types	Lower	Preferred	Upper
Tree (Shade Intolerant)	0.45	0.65	0.98
Shrub (Intermediate)	0.22	0.46	0.79
Herb (Shade Tolerant)	0.0	0.3	0.6

Figure 11. A scenario showing representations of different plant types competing for sunlight

Figure 12. A closer look at the same scenario showing the fitness of different plants under alternative level of sunlight

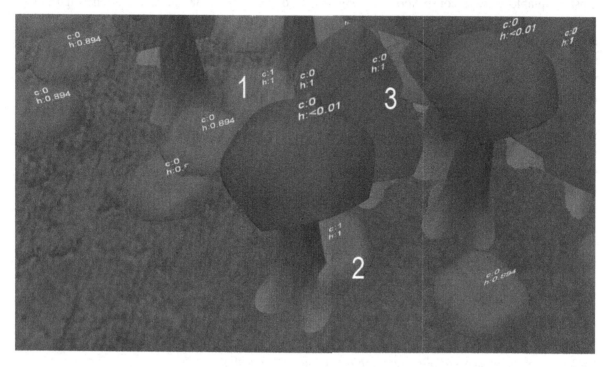

Figure 13. A scenario where plants with different moisture preferences are distributed across a landscape (a), the outcome (b) after a few simulation steps, and the outcome of a stricter rule (inset) showing clear ecotones

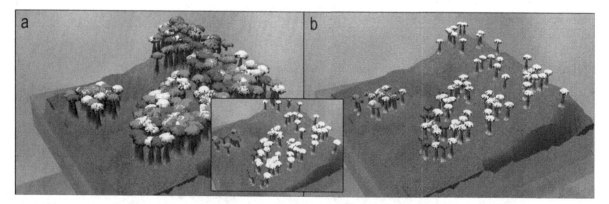

species) and white squares (hot climate species) are added later to clarify their positions, the rest are cold climate species.

The scenario demonstrates the ecotone of species, a term used by ecologists to describe the ecological niches of species adaptable to that specific condition. The population of the cold climate species showed a trend of growth towards the highest point of the terrain where conditions are in the extreme. In contrast, the realised niche of the hot climate species is at the lowest point of the terrain with gradual decline in higher altitudes.

Table 4. Genetic makeup of plant adaptability to soil moisture

Plant Types	Lower	Preferred	Upper
Yellow (Intolerant)	0.02	0.28	0.67
Green (Intermediate)	0.13	0.43	0.82
Blue (Tolerant)	0.3	0.58	0.96

The growth of the temperate climate species on the other hand, is at the peak in the middle section of the terrain with gradual decline towards the upper and lower altitude. The genetic makeup for resistance to temperature extremes of each of the species are listed in Table 5.

Behaviours on Generic Ground Info: Slope Conditions

This experiment uses the generic ground info to define slope angles on terrains. The genetic makeup of three different plants adaptable to levels of slope is defined in Table 6. The red species is the most tolerant to steep terrains followed by the green and blue species. Figure 15 demonstrates the patterns of growth on three different slope conditions on the terrain where the species are initially randomly distributed. The black dots (green species) and white squares (blue species) are added later to clarify their positions. Larger plants are older and parents to smaller ones. T1 is an initial condition of the landscape. At T4, the graph showed plant growth at all three slope conditions of the terrain. At T12, the adaptability of each plant towards different slope condition has become apparent. Due to its adaptability, the population of the red species are seen in all divisions of the landscape. It can also be observed that only the red species exists in the steep slopes. In the scenario, most of the green species populates the middle section whereas the blue species covers plots of flat lands in the terrain.

Layered Studies on Soil Types: Acidity, Depth and Texture

A scenario is created for testing species population on habitat based on different conditions of soil types. Three different soil types – soil acidity, soil depth, and soil texture were added into the factors affecting the plants in order to observe their behaviours. Higher concentration of whites yields higher values for each respective soil conditions. The soil layers represented as concentration maps are shown in Figure 16. Competition for space is also part of the equation. The genetic makeup for each species is shown in Table 7-10.

In the simulation, all species are distributed evenly across the landscape. T3 in Figure 17 shows an initial stable condition when the plants have found their niche. T10 shows the growth and population increase of existing species. At T17, the population has increased and the progenies of each species are beginning to spread into their realised niche. T22 is a condition prior to climax community. The distribution of species continued into habitable regions.

Reproduction, Seed Germination, and Crowd Tolerance

In this experiment, *Dryopteris filix-mas* (Male Ferns) and their spores were released onto a 5m² sampling of the test bed for observation (Figure 18). The adaptability of the Ferns can be seen in Table 11. The ecosystem conditions were set to be favourable to the growth, reproduction, and germination of the Fern species. T1 is the initial setting where some of the Ferns can be observed.

Figure 14. Population of species adaptable to extremes of temperatures in a high altitude terrain

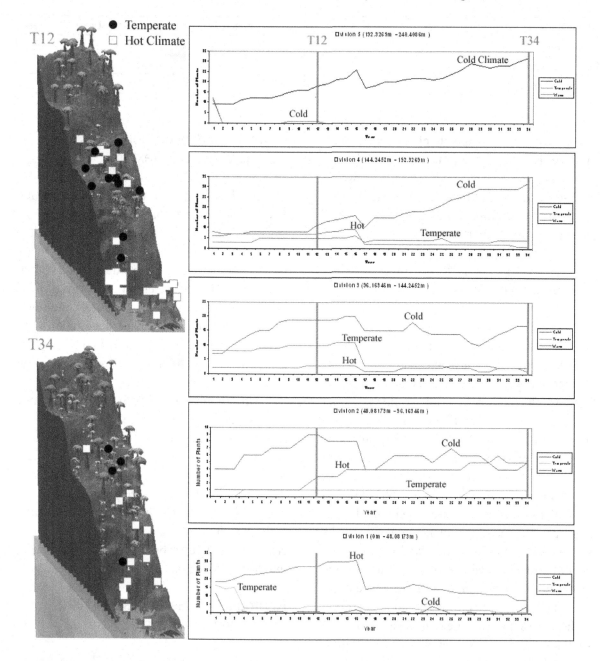

Table 5. Genetic makeup of plant resistance to extremes of temperatures

Plant Types	Lower	Preferred	Upper
Red (Hot Climate)	-15°C	8°C	25°C
Green (Temperate)	-7°C	10°C	27°C
Blue (Cold Climate)	-6°C	18°C	35°C

Table 6. Genetic makeup of plant adaptability to different levels of slope condition

Plant Types	Lower	Preferred	Upper
Red (Steep)	20°	70°	83°
Green (Moderate)	20°	45°	55°
Blue (Low)	0°	15°	35°

Figure 15. Graphs and time sequences of species adaptable to different terrain slopes

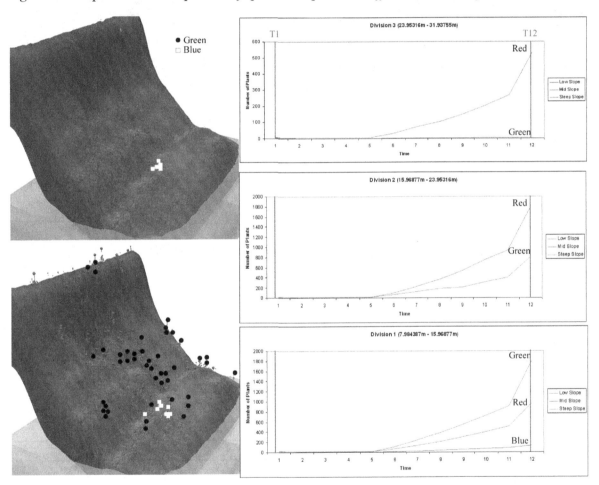

Table 7. Genetic makeup of plant adaptability to different levels of soil textures

Plant Types	Lower	Preferred	Upper
Red Species	0.3	0.8	0.95
Green Species	0.3	0.5	0.75
Blue Species	0	0.25	0.5

Figure 16. Concentration maps representing soil acidity, soil depth, and soil texture

Table 8. Genetic makeup of plant adaptability to different levels of soil acidity

Plant Types	Lower	Preferred	Upper
Red Species	0	4	8
Green Species	4	7	9
Blue Species	6	11	14

Table 9. Genetic makeup of plant adaptability to different levels of soil depth

Plant Types	Lower	Preferred	Upper
Red Species	0	0.2	0.7
Green Species	0.09	0.2	0.4
Blue Species	0.4	0.8	1

Table 10. Genetic makeup of plant adaptability to crowded spaces

Plant Types	Lower	Preferred	Upper
All Species	0	0.35	0.5

Table 11. Genetic makeup of species adaptability for Dryopteris filix-mas

Condition	Lower	Preferred	Upper
Sunlight	0.39	0.56	0.69
Temperature	-4°C	20°C	32°C
Moisture	0.08	0.21	0.62
Space	0.07	0.84	0.98

In T2, the growing Ferns began reproducing with some of the spores being dispersed around the terrain. From T2 onwards some of the offspring have germinated due to favourable conditions from the soil, temperature, sunlight, and moisture. The adaptability of the Male Fern species in crowded settings can be seen in T5-T6. From T6 onwards the emerging patterns arrived at a stable condition with very minor variations in the changing patterns.

Figure 19 is a landscape demonstrating crowding and hydrology. In Figure 19A, the pine species grows at a rather sparse condition. Beginning from T23, smaller and weaker Pines die from competition from sunlight and space as the trees reproduce and grow (T55). At T86, a comfortable Pine forest emerged. Young Pine trees can also be observed to thrive at open spaces where taller trees are sparse. Figure 19B is a similar scenario planted with Oak trees. Oaks, by nature, grow much further apart due to their characteristic broad shape and intolerance to crowding. As the trees grow, smaller and weaker Oaks are gradually replaced by larger ones. Figure 19C shows a Hazel landscape. The Hazel seedlings grow freely in T2. At T24 however, the setting has become denser. At T40, the water level is lowered to allow the seeds to spread in the foreground. At this stage, the shrubs have occupied all available spaces, leaving no space for the growth of younger plants.

Figure 17. Time sequence of species adaptable to soil acidity, depth, and texture

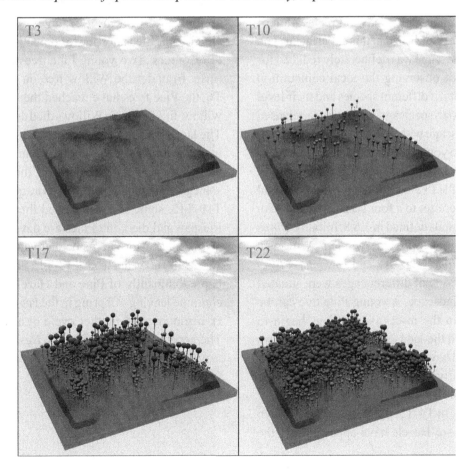

Figure 18. Growth of the Male Fern species

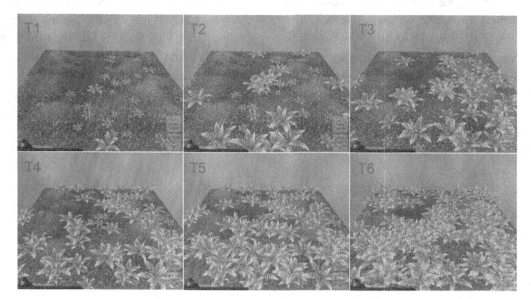

Growth and Competition

A 20m² landscape with a maximum elevation of one metre was established in this experiment. The size of the landscape was deliberately reduced for the purpose of observing the local competition amongst plants of different species and their level of growth. Four species of plants were released onto the landscape with different age groups from seed/spores to young plants. Figure 20 are screen-shots from a variable time steps T1-T15 of a total of 160 years. T1-T12 is a 100 years. Environmental conditions were set to a four seasonal cycle with ecological signals defined in 3.6.8. Initially, *Pinus Sylvestris* (Pine), *Salix Babylonica* (Willows), *Corylus Avellana* (Hazels), and *Dryopteris filix-mas* (Male Ferns) of different ages were situated around the landscape. A young Pine tree can be seen in T1. In the inset (a), seedlings begin to appear around the landscape. In T2, the Willows and the Hazel have grown to maturity. The plants continue to thrive around the landscape due to the availability of resources such as space, sunlight, and nutrients. In T4-T5, the Willows have grown larger and more Hazels have appeared. All the plants continue their reproduction by dispersing their seeds across the terrain. In T5, more Pine seedlings (also in inset c) have germinated, of which some died later due to competition and lack of resources. Two young Pine trees can be seen (inset b) under the Willow tree on the right. In T6, the Pine trees have reached the height of the willow. In T7-T8, the Willows died due to old age. The landscape has become denser in T9 as grow-ing trees occupy more spaces, leaving little space for the younger plants to develop. Inset d showed some young Pines developing more quickly. From T10-T12, some Hazels reached their maximum lifespan and died, the Pines are developing well at this stage. More Ferns begin to appear in T10. At 127 to 160 years from T13-T15, the landscape is predominantly of Pine and Hazel. The plants continue leaving offspring in the landscape (inset f), beginning yet another cycle of artificial life. The genetic makeup of *Pinus Sylvestris*, *Corylus Avellana*, and *Salix Babylonica* is defined in the tables below.

Figure 19. The density and patterns of distribution shown in a) A Pine landscape; b) An Oak landscape; and c) A Hazel landscape

Species Concentration: Grouping and Competition

In this experiment, three different species of herbaceous perennials were released onto a sampling of the Shotton River valley at five metres in width and length. Three species of plants – *Urtica dioica* (Stinging Nettles), *Hieracium gronovii L.* (Hairy Hawkweed), and *Dryopteris filix-mas* (Male Ferns) were observed. Adaptability for *Dryopteris filix-mas* is in Table 11. The adaptability for *Hieracium gronovii L.* and *Urtica dioica* is described in Table 15. The emerging patterns in the time steps demonstrate the adaptability and competition of the herbaceous plants.

In the image sequence (Figure 21), the Stinging Nettles and Hairy Hawkweeds species dominate the landscape with equal distribution of land-use due to the similarities in the genetic traits. The scenario showed that stronger plants – plants characterised by a higher level of adaptability and larger sizes are comparatively more dominant and that plants possessing similar adaptability will have equal opportunity in the struggle for resources, resulting in equal standing in terms of their growth and numbers.

Figure 22 shows other scenarios where species grouping emerged by reason of their niches and the way they distribute their seeds.

Figure 20. Growth and population amongst plants of different species

Hydrology and Competition

A terrain measuring 150m² and 50m at the highest point of the landscape relative to the river was sampled from the Shotton River Valley (Ch'ng, Stone, & Arvanitis, 2004). Equal number of seeds belonging to three species of vegetation – Pine, Hazel, and Willow were distributed across the landscape. The environmental setting simulates a typical Mesolithic landscape in the North Sea region. In the simulation (Figure 23), as virtual time progresses, seedlings belonging to the species begin germinating and growing. At year 71 the landscape has a healthy population. Willows began forming near the river banks where the condition is ideal. This reflects the Willow tree's

Figure 21. Herbaceous vegetation patterns on landscape demonstrating species groupings and competition

Table 12. Genetic makeup of species adaptability for Pinus Sylvestris

Condition	Lower	Preferred	Upper
Sunlight	0.4	0.5	0.7
Temperature	-20°C	20°C	35°C
Moisture	0.4	0.5	0.6
Space	0.07	0.62	0.92
Altitude	20m	728m	6394m

Table 13. Genetic makeup of species adaptability for Corylus Avellana

Condition	Lower	Preferred	Upper
Sunlight	0.4	0.5	0.6
Temperature	-6°C	20°C	36°C
Moisture	0.4	0.5	0.6
Space	0.01	0.25	0.55
Altitude	20m	50m	600m

preference in the natural world. Pine and Hazel appears to have an equal distribution across the landscape. From years 116 through to 179, the Pine and Hazel begin occupying most of the spaces, 'herding' the Willow towards the lower right corner of the river banks. At year 250 the Willow species disappeared entirely from the terrain. At year 500, the Pine species dominates the landscape. Each species' characteristics and their strength and preferences towards a typical environmental setting is observed. The habitat of the Willow trees is observable near the river

Table 14. Genetic makeup of species adaptability for Salix Babylonica

Condition	Lower	Preferred	Upper
Sunlight	0.57	0.69	0.84
Temperature	-5°C	20°C	36°C
Moisture	0.58	0.89	0.95
Space	0.01	0.25	0.55
Altitude	5m	22m	854m

Table 15. Genetic makeup of species adaptability for Hieracium gronovii L. and Urtica dioica

Condition	Lower	Preferred	Upper
Sunlight	0.21	0.46	0.78
Temperature	4°C	20°C	30°C
Moisture	0.14	0.3	0.52
Space	0.07	0.62	0.92

banks. The Hazel appeared to spread across the landscape faster than the other species, occupying spaces and competing with other plants. The Pine is a naturally slow-growing tree, even though its timeframe of growth is lengthy, spanning hundreds of years, its characteristics, adaptability, and height makes it the dominant species in the later stage of this particular scenario.

An observation of the same landscape planted only with the Willow species is at the bottom right of Figure 23. In comparison with previous observations, at year 282 without competition from Pines and Hazels, the Willow species showed a healthy population.

Temperature and Altitudinal Limits

In this experiment, three species of tree types were tested for their adaptability to temperature extremes and altitudinal limits. The experiment is carried out on a landscape 200m² with an altitude of 230.5m. The temperature-altitude ratio was set to decrease by -5°C per 100 metres to demonstrate the effects. Figure 24 are sequences of the simulation showing population densities in different altitudes.

The landscape has not reached climax community as seen in the open spaces and the population increase in the trends of the graphs. The graphs showed that the population of Pine is increased in the third and fourth divisions and fluctuates in the first division. The number of Hazel population remained constant in the third and fourth divisions while the first and second divisions showed a gradual population increase in the species. Willow exists only in the first and second divisions with a higher rate of increase in the first divisions near sources of water.

Effects of Sunlight and Shade

This experiment deals with the effects of sunlight and shade on different species of plants. In particular, the species growing in the undergrowth such as Ferns, Hairy Hawkweed, and Stinging Nettles are observed. Large trees such as *Betula* (Birch, Table 16) and *Quercus* (Oak, Table 17) are used as shade canopies. The genetic makeup of each species is listed in the tables below. Initially seeds and seedlings of Ferns, Hairy Hawkweed, Stinging Nettle, and Birch were scattered across the 20m² terrain (Figure 25). At T6, Birch seedlings

Figure 22. Various patterns on landscape demonstrating the clustering of similar species

have grown to a visible extent. The three earlier species did not survive the harsh sunlight. At T9, Oaks were planted on the landscape. Ferns were disseminated onto the landscape at year 10, Stinging Nettles at year 15, and Hairy Hawkweed at year 18. The latter two species persist for a little while and expired soon after year 25. The Ferns however begin spreading under the shade of the Oak tree. At T29, the two Birches under the oak tree expired due to competition for sunlight from the larger Oak tree. At year 26 the water level is lowered to create a more suitable condition for Birch seeds to germinate. At T38, a seed from the nearby Birch tree germinated (seen at foreground of T47). At T47, as the trees grow, the Ferns settled under their canopies, spreading from the Oak tree to the undergrowth of the clusters of Birches nearby.

Ecotones and Ecoclines

In landscape ecology, an ecotone is the transitional zone between two communities (Allaby, 1998). Examples of natural ecotones include the transitions from forest to open grasslands, forest to marshlands, or land-water transitions. An ecotone contains species from adjacent zones but often contains species not found in the adjacent communities. A characteristic of an ecotone is the richness of species (Walker et al., 2003). An ecocline is a landscape boundary where a gradual change in environmental conditions occurs. This continuous change causes the distribution of species across the boundary because certain species

Figure 23. Hydrology and species competition – Pine, Hazel, and Willow

survives better under certain conditions (Attrill & Rundle, 2002).

Ecotones and ecoclines can be observed throughout the simulation exercises. In Figure 14, three species of vegetation thrive in different ecoclines. Division 5 shows the blue species thriving in the extremes of a cold habitat where the population of the green and red species declined. In division 1, the red species survives better than the other species. Divisions 2, 3, and 4 show the

characteristic of an ecotone with richness of species. The boundary will be more apparent if the terrain is enlarged and more species included.

Figure 17 shows horizontal versions of ecotones and ecoclines. The zones on the landscapes where the concentration of a single species occurs are ecoclines. The transitional boundaries between each zones characterised by species richness are ecotones. In a vertical version in Figure 15, the various slope conditions of a landscape provided

Table 16. Genetic makeup of species adaptability for Betula

Condition	Lower	Preferred	Upper
Sunlight	0.33	0.5	0.98
Temperature	-6°C	20°C	30°C
Moisture	0.35	0.5	0.6

Table 17. Genetic makeup of species adaptability for Quercus

Condition	Lower	Preferred	Upper
Sunlight	0.3	0.69	1
Temperature	-6°C	20°C	36°C
Moisture	0.32	0.45	0.66

different niches for each species.

Examples of ecotones and ecoclines containing real plant representations can be seen in Figure 22 to 24.

FUTURE TRENDS

The imminent destruction of animal habitat in the near future requires rapid response from conservationist. Already, concerned government sectors in various countries are taking measures to ease the threat of biodiversity loss via establishments and conservation efforts. The media have also had its effects on public awareness and education.

The potentials of the emerging field of biodiversity informatics is yet unexplored but has promised the creation, integration, analysis, and understanding of information regarding biological diversity. Biodiversity informatics is distinct from Bioinformatics, which is "an established field that has made significant advances in the development of systems and techniques to organize contemporary molecular data" (Sarkar, 2007). A paper by Canhos *et al.* (Canhos, Souza, Giovanni, & Canhos, 2004) projected that the field has great potential in diverse realms, with applications ranging from prediction of distribu-

tions of known and unknown species, prediction of geographic and ecological distribution of infectious disease vectors, prediction of species' invasions, and assessment of impacts of climate change on biodiversity. Canhos *et al.* continues that "This potential nonetheless remains largely unexplored, as this field is only now becoming a vibrant area of inquiry and study."

The establishment of biodiversity informatics modelling principles related to vegetation in this chapter has laid the foundation for scientific explorations of disciplines that requires terrestrial plants in the model. There are great potentials from the perspective of applicable fields. The added advantage of the visualisation and interactive layer associated with Virtual Reality and interactive 3D will also open up a spectrum of opportunities in biodiversity informatics visualisation and education. Because of the nature of computer modelling and the presentation layers of Virtual Reality technology, simulation could provide us with an opportunity to observe what could not be observed because of our limitations (large spatial-temporal simulations). It should also be noted that any factors affecting biodiversity may be controlled in the model.

In the near future, it is foreseeable that research using the model presented in this chapter would

Figure 24. Temperature and altitudinal limits affecting plant species

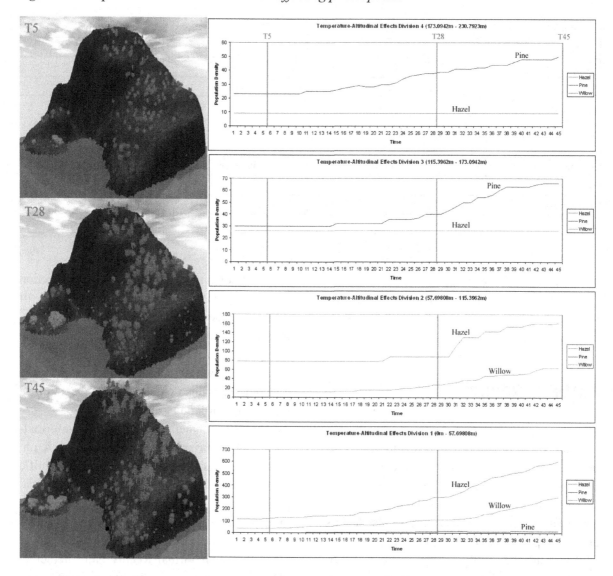

be to assist in biodiversity research for sustainable management of resources related to arthropods and other small organisms at the local level, the backyard biodiversity. Quoting Kim K.C. (Kim, 1993), Arthropods "must be preserved because of their inherent values but also because we need them for human survival… arthropods must become an important and necessary part of the conservation strategy at all levels of environmental organisation, from populations and species to ecosystems and landscapes." On the same note related to

Backyard Biodiversity, Kim and Byrne (2006) asserted that "Modern technology, particularly satellite technologies and computer models, has enabled contemporary ecology to study global changes in the Earth's systems and the effects of humans on these systems. Yet, we must also seek to understand how localized, 'on-the-ground' human activities (that can lead to global changes) affect smaller-scale biodiversity patterns in order to provide the information needed to guide local management of ecosystems by local human com-

Figure 25. Effects of sunlight and shade amongst species in the undergrowth

munities at the grassroots level."

The modelling approach presented here can also be used for determining the effects of climate change on biodiversity by segregating a biome into separate levels of life (taxonomic classification). Each levels (kingdom) or sub-levels (phylum, class, order, family, genus, species) may contain a subset of life form that exists in a single major ecological area. The foundation level may be the *Planta* layer, other important layers of the Phylum are the *Arthropoda* layer, the *Mollusca* layer, and the *Chordata* layer. The human layer may be added later to observe their destructive behaviours. Each layer can be strategically added or removed from within the phases of the simulation to demonstrate the effects of their presence or absence. The potentials of nature inspired informatics are extensive, and are limited only by our imagination.

CONCLUSION

This chapter presents a novel vegetation modelling approach for biodiversity informatics research. The approach, based on the emergence phenomenon that characterises natural systems, departs from the traditional top-down method by synthesising vegetation distribution on landscapes through the interaction of decentralised entities. The core of the technique lies in the simulation of natural selection – the distribution of autonomous agents on a landscape coupled with selection pressures in the environment. Rather than centralising decisions based on a global principle, the method imparts life and autonomy into individual vegetation that allows them to grow, compete, adapt, reproduce, and conquer plots of land for the survival of their progenies. Such method subtracts the manipulative human activity from the equation of life.

The core concepts of nature-inspired vegetation modelling have been introduced. A thorough review of literature related to vegetation modelling has also been given. The text identifies barriers that prevents the realistic modelling of vegetation and later provided a solution based on nature-inspired concepts. The methodology section explores the modelling process in detail and provided important scenarios for evaluating its usefulness in various studies. The results of the model investigated in this chapter have shown that correlations exist

between Artificial Life-based vegetation and their natural counterpart. In particular, characteristics known to occur in the interaction of vegetation communities and the effects of environmental change were observed in the detailed study of the model within the simulation:

- Variations in species and environmental selection pressures contribute to the selection of species on the landscape, excluding certain species and including others in the process of time
- Vegetation species migrate due to environmental change
- Migration of species suited to the local environment are observed to populate available spaces quickly, causing the decline of existing weaker species
- Population density of certain species increases in realised niche
- Seed reproduction and germination occur based on local conditions
- Crowd tolerant plants thrive in compact spaces
- Crowd intolerant plants are disadvantageous in their growth, reproduction, and distribution
- Shade tolerant plants constitute the undergrowth of forest canopies
- Smaller plants are at a disadvantage in comparison to larger plants due to competition for space and sunlight
- Similar species are observed to form communities over time
- Observable emergent dynamics in species distribution patterns such as the formation of ecotones, ecoclines and the realised niche of individual plant species.

Evaluations of the model in this research are based on observations of naturally occurring phenomena. It is important that the model is validated against real data to determine its strength in comparison to top-down approaches. Comparisons between the artificial and the natural could be made by modelling an existing landscape and evaluating the datasets produced by the model. If the accuracy of the model is inexact, parameters could be tuned to fit the real data. The validation measure for future application of the model should take into account the pattern formation of vegetation and the realised niche, temporal measures for seasonal changes in communities of vegetation, population dynamics in large time scale, and patterns of growth in different spatial scales.

The bottom-up approach investigated in this chapter has laid a foundation for the inclusion of vagile life forms. However, limitations discovered in the modelling method should first be resolved. Bottom-up approaches that take into account large population require extensive computational resources. The research presented here has its greatest limitation with regards to processing time for each simulation cycle. The methodology shows that simple rules in algorithm-driven entities do not equal simple implementation. The algorithms and calculations that have to be taken into account in modelling the species and its environment amounted to large numbers of variables and program structures. The real-time visualisation and the exponential growth of entities only add to the requirements. While a segmentation algorithm (Ch'ng, 2009) for efficient entity interaction developed during the study has helped reduced the time needed for each program cycle, landscapes larger than the ones presented in this chapter will require more resources. High-performance computing may be a solution in this case. Studies should also be conducted to see if the algorithms and certain environmental parameters could be simplified or removed without affecting the model results.

The experimental studies presented in this chapter have shown that the solution for overcoming barriers in the predictive modelling of vegetation distribution patterns is to emulate nature's intrinsic problem solving approach – by synthesising natural selection via environmental selection pressures and distributed autonomy with simple rules built into individual plant entities. The model has provided a base from which to build other simulations for the study of biodiversity and the loss of animal habitat and species. Future work will explore the model in these directions.

REFERENCES

Abrahamson, W. G. E. (1989). *Plant-Animal Interaction*. McGraw-Hill Inc.

Allaby, M. (1998). *Oxford Dictionary of Ecology*. New York, NY: Oxford University Press.

Aono, M., & Kunii, T. L. (1984). Botanical Tree Image Generation. *IEEE Computer Graphics and Applications*, 4(5), 10–34. doi:10.1109/MCG.1984.276141

Arvo, J., & Kirk, D. (1988). *Modeling Plants with Environment Sensitive Automata*. Paper presented at the Proceedings of AustGraph '88.

Attrill, M. J., & Rundle, S. D. (2002). Ecotone or ecocline: ecological boundaries in estuaries. *Estuarine, Coastal and Shelf Science, 55*, 929–936. doi:10.1006/ecss.2002.1036

Beaumont, L. J., Hughes, L., & Poulsen, M. (2005). Predicting species distributions: use of climatic parameters in BIOCLIM and its impact on predictions of species' current and future distributions. *Ecological Modelling, 186*(2), 251–270. doi:10.1016/j.ecolmodel.2005.01.030

Benes, B., & Cordoba, J. A. (2003). *Modeling virtual gardens by autonomous procedural agents*. Paper presented at the Proceedings of the Theory and Practice of Computer Graphics (TPCG'03).

Benes, B., & Millan, E. U. (2002). *Virtual Climbing Plants Competing for Space*. Paper presented at the Proceedings of Computer Animation.

Bjorkman, O. (1968). Further studies on differentiation of photosynthetic properties in sun and shade ecotypes of Solidago virgaurea. *Physiologia Plantarum, 21*, 84–99. doi:10.1111/j.1399-3054.1968. tb07233.x

Bonabeau, E., & Theraulaz, G. (2000). Swarm Smarts. *Scientific American, 282*, 72–79.

Busby, J. R. (1991). BIOCLIM - A Bioclimatic Analysis and Prediction System. In C. R. Margules & M. P. Austin (Eds.), *Nature Conservation: Cost Effective Biological Surveys and Data Analysis* (pp. 64-68). Canberra: CSIRO.

Cairns, D. M. (2001). A Comparison of Methods for Predicting Vegetation. *Plant Ecology, 156*, 3–18. doi:10.1023/A:1011975321668

Camazine, S., Deneubourg, J. L., Franks, N. R., Sneyd, J., Theraulaz, G., & Bonabeau, E. (2001). *Self-Organization in Biological Systems*. Princeton, NJ.: Princeton University Press.

Canhos, V., Souza, S., Giovanni, R., & Canhos, D. (2004). Global Biodiversity Informatics: setting the scene for a "new world" of ecological forecasting. *Biodiversity Informatics, 1*, 1–13.

Ch'ng, E. (2007a). Modelling the Adaptability of Biological Systems. *The Open Cybernetics and Systemics Journal, 1*, 13–20.

Ch'ng, E. (2007b). Using Games Engines for Archaeological Visualisation: Recreating Lost Worlds. *11th International Conference on Computer Games: AI, Animation, Mobile, Educational & Serious Games, CGames '07,* (pp. 26-30).

Ch'ng, E. (2009). An Efficient Segmentation Algorithm for Entity Interaction. *Biodiversity Informatics, 6*(1), 5-17.

Ch'ng, E., & Stone, R. J. (2006a). *3D Archaeological Reconstruction and Visualization: An Artificial Life Model for Determining Vegetation Dispersal Patterns in Ancient Landscapes*. Paper presented at the Computer Graphics, Imaging and Visualization (CGiV), Sydney, Australia.

Ch'ng, E., & Stone, R. J. (2006b). Enhancing Virtual Reality with Artificial Life: Reconstructing a Flooded European Mesolithic Landscape. *Presence (Cambridge, Mass.), 15*(3). doi:10.1162/pres.15.3.341

Ch'ng, E., Stone, R. J., & Arvanitis, T. N. (2004, 7-10 December 2004). *The Shotton River and Mesolithic Dwellings: Recreating the Past from Geo-Seismic Data Sources*. Paper presented at the The 5th International Symposium on Virtual Reality, Archaeology and Cultural Heritage, VAST04: Interdisciplinarity or "The Best of Both Worlds": The Grand Challenge for Cultural Heritage Informatics in the 21st Century, Brussels, Belgium.

Chapin, F. S. (1980). The mineral nutrition of wild plants. *Annual Review of Ecology and Systematics, 11*, 233–260. doi:10.1146/annurev.es.11.110180.001313

Clark, J. R., & Benforado, J. (1981). *Wetlands of Bottomland Hardwood Forests*. New York: Elsevier.

Clarkson, D. T., & Hanson, J. B. (1980). The mineral nutrient of higher plants. *Annual Review of Plant Physiology, 31*, 239–298. doi:10.1146/annurev.pp.31.060180.001323

Connell, J. H. (1961). The influence of interspecific competition and other factors on the distribution of the barnacle Chthamalus stellatus. *Ecology, 42*, 710–723. doi:10.2307/1933500

Crawley, M. J. (1992). Seed Predators and Plant Population Dynamics. In M. Fenner (Ed.), *Seeds: The Ecology of Regeneration* (2nd ed.): Cabi Publishing.

Crawley, M. J. E. (1986). *Plant Ecology*. Oxford: Blackwell Scientific Publications.

Cross, J. W. (2003). *Wearable Computing for Field Archaeology*. The University of Birmingham, UK.

Damer, B., Marcelo, K., & Revi, F. (1998). *Nerve Garden: A public terrarium in cyberspace.* Paper presented at the Proceedings of Virtual Worlds and Simulation Conference (VWSIM '99).

Darwin, C. (1858). On the tendency of species to form varieties; and on the perpetuation of varieties and species by natural means of selection. I. Extract from an unpublished work on species, II. Abstract of a letter from C. Darwin, Esq., to Prof. Asa Gray. J. *Proc Linn. Soc. London, 3*, 45–53.

Darwin, C. (1859). *The oigin of species by means of natural selection.* London: John Murray.

Davis, A. J., Jenkinson, L. S., Lawton, J. H., Shorrocks, B., & Wood, S. (1998). Making mistakes when predicting shifts in species range in response to global warming. *Nature, 391,* 783–786. doi:10.1038/35842

Davis, M. B., & Shaw, R. G. (2001). Range Shifts and Adaptive Responses to Quaternary Climate Change. *Science, 292,* 673–679. doi:10.1126/science.292.5517.673

Deussen, O., Hanrahan, P., Lintermann, B., Mech, R., Pharr, M., & Prusinkiewicz, P. (1998). *Realistic modeling and rendering of plant ecosystems.* Paper presented at the Proceedings of SIGGRAPH '98 Annual Conference Series 1998.

Doran, B., & Olsen, P. (2001, 24-26 September 2001). *Customizing BIOCLIM to investigate spatial and temporal variations in highly mobile species.* Paper presented at the Proceedings of the 6th International Conference on GeoComputation, University of Queensland, Brisbane, Australia.

Dubowsky, S., Lagnemma, K., Liberatore, S., Lambeth, D. M., Plante, J. S., & Boston, P. J. (2005). *A Concept Mission: Microbots for Large-Scale Planetary Surface and Subsurface Exploration.* Paper presented at the Space Technology and Applications International Forum.

Ebert, D., & Singer, M. (2004). GIS, Predictive Modelling, Erosion, Site Monitoring. *Assemblage, 8.*

Etterson, J. R., & Shaw, R. G. (2001). Constraint to adaptive evolution in response to global warming. *Science, 294,* 151–154. doi:10.1126/science.1063656

Farmer, D., & Packard, N. (1986). Evolution, Games, and Learning: Models for Adaptations in Machines and Nature. *Physica D. Nonlinear Phenomena, 22D*(1).

Firbank, F. G., & Watkinson, A. R. (1985). A model of interference within plant monocultures. *Journal of Theoretical Biology, 116,* 291–311. doi:10.1016/S0022-5193(85)80269-1

Fisher, J. B. (1977). How predictive are computer simulations of tree architecture. *International Journal of Plant Sciences, 153 (suppl.)*(1992), 137-146.

Fitter, A. H., & Haw, R. K. M. (1981). *Environmental Physiology of Plants.* London: Academic Press.

Fyfe, R. (2005). GIS and the application of a model of pollen deposition and dispersal: a new approach to testing landscape hypotheses using the POLLANDCAL models. *Journal of Archaeological Science, XXXIII*(4), 1–11.

Goldstein, J. (1999). Emergence as a Construct . *History and Issues, 1*(1), 49–72.

Gordon, R. (1999). *Ants at Work: How an Insect Society is Organized.* New York: Free Press.

Greene, N. (1989). *Voxel Space Automata: Modelling with Stochastic Growth Processes in Voxel Space.* Paper presented at the Proceedings of SIGGRAPH '89 Annual Conference Series.

Greene, N. (1991). *Detailing tree skeletons with voxel automata.* Paper presented at the SIGGRAPH '91, Course Notes on Photorealistic Volume Modeling and Rendering Techniques.

Grime, J. P., Hodgson, J. G., & Hunt, R. (1988). *Comparative Plant Ecology: A functional approach to common British species.* London: Unwin Hyman Ltd.

Guisan, A., & Zimmermann, N. E. (2000). Predictive habitat distribution models in ecology. *Ecological Modelling, 135*, 147–186. doi:10.1016/S0304-3800(00)00354-9

Gutowitz, H. (1991). Cellular automata: Theory and experiment. *Physica D. Nonlinear Phenomena, 45*, 1–3.

Hanan, J., Prusinkiewicz, P., Zalucki, M., & Skirvin, D. (2002). Simulation of insect movement with respect to plant architecture and morphogenesis. *Computers and Electronics in Agriculture, 35*(2-3), 255–269. doi:10.1016/S0168-1699(02)00022-4

Holland, J. H. (1995). *Hidden Order: How adaptation builds complexity*. Reading, MA: Helix Books, Addison-Wesley Publishing.

Holland, J. H. (1998). *Emergence from Chaos to order*. Oxford: Oxford University Press.

Holton, M. (1994). Strands, Gravity and Botanical Tree Imagery. *Computer Graphics Forum, 13*(I), 57–67. doi:10.1111/1467-8659.1310057

Honda, H. (1971). Description of the form of trees by the parameters of the tree-like body: Effects of the branching angle and the branch length on the shape of the tree-like body. *Journal of Theoretical Biology, 31*, 331–338. doi:10.1016/0022-5193(71)90191-3

Honda, H., Tomlinson, P. B., & Fisher, J. B. (1981). Computer simulation of branch interaction and regulation by unequal flow rates in botanical trees. *American Journal of Botany, 68*, 569–585. doi:10.2307/2443033

Howe, H. F. (1990). Seed dispersal by birds and mammals: Implications for seedling demography. In K. S. Bawa & M. Hadley (Eds.), *Reproductive Ecology of Tropical Forest Plants* (Vol. 7, pp. 191-218): Taylor & Francis Ltd.

Huth, A., & Wissel, C. (1992). The simulation of the movement of fish schools. *Journal of Theoretical Biology, 156*, 365–385. doi:10.1016/S0022-5193(05)80681-2

Johnson, S. (2002). *Emergence: The Connected Lives of Ants, Brains, Cities, and Software*. Sribner.

Kauffman, S. A. (1993). *The Origins of Order: Self-Organization and Selection in Evolution*. Oxford: Oxford University Press.

Kauffman, S. A. (1996). *At Home in the Universe: The search for laws of complexity*. Harmondsworth: Penguin.

Keller, E. F., & Segel, L. A. (1970). Initiation of Slime Mold Aggregation Viewed as an Instability. *Journal of Theoretical Biology, 26*, 399–415. doi:10.1016/0022-5193(70)90092-5

Kim, K. C. (1993). Biodiversity, conservation and inventory: why insects matter. *Biodiversity and Conservation, 2*, 191–214. doi:10.1007/BF00056668

Kim, K. C., & Byrne, L. B. (2006). Biodiversity loss and the taxonomic bottleneck: emerging biodiversity science. *Ecological Research, 21*, 794–810. doi:10.1007/s11284-006-0035-7

Kube, C. R., & Zhang, H. (1993). Collective robotics: From social insects to robots. *Adaptive Behavior, 2*(2), 189–219. doi:10.1177/105971239300200204

Lane, B., & Prusinkiewicz, P. (2002). *Generating Spatial Distribution for Multilevel Models of Plant Communities*. Paper presented at the Proceedings of Graphics Interface '02.

Lange, H., Thies, B., Kastner-Maresch, A., Dorwald, W., Kim, J. T., & Hauhs, M. (1998). *Investigating Forest Growth Model Results on Evolutionary Time Scales*. Paper presented at the Artificial Life VI: Proceedings of the Sixth International Conference on Artificial Life.

Langton, C. G. (1986, 20th-24th May 1985). *"Studying Artificial Life with Cellular Automata.* Paper presented at the Evolution, Games and Learning: Models of Adaptation in Machines and Nature, Proceedings of the Fifth Annual Conference of the Centre for Nonlinear Studies, Los Alamos.

Langton, C. G. (Ed.). (1989). *Artificial Life, Proceedings of an Interdisciplinary Workshop on the Synthesis and Simulation of Living Systems.* Redwood City: Addison-Wesley Publishing.

Langton, C. G. (1990). *Artificial Life.* Boston, MA: Addison-Wesley Longman Publishing Co., Inc.

Lewes, G. H. (1875). *Problems of Life and Mind* (Vol. 2). London: Kegan Paul, Trench, Turbner, & Co.

Lewin, R. (1993). *Complexity: Life on the Edge of Chaos.* London: Phoenix.

Lindenmayer, A. (1971a). Developmental systems without cellular interaction, their languages and grammar. *Journal of Theoretical Biology, 30,* 455–484. doi:10.1016/0022-5193(71)90002-6

Lindenmayer, A. (1971b). Mathematical models for cellular interaction in development, Parts I and II. *Journal of Theoretical Biology, 18*(1968), 280-315.

Luck, M., & Aylett, R. (2000). Applying Artificial Intelligence to Virtual Reality: Intelligent Virtual Environments. *Applied Artificial Intelligence, 14,* 3–32. doi:10.1080/088395100117142

Mandelbrot, B. (1982). *The Fractal Geometry of Nature.* San Francisco: W.H. Freeman and Co.

McLaughlin, B. P. (1992). *The Rise and Fall of British Emergentism. Emergence or Reduction?: Essays on the Prospects of Nonreductive Physicalism.* Berlin: Walter de Gruyter.

Mech, R., & Prusinkiewicz, P. (1996). Visual models of plants interacting with their environment. *SIGGRAPH, Proceedings of the 23rd annual conference on Computer graphics and interactive techniques* (pp. 397-410).

Mihata, K. (1997). The Persistence of 'Emergence'. In A. E. Raymond, Horsfall, S., Lee., M.E. (Eds.), *Chaos, Complexity & Sociology: Myths, Models & Theories* (pp. 30-38). California: Sage: Thousand Oaks.

Mill, J. S. (1843). *System of Logic* (8th ed.). London: Longmans, Green, Reader, and Dyer.

Miller, J., & Franklin, J. (2002). Modeling the distribution of four vegetation alliances using generalized linear models and classification trees with spatial dependence. *Ecological Modelling, 157,* 227–247. doi:10.1016/S0304-3800(02)00196-5

Mingers, J. (1995). *Self-Producing Systems: Implications and Applications of Autopoiesis.* New York and London: Plenum Press.

Moisen, G. G., & Frescino, T. S. (2002). Comparing five modelling techniques for predicting forest characteristics. *Ecological Modelling, 157,* 209–225. doi:10.1016/S0304-3800(02)00197-7

Morse, M. (1949). Equilibria in Nature. *Proceedings of the American Philosophical Society, 93,* 222–225.

Muñoz, J., & Felicísimo, Á. M. B. (2004). Comparison of statistical methods commonly used in predictive modelling. *Journal of Vegetation Science, 15,* 285–292.

Murdoch, A. J., & Ellis, R. H. (1992). Dormancy, Viability and Longevity. In M. Fenner (Ed.), *Seeds: The Ecology of Regeneration*: Cabi Publishing.

Nagel, E. (1961). *The Structure of Science.* New York: Harcourt, Brace and Wilson.

Nakagaki, T. (2000). Maze-solving by an amoeboid organism. *Nature, 407*, 470. doi:10.1038/35035159

Ng, W. K., Leng, G. S. B., & Low, Y. L. (2004). *Coordinated movement of multiple robots for searching a cluttered environment.* Paper presented at the IEEE/RSJ International Conference on Intelligent Robots and Systems (IROS 2004).

Niwa, H. S. (1994). Self-organizing dynamic model of fish schooling. *Journal of Theoretical Biology, 171*, 123–136. doi:10.1006/jtbi.1994.1218

Nix, H. A. (1986). Biogeographic analysis of Australian elapid snakes. In R. Longmore (Ed.), *Atlas of Elapid Snakes, Australian Flora and Fauna Series, 7*, 4-15. Canberra: Australian Government Publishing Service.

Nwana, H. S., & Ndumu, D. T. (1998). *A Brief Introduction to Software Agent Technology.* New York: Springer-Verlag.

Oppenheimer, P. (1986). *Real Time Design and Animation of Fractal Plants and Trees.* Paper presented at the Proceedings of SIGGRAPH '86 Annual Conference Series.

Pearson, R. G., & Dawson, T. P. (2003). Predicting the impacts of climate change on the distribution of species: are bioclimate envelope models useful? *Global Ecology and Biogeography, 12*, 361–371. doi:10.1046/j.1466-822X.2003.00042.x

Peterson, A. T., Sánchez-Corderob, V., Soberónc, J., Bartleyd, J., Buddemeierd, R. W., & Navarro-Sigüenza, A. G. (2001). Effects of global climate change on geographic distributions of Mexican Cracidae. *Ecological Modelling, 144*(1), 21–30. doi:10.1016/S0304-3800(01)00345-3

Prusinkiewicz, P., Hammel, M., Hanan, J., & Mech, R. (1996). Visual models of plant development. In G. Rozenberg, & A. Salomaa (Eds.), *Handbook of Formal Languages*: Springer-Verlag.

Prusinkiewicz, P., Hammel, M., Mech, R., & Hanan, J. (1995). *The Artificial Life of Plants.* Paper presented at the Artificial life for Graphics, Animation, and Virtual Reality Siggraph '95 Course Notes.

Prusinkiewicz, P., Hanan, J., & Mech, R. (1999). *An L-system-based plant modeling language.* Paper presented at the Proceedings of AGTIVE 1999, Lecture Notes in Computer Science 1779.

Prusinkiewicz, P., & Lindenmayer, A. (1990). *The algorithmic beauty of plants.* New York: Springer-Verlag.

Prusinkiewicz, P., & Remphrey, W. R. (2005). Characterization of architectural tree models using L-systems and Petri nets. In M. Labrecque (Ed.), *L'arbre -- The Tree* (pp. 177-186).

Reeves, W., & Blau, R. (1985). *Approximate and Probabilistic Algorithms for Shading and Rendering Structured Particle Systems.* Paper presented at the Proceedings of SIGGRAPH '85 Annual Conference Series.

Resnick, M. (1994). *Turtles, Termites, and Traffic Jams: Explorations in Massively Parallel Microworlds.* Cambridge, Massachusetts: MIT Press.

Resnick, M., & Silverman, B. (1996). *The Facts of Life.* Retrieved 3 January 2006, 2006, from http://llk.media.mit.edu/projects/emergence/life-intro.html

Reynolds, C. W. (1987). Flocks, Herds, and Schools: A Distributed Behavioral Model. *Computer Graphics, Siggraph '87 Conference Proceedings, 21*, 25-34.

Ricklefs, R. E. (1990). *Ecology.* New York: W.H. Freeman, (page 332).

Room, P. M., Maillette, L., & Hanan, J. (1994). Module and metamer dynamics and virtual plants. *Advances in Ecological Research, 25*, 105–157. doi:10.1016/S0065-2504(08)60214-7

Runions, A., Fuhrer, M., Lane, B., Federl, P., Rolland-Lagan, A. G., & Prusinkiewicz, P. (2005). Modeling and visualization of leaf venation patterns. *ACM Transactions on Graphics, 24*(3), 702–711. doi:10.1145/1073204.1073251

Sakaguchi, T., & Ohya, J. (1999). *Modeling and animation of botanical trees for interactive virtual environments.* Paper presented at the VRST 99, London, UK.

Sarkar, I. N. (2007). Biodiversity informatics: organizing and linking information across the spectrum of life. *Briefings in Bioinformatics, 8*(5), 347–357. doi:10.1093/bib/bbm037

Schaefer, L. A., Mackulak, G. T., Cochran, J. K., & Cherilla, J. L. (1998). *Application of a general particle system model to movement of pedestrians and vehicles.* Paper presented at the 1998 Winter Simulation Conference (WSC'98).

Segel, L. A. (2001). Computing an Organism. *Proceedings of the National Academy of Sciences of the United States of America, 98*(7), 3639–3640. doi:10.1073/pnas.081081998

Silander, J. A., & Antonovics, J. (1982). Analysis of interspecific interactions in a coastal plant community - a perturbation approach. *Nature, 298,* 557–560. doi:10.1038/298557a0

Sipper, M. (1998). Fifty years of research on self-replication: an overview. *Artificial Life, 4,* 237–257. doi:10.1162/106454698568576

Sipper, M., & Reggia, J. A. (2001). Go forth and replicate. *Scientific American, 285,* 34–43.

Slatyer, R. O. (1967). *Plant-Water Relationships.* London: Academic Press.

Smith, A. (1984). Plants, Fractals and Formal Languages. *Proceedings of SIGGRAPH '84 Annual Conference Series, 18*(3), 1-10.

Solbrig, O. T. (1981). Studies on the population biology of the genus Viola. II. The effect of plant size on fitness in Viola sororia. *Evolution; International Journal of Organic Evolution, 35,* 1080–1093. doi:10.2307/2408122

Soler, C., Sillion, F. X., Blaise, F., & Dereffye, P. (2003). An Efficient Instantiation Algorithm for Simulating Radiant Energy Transfer in Plant Models. *ACM Transactions on Graphics, 22*(2), 204–233. doi:10.1145/636886.636890

Spikins, P. (1999). *Mesolithic Northern England: Environment, Population and Settlement* (Vol. 283). England: Basingstoke Press.

Spikins, P. (2000). GIS Models of Past Vegetation: An Example from Northern England, 10,000-5000 BP. *Journal of Archaeological Science, 27,* 219–234. doi:10.1006/jasc.1999.0449

Spinney, L. (2008). The Lost World. *Nature, 454,* 151–153. doi:10.1038/454151a

Stacey, R. (1996). *Complexity and Creativity in Organizations.* San Francisco: Berrett-Koehler.

Taverna, K., Urban, D. L., & McDonald, R. I. (2005). Modeling landscape vegetation pattern in response to historic land-use: a hypothesis-driven approach for the North Carolina Piedmont, USA. *Landscape Ecology, 20,* 689–702. doi:10.1007/s10980-004-5652-3

Thomas, C. D., Bodsworth, E. J., Wilson, R. J., Simmons, A. D., Davies, Z. G., & Musche, M. (2001). Ecological and evolutionary processes at expanding range margins. *Nature, 411,* 577–581. doi:10.1038/35079066

Thompson & Morgan (2004). *Successful Seed Raising Guide*: Thompson & Morgan Inc.

Toffoli, T., & Margolus, N. (1987). *Cellular automata machines: A new environment for modelling.* Cambridge: MIT Press.

Vitousek, P. M. (1982). Nutrient cycling and nutrient use efficiency. *American Naturalist, 119*, 553–572. doi:10.1086/283931

von Neumann, J., & Burks, A. W. (1966). *Theory of Self-Reproducing Automata*. Urbana IL: University of Illinois Press.

Waldrop, M. M. (1993). *Complexity: The Emerging Science at the Edge of Order and Chaos*. London: Viking.

Walker, S., Barstow, W. J., Steel, J. B., Rapson, G. L., Smith, B., & King, W. M. (2003). Properties of ecotones: evidence from five ecotones objectively determined from a coastal vegetation gradient. *Journal of Vegetation Science, 14*, 579–590.

Wallace, A. R. (1858). On the tendency of species to form varieties; and on the perpetuation of varieties and species by natural means of selection. III. On the tendency of varieties to depart indefinitely from the original type. *J. Proc Linn. Soc. London, 3*, 53–62.

Weber, J., & Penn, J. (1995, August 6-11, 1995). *Creation and rendering of realistic trees*. Paper presented at the Proceedings of SIGGRAPH '95, Los Angeles, California.

Woodcock, S. (2000). Flocking: A Simple Technique for Simulating Group Behaviour. In M. A. DeLoura (Ed.), *Game Programming Gems*. Rockland, Massachusetts: Charles River Media, Inc.

Woodward, F. I. (1990). The impact of low temperatures in controlling the geographical distribution of plants. *Philosophical Transactions of the Royal Society of London. Series B, Biological Sciences, 326*(1237), 585–593. doi:10.1098/rstb.1990.0033

ENDNOTE

[1] Seed in this article also refers to candidate offspring as not all plants reproduce through seeds.

Chapter 5
Multimodal Genetic Algorithms for Craniofacial Superimposition

Oscar Ibáñez
European Centre for Soft Computing, Spain

Oscar Cordón
European Centre for Soft Computing, Spain

Sergio Damas
European Centre for Soft Computing, Spain

José Santamaría
University of Jaen, Spain

ABSTRACT

Craniofacial superimposition is a forensic process that aims to identify a missing person by overlaying a photograph and a model of the skull. This process is usually carried out manually by forensic anthropologists, thus being very time consuming and presenting several difficulties when trying to find a good fit between the 3D model of the skull and the 2D photo of the face. This contribution aims to provide both a detailed description of the problem and the proposal of two different designs of a multimodal (clearing) genetic algorithm to tackle it. The new proposals will be tested on superimpositions for different real-world identification cases from the Physical Anthropology lab at the University of Granada in Spain, including positive and negative cases, taking the manual and the basic genetic algorithm solutions as baselines for their quality.

INTRODUCTION

Photographic supra-projection (Iscan, 1993) is a forensic process that consists of comparing photographs or video shots of a missing person with the skull that is found. By projecting both photographs on top of each other (or, even better, matching a scanned three-dimensional skull model against the face photo/video shot), the forensic anthropologist can try to establish whether that is the same person.

To do so, an accurate 3D model of the skull is first demanded. Next, the matching of two sets of radiometric points (facial anthropometric (cephalometric) landmarks in the subject photograph, and

DOI: 10.4018/978-1-60566-705-8.ch005

cranial anthropometric (craniometric) landmarks in the obtained skull model) is considered to guide the superimposition of the skull 3D model and the photograph (Iscan, 1993). Then, a decision making stage starts by analyzing the different kinds of achieved matchings between landmarks. Some of them will perfectly match, some will partially do so, and finally some others will not. After the whole process, the forensic expert must declare whether the analyzed skull corresponds to the missing person or not.

As can be seen, the latter procedure is very time consuming and there is not a systematic methodology but every expert usually apply his/her particular process. Hence, there is a strong interest in designing automatic methods to support the forensic anthropologist to put it into effect.

In this chapter, we will focus our attention on the second stage of the identification task, known as craniofacial superimposition. It is fundamental to adopt a proper and robust technique to align the 3D model and the 2D image in a common coordinate frame by means of image registration (IR) techniques (Zitova & Flusser, 2003). The key idea of the IR process is to achieve the transformation that places different 2D/3D images in a common coordinate system.

Evolutionary Computation (EC) comprises global search algorithms with a general purpose that use principles inspired by natural genetics to solve problems. In the last few years, there is an increasing interest on applying EC fundamentals to IR (Cordón, Damas & Santamaría, 2007; Rouet, Jacq & Roux, 2000; Yamany, Ahmed & Farag, 1999).

As said, the superimposition process is one of the most time consuming tasks for the forensic experts. Therefore, software tools for the automation of their work are a real need. Unfortunately, we can find only few proposals to automate the process and, even worse, the results are not suitable for the forensic experts. We will address the problem by extending our previous approach (Ballerini, Cordón, Damas, Santamaría, Alemán

& Botella, 2007; Ballerini, Cordón, Damas & Santamaría, 2009), based on genetic algorithms (GAs) (Goldberg, 1989). These contributions aimed to automatize and drastically reduce the time of the superimposition task by means of a systematic method based on GAs. In spite of the good results achieved, there are some outcomes from our previous proposal that lead us to think we were dealing with a multimodal problem. In particular, the results analysis showed that both the standard deviation and the average fitness values of the best were too high. Hence, in this contribution we propose a multimodal GA aiming to improve the performance of the previous classical GA approach.

The structure of the chapter is as follows. The background section is devoted to introduce EC, the IR problem, the state of the art on craniofacial superimposition, and our previous GA for craniofacial superimposition. Our new proposal is detailed in the next section, where an experimental study is also described. Finally, some future works are outlined and concluding remarks are presented.

BACKGROUND

Evolutionary Computation

EC uses computational models of evolutionary processes as key elements in the design and implementation of computer-based problem solving systems (Bäck, Fogel & Michalewicz, 1997). GAs (Goldberg, 1989), based on the mechanisms of natural genetics and selection, are maybe the most known evolutionary algorithms. A GA works on a population of solutions. A fitness value, derived from the problem's objective function is assigned to each member of the population. Individuals that represent better solutions are awarded higher fitness values, thus giving them more chances to survive to the next generation. Starting with a random initial population, successive generations are created by the genetic operators: reproduction,

Figure 1. The IR optimization process

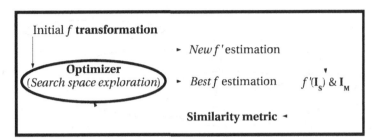

crossover and mutation. Finally, the best solution in the last population is given as output. To get more knowledge on EC and GAs, the interested reader can refer to recent books like (Goldberg, 2002; Eiben & Smith, 2003).

The Image Registration Problem

The key idea of the IR process is to achieve the transformation that places different 2D/3D images in a common coordinate system (Zitova & Flusser, 2003). There is not a universal design for a hypothetical IR method that could be applicable to all registration tasks, because various considerations of the particular application must be taken into account. Nevertheless, IR methods usually require the four following components: two input 2D or

3D Images named as Scene $Is = \left\{ \vec{p_1}, \vec{p_2}, \ldots, \vec{p_n} \right\}$ and Model $Im = \left\{ \vec{p_1}', \vec{p_2}', \ldots, \vec{p_m}' \right\}$, with $\vec{p_i}$ and $\vec{p_j}'$ being image points; a **Registration transformation** f, being a parametric function relating both images; a **Similarity metric function** F, in order to measure a qualitative value of closeness or degree of fitting between the scene and the model images; and an **Optimizer** which looks for the optimal transformation f within the defined solution search space.

Hence, IR is the process of finding the optimal spatial transformation f achieving the best fitting (measured using F) between the model and the transformed scene image points, $f(I_s)$. Such trans-

formation estimation is interpreted into an iterative optimization process in order to properly explore the search space. Figure 1 graphically represents the IR optimization process.

One of the most important components of any IR method is the similarity metric. This is considered as a function F that measures the goodness of a given registration solution, that is, the registration transformation f, and the final performance of any IR method will depend on its accurate estimation.

Each solution is evaluated by F applying its corresponding transformation f to one of the two images, usually to the scene image ($f(I_s)$). There are many approaches trying to define F depending on the dimensionality (2D or 3D) and the nature of the considered images. The most usual when following a feature-based IR approach, i.e. when the same relevant features are selected prior to tackling the IR problem, is the Mean Square Error (Santamaría, Cordón, Damas, Alemán & Botella, 2007; Besl & McKay, 1992; Zhang, 1994; Yamany, Ahmed & Farag, 1999):

$$F(Is, Im, f) = \frac{1}{r} \sum_{i=1}^{r} \left\| f(\vec{p_i}) - \vec{p_j}' \right\|^2 \qquad (1)$$

where r is the number of points in the scene image, $f(\vec{p_i})$ is the resulting point after the transformation is applied to the scene point $\vec{p_i}$, and $\vec{p_j}'$ is the closest model point to $f(\vec{p_i})$ of the scene.

State-of-the-Art on Craniofacial Superimposition

Successful comparison of human skeleton remains with artistic or photographic replicas has been achieved many times (Iscan, 1993), starting with the studies of the skeletal remains of Dante in the nineteenth century (Welcker, 1867), till the identification of victims of the recent Indian Ocean tsunami (Al-Amad, McCullough, Graham, Clement & Hill, 2006). Craniofacial identification is thus a challenging problem in forensic anthropology that has been tackled since long time ago (Iscan, 1993) following the photographic supra-projection process. Nevertheless, to date, no automatic method is used in practical applications despite the high number of cases examined (Ubelaker, 2000).

Recent papers confirm that some authors think the most advanced method is based on digital superimposition through the use of Adobe Photoshop® and Corel Draw® and the imaging tools provided by these software packages (Al-Amad, McCullough, Graham, Clement & Hill, 2006; Bilge, Kedici, Alakoc & Ilkyaz, 2003; Ross, 2004). We agree with these authors that working with digital images is definitely simpler and cheaper than with photographic or video superimposition equipments, but we should note that the methods they use are not automatic as they manually resize, shift and rotate the images by trial and error, thus dealing with a very time consuming and error affected process. It is worth mentioning that the forensic expert may employ approximately 24 hours for each case.

All the researchers agree that a key problem of photographic supra-projection is the size and orientation of the skull to correctly match that one of the head in the photo. Different methods for the craniofacial superimposition stage have been proposed. Some of these approaches were classified in a review by Aulsebrook, Iscan, Slabbert, & Becker (1995) according the technology they used, i.e. static photographic transparency, video

technology and computer graphics. In a previous paper (Ballerini, Cordón, Damas, Santamaría, Alemán & Botella, 2007) we updated that review both including different proposals published after 1995 and considering an up-to-date classification criterion, more related to the use of computers. We differentiated between automatic and not automatic methods.

Indeed, the differentiation between methods that do not use computer technology and methods that actually use it had already been proposed. In the literature, photographic and video superimposition has been considered to belong to the former category. Meanwhile, methods defined as digital or computer-aided superimposition had been considered to belong to the latter. We expanded the latter class by differentiating between computer-assisted and computer-based methods. The former ones use computers to support the superimposition process and/or to visualize the skull and the face. Nevertheless, the size and orientation of the skull is changed manually to correctly match the pose of the head in the photograph. This is achieved by either physically moving the skull, while computers are simply used to visualize it on the monitor, or (with the help of some commercial software) by moving its digital image on the screen until a good match is found. The works of Ubelaker, Bubniak & O'Donnel (1992), Yoshino, Matsuda, Kubota, Imaizumi, Miyasaka & Seta (1997), Ricci, Marella & Apostol (2006) are typical examples of what we call computer-assisted superimposition in the sense that a digital infrastructure is used, but not its potential utility.

The latter ones, i.e. computer-based craniofacial superimposition methods, automatically find the optimal superimposition between the 3D model of the skull and the 2D face photograph using computer algorithms. Up to our knowledge, there are only two proposals performing craniofacial superimposition in a fully automatic way, based on the use of neural networks (Ghosh & Sinha, 2001) and GAs (Nickerson, Fitzhorn, Koch & Charney, 1991), respectively. However, as we will see in the following, they are not suitable for the forensic experts.

The method proposed by Ghosh & Sinha (2001) was an adaptation of their previous proposal for face recognition problems (Sinha, 1998). The Extended Symmetry Perceiving Adaptive Neuronet (ESPAN) consisted of two neural networks to be applied to two different parts of the overlaying and allows the user to select fuzzy facial features to account for ambiguities due to soft tissue thickness. More in details, the system was able to implement an objective assessment of the symmetry between two nearly front images: the cranial image and the facial image that were the inputs as the source and the target images, respectively. The output was the mapped cranial image suitable for superimposition. Two networks needed to be trained separately because each of them was able to correctly map only a part of the cranial image. Two limitations, already pointed out by the authors, were: a part of the cranial image that would not be properly mapped and the need of a frontal view image. Moreover, this method was not fully applicable because of its long computation time and the need of separately applying two different networks to the upper skull contour and to frontal view cranial features, where the overlaying found by the first one could be disrupted by the second.

On the other hand, Nickerson, Fitzhorn, Koch & Charney's method (1991) used a GA to find the optimal parameters of the similarity and perspective transformation that overlays the 3D skull model on the face photograph. More in details, this method included the following tasks:

- 2D digitalization of an antemortem facial photograph.
- 3D digitalization of the surface mesh of the skull.
- Application of digital filtering techniques to the 2D photo image and the 3D model to reduce or eliminate systematic error.
- Selection of four landmark points on the digital facial image and four equivalent

noncoplanar landmarks on the skull surface mesh.
- Calculation of the near-optimal affine and perspective transformations required to map the skull surface mesh into two dimensions and onto the face image.
- Joint solid rendering of the digital facial photograph and transformed skull surface mesh for visual analysis.

A digital camera and a range scanner were used for 2D and 3D digitalizations, respectively. Well known image processing algorithms were considered for image enhancement (median filtering, histogram equalization, Wiener filtering (Gonzalez & Woods, 2002)). Rendering was done through computer graphics techniques, after polygonal texture mapping of the 2D image.

The most important novelty of this technique was the automatic calculation of the mapping of the skull surface mesh on the digital facial photograph. This mapping was achieved from the matching of the four landmarks previously identified both in the face and the skull. The landmarks used in their work were: the *glabella* or the *nasion*, the two *ectocanthion* points, and an upper mandibular dentition point, if present, or the *subnasal* point (see Figure 2).

Three approaches were considered to solve the problem: a heuristic, a classic numerical optimization and binary-coded GA methods. Results based on the GA outperformed the remainder.

According to Ghosh & Sinha, (2001), Nickerson, Fitzhorn, Koch & Charney's method (1991) did not gain much popularity due to the fact that it essentially required a digitalized 3D cranial image reconstruction, which could not be implemented either by an easy/simple procedure or by an economic hardware configuration. We think the reason for not finding practical applications of this method is probably also due to the difficulties for the forensic experts to understand the mathematical formulation of the registration problem and the evolutionary framework (es-

Figure 2. Cranial (craniometric) and facial (cephalometric) landmarks

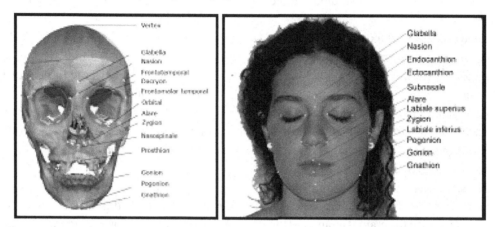

pecially considering there are important issues missing). A detailed description of these issues is provided in Appendix A.

Finally, we should mention that several automatic approaches regarding the 3D face model–2D face photograph superimposition have been also presented (Clarkson, Rueckert, Hill & Hawkes, 2001; Goos, Alberink & Ruifrok, 2006) and extensive reviews can be found like the one in (Bowyer, Chang & Flynn, 2006). However, they are out of the scope of this discussion, as they deal with face recognition that is a completely different problem.

Real-Coded Genetic Algorithm for Craniofacial Superimposition

First, we implemented Nickerson et al.'s approach, using the GAucsd package (Schraudolph & Grefenstette, 1992). We also made experiments by empirically changing GA parameters and using the gray coding provided by the package. None of these experiments gave acceptable results on our data (either synthetic or real ones), as our previous contribution (Ballerini, Cordón, Damas & Santamaría, 2009) shows.

The objective function to be minimized was the one originally proposed in Nickerson et al.'s proposal: the sum of the squared 2D Euclidean distances between the facial (cephalometric) landmarks (x_{fi}, y_{fi}) and the transformed cranial (craniometric) landmarks (x'_{ci}, y'_{ci}):

$$Fitness = \sum_{i-1}^{4} \sqrt{(x'_{ci} - x_{fi})^2 + (y'_{ci} - y_{fi})^2} \quad (2)$$

Then, we took this approach as a base and tried to solve its flaws. Therefore we made several adaptations of this proposal as follows: (1) improvement of the registration transformation; (2) use of a real coding scheme; (3) better design of GA components.

In order to properly match the 3D and 2D landmarks there are two processes to be considered regarding each of them, once similarity and perspective mapping have been applied (see Appendix A.). On the one hand, the transformed cranial landmarks $C^t = (x_{ci}^t, y_{ci}^t, z_{ci}^t, w_{ci}^t)$ must be mapped onto the 3D Euclidean plane by dividing the four components of every landmark by its fourth one: $C' = C^t / w_{ci}^t$. On the other hand, the coordinates of the 2D facial landmarks should be provided with respect to the origin located in the top-left corner of the digital image. Hence, they must be translated so that the origin is in the centre of the photo, mirrored in X so that we deal with the perspective assumptions, and normalized in [−1, 1]. The matrix M is not used in our implementation because of both the scanned cranial

3D mesh and the rendering software consider the same coordinate system (right-handed).

See Appendix A for a description of the parameters encoding the solution of our IR problem. Hence, every individual of our population will be defined by twelve genes $(g_1, g_2, ..., g_{12})$ given by:

$$r_x \; r_y \; r_z \; d_x \; d_y \; d_z \; \theta \; s \; \varphi \; t_x \; t_y \; t_z$$

The range of the transformation parameters (corresponding to genes in the chromosome) are calculated as follows:

$$r_i \in [C_i - radius, \; C_i + radius], i \in \{x,y,z\}$$

$$d_i^{MAX=MAX\sum_{i=1}^{N}\|f(Ci)-Fi\|}[-1,1], i \in \{x,y,z\}$$

$$\theta \in [0°, 360°]$$

$$s \in [0.25, 2]$$

$$\varphi \in [10°, 150°]$$

$$t_x \in [- legnth_{FB}, - (C_x + radius), legnth_{FB} - (C_x - radius)]$$

$$t_y \in [- legnth_{FB}, - (C_y + radius), legnth_{FB} - (C_y - radius)]$$

$$t_z \in [NCP - (C_z + radius), FCP - (C_z - radius)]$$

where $radius = max(d(C,L_j))$, with C being the centroid of the 3D landmarks, L_j being the jth 3D landmark, and d() being the Euclidean distance between two points,

$$\min_{FD} = \frac{1}{\tan\left(\dfrac{\varphi_{max}}{2}\right)} \tag{3}$$

(considering a 2 x 2 projection plane centered in the Z axis)

$$length_{FB} = \frac{(\min_{FD} + FCP) * \sin\left(\dfrac{\varphi_{max}}{2}\right)}{\sin\left(90° - \left(\dfrac{\varphi_{max}}{2}\right)\right)} \tag{4}$$

with FCP and NCP being the Far and Near Clipping Planes, respectively, FB the Frustrum Base and FD the Focal Distance.

In preliminary experiments, we considered a higher scaling upper bound but we did not achieve better results. On the other hand, we should note that the field of view of a typical camera is $\varphi = 45°$. However, in professional ones where even the lens can be changed, $\varphi \in [5°, 180°]$.

IR is an inherent real coding problem; therefore a real-coded GA is more suitable for craniofacial superimposition. It is reported by several authors that when dealing with real parameters, a real-coded GA performs better than a binary-coded one nine out of ten times (Bäck, Fogel & Michalewicz, 1997; Herrera, Lozano & Verdegay, 1998).

In our implementation, the IR parameters are represented by their natural form. This fact allows us to solve several difficulties associated to the use of a binary coding and let us avoid the mapping needed by Nickerson et al. between real-valued variables and fixed-length strings.

In this work, we also proposed the use of a different, more robust fitness function:

$$fitness = \beta_1 \cdot MSE + \hat{w} \cdot \beta_2 \cdot MAX \tag{5}$$

where:

$$MSE = \frac{\sum_{i=1}^{N}\|f(Ci) - Fi\|}{N} \tag{6}$$

and

$$MAX = MAX\sum_{i=1}^{N}\|f(Ci) - Fi\| \tag{7}$$

where $\|\cdot\|$ is the 2D Euclidean distance, N is the number of considered landmarks, $f(C_i)$ are the positions of the transformed 3D landmarks in the projection plane, and F_i are the 2D landmarks. Notice also that this function is to be minimized.

For each individual S_i of the initial population ($t = 0$) we calculate:

$$w_{S_i(t=0)} = \frac{MSE(S_i(t=0))}{MAX(S_i(t=0))} \quad (8)$$

Then the scaling factor $\hat{w}$ (used when $\beta_1 \neq 0$ and $\beta_2 \neq 0$) is obtained by averaging w_{Si} over the initial population ($t = 0$).

Based on the values of (β_1, β_2), we obtain different fitness functions. In this work we considered three different choices: (1) $(\beta_1, \beta_2) = (1, 0)$: the resulting fitness function becomes almost the same that the original one proposed by Nickerson et al., i.e. the mean distance between the corresponding landmarks; (2) $(\beta_1, \beta_2) = (0, 1)$: the resulting fitness function corresponds to the maximum distance between the corresponding landmarks; (3) $(\beta_1, \beta_2) = (0.5, 0.5)$: the fitness function is a weighted sum of the two previous ones.

In the first implementation with a binary-coded GA we used the roulette-wheel selection, two-point crossover and bit flipping mutation that were the typical GA components by the time that Nickerson et al.'s approach was proposed (Goldberg, 1989). Nowadays we can use more efficient genetic operators. In particular, we used the tournament selection (Blickle, 1997), the blend crossover (BLX-α) (Eshelman, 1993) and the random mutation operators (Bäck, Fogel & Michalewicz, 1997).

A MULTIMODAL GENETIC ALGORITHM FOR CRANIOFACIAL SUPERIMPOSITION IN FORENSIC IDENTIFICATION

Niching Genetic Algorithms

A simple GA (Goldberg, 1989) (SGA) is suitable for searching the optimum of unimodal functions in a bounded search space. However, both experiments and analysis show that this kind of GA cannot find the multiple global maxima of a multimodal function (Goldberg, 1989; Mahfoud, 1995). This limitation can be overcome by a mechanism that creates and maintains several subpopulations within the search space in such a way that each highest maximum of the multimodal function can attract one of them (Pétrowski, 1996). These mechanisms are referred to as "niching methods" (Mahfoud, 1995).

The main concept niching GAs are based on is similarity. The concept of closeness or remoteness (similarity) requires the calculation of a distance between solutions, which is problem-dependant. This distance is a measure of proximity between individuals.

Clearing Method

The clearing procedure (Pétrowski, 1996) is a niching method inspired by the principle stated by Holland (1975) that consists of sharing limited resources within subpopulations of individuals characterized by some similarities. However, instead of evenly sharing the available resources among the individuals of a subpopulation, the clearing procedure supplies these resources only to the best individuals of each subpopulation. Thus, the clearing is naturally adapted to elitist strategies. This can significantly improve the performance of GAs applied to multimodal optimization. Moreover, the clearing procedure allows a GA to efficiently reduce the genetic drift when used with an appropriate selection operator.

This procedure is applied after evaluating the fitness of individuals and before applying the selection operator. Like other niching methods, the clearing algorithm uses a dissimilarity measure between individuals to determinate whether they belong to the same subpopulation or not. This value could be either the Hamming distance for binary coded genotypes or the Euclidian distance for "real coded" genotypes. It could be also defined at the phenotype level.

Each subpopulation contains a dominant individual: the one with best fitness. If an individual belongs to a given subpopulation then its dissimilarity with the dominant individual is less than a given threshold θ: the clearing *radius*. The basic clearing algorithm preserves the fitness of the dominant individual while it resets the fitness of all the other members of the same subpopulation to zero. Thus, the clearing procedure fully attributes the whole resource of a niche to a single individual: the winner. The winner takes all rather than sharing resources with the other members of the same niche as is done in the sharing method.

It is also possible to generalize the clearing algorithm by accepting several winners chosen among the best individuals of each niche. The capacity of a niche *kappa*, is defined as the maximum number of winners that this niche can accept.

Clearing GA Design

We propose two different clearing designs based on the definition of two different distances. On the one hand a genotypic distance d_g (Eq 9), where an Euclidean distance between the alleles of each pair of genes is calculated. On the other hand a phenotypic distance d_f (Eq 10), where an Euclidean distance between each pair of transformed landmarks (phenotypic representation of the chromosome) is calculated.

$$d_g = \sum_{i=1}^{12} \sqrt{\left(g_i - g_i{'}\right)^2} \qquad (9)$$

where g_i is the i-th gene of one individual and $g_i{'}$ is the i-th gene of another individual.

$$d_f = \sum_{i=1}^{N} \sqrt{\left(\vec{f(C_i)} - \vec{f(C_i{'})}\right)^2} \qquad (10)$$

where $\vec{f(C_i)}$ is a vector whose components are the x and y coordinates of the transformed landmark C_i and $\vec{f(C_i{'})}$ refers to the transformed landmark of another individual.

Another important issue is the θ value (the clearing radius). As said, the radius is the parameter that will determine the size of the niches. The lower the clearing radius value, the lower the number of individuals in the niche. This is because, with small radius values, the individuals are forced to be more similar than those that would be included in the niche with a higher radius. In order to avoid the number of niches is highly dependant on both the population size and the fitness of the individuals, we define θ as:

$$\theta = d_{\min} + \theta_0 . (d_{\max} - d_{\min}) \qquad (11)$$

where $d_{\min}$ is the shortest distance between two individuals in the population, $d_{\max}$ is the longest distance between two individuals in the population and θ_0 is the radius initial value.

Furthermore, with the aim of promoting a similar clearing behavior along the whole evolutionary process, θ is recalculated when the number of niches is less than P*(σ/2), where P is the size of the population.

Experiments

Once the specific design of our multimodal GA proposal has been presented, its performance is tested with respect of that of our previous GA (Ballerini, Cordón, Damas & Santamaría, 2009). In that previous proposal, we studied the performance of a classical (monomodal) GA for different parameter

Table 1. GA Parameter settings used for craniofacial superimposition

GA Parameter settings			
Generations	600	Population size	600
Tournament size	2	Mutation probability	0.2
Crossover probability	0.9		

Figure 3. Negative case studies. From left to right. Skull 3D model (that do not correspond to the young women in the photograph). Photograph of the young women considered for the first and second negative superimposition cases. Landmarks selected by the forensic are also shown

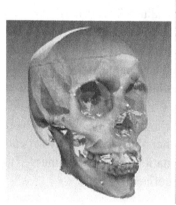 

combinations solving positive real identification cases. In this work, we will extend our previous scenario to tackle negative cases and compare the performance of the previous approach with the one using a multimodal GA.

Two positive identification cases will be considered, which were addressed by the staff of the Physical Anthropology lab at the University of Granada (Spain) in collaboration with the Spanish scientific police. They both were originally solved following a manual approach. We will consider the original 2D photographs and skull 3D models acquired at the lab using their Konica-Minolta 3D Lasserscanner VI-910.

On the other hand, we will also deal with two superimposition problems corresponding to two negative cases artificially generated by using the skull model of a young woman from one of the latter positive cases and a photograph of two fe-

male members of our centre (on around the same age than her).

The most suitable GA parameter values in that previous study are shown in Table 1.

In this contribution, we will restrict ourselves to consider the best performing variants of the fitness function (Ballerini, Cordón, Damas & Santamaría, 2009):

- $(\beta_1, \beta_2) = (1, 0)$, represented by $f=1$ in the first column of Tables 2, 3, 4, 5, 6, 7, 8, and 9
- $(\beta_1, \beta_2) = (0.5, 0.5)$, represented by $f=2$ in the first column of tables 2 to 9

Different values are considered for the α parameter related to the BLX-α crossover (0.1, 0.3 and 0.5) to study their influence in the GA behavior. In all the tackled problems, the GA is

Table 2. Negative case study 1. Results for the classical GA

f	α	Fitness				MSE				MAX			
		m	**M**	μ	σ	**m**	**M**	μ	σ	**m**	**M**	μ	σ
1	0,1	0,035	0,062	0,051	0,006	0,035	0,062	0,051	0,006	0,101	0,183	0,149	0,018
1	0,3	0,047	0,064	0,056	0,005	0,047	0,064	0,056	0,005	0,136	0,189	0,164	0,016
1	0,5	0,014	0,052	0,032	0,011	0,014	0,052	0,032	0,011	0,024	0,152	0,086	0,035
2	0,1	0,046	0,087	0,073	0,010	0,038	0,084	0,068	0,011	0,064	0,109	0,093	0,012
2	0,3	0,045	0,094	0,071	0,014	0,039	0,091	0,067	0,015	0,061	0,118	0,091	0,016
2	0,5	0,012	0,056	0,017	0,009	**0,010**	0,048	**0,014**	0,008	0,016	0,076	0,025	0,014

Figure 4. Negative case study 1. From left to right, top to bottom. Best and worst results achieved following a classical GA and a multimodal approach

run 30 different times for each parameter value combination to avoid any random bias. Tables 2 to 9 show the minimum (*m*), maximum (*M*), mean (*μ*) and standard deviation (*σ*) values of the MSE considering the Euclidean distances between the cephalometric landmarks that forensic experts identified in the photograph and the craniometric landmarks once they are transformed using the best solution achieved by the GA. We will analyze the results based on these MSE values. Besides,

Table 3. Negative case study 1. Results for the multimodal GAs

f	α	fC	θ	Fitness				MSE				MAX			
				m	M	μ	σ	m	M	μ	σ	m	M	μ	σ
1	0,1	d_f	0,05	0,009	0,047	0,014	0,008	0,009	0,047	0,014	0,008	0,023	0,137	0,035	0,024
1	0,1	d_f	0,15	0,008	0,026	0,015	0,005	**0,008**	0,026	**0,015**	**0,005**	0,021	0,081	0,038	0,017
1	0,1	d_f	0,25	0,008	0,054	0,016	0,010	**0,008**	0,054	0,016	0,010	0,023	0,156	0,041	0,033
1	0,1	d_g	0,05	0,038	0,073	0,066	0,007	0,038	0,073	0,066	0,007	0,113	0,219	0,184	0,027
1	0,1	d_g	0,15	0,020	0,068	0,050	0,012	0,020	0,068	0,050	0,012	0,048	0,199	0,141	0,039
1	0,1	d_g	0,25	0,014	0,068	0,049	0,014	0,014	0,068	0,049	0,014	0,034	0,200	0,141	0,041
1	0,3	d_f	0,05	0,009	0,023	0,013	0,003	0,009	0,023	0,013	**0,003**	0,022	0,050	0,029	0,006
1	0,3	d_f	0,15	0,009	0,024	0,014	0,003	0,009	0,024	0,014	**0,003**	0,021	0,057	0,030	0,008
1	0,3	d_f	0,25	0,008	0,020	0,011	0,003	**0,008**	0,020	**0,011**	**0,003**	0,023	0,055	0,028	0,006
1	0,3	d_g	0,05	0,023	0,078	0,068	0,010	0,023	0,078	0,068	0,010	0,040	0,222	0,191	0,036
1	0,3	d_g	0,15	0,025	0,076	0,060	0,012	0,025	0,076	0,060	0,012	0,066	0,219	0,174	0,036
1	0,3	d_g	0,25	0,011	0,075	0,047	0,017	0,011	0,075	0,047	0,017	0,025	0,220	0,133	0,055
1	0,5	d_f	0,05	0,010	0,028	0,016	0,004	0,010	0,028	0,016	**0,004**	0,020	0,077	0,034	0,010
1	0,5	d_f	0,15	0,009	0,040	0,018	0,007	0,009	0,040	0,018	0,007	0,020	0,092	0,043	0,019
1	0,5	d_f	0,25	0,008	0,046	0,014	0,007	**0,008**	0,046	**0,014**	0,007	0,020	0,136	0,035	0,021
1	0,5	d_g	0,05	0,054	0,078	0,067	0,008	0,054	0,078	0,067	0,008	0,145	0,232	0,192	0,027
1	0,5	d_g	0,15	0,011	0,070	0,051	0,017	0,011	0,070	0,051	0,017	0,026	0,209	0,145	0,053
1	0,5	d_g	0,25	0,016	0,075	0,055	0,015	0,016	0,075	0,055	0,015	0,039	0,222	0,157	0,045
2	0,1	d_f	0,05	0,012	0,024	0,016	0,003	**0,009**	0,022	**0,014**	**0,003**	0,017	0,033	0,023	0,004
2	0,1	d_f	0,15	0,012	0,030	0,016	0,004	0,010	0,028	0,015	0,004	0,016	0,041	0,023	0,006
2	0,1	d_f	0,25	0,013	0,035	0,016	0,005	0,011	0,034	0,015	0,005	0,017	0,047	0,021	0,007
2	0,1	d_g	0,05	0,033	0,104	0,083	0,016	0,028	0,099	0,075	0,016	0,047	0,144	0,110	0,020
2	0,1	d_g	0,15	0,030	0,104	0,072	0,019	0,027	0,101	0,068	0,018	0,040	0,133	0,094	0,024
2	0,1	d_g	0,25	0,013	0,073	0,042	0,020	0,011	0,079	0,042	0,021	0,025	0,115	0,070	0,032
2	0,3	d_f	0,05	0,013	0,021	0,015	0,002	**0,009**	0,019	**0,013**	**0,002**	0,017	0,031	0,022	0,003
2	0,3	d_f	0,15	0,012	0,016	0,013	0,001	0,010	0,017	0,012	0,001	0,016	0,027	0,019	0,002
2	0,3	d_f	0,25	0,012	0,015	0,013	0,001	**0,009**	0,014	**0,012**	**0,001**	0,016	0,025	0,018	0,002
2	0,3	d_g	0,05	0,036	0,110	0,091	0,016	0,031	0,103	0,081	0,017	0,050	0,162	0,122	0,023
2	0,3	d_g	0,15	0,037	0,096	0,068	0,018	0,035	0,092	0,066	0,018	0,051	0,133	0,094	0,024
2	0,3	d_g	0,25	0,013	0,091	0,053	0,024	0,012	0,095	0,051	0,026	0,018	0,127	0,079	0,034
2	0,5	d_f	0,05	0,012	0,025	0,017	0,003	**0,009**	0,023	**0,015**	**0,003**	0,017	0,034	0,025	0,004
2	0,5	d_f	0,15	0,013	0,020	0,014	0,002	**0,009**	0,018	**0,013**	**0,002**	0,017	0,029	0,021	0,003
2	0,5	d_f	0,25	0,012	0,021	0,014	0,002	0,010	0,021	0,013	0,002	0,015	0,026	0,019	0,003
2	0,5	d_g	0,05	0,059	0,110	0,092	0,014	0,054	0,103	0,081	0,015	0,076	0,167	0,124	0,021
2	0,5	d_g	0,15	0,017	0,101	0,078	0,021	0,015	0,099	0,073	0,022	0,024	0,129	0,103	0,027
2	0,5	d_g	0,25	0,012	0,095	0,064	0,024	0,012	0,096	0,063	0,026	0,017	0,134	0,094	0,034

Table 4. Negative case study 2. Results for the classical GA

f	α	Fitness				MSE				MAX			
		m	M	μ	σ	m	M	μ	σ	m	M	μ	σ
1	0,1	0,043	0,064	0,056	0,006	0,043	0,064	0,056	0,006	0,108	0,160	0,140	0,015
1	0,3	0,045	0,064	0,056	0,005	0,045	0,064	0,056	0,005	0,113	0,161	0,140	0,013
1	0,5	0,015	0,049	0,026	0,008	**0,015**	0,049	**0,026**	0,008	0,024	0,123	0,062	0,021
2	0,1	0,046	0,083	0,074	0,008	0,042	0,077	0,068	0,007	0,061	0,110	0,098	0,010
2	0,3	0,070	0,088	0,080	0,004	0,065	0,081	0,074	0,004	0,092	0,116	0,106	0,006
2	0,5	0,035	0,088	0,068	0,015	0,032	0,081	0,062	0,014	0,046	0,116	0,091	0,019

the m, M, μ and σ values are also provided for the corresponding fitness function (*fitness*) and for the maximum distance between the corresponding landmarks (*MAX*).

Referring the clearing experimental study, Tables 3, 5, 7 and 9 comprise both genotypic (d_g) and phenotypic (d_p) distance in the third column, as well as different initial clearing radius θ_0 (0.05, 0.15, 0.25) in the forth column.

Negative Case Study 1

This is a negative case, that is, the person in the picture does not correspond with the skull used for the superimposition. The skull 3D model (comprising 327.641 points) corresponds to a young woman different from the two ones in the photograph in Figure 3 (it is the skull of the subject in the positive case 2, see below). The 2D photograph is a 760 × 1050 RGB color image of two young women with a similar age to the said woman. We will use this image to tackle both negative case 1 (Figure 3, young woman on the left) and negative case 2 (Figure 3, young woman on the right). The forensic anthropologists identified seven cephalometric landmarks for the woman on the left in the photograph and the corresponding craniometric ones were manually extracted from the skull 3D model.

Table 2 shows the results using our previous approach (Ballerini, Cordón, Damas & Santamaría, 2009). Table 3 shows the corresponding ones

applying our clearing method. From the reported results we can observe that in all the cases the multimodal GA overcomes the classical GA. In the first case, phenotypic distance the behavior is very similar for all the parameter combinations (m ranging 0.008-0.009 and μ ranging 0.011-0.014), slightly better using fitness 1. Better results are obtained with α = 0.3. The phenotypic distance configuration always achieved better results than the genotypic one and there is not a fixed radius value associated to the best results. For all the configurations the standard deviation is very small, what demonstrates the robustness of the method. The better results of the classical GA are achieved when α is 0.5 and using fitness 2.

Figure 4 presents the superimposition results following the classical and multimodal GAs. In both cases the superimposition with the best MSE value is provided. In addition, we show the superimposition corresponding to the worst run, among the 30 runs performed, for the configuration achieving the solution with the best MSE.

Negative Case Study 2

In the second negative case, we used again the skull 3D model corresponding to the young woman in positive case 2. The 2D photograph is the one used in the previous negative case (see Figure 3) but we will consider the blond girl in this case (the one on the right). The forensic anthropologists identified ten cephalometric landmarks on her face and the

Table 5. Negative case study 2. Results for the multimodal GAs

f	α	fC	θ	Fitness				MSE				MAX			
				m	M	μ	σ	m	M	μ	σ	m	M	μ	σ
1	0,1	d_f	0,05	0,011	0,020	0,015	0,002	**0,011**	0,020	**0,015**	**0,002**	0,020	0,064	0,034	0,013
1	0,1	d_f	0,15	0,012	0,048	0,018	0,007	0,012	0,048	0,018	0,007	0,018	0,107	0,039	0,021
1	0,1	d_f	0,25	0,011	0,024	0,014	0,003	0,011	0,024	0,014	0,003	0,017	0,070	0,031	0,014
1	0,1	d_g	0,05	0,031	0,074	0,064	0,009	0,031	0,074	0,064	0,009	0,079	0,194	0,161	0,022
1	0,1	d_g	0,15	0,018	0,069	0,050	0,014	0,018	0,069	0,050	0,014	0,057	0,177	0,127	0,033
1	0,1	d_g	0,25	0,012	0,064	0,044	0,013	0,012	0,064	0,044	0,013	0,028	0,171	0,111	0,034
1	0,3	d_f	0,05	0,011	0,029	0,016	0,004	**0,011**	0,029	**0,016**	**0,004**	0,019	0,069	0,032	0,011
1	0,3	d_f	0,15	0,011	0,027	0,017	0,004	**0,011**	0,027	**0,017**	**0,004**	0,017	0,068	0,033	0,012
1	0,3	d_f	0,25	0,012	0,026	0,015	0,004	0,012	0,026	0,015	0,004	0,018	0,068	0,029	0,011
1	0,3	d_g	0,05	0,040	0,079	0,068	0,008	0,040	0,079	0,068	0,008	0,062	0,214	0,167	0,029
1	0,3	d_g	0,15	0,028	0,074	0,051	0,012	0,028	0,074	0,051	0,012	0,068	0,180	0,128	0,031
1	0,3	d_g	0,25	0,013	0,073	0,045	0,019	0,013	0,073	0,045	0,019	0,020	0,186	0,114	0,048
1	0,5	d_f	0,05	0,013	0,029	0,018	0,004	0,013	0,029	0,018	0,004	0,020	0,093	0,038	0,014
1	0,5	d_f	0,15	0,012	0,032	0,020	0,006	0,012	0,032	0,020	0,006	0,022	0,079	0,049	0,018
1	0,5	d_f	0,25	0,012	0,026	0,016	0,004	**0,012**	0,026	**0,016**	**0,004**	0,018	0,065	0,035	0,013
1	0,5	d_g	0,05	0,036	0,081	0,070	0,008	0,036	0,081	0,070	0,008	0,068	0,205	0,170	0,030
1	0,5	d_g	0,15	0,016	0,078	0,056	0,018	0,016	0,078	0,056	0,018	0,033	0,199	0,140	0,048
1	0,5	d_g	0,25	0,014	0,075	0,051	0,015	0,014	0,075	0,051	0,015	0,031	0,191	0,130	0,038
2	0,1	d_f	0,05	0,012	0,063	0,017	0,009	0,012	0,053	0,016	0,007	0,016	0,098	0,024	0,015
2	0,1	d_f	0,15	0,013	0,040	0,019	0,007	**0,011**	0,039	0,018	0,006	0,017	0,062	0,026	0,010
2	0,1	d_f	0,25	0,012	0,022	0,016	0,003	**0,011**	0,021	**0,016**	**0,003**	0,016	0,031	0,021	0,004
2	0,1	d_g	0,05	0,028	0,103	0,083	0,016	0,022	0,092	0,073	0,015	0,042	0,143	0,113	0,021
2	0,1	d_g	0,15	0,023	0,097	0,063	0,022	0,023	0,093	0,060	0,022	0,031	0,137	0,089	0,030
2	0,1	d_g	0,25	0,015	0,082	0,058	0,016	0,015	0,078	0,055	0,015	0,022	0,121	0,084	0,022
2	0,3	d_f	0,05	0,012	0,020	0,015	0,002	0,012	0,020	0,015	0,002	0,017	0,028	0,022	0,003
2	0,3	d_f	0,15	0,012	0,030	0,015	0,003	0,012	0,025	0,014	0,002	0,016	0,048	0,020	0,006
2	0,3	d_f	0,25	0,012	0,017	0,013	0,001	**0,011**	0,018	**0,013**	**0,002**	0,016	0,021	0,018	0,001
2	0,3	d_g	0,05	0,049	0,103	0,090	0,013	0,047	0,093	0,078	0,012	0,063	0,143	0,124	0,019
2	0,3	d_g	0,15	0,032	0,098	0,072	0,018	0,032	0,090	0,068	0,018	0,043	0,141	0,101	0,024
2	0,3	d_g	0,25	0,014	0,086	0,061	0,022	0,015	0,088	0,061	0,022	0,019	0,128	0,091	0,032
2	0,5	d_f	0,05	0,013	0,024	0,018	0,003	0,013	0,022	0,016	0,003	0,019	0,039	0,027	0,004
2	0,5	d_f	0,15	0,012	0,019	0,015	0,002	0,012	0,019	0,014	0,002	0,015	0,031	0,021	0,004
2	0,5	d_f	0,25	0,012	0,019	0,015	0,002	**0,011**	0,019	**0,015**	**0,002**	0,016	0,026	0,020	0,003
2	0,5	d_g	0,05	0,073	0,104	0,090	0,007	0,059	0,091	0,077	0,009	0,096	0,142	0,125	0,010
2	0,5	d_g	0,15	0,015	0,097	0,076	0,018	0,014	0,094	0,072	0,018	0,022	0,143	0,110	0,026
2	0,5	d_g	0,25	0,012	0,088	0,059	0,024	0,013	0,091	0,061	0,025	0,016	0,144	0,092	0,037

corresponding craniometric ones were manually extracted from the skull 3D model.

Table 4 shows the results obtained for this case using the classical GA while Table 5 does so for the clearing GAs. From the reported results we can observe that, as in the previous cases, the multimodal approach always overcomes the classical GA. In the first case, phenotypic distance, the behavior is very similar again for all the parameter combinations (m ranging 0.011-0.012 and μ ranging 0.013-0.016), slightly better using fitness 2. Good results are achieved considering different values for the α parameter. Hence, it seems there are other more influencing parameters than α. The phenotypic distance configuration always achieved better results than the genotypic one and again there is not a fixed value for the niche radius providing the best results. For all the configurations the standard deviation is very small. For the case of the classical GA, better results are achieved when α is 0.3 and using fitness 1.

Figure 5 presents the superimposition results following the classical and multimodal GA-based approaches. In both cases the superimposition with the best MSE value is provided. In addition, we show the superimposition corresponding to the worst run, among the 30 runs performed, for the configuration providing the best solution.

Positive Case Study 1

The facial photographs of this missing lady found in Malaga, Spain, were provided by the family. Her identity was confirmed using manual photographic supra-projection. We studied this real case with the consent of the relatives. The 2D image used by anthropologists is a 290 × 371 color image. The 3D model of the skull comprises 243.202 points (Figure 6).

The forensic anthropologists identified six cephalometric landmarks. The counterpart craniometric ones were manually extracted from the skull 3D model.

Table 6 shows the results obtained for this case as in the previous cases. When working with the classical GA, better results are achieved when α is 0.5 and using fitness 1, i.e. $(\beta_1, \beta_2) =$ (1, 0). Table 7 shows the corresponding ones applying our clearing method. From the reported results we can observe that the multimodal GA clearly overcomes the classical one. Using the phenotypic distance the behavior is similar for all the parameter combinations. The best m values ranging 0.018-0.024 and μ ranging 0.024-0.039. Good results are achieved considering different values for the α parameter. Hence, it seems there are other more influencing parameters than α. The phenotypic distance configuration always achieved better results than the genotypic one. Higher values for the niche radius allows the GA to get the best results.

Figure 7 presents the superimposition results obtained by the classical and multimodal GAs. In both cases the superimposition with the best MSE value is provided, as well as the one associated to the worst run of that configuration.

Positive Case Study 2

The second positive case is again a real-world one happened in Puerto de Santa María, Spain. The considered photo shows a frontal view of the young woman involved. Notice that it has been processed in order the woman cannot be recognized due to legal reasons as she had no relatives to provide us with the consent to handle it. The skull 3D model comprises 327,641 points and the 2D photograph is a 744 × 1147 RGB color image (see Figure 8). As in the previous case, the anthropologists identified eight cephalometric landmarks and the corresponding craniometric ones were manually extracted from the skull 3D model.

Table 8 shows the classical GA results obtained for this case as in the previous cases. The best results are achieved when α is 0.5 and using fitness 1, i.e. $(\beta_1, \beta_2) = (1, 0)$. Table 9 shows the

Figure 5. Negative case study 2. From left to right, top to bottom. Best and worst results achieved following a classical GA and a multimodal approach

Figure 6. Real world positive case study 1: 3D skull model (left) and photograph of the missing person: original image where the person is sitting at the left side of the table (middle), and a cropped image (the one used for doing the superimposition) of the person where we can see the identified landmarks highlighted

Table 6. Positive case study 1. Results for the classical GA

f	α	Fitness				MSE				MAX			
		m	M	μ	σ	m	M	M	σ	m	M	μ	σ
1	0,1	0,232	0,251	0,244	0,004	0,232	0,251	0,244	0,004	0,387	0,417	0,404	0,007
1	0,3	0,231	0,256	0,247	0,006	0,231	0,256	0,247	0,006	0,384	0,425	0,409	0,010
1	0,5	0,090	0,259	0,233	0,038	**0,090**	0,259	**0,233**	0,038	0,149	0,429	0,386	0,060
2	0,1	0,238	0,260	0,250	0,005	0,243	0,263	0,254	0,005	0,332	0,366	0,350	0,008
2	0,3	0,241	0,263	0,256	0,005	0,242	0,265	0,258	0,006	0,336	0,364	0,355	0,007
2	0,5	0,158	0,262	0,252	0,020	0,154	0,268	0,257	0,022	0,234	0,367	0,354	0,025

corresponding results for the clearing method. We can observe that the multimodal GA overcomes the classical one. In the first case, phenotypic distance, the behavior is similar for all the parameter combinations (*m* ranging 0.031-0.047 and *μ* ranging 0.040-0.056), being slightly better using fitness 1. Good results are achieved considering different values for the α parameter. Hence, it seems there are other more influencing parameters than α. The phenotypic distance configuration always achieved better results than the genotypic one and again there is not a single radius niche value providing the best results.

Figure 9 presents the superimposition results obtained by the classical and multimodal GAs with and without clearing. In both cases the superimposition with the best MSE value and its associated worst run are provided.

FUTURE WORK

Craniofacial superimposition is a very challenging problem. As said, most of the landmarks are nearly coplanar, resulting in a system of indeterminate equations. Moreover, a large range of parameters needs to be used, in order to consider one of the worse possible settings of the camera. This makes the search space of the GA much bigger than any possible real identification problem. Finally, as we

Figure 7. Positive case study 1. From left to right. Best and worst results achieved following a classical GA and a multimodal approach

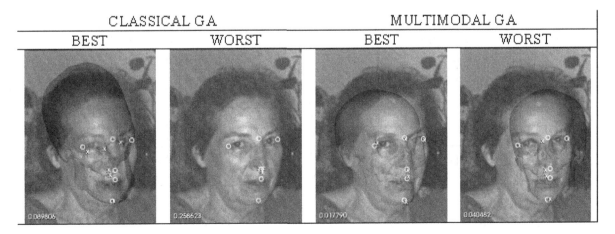

Table 7. Positive case study 1. Results for the multimodal GAs

f	α	fC	θ	Fitness				MSE				MAX			
				m	M	μ	σ	m	M	μ	σ	m	M	μ	σ
1	0,1	d_f	0,05	0,022	0,115	0,039	0,018	0,022	0,115	0,039	0,018	0,031	0,262	0,076	0,043
1	0,1	d_f	0,15	0,019	0,048	0,026	0,006	**0,019**	0,048	**0,026**	**0,006**	0,032	0,107	0,053	0,020
1	0,1	d_f	0,25	0,019	0,045	0,026	0,007	**0,019**	0,045	0,026	0,007	0,030	0,121	0,050	0,019
1	0,1	d_g	0,05	0,112	0,267	0,238	0,032	0,112	0,267	0,238	0,032	0,196	0,437	0,387	0,057
1	0,1	d_g	0,15	0,065	0,261	0,206	0,050	0,065	0,261	0,206	0,050	0,095	0,430	0,337	0,085
1	0,1	d_g	0,25	0,104	0,246	0,183	0,045	0,104	0,246	0,183	0,045	0,194	0,409	0,318	0,062
1	0,3	d_f	0,05	0,020	0,032	0,024	0,003	**0,020**	0,032	**0,024**	**0,003**	0,031	0,056	0,043	0,007
1	0,3	d_f	0,15	0,020	0,038	0,027	0,004	**0,020**	0,038	0,027	**0,004**	0,030	0,076	0,047	0,011
1	0,3	d_f	0,25	0,018	0,040	0,027	0,006	0,018	0,040	0,027	0,006	0,037	0,169	0,056	0,024
1	0,3	d_g	0,05	0,079	0,268	0,229	0,048	0,079	0,268	0,229	0,048	0,162	0,488	0,371	0,078
1	0,3	d_g	0,15	0,028	0,268	0,211	0,055	0,028	0,268	0,211	0,055	0,079	0,451	0,355	0,087
1	0,3	d_g	0,25	0,043	0,246	0,198	0,049	0,043	0,246	0,198	0,049	0,094	0,420	0,338	0,074
1	0,5	d_f	0,05	0,021	0,032	0,025	0,003	0,021	0,032	**0,025**	**0,003**	0,029	0,074	0,046	0,010
1	0,5	d_f	0,15	0,027	0,051	0,035	0,006	0,027	0,051	0,035	0,006	0,041	0,122	0,067	0,022
1	0,5	d_f	0,25	0,018	0,054	0,035	0,009	**0,018**	0,054	0,035	0,009	0,039	0,151	0,072	0,026
1	0,5	d_g	0,05	0,066	0,275	0,239	0,039	0,066	0,275	0,239	0,039	0,196	0,496	0,389	0,056
1	0,5	d_g	0,15	0,035	0,263	0,193	0,067	0,035	0,263	0,193	0,067	0,052	0,433	0,320	0,110
1	0,5	d_g	0,25	0,040	0,263	0,190	0,071	0,040	0,263	0,190	0,071	0,074	0,434	0,321	0,109
2	0,1	d_f	0,05	0,021	0,055	0,033	0,009	0,022	0,057	0,033	0,009	0,028	0,086	0,049	0,015
2	0,1	d_f	0,15	0,021	0,042	0,027	0,005	0,021	0,038	**0,027**	**0,004**	0,026	0,065	0,039	0,010
2	0,1	d_f	0,25	0,019	0,044	0,026	0,006	**0,019**	0,044	0,027	0,006	0,025	0,065	0,037	0,010
2	0,1	d_g	0,05	0,218	0,273	0,251	0,016	0,218	0,273	0,252	0,017	0,307	0,397	0,359	0,022
2	0,1	d_g	0,15	0,115	0,268	0,226	0,036	0,124	0,276	0,232	0,039	0,158	0,386	0,324	0,050
2	0,1	d_g	0,25	0,053	0,260	0,204	0,050	0,049	0,276	0,213	0,057	0,091	0,381	0,303	0,070
2	0,3	d_f	0,05	0,019	0,030	0,023	0,003	**0,020**	0,032	**0,024**	**0,003**	0,025	0,045	0,034	0,005
2	0,3	d_f	0,15	0,022	0,044	0,029	0,006	0,022	0,043	0,030	0,006	0,030	0,066	0,042	0,009
2	0,3	d_f	0,25	0,018	0,050	0,026	0,006	**0,020**	0,054	0,027	0,007	0,024	0,067	0,035	0,009
2	0,3	d_g	0,05	0,137	0,282	0,255	0,034	0,134	0,281	0,252	0,035	0,193	0,394	0,358	0,046
2	0,3	d_g	0,15	0,122	0,262	0,226	0,041	0,105	0,270	0,231	0,044	0,196	0,372	0,323	0,056
2	0,3	d_g	0,25	0,029	0,258	0,193	0,074	0,028	0,268	0,200	0,076	0,045	0,373	0,279	0,107
2	0,5	d_f	0,05	0,020	0,032	0,026	0,003	**0,020**	0,033	**0,025**	**0,004**	0,030	0,051	0,039	0,006
2	0,5	d_f	0,15	0,024	0,059	0,036	0,008	0,024	0,059	0,035	0,009	0,033	0,085	0,052	0,012
2	0,5	d_f	0,25	0,019	0,050	0,032	0,010	**0,019**	0,050	0,033	0,009	0,024	0,089	0,047	0,016
2	0,5	d_g	0,05	0,185	0,280	0,254	0,027	0,177	0,285	0,251	0,031	0,275	0,432	0,366	0,036
2	0,5	d_g	0,15	0,070	0,268	0,232	0,050	0,049	0,277	0,236	0,055	0,104	0,384	0,334	0,068
2	0,5	d_g	0,25	0,044	0,270	0,223	0,057	0,040	0,274	0,227	0,058	0,065	0,390	0,315	0,080

Figure 8. Positive case study 2. From left to right: skull 3D model and the photograph of the missing person. Notice that the original face photograph has been processed to hide the identity of the woman due to legal reasons

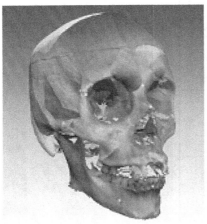 

Table 8. Positive case study 2. Results for the classical GA

f	α	Fitness				MSE				MAX			
		m	M	μ	σ	m	M	μ	σ	m	M	μ	σ
1	0,1	0,105	0,126	0,115	0,006	0,105	0,126	0,115	0,006	0,271	0,327	0,299	0,015
1	0,3	0,097	0,123	0,115	0,006	0,097	0,123	0,115	0,006	0,248	0,321	0,298	0,018
1	0,5	0,039	0,092	0,051	0,009	**0,039**	0,092	**0,051**	0,009	0,078	0,229	0,101	0,028
2	0,1	0,074	0,159	0,146	0,016	0,066	0,151	0,138	0,016	0,107	0,215	0,197	0,021
2	0,3	0,097	0,165	0,152	0,012	0,083	0,156	0,144	0,013	0,143	0,224	0,208	0,014
2	0,5	0,057	0,162	0,106	0,041	0,049	0,152	0,095	0,040	0,077	0,216	0,146	0,053

are dealing with real craniofacial superimposition cases, the thickness of the soft tissue as well as the uncertainty of localizing landmarks will both influence the final results of our automatic approach based on multimodal GA.

We have found that there is still room for improvement on our proposal. We plan to extend this study by improving the GA design using other advanced approaches such as the scatter search algorithm (Laguna & Martí, 2003) that we already applied to medical IR and RIR real-world problems with very successful results (Santamaría, Cordón,

Damas, Alemán & Botella, 2007; Cordón, Damas & Santamaría, 2006a and 2006b; Santamaría, Cordón & Damas, 2007). One important future work is initializing the algorithm and restricting the parameter ranges using problem-specific information (domain knowledge). We are also planning to consider a higher number of real cases of identification provided and solved by the Physical Anthropology Lab at the University of Granada in Spain.

Lastly, we also aim to tackle the final identification stage, i.e. the decision making by using

Figure 9. Positive case study 2. From left to right. Best result achieved by the classical and the multimodal GA

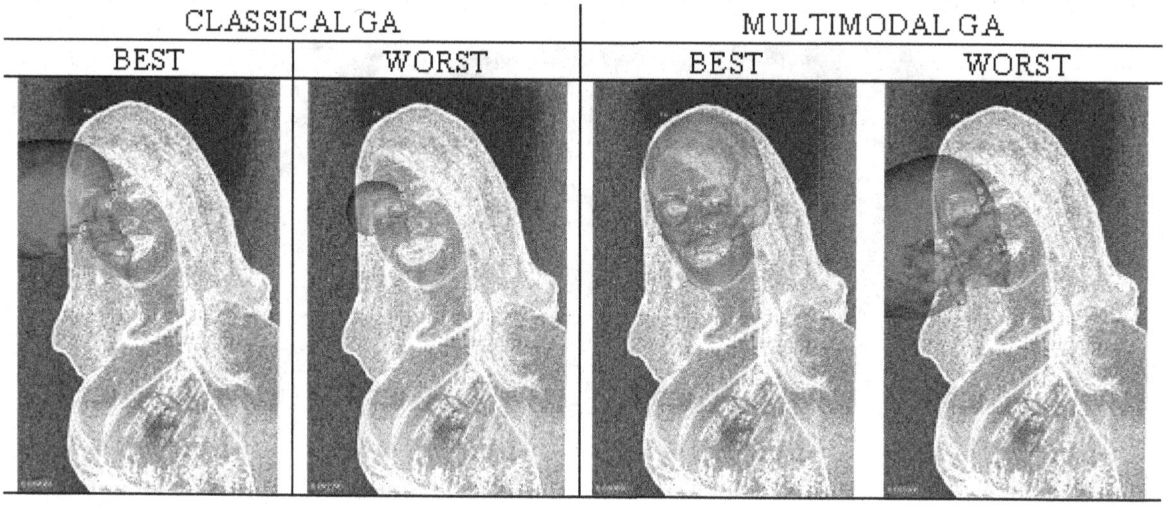

CLASSICAL GA		MULTIMODAL GA	
BEST	WORST	BEST	WORST

fuzzy logic, in order to assist the forensic expert to take the final identification decision.

CONCLUSION

This work represents part of a project that aims to design a complete, automatic, soft computing-based procedure to aid the forensic anthropologist in the identification task of photographic supra-projection. In this chapter, we described the craniofacial superimposition problem and formulated it as an IR problem. We also proposed and validated the use of a multimodal GA following a clearing approach to improve the behavior of our previously developed GAs for craniofacial superimposition.

We presented and discussed superimposition results obtained on real-world cases, both negatives and positives ones. The proposed method is fast (i.e. it always takes less than 20 seconds) and automatic, and therefore very useful for solving one of the most tedious works (requiring around 24 hours) performed by the forensic anthropologists. In addition, this method supposed a systematic ap-

proach to solve the superimposition problem and in spite of its need for improvements, it could be used now as a tool for obtaining a previous automatic superimposition before a manually one.

We can conclude that using clearing over the population of individuals, the behavior of the GA is more robust. Furthermore, both the mean and the minimum values achieved by following a multimodal approach are much better than the ones reached by our previous proposal. From the visualization of the images we can remark that the multimodal GA achieved better and more robust superimpositions. However, we also observed that the search space is so big that at times the GA is trapped in local minima. We aim to solve this problem in future work by considering problem-specific information to both generating the initial GA population and restricting the parameter ranges to reasonable sizes.

ACKNOWLEDGMENT

This work is supported by the Spanish Ministerio de Educación y Ciencia (ref. TIN2006-00829), and

Table 9. Positive case study 2. Results for the multimodal GAs

f	α	fC	θ	Fitness				MSE				MAX			
				m	M	μ	σ	m	M	μ	σ	m	M	μ	σ
1	0,1	d_f	0,05	0,035	0,097	0,045	0,012	0,035	0,097	0,045	0,012	0,078	0,245	0,103	0,030
1	0,1	d_f	0,15	0,032	0,086	0,040	0,010	**0,032**	0,086	**0,040**	**0,010**	0,080	0,219	0,099	0,024
1	0,1	d_f	0,25	0,032	0,087	0,042	0,012	**0,032**	0,087	**0,042**	0,012	0,085	0,226	0,104	0,033
1	0,1	d_g	0,05	0,048	0,134	0,111	0,021	0,048	0,134	0,111	0,021	0,113	0,351	0,280	0,052
1	0,1	d_g	0,15	0,037	0,119	0,100	0,018	0,037	0,119	0,100	0,018	0,093	0,309	0,253	0,049
1	0,1	d_g	0,25	0,052	0,127	0,095	0,019	0,052	0,127	0,095	0,019	0,100	0,335	0,240	0,058
1	0,3	d_f	0,05	0,034	0,052	0,040	0,004	**0,034**	0,052	**0,040**	**0,004**	0,081	0,117	0,095	0,007
1	0,3	d_f	0,15	0,035	0,050	0,041	0,004	0,035	0,050	0,041	0,004	0,076	0,134	0,095	0,010
1	0,3	d_f	0,25	0,033	0,051	0,040	0,005	**0,033**	0,051	**0,040**	**0,005**	0,069	0,107	0,096	0,008
1	0,3	d_g	0,05	0,076	0,135	0,121	0,013	0,076	0,135	0,121	0,013	0,138	0,364	0,302	0,045
1	0,3	d_g	0,15	0,075	0,134	0,111	0,014	0,075	0,134	0,111	0,014	0,196	0,349	0,287	0,040
1	0,3	d_g	0,25	0,044	0,132	0,093	0,022	0,044	0,132	0,093	0,022	0,088	0,348	0,233	0,066
1	0,5	d_f	0,05	0,034	0,052	0,040	0,004	**0,034**	0,052	**0,040**	**0,004**	0,072	0,129	0,100	0,010
1	0,5	d_f	0,15	0,038	0,057	0,048	0,005	0,038	0,057	0,048	0,005	0,081	0,122	0,100	0,010
1	0,5	d_f	0,25	0,031	0,056	0,045	0,006	**0,031**	0,056	**0,045**	**0,006**	0,079	0,140	0,096	0,012
1	0,5	d_g	0,05	0,076	0,139	0,116	0,019	0,076	0,139	0,116	0,019	0,117	0,364	0,278	0,069
1	0,5	d_g	0,15	0,055	0,136	0,110	0,021	0,055	0,136	0,110	0,021	0,122	0,353	0,283	0,061
1	0,5	d_g	0,25	0,053	0,129	0,100	0,021	0,053	0,129	0,100	0,021	0,118	0,340	0,257	0,060
2	0,1	d_f	0,05	0,045	0,071	0,051	0,006	0,037	0,067	0,049	0,006	0,060	0,096	0,070	0,011
2	0,1	d_f	0,15	0,047	0,058	0,051	0,004	0,037	0,053	0,046	0,004	0,063	0,098	0,073	0,010
2	0,1	d_f	0,25	0,045	0,058	0,051	0,003	**0,034**	0,051	**0,044**	**0,005**	0,062	0,093	0,077	0,011
2	0,1	d_g	0,05	0,109	0,167	0,147	0,018	0,093	0,157	0,133	0,019	0,146	0,241	0,203	0,024
2	0,1	d_g	0,15	0,067	0,160	0,121	0,023	0,058	0,155	0,116	0,025	0,098	0,222	0,169	0,030
2	0,1	d_g	0,25	0,053	0,160	0,098	0,033	0,048	0,163	0,096	0,035	0,081	0,229	0,145	0,045
2	0,3	d_f	0,05	0,046	0,054	0,049	0,001	0,042	0,050	0,045	0,002	0,062	0,075	0,067	0,003
2	0,3	d_f	0,15	0,046	0,059	0,050	0,004	0,037	0,057	0,046	0,005	0,061	0,093	0,073	0,010
2	0,3	d_f	0,25	0,046	0,057	0,051	0,003	**0,033**	0,052	**0,045**	**0,005**	0,064	0,091	0,077	0,009
2	0,3	d_g	0,05	0,111	0,174	0,148	0,020	0,101	0,164	0,136	0,020	0,153	0,238	0,203	0,026
2	0,3	d_g	0,15	0,051	0,155	0,111	0,039	0,054	0,157	0,107	0,039	0,067	0,218	0,158	0,053
2	0,3	d_g	0,25	0,046	0,139	0,095	0,030	0,036	0,146	0,093	0,033	0,071	0,209	0,153	0,046
2	0,5	d_f	0,05	0,048	0,058	0,052	0,003	0,038	0,053	0,048	0,004	0,060	0,092	0,072	0,009
2	0,5	d_f	0,15	0,046	0,062	0,054	0,004	**0,033**	0,060	**0,048**	**0,006**	0,064	0,098	0,081	0,010
2	0,5	d_f	0,25	0,046	0,058	0,052	0,004	0,034	0,054	0,047	0,005	0,058	0,091	0,078	0,010
2	0,5	d_g	0,05	0,097	0,177	0,153	0,022	0,079	0,163	0,138	0,021	0,124	0,247	0,208	0,030
2	0,5	d_g	0,15	0,054	0,169	0,138	0,031	0,041	0,161	0,130	0,032	0,087	0,230	0,190	0,039
2	0,5	d_g	0,25	0,048	0,154	0,115	0,030	0,035	0,156	0,113	0,033	0,089	0,217	0,168	0,039

by the Andalusian Dpt. of Innovación, Ciencia y Empresa (ref. TIC-1619), both including EDRF fundings.

REFERENCES

Al-Amad, S., McCullough, M., Graham, J., Clement, J., & Hill, A. (2006). Craniofacial identification by computer-mediated superimposition. *The Journal of Forensic Odonto-Stomatology, 24*, 47–52.

Aulsebrook, W.A., Iscan, M.Y., Slabbert, J.H., & Becker, P. (1995). Superimposition and reconstruction in forensic facial identification: a survey. *Forensic Science International, 75*(2-3), 101–120. doi:10.1016/0379-0738(95)01770-4

Bäck, T., Fogel, D. B., & Michalewicz, Z. (1997). (Eds.) *Handbook of evolutionary computation*. IOP Publishing Ltd and Oxford University Press.

Ballerini, L., Cordón, O., Damas, S., & Santamaría, J. (2008). *Craniofacial superimposition in Forensic identification using genetic algorithms*. Technical Report ECSC AFE 2008-03, European Center for Soft Computing.

Ballerini, L., Cordón, O., Damas, S., Santamaría, J., & Alemán, I. & Botella. M. (2007). Craniofacial superimposition in forensic identification using genetic algorithms. *Proceedings of the IEEE International Workshop on Computational Forensics* (pp. 429–434), Manchester, UK.

Ballerini, L., Cordón, O., Damas, S., Santamaría, J., Alemán, I., & Botella, M. (2007). *Identification by computer aided photographic supra-projection: a survey*. Technical Report AFE 2007-04, European Centre for Soft Computing.

Besl, P. J., & McKay, N. D. (1992). Iterative point matching for registration of free-form curves and surfaces. *IEEE Transactions on Pattern Analysis and Machine Intelligence, 14*, 239–256. doi:10.1109/34.121791

Bilge, Y., Kedici, P., Alakoc, Y. U. K., & Ilkyaz, Y. (2003). The identification of a dismembered human body: a multidisciplinary approach. *Forensic Science International, 137*, 141–146. doi:10.1016/S0379-0738(03)00334-7

Blickle, T. (1997). *Tournament selection*. In T. Bäck, D. B. Fogel, & Z. Michalewicz (Eds.), *Handbook of Evolutionary Computation*, IOP Publishing Ltd and Oxford University Press, C2.3.

Bowyer, K. W., Chang, K., & Flynn, P. (2006). A survey of approaches and challenges in 3D and multi-modal 3D + 2D face recognition. *Computer Vision and Image Understanding, 101*, 1–15. doi:10.1016/j.cviu.2005.05.005

Clarkson, M. J., Rueckert, D., Hill, D. L. G., & Hawkes, D. J. (2001). Using photo-consistency to register 2D optical images of the, human face to a 3D surface model. *IEEE Transactions on Pattern Analysis and Machine Intelligence, 23*(11), 1266–1280. doi:10.1109/34.969117

Cordón, O., Damas, S., & Santamaría, J. (2006a). A fast and accurate approach for 3D image registration using the scatter search evolutionary algorithm. *Pattern Recognition Letters, 27*(11), 1191–1200. doi:10.1016/j.patrec.2005.07.017

Cordón, O., Damas, S., & Santamaría, J. (2006b). Feature-based image registration by means of the CHC evolutionary algorithm. *Image and Vision Computing, 24*(5), 525–533. doi:10.1016/j.imavis.2006.02.002

Cordón, O., Damas, S., & Santamaría, J. (2007). A practical review on the applicability of different EAs to 3D feature-based registration. In S. Cagnoni, E. Lutton, & G. Olague (Eds.), *Genetic and Evolutionary Computation in Image Processing and Computer Vision*, EURASIP Book Series on SP&C (pp. 241–263).

Eiben, A. E., & Smith, J. E. (2003). *Introduction to evolutionary computation*. Springer Verlag.

Eshelman, L. J. (1993). Real-coded genetic algorithms and interval schemata. In L. D. Whitley (Ed.), *Foundations of Genetic Algorithms 2*, (pp. 187–202) Morgan Kaufmann, San Mateo.

Ghosh, A.K., & Sinha, P. (2001). An economised craniofacial identification system. *Forensic Science International, 117*(1-2), 109–119. doi:10.1016/S0379-0738(00)00454-0

Goldberg, D. E. (1989). *Genetic algorithms in search, optimization, and machine learning.* Reading, MA: Addison-Wesley.

Goldberg, D. E. (2002). *The design of innovation: lessons from and for competent genetic algorithms.* Boston: Kluwer Academic.

Gonzalez, R., & Woods, R. (2002). *Digital image processing* (2nd Edition)., Upper Saddle River, NJ: Prentice Hall.

Goos, M. I., Alberink, I. B., & Ruifrok, A. C. (2006). 2D/3D image (facial) comparison using camera matching. *Forensic Science International, 163*, 10–17. doi:10.1016/j.forsciint.2005.11.004

Herrera, F., Lozano, M., & Verdegay, J. L. (1998). Tackling real-coded genetic algorithms: operators and tools for the behavioral analysis. *Artificial Intelligence Review, 12*(4), 265–319. doi:10.1023/A:1006504901164

Holland, J. H. (1975). *Adaptation in natural and artificial systems.* Ann Arbor, MI: University of Michigan Press.

Ibáñez, O., Cordón, O., Damas, S., & Santamaría, J. (2008). Craniofacial superimposition by means of genetic algorithms and fuzzy location of cephalometric landmarks. *Hybrid Artificial Intelligence Systems, LNAI, 5271,* 599–607. doi:10.1007/978-3-540-87656-4_74

Iscan, M. Y. (1993). Introduction to techniques for photographic comparison. In M. Y. Iscan, & R. Helmer (Eds.), *Forensic Analysis of the Skull* (pp. 57-90). Wiley. Laguna, M., & Martí, R. (2003). *Scatter search: methodology and implementations in C.* Kluwer Academic Publishers.

Mahfoud, S. W. (1995). *Niching methods for genetic algorithms.* Doctoral dissertation. University of Illinoisat Urbana-Champaign.

Nickerson, B. A., Fitzhorn, P. A., Koch, S. K., & Charney, M. (1991). A methodology for near-optimal computational superimposition of two-dimensional digital facial photographs and three-dimensional cranial surface meshes. *Journal of Forensic Sciences, 36*(2), 480–500.

Pétrowski, A. (1996). A clearing procedure as a niching method for genetic algorithms. *Proceedings of IEEE International Conference on Evolutionary Computation* (pp. 798–803).

Ricci, A., Marella, G. L., & Apostol, M. A. (2006). A new experimental approach to computer-aided face/skull identification in forensic anthropology. *The American Journal of Forensic Medicine and Pathology, 27*(1), 46–49. doi:10.1097/01.paf.0000202809.96283.88

Ross, A. H. (2004). Use of digital imaging in the identification of fragmentary human skeletal remains: A case from the Republic of Panama. *Forensic Science Communications, 6*(4), [online].

Rouet, J. M., Jacq, J. J., & Roux, C. (2000). Genetic algorithms for a robust 3-D MR-CT registration. *IEEE Transactions on Information Technology in Biomedicine, 4*(2), 126–136. doi:10.1109/4233.845205

Santamaría, J., Cordón, O., & Damas, S. (2007). Evolutionary approaches for automatic 3D modeling of skulls in forensic identification. *Applications of Evolutionary Computing, LNCS, 4448,* 415–422.

Santamaría, J., Cordón, O., Damas, S., Alemán, I., & Botella, M. (2007). A scatter search-based technique for pair-wise 3D range image registration in forensic anthropology. *Soft Computing, 11*(9), 819–828. doi:10.1007/s00500-006-0132-0

Schraudolph, N. N., & Grefenstette, J. J. (1992). *A user's guide to GAucsd 1.4.* Technical Report CS92-249, Computer Science and Engineering Department, University of California, San Diego, La Jolla, CA.

Sinha, P. (1998). A symmetry perceiving adaptive neural network and facial image recognition. *Forensic Science International, 98*(1-2), 67–89. doi:10.1016/S0379-0738(98)00137-6

Ubelaker, D. H. (2000). A history of Smithsonian-FBI collaboration in forensic anthropology, especially in regard to facial imagery. *Forensic Science Communications, 2*(4), [online].

Ubelaker, D. H., Bubniak, E., & O'Donnel, G. (1992). Computer-assisted photographic superimposition. *Journal of Forensic Sciences, 37*(3), 750–762.

Welcker, H. (1867). Der schädel Dantes. In K. Witte, & G. Boehmer (Eds.), *Jahrbuch der deutschen Dantegesellschaft*, 1, 35–56, Brockhaus, Liepzig.

Yamany, S. M., Ahmed, M. N., & Farag, A. A. (1999). A new genetic-based technique for matching 3D curves and surfaces. *Pattern Recognition, 32*, 1817–1820. doi:10.1016/S0031-3203(99)00060-6

Yoshino, M., Matsuda, H., Kubota, S., Imaizumi, K., Miyasaka, S., & Seta, S. (1997). Computer-assisted skull identification system using video superimposition. *Forensic Science International, 90*, 231–244. doi:10.1016/S0379-0738(97)00168-0

Zhang, Z. (1994). Iterative point matching for registration of free-form curves and surfaces. *International Journal of Computer Vision, 13*(2), 119–152. doi:10.1007/BF01427149

Zitova, B., & Flusser, J. (2003). Image registration methods: a survey. *Image and Vision Computing, 21*, 977–1000. doi:10.1016/S0262-8856(03)00137-9

APPENDIX A. NICKERSON ET AL.'S PROPOSAL

In Nickerson, Fitzhorn, Koch & Charney's proposal (1991) the mapping between the skull surface mesh and the digital facial photograph was developed from sets of similarity transformations and a perspective projection. These transformations consisted of the following steps performed on the skull mesh:

1. general rotation about an arbitrary 3D point and rotation axis;
2. uniform scaling;
3. arbitrary translation in 3D space;
4. mirroring about the z-axis;
5. perspective projection from 3D to 2D as a function of angle of view.

This mapping problem was specified as a set of eight equations in twelve unknowns. The unknowns were:

(r_x, r_y, r_z) = origin of the general 3D rotation
(d_x, d_y, d_z) = direction cosines of the axis of rotation
θ = general angle of rotation of the cranial mesh
s = constant 3D mesh scaling factor
(t_x, t_y, t_z) = general 3D mesh translation vector
φ = perspective angle of view

The known quantities were the set of landmark points:

$(x_{fi}, y_{fi}, 1)$ = facial landmarks

(x_{ci}, y_{ci}, z_{ci}) = cranial landmarks

The total sum of bits required to encode the twelve discretized unknowns (chromosome size) was then 141. Unfortunately the authors did not specify any other component of the GA. Their system required from 4 to 6 hours to converge. Finally, they showed only qualitative results on a few of the twelve cases they claimed to have studied.

Chapter 6
Neural Networks in Medicine:
Improving Difficult Automated Detection of Cancer in the Bile Ducts

Rajasvaran Logeswaran
Multimedia University, Malaysia

ABSTRACT

Automatic detection of tumors in the bile ducts of the liver is very difficult as often, in the defacto non-invasive diagnostic images using magnetic resonance cholangiopancreatography (MRCP), tumors are not clearly visible. Specialists use their experience in anatomy to diagnose a tumor by absence of expected structures in the images. Naturally, undertaking such diagnosis is very difficult for an automated system. This chapter proposes an algorithm that is based on a combination of the manual diagnosis principles along with nature-inspired image processing techniques and artificial neural networks (ANN) to assist in the preliminary diagnosis of tumors affecting the bile ducts in the liver. The results obtained show over 88% success rate of the system developed using an ANN with the multi-layer perceptron (MLP) architecture, in performing the difficult automated preliminary detection of the tumors, even in the robust clinical test images with other biliary diseases present.

INTRODUCTION

There are a large number of algorithms and applications that have been and are actively being developed to assist in medical diagnosis. As medical problems are biological in nature, it is expected that nature-inspired systems would be appropriate solutions to such problems. Among the most popular of such nature-inspired tools is the artificial neural network (ANN), which has lent itself to applications in a variety of fields ranging from telecommunications to agricultural analysis. There is a large amount of literature on the use of ANN in medical applications. Some examples of medical systems developed employing neural networks include those for screening of heart attacks (Furlong et al., 1991) and coronary artery disease (Fujita et al., 1992), facial pain syndromes (Limonadi et al., 2006), diabetes mellitus (Venkatesan & Anitha, 2006), psychiatric diagnosis (NeuroXL, 2003), seizure diagnosis

DOI: 10.4018/978-1-60566-705-8.ch006

(Johnson et al., 1995), brain injuries (Raja et al., 1995), and many more.

There is an increasing number of cancer cases in most countries, with an increasing variety of cancers. Over the years, ANN has been actively employed in cancer diagnosis as well. ANN systems have been developed for cancer of the breast (Degenhard et al., 2002), skin (Ercal et al., 1994), prostate (Brooks, 1994), ovaries (Tan et al., 2005), bladder (Moallemi, 1991), liver (Meyer et al., 2003), brain (Cobzas et al., 2007), colon (Ahmed, 2005), lung (Marchevsky et al., 2004), eyes (Maeda et al., 1995), cervix (Mango & Valente, 1998) and even thyroid (Ippolito et al., 2004). ANN has also been used for cancer prognosis and patient management (Naguib & Sherbet, 2001).

Although there has been extensive development of ANN systems for medical application, there are still many more diagnostic systems for diseases and organs that would be able to gain from this nature-inspired technology. This chapter proposes a multi-stage nature-inspired detection scheme that mimics the radiologist's diagnosis strategy, where most of the algorithms employed are themselves nature-inspired. The scheme is augmented with the nature-inspired neural networks to improve the system performance in tackling automatic preliminary detection of a difficult and much less researched set of tumors affecting the bile ducts, using the defacto diagnostic imaging technology for the liver and pancreato-biliary system.

BACKGROUND

Bile is used in the digestion and absorption of fat-soluble minerals and vitamins in the small intestines. In addition, it also has the function of removing soluble waste products from the body, including cholesterol. Diseases affecting the biliary tract cause distension (swelling) in the bile ducts, blockages, swelling of the liver and build up of toxic waste in the body, which can be fatal.

Tumor of the bile ducts, medically known as cholangiocarcinoma, is the second most common primary malignant tumor of the liver after hepatocellular carcinoma and comprises approximately 10% to 15% of all primary hepatobiliary malignancies (Yoon & Gores, 2003). The incidence of this disease has been on the rise in recent decades (Patel, 2002). It is highly lethal as most tumors are locally advanced at presentation (Chari et al., 2008). These tumors produce symptoms by blocking the bile duct, often seen in clinical diagnosis as clay colored stools, jaundice (yellowing of the skin and eyes), itching, abdominal pain that may extend to the back, loss of appetite, unexplained weight loss, fever, chills (UCSF, 2008) and dark urine (Chari et al., 2008).

The clinical diagnosis of the biliary tumor depends on appropriate clinical, imaging, and laboratory information (Yoon & Gores, 2003). Generally, after taking the medical history and performing a physical examination, the doctor would order one or more tests to get a better view of the affected area before making the diagnosis. The common follow-up test for biliary tumors include non-invasive medical imaging tests such as computed tomography (CT) scans, magnetic resonance imaging (MRI) scans or ultrasound; (minimally) invasive imaging tests such as endoscopic retrograde cholangiopancreatography (ERCP), endoscopic ultrasound (EUS) or percutaneous transhepatic cholangiography (PTC); or even a bile duct biopsy and fine needle aspiration (UCSF, 2008). Treatments for this disease include surgery, liver transplantation, chemotherapy, radiation therapy, photodynamic therapy and biliary drainage (Mayo, 2008).

Medical imaging has become the vital source of information in the diagnosis of many diseases, work-up for surgery, anatomical understanding of the body's internal systems and functions etc. It is also the preferred technological method in aiding diagnosis as most of the medical imaging techniques are either non-invasive or minimally-invasive, thus causing minimal discomfort to

Figure 1. Location of the biliary tract in the abdomen

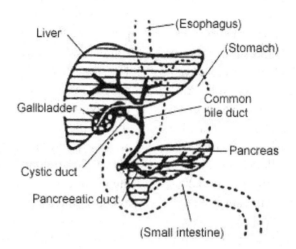

the patient and does not involve long (or any) hospitalization for recovery. Magnetic resonance cholangiopancreatography (MRCP) is a special sequence of magnetic resonance imaging (MRI) that is used to produce images of the pancreato-biliary region of the abdomen. This area covers the biliary system within and just outside the liver, as shown in Figure 1 (NIDDK, 2008).

MRCP is now the preferred imaging test for biliary diseases as it is non-invasive, non-ionizing, has no side-effects nor requires any hospitalization. However, as MRI uses electromagnets, this technique is not applicable to any patients with implants affected by magnets. So far, there has been very little work done on developing auto-mated computer-aided diagnosis (CAD) systems for tumor detection in MRCP images due to the high complexity in accurately identifying such diseases in a relatively noisy image. Although there are articles on clinical work, case studies and on the MRCP technology, the only automated biliary tumor detection scheme using MRCP images readily available in the literature to date is the one developed by Logeswaran & Eswaran (2006). The performance of the ANN model proposed in this chapter will be compared against the published non-ANN model, in the Results section.

To illustrate the complexity faced in automatic detection of tumors affecting the bile ducts, let us look at an example. Figure 2 shows a sample MRCP image containing a tumor at the indicated area. It is observed that there is no apparent identifiable structure in the area of the tumor, nor is the tumor boundary distinguishable from the background. Secondly, it should be observed that the image is noisy and affected by a lot of background tissue. Very often MRCP images are severely influenced by the presence of other organs (e.g. stomach and intestines) and tissue (e.g. liver). In addition, MRCP images are also prone to artifacts and bright spots. The orienta-tion of the image during acquisition may also not be optimal in detecting a tumor, as there may be parts of the biliary structure itself overlapping the tumor. The intensity ranges of MRCP images are very susceptible to parameter settings, which are routinely tweaked by the radiographer in an attempt to best visualize the regions of interest. The signal strength or signal to noise ratio (SNR) decreases with the thickness of the image slices, but thicker slices are subject to greater partial volume effect (where larger amounts of the 3D volume is squashed into a 2D image causing loss of depth, and thus, structural information).

Figure 2. MRCP image containing tumor of the bile duct (indicated by the arrow)

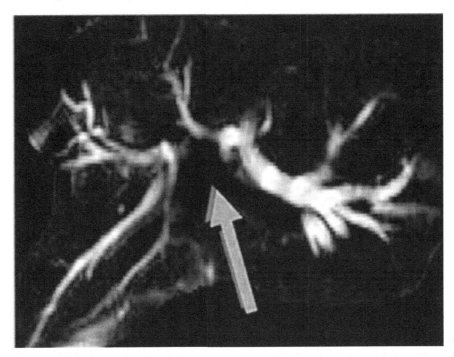

ANN Tumor Detection System

With the complexities described in the previous section, conventional image processing techniques for structure detection and modeling would be hard-pressed to detect the presence of the tumor. As such, it was decided that it would be best to attempt to mimic as much of the processes involved in the natural methodology of diagnosis of such diseases by the specialists, and adapt them for implementation in computer systems. Through collaboration with a leading medical institution in Malaysia, which is also the liver diseases referral center of the country and a modern paperless hospital, radiologists were interviewed and observed on the diagnosis patterns used for identifying tumors in these MRCP images. Their diagnoses stemmed from their educational background and experience, the human visual system and biological neural network system in the brain, allowing for powerful noise compensation and making associations within structures in an image.

The important aspects observed that were vital in the diagnosis were basic knowledge of identifying characteristics, the ability to seek out important structures through the image noise and artifacts in the MRCP images, being able to compensate for inter-patient variations and inhomogeneity in intra-patients images (e.g. different orientations), in addition to the issues raised in the previous section. Based on the observed radiologist diagnosis methodology, a nature-inspired scheme comprising various nature-inspired components is proposed in an attempt to adapt computer systems, albeit in a rudimentary fashion, to mimic parts of their diagnosis method. The computer-aided system to be developed should be automatic as far as possible for ease of use and to allow automatic detection of the tumors. It is not meant to replace the medical experts in diagnosis but instead to assist them in screening large numbers of images and tagging those with potential tumors. Such a system can then be extended to highlight, navigate and manipulate pre-processed information, structures

Figure 3. Flowchart of algorithm for tumor detection

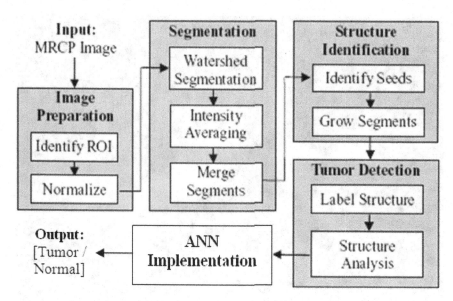

and parts of images, to aid the medical practitioners further in their diagnosis. Enabling an interactive interface also allows such a system to operate in a semi-automatic fashion, thus allowing the medical practitioner to correct or modify the parameters and results at various stages of the implementations to overcome weaknesses of the automated system, for instance when faced with the inability to handle a very difficult pathology.

Essentially, the algorithm involves several parts, as shown in Figure 3. Firstly, some image preparation or pre-processing is required to highlight the region(s) of interest and reduce the influence of noise in the image. Then, segmentation is required for preliminary abstraction of the objects from the background. Structure identification would be required for refining the segmentation process and labeling the biliary structures of interest. This will then be followed by the tumor detection phase, and finally enhanced with decision-making via the ANN implementation.

Although at first glance the above steps may appear to be standard computer-aided methodology, each step taken consists of nature-inspired components. Some of the steps above are taken for granted by many as our natural human vi-

sual system undertakes them automatically. For instance, noise reduction, brightness and contrast compensation and image enhancement are all handled by our visual cortex such that when a radiologist studies MRCP images with such "problems", he/she will not face much difficulty or conscious effort in overcoming them and analyzing the important information within the images. Similarly, although the method of segmentation differs, when observing a picture we do naturally break it up into smaller regions to which we can assign some meaning, in order to understand the different parts of the picture and get a better sense of the entire picture. The segmentation algorithm employed in this work is nature-inspired by rainfall on mountains, as will be described later. Structure identification is usually a conscious task as we identify the structures of interest (in this case the biliary ducts and tract) from other structures in the image (blood vessels, fat, tissue, artifacts, noise, organs etc.). The algorithm used in the structure identification consists of modified region-growing, which is inspired by fluid spreading to areas with desired characteristics (e.g. down a stream). From these structures, the next step, naturally, is to shortlist the potential tumor areas for further analysis. The final decision is made using the ANN. Although now more associated with their mathematical algorithms (Sarle, 1994), ANNs were originally nature-inspired after a crude model of the brain. It is used in this scheme to incorporate some intelligence, tolerance to data inconsistencies, and as a tool to incorporate "learning" and storage of adaptive knowledge through training.

In the interest of faster processing and reduced complexity, one major aspect of the natural diagnosis is not undertaken in the proposed scheme, which is the use of multiple MRCP slice images to conduct the diagnosis. A typical MRCP examination consists of a number of series of images, composed of locator slices, axial T2 sequence series, axial in-phase (fat saturation) series, MRCP thin slice series and MRCP thick slab images (Prince, 2000), and additional series as deemed necessary by the radiologist. Often, the total number of images acquired by the radiographer during a single examination may be in excess of a hundred images. In the event of doubt and for better understanding of the anatomy, a radiologist would scan through a number of the images, if not all of them. Implementing such ability in a CAD system is very tedious due to the large amount of variations in orientations and even sequences that may be used in a single examination, in addition to the need to approximate volumetric information lost due to the partial volume phenomenon during acquisition. Furthermore, it would be very processing intensive, taking up a lot of resources and time. Although not undertaken in this implementation, some recent work towards more rigorous 3D reconstruction of the biliary tract has been done in Robinson (2005) and with sufficient resources such as GPU (graphic processing unit) programming, may be undertaken in the near future to enhance the system proposed here. Such considerations will be described in the Discussion and Future Trends sections later in this chapter.

Image Preparation

Image preparation essentially consists of two parts. Firstly, the region of interest (ROI) in the images should be determined, and then the image needs to be normalized it so that it is more consistent with the other images. ROI identification may be undertaken in several ways. A popular manual method is by a rectangular selection box. Another method, in the case that the ROI is spread throughout most of the image, is to remove the parts that are not of interest, such as other organs. The image shown in Figure 2 is the result of a freehand selection area (not box), with obvious organs and artifacts removed from the boundary areas. For the ROI stage, it will be assumed that only appropriate MRCP images focusing on the biliary tract would be presented to the system. The images should have good orientation where the structures of interest are not unduly obstructed. Ideally, only perfectly oriented, clear, high quality images would be presented to the system, but that would be an unrealistic expectation even if most of the images were manually selected. So the system and consecutive stages in the algorithm will be developed to handle various imperfections in the images presented.

The most popular method of normalization, which often reveals acceptable noise reduction, is via thresholding. However, due to the nature of MRCP, fixed values cannot be used as there is often a lot of inter-image variation, especially in terms of brightness and contrast. Instead, the thresholds need to be dynamically determined in each of the non-normalized MRCP images due to their varying intensity ranges and parameter settings. When a radiologist analyzes MRCP images with different intensity distributions (i.e. change in brightness and/or contrast), the relative information within the intensities is usually used, as opposed to the absolute intensity value. The human visual system compensates for this, and also fills in missing details to reconstruct the whole

Figure 4. Dynamic histogram thresholding of an MRCP image

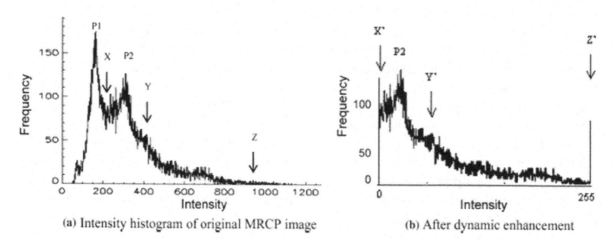

(a) Intensity histogram of original MRCP image   (b) After dynamic enhancement

picture. A similar facility has to be implemented in the proposed system.

First, histogram analysis is used to collect information relating to the image. Robinson (2005) studied typical MRCP images and found that the patterns in the histogram provided good estimates of the intensity range of the biliary structures in the image. The frequency histogram of the intensities in an MRCP image is shown in Figure 4(a). From an analysis of a large number of images, it was found that the first global peak (P1) in an MRCP image corresponded to the intensity of most of the air present in the abdominal area, whilst the second peak (P2) corresponded to the intensity of the soft tissues (which includes the lower intensity biliary ducts). As such, the intensity distribution, if not the exact values, could be used to normalize the brightness and contrast between images. The minimum point between the two peaks (i.e. the trough, X) is used as the threshold intensity (the value of which varies for each image) to remove most of the air. The rest were found to be different intensities of the various parts corresponding to the biliary tract (as well as some noise, artifacts, background and other structures). The very high intensities (after Z) tend to be a few very bright spots, which make the rest of the image appear dull in comparison. Adapting these thresholds, by

truncating to the right of Z, the biliary structures could be enhanced. To improve the enhancement, the middle area between Y (a point estimated 2/3 ways down the slope, considered as the beginning intensity of the more significant parts of the bile ducts) and Z are stretched so that the histogram between X and Z stretches to cover the original x-axis, enhancing the intensities of the main parts of the biliary ducts in the image.

In practical implementations, the x-axis (intensity) would be scaled down from the original 12 bits per pixel (bpp) representation (i.e. 2^{12} intensity range) in the images to the 8 bpp resolution of the conventional computer monitor (i.e. 2^8 intensities, ranging from 0-255). The processed histogram is shown in Figure 4(b). This represents the normalized intensities correctly on the conventional monitor. If the scaling is not done, there is a tendency for the monitors and programs to represent the 12 bpp intensities as cycles of the 0-255 intensity, i.e. intensity 256 in the 12 bit format would be displayed as 0 on the conventional monitor, thus wrongly representing the image. The outcome of this stage on a sample MRCP image is shown in a later section (in Figure 5).

Figure 5. Effects of image preparation, segmentation and biliary structure detection

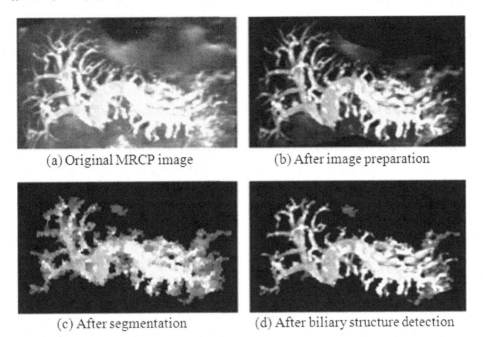

(a) Original MRCP image

(b) After image preparation

(c) After segmentation

(d) After biliary structure detection

Segmentation

Good segmentation allows an image to be broken up into meaningful homogenous sections. Although infamous for its over-segmentation problem where images tend to be broken up into too many segments, the watershed algorithm (Vincent & Soille, 1991) does produce relatively accurate segmentation of edges. This morphological (shape based algorithm) is also nature-inspired as it was derived from the idea of watersheds formed in mountain ranges during rainfall. The topography (elevation) of the mountain represents the image intensity. The flow of the water down the gradients is the inspiration behind how the intensity flows in the image is analyzed. The water catchment basins (which are very often lakes) is the central idea of the segments. Taking the intensity gradient image, the watershed algorithm produces segment boundaries at the steepest points of the gradient. This allows the image to be separated into semi-homogeneous segments.

Once the image has been segmented, as is expected with watershed, small spurious seg-

ments (cf. puddles) may occur in various parts of the image, most notably in the background. Also, as the intensity of the biliary structures do fluctuate throughout its length and width, which often makes it difficult to differentiate parts of the structure from the background, the spurious and very small segments need to be consolidated into the larger structures (either background or bile ducts). In order to overcome inter-pixel variations in a segment, the segments (instead of pixels) are considered as the minimal unit, and each segment's average intensity is calculated, and all pixels within the segment are assigned this average intensity value. This is then followed by region merging, where small segments that are similar in terms of average intensity are merged to form larger, more meaningful segments.

The segments that merge most in this phase are those of the background. Ideally, the segmentation identifies all the background with a single label 0 and removes it. The intensity averaging and merging, although very useful in simplifying processing and overcoming intra-segment inconsistencies, should be taken with utmost caution as it could lead to elimination of parts of the biliary structure. In practice, using a test set of 256x256 MRCP images, it was found that the segments that generally fit the criteria for merging were those that were less than 30 pixels in size, and are merged to other segments with intensities within 10% of their own.

Biliary Structure Identification

In the case of most of the tumors, the bile ducts that are of interest (in nearby locations) are those that are distended (enlarged) from the bile buildup due to the blockage caused by the tumor. As such, the first clue to the possible existence of a tumor (and for that matter, many of the diseases affecting the biliary ducts) is the presence of uncommonly large biliary structures in the MRCP image. The segmentation should, ideally, have identified each meaningful segment as a separate biliary structure. However, due to the nature of the MRCP images, partial volume problems and intensity inconsistencies, some parts of the background may appear to be bile ducts and vice versa.

Several strategies including scale-space analysis (another nature-inspired algorithm based on the human visual system) were attempted. Scale-space examines the same image at different scales (implemented as different levels of blurring of the image) in order to discern the significance of the different parts of the image. This is likened to looking at a picture of a fruit tree and first just seeing the overall shape of the tree, before focusing on the fruits, type of leaves etc. This method is effective in hierarchical analysis of an image, but only moderate results were achieved as the blurring process (even anisotropic blurring) caused too much loss of information. A related scheme using multiresolution analysis through directional wavelets such as contourlets also failed to produce sufficiently accurate results.

A more promising yet simple approach of merging the segments meaningfully, and discarding non-biliary segments, was segment growing

(i.e. an adaptation of the region growing algorithm at the segment level). The region-growing strategy too is nature-inspired as it mimics the natural expansion to areas or materials of similar characteristics. Such a growing strategy requires identification of appropriate starting source or seed segments. As the proposed system is to be able to undertake automatic detection, automatic seed selection is required.

To identify the characteristics for determining the appropriate seed selection, test MRCP images were segmented and manually labeled into background and bile ducts, to collect the statistics and identify the characteristics for merging. Out of the many features analyzed in Logeswaran (2005), it was found that only average intensity, location and size influenced the correct selection of seed segments. A seed segment, it was found, is usually a segment within the top 20% highest intensity, close to the middle of the image (i.e. the focus of the region of interest) and not too small (minimum 10 pixels in size). Using the characteristics above, all seeds meeting the criteria are selected automatically and grown. Many seeds are used due to the disjoint nature in tumor affected biliary ducts, where in a typical 2D MRCP image, the tumor obscures parts of the biliary tree structure, causing them to appear disjoint. Also, in the case of patients with other biliary diseases and prior biliary surgeries, as well as to compensate for possible low intensity areas of the biliary structures in the MRCP image, several seeds allow for all potential biliary structure areas to be identified.

To grow the segments, once again appropriate characteristics had to be identified. These characteristics were discerned from the previously manually labeled images. Grown segments had to meet the criteria of having similar high average intensities (i.e. intensity greater than 200 with a intensity difference of less than 20%), small segment size (less than 100 pixels as larger segments were usually background), located nearby (maximum distance between the centers of gravity of the two corresponding segments was 10 pixels apart) and sharing a small border (maximum 30 pixels). Large segments with large borders often tend to be background or noise.

For clarity, the effects of steps above until the structure detection of part of the biliary tract in an MRCP image are shown in Figure 5 (Logeswaran, 2006). Take note that the MRCP image in Figure 5(a) is that of a 50mm thick slab (i.e. 50mm volume squashed into 1 pixel thickness in a 2D image). Figure 5(c) shows the segments with each pixels assigned its average segment intensity. Through the various steps, the algorithm managed to successfully eliminate most of the background and even provide better 3D information approximation. The lower intensities usually represent parts further away; although lower intensities also represent structures deeper in the body and those influenced by some obstructions (e.g. fat). It should be observed that although most of the background was removed, some still remains between the biliary tree branches on the right side of Figure 5(d). Increasing the thresholds or making the segment growing more stringent will not be able to completely remove such influences, as minor branches of the biliary tree are already adversely affected by the processing (see missing minor ranches on the left side of the same image).

Tumor Detection

A tumor affects the bile ducts by impeding the flow of bile in the ducts, causing the mentioned swelling or distention in the biliary structures around the tumor. The tumor itself is not seen clearly in a T2 MRCP image, as it is solid and appears to be black (fluid is represented by higher intensities in such images). In radiological diagnosis, the presence of a tumor is suspected if the distended biliary structure appears disjoint (i.e. a black object overlapping part of the biliary structure). In the typical radiological diagnosis, the suspicion is confirmed by examining the appropriate series of MRCP images, other series (different orientations and even different sequence) and possibly ordering more tests and/or images, if necessary. As the proposed system is a preliminary detection system to aid in the diagnosis of the tumor, without implementing sophisticated and rigorous processing or requiring intensive processing power, the system is required at this stage to only shortlist images with potential tumors for further analysis, whilst discarding those that do not fit the profile.

The algorithm looks for two or more disjoint biliary structures in moderately close proximity. The distance information to be incorporated is very subjective as the orientation of the images in the 3D plane heavily influences the way disjoint sections are viewed in a 2D plane. For example, two disjoint sections as seen in the coronal (front) view may appear joined in the sagital (side) view, with decreasing distance between the disjoint sections in the rotational angles between the coronal and sagital views. A sample of this problem is given in the Discussion section later. As such, only the worst case scenario for distance, i.e. maximum distance, is used. From the test images, the sizes of the tumors were found to be less than 50 pixels wide, and consequently the maximum distance is set likewise.

Each structure has to be sufficiently large to be considered as distended. As such, structures less than 50 pixels in size were not considered as a significant biliary structure. In the case of Figure 5(d), the small patch above the biliary structure could be eliminated this way. Ideally, the duct thickness (or a simple approximation of area divided by length) would be used as a measure of the distension, but it was found that the distension of the biliary structures in the case of biliary tumors were not significant enough (see Figure 2) to be incorporated as a criteria, as opposed to other biliary diseases such as cyst. So, the area (i.e. total number of pixels in a biliary segment) is used as the criterion. The actual structure analysis implementation in the developed system labels each biliary segment (i.e. after the segment merging and growing above) with different numbers. The size (in pixels) of each biliary segment is then calculated. If two or more sufficiently large biliary segments exist in the MRCP image, the image is considered as possibly containing a tumor.

ANN Implementation Issues

Unfortunately, assumption of the size of disjoint segments can vary depending on the orientation of the acquired image. Furthermore, it is also greatly influenced by the size of the focus area in the image. To add to the complication, not all disjoint structures necessarily indicate cancer. An ANN is employed to improve the automatic learning and decision-making performance of the system. Inspired by the crude model of the brain, the ANN is powerful in detecting patterns in data and predicting meaningful output. For the purposes of this work, a training set of images are ascertained, both with tumors and without. However, medical diagnosis is rarely that straightforward, as patients often suffer from more than one disease, and even preliminary detection should be able to exclude other common diseases present in the type of images being analyzed. To make the implementation realistic and applicable in the clinical environment, MRCP images with other biliary diseases present (such as stones, cyst and non-tumor swelling in the bile duct) are also included in the training and test sets.

An ANN essentially approximates functions, and the characteristics pivotal to its performance rely very much on its architecture or network topology. Lately, there have also been many architectures of ANN introduced for specific problems. In addition to the very popular multi-layer perceptron (MLP) network, linear networks, recurrent networks, probabilistic networks, self-organizing maps (SOM), clustering networks, Elman, Kohonen and Hopfield networks, regression networks, radial basis functions, temporal

networks and fuzzy systems, are just a few of the many existing ANN architectures that have been developed and incorporated into numerous applications to handle different classes of problems. Choosing the best network topology for the ANN allows it to produce the best results, but this is rarely obvious and certainly not easy. Literature such as (Sima & Orponen, 2003) and (Ripley, 1995) may be referred for a more detailed discussion on choosing an appropriate ANN architecture for specific problems, while there are numerous books and even Wikipedia (2008) providing information on the architectural configuration, learning algorithms and properties of the ANN. In the case of multi-layered architectures, the number of hidden layers corresponds to the complexity of problems that the network is able to process, while the number of neurons generally denotes the number of patterns that may be handled.

Many of these networks are able to ascertain patterns in the input automatically, through supervised or unsupervised learning algorithms, making them a powerful tool in data analysis and prediction. Decision-making information is usually stored as weights (coefficients) and biases that influence the neurons and the connections between them. There are many different learning algorithms as well as activation / transfer / squashing functions that may be used in the neurons. The learning or training algorithms determine how the appropriate values of the weights and biases are assigned to each neuron and connection, based on the data it is given during training (or at run-time, in the case of unsupervised or adaptive networks). The speed and quality of training is determined by a learning rate, whilst a learning goal (i.e. and error rate) is set to indicate that the network should be trained until the error achieved is below the set training goal. An important aspect with regards to the training of an ANN is that over-training an ANN makes it rigid and hinders its ability to handle unseen data. The error tolerance property of the ANN is very much dependent on its generalization ability, which is the strength of the

ANN. As such, caution must be exercised during training such that over-zealous training to achieve high precision output must not render the ANN rigid. At the same time, the choice of training data is significant, and a good distribution of data covering typical and atypical scenarios improves the ANN's ability in decision-making for a larger group of unseen data. In many cases, a maximum number of iterations (epochs) is also set to forcibly terminate training, thus preventing it from going on indefinitely, even when the desired training goal is not achieved.

Bender (2007) states that when testing a large number of models, especially when using flexible modeling techniques like ANN, one that fits the data may be found by pure chance (Topliss & Edwards, 1979). A discussion on this issue, with regards to ANN can be found in Livingstone & Salt (2005). It is recommended that feature selection be used and refined until the "best" model is found. Good classification or regression result may be obtained by shortlisting possible features, generating many models, conducting validation, and repeating the process until the "best" model based on the user's preference is found. The rational is that very often, the actual feature may not be known at the onset, and will only be realized through such a refining process. The initial features in this work were selected manually through the observations described in the previous section.

The model significance, often measured through metrics such as the "F measure" has been shown to vary with feature selection (Livingstone & Salt, 2005) and thus, such correlation coefficients and RMSE by themselves may not reflect the performance of the model. The necessary factors to be taken into account to reflect the model's performance include the number of descriptors (parameters), the size of the dataset, the training/test/validation set split, the diversity of structures (in this work reflect the cancerous bile ducts), and the quality of the experimental data (Bender, 2007). Model validation requires splitting the data into 3 sets: training (to derive the parameters), validation (assess model quality) and testing (assess model performance). Such splitting is undertaken in this work. Alternatives to this method, especially for small datasets, include using cross-validation (split data to multiple equal parts – use one for testing and the rest for training) or leave-multiple-out splits. K-fold validation or receiver operating characteristic (ROC) curve could be used as well, to evaluate the statistical significance of a classifier. Ideally a clean dataset, measured by a single, well-defined experimental procedure, should be used in any experiment. This is not possible in this work as when dealing with typical medical data, it involves a variety of radiographers, patients, diseases and their many inconsistencies. However, the training, validation and test sets will each encompass a representative sample of the structure diversity of the data.

ANN Setup & Training

The issues discussed in the previous section are those that should be taken into account when developing an optimal ANN system. However, very often, some compromises are made depending on the objectives of the work, available resources and other compounding factors. The objective of this chapter is not to produce the best bile duct tumor detection system, as that requires much more in-depth research and implementation, but rather to show that the nature-inspired ANNs could be a possible solution in the ultimate development of a CAD system for that purpose using MRCP images. As such, this section concentrates on employing a popular but relatively simple ANN to the task and showing that even such an implementation with low resource requirements could provide good results, as will be discussed further in the following sections.

Although facing many valid critiques in recent times, such as those in Roy (2000), Thornton (1994) and Smagt & Hirzinger (1998), the feedforward MLP ANN is still arguably the most popular ANN. It has, over the decades, provided good performance in a large number of applications with a broad base of data types. Easy availability, convenient and intuitive setup, automatic setting of weights and biases, and ability to be instructed on expected outcomes through supervised training, are among the reasons the MLP is set up as the final component of the proposed system to make the binary selection between tumor and non-tumor cases. The reader, however, is advised that alternative architectures and ANN setups may be experimented with for improved results. Some possible alternatives that may be implemented in the near future are discussed later in the chapter.

The ANN used in this implementation is set up as shown in Figure 6. Figure 6(a) shows the basic architecture of a single perceptron model taking in j number of input streams or parameters. Each input is multiplied by its weight coefficient (w) acting on that stream, before being sent to the perceptron node (i.e. the black circular node). The node itself will be subjected to a constant bias (b), producing the result $f(x)$ as given by the formula in the figure. The output is dependent on the activation function that is used in the node. The output of a traditional hardlimiter (step activation function) perceptron is binary, so $O(x)$ would be a 0 or 1 depending on a set threshold of the result $f(x)$. Note that the output is usually denoted by $f(x)$ itself as that is the activation function, but we are splitting it here and denoting a separate term $O(x)$ to describe the calculation and the output individually.

An MLP is made up of multiple layers of one or more perceptrons in each layer, as shown in Figure 6(b) for a fully connected MLP architecture. The nodes of the input layer in Figure 6(b) are shown in a different color (grey instead of black) as these are usually not perceptrons but merely an interface to accept the input values in their separate streams. The input layer of the MLP used for this work consists of a neuron for each of the parameters identified in the previous section, namely, the average segment intensities and sizes of the two largest biliary segments, thus four neurons.

Additional sets of input neurons could be used if more than two biliary segments are to be analyzed, although this was found to be unnecessary in the test cases. Depending on the stringent control of images being presented to the system, further input neurons to incorporate parameters including distance between the midpoint of the segments, thickness of each segment (can be approximated by dividing the area of the segment by its length), as well as shape characteristics, could be added. This was not undertaken in the proposed system as the available images were retrieved from the radiological archives spanning a number of years. The acquisitions were by various radiographers under the supervision of various radiologists, and thus, were not taken under a stringent enough control environment for a more precise study.

A priority in the setup is low computing power requirements and fast processing time. Since the features used as input to the system were few and of low complexity, a single hidden layer sufficed. 10 neurons were used to delineate the network in this layer, the number found experimentally to be suitable in producing the best results. Lesser number of hidden neurons caused the overall detection rate to deteriorate, whilst increasing the number of neurons (only up to 20, as the complexity was to be kept low) did not cause any appreciation of the results. As for the output, only a single neuron was required as the output would be binary, i.e. 0 indicating negative tumor detection or 1 indicating possible tumor detection. All neurons used were standard. For generalization and function approximation, the activation functions used in the neurons were sigmoidal and linear, in the hidden and output layers, respectively. No activation function is used in the input layer, but the input is normalized to a range of 0.0-1.0, where the maximum size would be the size of the image and the maximum intensity 255.

As the ANN used is a supervised network, a set of training data and confirmed diagnosis results are required. 20% (120 images) of the acquired 593 MRCP images (see next section) were used as

Figure 6. Fully-connected feedforward MLP ANN with one hidden layer

(a) Single perceptron

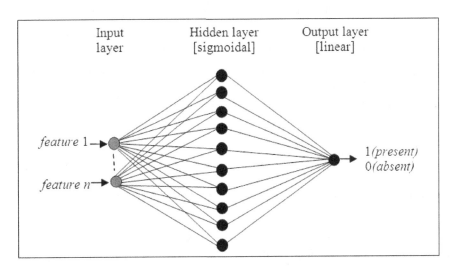

(b) Complete network

the training set. The images were selected pseudo-randomly to include a distribution comprising proportionately of images consider as normal (healthy), diagnosed as bile duct tumor, and those with other diseases. The confirmed diagnoses for these images were used to determine the binary expected output which was fed to the MLP during training, labeled as 1 (containing tumor) or 0 (no tumor), for the corresponding image. The MLP uses the backpropagation learning algorithm to adjust the coefficients (weights) on each neuron interconnection (lines in the figure), such that the error between the actual results produced by the network and the expected result is minimized. There are several variants but the basic gradient descent backpropagation was used in this work. The system is trained until the training converges

to the training goal (mean squared error of 0.05) or maximum limit of training cycles (30,000 epochs) to prevent the training from going on indefinitely if it does not converge. In handling robust data, as the case was in this work, some cases of non-convergence is to be expected. The maximum training limit was set to 30,000 as there was no observable improvement in the convergence beyond that. Based on past experience, a learning rate of 0.15 was used in this work as it was found that minor changes in the learning rate did not affect the outcome for these images, whilst large learning rates produced poor results.

RESULTS

Before the system is tested in a robust clinical environment, it should be first tested for proof of concept. For this test, the algorithm is evaluated on its ability to differentiate images containing tumor from images of healthy patients. It must be remembered that the tumor may be present in different parts of the bile ducts, and that in biological systems, even the images of healthy patients can differ considerably. The choice of parameters, intensity thresholds, values of the segment sizes for merging and growing, and biliary segment size for tumor detection were varied and tested. The performance of the proposed system is very dependent on the choices made, which is in turn dependent on the quality of MRCP images obtained. The configuration and results presented in this chapter are for the setup that performed the best for the available 2D MRCP images.

All the images used in this work, inclusive of the training and test data, were obtained from the archives of the collaborating medical institution. As the images were acquired there, and the patients were also treated at the same place, the actual medical records and diagnosis information (in some cases further confirmed through ERCP or biopsy) were available. The presence and absence of tumors and other biliary diseases was further confirmed by the expert medical consultant, who is the senior radiologist heading the digital imaging department where the clinical and radiological diagnoses were made.

The proposed ANN system is trained with 20%

of the clinical 2D MRCP images acquired from the collaborating hospital, containing a distribution of diseases. The results obtained for 55 images in this first test using the trained ANN above are given in Table 1. As is observed from the table, the accuracy level is very good when validating the detection against normal healthy images. In cases where the classification was inaccurate, the description of the reason for the error is given in the table. In one of the cases where the tumor was not identified correctly, it was due to lack of distention which made the structures appear to be that of a healthy patient, whilst in the other case, the orientation made the biliary structures appear joint, indicating other biliary diseases. The normal image that was detected wrongly was not detected as a tumor, but merely as distended (dilated), as the biliary structure appeared unusually large, possibly due to some zooming during image acquisition. Such cases are unavoidable through a simple detection system using a single image.

Next, for realistic medical diagnosis, all the available images (including those of healthy patients as well as those of patients with various biliary diseases) were used in the second test. Many patients suffer from more than one biliary affliction, and as such, many of the test images were influenced by more than one disease. This kind of testing allows for robust evaluation of the proposed system in the clinical environment for which it is targeted. This set of 593 images contained 248 healthy (normal), 61 tumor and the remainder images with other biliary diseases such as stones, cyst, residual postsurgery dilation,

Table 1. Results of the tumor detection validation testing

	Normal	Tumor
Medically Diagnosed	27	28
Detected	26	26
Accuracy %	96.3%	92.8%
Error	1	2
Description of Error	Large biliary structures	1 normal, 1 non-tumor dilation

Klatskin's disease, Caroli's disease, strictures, and obstruction from other liver diseases. In some of the images with more than one disease, some of the visual characteristics were very similar between the different afflictions (e.g. dilation / swelling / distention is common in most biliary diseases).

The results obtained are given in Table 2. As this is a robust testing, the evaluation criterion known as "Overall accuracy" is calculated as the percentage of the sum of the true positives and true negatives over the total test set. This overall accuracy takes into account how well the system performed in detecting the correct disease, as well as in rejecting the wrong diagnosis. For comparison, results from the earlier published work on automated tumor detection using MRCP images is given in the last row. As is observed from the table, the ANN implementation successfully improved the detection results for both the cases with tumor as well as for the healthy normal images. In terms of specificity (i.e. the non-tumor images correctly identified as not containing tumor), the ANN implementation performed well too, achieving 94.70% (an improvement from 89.85% without ANN).

The algorithm prototype was developed in IDL as it allowed for fast development with readily available tools and libraries, without incorporating any significant optimization. In terms of timing performance, the entire process from pre-processing until ANN output for each image on a standard Pentium IV desktop personal computer took less than a minute. IDL is a matrix-based software, and programs running in its run-time environment would not be as fast as those com-

piled into machine language. Thus, the timing performance could be dramatically enhanced by changing the platform and using optimized code in a language that allowed compilation to machine code, e.g. C or C++. The timing performance enhancement falls out of the scope of this chapter and is left for the reader to experiment with. The classifier's performance could also be analyzed using machine learning research tools such as MLC++, WEKA etc.

DISCUSSION

The results obtained show good overall accuracy for the ANN system, proving that the nature-inspired strategy employed has merit. Although errors were present, the accuracy achieved is amicable taking into account that even visual diagnosis using single 2D MRCP images is very difficult and impossible in certain cases. This is compounded by the fact the test data contained a large number of images with various diseases, in which accurate detection algorithms had not been developed. Very often, even experienced radiologists would look through a series of images before confidently making a diagnosis.

In most of the failed cases, the influence of other diseases and inconsistency in image acquisition by various radiography technologists affected the detection. Examples of some of the failed cases are shown in Figure 7. The image in Figure 7(a) was acquired in the very same MRCP examination of the patient in Figure 2, taken at a different orientation that makes it impossible for

Table 2. Results of robust testing using multi-disease clinical MRCP images

	Normal	Tumor	Others	TOTAL
Test images	248	61	284	593
Overall accuracy (ANN)	83.64%	88.03%	-	-
Overall accuracy (Non-ANN)*	76.90%	86.17%	-	-

* Based on results from (Logeswaran & Eswaran, 2006)

Figure 7. Example MRCP images that caused tumor detection inaccuracies

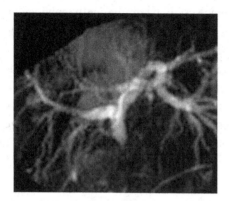

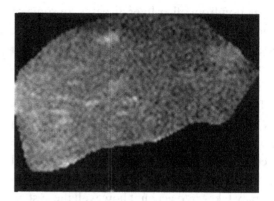

(a) Problematic orientation of Figure 2 patient   (b) Background intensity masks biliary structures

the developed system and even a human observer to conclusively diagnose the tumor. In the case of Figure 7(b), the signal strength for the acquisition was poor (a norm with MRCP thin slices) and the liver tissue intensity masked the biliary structures. Again, such images would defeat the human as well. Although the proposed algorithm does incorporate several features at various stages to minimize the influence of a certain amount of weaknesses in the acquired images, problems due to cases as shown in Figure 7 are too severe.

Overcoming such problems requires strict adherence of image acquisition standards and uniformity, which is beyond the scope of the work conducted. Some information relating to the MRCP protocol, examination and relevant information can be found at (Prince, 2000). What is important in the presented results is that even when faced with a difficult test set of mostly unseen data, a simplified implementation of a non-optimal ANN was able to perform well through its nature-inspired learning and processing capabilities, as the improvement in results obtained against the system in the literature relied entirely on the ANN's learning abilities from the parameters fed into it. The non-ANN implementation used experimental hard-coded decision-making.

Further benchmarking may be possible once such automated cholangiocarcinoma detection

using MRCP implementations using other algorithms (possibly those employing advanced classifiers such as Support Vector Machine, Adaboost etc.) are available. Of course, to be fair for the purposes of benchmarking, an optimally selected and configured ANN topology with appropriate customizations should be the used in the tests. Performance comparisons would also need to be undertaken under a controlled environment, implemented on the same platform, and using the same set of images.

Of interest to this discussion is also the appropriate and correct use of the ANN in medical applications. There have been issues raised on the misuse of ANN in oncology / cancer in the past, as highlighted by Schwarzer et al. (2000). In the article, the authors studied literature published between 1991-1995 where ANN were used in oncology classifications (43 articles) and identified several common shortcomings in those articles. These include:

- mistakes in estimation of misclassification probabilities (in terms of biased estimation due to neglecting the error rate, and inefficient estimation due to very small test sets).
- fitting of implausible functions (often leading to "overfitting" the ANN with too many hidden nodes)

- incorrectly describing the complexity of a network (by considering the complexity to only cover only one part of the network, leading to underestimating the danger of overfitting),
- no information on the complexity of the network (when the architecture of the network used in terms of number of hidden layers and hidden nodes are not identified),
- use of inadequate statistical competitors (feedforward ANN are highly flexible classification tools and as such, it should only be compared against statistical tools of similar flexibility),
- insufficient comparison with statistical methods, and
- naïve application of ANN to survival data (building and using ANN with shortcomings to the data and situations being modeled, such as not guaranteeing monotonicity of estimated survival curves, omission of censored data, or not providing data with the proper relationships).

The above problems are still very common and should be taken into account for better understanding and use of ANNs. Care must always be taken, especially in developing medical applications, such that they are rigorously tested for accuracy and robustness before being adapted to the clinical environment. Pertinently, it must always be remembered that no matter how good a tool is, it is just a tool to facilitate the medical practitioner in obtaining the necessary information so that he/she can made the diagnosis. A tool, such as the proposed system, is never to be used to replace the medical practitioner's responsibility in making the final diagnosis. The objective of such a tool as the one proposed here is to help flag suspicious images so that the medical practitioner may proceed with further analysis as necessary.

FUTURE TRENDS

From its humble beginnings of a single layered, hardlimiter / step activation function and binary output perceptron, the ANN has evolved impressively over the years. In the Introduction section of this chapter, a very small number of examples of the vast work that has been done in employing ANN in medical applications were mentioned. From this, it is obvious that ANN is already a very established nature-inspired informatics tool in medical applications, in addition to its contributions in many other fields. More interesting is the development of hybrid networks that allow the strengths of various architectures and algorithms to be combined into a single network, giving it the ability to handle a greater variety of data and highly complex pattern recognition, apt for the increasingly complex modern systems. Such optimized ANNs boast of superior performance to traditional architectures.

In addition to the ANN, there has been a marked increase in development of other nature-inspired algorithms and tools as well. Some of the popular ones include simulated annealing (mimics the crystallization process), genetic algorithms (mimics population growth), particle swarm optimization (mimics social behavior of birds flocking), ant colony algorithm and many more. These state-of-the-art algorithms often provide solutions to difficult problems. In this author's opinion, many such algorithms can be adapted to collaboratively work with ANNs, to develop even more powerful tools. As such, there is definitely a trend for nature-inspired informatics in general, and neural networks specifically, to be used in larger proportions in the foreseeable future.

A majority of implementations of ANN systems treat the ANN as a "black box" system where the ANNs, through the training routine, determine its internal coefficient values. The setup proposed in this chapter is an example of that. Lately, there have been efforts for possible rule extraction from the trained network. Once the rules are known, they may be further optimized and/or be applied for other similar problems. Once perfected, such rule extraction becomes a powerful companion to the ANN systems.

There has been a lot of work done in the handling of 3D data. Although most of the frontiers in this technology appear in the computer gaming as well as the film and animation worlds, the medical field has also begun employing more of such technology. Conventional MRI equipment visualizes 3D volume as a static series of 2D images, such as those used in this work. Although this is still the norm at most medical institutions worldwide, technological advancement has seen the introduction of many real-time and 3D systems such as 3D ultrasound, 3D CT, fMRI and many others. Furthermore, computer processing power, technology and memory are increasing dramatically. New paradigms in programming, such as those for the graphics processing units (GPU), are becoming popular. All these enable more 3D volume reconstruction and manipulation. The future in medical diagnosis is in 3D and as such, the next step is to upgrade systems such as the proposed one to become a complete 3D graphical user interface (GUI) ANN CAD system.

CONCLUSION

This chapter started off by providing a brief introduction to the increasing efforts in incorporating automated and computerized technology that employs nature-inspired artificial neural networks (ANN) to undertake difficult diagnosis of various diseases in different organs. It then proceeded to the disease of interest, i.e. cancer, which is fast becoming a serious threat and cause of death in many nations. It is expected that there will a significant increase in cancer deaths in the years to come.

The central focus of the chapter was to introduce a nature-inspired algorithm mimicking the natural diagnosis strategies of medical specialists, aided

by the nature-inspired methods and technology, for the preliminary detection of tumors affecting the bile ducts. The algorithm developed consisted of image enhancement, watershed segmentation, region growing, diagnosis-based evaluation, and ANN pattern recognition for detection. Almost all steps employed were inspired in one way of another by natural systems. The results obtained prove that such a nature-inspired approach can provide improved detection of difficult to observe tumors in 2D MRCP images in a clinically robust multi-disease test set, even when using a non-optimized simplistic setup.

From the trends observed, it is expected that many more successful systems would be developed in the future, gaining from a broader outlook at various natural systems. With the formidable track record, ANNs are sure to lead the way to many more accomplishments. It is hoped that this chapter contributes ideas and examples that propagate such advancement to nature-inspired systems, especially in developing and improving much needed medical applications that would benefit from computer-aided technology.

ACKNOWLEDGEMENT

This work is supported by the Ministry of Science, Technology and Innovation, Malaysia, the Academy of Sciences Malaysia, and the Brain Gain Malaysia program. The author would like to express his appreciation to Dr. Zaharah Musa and Selayang Hospital, Malaysia for the medical consultation and clinical data (MRCP images and medical diagnosis) used in this research work.

REFERENCES

Ahmed, F. E. (2005). Artificial neural networks for diagnosis and survival prediction in colon cancer. *Molecular Cancer*, *4*, 29. http://www.molecular-cancer.com/content/4/1/29. doi:10.1186/1476-4598-4-29

Bender, A. (2007, October). A Primer on Molecular Similarity in QSAR and Virtual Screening. Part III – Connecting descriptors and experimental measurements – model generation. *QSARWorld Strand Life Sciences*, (pp. 1-4).

Brooks, A. C. (1994, December). Prostate cancer: diagnosis by computer - neural network trained to identify men with prostate cancer and to predict recurrence. *Brief ArticleScience News*. Retrieved February 21 2008, from http://findarticles.com/p/articles/mi_m1200/ is_n23_v146/ai_15972193.

Chari, R. S., Lowe, R. C., Afdhal, N. H., & Anderson, C. (2008). Clinical manifestations and diagnosis of cholangiocarcinoma. *UpTo-Date*. Retrieved May 24 2008, from http://www.uptodate.com/patients/content/topic.do?topicKey=gicancer/23806.

Cobzas, D. Birkbeck, N., Schmidt, M., Jagersand, M., & Murtha, A. (2007). 3D Variational Brain Tumor Segmentation using a High Dimensional Feature Set. *Workshop on Mathematical Methods in Biomedical Image Analysis*, (pp. 1-8).

Degenhard, A., Tanner, C., Hayes, C., Hawkes, D. J., Leach, M. O., & Study, T. U. M. B. S. (2002). Comparison between radiological and artificial neural network diagnosis in clinical screening. *Physiological Measurement*, *23*(4), 727–739. doi:10.1088/0967-3334/23/4/311

Ercal, F., Chawla, A., Stoecker, W. V., Lee, H.-C., & Moss, R. H. (1994). Neural network diagnosis of malignant melanoma from color images. *IEEE Transactions on Bio-Medical Engineering*, *41*(9), 837–845. doi:10.1109/10.312091

Fujita, H., Katafuchi, T., Uehara, T., & Nishimura, T. (1992). Application of Artificial Neural Network to Computer-Aided Diagnosis of Coronary Artery Disease in Myocardial SPECT Bull's-eye Images. *Journal of Nuclear Medicine*, *33*(2), 272–276.

Furlong, J., Dupuy, M., & Heinsimer, J. (1991). Neural Network Analysis of Serial Cardiac Enzyme Data. *American Journal of Clinical Pathology*, *96*(1), 134–141.

Ippolito, A. M., Laurentiis, M. D., Rosa, G. L. L., Eleuteri, A., Tagliaferri, R., & Placido, S. D. (2004). Immunostaining for Met/HGF Receptor May be Useful to Identify Malignancies in Thyroid Lesions Classified Suspicious at Fine-Needle Aspiration Biopsy. *Thyroid*, *14*(12), 1065–1071. doi:10.1089/thy.2004.14.1065

Johnson, M. A., & Kendall, G. Cote, P.J., & Meisel, L.V. (1995). Neural Networks in Seizure Diagnosis. *Report no. A926592 (Army Armament Research Development and Engineering Center Watervliet NY Benet Labs)*. Retrieved February 21 2008, from http://www.stormingmedia.us/92/9265/A926592.html.

Limonadi, F. M., McCartney, S., & Burchiel, K. J. (2006). Design of an Artificial Neural Network for Diagnosis of Facial Pain Syndromes. *Stereotactic and Functional Neurosurgery*, *84*(5-6), 212–220. doi:10.1159/000095167

Livingstone, D. J., & Salt, D. W. (2005). Judging the significance of multiple linear regression models. *Journal of Medicinal Chemistry*, *48*(3), 661–663. doi:10.1021/jm049111p

Logeswaran, R. (2005). Scale-space Segment Growing For Hierarchical Detection of Biliary Tree Structure. *International Journal of Wavelets, Multresolution, and Information Processing*, *3*(1), 125–140. doi:10.1142/S0219691305000750

Logeswaran, R. (2006). Neural Networks Aided Stone Detection in Thick Slab MRCP Images. *Medical & Biological Engineering & Computing*, *44*(8), 711–719. doi:10.1007/s11517-006-0083-8

Logeswaran, R., & Eswaran, C. (2006). Discontinuous Region Growing Scheme for Preliminary Detection of Tumor in MRCP Images. *Journal of Medical Systems, 30*(4), 317–324. doi:10.1007/s10916-006-9020-5

Maeda, N., Klyce, S. D., & Smolek, M. K. (1995). Neural Network Classification of Corneal Topography Preliminary Demonstration. *Investigative Ophthalmology & Visual Science, 36*, 1327–1335.

Mango, L. J., & Valente, P. T. (1998). Comparison of neural network assisted analysis and microscopic rescreening in presumed negative Pap smears. *Acta Cytologica, 42*, 227–232.

Marchevsky, A. M., Tsou, J. A., & Laird-Offringa, I. A. (2004). Classification of Individual Lung Cancer Cell Lines Based on DNA Methylation Markers Use of Linear Discriminant Analysis and Artificial Neural Networks. *The Journal of Molecular Diagnostics, 6*(1), 28–36.

Mayo Clinic. (2008). Bile Duct Cancer. Retrieved May 24 2008, from http://www.mayoclinic.org/bile-duct-cancer/.

Meyer, C. R., Park, H., Balter, J. M., & Bland, P. H. (2003). Method for quantifying volumetric lesion change in interval liver CT examinations . *Medical Imaging, 22*(6), 776–781. doi:10.1109/TMI.2003.814787

Moallemi, C. (1991). Classifying Cells for Cancer Diagnosis Using Neural Networks . *Intelligent Systems and Their Applications, 6*(6), 8–12.

Naguib, R. N. G. (Ed.) & Sherbet, G.V. (Ed.) (2001). *Artificial Neural Networks in Cancer Diagnosis, Prognosis, and Patient Management (Biomedical Engineering Series)*. CRC.

Neuro, X. L. (2003). Neural networks for medical and psychiatric diagnosis. Retrieved February 21 2008, from http://www.neuroxl.com/neural_networks_psychiatry.htm.

NIDDK – National Institute of Diabetes and Digestive and Kidney Diseases. (2008). Digestive diseases dictionary A-D: biliary track. *National Digestive Diseases Information Clearinghouse (NDDIC)*. Retrieved February 21 2008, from http://digestive.niddk.nih.gov/ddiseases/pubs/dictionary/pages/a-d.htm.

Patel, T. (2002). Worldwide trends in mortality from biliary tract malignancies. [PMID 11991810.]. *BMC Cancer, 2*, 10. doi:10.1186/1471-2407-2-10

Prince, M. R. (2000). MRCP Protocol. Retrieved 2008 May 25, from http://www.mrprotocols.com/MRI/Abdomen/MRCP_Dr.P_Protocol.htm.

Raja, A., Meister, A., Tuulik, V., & Lossmann, E. (1995). A neural network approach to EEG classification in brain chemical injuries diagnosis. *MEDICON'95: VII Mediterranean Conference on Medical & Biological Engineering (IFMBE)* (pp. 133–133), Jerusalem, Israel.

Ripley, B. D. (1995). Statistical ideas for selecting network architectures. *Neural Networks: Artificial Intelligence and Industrial Application* (pp. 183-190). Springer.

Robinson, K. (2005). Efficient pre-segmentation. *PhD thesis, Dublin,* from http://www.eeng.dcu.ie/~robinsok/pdfs/Robinson PhDThesis2005.pdf

Roy, A. (2000). Artificial neural networks – a science in trouble. *Special Interest Group on Knowledge Discovery and Data Mining, 1*, 33–38.

Schwarzer, G., Vach, W., & Schumacher, M. (2000). On the misuses of artificial neural networks for prognostic and diagnostic classification in oncology. *Statistics in Medicine, 19*, 541–561. doi:10.1002/(SICI)1097-0258(20000229)19:4<541::AID-SIM355>3.0.CO;2-V

Sima, J., & Orponen, P. (2003). General purpose computation with neural networks: A Survey of Complexity Theoretic Results. *Neural Computation, 15,* 2727–2778. doi:10.1162/089976603322518731

Tan, T. Z., Quek, C., & Ng, G. S. (2005). Ovarian cancer diagnosis by hippocampus and neocortex-inspired learning memory structures. *Neural Networks, 18*(5-6), 818–825. doi:10.1016/j.neunet.2005.06.027

Thornton, C. (1994). The worrying statistics of connectionist representation. *Technical Report CSRP 362, Cognitive and computing sciences.* University of Sussex. United Kingdom.

Topliss, J. G., & Edwards, R. P. (1979). Chance factors in studies of quantitative structure-activity relationships. *Journal of Medicinal Chemistry, 22*(10), 1238–1244. doi:10.1021/jm00196a017

UCSF Medical Center. (2008). *Cholangiocarcinoma.* Retrieved May 24 2008, from http://www.ucsfhealth.org/adult/medical_services/gastro/cholangiocarcinoma/conditions/cholang/signs.html.

v Smagt, P. d., & Hirzinger, G. (1998). Why feedforward networks are in bad shape. *Proceedings 8th International Conference on Artificial Neural Networks* (pp. 159-164).

Venkatesan, P., & Anitha, S. (2006). Application of a radial basis function neural network for diagnosis of diabetes mellitus. *Current Science, 91*(9), 1195–1198.

Vincent, L., & Soille, P. (1991). Watersheds in digital spaces: an efficient algorithm based on immersion simulations. *Transactions on Pattern Analysis and Machine Intelligence, 13,* 583–598. doi:10.1109/34.87344

Wikipedia (2008). *Artificial neural network.* Retrieved September 17 2008, updated September 14 2008, from http://en.wikipedia.org/wiki/Artificial_neural_network.

Yoon, J.-H., & Gores, G. J. (2003). Diagnosis, staging, and treatment of cholangiocarcinoma. *Current Treatment Options in Gastroenterology, 6,* 105–112. doi:10.1007/s11938-003-0011-z

Chapter 7
Solving Complex Problems in Human Genetics Using Nature-Inspired Algorithms Requires Strategies which Exploit Domain-Specific Knowledge

Casey S. Greene
Dartmouth College, USA

Jason H. Moore
Dartmouth College, USA

ABSTRACT

In human genetics the availability of chip-based technology facilitates the measurement of thousands of DNA sequence variations from across the human genome. The informatics challenge is to identify combinations of interacting DNA sequence variations that predict common diseases. The authors review three nature-inspired methods that have been developed and evaluated in this domain. The two approaches this chapter focuses on in detail are genetic programming (GP) and a complex-system inspired GP-like computational evolution system (CES). The authors also discuss a third nature-inspired approach known as ant colony optimization (ACO). The GP and ACO techniques are designed to select relevant attributes, while the CES addresses both the selection of relevant attributes and the modeling of disease risk. Specifically, they examine these methods in the context of epistasis or gene-gene interactions. For the work discussed here we focus solely on the situation where there is an epistatic effect but no detectable main effect. In this domain, early studies show that nature-inspired algorithms perform no better than a

DOI: 10.4018/978-1-60566-705-8.ch007

simple random search when classification accuracy is used as the fitness function. Thus, the challenge for applying these search algorithms to this problem is that when using classification accuracy there are no building blocks. The goal then is to use outside knowledge or pre-processing of the dataset to provide these building blocks in a manner that enables the population, in a nature-inspired framework, to discover an optimal model. The authors examine one pre-processing strategy for revealing building blocks in this domain and three different methods to exploit these building blocks as part of a knowledge-aware nature-inspired strategy. They also discuss potential sources of building blocks and modifications to the described methods which may improve our ability to solve complex problems in human genetics. Here it is argued that both the methods using expert knowledge and the sources of expert knowledge drawn upon will be critical to improving our ability to detect and characterize epistatic interactions in these large scale biomedical studies.

INTRODUCTION

Nature-inspired algorithms are a natural fit for solving problems in biological domains, not just because of the connection between method and application but also because many of the problems natural systems solve are common to biological data. Biological organisms evolve in a noisy environment with a rugged fitness landscape. Many of the interesting problems in human genetics also likely involve a rugged fitness landscape where models that contain some but not all of the relevant attributes may not have an accuracy greater than that of the surrounding noise. In addition these data are frequently noisy, in the sense that two individuals with the same values at the relevant attributes may have different disease states. In this context it is no surprise that we look to natural systems for inspiration when designing algorithms which succeed in this domain. Wagner discusses the role of robustness and evolvability in living systems (Wagner, 2005). We must design and use algorithms that, like living systems, are both robust to the noise in the data and evolvable despite the rugged fitness landscape. We briefly discuss the Relief family of machine learning methods which are useful for separating signals from noise in this type of data and then focus on approaches

that exploit this information. The nature-inspired methods we examine here are genetic programming (GP), a computational evolution system (CES), and ant colony optimization (ACO).

GP is an automated computational discovery tool inspired by Darwinian evolution and natural selection (Koza, 1992, 1994; Koza, Andre, Bennett & Keane, 1999; Koza, 2003; Banzhaf, Nordin, Keller & Francone, 1998; Langdon & Koza, 1998; Langdon & Poli, 2002). The goal of GP is to evolve computer programs which solve problems. This is accomplished by generating programs composed of the building blocks needed to solve or approximate a solution and then iteratively evaluating, selecting, recombining, and mutating these programs to form new computer programs. This process repeats until a best program or set of programs is identified. Genetic programming and its many variations have been applied successfully to a wide range of different problems including data mining, knowledge discovery (Freitas, 2002), and bioinformatics (Fogel & Corne, 2003). Despite the power of this method, there remain a number of challenges that GP practitioners and theorists must address before this computational discovery tool becomes a standard in the modern problem solver's toolbox. Yu et al. list 22 such challenges (Yu, Riolo & Worzel, 2006). We discuss here methods that address some of these challenges, in particular those related to practice. We specifically discuss methods that use information from pre- and post- processing, methods for handling large high dimensional datasets, and methods for integrating domain knowledge. We argue that these methods will be critical if we are to successfully and reliably analyze these genetic data for epistasis.

Spector, as part of an essay regarding the roles of theory and practice in genetic programming, discusses the push towards biology by GP practitioners (Spector, 2003). Banzhaf et al. propose the transformation of overly simplistic and abstracted artificial evolution methods such as GP into computational evolution systems (CES) that more closely resemble the complexity of real biological and evolutionary systems (Banzhaf et al., 2006). We review work here regarding a CES developed for this domain. The working hypothesis addressed in the papers we discuss is that a GP-based genetic analysis system will find better solutions faster if it is implemented as a CES that can evolve a variety of complex operators that in turn generate variability in solutions. This is in contrast to an artificial evolution system that employs a fixed set of operators. Unlike the other two systems we discuss, the goal here is to both identify attributes and discover a mathematical model that correctly classifies individuals with regard to their disease state.

The final nature-inspired approach we discuss, ACO, is a positive feedback approach to search modeled on the behavior of ants (Dorigo, Maniezzo & Colorni, 1991). ACO is attractive for the area of human genetics because it is a straightforward population based approach which is easily parallelizable, and there is some history of applying ant based approaches to biological data. Parpinelli et al. demonstrated their AntMiner system as a rule discovery method on biological data (Parpinelli, Lopes & Freitas, 2001). We discuss a nature-inspired ant system for attribute selection in the domain of human genetics. ACO is a particularly

appropriate framework for this problem because of the ease with which expert knowledge can be included. For example, Merkle et al. showed that dynamically altering a heuristic weighting factor during the search can lead to greater success for a resource-constrained project scheduling problem (Merkle, Middendorf & Schmeck, 2002). If ACO is successful here, we can draw from and implement methods described in the wide body of ACO literature to improve our ant system for this human genetics problem.

The wealth of data now available to biological and biomedical researchers necessitates the application of these nature-inspired approaches. With chip-based technologies it is now economically feasible to measure over one million DNA sequence variations in the human genome. The work we review specifically focuses on the analysis of single nucleotide polymorphisms (SNPs). A SNP is a single nucleotide or point in the DNA sequence that differs among people. At least one SNP is anticipated to occur approximately every 100 nucleotides across the 3×10^9 nucleotide human genome. An important goal in human genetics is determining which of these SNPs are useful for predicting an individual's risk of common diseases. This "genome-wide" approach is expected to revolutionize the genetic analysis of common human diseases. Despite the promise of this broad approach, success in this endeavor will be difficult due to nonlinearity in the genotype to disease mapping relationship that is due, in part, to epistasis. The implication of epistasis from a data mining point of view is that SNPs need to be considered jointly in learning algorithms rather than individually. Moore argues that epistasis, far from being a corner case, is likely to be ubiquitous in common human diseases (Moore, 2003). The challenge of modeling attribute interactions in data mining has been previously described (Freitas, 2001). Due to the combinatorial magnitude of this problem, analysis strategies which can use outside knowledge are crucial.

Combining the difficulty of modeling nonlinear

attribute interactions with the challenge of attribute selection yields, for this domain, what Goldberg calls a needle-in-a-haystack problem (Goldberg, 2002). That is, there may be a particular combination of SNPs that, together with the right nonlinear functions, are a significant predictor of disease susceptibility. Considered individually they may not look any different than thousands of other irrelevant SNPs. Under these models the learning algorithm is truly looking for a genetic needle in a genomic haystack. A recent report from the International HapMap Consortium suggests that approximately 300,000 carefully selected SNPs may be necessary to capture all of the relevant variation across the Caucasian human genome (The International HapMap Consortium, 2005). Assuming this is true, it is probably a lower bound, we would need to scan 4.5×10^{10} pair-wise combinations of SNPs to find a genetic needle. The number of higher order combinations is astronomical. We discuss preliminary work which shows that without expert knowledge these approaches perform no better than a random search. We follow with a discussion of methods that integrate expert knowledge into the search strategy and which succeed in this domain (White, Gilbert, Reif & Moore, 2005; Moore & White, 2007a). Each of these successful approaches exploit knowledge gained by pre-processing the data with the Relief family of algorithms which are capable of detecting epistatic interactions in this type of data.

BUILDING BLOCKS FROM THE TUNED RELIEFF ALGORITHM (TURF)

For these nature-inspired methods we require a source of outside knowledge capable of pre-processing the input data and weighting attributes (SNPs) on how well they, in the context of other SNPs, are able to differentiate individuals with disease from those without. Kira and Rendell developed Relief which is capable of detecting

attribute dependencies (Kira & Rendell, 1992). The approach Relief uses to detect interactions is conceptually simple. SNPs that distinguish similar individuals in different classes are likely to be of interest. For any random individual, R_i, the nearest individual of the same class (H_i) and the nearest individual of the other class (M_i) are found. For each SNP, A, if R_i shares a value with H_i but not with M_i, the weight of A is increased. If R_i shares A with M_i but not with H_i, the weight of A is decreased. If R_i shares A with or differs from both H_i and M_i, the weight remains unchanged. This process of weighting attributes can be repeated for all individuals in the dataset. This neighbor-based process allows Relief to discover attribute dependencies when an interaction with no main effect exists. The algorithm produces weights for each attribute ranging from -1 (worst) to +1 (best). Kononenko improved upon Relief by choosing n nearest neighbors instead of just one (Kononenko, 1994). This new algorithm, ReliefF, has been shown to be more robust to noisy attributes and missing data and is widely used in data mining applications (Robnik-Sikonja & Kononenko, 2003). Unfortunately the power of ReliefF is reduced in the presence of a large number of noisy attributes. This drove the development of Tuned ReliefF (TuRF). The TuRF algorithm systematically removes attributes that have low quality estimates so that the weights of the remaining attributes can be re-estimated. TuRF is significantly better than ReliefF in the domain of human genetics (Moore & White, 2007b). The nature-inspired methods we discuss here use TuRF as their source of expert knowledge.

MULTIFACTOR DIMENSIONALITY REDUCTION (MDR)

Within the GP and ACO approaches we wish to first focus solely on attribute selection. We therefore need a method to identify whether or not the attributes selected are relevant. For this we

Figure 1. Example GP trees for solutions from these studies (A). Examine of a more complex tree we hope to address in future studies (B).

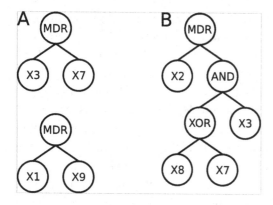

use multifactor dimensionality reduction (MDR) which has been developed as a nonparametric and model-free genetic data mining strategy for identifying combinations of SNPs that are predictive of a discrete clinical endpoint (Ritchie et al., 2001). At the core of the MDR approach is an attribute construction algorithm that creates a new attribute by pooling genotypes from multiple SNPs. Constructive induction using the MDR kernel is accomplished in the following way. Given a threshold T, a multilocus genotype combination is considered high-risk if the ratio of cases (subjects with disease) to controls (healthy subjects) exceeds or equals T, otherwise it is considered low-risk. Genotype combinations considered to be high-risk are labeled G1 while those considered low-risk are labeled G0. This process constructs a new one-dimensional attribute with levels G0 and G1. It is this new single variable that is returned by the MDR function in the GP root node and the quality measure for depositing pheromone in the ACO approach. The CES approach discussed here solves this problem without employing the MDR function. MDR is described in more detail by Moore et al., (2006).

GENETIC PROGRAMMING WITH MDR AND EXPERT KNOWLEDGE BUILDING BLOCKS

We have developed GP-MDR which is MDR wrapped in a GP framework for attribute selection. Figure 1A illustrates an example GP tree for this problem. In this work the solution representation is kept simple with one function in the root node and two leaves to evaluate the best GP parameterization for attribute selection. More complex trees (e.g. Figure 1B) can be explored once the principles of how the GP performs attribute selection in simpler trees are understood. By first focusing on attribute selection, we separate the task of finding good attributes from the task of generating good models. To these ends the MDR approach is used at the root node because it is able to capture interaction information. In this representation each tree has two leaves or terminals consisting of attributes.

Given that the challenge has been described as a needle in a haystack, we were not surprised to discover that without building blocks from expert knowledge the GP approach performed no better than a random search (Moore & White, 2007a). Goldberg describes a class of genetic algorithms called ``Competent Genetic Algorithms" (Goldberg, 2002). These are genetic algorithms that solve specific problems quickly, reliably, and accurately and which exploit knowledge about the task or dataset to the fullest extent possible.

A Competent Fitness Function

Our initial work integrating expert knowledge focused on developing a fitness function that could be part of a competent genetic algorithm (Moore & White, 2007a). We used a multiobjective fitness function that consisted of two pieces in a simple linear combination of the form $\alpha * A + \beta * Q$. Here, A is a normalized measure of accuracy obtained from the analysis of the single constructed attribute from the GP tree using a naïve Bayes classifier. The parameter α is used to weight the accuracy measures. Q in this function represents a normalized measure of attribute quality obtained from pre-processing the attributes using the TuRF algorithm. The parameter β is used to weight the quality measures. The algorithm can identify useful building blocks because information from TuRF is used.

We found that a GP with accuracy (A) as the fitness function does no better than random search (R) across all genetic models and all genetic effect sizes. In a few cases random search was significantly better ($p < 0.05$) than a GP strategy using accuracy for fitness. This is not unexpected because random search is able to explore a greater diversity of trees than GP. At a heritability of 0.05 and greater there is clear difference between the GP that uses attribute quality (Q) in the fitness function versus the GP that only uses accuracy (A). This difference was statistically significant ($p < 0.05$) across most models and most heritabilities. Here, GP is also outperforming random search ($p < 0.05$). This is clear evidence that learning is occurring. It is interesting to note that increasing the weight of the attribute quality to twice that of accuracy ($\alpha = 1$ and $\beta = 2$) performed no better than equal weighting ($\alpha = 1$ and $\beta = 1$), thus it is clearly important to provide expert knowledge but a higher weighting of expert knowledge is not necessarily better.

Sensible Operators

While a fitness function is one way to exploit expert knowledge in an evolutionary search, it is also possible to utilize expert knowledge via operators tuned to exploring areas of the search space thought to be beneficial. Work has been done to develop such operators. Majeed and Ryan have, in a series of papers (Majeed & Ryan, 2006a, 2006b), developed and examined a context aware crossover operator. This operator efficiently mitigates much of the destructiveness of the crossover operation in GP (Majeed & Ryan, 2007b). Both

have also developed a context aware mutation operator which, operating on similar principles, also attempts to improve the usefulness of sub-trees (Majeed & Ryan, 2007a). Here we employ similar principles as we use TuRF scores from pre-processing to direct the GP to areas of the search space which the scores indicate are likely to be useful. We have titled these "sensible" operators as they make sense in our context and heavily exploit dataset specific information. Here we examine three of these operators which could be useful for building "Competent Genetic Algorithms" for this domain, and then discuss results obtained using these operators.

Sensible Initialization

With our sensible initializer we focus on using expert knowledge for the initialization of terminals in this GP tree structure. O'Neill and Ryan discuss the importance of initialization and the negative impact of a lack of diversity on final solutions (O'Neill & Ryan, 2003). We apply their principles of sensible initialization in two different initialization operators (Greene, White & Moore, 2008b). The first is an exhaustive initializer focused on diversity and the second is an expert knowledge based initializer focused on exploiting pre-processing information for population initialization. The exhaustive initializer insures maximal diversity by selecting attributes to be leaves without replacement until all attributes have been used, at which point it replenishes the pool from which attributes are selected. This insures that all attributes are used once before any are used a second time. The expert knowledge aware probabilistic initializer selects attributes for terminals via a biased roulette wheel. The same attribute is not allowed to be used twice within the same tree, but it may be used any number of times within the generated population. We compare both to a random initializer.

Sensible Recombination

Our sensible recombination operator heavily exploits expert knowledge building blocks (Moore & White, 2006). We modified this operator by first selecting the top 1% or 5% of trees according their maximum TuRF score. Each possible pair of these selected trees is recombined and the children are included in the next generation. For example, with a population size of 500 either 5 or 25 trees are selected. There are 5 choose 2 (10) and 25 choose 2 (300) possible recombination events. Thus, the new population consists of either 10 or 300 recombined trees generated from those with the maximum TuRF scores. The remaining 490 or 200 individuals in the population are generated using the standard binary tournament operator. This new selection operator ensures that the best trees as measured by pre-processed expert knowl-

edge are selected and recombined. Generating the remaining trees by binary tournament ensures that functional attributes not assigned a high quality by TuRF still have a chance of being evaluated.

Sensible Mutation

The sensible mutation operator is based on the principles of the sensible recombination operator (Greene, White & Moore, 2007). It aggressively applies information from pre-processing to generate solutions. One potential weakness of the recombination operator is that it can only use attributes still in the population. Sensible mutation, on the other hand, can exploit attributes that are not currently in the population. This operator mutates individuals with the greatest difference in TuRF scores between the leaves, changes the leaf in that individual with the lowest TuRF score,

Figure 2. A schematic diagram showing the operators in GP and the population flow between them. The notation on the right shows where expert knowledge has been applied to the system.

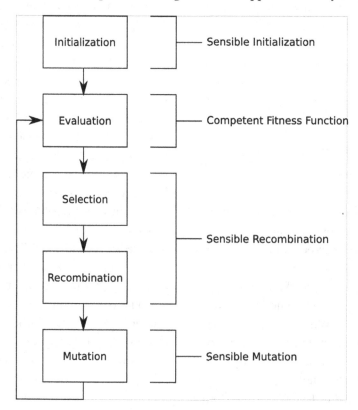

evaluates trees where the changed leaf is replaced with high TuRF scoring attributes, and retains the best individual for the next generation. This sensible mutator ensures that poor building blocks are replaced by good building blocks throughout evolution. This method is designed to change leaves which are unlikely to lead to success and provide attributes likely to be involved in successful models. For comparison with a random mutator, the percentage of the population chosen for mutation is adjusted to account for the iterative replacement attempts (see Figure 2).

Sensible Operators Results and Conclusions

Both sensible recombination and sensible mutation were extremely successful. Despite exploring less search space (1% vs. 10%) relative to the "competent fitness function," the power of each method was similar. Sensible recombination performed slightly better than sensible mutation, potentially due to its role in both selection and recombination. Sensible initialization was not as successful in its own right, but using the expert knowledge driven probabilistic initialization operator did improve the power of a GP also using the ``competent fitness function." The diversity focused initializer did not outperform a random initialization operator. From these results we can gain a number of insights. Firstly, expert knowledge building blocks must be exploited to find the genetic needle in the genomic haystack. Secondly, operators which strongly exploit this expert knowledge can explore a smaller part of the search space and retain high power. The sensible mutation and sensible recombination approaches both consistently return good results. One area that remains to be explored is how well these approaches work cooperatively. Are there any interactions between them that can increase the power of GP for attribute selection? Also, is it possible to use expert knowledge in initialization

to improve the power of these methods? One potential issue with the sensible operator approach is that the operators are rigid and pre-defined. They work for this problem, but will they generalize to other problems? The work we discuss in the next section addresses this concern by creating a system able to evolve its own sensible operators.

A COMPUTATIONAL EVOLUTION SYSTEM

The GP method discussed thus far is an effective approach for attribute selection, but how does a comparable system perform when asked to both identify good attributes and build a model predicting disease status? In addition, instead of providing pre-defined ``sensible" operators to enhance the GP, is there a way to allow the method to discover good operators on its own? It may be possible to evolve complex operators which tune themselves to the specific problem, outside knowledge, or dataset. Previous work in this area of GP has been performed by Edmonds as Meta-GP and Spector as PushGP (Edmonds, 1998; Spector, 2001; Spector & Robinson, 2002). Both systems are able to evolve their own methods to generate variability and, as such, can tune the analysis. PushGP does not differentiate between operators and solutions, while Meta-GP is more similar to the approach we propose with separate groups for operators and solutions.

To address these questions we developed a prototype of a CES for human genetics. This prototype, as shown in Figure 3, is structured in a four layer grid. At the lowest level of this grid are the solutions. These are postfix solutions which are evolved to explain the relationship between case and control in the data. They act as classifiers by taking attributes from the data, applying mathematical functions to those attributes, and producing a score. The goal of these classifiers is to accept as input two or more SNPs and pro-

Figure 3. Visual overview of the prototype CES. The hierarchical structure is shown on the left while some specific examples at each level are shown on the right. The top two levels of the hierarchy (A and B) exist to generate variability in the operators that modify the solutions. Shown in C is an example solution operator. These solution operators can act similarly to sensible operators from our GP work and can exploit expert knowledge to modify the classifiers (level D).

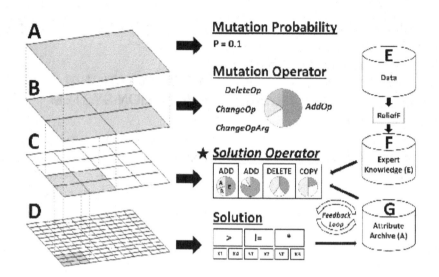

duce a discrete output that can be used to predict disease state. Here, we used symbolic discriminant analysis or SDA as our classifier. The SDA method has been described previously for this problem domain (Moore, Parker, Olsen & Aune, 2002; Moore, Andrews, Barney & White, 2008; Moore et al., 2007; Moore & White, 2007a). SDA models consist of a set of attributes and constants as input and a set of mathematical functions that produce a score for each instance in the dataset. Here, the SDA function set is +, -, *, /, %, <, <=, >, >=, ==, != where the % operator is a mod operation and / is a protected division. The next level of the grid contains the solution operators. These operators act upon solutions as the instruments of generating diversity. They can perform much the same role as the sensible recombination and sensible mutation operators. These operators consist of six building blocks: AddOperator, DeleteRangeOperator, CopyRangeOperator, PermuteRangeOperator, PointMutationOperator, and PointMutationExpertKnowledgeOperator.

With these building blocks the system is able to generate operators that can perform recombination, mutation, and many other complex operations. The system can use expert knowledge, but to do so it must first evolve the ability to exploit the PointMutationExpertKnowledgeOperator, which replaces a function and its arguments with a randomly selected function and arguments chosen by an expert knowledge source.

Preliminary CES Results

Mutation alone only approximated the correct answer once out of 100 runs while the full CE system approximated the correct answer more than 5% of the time. In both cases, the mean accuracy was significantly higher for the full system ($p < 0.05$). These preliminary results indicate that, for this specific domain, a CES with the ability to evolve operators of any size and complexity does indeed identify better solutions than a baseline system that uses a fixed mutation operator. An important question is whether more complex operators were actually used to generate the best models discovered by the CE system. We evaluated the operators discovered during each run that contributed to a best model and found that all six operators and operator building blocks were used at least once in each of the 100 runs. This demonstrates that complex operators were discovered and used to generate better solutions than a simple mutation operator.

Evolving Expert-Knowledge Driven Operators

The CES described above succeeds in this domain, but it begins by building operators from fairly complex operator building blocks. The next step was to simplify the operator building blocks (Moore et al., 2009). In this modified system the solutions are stack based but still act as classifiers. The operators are analogous to those in the previous system but are composed of only three much simpler building blocks (Add, Delete, and Copy). Each operator building block has a vector of three probabilities. The probabilities in the vector specify the chance that the function being added, deleted, or copied is determined stochastically, by using the archive, or by using TuRF. As we have discussed the ability to use expert knowledge from TuRF is important in this domain, and this is consistent with Goldberg's ideas about exploiting good building blocks in competent genetic algorithms (Goldberg, 2002). The archive creates a feedback loop between the solutions and the solution operators. Operators built from these blocks can take advantage of both what we think we know before the approach starts in the form of TuRF scores and what we learn during the run through the archive.

Further Results from the CES

The use of both the archive and the pre-processed expert knowledge significantly improve perfor-

mance of the system as measured by accuracy of the best classifiers discovered in each run ($p < 0.0001$). A Tukey's post-hoc analysis showed that including the archive was better than random attribute selection ($p = 0.0001$) and that including expert knowledge was better than both random selection ($p < 0.0001$) and the archive ($p < 0.0001$). These results suggest that the solution operators are able to evolve the ability to utilize information from both the continuously updated attribute archive and pre-processed expert knowledge and that this ability leads to improved performance of the system. The observation that operators succeed when they are able to use TuRF information is consistent with our results from GP. The ability to archive and use information about the frequency with which different attributes are represented in solutions creates an important feedback loop in the system. In addition it leads to classifiers which are better able to predict disease state when used in addition to random choices. Figure 4 shows an evolved tree which successfully classifies 87.25% of the individuals in the dataset. This accuracy matches that obtained with MDR using these chosen attributes. There are non-functional nodes in the tree but pareto optimization or multiobjective fitness with a preference towards smaller solutions could be integrated into the CES. This would encourage evolution towards smaller classifiers with equal accuracy.

ANT COLONY OPTIMIZATION

Another nature-inspired approach that has been applied to the epistasis problem in human genetics is ACO. Ants explore the search space and leave pheromone in quantities relative to the quality of their solution. Over time the pheromone evaporates. The quantity of this pheromone determines the chance that ants will explore similar regions in the future. With this addition and evaporation of pheromone, ant systems balance exploration of new areas and exploitation of areas that have

Figure 4. The tree representation of a successful solution evolved with the CES using pre-processing based knowledge from TuRF and information from the archive. Gray portions of the tree have no effect on the accuracy of the classifier and could be trimmed. A pareto or multiobjective approach assessing simplicity of solutions in addition to accuracy may help evolve trees lacking these unnecessary sections.

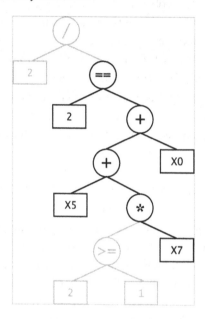

previously contained good solutions. These ant-based approaches were first applied to the traveling salesman problem (Dorigo et al., 1991) but have since been applied to areas from scheduling (Colorni, Dorigo, Maniezzo & Trubian, 1994) to machine learning (Parpinelli et al., 2001).

Here we apply this technique to the epistasis problem in human genetics. We discovered in our work with GP that expert knowledge is critical for machine learning algorithms to be successful with this problem (Moore & White, 2007a). Here we apply these principles to the ACO arena and structure our pheromone updating rule to include expert knowledge. The pheromone is updated for each SNP according to both the MDR accuracy of models containing that attribute and information from TuRF. This method of including expert

knowledge is effective (Greene, White & Moore, 2008a). Our results show that ACO is a viable approach to this problem when pre-processing based expert knowledge is added to the pheromone updating rule. This suggests that ACO might be an appropriate search strategy when exhaustive analysis is impossible. These results are also encouraging because of the simplicity and high power of this approach. In fact, these results indicated a power moderately greater than the genetic programming approaches we have already discussed for attribute selection.

Work in this area should focus on adapting other advancements in ant systems to human genetics. Merkle et al. dynamically alter the heuristic weighting factor to more effectively balance exploration and exploitation (Merkle et al., 2002). This could now be applied to our problem. In addition to this heuristic weighting approach, modifications such as a rank based ant system or a *MIN-MAX* ant system warrant investigation (Bullnheimer, Hartl & Strauss, 1999; Stützle & Hoos, 1997; Stützle & Hoos, 2000). Now that a prototype has succeeded in this domain, additional ant methods should be adapted and examined to determine whether they help solve these important human genetics problems.

DISCUSSION

It is clear that work in this area will require the use of expert knowledge if nature-inspired approaches are going to successfully find predictors of common human diseases. Now the charge is to develop simple and efficient methods for attribute selection, implement and evaluate low parameter approaches for both attribute selection and epistasis modeling, and improve and develop new and better sources of expert knowledge. Developing systems with fewer parameters but high power will make the application of these systems to real biological problems more routine. Better expert knowledge should speed the search in these algorithms making them much more efficient. Together these will help put this class of methods in the modern geneticist's toolbox.

We can improve our expert knowledge component by improving our pre-processing methods or by using information derived from other biological data. Improvements to the power of ReliefF or TuRF will play a crucial role in our ability to find answers using nature-inspired algorithms. Using biological expert knowledge from protein-protein interaction databases, the Gene Ontology, or known biochemical pathways we should be able to identify SNPs predictive of disease risk. For example, Pattin and Moore argue that once we successfully develop the methods to extract expert knowledge from protein-protein interaction databases, we will improve our ability to identify important epistatic interactions in genome-wide studies (Pattin & Moore, 2008). By using biological knowledge to drive this search, the potential exists to enhance our comprehension of common human diseases. Eventually this could lead to an improvement in the prevention, diagnosis, and treatment of these diseases.

To develop parameter free or parameter robust approaches we should explore methods that minimize or avoid user-defined parameters. While parameter sweeps are one way to approach the problem they are time consuming and cumbersome. Another option is to make all parameters evolvable. In this way the system can learn the appropriate parameters from the data. The CES approach we discuss is a step in this direction. Using the CES with an island model and entirely evolvable parameters could lead to a situation where the only two parameters are how many CPUs should be used and how long the run should continue. The goal of this work is to develop techniques which solve hard problems with minimal tweaking. If these nature-inspired approaches are to become widespread in the biological and biomedical sciences, methods that powerfully analyze genome-wide datasets with minimal parameter sweeping will be critical.

REFERENCES

Banzhaf, W., Beslon, G., Christensen, S., Foster, J. A., Kepes, F., & Lefort, V. (2006). From artificial evolution to computational evolution: a research agenda. *Nature Reviews. Genetics*, 7, 729–735. doi:10.1038/nrg1921

Banzhaf, W., Nordin, P., Keller, R. E., & Francone, F. D. (1998). *Genetic Programming: An Introduction: On the automatic evolution of computer programs and its applications*. San Francisco, CA, USA: Morgan Kaufmann Publishers Inc.

Bullnheimer, B., Hartl, R., & Strauss, C. (1999). A new rank-based version of the ant system: a computational study. *Central European Journal for Operations Research and Economics*, 7(1), 25–38.

Colorni, A., Dorigo, M., Maniezzo, V., & Trubian, M. (1994). Ant system for job-shop scheduling. *JORBEL – Belgian Journal of Operations Research. Statistics, and Computer Science*, 34(1), 39–53.

Dorigo, M., Maniezzo, V., & Colorni, A. (1991). Positive feedback as a search strategy. *Technical report 91-016, Dipartimento di Elettronica e Informatica, Politecnico di Milano*.

Edmonds, B. (1998). Meta-genetic programming: *Co-evolving the operators of variation (CPM Report 98-32)*. Aytoun St., Manchester, M1 3GH. UK: Centre for Policy Modelling, Manchester Metropolitan University, UK.

Fogel, G., & Corne, D. (2003). *Evolutionary computation in bioinformatics*. Morgan Kaufmann Publishers.

Freitas, A. A. (2001). Understanding the crucial role of attribute interaction in data mining. *Artificial Intelligence Review*, 16(3), 177–199. doi:10.1023/A:1011996210207

Freitas, A. A. (2002). *Data mining and knowledge discovery with evolutionary algorithms*. Secaucus, NJ, USA: Springer-Verlag New York, Inc.

Goldberg, D. E. (2002). *The design of innovation: Lessons from and for competent genetic algorithms*. Norwell, MA, USA: Kluwer Academic Publishers.

Greene, C. S., White, B. C., & Moore, J. H. (2007). An expert knowledge-guided mutation operator for genome-wide genetic analysis using genetic programming. *Lecture Notes in Bioinformatics, 4774*, 30–40.

Greene, C. S., White, B. C., & Moore, J. H. (2008a). Ant colony optimization for genome-wide genetic analysis. *Lecture Notes in Computer Science, 5217*, 37–47. doi:10.1007/978-3-540-87527-7_4

Greene, C. S., White, B. C., & Moore, J. H. (2008b). Using expert knowledge in initialization for genome-wide analysis of epistasis using genetic programming. *Gecco '08: Proceedings of the 10th annual conference on genetic and evolutionary computation* (pp. 351–352). New York, NY, USA: ACM.

Kira, K., & Rendell, L. A. (1992). A practical approach to feature selection. *Proceedings of the 9th International Workshop on Machine Learning* (pp. 249-256). Morgan Kaufmann Publishers.

Kononenko, I. (1994). Estimating attributes: Analysis and extension of relief. *Proceedings of European Conference on Machine Learning* (pp. 171-182).

Koza, J. R. (1992). *Genetic programming: on the programming of computers by means of natural selection*. Cambridge, MA, USA: MIT Press.

Koza, J. R. (1994). *Genetic programming II: automatic discovery of reusable programs*. Cambridge, MA, USA: MIT Press.

Koza, J. R. (2003). *Genetic programming IV: Routine human-competitive machine intelligence*. Norwell, MA, USA: Kluwer Academic Publishers.

Koza, J. R., Andre, D., Bennett, F. H., & Keane, M. A. (1999). *Genetic programming III: Darwinian invention & problem solving*. San Francisco, CA, USA: Morgan Kaufmann Publishers Inc.

Langdon, W. B., & Koza, J. R. (1998). *Genetic programming and data structures: Genetic programming + data structures = automatic programming!* Norwell, MA, USA: Kluwer Academic Publishers.

Langdon, W. B., & Poli, R. (2002). *Foundations of genetic programming*. Springer-Verlag.

Majeed, H., & Ryan, C. (2006a). A less destructive, context-aware crossover operator for GP. *Lecture Notes in Computer Science, 3905*, 36–48. doi:10.1007/11729976_4

Majeed, H., & Ryan, C. (2006b). Using context-aware crossover to improve the performance of GP. *GECCO '06: Proceedings of the 8th annual conference on Genetic and evolutionary computation* (pp. 847-854). New York, NY, USA: ACM.

Majeed, H., & Ryan, C. (2007a). Context-aware mutation: a modular, context aware mutation operator for genetic programming. *GECCO '07: Proceedings of the 9th annual conference on Genetic and evolutionary computation* (pp. 1651-1658). New York, NY, USA: ACM.

Majeed, H., & Ryan, C. (2007b). On the constructiveness of context-aware crossover. *GECCO '07: Proceedings of the 9th annual conference on Genetic and evolutionary computation* (pp. 1659–1666). New York, NY, USA: ACM.

Merkle, D., Middendorf, M., & Schmeck, H. (2002). Ant colony optimization for resource-constrained project scheduling. *IEEE Transactions on Evolutionary Computation, 6*(4), 333–346. doi:10.1109/TEVC.2002.802450

Moore, J. H. (2003). The ubiquitous nature of epistasis in determining susceptibility to common human diseases. *Human Heredity*, *56*, 73–82. doi:10.1159/000073735

Moore, J. H. (2004). Computational analysis of gene-gene interactions using multifactor dimensionality reduction. *Expert Review of Molecular Diagnostics*, *4*(6), 795–803. doi:10.1586/14737159.4.6.795

Moore, J. H. (2007). Genome-wide analysis of epistasis using multifactor dimensionality reduction: feature selection and construction in the domain of human genetics. In D. Zhu (Ed.), *Knowledge Discovery and Data Mining: Challenges and Realities with Real World Data,* IGI Global, in press.

Moore, J. H., Andrews, P. C., Barney, N., & White, B. C. (2008). Development and evaluation of an open-ended computational evolution system for the genetic analysis of susceptibility to common human diseases. *Lecture Notes in Computer Science*, *4973*, 129–140. doi:10.1007/978-3-540-78757-0_12

Moore, J. H., Barney, N., Tsai, C. T., Chiang, F. T., Gui, J., & White, B. C. (2007). Symbolic modeling of epistasis. *Human Heredity*, *63*(2), 120–133. doi:10.1159/000099184

Moore, J. H., Gilbert, J. C., Tsai, C. T., Chiang, F. T., Holden, T., Barney, N., & White, B. C. (2006). A flexible computational framework for detecting, characterizing, and interpreting statistical patterns of epistasis in genetic studies of human disease susceptibility. *Journal of Theoretical Biology*, *241*(2), 252–261. doi:10.1016/j.jtbi.2005.11.036

Moore, J. H., Greene, C. S., Andrews, P. C., & White, B. C. (2009). Does complexity matter? Artificial evolution, computational evolution and the genetic analysis of epistasis in common human diseases. In R. Riolo, T. Soule & B. Worzel (Eds.), *Genetic programming theory and practice VI* (pp. 125-144). Springer.

Moore, J. H., Parker, J. S., Olsen, N. J., & Aune, T. (2002). Symbolic discriminant analysis of microarray data in autoimmune disease. *Genetic Epidemiology*, *23*, 57–69. doi:10.1002/gepi.1117

Moore, J. H., & White, B. C. (2006). Exploiting expert knowledge in genetic programming for genome-wide genetic analysis. *Lecture Notes in Computer Science*, *4193*, 969–977. doi:10.1007/11844297_98

Moore, J. H., & White, B. C. (2007a). Genome-wide genetic analysis using genetic programming: The critical need for expert knowledge. In R. Riolo, T. Soule, & B. Worzel (Eds.), *Genetic programming theory and practice IV* (pp. 11-28). Springer.

Moore, J. H., & White, B. C. (2007b). Tuning ReliefF for genome-wide genetic analysis. *Lecture Notes in Computer Science*, *4447*, 166–175. doi:10.1007/978-3-540-71783-6_16

O'Neill, M., & Ryan, C. (2003). *Grammatical evolution: Evolutionary automatic programming in an arbitrary language*. Norwell, MA, USA: Kluwer Academic Publishers.

Parpinelli, R., Lopes, H., & Freitas, A. (2001). An Ant Colony Based System for Data Mining: Applications to Medical Data. *Proceedings of the Genetic and Evolutionary Computation Conference* (pp. 791-797).

Pattin, K., & Moore, J. (2008). Exploiting the proteome to improve the genome-wide genetic analysis of epistasis in common human diseases. *Human Genetics*, *124*(1), 19–29. doi:10.1007/s00439-008-0522-8

Ritchie, M. D., Hahn, L. W., Roodi, N., Bailey, L. R., Dupont, W. D., & Parl, F. F. (2001). Multifactor dimensionality reduction reveals high-order interactions among estrogen metabolism genes in sporadic breast cancer. *American Journal of Human Genetics*, *69*, 138–147. doi:10.1086/321276

Robnik-Sikonja, M., & Kononenko, I. (2003). Theoretical and empirical analysis of relieff and rrelieff. *Machine Learning*, *53*(1/2), 23–69. doi:10.1023/A:1025667309714

Spector, L. (2001). Autoconstructive evolution: Push, pushGP, and pushpop. *Proceedings of the Genetic and Evolutionary Computation Conference* (pp. 137–146). San Francisco, California, USA: Morgan Kaufmann.

Spector, L. (2003). An essay concerning human understanding of genetic programming. In R. L. Riolo & B. Worzel (Eds.), *Genetic programming theory and practice* (pp. 11-24). Kluwer.

Spector, L., & Robinson, A. (2002). Genetic programming and autoconstructive evolution with the push programming language. *Genetic Programming and Evolvable Machines*, *3*(1), 7–40. doi:10.1023/A:1014538503543

Stützle, T., & Hoos, H. H. (1997). MAX-MIN Ant System and local search for the traveling salesman problem. *Proceedings of the IEEE International Conference on Evolutionary Computation* (pp. 309–314).

Stützle, T., & Hoos, H. H. (2000). MAX-MIN ant system. *Future Generation Computer Systems*, *16*(8), 889–914. doi:10.1016/S0167-739X(00)00043-1

The International HapMap Consortium. (2005, October 27). A haplotype map of the human genome. *Nature*, *437*(7063), 1299–1320. doi:10.1038/nature04226

Wagner, A. (2005). *Robustness and evolvability in living systems (Princeton studies in complexity)*. Princeton, NJ: Princeton University Press.

White, B. C., Gilbert, J. C., Reif, D. M., & Moore, J. H. (2005). A statistical comparison of grammatical evolution strategies in the domain of human genetics. *Proceedings of the IEEE Congress on Evolutionary Computing* (pp. 676–682).

Yu, T., Riolo, R., & Worzel, B. (2006). *Genetic programming: Theory and practice*. Springer.

Section 4
Nature–Inspired Solutions in Computing & Engineering

Chapter 8
AGE–P:
An Evolutionary Platform for the Self-Organization of Smart-Appliance Ensembles

Ralf Salomon
University of Rostock, Germany

Stefan Goldmann
University of Rostock, Germany

ABSTRACT

Smart-appliance ensembles consist of intelligent devices that interact with each other and that are supposed to support their users in an autonomous, non-invasive way. Since both the number and the composition of the participating devices may spontaneously change at any time without any notice, traditional approaches, such as rule-based systems and evolutionary algorithms, are not appropriate mechanisms for their self-organization. Therefore, this chapter describes a new evolutionary framework, called appliances-go-evolution platform (AGE-P) that accounts for the inherent system dynamics by distributing all data structures and all operations across all participating devices. This chapter illustrates the behavior of this framework by presenting several results obtained from simulations as well as real-world case studies.

INTRODUCTION

Evolutionary algorithms of various sorts solve technical problems by utilizing some selected concepts from natural evolution (Back et al., 1997; Fogel, 1995; Goldberg, 1989; Rechenberg, 1994; Schwefel, 1995). They describe a technical (optimization)

problem as a set of n problem-specific parameters x_i, also called genes. The set of genes is called a genome and is tightly embedded into an object, called an individual. Typically, an evolutionary algorithm applies its random variation operators, such as mutation and recombination, to an individual's genes. As a consequence, these random variations change the individual's fitness values. A subsequent selection process exploits these fitness variations in

DOI: 10.4018/978-1-60566-705-8.ch008

order to gain some progress. It should be obvious that both the fitness evaluation and the selection process consider the genomes as atomic entities. In summary, the notion of an *individual* as the container of its genome is a very fundamental concept in all evolutionary algorithms.

The concepts described above are quite generic by their very nature. The pertinent literature on evolutionary algorithms presents a huge number of successful applications that can be found in areas as diverse as machine learning, combinatorial problems, VLSI design, breast cancer detection, evolutionary robotics, and numerical optimization in general. However, in its canonical form, the concept of an individual is not suitable for all types of applications. For example, when evolving structures, such as the topology of a neural network, the number n of parameters x_i is generally not known in advance. Rather, the number n of parameters itself is the result of the actual evolutionary process. As a relief, previous research has developed the concept of variable-length genomes (Lee & Antonsson, 2000; Ramsey et al., 1998; Schiffmann et al., 1993). This option allows an individual to grow and shrink its genome, and thus to adapt to changing demands. But still, with its genome, an individual constitutes a solid, atomic, and monolithic entity, which is fundamental to all evolutionary algorithms.

Even with the concept of variable-length genomes, evolutionary algorithms cannot be directly utilized in all application domains. Section 2 briefly describes an example of smart-appliance ensembles (Aarts, 2004; Saha & Mukherjee, 2003; Weiser, 1993). The term "smart-appliance ensemble" refers to everyday-life devices that are equipped with some computational resources and that are supposed to self-organize according to the users' needs. The following properties are closely linked to smart-appliance ensembles: (1) they are dynamic by their very nature in that devices may join or leave the ensemble at any time without notice; (2) the physical properties of every device are known only to itself and *not* to the rest of

the system; and (3) a smart-appliance ensemble should not induce any user-based modeling and/or administration; rather, devices might be freely added and be freely removed, which also includes device failures.

The discussion presented above suggests that the conventional usage of individuals and genes does not match the dynamic and model-free nature of smart-appliance ensembles. Therefore, Section 3 proposes a new evolutionary framework, called the appliances-go-evolution platform (AGE-P). A key feature of AGE-P is that it physically distributes the genome as well as the variation operators across all the appliances. This way, the genome grows and shrinks as devices come and go, and thus is naturally adapting to an ensemble's dynamics. It should be mentioned, that the idea of distributed evolution is not new. For a good overview, the interested reader is referred to the literature (Alba & Tomassini, 2002; Cahon et al., 2004). In order to gain performance, these methods work on several subpopulations simultaneously, but nonetheless handle genomes in the form of assembled individuals. In contrast, AGE-P abolishes the concept of assembled individuals, not to gain performance, but to ensure consistency.

For validation purposes, Section 4 evaluates the algorithm in the office lighting scenario in which several light sources are distributed within a typical office space. The light sources are supposed to autonomously dim themselves such that all users have the specified illuminations at their desks. In this educational example, neither the number of light sources nor their physical properties are known to the system. Rather, all light sources randomly change their activation, and the resulting effects are subsequently fed back by the sensors. The simulation results indicate that the proposed AGE-P approach is able to solve the office lighting problem and that it is able to cope with all the mentioned system dynamics.

Because of the encouraging simulation results, further research is focusing on a physical real-world example. Section 5 briefly describes the used hardware components; further detail can be found in Appendix A. The experimental results support the simulations to a large extent. However, the real-world experiments have also indicated certain peculiarities that are due to the application's physical limits, which should be addressed by future research. Finally, Section 6 concludes this chapter with a brief discussion.

PROBLEM DESCRIPTION: SMART-APPLIANCE ENSEMBLES

Smart-appliance refers to devices, such as laptops, personal digital assistants, cellular phones, beamers, window blinds, light bulbs, and the like, that are present in everyday life and that are equipped with some communication interface as well as a processing unit. The devices are considered *smart* in that each one executes a program in order to measure and change physical modalities, and they are also able to communicate with others. Smart appliances are called an *ensemble* if the execution of these programs results in a coherent cooperation such that they support their users in an autonomous and non-invasive way (Aarts, 2004; Saha & Mukherjee, 2003; Weiser, 1993).

The smart conference room is a good educational example (Encarnacao & Kirste, 2005). It may consist of a certain number of laptops, a few beamers, some light sources, and window blinds. Suppose that a user is about to do a presentation and that the room is illuminated too much. Then, the ensemble is supposed to properly dim the lights and/or close the window blinds. Other examples include situations from everyday life such as beepers reminding senior persons to take their medicine at the right time.

A common approach for solving this task is to utilize rule-based methods, such as ontologies (Bry et al., 2005; Chen et al., 2004). These approaches require a precise model of the world under consideration. A description would include all dependencies between actuators and sensors, as well as a rule set that describes all possible ensemble actions as responses to the observable user behavior. During operation, the devices choose rules from sensor readings and set the actuators accordingly.

Though modeling may be usable for purely static environments, i.e., statically mounted devices, it can easily fail to work in more dynamic setups, which become more and more common today. For example, attendees may suddenly join or leave a meeting. These users add or remove electronic devices with varying computational resources and capabilities. It might be, for example, that a joining attendee carries a device with superb audio capabilities, which other attendees might wish to use for their own presentation. These system dynamics make it hard or even impossible to centrally care for all possible ensemble combinations. Rather, the present devices should dynamically evaluate their capabilities as a group, and should establish a suitable cooperation.

The brief discussion presented above has already given a first impression of the dynamics of smart-appliance ensembles. In order to allow for the evaluation of a new self-organization concept, this chapter focuses on a simplification, the office lighting scenario. Figure 1 shows a typical office that is equipped with some light sensors and a number of light sources, all being "smart" in the aforementioned manner. Each sensor is tagged with a target value that defines the working level brightness at the associated desk. These target values may arise from a higher-level intention module or may be specified by the user. The goal of the entire system is to set the lights such that the sensors measure the desired values. This scenario already imposes several issues due to unknown facts about the appliances:

- Their number and locations;
- Their properties, such as power or characteristic curves;

Figure 1. The office lighting scenario consists of a number of light sensors and light sources (two and four in this example). The goal is to reach the specified target value at each sensor.

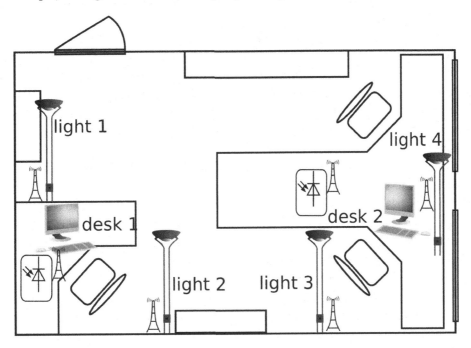

- Their current working states, e.g., working, broken, current brightness, current target value;
- And external influences, such as the current sunlight and the state of the window blinds.

In addition to these issues the following one is fundamental to smart-appliance ensembles: *Any aspect of the entire ensemble may change at any time without any notice.* For example, a light source might be moved (and not moved back) by a housekeeper, or a sensor target value might change due to a different person starting to work at a desk.

Modeling an instance of the office lighting scenario in a static context would be possible, though already difficult, as the dependencies between sensors and light sources may be difficult to determine, due to strong non-linearity in the underlying characteristic curves. However, due to the dynamic nature of smart-appliance ensembles,

every change, e.g., every joining or leaving device, would impose administrative work, which is but desirable and therefore makes modeling not feasible.

Rather, the ensemble should employ a self-organization process in order to work for the users and not vice versa. Derived from the above illumination example, such a self-organization process should be able to cope at least with the following issues:

- The scenario is not observable in terms of missing facts about the devices. Especially, the dependencies (influence) between actuators and sensors are not given explicitly. This prohibits any analytical or semi-analytical, and therefore also modeling-based, method, such as Steepest Descent or Folded Spectrum. Instead, heuristic, black-box optimization methods seem more appropriate.
- The problem to solve is dynamic, as

any aspect or property may change. Furthermore, these changes can appear at any time without notice.

- It is a multi-objective problem, as each sensor constitutes its own objective. Furthermore, objectives may be contradictory to each other. For example, when sensors that are close to each other measure the same physical modality but have very different target values.

- All parameters are constrained as real-world devices can only work in a limited range.

- Human perception is long-lasting tolerant for small errors, whereas large errors are annoying even for short periods. Therefore, a good solution found in short time is preferred over the perfect solution found after a long time. Such human-based expectations exclude basic brute force methods, such as Exhaustive Search or Monte Carlo optimization.

- Human perception is sensible for fast, large changes of physical modalities. Therefore, solutions should be found in a smooth process. This property excludes any method, where successive candidate solutions vary strongly through the parameter space, such as the Monte Carlo method.

To a large extend, evolutionary algorithms seem to be a good choice for the optimization problem at hand; they provide smooth transitions between parents and offspring, they can cope with parameter bounds, they can adapt to changing environmental conditions, and they are able to handle a dynamically changing number of parameters. However, the concept of individuals as containers for genomes requires that they are *aware* of the number of parameters, which is not guaranteed for the given problem. Therefore, Section 3 proposes a modification that allows evolutionary algorithms to even cope with this application type.

THE APPLIANCES-GO-EVOLUTION PLATFORM

This section describes the *appliances-go-evolution platform*, or AGE-P in short, in full detail. The description consists of a brief overview, the distributed setup, the processing loop, the available options to cope with changes, and the options to handle timing and physical constants.

The AGE-P Algorithm: Overview

The key idea of AGE-P is to abandon any central processing; rather, AGE-P *physically* distributes all the operations as well as involved data structures across all devices, i.e., actuators and sensors. This means, for example, that in AGE-P, every gene only resides in the actuator to which it belongs. Consequently, every actuator hosts its own mutation operator, which is applied by the actuator to only its private gene. In other words, none of the other components has any knowledge about an actuator's gene value or its particular variation operator. Similarly, AGE-P distributes the fitness evaluation across the sensors present in a scenario. A consequence of the chosen approach is that removing or adding actuators automatically removes or adds the associated genes from or to the genome. Similarly, removing or adding sensors automatically removes or adds the associated objectives from the fitness evaluation.

The distributed handling of data and operations prohibits some complex evolutionary algorithms, such as the Covariance Matrix algorithm (Hansen & Ostermeier, 2001) or the Smart Hill Climbing algorithm (Xi et al., 2004). These methods require data structures with complete genome information in order to perform a single mutation of a single gene. Storing such data structures on every device and keeping them synchronized contradicts AGE-P's automatic adaption to changes of the ensemble. Therefore, in this first prototype, AGE-P is restricted to simple $\mu + \lambda$-evolution strategies. Furthermore, to ensure smoothness and hence visual acceptance, as discussed in Section 2, AGE-P operates in $1 + \lambda$-mode.

The AGE-P Algorithm: The Distributed Scheme Setup

With the aforementioned conceptual modifications in mind, AGE-P assumes the following setup:

1. All devices are split into two classes, sensors s_i and actuators a_j. Actuators are those devices that influence principal modalities, such as brightness, heat, sound volume, and the like. Sensors, on the other hand, measure modalities.
2. Each sensor hosts its own, private, target value s_i^t. The overall goal of the AGE-P system is that all the differences between the actual sensor measurements s_i and sensor targets s_i^t vanish, i.e., all partial fitness values $d_i = s_i - s_i^t \rightarrow 0$.

It is generally assumed that the target values originate from either higher abstraction levels, such as an intention module, or given user settings. The discussion of the intension module, which is part of the ensemble's infrastructure, is beyond the scope of this chapter.

3. In order to allow for the utilization of a $1 + \lambda$-evolution strategy, every actuator hosts $1+\lambda$ instances (genes) of its activation a_j and the associated fitness values, as well as its private mutation operator m_j.
4. An aggregation function *agg(.)* is used to evaluate the total fitness for the actuator activations a_j, i.e., a solution, from the partial fitness values d_i.

As with the target values, this function is assumed to arise from an intention module or given user settings.

5. AGE-P assumes that a proper communication infrastructure, such as Bluetooth, WLAN, DECT, or the like, is in place and ready to be used.

This setup implies the following generic fitness function to be minimized:

$$f = agg(...,d_i = s_i - s_i^t,...). \qquad (1)$$

with

$$s_i = s_i(...,a_j,...). \qquad (2)$$

The distributed setup is illustrated in Figure 2 for the office illumination scenario and a basic (1+1)- evolution strategy.

The AGE-P Algorithm: The Processing Loop

The processing loop works as follows:

1. Initially, all sensors are tagged with reasonable target values s_i^t. Similarly, all actuators choose suitable activations a_j. In case of light sources, these values might correspond to zero illumination.
2. Periodically, all sensors determine their current sensor values s_i, and broadcast the differences $d_i = s_i - s_i^t$ (Figure 3).
3. On the arrival of new differences d_i, each actuator calculates the fitness of its current activation, i.e., gene, using the aggregate function *agg(.)*. The actuator selects the best genes according to the selection strategy and applies its private mutation operator m_j, i.e., $a_j \leftarrow a_j + m_j$, in order to generate offspring genes for the next generation. As a consequence, the actuators' activations (randomly) change. The physics mediate these changes, which the sensors s_i feed back in the next

Figure 2. The distributed setup of AGE-P. Each sensor hosts its own target value s_i^t. Each actuator hosts $1+\lambda$ instances of its activations a_j (genes), along with the associated fitness values, as well as a private mutation operator m_j.

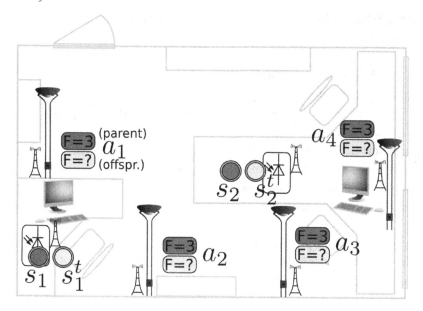

cycle. Please recall that all actuators perform these steps in parallel (Figure 4).

4. The process continues with step 2. Please note that the terms generation and cycle only denote the same, if the (1+1)-evolution strategy is used. Otherwise, the term "cycle" denotes each time the sensors broadcast their partial fitness values, whereas "generation" denotes each time the actuators have completely evaluated their genes and perform selection and mutation.

In AGE-P, the broadcast of the sensor values is the only data exchange, whereas all actuator updates happen asynchronously and hence self-organized. As all actuators work according to the same evolution strategy, they all evaluate the same fitness for a specific genome, and they all come to the same selection decisions. Therefore, this method resembles the traditional evolutionary scheme, but in an entirely distributed manner.

The AGE-P Algorithm: Coping with Dynamic Changes

Dynamic changes, such as changing sun light, broken actuators, changed locations of the actuators and/or sensors, changing sensor targets, new devices, and so forth, might invalidate the previously collected gene-fitness value pairs. To cope with these changes, AGE-P periodically skips the selection process and re-evaluates the best so far values.

Some changes can be detected, such as changing sensor targets, new sensors or new actuators. In these cases, the affected device should broadcast a special trigger message in order to enable the re-establishment of a consistent state.

Other changes may not be detectable, for example failing devices, external influences such as sun light, or changes in the location of devices. To cover these cases, AGE-P applies the fitness re-evaluation at regular time intervals, for example every c cycles, with c being some system con-

Figure 3. Periodically, the sensors broadcast their differences, i.e., partial fitness values, $d_i = s_i - s_i^t$. This is the only data exchange between devices in AGE-P.

stant. Small values of c allow for fast "detection", whereas larger values increase the algorithm's efficiency during the normal working phase.

The AGE-P Algorithm: Timing and Physical Constants

The timing of the sensors, i.e., the frequency of the sensor broadcasts, highly depends on the specifically used devices. For example, filament-based light sources can change only much slower than LED-based light sources, due to inertia of their glowing wire. The easiest solution for this problem is to adapt the broadcast frequency to the slowest device. For the real-world results of the exemplary office lighting scenario, presented in Section 5, this adaption has been realized by hard-coding the frequency into the sensors. Automatic adaption and other timing schemes are subject to further research.

SIMULATION

In order to validate the core concepts of the AGE-P framework, this section considers several simulations that model the main aspects of the office illumination scenario introduced in Section 2.

Methods

The simulations presented in this section model the illumination of a certain number of sensors by a certain number of light sources. The focus of these simulations is not on a realistic modeling of all the physical properties but rather on the consideration of those aspects that are technically relevant for the algorithm. The remainder of this section presents a description of the used parameter settings as well as the considered scenarios.

Configuration of AGE-P: All experiments have been done with (1+1)-AGE-P. This notation indicates that each actuator generates one offspring from one parent and that it selects the better one as the parent for the next generation.

Figure 4. On the arrival of new differences, each actuator independently determines the overall fitness of its current activation a_j. It then selects the best for the next generation and applies its private mutation operator m_j in order to generate new offspring genes.

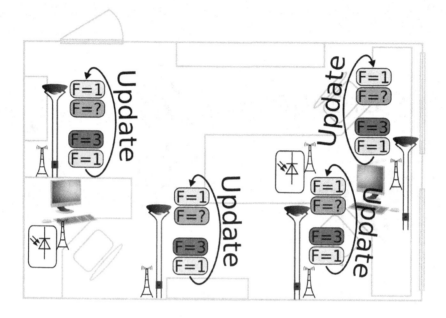

Sensors s_i: AGE-P employs a user-specified number k of sensors s_i. In the validation study presented in Section 4.2, these sensors measure the illumination at various locations, e.g., the users' desks.

Fitness function f: All sensors calculate the difference $d_i = s_i - s_i^t$ as their partial fitness contribution. By means of a global communication infrastructure, all sensors broadcast their differences d_i across the system. Each actuator uses the sum of the squared differences to calculate the ensemble's total fitness:

$$f = \sum_{i=1}^{k} d_i^2 = \sum_{i=1}^{k} (s_i - s_i^t)^2 \qquad (3)$$

This choice of the least square method gives every sensor the same importance, and therefore results in a fair compromise in case of contradicting sensor targets.

Actuators a_j: The simulation employs l actuators a_j, which represent l light sources that are distributed in the environment. Every actuator employs its private mutation operator $a_j \leftarrow a_j + \sigma \cdot N(0,1)$, with σ denoting a private step size and $N(0,1)$ being a gaussian distributed random number. Without loss of generality, all actuator values a_j are bound to $0 \leq a_j \leq 1$. Unless otherwise stated, the step size is set to $\sigma = 0.1$ in all simulation scenarios. Please remember that these actuators are not explicitly known to the sensors, the fitness evaluation, or the system in general. Rather, the environment, i.e., the physics, autonomously mediates their modalities towards the sensors s_i.

Simulation setup: The simulation setup resembles a typical workplace situation as shown in Figure 1, with two light sensors and a certain number of light sources.

For the sake of simplicity, the simulation uses idealized sensors that respond linearly to the incoming brightness. Therefore, the effect of light source a_j on sensor s_i can be modeled by a weight w_{ji}. These weights subsume all the relevant physical effects, such as the light sources' positions, their brightness, their illumination characteristics, etc. In addition, most rooms have one or several windows through which the sun might contribute some global illumination g. In mathematical terms, this chapter utilizes the following (simplified) physical model:

$$s_i = g + \sum_{j=1}^{l} w_{ij} \cdot a_j \qquad (4)$$

with w_{ji} set to values plausible for the scenario depicted in Figure 1. As a result, the overall fitness function in the simulation corresponds to a quadratic function, which is solvable by numeric optimization methods. It might be mentioned again, that the mathematical model of Eq. (4) is *not* part of AGE-P, but solely used for validation purposes within the simulation setup.

Depending on the chosen scenario (please, see below), the weights, the global illumination, the target sensor values, and the number of actuators spontaneously change over time, i.e., $w_{ji}(t)$, $g(t)$, $s_i^t(t)$, and $l(t)$ are all time dependent. For the purpose of readability, the time t is omitted.

Scenario 1, System Startup: At startup time, all actuator values are set to $a_j = 0$ and $g = 0$, i.e., total darkness, and the target sensor values are set to $s_1^t = 0.7$ and $s_2^t = 1.2$. These target values have been chosen deliberately. They model some desired brightness, but have no specific physical interpretation. The ensemble is then responsible to power up the light sources to the desired level. This situation resembles an early winter morning, when the users enter the dark office.

Scenario 2, Scalability: This scenario increases the number of actuators from $l = 2$ to $l = 100$. The goal of this scenario is to test the scaling behavior of AGE-P.

Scenario 3, System Dynamics: This scenario focuses on the ensemble behavior in more dynamic setups. It starts off with two light sources per desk, i.e., $l = 4$. In generation $G = 150$, a light source of each desk fails. Then, in generation $G = 300$, the target sensor value of desk 2 is increased from $s_2^t = 1.2$ to $s_2^t = 1.5$. This might model a situation in which a different person starts working and might prefer a brighter desk. This situation implies that the illumination of the other desk should remain unchanged.

Scenario 4, External Effects: This scenario starts off like the first one. However, in generation $G = 150$, the external (sunshine) illumination is set to $g = 1$, and is reduced to $g = 0.5$ in generation $G = 300$. This scenario models the influence of external modalities, which are outside the control of the ensemble. A further challenge is that during generations $150 < G < 300$, the ensemble cannot reach the specified target values, since the external illumination already exceeds target value s_1^t.

Results

The simulation results of the four experiments are summarized in Figures 5 to 8. On the x-axis, the figures show the generation, and on the y-axis, they show the target sensor values s_i^t, their actual readings s_i, and the global ensemble fitness f (Eq.3). All data were obtained from 500 independent runs. From all these runs, the figures always present the average value of the corresponding generation.

All figures clearly indicate that the global system error closely follows an exponential decrease, and that thus after some adaption time, the AGE-P algorithm arrives at the specified target values, i.e., $s_i \approx s_i^t$. This is not only observable in the simple scenarios 1 and 2, but also in the more dynamic one (Figure 7) in which the target values change over time. The only exception occurs in the fourth scenario (Figure 8) between generations 150 and 300. However, it has already been discussed above that AGE-P cannot reach the target values, since the external illumination is brighter than the specification demands. In other words, the small deviation from the optimum is not due to AGE-P, but due to the physical limitations; but even in this case, AGE-P returns to the optimum shortly after the reduction of the external illumination in generation $G = 300$.

It might be quite interesting to take a look at the

Figure 5. Scenario 1 resembles the basic situation of powering up the light sources from darkness to a desired brightness

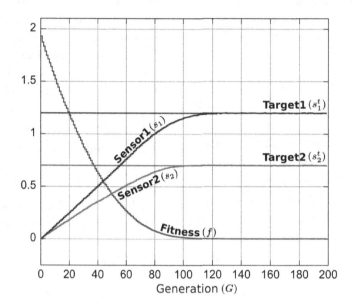

Figure 6. Scenario 2 resembles Scenario 1, but with 100 instead of only 2 light sources

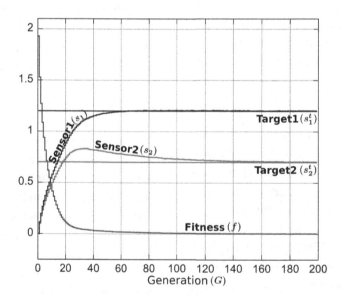

scaling behavior of the proposed self-organization algorithm. Normally, an increasing number of components slow down the system convergence speed. However, a comparison of Figure 5 and Figure 6 indicates that a larger ensemble (i.e., 50 light sources per desk) reaches the optimum even faster than a smaller one (i.e., 2 light sources per desk). This effect is counter-intuitive, but probably due to a significantly increased number of actuator configurations that match the optimum sensor readings.

Another interesting aspect of AGE-P's scaling

Figure 7. Scenario 3 focuses on the ensemble behavior in more dynamic setups. In generation G = 150 two of four light sources fail, in generation G = 300 the second sensor target value is increased from $s_2^t = 1.2$ to $s_2^t = 1.5$

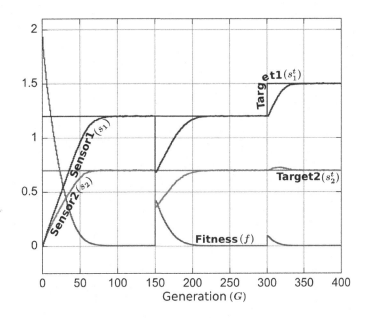

behavior is the independence of the number of actuators with respect to the cost of fitness calculation, selection, and mutation. As each actuator brings in its own processing unit, the fitness calculation cost only depends on the number k of sensors, whereas selection and mutation cost are entirely independent of the ensemble's size.

Rather than focusing on convergence speed, the application at hand focuses on a smooth adaption of its actuators. To this end, the step size σ should be set to rather small values; larger values would speed up the adaptation process, but would also induce significant fluctuations around the optimum, which might be rather annoying in real-world applications. Furthermore, a larger number of actuators, such as a total of 100 light sources used in Scenario 2, requires a smaller step size, such as $\sigma = 0.02$. Otherwise, the fluctuations would be way too large to be acceptable. Therefore, future research will be devoted to a proper distributed self-adaption scheme of the step size σ.

It should be mentioned that the simulation results do not allow conclusions on the real-time behavior of AGE-P. Physical devices suffer from inertia, whereas the simulated devices changed their state with the computer's calculation speed. This issue is addressed in the next section.

PROOF-OF-CONCEPT IN A REAL-WORLD SCENARIO

The *simulations* presented in Section 4 have shown that the AGE-P framework is suitable for the office lighting problem. In addition to these simulations, which consider only selected real-world aspects by their very nature, this section discusses the setup and results of a physical instance of the same application. The details of the used hardware components, which include the wireless communication infrastructure, the light sensors, and the light source controllers, can be found in Appendix A.

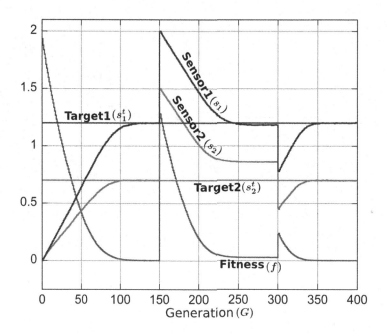

Figure 8. This scenario models the influence of external modalities, which are outside the control of the ensemble. Especially, between G = 150 and G = 300, the external influence already exceeds the target value s_1^t and therefore prevents the system to reach the specified goal.

Office Setup and Methods

Figure 1 has already shown the floor plan of the authors' office space, which has been used to perform the real-world experiments. Two light sensors have been deliberately placed on the desks near the keyboards. Four light sources (standard lamps) have been deliberately placed according to the available space. Finally, a PC is used as a global radio communication router. The remainder of this subsection presents a description of the considered scenarios as well as the used parameter settings.

Configuration of AGE-P: As with the simulation, all experiments have been done with (1+1)-AGE-P. In order to simplify testing and benchmarking, this first real-world version of AGE-P has been realized on a PC. Nonetheless, AGE-P has *not* been configured in any way to match the specifics of the room setup. Though the test system knows about the sensors and light sources, it does not know about their relation, i.e.,

brighter light sources cause higher sensor readings. Furthermore, it is not aware of the light sources' positions, nor does it know whether or not a light source is plugged in.

Light sensors: The light sensors read their values from their analog-to-digital converters, and send these 10-bit values to the PC, where they are linearly transformed to values ranging from 0 to 1. A value of 0 corresponds to almost total darkness, whereas a value of 1 corresponds to high brightness. In the authors' office, the typical room brightness on a cloudy day ranges from values between 0.6 (desk 1) and 0.8 (desk 2).

Light sources: The brightness values of the light sources are normalized and bound to [0,1], and are also hosted on the central PC. These values are linearly transformed to timer values for the light sources' phase angle controls, and then send to the light sources.

Fitness function: Fitness calculation happens exactly the same way as has been done in the simulation (Eq.(3)). However, this time, the overall fitness function is way more complicated than in the simulation, due to strong non-linearity in the characteristic curves of light sources and sensors.

Mutation: The module of every light source employs its private mutation operator $a_j \leftarrow a_j + \sigma \cdot N(0,1)$, with a_j denoting the internal representation of the jth light source's brightness. After mutation, the value is rebound to $[0,1]$. In the mutation operator, σ denotes a private step size. It has been deliberately set to 0.2 for all scenarios and all light sources. $N(0,1)$ denotes a gaussian distributed random number.

Re-evaluation: Each second step, mutation is left out in favor of re-evaluation.

Scenarios: In this setup, all experiments from Section 4 have been performed, except the scalability test, as 100 light sources were not at the authors' disposal. Due to the strong nonlinearity of the sensors, brightness could only be measured sufficiently for quit dark scenarios. Otherwise, the normal daylight already dominates the office's illumination. Therefore, the office's window blinds had been closed and a very cloudy day had been chosen for the experiments, as sunny days turned out to be too bright even with closed window blinds.

For all scenarios, the target values of the sensors have been deliberately chosen, such that the light sources could theoretically provide the desired brightness levels.

Scenario 1, System Startup: This scenario directly corresponds to Scenario 1 of the simulation. Light sources 1 and 3 are used, each set to darkness at the beginning. The target sensor value for desk 1 and 2 are set to $s_1^t = 0.45$ and to $s_2^t = 0.6$, respectively.

Scenario 2, System Dynamics: This is the equivalent of Scenario 3 of the simulation. All four light sources are used. It starts off with all light sources set to darkness. After 40 generations, one light source of each desk fails. In generation 80, the target value of sensor 2 is decreased from $s_2^t = 0.6$ to $s_2^t = 0.5$. The target value of sensor 1 is set to $s_1^t = 0.5$ for the entire run.

Scenario 3, External Effects: This scenario is the pendant of the fourth simulation scenario. Again, only light sources 1 and 3 are used. The scenario starts off like the first one. However, after 40 generations, the ordinary room illumination is switched on, and after 80 generations switched off again. This scenario focuses on the ensembles behavior in the presence of external modalities that are beyond the control of the system. A further challenge is that the ensemble cannot reach the optimum during this time, as the room illumination is too bright. However, after generation 80 the system must find the optimum again.

Results

The results of the real-world experiments are summarized in Figs. 9 to 11. On the x-axis, these figures show the generation, and on the y-axis they show the target sensor values s_i^t, their actual readings s_i, and the overall ensemble fitness f, i.e., the global error. The figures show the average values of 50 independent runs.

In all figures the error closely follows an exponential decrease, such that after some adaption time, AGE-P approaches the optimum, i.e., $s_i \approx s_i^t$. This is not only observable in the simple Scenario 1, but also in the more dynamic Scenarios 2 and 3, where some target sensor values change and external influences appear. The only major exception occurs in the middle of Scenario 3, where the room illumination is switched on. Even though AGE-P was completely switching off all light sources, expressed in the slight decrease of the error between generations 40 and 80, the room illumination itself exceeds the desired brightness levels by far. Nevertheless, after the room illumination was switched off again in generation 80, AGE-P quickly returns back to the original optimum.

Another minor exception occurred in generation 40 in Scenario 2, where two of the four light sources failed. Even though AGE-P was setting all light sources to their maximum values, they

Figure 9. Scenario 1 resembles the basic situation of powering up the light sources from darkness to the desired brightness

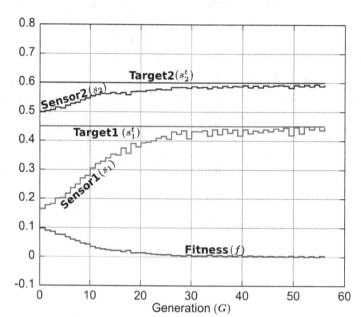

are simply not powerful enough to satisfy the user demands. Both exceptional cases are not due to limitations of AGE-P, but due to physical limitations themselves.

Inertia of the used light sources and sensors allowed only about 5 changes per second, which corresponds to 1/5 seconds per generations. This is the time constant that has been used for the experiments presented above. Therefore, it took AGE-P about 10 seconds to converge, respectively to reconverge after changes. During this time, no step size adaption was performed and flickering of the light sources was clearly noticeable. Obviously, 10 seconds of flickering is unacceptable for humans. Therefore, AGE-P should exploit further options to integrate a step size adaption method into its distributed processing scheme, starting with very large steps in order to find a good solution within the first few seconds. Fine-adjustment could then be performed at slow speed, i.e., small step sizes, that do not cause noticeable flickering. Furthermore, AGE-P should exploit the fact that devices, such as lamps, can perform small changes

faster than large changes. This could be used to speed up the fine-adjustment phase.

CONCLUSION

This chapter has proposed a distributed evolutionary algorithm, called AGE-P, for the self-organization of smart-appliance ensembles. A key feature of this algorithm is that it does not maintain assembled genomes in the traditional sense. Rather, AGE-P physically distributes all gene values across all devices, and evaluates only the resulting sensor modalities. Furthermore, the application of the variation operators is done by the actuators rather than a central processing instance.

The presented results from simulation and real-world experiments indicate that the proposed method is suitable as the self-organization mechanism for smart-appliance ensembles. In addition to the required basic adaptation capabilities, the AGE-P framework scales well, as has been shown

Figure 10. Scenario 2 focuses on the ensemble's behavior in more dynamic setups. At generation $G = 40$, two of the four light sources failed, and at generation $G = 80$, the second target sensor value was decreased from $s_2^t = 0.6$ to $s_2^t = 0.5$.

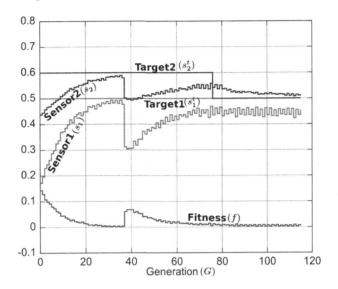

Figure 11. This scenario examines the influence of external modalities, which are outside the control of the ensemble. Between $G = 40$ and $G = 80$, the room illumination, which is external to the system, already exceeds the target sensor values and therefore prevents the system to reach the specified goal

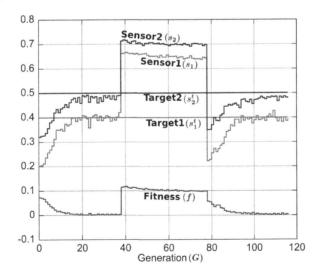

in the simulation. Furthermore, AGE-P is also able to cope with the inherent system dynamics of those ensembles, such as failing lights and changing user demands.

Obviously, the office lighting scenario covers only a fraction of the possible everyday life scenarios. Therefore, future research will be devoted to the integration of further modalities, such as sound, which is orthogonal to light, or power consumption, which is even opposed to both light and sound. As most devices, light sources operate non-linearly. Thus, different configurations result in equivalent outcomes but with different power consumptions. In order to exploit this phenomenon, AGE-P will explore further aggregation functions, such as weighted sums, hierarchies or Pareto Fronts (Veldhuizen & Lamont, 1998).

As has been said above, not all modalities interact with each other; examples are light and sound. On the other hand, the AGE-P algorithm currently varies all actuators in order to find solutions, which can be very disturbing. Therefore, future versions of AGE-P will be enhanced with an ontology-learning component. If, for example, the Covariance Matrix algorithm could somehow be applied to AGE-P, then, after a while, its matrix could be used to derive an ontology that would consist of a clustering of the actuators with respect to the sensors they influence. Such a "learned" ontology might enable the entire system to significantly improve the system's adaptation speed and actuator smoothness. Furthermore, with cluster-learning capabilities, AGE-P could be used as a pre-configuration system, for example in large event halls with many speakers and light sources. Given a night or so before the event and a number of sensors within the hall, AGE-P could provide useful information for the adjustment of light sources and speakers.

The results also show that the behavior of AGE-P depends on the chosen step size σ of the mutation operators, privately employed in every actuator. Obviously, larger values of σ speed up the adaption process, but also induce significant fluctuations around the optimum. To this end, the step size was chosen as a compromise between adaption time and fluctuation. However, the real-world experiments revealed that (1) even small brightness fluctuations are noticeable and annoying, and (2) any time longer than a few seconds to adjust the lights is unacceptable. Furthermore, the real-world experiments have shown that AGE-P has to cope with varying time constants. For example, slight brightness changes can be performed faster than drastic brightness changes. These tim-

ing constants depend on the chosen devices and potentially other system parameters. Therefore, future research will be devoted to the development of an adequate self-adaption mechanism.

ACKNOWLEDGMENT

The authors gratefully thank Ralf Joost and Ulf Ochsenfahrt for encouraging discussions and valuable comments on draft versions of this chapter, as well as Mathias Haefke for building up the hardware. This work was supported in part by the DFG graduate school 1424.

REFERENCES

Aarts, E. H. L. (2004). Ambient intelligence: A multimedia perspective. *IEEE MultiMedia, 11*(1), 12–19. doi:10.1109/MMUL.2004.1261101

Alba, E., & Tomassini, M. (2002). Parallelism and evolutionary algorithms. *IEEE Transactions on Evolutionary Computation, 6*(5), 443–462. doi:10.1109/TEVC.2002.800880

Back, T., Hammel, U., & Schwefel, H.-P. (1997). Evolutionary computation: Comments on the history and current state. *IEEE Transactions on Evolutionary Computation, 1*(1), 3–17. doi:10.1109/4235.585888

Bry, F., Hattori, T., Hiramatsu, K., Okadome, T., Wieser, C., & Yamada, T. (2005). Context modeling in owl for smart building services. In S. Brass & C. Goldberg (Eds.), *Tagungsband zum 17. GI-Workshop über Grundlagen von Datenbanken (17th GI-Workshop on the Foundations of Databases)* (pp. 38–42).

Cahon, S., Melab, N., & Talbi, E.-G. (2004). Building with paradiseo reusable parallel and distributed evolutionary algorithms. *Parallel Computing, 30*(5-6), 677–697. doi:10.1016/j.parco.2003.12.010

Chen, H., Perich, F., Finin, T., & Joshi, A. (2004). Soupa: Standard ontology for ubiquitous and pervasive applications. In *Proceedings of the International Conference on Mobile and Ubiquitous Systems: Networking and Services* (pp. 258–267).

Chipcon (2004). *Cc1010 data sheet revision 1.3.* Available at www-mtl.mit.edu/Courses/6.111/labkit/datasheets/CC1010.pdf.

Encarnacao, J. L., & Kirste, T. (2005). Ambient intelligence: Towards smart appliances ensembles. In *From Integrated Publication and Information Systems to Information and Knowledge Environments*, volume 3379 of *Lecture Notes in Computer Science* (pp. 261–270). Springer-Verlag.

Fogel, D. B. (1995). *Evolutionary Computation: Toward A New Philosophy of Machine Intelligence.* IEEE Press, Piscataway, NJ, USA.

Goldberg, D. E. (1989). *Genetic Algorithms in Search, Optimization and Machine Learning.* Addison-Wesley Longman Publishing Co., Inc., Boston, MA, USA.

Hansen, N., & Ostermeier, A. (2001). Completely derandomized self-adaptation in evolution strategies. *Evolutionary Computation, 9*(2), 159–195. doi:10.1162/106365601750190398

Lee, C.-Y., & Antonsson, E. K. (2000). Variable length genomes for evolutionary algorithms. In *Proceedings of the Genetic and Evolutionary Computation Conference (GECCO '00)*, (p. 806).

Ramsey, C. L., Jong, K. A. D., Grefenstette, J. J., Wu, A. S., & Burke, D. S. (1998). Genome length as an evolutionary self-adaptation. In *PPSN V: Proceedings of the 5th International Conference on Parallel Problem Solving from Nature* (pp. 345–356), London, UK: Springer-Verlag.

Rechenberg, I. (1994). *Evolutionsstrategie.* Frommann-Holzboog Verlag, Stuttgart, Germany.

Saha, D., & Mukherjee, A. (2003). Pervasive computing: A paradigm for the 21st century. *Computer, 36*(3), 25–31. doi:10.1109/MC.2003.1185214

Schiffmann, W., Joost, M., & Werner, R. (1993). Application of genetic algorithms to the construction of topologies for multilayer perceptrons. In *Proceedings of the International Conference on Artificial Neural Nets and Genetic Algorithms* (pp. 676–682).

Schwefel, H.-P. P. (1995). *Evolution and Optimum Seeking: The Sixth Generation.* John Wiley & Sons, Inc., New York, NY, USA.

Veldhuizen, D. A. V., & Lamont, G. B. (1998). Evolutionary computation and convergence to a pareto front. In *Stanford University, California* (pp. 221–228). Morgan Kaufmann.

Weiser, M. (1993). Some computer science issues in ubiquitous computing. *Communications of the ACM, 36*(7), 75–84. doi:10.1145/159544.159617

Xi, B., Liu, Z., Raghavachari, M., Xia, C. H., & Zhang, L. (2004). A smart hill-climbing algorithm for application server configuration. In S. I. Feldman, M. Uretsky, M. Najork & C. E. Wills (Eds.), *Proceedings of the 13th international conference on World Wide Web, (WWW 2004)* (pp. 287–296). ACM Press.

APPENDIX A

Hardware Components

Figure 12 depicts the general hardware configuration used in the real-world experiments. It can be seen that the hardware components consist of several radio communication modules as well as controllable light sources and light sensors. For the light sources, customary standard lamps have been used, enhanced by a circuitry for controlling the brightness, which itself is connected to a radio unit. The light sensors have been realized using simple photo diodes, which have also been connected to radio units. Finally, a standard PC has been connected to such a radio unit via a serial communication line. This enables the PC to act as a global router for all radio transmission, which in turn allows easy shifting of tasks between the distributed units and the central PC. During development, this property has been strongly utilized, as the current initial testing version performs the majority of all tasks on the PC, having full control over all processing and data, whereas the final version will merely use the PC to set target values at the sensors and to read all the state information from the ensemble, in order to create statistical results.

Radio Communication

The required radio communication has been realized with the CC1010 microcontrollers (Figure 12), which are widely used and manufactured by Chipcon (Chipcon, 2004). This controller contains an integrated radio unit, and is shipped with a well-documented standard software library, which allows programming of the radio unit by means of a simple datagram-socket protocol. This relieves the developer from additional hardware and software tinkering work, especially from connecting a stand-alone radio unit to a general-purpose microcontroller. The CC1010 radio module achieves a data rate of up to 76.8Kbit/s, which is sufficient for the task at hand. Furthermore, the on-board 8-bit controller is clocked at 14.7MHz, which is certainly powerful enough not only to serve as a mere radio unit, but also to perform the other required tasks, such as controlling a light source, reading and processing the sensor readings, and executing the required evolutionary operators, at the same time (see Figure 13).

Figure 12. The hardware setup consists of photo diodes, standard lamps, and a PC, that are all connected to radio communication modules. The PC acts as a global router for all the radio messages.

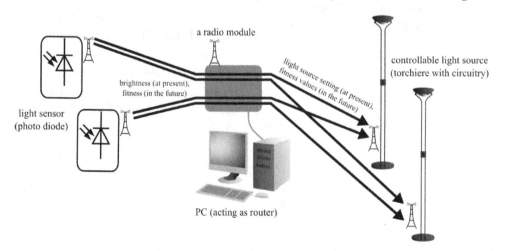

Figure 13. The radio communication is realized by the widely used CC1010 controller from Chipcon

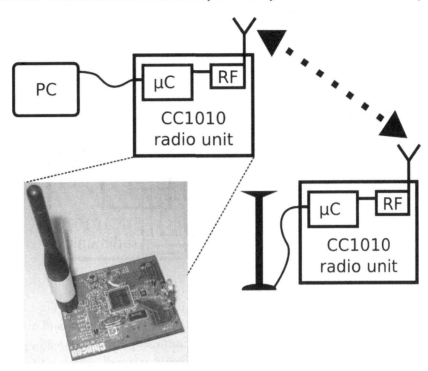

The Light Sensor

Figure 14 shows the realization of the light sensor. A simple photo diode of type A1060-12 along with a 10KΩ resistor is directly connected to the on-board analog-to-digital converter of a CC1010. Again, the standard software library provides functions that allow comfortable access to the converter.

Light Source Control

The task of this controller is to set a light source's brightness according to an incoming integer value. A main challenge is that both parties operate at very different voltages: the radio unit has a power supply of 3.3V, whereas the light source operates at 220V AC and 50Hz. This challenge is normally solved by using two modules: a power module and a zero-crossing-detection module. For safety reasons, these modules are entirely detached from the radio unit via two opto-couplers.

Figure 15 depicts the entire controller. The top part shows the 3.3V power supply for the radio unit. The lower part depicts the aforementioned zero-crossing-detection module and the power module. The TIC206M triac is the main component of the power module. After it has been activated it delivers the 220V to the light bulb. However, once the high-voltage AC current crosses the zero line, the triac blocks the power supply until it is activated again. For the triac's activation a very short pulse is sufficient which is transferred from the radio unit to the triac via the opto-coupled MOC3020 diac.

The zero-crossing-detection module sends a signal to the radio unit whenever the 220AC voltage drops to zero, which happens a hundred times per second. The zero voltage detection is done as follows.

Figure 14. Brightness is measured with a simple photo diode and a resistor, which are directly connected to the on-board analog-to-digital converter

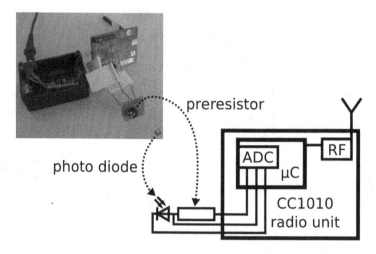

First of all, the alternate current is converted to a direct current, which drives the LED of a standard 4N25 opto-coupler. Due to the driving alternate current, this LED switches on and off a hundred times per second, which is detected by a light-sensitive transistor (also part of the 4N25 opto-coupler). The transistors signal is then attenuated by two 74HC14N Schmitt triggers, which activate the microcontroller's interrupt request line. After the occurrence of an interrupt, the microcontroller waits the time as specified by the internal integer value, and then activates the triac as described above.

Figure 16 shows the controller's overall behavior. At regular times, it switches the light source's power supply on and off. Since this happens a hundred times per second and since the physical time constants of the light bulbs are quite high, the light source emits a constant illumination with a controllable intensity. Figure 17 shows the actual hardware.

Figure 15. The light source controller connects the low-voltage radio unit with the high-voltage light source. Details can be found in the text.

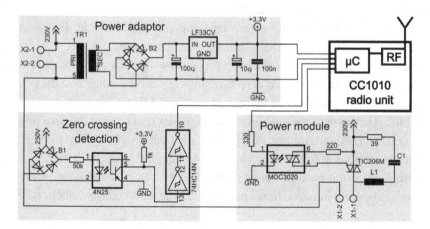

Figure 16. The phase angle control sets the light bulb's brightness by switching on and off the power supply a hundred times per second. Due to physical reasons no flickering is noticeable.

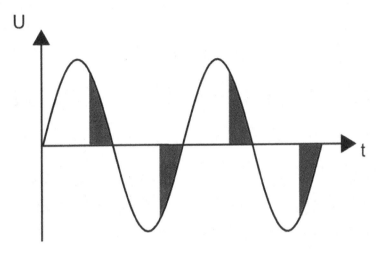

Figure 17. The developed hardware safely mounted in a CD spindle

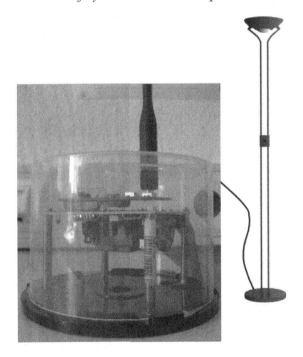

Chapter 9

Modelling Biological Processes Naturally using Systemic Computation:
Genetic Algorithms, Neural Networks, and Artificial Immune Systems

Erwan Le Martelot
University College London, UK

Peter J Bentley
University College London, UK

ABSTRACT

Natural systems provide unique examples of computation in a form very different from contemporary computer architectures. Biology also demonstrates capabilities such as adaptation, self-repair, and self-organisation that are becoming increasingly desirable for our technology. To address these issues a computer model and architecture with natural characteristics is presented. Systemic computation is Turing Complete; it is designed to support biological algorithms such as neural networks, evolutionary algorithms and models of development, and shares the desirable capabilities of biology not found in conventional architectures. In this chapter the authors describe the first platform implementing such computation, including programming language, compiler and virtual machine. They first demonstrate that systemic computing is crash-proof and can recover from severe damage. The authors then illustrate various benefits of systemic computing through several implementations of bio-inspired algorithms: a self-adaptive genetic algorithm, a bio-inspired model of artificial neural networks, and finally we create an "artificial organism" - a program with metabolism that eats data, expels waste, clusters cells based on data inputs and emits danger signals for a potential artificial immune system. Research on systemic computation is still ongoing, but the research presented in this chapter shows that computers that process information according to this bio-inspired paradigm have many of the features of natural systems that we desire.

DOI: 10.4018/978-1-60566-705-8.ch009

INTRODUCTION

Does a biological brain compute? Can a real ant colony solve a travelling salesman problem? Does a human immune system do anomaly detection? Can natural evolution optimise chunks of DNA in order to make an organism better suited to its environment?

The intuitive answer to these questions is increasingly: we think so. Indeed, researchers are so impressed by the capabilities of nature that biological systems have become highly significant to computer science as examples of highly complex self-organising systems that perform tasks in parallel with no centralised method of control and show homeostatic behaviour. For example, in nature, old and potentially damaged cells are constantly being replaced and DNA repaired (Darnell, 1990). The lifespan of cells is shorter than the life of an organism, so fault-tolerance and self-maintenance are essential for the survival of the organism. The failure of some components does not destroy the overall organism; cell death is an important part of staying alive.

Features such as self-organisation, fault-tolerance or self-repair, found in natural computation, would be of great interest for our technologies. Today, software regularly crashes, top of the line robots break down on the wrong kind of ground, power distribution networks fail under unforeseen circumstances (Bentley, 2007a). With the increasing performance, potential and complexity in machines and software, it has become increasingly difficult to ensure reliability in systems.

But how can useful biological features be achieved in computers? While the theory of computation is well understood through the concept of the Universal Turing Machine (UTM) (Turing, 1936), practical issues of architecture remain problematical for computer science and computer-based technologies. The apparent dichotomy between systems of "natural computation" such as the brain, and computer systems based on classical designs shows that even though the two

systems of computation might be mathematically equivalent at a certain level of abstraction, they are practically so dissimilar that they become incompatible.

We can state that natural computation is stochastic, asynchronous, parallel, homeostatic, continuous, robust, fault tolerant, autonomous, open-ended, distributed, approximate, embodied, has circular causality, and is complex. The traditional von Neumann architecture is deterministic, synchronous, serial, heterostatic, batch, brittle, fault intolerant, human-reliant, limited, centralised, precise, isolated, uses linear causality and is simple. The incompatibilities are clear.

Just as the development of Prolog enabled elegant and precise implementations of logical expressions, so the development of a paradigm where systems could be defined in a manner that resembles their true structures would improve our ability to implement bio-inspired systems.

To address these issues, (Bentley, 2007b) introduced Systemic Computation (SC), a new model of computation and corresponding computer architecture based on a systemics world-view and supplemented by the incorporation of natural characteristics (listed above). Such characteristics are not natively present in current conventional paradigms and models of natural processes that run on conventional computers must simulate these features. This often leads to slower and less straightforward implementations compared to analytical or linear algorithms for which computers are well suited. Also in contrast, systemic computation stresses the importance of structure and interaction, supplementing traditional reductionist analysis with the recognition that circular causality, embodiment in environments and emergence of hierarchical organisations all play vital roles in natural systems.

In this chapter we present the first platform implementing systemic computation, including programming language, compiler and virtual machine. Using this platform we first show by implementing a genetic algorithm how systemic computing enables fault-tolerance and easily integrated self-repair, fundamental properties of natural computing and highly desirable features in modern computational systems. Then, to demonstrate further benefits of SC programming, we provide several implementations of bio-inspired algorithms: genetic algorithms, artificial neural networks and artificial immune systems. These illustrate how SC enables ease, clarity and fidelity in the modelling of bio-inspired systems, but also respectively illustrate advanced and desirable features provided natively by SC.

Reusing the genetic algorithm, we show how self-adaptation can be added with the minimum of additional code. We then present an artificial neural network model, designed to exploit local knowledge and asynchronous computation, significant natural properties of biological neural networks and naturally handled by SC. Exploiting these built-in properties, which come for free, the model enables neural structure flexibility without reducing performance. Finally, we describe an implementation of an Artificial Immune System in SC, presenting an original kind of program, relying on a metabolism that can eat data, expel waste, and shows excellent abilities to detect anomalies in its diet.

Research on systemic computation is still ongoing, but the research presented in this chapter shows that computers that process information according to this bio-inspired paradigm have many of the features of natural systems that we desire.

BACKGROUND

Systemic computation (SC) is not the only model of computation to emerge from studies of biology. The potential of biology had been discussed in the late 1940s by Von Neumann who dedicated some of his final work to automata and self-replicating machines (von Neumann, 1966). Cellular automata have proven themselves to

be a valuable approach to emergent, distributed computation (Wolfram, 2002). Generalisations such as constrained generating procedures and collision-based computing provide new ways to design and analyse emergent computational phenomena (Holland, 1998; Adamatzky, 2001). Bio-inspired grammars and algorithms introduced notions of homeostasis (for example in artificial immune systems), fault-tolerance (as seen in embryonic hardware) and parallel stochastic learning, (for example in swarm intelligence and genetic algorithms) (Bentley, 2007b; Fogel and Corne, 2003).

However, most researchers in this area do not concern themselves with the nature of computation. Instead they focus on algorithm development for traditional processors. Many algorithms or exploration techniques were developed over the past decades, whether inspired from evolution with genetic algorithms and evolutionary strategies, the human immune system with artificial immune systems, flocking and insect swarming with swarm intelligence, the brain with artificial neural networks, competition for survival with Core Wars (Dewdney, 1984) and self-replication and speciation with Tierra (Ray, 1990) or Avida (Ofria and Wilke, 2004). Dedicated languages and frameworks such as Push and PushGP (Spector, 2001) were also designed and developed to assist implementation of evolutionary algorithms. However, without tackling the underlying architecture, the underlying incompatibilities of conventional computation cause significant problems – even modern supercomputers struggle to provide sufficient flexibility and power to enable the desired natural characteristics.

Significant research is underway to develop new computer architectures, whether distributed computing (or multiprocessing), computer clustering, grid computing, ubiquitous computing or speckled computing (Arvind and Wong, 2004). Specific hardware has also been designed to integrate natural features, for example the POEtic project (Tempesti et al., 2002), which aimed at creating a platform organised with a similar hierarchy as found in biological systems, and capable of implementing systems inspired by all the three major axes (phylogenesis, ontogenesis, and epigenesis) of bio-inspiration in digital hardware. An improved version of this platform, currently under development, is known as Perplexus (Upegui et al., 2007). The Embryonics project (Tempesti et al., 2007) is also another project that investigated such hardware for reliability, involving self-replicating hardware. Looking at more generic hardware, FPGAs and wireless sensor networks offer crucial features for distributed and parallel computation; Reaction-diffusion Computing (Adamatzky, 2002) or DNA Computing (Adleman, 1994) also provide platforms able to host certain types of bio-inspired computation.

Both inside and outside of the research laboratories, computation is increasingly becoming more parallel, decentralised and distributed. However, while hugely complex computational systems will be soon feasible and more and more technologies become available, their organisation and management is still the subject of research. Ubiquitous computing may enable computation anywhere, and bio-inspired models may enable improved capabilities such as reliability and fault-tolerance, but there has been no coherent architecture that combines both technologies.

To unify notions of biological computation and electronic computation, (Bentley 2007b) introduced SC as a suggestion of necessary features for a computer architecture compatible with current processors, yet designed to provide native support for common characteristics of biological processes. Systemic computation provides an alternative approach. With SC, organisms and software programs now share a common definition of computation. In this chapter we show how this paradigm leads to native fault-tolerance, easily-implemented self-maintaining programs, fidelity and clarity of modelling, and how program improvement can simply emerge from adding a small number of new systems to some existing code, in contrast to redesigning and rewriting a traditional implementation.

SYSTEMIC COMPUTATION

"Systemics" is a world-view where traditional reductionist approaches are supplemented by holistic, system-level analysis. Instead of relying on a notion of compartmentalising a natural system into components, analysing each in isolation, and then attempting to fit the pieces into a larger jigsaw, a systemic approach would recognise that each component may be intricately entwined with the other components and would attempt to analyse the interplay between components and their environment at many different levels of abstractions (Eriksson, 1997).

Systemic computation (Bentley, 2007b) is a method of computation which uses the systemics world-view and incorporates all of the attributes of natural computation listed previously. Instead of the traditional centralised view of computation, here all computation is distributed. There is no separation of data and code, or functionality into memory, ALU, and I/O.

Systemic computation stresses the importance of structure and interaction, supplementing traditional reductionist analysis with the recognition that circular causality, embodiment in environments and emergence of hierarchical organisations all play vital roles in natural systems. Systemic computation makes the following assertions:

- Everything is a system
- Systems can be transformed but never destroyed or created from nothing
- Systems may comprise or share other nested systems
- Systems interact, and interaction between systems may cause transformation of those systems where the nature of that transformation is determined by a contextual system

- All systems can potentially act as context and affect the interactions of other systems, and all systems can potentially interact in some context
- The transformation of systems is constrained by the scope of systems, and systems may have partial membership within the scope of a system
- Computation is transformation

Computation has always meant transformation in the past, whether it is the transformation of position of beads on an abacus, or of electrons in a CPU. But this simple definition also allows us to call the sorting of pebbles on a beach, or the transcription of protein, or the growth of dendrites in the brain, valid forms of computation. Such a definition is important, for it provides a common language for biology and computer science, enabling both to be understood in terms of computation. Previous work (Bentley, 2007b) has analysed natural evolution, neural networks and artificial immune systems as systemic computation systems and shown that all have the potential to be Turing Complete and thus be fully programmable. In this chapter we present the state of the art of the research in SC, focussing on the more applied use of SC, for computer modelling.

In systemic computation, everything is a system, and computations arise from interactions between systems. Two systems can interact in the context of a third system. All systems can potentially act as contexts to determine the effect of interacting systems. Systems have some form of "shape" that determines which other systems they can interact with, and the nature of that interaction. In a digital environment, one convenient way to represent and define a system (i.e. its "shape") is as a binary string. (Note that the choice of binary strings for the systems is a suggestion of implementation compatible with current electronic hardware. Implementing SC using alternative computational units like with DNA-Computing (Adleman, 1994) or Reaction-

diffusion Computing (Adamatzky, 2002) would clearly lead to a different type of implementation.) Each system (i.e. here string) is divided into three parts: two schemata and one kernel. These three parts can be used to hold anything (data, typing, etc) in binary as shown in Figure 1.

The primary purpose of the kernel is to define an interaction result (and also optionally to hold data). The two schemata define which subject systems may interact in this context as shown in Figure 2. The schemata thus act as shape templates, looking for systems matching its shape. The resultant transformation of two interacting systems is dependent on the context in which that interaction takes place. A different context will produce a different transformation. How templates and matching is done precisely is explained later in the platform section.

Thus, each system comprises three elements: two schemata that define the possible systems that may interact in the context of the current system, and a kernel which defines how the two interacting systems will be transformed. This behaviour enables more realistic modelling of natural processes, where all behaviour emerges through the interaction and transformation of components in a given context. It incorporates the idea of circular causality (e.g. 'A' may affect 'B' and simultaneously 'B' may affect 'A') instead of the linear causality inherent in traditional computation (Wheeler and Clark, 1999). Such ideas are vital for accurate computational models of biology and yet currently are largely ignored. Circular causality is the norm for biological systems. For example,

Figure 1. A system used primarily for data storage. The kernel (in the circle) and the two schemata (at the end of the two arms) hold data

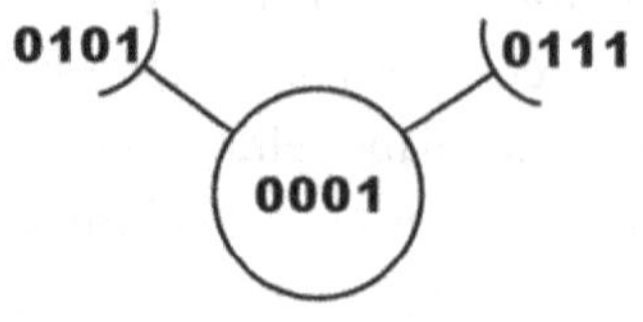

Figure 2. (a) A system acting as a context. Its kernel defines the result of the interaction while its schemata define allowable interacting systems (using a given code discussed later). (b) An interacting context. The contextual system S_c matches two appropriate systems S_1 and S_2 with its schemata (here "abaa" and "aaba" respectively matched S1 and S2) and specifies the transformation resulting from their interaction as defined in its kernel

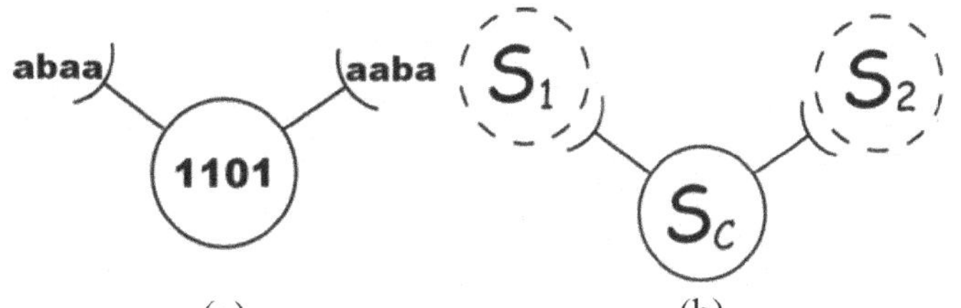

(a)   (b)

consider two plants growing next to each other, the leaves of each affecting the growth of the leaves of the other at the same time; in the interaction of any two systems there is always some effect to both systems.

Systemic computation also exploits the concept of scope. In all interacting systems in the natural world, interactions have a limited range or scope, beyond which two systems can no longer interact (for example, binding forces of atoms, chemical gradients of proteins, physical distance between physically interacting individuals). In cellular automata this is defined by a fixed number of neighbours for each cell. Here, the idea is made more flexible and realistic by enabling the scope of interactions to be defined and altered by another system. Thus a system can also contain or be contained by other systems. Interactions can only occur between systems within the same scope. Therefore any interaction between two systems in the context of a third implies that all three are contained within at least one common super-system, where that super-system may be one of the two interacting systems.

From a more philosophical approach, systems can be regarded as holons (Koestler, 1989), being a whole but also parts (building blocks) of a bigger whole, being autonomous, self-reliant and independent, affecting and being affected by a hierarchy (holarchy).

SYSTEMIC COMPUTATION CALCULUS VS STOCHASTIC PI-CALCULUS

Systemic computation can be expressed using a graph notation and a more formal calculus. Methods such as Stochastic PI-Calculus provide an alternative way of expressing biological processes formally. However, the origins of PI-Calculus lie in computer science and communications theory, which is evident from the non-intuitive method of expressing the interaction and transformation of entities. For example, the binding model *H + Cl <--> HCl* (used by (Phillips and Cardelli, 2004) to introduce and teach Stochastic PI-Calculus) shows the difference in clarity of expression very clearly. In the Stochastic PI-Calculus model (Figure 3) H donates its electron which is shared between H and Cl. Cl then loses an electron and H gains it to break the bond. Binding of H and Cl is never explicit – they are never actually linked in the model, simply transformed from H to H_Bound and Cl to CL_Bound. This confusion of abstractions (are atoms being modelled or electrons, protons and neutrons?) and confusion of bindings (which atom is bound to which?) results in a partial and somewhat cryptic model.

In contrast, when using SC we can remain at one level of abstraction – the atom. We do not need to model individual electrons for such a simple

Figure 3. Graphical representation of Stochastic PI-Calculus model and corresponding notation of binding model H + Cl <--> HCl (from (Phillips and Cardelli, 2004)). It is not obvious that H and Cl become bound to each other, despite this being the purpose of the model

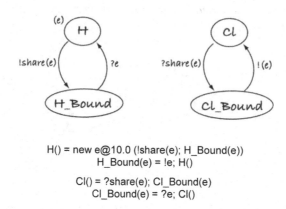

H() = new e@10.0 (!share(e); H_Bound(e))
H_Bound(e) = !e; H()

Cl() = ?share(e); Cl_Bound(e)
Cl_Bound(e) = ?e; Cl()

model of binding. All we need to do is ensure the scopes of each atom overlap. The result in SC graph form (Figure 4) looks like a familiar representation of the molecular model for HCl (Figure 5), making the model remarkably intuitive and simple to understand. But most significantly, the systemic computation version includes the cause of the binding – energy. The whole reaction between the two atoms is impossible without sufficient energy – a detail that is necessary to include in SC (the interaction between the atoms

must occur in some context) but can be and has been ignored in Stochastic PI Calculus, resulting in an incomplete model.

Both approaches enable multiple atoms and bindings to be modelled by the addition of parameters. But only SC permits the modelling of this process in more detail by revealing the deeper systems (protons, neutrons and electrons) hidden within the H and Cl systems without changing the overall structure of the model. It should thus be evident that by designing systemic computation

Figure 4. Systemic computation graph model and corresponding notation of binding model H + Cl <--> HCl. Note that the diagram closely resembles standard diagrammatic representations of this chemical process (Figure 5) and clearly shows how H and Cl become bound in a symmetrical way

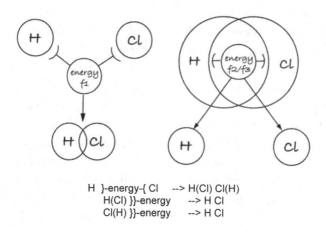

H }-energy-{ Cl   --> H(Cl) Cl(H)
H(Cl) }}-energy   --> H Cl
Cl(H) }}-energy   --> H Cl

Figure 5. Molecular model of HCl (Hydrogen Chloride)

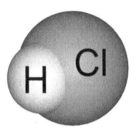

explicitly for natural and biological computation, real advantages of clarity can be obtained compared to other modelling approaches.

PART 1: PLATFORM PRESENTATION AND TUTORIAL

Systemic computation has been designed to support models and simulations of any kind of nature-inspired system, improving the fidelity and clarity of such models. In the first major section of the chapter, in order to show how SC can be implemented, we present the first platform for systemic computation. This platform models a complete systemic computer as a virtual machine within a conventional PC. It also provides an intuitive language for the creation of SC models, together with a compiler.

To illustrate the modelling and the mechanism of SC, we present an implementation of a simple genetic algorithm. We discuss the structure of the systems chosen and the accuracy when various selection and evolution methods are used. We then show how such a SC model can simply be turned into a self-adaptive one. (More details of the platform can be found in Le Martelot, Bentley and Lotto (2007a).)

Note that SC is a computational model as well as a computer architecture. This platform is therefore a proof-of-concept implementation with which we can carry experiments on modelling and programs' behaviour within the SC

paradigm. Further development of SC will lead to the creation of a hardware systemic computer. A hardware systemic computer using sensor networks has been investigated in Bentley (2008) to provide native hardware support using a wireless network of sensors where our platform still relies on emulation.

Virtual Machine

A systemic computer (or an SC virtual machine on a conventional computer) runs the "Building Blocks" of systemic computation: the systems. Compiled from the program, the systems carry out all computation according to the natural rules of SC.

An SC program differs subtly from conventional logic, procedural or object-oriented program both in its definition and in its goals. A procedural program contains a sequence of instructions to process whereas an SC program needs, by definition, to define and declare a list of agents (the systems), in an initial state. The program execution begins by creating these systems in their initial state and then continues by letting them behave indefinitely and stochastically. The outcome of the program is created from an emergent process rather than a deterministic predefined algorithm.

Since an SC program runs indefinitely, the virtual machine (VM) has to run an infinite loop. SC is based on parallel, asynchronous and independent systems; therefore the VM can simulate this by randomly picking a context system at each iteration. Once a context is selected, eligible subject systems in the same scope(s) are identified. If any are found, two of them are randomly chosen. A subject is eligible if its definition sufficiently matches the schema of a context. The VM then executes the context interaction instructions to transform the interacting systems and thus process a computation.

A context may be isolated from its potential subjects, so a computation may not occur at each iteration. It may also not occur if the computing function had nothing to compute from the context and systems it was provided with.

Language and Compiler

To enable the creation of effective programs for the VM, a language intuitively very close to the SC model has been created together with a compiler translating source code into byte-code for the virtual machine. The aim of the SC language is thus to aid the programmer when defining systems, declaring instances of them and setting scopes between them. The main characteristics of the language are listed below:

- **Defining a system** involves defining its kernel and its two schemata. When a system acts as a context, the two schemata are used as the two templates of the systems to interact with, and the kernel encodes the context behaviour. This raises the problem of coding a schema knowing that it has to specify complete systems (defined by a kernel and two schemata). The method chosen was to compress information making up each schema (Bentley, 2007b). A compression code is used for this purpose, coding three bits (where each bit may be '1', '0' or the wildcard '?') into one character. This allows the complete description of a system (kernel and two schemata) in one single schema, as shown in Figure 2. Here "abaa" and "aaba", in a compression code, describe S1- and S2-like systems respectively. Bits to be compressed are placed within the '[ ]' compression operator.
- **Computing function.** The kernel of each system defines the function(s) to be applied to matching interacting systems (and stores associated parameter values). A lookup table matches binary values with the corresponding binary, mathematical, or procedural call-back functions (defined in the encoding section, see later). These

transformation functions are applied to the matching systems in order to transform their values.

- **Labels.** In order to make the code more readable, string labels can be defined and then used in the program instead of their value. These labels must have the correct word length. Since the length bounds the amount of information a system can store, the choice of the length is left to the user. To combine labels, an OR operator is used in combination with the wildcard symbol. Labels defining different bits within the same schema can then be combined using the '|' operator. For instance if "LABEL_1" and "LABEL_2" are respectively set to "10??" and "??01" then "LABEL_1 | LABEL_2" means "1001". Note that '|' is not a "binary or" since an operation such as "0011 | 1100" is not allowed.
- **Basic system definition.** To illustrate the SC language, Program 1 provides code defining a system similar to the one in Figure 1. Labels and the "no operation" function NOP, are first defined. The system declaration follows where each line successively defines the first schema, the kernel and the second schema. Any definition is given a name, here "MySystem" to be later referenced when instantiating. In this example, MY_SYSTEM could be a type identifier and MY_K_DATA and MY_S_DATA would be data. NOP represents the nil function making this system unable to behave as a context system. This first system would thus be stored in memory using a string of three words: "0101 0001 0111".
- **Context system definition.** Program 2 gives an example of a definition for a system that will behave as context, like the one in Figure 2. In this example, "My_Function" refers to the function to call when two systems interact in the current context. This fragment of program assumes

the code of Program 1 is also included. It also assumes the definition of another similar system referred to as "MY_OTHER_SYSTEM". The use of the label "ANY" in the template indicates that here the value of the kernel and the right schema do not matter in the search for systems to interact with. The other use of the wildcard is shown when combining "My_Function" and "MY_CTX_DATA" using the operator '|'. (see Table 1) Each function defined in a system's kernel must refer to an existing call-back function. In the current platform implementation these call-back functions are written in C++ and compiled as plug-ins of the virtual machine. (The only

exception is the NOP function.)

- **System and scope declarations.** Once all the systems have been defined, the last aim of the SC language is to allow the declaration of system instances and their scopes (reminiscent of variable declarations and function scopes in a procedural program). Since scopes are relationships between instances, we propose to handle all this in a "program body". An example, following the previous ones, is given in Program 3. The first part of the program body declares instances, one by one or in a group (array notation). Note that a system definition name (left part of a declaration) is not a type. An instance (right part of a declaration) is

Figure 6. Human-program interaction in the context of the Systemic Computer

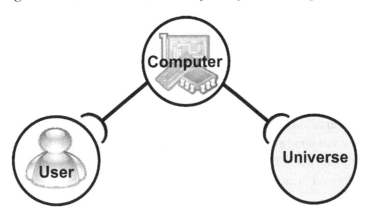

Table 1. Programs 1 and 2

Program 1. Definition of a non-context system	Program 2. Definition of a context system

label   MY_SYSTEM 0101
label   MY_K_DATA ??01
label   MY_S_DATA 0111
 	
function NOP 00??
 	
system MySystem {
     MY_SYSTEM ,
     NOP | MY_K_DATA ,
     MY_S_DATA
 	
}
	label ANY ????
	label MY_CTX_DATA ??01
	
	function My_Function 11??
	
	system MyContext {
	     [MY_SYSTEM, ANY, ANY],
	     My_Function | MY_CTX_DATA,
	     [MY_OTHER_SYSTEM, ANY, ANY]
	}

always a system instance initialised with a system definition (triple string value) previously defined and identified by the left name (e.g. MySystem, MyContext). These system values are by definition only initial values which during computation are likely to change. Only inner data such as "MY_ SYSTEM" in Program 1 can be used as a method of typing. The second part of the program body then sets the scopes between the instances. This notion of scopes refers to embedded hierarchies. An SC program is a list of systems behaving in and belonging to systems which themselves behave in and belong to others and so on. Since the SC definition considers everything as a system, the program is a system, the computer running a program is a system, the user is a system, etc. The human-program interaction can thus be seen as in Figure 6. (see Table 2)

A user can interact with a program in the context of a computer. Therefore the program needs to be embedded in a single entity. This leads us to introduce the notion of "universe". Any SC program should have a universe containing everything but itself and being the only one not to be contained. This universe can be defined in any manner, but

Table 2. Program 3

Program 3. Systems instantiations and scopes setup

program {
        // Declarations
        Universe universe ;
        MySystem ms[1:2] ;
        MyOtherSystem mos[1:2];
        MyContext cs[1:2] ;
 	
        // Scopes
        universe { ms[1:2] , mos[1:2] , cs[1:2] }
 	
}

since it contains everything it cannot interact by itself with the program. Therefore there is no constraint on its definition and no need for it to act as a context. However, it is the only system a user can interact with. The universe is therefore where user's parameters, to be changed at runtime, should be placed. It is also the place where the program can output its results.

Program 3 assumes a system named "Universe" has been defined, although having a dedicated system definition is not mandatory. In this example the universe contains the two instances of MySystem, the two of MyOtherSystem and the two of MyContext, namely everything but itself. This hierarchy is shown in Figure 7.

Figure 7. Visualisation of a simple program. The universe encompasses everything

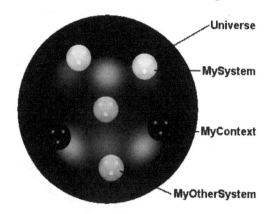

SYSTEMIC ANALYSIS, ILLUSTRATED WITH A GENETIC ALGORITHM

Systemic computation is an alternative model of computation. Before any new program can be written, it is necessary to perform a systemic analysis (Le Martelot, Bentley and Lotto, 2007a) in order to identify and interpret appropriate systems and their organisation. The systemic analysis provides a method for analysing and expressing a given problem or biological system more formally in SC. When performed carefully, such analysis can itself be revealing about the nature of a problem being tackled and the corresponding solution. A systemic analysis is thus the method by which any natural or artificial process is expressed in the language of systemic computation. The steps are in order:

- Identify the systems (i.e. determine the level of abstraction to be used, by identifying which entities will be explicitly modelled as individual systems),
- Analysis of interactions (which system interacts with which other system in which context system),
- Determine the order and structure (scopes) of the emergent program (which systems are inside which other systems) and the values stored within systems.

We now illustrate this by creating a genetic algorithm (GA) in SC.

The first stage is to identify the systems. The use of a GA implies we need a population of solutions, so a collection of systems, with each system corresponding to one solution, seems appropriate. (A lower-level abstraction might use one system for every gene within each solution, but for the purposes of this investigation, this would add unnecessary complexity.)

The identification of appropriate low-level systems is aided by an analysis of interactions. In a GA, solutions interact in two ways: they compete for selection as parents, and once chosen as parents, pairs produce new offspring. The use of contextual systems (which determine the effects of solution interaction) for the genetic operations therefore seems highly appropriate, as shown in Figure 8.

Program 4 provides an example for the definition of solutions and operators. The "SelectAndEvolve" function (defined elsewhere) computes new solutions using the two solutions provided. Any selection and evolution methods may be used. For simplicity, here we perform the selection and reproduction at the same time with the pair of interacting solutions. (All conventional operators could be implemented, e.g. using 'selection' systems to move solutions inside a 'gene pool' system, from which other 'reproduction' systems would control the interaction of parents to make

Figure 8. An operator acts as a context for two interacting solutions

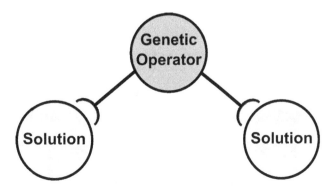

offspring. Such complexity is unnecessary here, however.)

Once the systems and interactions are understood, it is necessary to determine the order and structure of the emergent program. For this we need to determine scopes (which systems are inside which other systems) and the values stored within systems. In a GA, the population is usually initialised with random values, before any other kind of interaction can take place. This implies a two-stage computation: first all solutions must be initialised, then they are permitted to interact and evolve. One way to achieve this is to use a 'supersystem' as a computation space, and an initialiser system. If all solutions begin outside the computation space, then the initialiser acts as context for interactions between the empty solutions and the space, resulting in initialised solutions being pushed inside the space ready for evolution, see Figure 9. The computation space and initialiser can be defined as in Program 5. (When declaring the initialiser, the wildcard word ANY is used to fill in the schemata.)

Finally, as in the example of Program 3, all our program's systems can be wrapped, contained in a super-system "Universe". As illustrated in Figure 6, this universe can be the layer of communication with a user. Therefore in the case of our GA, the program must output on the universe its results, or state, which can be

here the best solution found so far. This has two implications: first we need a "transfer" system, for instance in the universe, interacting between the universe and solutions, and transferring to the universe the current solution if outranking the best known so far. The second implication is that solutions must remain accessible to this transfer system, thus when solutions are pushed into the computation space, they also remain within the universe.

Scopes can be seen as dimensions. Here initialised solutions do exist within a computation space, where they interact in some genetic operators contexts, but they also co-exist in the universe where they interact with it in a solution transfer context. Figure 10 summarises the organisation of the GA.

In the computation space, when two solution systems interact in the context of an operator, the operator applies two functions in succession: selection and reproduction. It is noticeable that our configuration has many similarities with steady-state GAs. However, the systemic selection chooses two competing solutions at random rather than from a fitness sorted set, which makes it subtly different. (It would be possible to sort and order solutions using 'sort' systems and 'linking' systems to produce an ordered chain of solutions, but again this was deemed unnecessary complexity here.)

Figure 9. Left: The "Initialiser" acts as context for interactions between non-initialised solutions and a computation space. Right: The result of the interaction, as defined by the Initialiser, is an initialised solution pushed inside a computation space where it can then interact with other solutions in the context of operators (not shown)

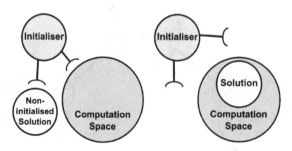

Table 3. Programs 4 and 5

Program 4. GA Solution and Operator system declaration	Program 5. GA Computation Space and Initialiser definition.

system Solution {
    ANY ,
    NOP | SOLUTION ,
    ANY
}
	system ComputationSpace {
	    ANY ,
	    NOP | COMPUTATION_SPACE ,
	    ANY
	}

system Operator {
    [ANY , NOP | SOLUTION , ANY] ,
    SelectAndEvolve ,
    [ANY, NOP | SOLUTION , ANY]
}
	system Initialiser {
	    [ANY , NOP | SOLUTION , ANY] ,
	    Initialise ,
	    [ANY , NOP | COMPUTATION_SPACE , ANY]
	}

More information about the creation of a GA within SC can be found in Le Martelot, Bentley and Lotto (2007a) with an application to the travelling salesman problem, and in Le Martelot, Bentley and Lotto (2008a).

The systemic analysis is complete when all systems and their organisation have been designed for the given problem (or biological process or organism), providing an easy to understand graph-based model. This model can be used on its own as a method of analysis of biological systems, e.g. to understand information flow and transition states. However, a systemic model is best understood when executed as a program. To turn this model into a working program, the data and functions need to be specified for each system in a systemic computation program.

Figure 10. GA program with 1 computation space, 1 initialiser, 1 solution-transfer, 2 operators and 4 solutions (3 initialised and 1 non-initialised). We can see: at the top an initialisation (the solution will then become also part of the computation space); within the computation space two solutions are interacting within the context of a genetic operator; at the bottom left a solution transfer between a solution and the universe. Note that the representation of solution systems between the universe and a computation space means here that the solution systems are part of both.

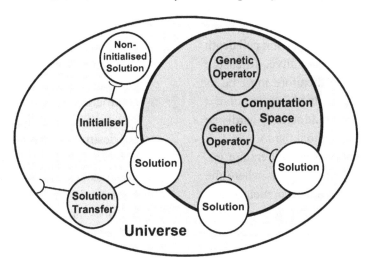

PART 2: CRASH PROOF COMPUTATION

While biology has become very popular in modern computation, fault-tolerant programming is still generally handled in a manner fundamentally different from the methods used in nature. N-version programming (NVP) (Avizienis, 1985), or multi-version programming, is a software engineering process that was introduced to incorporate fault-tolerance. Various functionally equivalent programs are generated from the same specifications and compared by the NVP framework. The method thus introduces functional redundancy in order to improve software reliability. However it does not guarantee that the alternative programs are not facing the same issues. It can also make mistakes when, in case of errors, deciding which program version is providing the right answer. Finally, the development and cost overheads are important (several programs for one specification). Another technique that faces the same issues is known as Recovery blocks (Horning et al, 1974), which provides alternative code blocks for code that fails to work properly.

In nature, old and potentially damaged cells are constantly being replaced and DNA repaired (Darnell et al, 1990). The lifespan of cells is shorter than the life of an organism, so fault-tolerance and self-maintenance are essential for the survival of the organism. The failure of some components does not destroy the overall organism; cell death is an important part of staying alive. To ensure durability, fault tolerance therefore must be as mandatory in a system as its ability to solve a given problem. The latter could actually hardly be trusted or even possible without the former.

In contrast, conventional computers are examples of non fault-tolerant systems where the smallest error in code, corruption in memory, or interference with electronics can cause terminal failures (Bentley, 2005). Software regularly crashes, top of the line robots break down on the wrong kind of ground, power distribution networks fail under unforeseen circumstances (Bentley, 2007a).

In this section, we show using a genetic algorithm (GA) implementation on the systemic computation platform, that SC programs have the native property of fault-tolerance and can be easily modified to become self-maintaining. We compare several variations of the program, involving various faults and self-maintenance configurations, demonstrating that software can repair itself and survive even severe damage.

Motivation

SC programming differs subtly from conventional logic, procedural or object-oriented programming both in its definition and in its goals (Bentley, 2007b; Le Martelot, Bentley and Lotto, 2007a). A procedural program contains a sequence of instructions to process whereas an SC program needs, by definition, to define and declare a list of agents (the systems), in an initial state. The program execution begins by creating these systems in their initial state and then continues by letting them behave indefinitely and stochastically. The outcome of the program is created from an emergent process rather than a deterministic predefined algorithm.

Programming with SC has various benefits when regarding fault-tolerance:

- The parallelism of SC means that a failed interaction does not prevent any further interactions from happening
- A program relies on many independent systems and the failure of one of them cannot destroy the whole program. Like cells in biology, one system collapsing or making mistakes can be compensated by other systems working correctly,
- SC does not permit memory corruption, and even if individual systems contained fatal errors (e.g. divide by zero) the whole program would not halt; every SC program

is already in an infinite, never-ending loop of parallel processes so it cannot crash in the conventional sense,

- Having multiple instances of similar systems not only provides redundancy, it also makes it easy to introduce a self-maintenance process which allows similar systems to fix each other, including the self-maintenance systems themselves.

Fault-Tolerance: Experiments and Results

To assess the fault tolerance of an SC program, we implemented a genetic algorithm as described previously, with a simple fitness function. In order to observe the progression of the GA in a visually convenient way, here the objective is simply to evolve a string of bits that matches a target pattern -a bit string of 256 '1's. (Any other fitness function could have been used instead.) More about this implementation can be found in Le Martelot, Bentley and Lotto (2008a). While any program could be used for the demonstration of fault-tolerance and self-repair, we chose a GA as its natural parallelism simplifies the implementation in SC.

Simulating Faults

The aim of this first set of experiments is to study the fault tolerant behaviour of our program. To achieve this, faults first have to be modelled.

Hardware or software faults can be simulated by randomly altering a memory state (replacing its value with any possible value) with a given rate. By this we provide unpredictable random mistakes that can occur anywhere at any time in the program.

These faults should be modelled so that their "systemic existence" (i.e. the fact that the systems involved in their modelling exist) does not disrupt the inner organisation of the program. In other words, if we introduce the 'fault simulation sys-

tems' in the program with a null fault probability, the program should behave perfectly normally as if the fault systems were absent.

We can state that a fault is due to an unexpected phenomenon which interacts with a component. Whether this phenomenon is an increase of temperature leading to a hardware failure or a programming mistake in memory addressing, the result is the alteration of the memory state in the context of the laws of physics that made this physical change possible. Any program system is therefore susceptible to faults, whether software or hardware initiated.

In SC modelling, the above can be achieved by putting any program system (i.e. system part of our initial program) within a "phenomenon system" also containing the "laws of physics", as shown in Figure 11. The unexpected phenomenon can thus interact with a program system within the context of the laws of physics (the same laws of physics system is within the scope of all phenomena). In the case of our program, a program system can therefore be a computation space, a solution, an operator, a solution transfer or an initialiser. The user provides parameters to the universe and reads what the program returns from it. Also, the phenomena and the laws of physics are not part of the "tested program". Therefore we do not consider here the universe, the laws of physics or the phenomena as fallible components.

Experiments

Previous work by one of the authors (Bentley, 2005) showed that programs evolved using fractal gene regulatory networks cope better with code damage than human-designed or genetic programming generated programs. In the following experiments, we focus on how human-designed programs for SC can natively cope with code damage.

In the following, *iterations*, *systems*, *contexts* and *simple* respectively refer to the number of iterations, systems, context systems and non-context

Figure 11. Interaction between an external unexpected phenomenon and a program system in the context of the laws of physics and within the scope of the phenomenon (i.e. the system is encompassed in the field of interaction of the phenomenon).

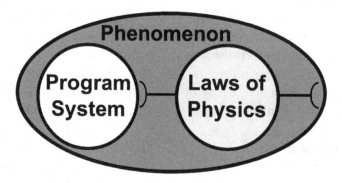

systems. In all experiments, the solutions are 256 bits long. The best solution's fitness is thus 256. To fit solutions within the systems we chose a kernel and schema length of 256 characters. The total length of a system is thus

Ls = 256 × 3 =768

In the following experiments, all runs for a particular configuration are repeated 10 times, and the presented results are averaged over the 10 runs.

To measure the quantity of errors introduced in the programs we use the following:

- p_c: character-wise fault probability,
- $p_s = 1 - (1 - p_c)^{ls}$: system corruption probability,
- $q = p_c \cdot l_s \dfrac{iterations}{contexts}$: quantity of corrupted bits over an execution.

The ratio $\dfrac{iterations}{contexts}$ is the number of times each fallible context system can attempt an interaction. It depends on each program configuration and we provide for each experiment an average number that experiments showed to be required for the program to finish.

Also, damages made to context systems have a stronger impact, although as likely to happen as for any other system. Indeed other systems can be scopes and hold no or little data, or data systems usually using less crucial characters than the contexts. It is therefore a useful measure to calculate the "quantities" q_c and q_s of damage respectively made to fallible context and simple (non context) systems:

$q_c = q \cdot \dfrac{contexts}{systems}$: Number of context system bits corrupted in one run,

$q_s = q \cdot \dfrac{simple}{systems}$: Number of simple (non-context) system bits corrupted in one run.

Experiment 1

Program setup with a minimalist configuration:

- 1 initialiser,
- 25 solutions,
- 1 computation space,
- 1 crossover operator,
- 1 solution transfer,
- 1 mutation operator.

Here *contexts* = 4, *systems* = 30.

10 runs of the program were performed with no fault and 10 runs were performed with faults injected with $p_c = 0.0001$ giving $p_s = 0.0739$

We consider here $\dfrac{iterations}{contexts} \approx 3700$. Thus, $q(p_c = 0.0001) = 284.16$.

We have an estimation of about 284 bits damaged during the program execution, divided amongst the different types of systems as:

$$q_c = q \cdot \frac{4}{30} \approx 38 \text{ and } q_s = q \cdot \frac{26}{30} \approx 246.$$

Figure 12 shows the program progression with and without faults.

Experiment 2

The previous program was performing correctly for a very short time due to the single instantiation of all the systems (except the "solution" systems since a GA by definition uses a population of solutions). The second experiment thus used duplicated systems:

- 5 initialisers,
- 25 solutions,
- 3 computation spaces,
- 10 crossover operators,
- 10 solution transfers,
- 10 mutation operators.

Here *contexts* = 35 and *systems* = 63. Like in experiment 1, 10 runs of the program were performed with no fault and 10 runs were performed with faults injected with the same probability. We have an estimation of about 31 bits damaged during the program execution divided in:

$$q_c = q \cdot \frac{35}{63} \approx 17 \text{ and } q_s = q \cdot \frac{28}{63} \approx 14.$$

Figure 13 shows the results of such configuration tested over 10 runs.

We can now observe that the program performed well in its task in spite of the faults. However, if the execution had required to last longer (e.g. more difficult problem), or if more faults were to occur, the program could stop working before reaching its goal like in experiment 1. This hypothesis is verified in the following experiment.

Figure 12. Experiment 1: GA progression without and with faults averaged over 10 runs using a minimalist system configuration. With this first configuration we can see that our GA stops evolving at a very early stage when its program is corrupted by faults. However, it is noteworthy that when injecting faults, the program does not crash; it merely stops evolving properly. The systemic computer is crash-proof as systems deterioration can only stop or corrupt individual interactions, but as the whole program consists of systems interacting in parallel, the other uncorrupted individual interactions will continue as normal.

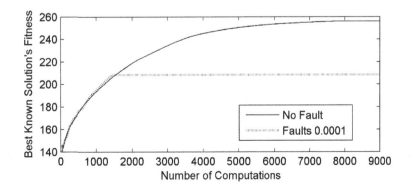

Figure 13. Experiment 2: GA progression without and with faults averaged over 10 runs with a program configuration using redundant systems.

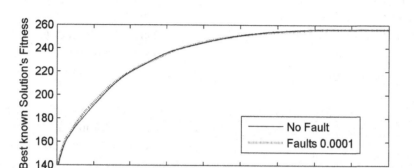

Experiment 3

We use the same systems configuration as in the previous experiment but we rise the character-wise fault probability to $p_c = 0.0005$ giving $p_s = 0.3189$. This system fault probability is comparable to a simultaneous erroneous state of a third of the computer components.

$$q(p_c = 0.0005) = 153.6$$

$$q_c = q \cdot \frac{35}{63} \approx q \cdot 56\% \approx 85$$

$$q_s = q \cdot \frac{28}{63} \approx q \cdot 44\% \approx 68 .$$

Figure 14 shows the obtained results. We can see that the program, although using duplicated systems, stops evolving before reaching its goal. If we try to analyse the reasons of this program failure we can guess that "solution transfer" systems are the first not to fulfil their role anymore. Initialisers are indeed only required at the beginning, computation spaces are just encompassing systems so have no context nor data holding role, and solutions and operators (crossover or mutation) are more numerous than solution transfers. Analysing the results, looking at the systems memory state evolution through time, showed indeed that each

program failure is due in the first place to the corruption of all transfer systems. If solution transfers were more numerous than operators for instance we could then expect solution evolution to stop working first. As soon as one program subtask (e.g. solution transfer, solution evolution, etc) is not fulfilled anymore, the program stops working. In the case of our GA, the subtask in charge of transferring solutions to the universe is not executed anymore once all transfer systems are corrupted. Once such a subtask is down, it does not matter what the others can do as the program requires all of them to work properly.

These experiments showed up to now that we always have a graceful degradation (solutions are evolved normally until evolution fails because of damage, but the solutions are not lost) but sooner or later the GA fails to work properly. We can delay the program failure point by providing enough systems to survive for a while (e.g. as long as we need the program to run, see experiment 2) but we cannot prevent this failure if faults keep happening.

To slow down the degradation without adding too many systems (or even avoid this failure point) the program could be repaired. An elegant way to have a program repaired would be an "on-line" self-maintenance of the program. The program would repair itself. No external intervention would

Figure 14. Experiment 3: GA progression without and with faults averaged over 10 runs with a configuration using redundant systems and facing a strong fault probability.

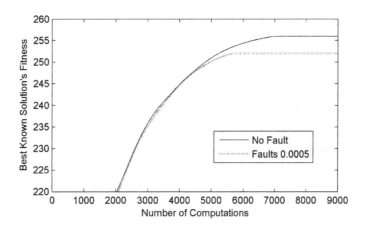

then be required as the program would show a homeostatic behaviour.

SELF-MAINTENANCE: EXPERIMENTS AND RESULTS

Implementing Self-Maintenance

System definitions in our program can be instantiated several times, and need to be in order to provide fault-tolerance. Therefore interacting instances could try to fix each other in a "self-maintenance" context, as shown in Figure 15.

Indeed, if the two systems are similar on their healthy parts, then they can replace the damaged parts of each by the ones of the other if these are healthy. The self-repair ability of the program then arises from its conception in independent and multiple times instantiated systems. For this reason, the self-maintenance context systems should also be instantiated several times. The more redundant the information (the more duplicated systems) the more likely systems are to be able to fix each other and the more likely the function they play in the program is reliable.

Experiment 4

In this experiment, we repeat over 10 runs the same setup as experiment 3 but we inject 7 self-maintenance systems. We now get *context*s = 42 and *system*s = 70. The amount of self-maintenance systems thus represents 10% of the total amount of systems We consider here $\frac{iterations}{contexts} \approx 535$, thus $q(p_c = 0.0005) = 205.71$.

We have an estimation of about 205 bits damaged during the program execution divided in:

$$q_c = q \cdot \frac{42}{70} \approx q.60\% \approx 123$$

$$q_s = q \cdot \frac{28}{70} \approx q.40\% \approx 82 \,.$$

Note that q_c increased with respect to q as this configuration involved additional fallible context systems for self-maintenance. Figure 16 shows the program progression without faults, with faults and then with faults and self-maintenance.

We can observe that the program is working fine in spite of the high amount of faults (e.g. very unreliable hardware or very buggy software), and

Figure 15. Two program systems interacting within a context of self-maintenance.

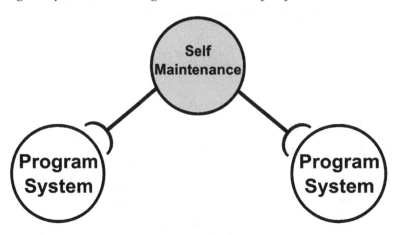

Figure 16. Experiment 4: GA progression with no fault, with faults and with faults and self-maintenance, all averaged over 10 runs with configurations using redundant systems and facing a strong fault probability.

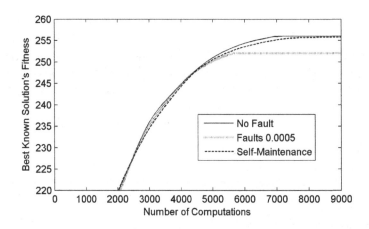

using a reasonable amount of systems dedicated to fault repair.

Discussion

It should be noted that the more contexts there are in an SC program, the more iterations are required to make all contexts create an interaction once. Therefore, if the "laws of physics" system interacts once in a cycle, then the more systems there are, the less likely each individual system is to be damaged, but still the probability that something happens within the whole system is the same. We

can thus say that faults happen depending on the usage of a system. This bias is part of SC, just as any other paradigm can have inner biases due to their properties.

However, to remove this bias in the experiments, some dummy systems can be added to ensure that experiments with different needs of systems still have the same amount of systems (same amount of context systems and same amount of non-context systems).

To confirm this, experiment 3 was conducted again using 7 dummy context systems in order to have 42 context and 28 non-context systems as in experiment 4. This way the comparison between the two experiments was strictly unbiased. The results showed that the program running with faults performed on average only slightly better than in the dummy-less version, confirming that the bias had no significant impact on the overall outcome of the experiment.

PART 3: SYSTEMIC COMPUTATION MODELLING, ADVANTAGES AND BENEFITS

Ease of Program Evolution: Making a Genetic Algorithm Self-Adaptive

In the GA model previously presented, a novel opportunity for parameter tuning is provided because operators exist as entities within the computation space in the same way that solutions do. Since SC randomly picks a context, changing the proportion of operator instances changes the probability of different operator types being chosen. The probability of being chosen, and therefore the impact, of an operator O is thus given by the ratio:

$$impact(O) = \frac{\text{instances of O}}{\text{total number of operator instances}}$$

Indeed, when the contribution of each operator is analysed in more detail (by assessing how frequently each operator produced a fitter solution over time), it becomes apparent that all enable convergence to solutions at different rates, and that those rates all vary over time. Indeed, it can be seen that different combinations of operators would be more appropriate at different times during evolution.

Therefore, it is clear that when solutions interact in the right context at the right times, the speed of evolution can be increased, or the ability of evolution to continue making progress can be improved. In nature, factors affecting the progression of evolution (whether part of the evolving organisms, or of the environments of the organisms), are also subject to evolution. The contexts that affect evolutionary progress may co-evolve, giving evolution of evolvability.

If we perform a new systemic analysis and identify the systems, interactions and structure, it is clear that the evolution of evolvability implies new interactions and new systems. Similarly to the introduction of self-maintenance with only one additional system, an elegant way to introduce this new evolution of evolvability functionality is to top-up the existing model with a new system in charge of this function. In this case the genetic operator systems must interact with each other in the context of new operator adapter systems, see Figure 17. This enables the genetic operators to evolve in parallel to the solutions they modify.

We implemented this new feature with a new context system which adapts the operator type between the different approaches. When two operators interact in the context of this system, a fitter operator has on average a higher chance of replacing a less fit one, thus making the number of fitter operators more numerous in the population. The average fitness of a genetic operator can be measured within a window of size W last operations. This grows in time following the distribution $W = A \cdot (1 - e^{-k \cdot n})$ where n is the total number of computations performed and A and k are constants to be set by the user to determine how the size of the window changes over time.

This additional feature for a GA shows how systemic computation enables self-adaptation with the minimum of additional code. More about turning a regular GA into a self-adaptive one can be found in Le Martelot, Bentley and Lotto (2007a), investigating for the travelling salesman problem the impact of evolutionary operators.

Neural Networks: Natural Modelling Enables Free Properties

In this section of the chapter, we focus on two other natural properties of systemic computation: local

Figure 17. A Genetic Operator Adapter is added to the current interaction scheme to adapt or evolve genetic operators during computation.

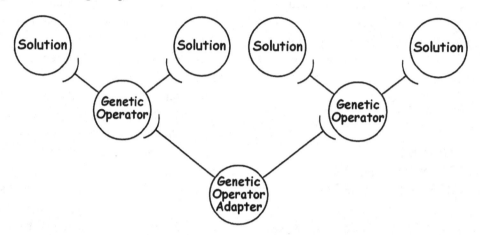

knowledge and asynchronous computation, applying them to a common bio-inspired paradigm: artificial neural networks (ANN). Local knowledge and asynchrony do not suit conventional computer architectures, so classical ANN models often employ global algorithms, constraining the network structure and making them less biologically plausible. Real biological NN imply a more flexible model without the structural limitations imposed by conventional approaches. We thus suggest an ANN implementation using SC to further illustrate the benefits of this paradigm. The use of SC requires the use of local knowledge and asynchronous computation. We show that such a model enables the implementation of the same networks as those implemented using conventional global and synchronous approaches, but the SC implementation does not constrain the network structure.

MOTIVATION

ANN are suitable to highlight the properties of built-in asynchronous computation and local knowledge as:

- Neurons are organised to create a whole (the network) that solves problems,
- Neurons are computing locally, yet the result is global,
- Neurons are independent (in timing and internal knowledge).

Classical backpropagation (BP) (Tang et al, 2007) constrains the network to be layered and feed-forward; therefore no change in the neurons' organisation breaking this requirement can be made. Recurrent BP was introduced to overcome one of these constraints and cope with backward connections (Tang et al, 2007). Other more biologically plausible techniques, like contrastive Hebbian learning for deterministic networks (Peterson and Anderson, 1987; Hinton, 1990), generalised recirculation (O'Reilley, 1996), or spiking neurons networks (Maass, 1997) were introduced and showed successful results. Still, these approaches all define global algorithms, coping with various specific network structures, giving neurons more and more realistic computational abilities, but do not give the neuron entity the ability to be autonomous (i.e. inner data processing) in whatever situation (i.e. disregarding the position in the structure). Such natural flexibility reflects, from our modelling point of view, what is desirable and missing in approaches using conventional computation. The reason for using SC at all is to move beyond simply attempting to mimic the functional behaviour of natural systems through global algorithmic approximations, and instead (as much as is feasible) duplicate the functional behaviour through mirroring the underlying systems, organisations and local interactions. SC is thus intended to be a truer representation and thus an improved model of natural systems implemented following its paradigm, compared to other approaches. More about this work can be found in (Le Martelot, Bentley and Lotto, 2007b).

ANN Model

Modelling a neural network keeping all its natural characteristics should involve the same entities that form a real one: neurons, their inner mechanism and their communication mechanism. These mechanisms could be modelled a priori at several levels. One model could represent the interaction of neurons using synapses to make the link between axon and dendrites. Another one could involve pre-synapse, post-synapse, protein exchange, protein transfer, etc. We chose to study and create our model at the neuron level of abstraction and not explicitly represent protein interactions. A neuron receives inputs from its dendrites that are processed in the soma; the resulting signal is then sent through the axon (Kandel et al, 1991). Axon signals are weighted and transmitted to further neurons through synapses which communicate with their dendrites. The signal will thus be a value transmitted across the network rather than many molecular and electrical entities.

Systemic Analysis

The synapse which transfers signals from axon to dendrites can be chosen as a context of interaction between neurons. However, neurons interactions do not provide information regarding the signal flow direction. This flow is by definition directional from axons to dendrites. Therefore the model should have the more precise notions of axons and dendrites to precise the signal direction. Dendrites can be modelled as one system representing the dendritic tree rather than one system per dendrite which would add unnecessary complexity to the model. A synapse connects an axon with a dendrites system, each systems triplet belongs to the scope of a connection (Figure 18(a)).

Two types of synapses could be considered here: excitatory and inhibitory synapses (Kandel et al, 1991); not to mention that synapses can be electrical or chemical (Kandel et al, 1991), which we do not explicitly model here. For modelling simplicity and not to introduce inconsistencies we chose to allow both excitatory and inhibitory excitations within one synapse. This is modelled by a weight taken within $[-1; 1]$. A positive weight simulates an excitatory synapse and a negative weight an inhibitory one.

To model the signal processing between dendrites and axon inside a neuron, we can consider the ionic transmissions in the membrane and the membrane as a whole and define the membrane as context of interaction between dendrites and axon, as shown in Figure 18(b). A membrane also owns a threshold of signal activation, real value also taken within $[-1; 1]$.

To keep neuronal integrity, scopes are used to group what is part of a neuron, of the outside or of both. All the inherent neuron interactions happen within its soma. A neuron is therefore represented as dendrites, a soma, a membrane and an axon. However, dendrites and axons also belong to the outside (they are exposed to the outside of the soma) as their role is to receive and transmit signals from or to other neurons. Therefore, neurons can be modelled as shown in Figure 18(b).

Neurons belong to a NN, therefore it is sensible for integrity to encompass them in a "network" system itself contained in the systemic "universe".

Figure 18. (a) Axon-dendrites interaction in the context of a synapse. (b) Systemic model of a neuron showing the dendrites-axon interaction in the context of a membrane, and within a soma.

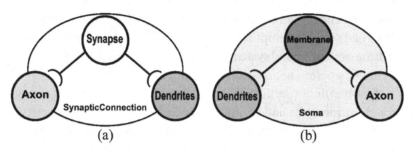

The universe is here a system which encloses everything within the program. It is also used as the interface between the program and the user (Figure 6). However, the network inputs and outputs as well as the data transfer between them and the universe are still to be defined. A real brain receives axons from neurons located outside, like visual inputs, and sends signals also outside, like to muscles. Thus, axons can naturally also play the role of network inputs and outputs. Then "Input-Transfer" (IT) and "OutputTransfer" (OT) context systems transfer data between the universe and the input and output axons. Figure 19 shows a single neuron systemic neural network.

So far, this model can organise interactions disregarding the physical location of the neurons. Nonetheless, the notion of neuron neighbourhood can be easily handled using scopes. An "area" system can encompass neurons and neurons can belong to several areas (the network itself being an "area"). This partition and sharing of neurons would thus create neighbourhoods in the network. Note that the physical neighbourhood is defined by relationships between systems rather than by physical coordinates. Figure 20 shows a more complex network using areas.

This network partitioning into areas using scopes also offers potential interest for future work. Some more interaction possibilities could then be added, injecting new context systems in specific areas, thus giving one a different potential

and behaviour from another. In addition, from a biological modelling point of view, partitioning the network into areas is of relevance (Kandel et al, 1991).

Rules

The organisation of neurons is based on observations taken from biological studies (Kandel et al, 1991). However, knowing the organisation does not explain the inner behaviour of the entities involved. Unfortunately, this is not well understood yet how everything happens at this stage. We are thus forced to use methods that may or may not be biologically plausible, and use an adaptation for asynchronous and local computation of the gradient back propagation (BP) method (Tang et al, 2007) for learning. BP is often described as a global algorithm relying on some precise network structure (Tang et al, 2007). The aim of our adaptation is to keep the principle of this method but adapt it to be a local-rule based principle.

BP relies on the concept of layers to group independent neurons together, which provides an easy control of the flow of information from layer to layer and therefore suits a global and serial algorithm. In the SC paradigm, we can use the very same principle without any structure hypothesis by defining the information flow process locally. Equations 1 to 3 give the BP rules with a momentum factor:

Figure 19. Systemic NN with 2 inputs and 1 neuron

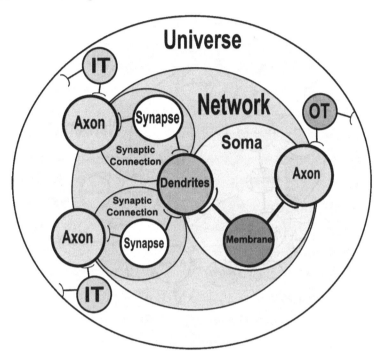

$$x_i = g(h_i) = g(\sum_{k \in K_i} w_{ik} \cdot x_k) \qquad (1)$$

$$\Delta w_{ik}(t) = \lambda \cdot e_i \cdot x_k + \alpha \cdot \Delta w_{ik}(t-1), \forall k \in K_i \qquad (2)$$

$$e_i = g'(h_i) \cdot \sum_{j \in J_i} w_{ji} \cdot e_j = \sum_{j \in J_i} (g'(h_i) \cdot w_{ji} \cdot e_j) \qquad (3)$$

with:

- i: the neuron for which a value is being processed,
- x_n: the signal output of a neuron n,
- g: the transfer function,
- h_n: the weighted input sum of a neuron n,
- K_n: the set of neurons firing into a neuron n,
- w_{mn}: the weight of the connection from a neuron n to a neuron m,

- $w_{mn}(t)$: the weight of the connection from a neuron n to a neuron m at a time t,
- Δw_{mn}: the variation of the weight from a neuron n to a neuron m,
- λ: the learning rate,
- α: the momentum term,
- e_n: backpropagated error value of a neuron n,
- g': the transfer function's gradient,
- J_n: the set of neurons a neuron n is firing into.

The mathematical principles of the rules can be kept. However their implementation needs to be local. Equation (3) shows that the error can be written as a sum. It can therefore be performed by a sequence of independent computations as long as their common term $g'(h_i)$ remains constant during computations. Figure 21 shows a flowchart of the error backpropagation and delta weight update.

Each neuron keeps a current error value where

Figure 20. Network with four inputs, one output and three areas sharing neurons. Each area defines a neighbourhood for the neurons inside.

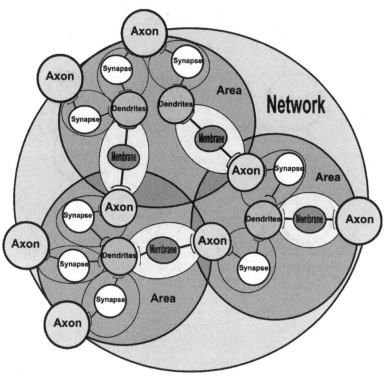

further neurons can add their backpropagated error contribution. To avoid reusing twice any information, a neuron resets to zero its error value as soon as it is backpropagated. To assert the constancy of the terms $g'(h_i)$, the weights are updated only at the end of the computation (like in a classical BP) when a new sample is presented.

Neurons and synapses are therefore autonomous and responsible for their own local data. These local rules imply that no global algorithm is defined and therefore no constraint is imposed on the network structure. This model can be used to design feed-forward networks as well as recurrent NN as shown in Figures 22(a) and (b). The biological plausibility comes in this work from the autonomy and organisation of the systems, caused by the natural characteristics of asynchrony and local knowledge built into SC, leading to an emerging global behaviour, like the global learning. Also, the model could use any other kind of

learning within the neuron and synapse systems, still keeping the very same organisation.

Note that a stabilised network could easily have its weak synapses trimmed by the injection of a new context system, programmed for instance to kill settled redundant synapses. This illustrates again how the model could be improved by easy addition of new systems rather than requiring modifications of the code at its core.

This ANN model gives a new illustration of SC modelling. The example implementation contrasts significantly with classical approaches where data and algorithm are interdependent separate parts making network implementations more rigid and less biologically plausible. Using SC modelling and its intrinsic (non-simulated) properties of local knowledge and asynchrony, our implementation gives full autonomy to neurons, thus enabling flexibility in neural structure, and is compatible with any neuron model (first, second, third generation

Figure 21. Neuron k receives error values from ahead neurons i and j and backpropagates error values to neurons m and n. Error is transmitted between dendrites (De) and axons (Ax) by the context systems membrane (Me) and synapse (Sy). A synapse updates its delta weight (dw), a membrane its delta threshold (dth), L is the learning rate and e is the error. The momentum term is not shown for simplicity and readability.

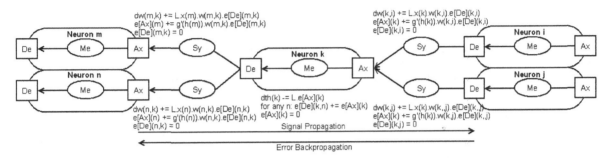

(Maass, 1997)). Experiments carried out in (Le Martelot, Bentley and Lotto, 2007b) on various machine learning problems showed that SC neural networks perform as well as, if not better than, conventional implementations such as Matlab ANN toolbox and therefore enable flexibility with no trade-off with performance.

Artificial Metabolism, Modelling Tissue for Artificial Immune Systems: Towards a New Kind of Program

An increasingly popular view in the field of Artificial Immune Systems (AIS) holds that innate immunity (as enabled by non-adaptive cells such as dendritic cells) can play a significant role in maintaining immunity in computer systems (Aickelin and Greensmith, 2007). Notions such as the Danger Theory suggest that normal self cells may provide signals when damaged, thus helping to encourage the response of immune cells in the right areas of the tissue of an organism at the right time (Matzinger, 1994). Previous work by one of the authors has investigated the development of an artificial tissue to serve this function, providing an interface between data and AIS, and performing preliminary data processing

and clustering (Bentley et al, 2005).

In the final section of this chapter we extend the previous work on tissue for AIS, and investigate a different implementation based on systemic computation. In contrast to previous implementations of tissue, which largely ignore the relationships between real organisms and their environments, here we present a model of organism, implemented as a systemic computation program with its own metabolism that eats data, expels waste, self-organises its cells depending on the nature of its food and can emit danger signals for an AIS. The implementation is tested by application to a standard machine learning set (Breast Cancer data (Wolberg et al, 1992)) and shows excellent abilities to recognise anomalies in its diet.

Motivation

Although not commonly modelled, the notion of tissue is fundamental to immunity. The immune system within an organism defends the tissue of that organism. The concept of artificial tissue has been used for instance in the POEtic project, aiming at creating a hardware platform organised with a similar hierarchy as found in biological systems (Tempesti et al, 2002), and using reconfigurable circuits to simulate tissue growth (Thoma et al,

Figure 22. (a) A feed forward network. (b) Same network with a recursive synapse. The program is initially the same but then topped up with one more synapse. (Synaptic Connection systems are made discreet for readability but the synapses' schemata clearly indicate the interacting systems).

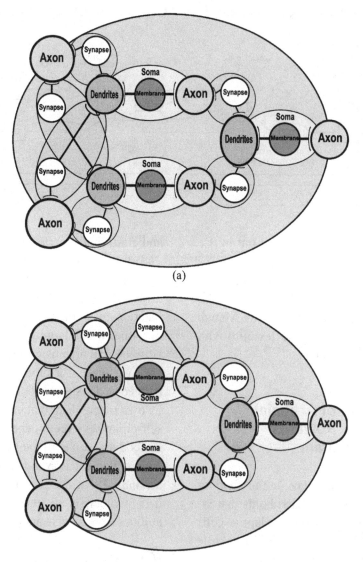

(a)

2004). It has also been used in work that implemented an AIS in a sensor network, the sensor nodes taking on the role of tissue cells (Wallenta et al, 2008).

In biology, tissue is a crucial part of the immune system and its importance was particularly highlighted by Polly Matzinger when introducing the Danger Model (Matzinger, 1994). This view rejected the notion that the immune system differentiates self from non-self and suggested that it instead responds to cellular damage. It thus suggests that cells that die abnormally release signals which encourage immune cells to converge on that location and become more active.

This theory was adopted in Bentley et al (2005) to propose two ways of growing tissues where damaged cells would release danger signals exploitable by an AIS. Tissue was defined as the interface between a problem to solve and the AIS. Here we follow a similar view, but attempt to improve the tissue model and its potential advantages by implementing a tissue-growing program designed for AIS using systemic computation.

In this section of the chapter we use an approach similar to Bentley et al (2005) and deepen the biological analogy by modelling an artificial organism as a program with metabolism. The program does not only mimic some tissue features but also mimics many fundamental properties of living organisms: eating data as food and expelling waste, while growing tissue, and releasing danger signal when its cells die in an abnormal way.

To implement such program SC provides a suitable alternative approach to traditional computation. Indeed with SC, organisms and software programs now share a common definition of computation. The work illustrates how organisms and programs can behave similarly, sharing the notion of metabolism, using SC. More about this work can be found in Le Martelot, Bentley and Lotto (2008b).

An SC Program with Metabolism

Systemic Analysis

As described in earlier sections, when programming with SC it is necessary to perform a systemic analysis in order to identify and interpret appropriate systems and their organisation (Le Martelot, Bentley and Lotto, 2007a). The first stage is to identify the low-level systems (i.e. determine the level of abstraction to be used).

In most artificial immune systems, the level of abstraction is the cell: few approaches require modelling of the internal organelles or genome of cells, and few require modelling of populations of organisms. Here we intend to model the growth of tissue cells, the consumption of "food" (data items), the expulsion of waste and the emission of danger signals. Thus an abstraction at the cellular level is appropriate, with systems being used to explicitly model each element.

The identification of appropriate low-level systems is aided by an analysis of interactions. The organism should be able to eat food from its environment, use this food to grow organs (clusters of cells) by creating new cells and expel waste into the environment.

To prevent being overloaded with systems, the waste can be recycled into new food (a simple ecosystem model). Food and waste could therefore be seen as different states of the same system (in SC systems can be transformed, but never created from nothing or destroyed). Also, the food is what the organism takes from its environment to be able to grow. Therefore cells and all the necessary matter for the growth should also derive from the food systems.

We can thus visualise the ecosystem between the organism and the environment as shown in Figure 23.

Looking within the organism, it takes food as input and this food must be sufficient to grow tissue. One simple way to model this is by using the approximation that the food is transformed into cells when absorbed by the organism. However, to enable cells to adhere to each other (rather than float free), cells need some sticky adhesion molecules. Here we do not need to explicitly model all these molecules but an "adhesion surface" is at least required to bind two or more cells together. As SC forbids the creation of systems from nothing, the adhesion surfaces must be obtained either from incoming food or from the cells themselves. In a biological organism each cell has a limited lifespan and thus dies at some point. It may then be consumed by macrophages or dendritic cells and its energy is partially recycled. In the model dead cells can thus be recycled to make adhesion surfaces. A growth process can now attach cells to each other by using adhesion surfaces to create tissue. To regulate this growth and introduce the notion of time, a decay process simulates the aging of cells. When cells die, a split process splits them from the adhesion surfaces they are bound to.

Figure 23. 'Food to waste' cycle for an organism within its environment: Food is absorbed by the organism, processed as energy to grow tissues before being expelled when the organism cannot make use of it any more.

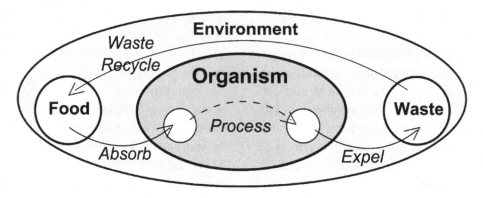

Table 4.

organism }-absorb-{ food	→	organism(cell)
cell }-growth-{ adhesion_surface	→	cell(adhesion_surface)
cell(adhesion_surface) }}-split	→	(cell adhesion_surface)
organism(cell) }}-cell_recycling	→	organism(adhesion_surface or danger_signal)
X[age](time) }}-decay	→	X[age+1](time), X = cell or adhesion_surface or danger_signal
organism(X) }}-expel	→	(organism waste), X = adhesion_surface or danger_signal
universe(waste) }}-waste_recycling	→	universe(food[data])

So the organism eats new data, converts each data item into a new cell, and attempts to bind that cell to itself, with cells made from similar data items binding to each other. Thus, a cell unable to bind to any group of cells reveals itself to be significantly different from them – more like the result of an invading pathogen than part of the organism. If this abnormal cell dies unbound, it can therefore be spotted as a potential anomaly. In that case, the death of the cell can entail that cell releasing a Danger signal (i.e. the cell can be converted into a signal). This signal can then be used by an AIS algorithm which can be implemented through the addition of systems corresponding to immune cells (here we focus on the organism).

The organism can also make use of a hunger parameter defining a maximum amount of alive cells it can contain at a time. This parameter can be stored in the organism system and the absorption context then only allows food absorption if the organism is "hungry". This parameter can be useful to avoid having the organism growing too big and using too much memory/data at a time. A bad usage of memory could indeed to some extend slow down the computation process significantly.

The organism food to waste chain is therefore as shown in Figure 24.

From this defined cycle, the interactions and systems in the model can be written as in Table 4 (also see .Figure 25):

Each system models a biological entity:

- absorb: endocytosis (e.g. via cell receptors)
- growth: organism's genome;

Figure 24. 'Food to Waste' cycle within the organism: Food is absorbed, transformed into cells. When dying cells can be recycled into adhesion surfaces if they were part of a tissue or turned into a danger signal if they were single. Cells, adhesion surfaces and danger signals have a limited lifespan and decay over time (i.e. when they reach a certain age they die). When dying, cells also need a split process to detach them from the tissue they were part of.

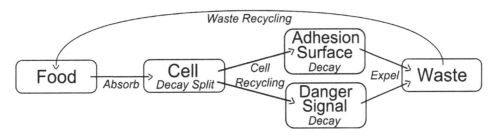

Figure 25. Systemic organisation of the organism. The universe contains a waste recycling system, some waste and food, and an organism. The organism shares with the universe the absorption context. It contains cells, adhesion surfaces, danger signals, growth contexts, cells recycling contexts and expelling contexts. Finally cells (and thus all derived system states like adhesion surfaces and danger signals) contain the time system, a decay process and a split process. The schemata appear on context systems to show the allowable interactions between systems. The dashed arrows indicate the potential transformation of some systems during an interaction. For instance on the far left we can observe a food system interacting with an organism in an absorption context: the food is turned into a cell and injected into the organism.

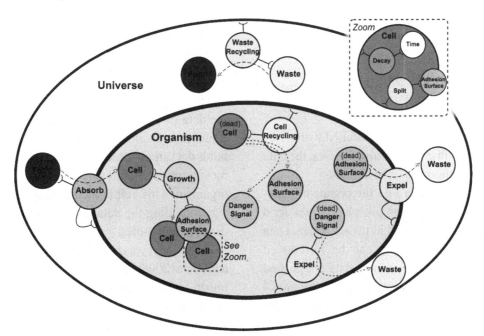

- decay: aging (progression along the axis of time);
- split: chemical breakdown between adhesion molecules and cell wall;
- cell recycling: phagocytes;
- expel: exocytosis;
- waste recycling: ecosystem;
- universe: environment;
- organism: boundary between tissue and environment;
- food: nutrients;
- cells: tissue cells;
- adhesion surfaces: adhesion molecules;
- danger signal: Matzinger's danger signals;
- waste: cell waste (unused or unusable compounds);
- time: dimension of time.

Figure 25 summarises the organism's organisation and shows the potential interactions.

Note that waste recycling, absorption, cell recycling, and expel systems should have the same amount of instances. Indeed, on average if one food system can be created at a time, then only one can be absorbed, then recycled and finally expelled at a time.

Data Organisation within the Artificial Organism

So far an organism has been modelled within SC. To use this organism to organise the data, the data processing method has to be defined.

To incorporate data into the organism's metabolism, new data items are placed into food systems, where it is stored in the schemata. Data from an incoming stream can be introduced when recycling waste (i.e. new data are pushed into the resulting food systems). The amount of waste recycling and absorption systems gives the data introduction rate (the more food can be absorbed at a time, the more data are introduced). The data are then absorbed into the organism and transformed to cells. When a growth interaction

occurs between a cell and an adhesion surface, the two are bound based on their data similarity. Algorithm 1 describes in pseudo-code the binding method. For binding a cell to an adhesion surface the adhesion surface is injected into the cell but remains also part of the organism so that more cells can bind to it.

Algorithm 1 Pseudo-code for the growth context binding method. τ is a given threshold. The distance function calculates the Euclidian distance of two vectors.

```
if adhesion surface not bound to
anything then
    Bind cell and surface
    Surface data value ← Cell
data value
else if distance(Cell data, Sur-
face data) ≤ τ then
    Bind cell to surface
    Surface data value ←
Average(Surface data, Cell data)
end if
```

The measure chosen in this implementation to compare data is the Euclidian distance (as was used in Bentley et al (2005)). In the organism, cells bind together according to their values, and various clusters may emerge from this, thus reflecting the data distribution. If a cell is left single then it means it cannot bind anywhere and therefore holds data significantly different from the current most common data values contained within the organism. This cell is then turned into a danger signal holding the data that an AIS could use to develop antibodies.

The model was tested in Le Martelot, Bentley and Lotto (2008b). Starting from scratch and working on-line the organism was able to organise data according to its similarities and provide danger signals when cells die in an abnormal way for the current organism. The organism proved to be able to detect anomalous UCI Breast Cancer data (Wolberg et al, 1992) with better accuracy than in previous work (Bentley et al, 2005). Also the study of the evolution over time of the organism showed that its inner organisation reflects the data distribution of the current flow.

As the organism is designed to grow to match the data rate, such a program is therefore able to cope with various (unexpected) parameter changes, self-(re)organising with the data flow, and providing information over time regarding detected potentially abnormal data items. When used in conjunction with an artificial immune algorithm, the good accuracy of detection (albeit with a high false positive rate), and the automatic organisation of similar data into clusters should enable excellent performance overall. While temporal information is currently lost because of the stochastic computation of SC, this could be added as additional features of data items, enabling the clustering according to similar timings in addition to data values.

One advantage of SC is the simplicity of modelling new stochastic systems, so an immune algorithm could be added to this model by simply adding two or three new types of system (e.g. B-cell, T-cell, antibody) that would then automatically interact with the existing tissue systems. Another valuable advantage of using SC in our approach is the fault-tolerance and self-repair ability an SC model can naturally have, as described earlier (and investigated in Le Martelot, Bentley and Lotto (2008a)). Having robust software can indeed be an important feature in network security to ensure the program can survive even severe damage provoked for instance by hacking.

FUTURE TRENDS

Biological computation (i.e. the behaviour of living organisms) may or may not be Turing Complete, but it is clearly organized differently from traditional von Neumann architectures. Computation (whether in a brain or an ant colony) is distributed, self-organising, autonomous and embodied in its environments. Systemic computation is a model of computation designed to follow the "biological way" of computation: it relies on the notion that systems are transformed through interaction in some context, with all computation equivalent to controlled transformations. This model implies a distributed, stochastic architecture. One suitable physical implementation of this architecture could be achieved through the use of wireless devices produced for sensor networks. A useful, fault-tolerant and autonomous computer could exploit all the features of sensor networks, providing benefits for our understanding of "natural computing" and robust wireless networking.

However, SC is an alternative approach to computation, and can be implemented on any interacting systems, electronic, biological, or mechanical. In addition to being a model of computation, it may also be viewed as a method of analysis for biological systems, enabling information flow, structure and computation within biology to be formulated and understood in a more coherent manner. Work is underway on more advanced visualisation of systemic computation models to enable more detailed analysis of structure, interactions and behaviours of SC models and the biological systems they represent.

Work is still ongoing in this area. It is anticipated that in the future systemic computation may even enable a clear formalism of 'complex system' enabling more coherent investigations and engineering designs to be made.

CONCLUSION

Biological computation has many significant characteristics that help give it desirable properties. Systemic computation is a model of computation that incorporates those characteristics and suggests a non-von Neumann architecture compatible with conventional hardware and able to support biological characteristics natively.

This chapter presented a platform for the

newly introduced systemic computation model including a virtual machine, language, compiler and visualiser. This permits us to design, run and test systems with natural characteristics. This platform was presented together with several concrete applications.

We showed how bio-inspired programming using SC can natively provide fault-tolerant behaviour and easy self-maintenance to a program with minimal software conception overhead: fault tolerance is achieved by duplicating system instances and self maintenance by introducing a new system using existing systems to repair each other. The fault-tolerant self-maintaining GA used in the last experiment showed that we have a crash-resistant computer able to run fault-tolerant self-maintaining programs in spite of a high probability of fault occurrence and allocating only 10% of its resource to maintenance. Therefore, compared to conventional software which crashes immediately, the SC programs are clearly better.

The overall fault-tolerance is due to the massively distributed architecture and independent computations of the systemic computer making it by definition crash proof, and then to the multiple instantiations of all the systems involved. Finally the self-maintenance systems making use of healthy parts of systems to fix damaged parts of others enabled a homeostatic behaviour.

With this method, fault detection and fault correction are done automatically and are fully integrated into the core of the program. In addition, the fault detection mechanism is independent from the kind of systems being repaired and could therefore be used as it is in any SC program. Similar to a biological organism, this process is part of the whole and just as any other constituent is a regular and autonomous running task.

We then illustrated the advantages and benefits of SC modelling, giving an overview and the outcome of past achieved work in this area. We showed, based on the presented genetic algorithm, how it could be made self-adaptive with minimal extra code, by just "topping-up" the existing model with one additional context system.

We continued our exploration of systemic computation showing how its intrinsic (non-simulated) properties of local knowledge and asynchrony naturally provide more flexibility for artificial neural network structures. The example implementation contrasts significantly with classical approaches where data and algorithm are interdependent separate parts making network implementations more rigid and less biologically plausible. Our implementation gave full autonomy to neurons, and is compatible with any neuron model (first, second, third generation). It thus highlights the potential of SC for the modelling of such natural processes, providing additional properties to our model for free.

Finally we presented the notion of artificial metabolism using systemic computation to create an organism for clustering data that is suitable for an artificial immune system. This work is inspired by Matzinger's Danger Theory and uses the notion of danger signals. Starting from scratch and working on-line our organism is able to cluster data according to its similarities and can provide danger signals when cells die in an abnormal way for the current organism.

In summary, the research described in this chapter has presented the state of the art in research on systemic computation, illustrating this new method of crash-proof computation which is designed to express models of natural processes naturally, and showing benefits demonstrated in several bio-inspired models.

REFERENCES

Adamatzky, A. (2001). *Computing in nonlinear media and automata collectives*. IoP Publishing, Bristol.

Adamatzky, A., & De Lacy Costello, B. (2002). Experimental logical gates in a reaction-diffusion medium: The XOR gate and beyond. *Physical Review E, 66*(2), 046112.1–046112.6.

Adleman, L. M. (1994). Molecular computation of solutions to combinatorial problems. *Science, 266*, 1021–1024. doi:10.1126/science.7973651

Aickelin, U., & Greensmith, J. (2007). Sensing danger: Innate immunology for intrusion detection. *Elsevier Information Security Technical Report,* (pp. 218–227).

Arvind, D. K., & Wong, K. J. (2004). Speckled computing: Disruptive technology for networked information appliances. In *Proceedings of the IEEE International Symposium on Consumer Electronics* (pp. 219-223), UK.

Avizienis, A. (1985). The N-version approach to fault-tolerant software. *IEEE Transactions on Software Engineering*, SE-111491–SE-111501.

Bentley, P. J. (2005). Investigations into graceful degradation of evolutionary developmental software. *Journal of Natural Computing, 4*, 417–437. doi:10.1007/s11047-005-3666-7

Bentley, P. J. (2007a). Climbing Through Complexity Ceilings. In A. Burke & T. Tierney (Eds.), *Network Practices: New strategies in architecture and design* (pp. 178-197). NJ: Princeton Architectural Press.

Bentley, P. J. (2007b). Systemic computation: A model of interacting systems with natural characteristics. *International Journal of Parallel . Emergent and Distributed Systems, 22*(2), 103–121. doi:10.1080/17445760601042803

Bentley, P. J. (2008). Designing biological computers: Systemic computation and sensor networks. In P. Liò et al (Eds.), *Bio-inspired computing and communication* (LNCS 5151, pp. 352-363). Springer-Verlag.

Bentley, P. J., Greensmith, J., & Ujjin, S. (2005). Two ways to grow tissue for artificial immune systems. In *Proceedings of the Fourth International Conference on Artificial Immune Systems* (LNCS 3627, pp. 139–152). Springer-Verlag.

Darnell, J. E., Lodish, H. F., & Baltimore, D. (1990). *Molecular cell biology*. New York: Scientific American Books.

Dewdney, A. K. (1984). Computer recreations: In the game called core war hostile programs engage in a battle of bits. *Scientific American, 250*(5), 14–22.

Eriksson, D. (1997). A principal exposition of Jean-Louis Le Moigne's systemic theory. *Review Cybernetics and Human Knowing, 4*(2-3), 35–77.

Fisher, R. A., & Marshall, M. (1988). *Iris plants database*. UCI Machine Learning Repository [http://www.ics.uci.edu/mlearn/MLRepository.html]

Fogel, G. B., & Corne, D. W. (2003). (Eds.). *Evolutionary computation in bioinformatics.*, San Francisco Morgan Kaufmann.

Hinton, G. E. (1989). Deterministic Boltzmann learning performs steepest descent in weight-space. *Neural Computation, 1*, 143–150. doi:10.1162/neco.1989.1.1.143

Holland, J. H. (1998). *Emergence. from chaos to order*. UK: Oxford University Press.

Horning, J. J., Lauer, H. C., Melliar-Smith, P. M., & Randell, B. (1974). A program atructure for error detection and recovery. In *Proceedings of an International Symposium on Operating Systems* (LNCS 16, pp. 171-187). Springer-Verlag.

Kandel, E. R., Schwartz, J. H., & Jessel, T. M. (1991). (Eds.). *Principles of neural science* (3rd Edition).New York: Elsevier.

Koestler, A. (1989). *The ghost in the machine.* London: Arkana Books.

Le Martelot, E., Bentley, P. J., & Lotto, R. B. (2007a). A systemic computation platform for the modelling and analysis of processes with natural characteristics. In *Proceedings of the 9th Genetic and Evolutionary Computation Conference (GECCO 2007) Workshop: Evolution of Natural and Artificial Systems - Metaphors and Analogies in Single and Multi-Objective Problems* (pp. 2809-2819), London, UK.

Le Martelot, E., Bentley, P. J., & Lotto, R. B. (2007b). Exploiting natural asynchrony and local knowledge within systemic computation to enable generic neural structures. In *Proceedings of the 2nd International Workshop on Natural Computing (IWNC 2007)*(pp. 122-133), Nagoya University, Nagoya, Japan.

Le Martelot, E., Bentley, P. J., & Lotto, R. B. (2008a). Crash-proof systemic computing: A demonstration of native fault-tolerance and self-maintenance. In *Proceedings of the 4th IAS-TED International Conference on Advances in Computer Science and Technology* (pp. 49-55), Langkawi, Malaysia.

Le Martelot, E., Bentley, P. J., & Lotto, R. B. (2008b). Eating data is good for your immune system: An artificial metabolism for data clustering using systemic computation. In *Proceedings of the 7th International Conference on Artificial Immune Systems* (LNCS 5132, pp. 412-423). Springer-Verlag.

Maass, W. (1997). Networks of spiking neurons: The third generation of neural network models. *Neural Networks, 10,* 1659–1671. doi:10.1016/S0893-6080(97)00011-7

Matzinger, P. (1994). Tolerance, danger and the extended family. *Annual Review of Immunology, 12,* 991–1045.

O'Reilly, R. C. (1996). Biologically plausible error-driven learning using local activation differences: The generalized recirculation algorithm. *Neural Computation, 8,* 895–938. doi:10.1162/neco.1996.8.5.895

Ofria, C., & Wilke, C. O. (2004). Avida: A software platform for research in computational evolutionary. *Biology, 10,* 191–229.

Peterson, C., & Anderson, J. R. (1987). A mean field theory learning algorithm for neural networks. *Complex Systems, 1,* 995–1019.

Phillips, A., & Cardelli, L. (2004). A correct abstract machine for the stochastic PI-calculus. In *Proceedings of the Workshop on Concurrent Models in Molecular Biology (BioConcur 2004),* London, UK.

Ray T. S. (1990). http://life.ou.edu/tierra

Spector, L. (2001). Autoconstructive evolution: Push, PushGP, and Pushpop. In *Proceedings of the Genetic and Evolutionary Computation Conference* (pp. 137-146). San Francisco: Morgan Kaufmann.

Tang, H., Tan, K. C., & Yi, Z. (2007). *Neural networks: Computational models and* applications. Berlin: Springer-Verlag.

Tempesti, G., Mange, D., Mudry, P.-A., Rossier, J., & Stauffer, A. (2007). Self-replicating hardware for reliability: The embryonics project. *ACM Journal on Emerging Technologies in Computing Systems, 3*(2), 9. doi:10.1145/1265949.1265955

Tempesti, G., Roggen, D., Sanchez, E., & Thoma, Y. (2002). A POEtic Architecture for Bio-Inspired Hardware. In *Artificial Life VIII: Proceedings of the 8th International Conference on the Simulation and Synthesis of Living Systems* (pp. 111-115). MIT Press, Cambridge, MA.

Thoma, Y., Tempesti, G., Sanchez, E., & Moreno Arostegui, J.-M. (2004). POEtic: An electronic tissue for bio-inspired cellular applications. *Bio Systems*, *76*, 191–200. doi:10.1016/j.biosystems.2004.05.023

Turing, A. (1936). On computable numbers, with an application to the Entscheidungsproblem. *Proceedings of the London Mathematical Society*, *2*(42), 230–265.

Upegui, A., Thoma, Y., Sanchez, E., Perez-Uribe, A., Moreno, J.-M., & Madrenas, J. (2007). The perplexus bio-inspired reconfigurable circuit. In *Proceedings of the Second NASA/ESA Conference on Adaptive Hardware and Systems* (pp. 600-605). IEEE Computer Society Press, Washington, DC.

von Neumann, J. (1966). *The theory of self-reproducing automata*. A. Burks (ed.), Urbana: University of Illinois Press.

Wallenta, C., Kim, J., Bentley, P. J., & Hailes, S. (2008). (to appear). Detecting interest cache poisoning in sensor networks using an artificial immune algorithm. *Applied Intelligence*.

Wheeler, M., & Clark, A. (1999). Genic representation: Reconciling content and causal complexity. *The British Journal for the Philosophy of Science*, *50*, 103–135. doi:10.1093/bjps/50.1.103

Wolberg, W. H., Street, W. N., & Mangasarian, O. L. (1992). *Breast Cancer Wisconsin (Diagnostic) Data Set*. UCI Machine Learning Repository [http://archive.ics.uci.edu/ml/]

Wolfram, S. (2002). *A new kind of science*. Wolfram Media, Inc.

Chapter 10
Noble Ape's Cognitive Simulation:
From Agar to Dreaming and Beyond

Thomas S. Barbalet
Noble Ape, USA

ABSTRACT

Inspired by observing bacterial growth in agar and by the transfer of information through simple agar simulations, the cognitive simulation of Noble Ape (originally developed in 1996) has defined itself as both a philosophical simulation tool and a processor metric. The Noble Ape cognitive simulation was originally developed based on diverse philosophical texts and in methodological objection to the neural network paradigm of artificial intelligence. This chapter explores the movement from biological observation to agar simulation through information transfer into a coherent cognitive simulation. The cognitive simulation had to be tuned to produce meaningful results. The cognitive simulation was adopted as processor metrics for tuning performance. This "brain cycles per second" metric was first used by Apple in 2003 and then Intel in 2005. Through this development, both the legacy of primitive agar information-transfer and the use of this as a cognitive simulation method raised novel computational and philosophical issues.

ARTIFICIAL LIFE, NOBLE APE AND AGAR

There is no coherent, universally accepted history of artificial life. The term artificial life was coined by Christopher G. Langton in the late 1980s (Langton, 1997). From the late 1980s to the early 1990s a number of popular and academic books covered the topic of artificial life either as a surveying of the art (Emmeche, 1991; Levy, 1992) or covering the author's particular interests in artificial life (Dawkins, 1987). Contemporary practitioners of artificial life tend to attribute one of these books as the basis for their development - Dawkins' Biomorphs (1987) or Dawkins' inspired possibilities (Ventrella, 2005; Barbalet & Stauffer, 2006; Barbalet & De Jong, 2007) or Sims' Blockies (1994) (Barbalet & Klein, 2006). Dawkins, Sims and the inspired practitioners'

DOI: 10.4018/978-1-60566-705-8.ch010

simulations were based on genetic algorithms.

Noble Ape was framed in the broadest possible surveying of these books. No particular book was the focused basis for the development. In fact, Dawkins' earlier work (1976) was considered over Dawkins' later work (1987) with regard to the social framing of Noble Ape. Without any guiding artificial life text, the foundational theme of Noble Ape was that artificial life empowered the developer to take from any area of interest and assemble a testable simulation environment to see how these theories inter-played. This was a view born in isolation.

In 1996, the open source Noble Ape Simulation was created to produce a rich biological environment and to simulate the movement and cognitive processes of the Noble Apes, a sentient ape-like creature that wandered through the simulated environment (Barbalet, 2005c). One of the primary interests of the Noble Ape Simulation was the development of simple societies and whether the environment could contribute to the structure of the societies created. Would a harsh environment with limited food and water create an authoritarian society? Would an environment teeming with food and water produce a casual and contemplative society? What would happen through transitions of famine or war? How would the societies develop through these experiences?

If there was a seminal theme through the original development of Noble Ape it was through the ideas of Logical Atomism (Russell, 1956). These ideas were not developed in the age of contemporary computing however they appeared applicable through the description of sense-data processing and the idea of atomic sense information. Logical Atomism presented the idea that sense data was provided in discrete processable quantities. Through providing sense data over time, the development of a coherent self could be generated. These ideas were further refined in Noble Ape Philosophic (Barbalet, 1997) into a coherent means of taking the external world and making an internal created representation. It is

important to note that this internal representation can be without observable reference in terms of relationships between the external information (or the sense data presentation of the external information) and the internal representation. This still gave no indication of the method of processing. In terms of the cognitive simulation it defined vision (shorthand for all external sense data), the identity which was the material of the cognitive simulation, fear and desire. Fear and desire were the two operators that acted on the identity to manipulate the vision information over time.

The artificial life project closest to Noble Ape was PolyWorld (Yaeger, 1994). Like Noble Ape, PolyWorld was an example of the "intelligent agents in a simulated environment" class of artificial life simulations. Although the projects were completely independent, they shared a number of the same high-level concepts - computational genetics, physiology, metabolism, learning, vision and behavior.

The primary distinctions between Noble Ape and PolyWorld related to two components. Noble Ape contained a more detailed simulated environment, including an undulating topography, a changing weather simulation and a biological simulation containing a diversity of simulated flora and fauna. The other distinction, and the subject of this chapter, was the means of simulating the intelligent behavior of the agents. PolyWorld used a neural network model of intelligence. Noble Ape did not.

The motivation not to use a neural network intelligent agent model in Noble Ape was due to Kirsh (1991). Kirsh asserted that simple processes could provide "concept-free" intelligence which was shared through all intelligent life from simians to insects. This seemed plausible and also linked well with Russell's account of Logical Atomism. Kirsh's position was highly critical of traditional artificial intelligence methods. Whilst Kirsh did not name neural networks explicitly, the tenor of his text was clearly against "highly cerebral activities" in intelligence modeling. Rather than being a technical paper, Kirsh wrote a philosophical critique of artificial intelligence which motivated much of the early cognitive simulation development in Noble Ape.

Without any clear technical description of the means of concept-free sense-data processing based on these foundational ideas in the initial Noble Ape development, the only other simulation mechanism available to the author was agar simulations that had been developed prior to the Noble Ape development as a means of learning to program real-time graphics applications.

Through high school, the author took biology courses that utilized agar studies. Materials like the author's hand and contact swabs had been place in agar dishes. The contaminated agar dishes had then been left to grow in warm, dark environments. These agar dishes were studied in terms of population growth and levels of bacteria based on the known population growth rates. These kinds of agar studies gave the author an early insight into the agar medium and bacterial growth.

With the author's interest in computer simulations, agar simulations had been particularly useful as they provided real-time movement over the screen as the agar's simulated bacterial plumes took hold and died back. These simulations represented an idealized biological environment where one or potentially more populations of organisms colonized the energy rich agar environment. In its simplest form, there was a numerical array representation of the energy stored in each agar cell and a population number indicating the population density at that particular agar cell. Various algorithms were used to produce population growth, energy consumption and movement into adjacent agar cells. These agar simulations were a population cell occupation step from simpler cellular automaton simulations. Although the agar simulations did share some of the same spatial spread processes.

In addition to artificial life books, the early Noble Ape development was also heavily influenced by "write your own computer game" books

(Isaaman & Tyler, 1982; Howarth & Evans, 1984). These books discussed how to create fictional environments and related mythos associated with these kinds of games. From the inception of Noble Ape, there needed to be a strong narrative relating to the simulation. If the entities in the environment were merely agent dots on the screen, the user would be less likely to bond with the agents and the simulation. The agents had to be humanoid and the name "Noble Ape" gave a strong emotive resonance with the user.

The development of the cognitive simulation followed a familiar pattern to other aspects of the Noble Ape development. A philosophical vision directed by apparently unrelated source code that converged back on the philosophical vision. It is this element of cyclically re-enforced philosophical experimentation through source code that has kept the author's interest in the Noble Ape Simulation for more than a decade and quite possibly many more decades to come.

The development of the cognitive simulation through agar simulation methods required a clear vision with regards to the two primary elements, fear and desire. Once the algorithm was established, the cognitive simulation needed to be tuned and the method chosen to tune the simulation required a three dimensional, real-time visual description of the cognitive simulation. Once the simulation was tuned, it was adopted by Apple and then Intel as a means of providing a rich processor metric.

The cognitive simulation development did not end after tuning or corporate use. It continues to this day and offers a number of interesting future projects both through Noble Ape and by third-parties. Like PolyWorld and a number of other contemporary mature artificial life simulations, Noble Ape is intended to continue development for many decades to come. It is not intended to be a stand-alone complete project subject to conclusion-testing. It continues to provide insights to users and developers alike. Some of these aspects will be discussed here, however

Noble Ape should not be thought of as a static or historical work.

This chapter is offered as an example of how to take a divergent set of concepts from a number of sources, including inspiration from the natural world, and produce a coherent and unique solution. It is intended to show not only the particular use in the Noble Ape Simulation but also the potential for this method to be used in other applications.

AGAR INFORMATION TRANSFER AND COGNITION

The author's interest in agar simulation predated Noble Ape. It came from three sources - high school biology coursework (as discussed), developing computer anti-virus software and as a means of showing time-evolving graphics. Writing anti-virus software created an interesting byproduct - a fascination in the heuristic analysis of infections over networks and how these infections appeared to replicate biological viruses. The computational and biological infection graphs showed similar properties and it intrigued the author sufficiently to write simple agar simulations to confirm that the simulated biology could replicate these growth rates.

As with the similarities between Noble Ape and PolyWorld, the agar simulations shared a number of traits with cellular automaton simulations (von Neumann & Burks, 1966). Rather than single cellular automaton inhabiting each array cell, a population of bacterial agents and a corresponding energy value for that agar cell over an array of agar cells was the basis of the agar simulations.

At the same time, the author began to experiment with simple real-time graphics and in particular the color capabilities of VGA. This produced colorful agar bacterial growth simulations that showed the growth and infection patterns on a fullscreen display.

As an enhancement to the long-term visual interaction, the agar simulations had end wrap-around properties. This eliminated most problems with boundary conditions and created effectively an infinite simulation space for the simulated bacterial spread. In addition to simulated bacterial consumption of energy, energy regeneration and growth was added. The idea that the simulated agar including the bacteria and energy in the system resulted in a zero sum was critical. The bacteria once dead would be the food of the next generation. The bacteria-rich agar had to flourish through wave after wave of bacterial plume. These agar simulations were integer-based both in terms of the energy level and the bacterial population but also in terms of the grid coordinates. Each grid coordinate represented an integer value of bacteria population and energy.

Through these experiments many algorithms to produce regenerating agar growth for great visual effect were developed. All the simulations had an information transfer function similar to:

$$I_{t+1}(x,y) = (\ I_t(x\text{-}1,y\text{-}1) + I_t(x,y\text{-}1) + I_t(x\text{+}1,y\text{-}1) \\ + I_t(x\text{-}1,y) + (a * I_t(x,y)) + I_t(x\text{+}1,y) + I_t(x\text{-}1,y\text{+}1) \\ + I_t(x,y\text{+}1) + I_t(x\text{+}1,y\text{+}1)\ )\ /\ b \qquad (1)$$

where *I* was the information transfer meta-agar, *a* was a weighting value to show the primacy of the central reference and *b* is a normalizing value. *x* and *y* were the cell coordinates. Whilst not referring to cellular automaton, this equation is the simulated-agar equivalent of a Moore neighborhood (1962).

This formula did not exactly replicate the random fluctuations in the agar simulation but it gave a good general equation for information transfer over time. The experimentation with agar simulations continued. The parameters that went into the growth and death of the agar simulation and the algorithms associated with energy consumption and bacterial survival became less important. The agar simulations all shared a similar pattern of information transfer between the distinct population and energy cells. This information transfer became more interesting than the underlying agar simulation.

This required a new mathematical method to describe the information transfer rather than the traditional agar simulation metrics of population and energy fluctuation.

Over time the agar populations would move outward through the agar at a rate of spread which was algorithm dependent but always adhered to the same characteristics. The spread described a spatial wave-like property of the agar. This population information transfer was an ethereal property of the agar. This analysis begged the question - what would happen if other kinds of information were placed into this meta-agar information transfer environment?

This meta-agar had both time resistive qualities and also dissipation qualities which could be represented through quantized spatial and temporal units as follows:

$$dI_{t+1}(x,y)/ds = I_t(x-1,y) + I_t(x+1,y) + I_t(x,y-1) + I_t(x,y+1) \qquad (2)$$

$$dI_{t+1}(x,y)/dt = I_t(x,y) - I_{t-1}(x,y) \qquad (3)$$

where x and y were the cell coordinates. I was the information transfer meta-agar. *dI/ds* referred to the spatial derivative and *dI/dt* was the time derivative. Obviously through various simulations there were constants of environment applied to both *dI/ds* and *dI/dt*. This did not change the underlying spatial and temporal properties. The *dI/ds* algorithm is analogous to a Von Neumann neighborhood (1966).

It is important to understand these two equations in terms of information transfer.

dI/ds propagates information through the meta-agar and also defines how information can be collected through the meta-agar. Aside from information flowing from the center, there is also

a collection of information where the information gradient is particularly favorable. There is nothing that says that the total information has to remain constant through these functions. The dI/ds can be tuned to favor optimizing information piling around like values. This is analogous to simplification and amplification.

dI/dt can also be tuned to allow for cyclical resonance which, in concert with dI/ds, can propagate particular information with greater intensity. This is analogous to wave mechanics in physics and the primary reason the physics algebraic conventions are adhered to in describing the derivatives.

Noble Ape was created relatively rapidly. It was formulated and first announced within a three week period. This was achieved as a number of the components of Noble Ape had been developed through other coding projects. These components included the terrain visualization, the real-time mouse and keyboard interface and also file parser code. Part of the underlying rationale behind developing Noble Ape was to take the divergent pieces of software the author had developed and put them together.

The cognitive simulation was no exception. It could have gone one of two ways. Prior to Noble Ape in 1994, the author travelled through Malaysia and Thailand. This provided a trilingual transfer between the English language in the larger cities to the Bahasa (Malay) language in the regional parts of Malaysia to the Thai language. The three languages were distinctly different but they all mapped onto the same underlying meaning. This begged the question - could a general language analysis algorithm be developed to parse vast quantities of a particular language and generate a syntactical-check? More importantly also a meaning-check to construct meaning from a substantial body of text. This idea became LaSiE (the LAnguage Simplification Engine). As the Philosophy of Language was also alluring to the author through reading Bertrand Russell and his student, Ludwig Wittgenstein (1953), Noble Ape's cognitive simulation could have been an abstract engineering of LaSiE. LaSiE was in part a specialized neural network algorithm, but also as the name suggests it had a substantial phoneme reduction component to simplify the neural network. Following extensive algorithm testing and modification relating to the best and most substantial electronic texts of the time (Starr, 1994) amongst others, the results were inconclusive. In contrast, the meta-agar simulation provided more positive results. The potential for this meta-agar to yield an abstract but successful cognitive simulation seemed likely.

There were still a number of problems. The information transfer did not map well to visualization information. A considerable amount of time was spent exploring how the spatial visual information could be translated into a two dimensional cognitive simulation. The original vision method had an eye simulator creating both simulated eyes' two dimensional photographic renderings of the outside world back into the cognitive simulation. This was not feasible computationally.

The solution was to translate the outside world into a scanning obstacle line - not like a radar or sonar - but like a piece of string that stretched to the nearest obstacle as a radial scan of the vision. This idea was central to the development of the Psi visualization method (Rushkoff, 1999).

It became evident that what was missing was an additional dimension in the cognitive simulation - it needed to be three dimensional (plus time evolution, obviously). The addition of a third dimension clouded how the visualization information would be put into the cognitive simulation and also how point and line (versus linear) actuators would be placed in the cognitive simulation.

In three dimensions, the Noble Ape cognitive simulation was transformed to:

$$I_{t+1}(x,y,z) = (p * I_t(x,y,z)) + (q * dI_t/ds(x,y,z)) + (r * dI_t/dt(x,y,z)) \tag{4}$$

where

$$dI_t(x,y,z)/ds = I_t(x-1,y,z) + I_t(x+1,y,z) + I_t(x,y-1,z) + I_t(x,y+1,z) + I_t(x,y,z-1) + I_t(x,y,z+1) \tag{5}$$

$$dI_t(x,y,z)/dt = I_t(x,y,z) - I_{t-1}(x,y,z) \tag{6}$$

where x, y and z were the cell coordinates. p, q and r were weightings to produce a normalized value for I_{t+1}. dI/ds was labelled "desire" and dI/dt was labelled "fear". The origins of these names have already been discussed with regards to the Noble Ape Philosophic document. The algorithmic distinction of these two components were subdivided and named for both methodological and emotive reasons.

The methodological reasons related to the mathematical primitives that also came through the biological simulation. Noble Ape's biological simulation was based on quantum mechanics. The landscape provided the wave function for operators to be applied to determine the surface area, directional gradient and other factors similar to a wave function in quantum mechanics. The landscape height map could be operated on to provide additional biological information. The surface area of the landscape at a particular point indicated the amount of grass or moss that was present. A greater surface area (characterized by steep angles) meant trees could not grow. Similarly the east/west traversing of the simulated sun provided an accurate indication of insect movement and also where the most sun would be found over the land area. These biological operators resolved down to basic orthogonal primitives.

The same was observed with fear and desire. The algorithmic effect of fear was a very rapid time evolving reaction. Desire in contrast dissipated in all directions leaving a shadow of previous information. Fear and desire were orthogonal and they contributed different properties to the information transfer.

The final orthogonal component was the representation of the information transfer itself. This could be represented by contour lines through three dimensional space. This captured the shape of the evolving information transfer and indicated the stability of the cognitive simulation. It was that information transfer contour that was so useful in tuning the cognitive simulation.

The emotive reasons behind naming the two components of the equation fear and desire was it allowed someone who was a mathematical novice to get a clear understanding of what these properties did in the cognitive simulation. The description of fear as an instantaneous reaction to rapid changes in stimulus gave a solid emotive connection to both what the algorithm was attempting to model in the cognitive simulation but also with the user's own experience. Similarly the discussion of desire as being something which motivated future judgements, future expectations, future understanding and also desire as the great simplifier, seemed to both describe the algorithmic reality and resonate with the user's experience and understanding.

TUNING AN INSTRUMENT IN A NON-LINEAR KEY

There is an ethereal quality in tuning a detailed non-linear simulation that combines elements of art, science and experience. Other simulators, too, find it difficult to describe what is explicitly needed to be able to tune artificial life simulations (Barbalet & Stauffer, 2006; Barbalet & Daigle, 2006). Before exploring the tuning of the cognitive simulation, it is important to explore the basics in simulation tuning and then discuss the importance of visualization to give accurate feedback.

In 1997, a high school science teacher in rural Australia contacted the Noble Ape development to ask if it would be possible to take just the ecological simulation component of Noble Ape and put it in a program that his high school students could use. The ecological simulation in Noble Ape contained the animal groups found through the

author's travels in Malaysia (Cranbrook, 1987). As already noted, the biological simulation dynamics were based in principles from quantum mechanics. The transition in simulated flora and fauna populations were covered with surface area integrals and convolutions. The teacher's requirements were better served with extended Lotka-Volterra equations (Volterra, 1931) where the notion of predator-prey was expanded to include plants, herbivores, carnivores and omnivores. From this the collected species were phylum-grouped into bushes, grass, trees, seed eating birds, sea birds, birds of prey, insect eating birds, insects, mice, frogs, lizards, apes, cats and fish. The fish represented the ocean fish population surrounding the Noble Apes' island and thus could be maintained as a constant food source. This provided a rich and complicated set of non-linear interactions that evolved over time.

The feedback provided to the high school teacher, in terms of teaching his students how to tune the biological simulation, was to start with a reduced subset of the species and look at how these groups interacted over time. This in some regard was analogous to learning to juggle by starting with a couple of balls. Traditionally Lotka-Volterra mathematics had been taught with two dimensional plotting to show stability conditions in joining cycles. For so many species interactions, this was impossible. The method of finding reoccurring values for all populations at known time deltas was not applicable with plant, herbivore, carnivore and omnivore interactions. After tens of hours of play, the author was able to get five species stability with occasional bursts into six or seven species stability. It was a bridge too far for the high school teacher and students.

Lotka-Volterra equations related to scalar population numbers. This was in contrast to the Noble Ape Simulation method which used area-integration to show population predation through overlapping habitat. The property of stability of simulation over areas and volumes is a different technique, but with similarities to the scalar analysis in terms of time-cycle changes.

When development began on Noble Ape, the visualization of the cognitive simulation was achieved with planar scans through the three dimensional brain representation. This provided little meaningful information bar a great aesthetic draw to the user.

By 2000, a real-time rotating three dimensional visualization method that showed the changes in the cognitive simulation to a high level of detail was implemented (Barbalet, 2004). This, in turn, enabled the cognitive simulation variables to be tuned with real-time graphical feedback. Whilst this was not analogous to the cyclical graphs of Lotka-Volterra tuning, it enabled stable constants to be found for both the awake and asleep aspects of the cognitive simulation)(Figure 1).

The simulation needed to model the properties of sleep in terms of dreaming and problem resolution analogous to human and mammalian sleep cycles. The Noble Apes would need to be able to have some dreams they could remember and use the sleep environment to distill long-term goals. Ideally the quantifiable transition between awake and asleep could be transitioned for additional feedback.

The elements of the cognitive simulation had already been defined through the Noble Ape Philosophic document. The implementation of constants for the sleep and awake states of the cognitive simulation had to be regulated around those orthogonal ideas. This created an interesting mix of applied method weighed against philosophical methodology.

This method of creating graphically stable simulations with applied theories was well defined through the biological simulation tuning and the author's earlier work with agar simulations. The constants that emerged would ultimately be scalar weightings to multi-dimensional equations. The philosophy of fear and desire, the identity and ultimately Logical Atomism was also a heavy consideration in the simulation tuning but the simulation needed to operate with stability first and foremost. With these apparently competing

ideas, the simulation constants found in March 2001 following months of simulation tuning were particularly interesting (Barbalet, 2008).

In the awake brain simulation:

$$I_{t+1} = ((I_t * 0) + (dI_t/ds * 171) + (dI_t/dt * 146)) / 1024 \qquad (7)$$

In the asleep brain simulation:

$$I_{t+1} = ((I_t * 501) + (dI_t/ds * 86) + (dI_t/dt * 73)) / 1024 \qquad (8)$$

Whilst awake the cognitive simulation existed purely on instinct coming from desire (the *dI/ds* multiplier) and fear (the *dI/dt* multiplier). Desire played a slightly heavier role in both awake and asleep states, but the fear and desire elements were both roughly halved during sleep with a substantial residual identity maintaining through the sleep versus none in the awake state.

For Noble Apes that were unable to sleep, in conditions of drowning or for other similar extreme reasons, the effects in the cognitive simulation would be quite dramatic indicating the level of trauma the Noble Ape was suffering.

Two important points should be noted with the final six constants that came through the applied analysis of the three dimensional graphical output of the cognitive simulation.

These results may not be unique. In fact there is a good range around the constants (tested to +/- 5 in all cases) that yielded the same kind of stability. It is to be determined if there are unique properties associated with these number ranges. It has been a useful byproduct to allow users the freedom to choose their own constant weighting or variations of cognitive simulation constants to allow experimentation with the outcome through these ranges and their range boundaries.

The subjective nature of the non-mathematical to mathematical mapping of fear and desire and the narrative historical description of the Noble Ape Simulation development could indicate an

Figure 1. An example of the Noble Ape cognitive simulation visualization through general movement paused at 11.25 degree rotations

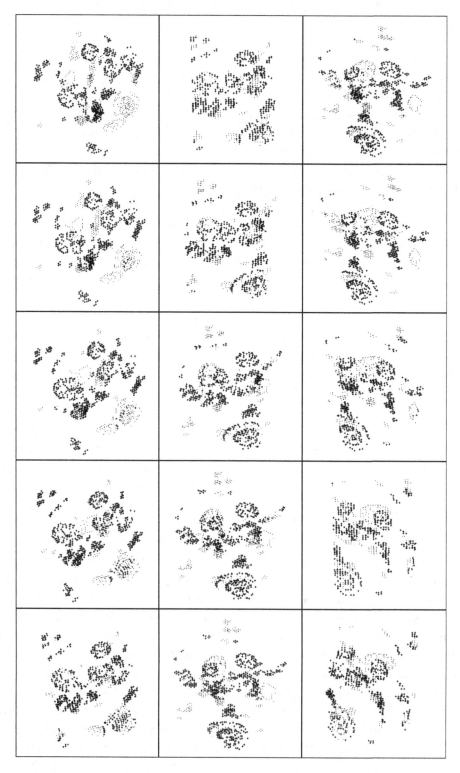

implicit yet predetermined outcome. This is a fair criticism. The results captured the almost circular philosophical outcomes of creating a mathematical modeling method that described two orthogonal operators and the insight into awake and asleep states of the resultant mathematical simulation.

Both these points merit further investigation.

The apparent dampening of the cognitive simulation through the large total divisor (1024) may appear a point of concern for information persistence. This analysis comes through passive observation. It should be noted that this dampening actually forces dynamic structure propagation through the cognitive simulation which explicitly beats this dampening. This can be observed in the Noble Ape Simulation but merits further descriptive investigation and analysis (Figure 2).

Through tuning the cognitive simulation, the description of sleep in a quantifiable sense may be considered with some interest. The sleeping Noble Ape has a roughly halved awake-state combination of fear and desire but also maintains a half residual identity component which doesn't exist when awake. As with real animals, the Noble Apes remain relatively paralyzed during sleep. It would be an interesting experiment to simulate the dreamt movements of Noble Apes as an additional psychological tool to understand the Noble Apes thought processes a little better.

APPLIED USE OF THE COGNITIVE SIMULATION

Without the interest of two engineers at Apple, Nathan Slingerland and Sanjay Patel, Noble Ape's cognitive simulation would have continued as an open source curio. In early 2003, they asked to use Noble Ape as an example for new optimization techniques that Apple wanted to display to their third party developers. The two techniques related to thread balancing the cognitive simulation and rewriting the cognitive simulation optimized for AltiVec vector processing (Barbalet, 2005b).

The cognitive simulation had been optimized heavily to minimize the mathematical instructions that went into the tight loop focused around quadrants characterized as positive and negative, lower and upper halves (Barbalet, 2008). These minimized the use of binary ANDs on edge limits. The brain is defined as a 32 x 32 x 32 byte array (32768 bytes) with a previous time cycle cached brain (old brain).

```
#define   B_SIZE  (32768)
#define   B_WR  (B_SIZE - 1)
#define   F_X  (1)
#define   F_Y  (32)
#define   F_Z  (1024)
#define   B_Z  (B_SIZE - F_Z)
#define   B_Y  (B_SIZE - F_Y)
#define   B_X  (B_SIZE - F_X)
/*
 *  The basic brain formula is;
 *      b(t+1) = a*l + b(t)*m + (b(t)-b(t-
1))*n;
 *
 *  The waking mind works differently to the
sleeping mind. This is quantified
 *  with two distinct but similar equations.
There are two versions for the awake
 *  and asleep states, in this function it
is simplified to;
 *      b(t+1) = a*l_a + b(t)*l_b - b(t-
1)*l_c;
 *
 *      where, l_a = 1, l_b = m+n, l_c = n
 */
#define   B_FN(ave, bra, obra)
((((ave)*l_a)+((bra)*l_b)-((obra)*l_c))>>10)
/* positive and negative, lower and upper
halves */
#define   B_P_LH  (br[loc+F_X]+br[loc+F_Y]+b
r[loc+F_Z])
#define   B_P_UH  (br[loc-F_Z]+br[loc-
F_Y]+br[loc-F_X])
#define   B_N_LH  (br[(loc+F_X)&B_
WR]+br[(loc+F_Y)&B_WR]+br[(loc+F_Z)&B_WR])
#define   B_N_UH  (br[(loc+B_Z)&B_
WR]+br[(loc+B_Y)&B_WR]+br[(loc+B_X)&B_WR])
typedef   unsigned char   n_byte;
typedef   unsigned short   n_byte2;
typedef   long   n_int;
void brain_cycle(n_byte * local, n_byte2 *
constants) {
  n_byte  *br = local, *obr = &local[B_
SIZE];
  n_int   l_a = constants[0], l_c = con-
stants[2];
  n_int   l_b = constants[1] + l_c, loc = 0;

    while (loc < F_Z) {
```

Figure 2. An example of the Noble Ape cognitive simulation visualization resolving multiple dynamic structures paused at 11.25 degree rotations

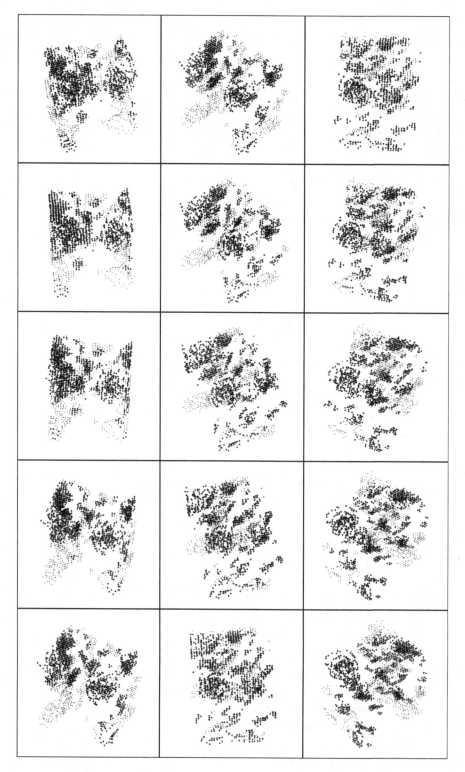

```
  n_int  average = (B_P_LH + B_N_UH);
  n_byte  obr_tmp = obr[loc];
  n_byte  br_tmp;
  obr[loc] = br_tmp = br[loc];
  br[loc++] = (n_byte)(B_FN(average, br_
tmp, obr_tmp));
  }
  while (loc < B_Z) {
    n_int  average = (B_P_LH + B_P_UH);
    n_byte  obr_tmp = obr[loc];
    n_byte  br_tmp;
    obr[loc] = br_tmp = br[loc];
    br[loc++] = (n_byte)(B_FN(average, br_
tmp, obr_tmp));
  }
  while (loc < B_SIZE) {
    n_int  average = (B_N_LH + B_P_UH);
    n_byte  obr_tmp = obr[loc];
    n_byte  br_tmp;
    obr[loc] = br_tmp = br[loc];
    br[loc++] = (n_byte)(B_FN(average, br_
tmp, obr_tmp));
  }
}
```

The Apple engineers took a single cycle of the brain calculation and optimized it into a 16-bit pipeline which allowed eight independent brain cycles to be calculated simultaneously (Barbalet, 2005b).

```
  average = br[loc_MINUS_X] + br[loc_
MINUS_Y]; // 16-bit precision
  average += br[loc_MINUS_Z] + br[loc_
PLUS_X]; // 16-bit precision
  average += br[loc_PLUS_Y] + br[loc_
PLUS_Z]; // 16-bit precision
  obr_tmp = obr[loc]; // 8-bit precision
  obr[loc] = br_tmp = br[loc]; // 8-bit
precision
  nbr_tmp = var_a * average; // 32-bit
precision
  nbr_tmp += var_b * br_tmp; // 32-bit
precision
  nbr_tmp -= var_c * obr_tmp; // 32-bit
precision
  nbr_tmp = nbr_tmp >> 10; // 32-bit pre-
cision

  br[loc] = nbr_tmp; // 8-bit precision
```

The Apple engineers proposed a 16-bit arithmetic pipe where the following was divided into high 16-bit and low 16-bit arithmetic.

```
  nbr_tmp = var_a * average; // 32-bit
precision
  nbr_tmp += var_b * br_tmp; // 32-bit
precision
```

```
  nbr_tmp -= var_c * obr_tmp; // 32-bit
precision
  nbr_tmp = nbr_tmp >> 10; // 32-bit pre-
cision
```

The brain cycles per second is equal to the number of individual brain cycles calculated every ten seconds divided by ten. If there were a troop of sixty apes and in ten seconds there were six full simulation cycles, the ape brain cycles per second would be;

60 * 6 / 10 = 36 ape brain cycles per second.

There were two reasons the ape brain cycles per second metric was useful. It provided a thorough arithmetic pipeline through the vector implementation which indicated the processor was heavily loaded. Similarly Noble Ape's multi-window real-time graphical feedback environment shared the processor load with the ape brain calculations. This showed the impact the GUI interaction had on a separate but interdependent section of the code.

Intel's optimization for SSE, implemented by Justin Landon, Michael Yi and Pallavi Mehrotra, also included a simplification in the desire calculation to limit the switching between referencing the current brain and the previous brain cycle's memory. This minimized the memory traversal through the calculation.

```
static inline void brain_avg( __m128i *avg_
hi, __m128i *avg_lo, int loc, char *br, char
*obr ) {
  int _v1 = ( loc + F_X ) & B_WR;
  int _v2 = ( loc + F_Y ) & B_WR;
  int _v3 = ( loc + F_Z ) & B_WR;
  int _v4 = ( loc + B_Z ) & B_WR;
  int _v5 = ( loc + B_Y ) & B_WR;
  int _v6 = ( loc + B_X ) & B_WR;
  int _v1_lo = _v1 & ~0x0F;
  int _v6_lo = _v6 & ~0x0F;
  int _v1_hi = ( _v1_lo + 0x10 ) & b_eand;
  int _v6_hi = ( _v6_lo + 0x10 ) & b_eand;
  __m128i a_hi = _mm_load_si128( (__m128i*)
(( _v1_hi < loc ? obr : br ) + _v1_hi) );
  __m128i a_lo = _mm_load_si128( (__m128i*)
(( _v1_lo < loc ? obr : br ) + _v1_lo) );
  __m128i a = _mm_or_si128( _mm_srli_si128(
```

```
a_lo, 1 ), _mm_slli_si128( a_hi, 15 ) );
  __m128i b = _mm_load_si128( (__m128i*)((
_v2 < loc ? obr : br ) + _v2) );
  __m128i c = _mm_load_si128( (__m128i*)((
_v3 < loc ? obr : br ) + _v3) );
  __m128i d = _mm_load_si128( (__m128i*)((
_v4 < loc ? obr : br ) + _v4) );
  __m128i e = _mm_load_si128( (__m128i*)((
_v5 < loc ? obr : br ) + _v5) );
  __m128i f_hi = _mm_load_si128( (__m128i*)
(( _v6_hi < loc ? obr : br ) + _v6_hi) );
  __m128i f_lo = _mm_load_si128( (__m128i*)
(( _v6_lo < loc ? obr : br ) + _v6_lo) );
  __m128i f = _mm_or_si128( _mm_srli_si128(
f_lo, 15 ), _mm_slli_si128( f_hi, 1 ) );
  __m128i zer = _mm_setzero_si128();
  __m128i tmp1 = _mm_add_epi16( _mm_unpack-
hi_epi8( a, zer ), _mm_unpackhi_epi8( b, zer
) );
  __m128i tmp2 = _mm_add_epi16( _mm_unpack-
hi_epi8( c, zer ), _mm_unpackhi_epi8( d, zer
) );
  __m128i tmp3 = _mm_add_epi16( _mm_unpack-
hi_epi8( e, zer ), _mm_unpackhi_epi8( f, zer
) );
  *avg_hi = _mm_add_epi16( _mm_add_epi16(
tmp1, tmp2 ), tmp3 );
  tmp1 = _mm_add_epi16( _mm_unpacklo_epi8(
a, zer ), _mm_unpacklo_epi8( b, zer ) );
  tmp2 = _mm_add_epi16( _mm_unpacklo_epi8(
c, zer ), _mm_unpacklo_epi8( d, zer ) );
  tmp3 = _mm_add_epi16( _mm_unpacklo_epi8(
e, zer ), _mm_unpacklo_epi8( f, zer ) );
  *avg_lo = _mm_add_epi16( _mm_add_epi16(
tmp1, tmp2 ), tmp3 );
}
static inline __m128i SSE_B_FN ( __m128i
aver_hi, __m128i aver_lo, __m128i sse_
local_a, __m128i sse_local_b, __m128i
sse_local_c, __m128i sse_br_tmp, __m128i
sse_obr_tmp )
{
  const __m128i mask = _mm_set1_epi32(0xff);
  __m128i sse_zero = _mm_setzero_si128( );
  __m128i brain_lo, brain_hi, obrain_lo,
obrain_hi;
  __m128i result_01, result_02, result_03,
result_04, result_05, result_06;
  brain_lo = _mm_unpacklo_epi8 ( sse_br_tmp,
sse_zero );
  brain_hi = _mm_unpackhi_epi8 ( sse_br_tmp,
sse_zero );
  obrain_lo = _mm_unpacklo_epi8 ( sse_obr_
tmp, sse_zero );
  obrain_hi = _mm_unpackhi_epi8 ( sse_obr_
tmp, sse_zero );
  result_01 = _mm_unpacklo_epi16 ( sse_
local_a, sse_local_b );
  result_02 = _mm_unpacklo_epi16 ( aver_lo,
brain_lo );
  result_02 = _mm_madd_epi16 ( result_01,
result_02 );
  result_03 = _mm_unpackhi_epi16 ( aver_lo,
brain_lo );
  result_03 = _mm_madd_epi16 ( result_01,
result_03 );
  result_05 = _mm_mullo_epi16 ( obrain_lo,
sse_local_c );
  result_04 = _mm_mulhi_epi16 ( obrain_lo,
sse_local_c );
  result_02 = _mm_sub_epi32 ( result_02,
_mm_unpacklo_epi16 ( result_05, result_04 )
);
  result_02 = _mm_srli_epi32 ( result_02, 10
);

  result_03 = _mm_sub_epi32 ( result_03,
_mm_unpackhi_epi16 ( result_05, result_04 )
);
  result_03 = _mm_srli_epi32 ( result_03,
10 );
  result_02 = _mm_packs_epi32 ( _mm_
and_si128(result_02, mask), _mm_and_
si128(result_03, mask) );
  result_03 = _mm_unpacklo_epi16 ( aver_hi,
brain_hi );
  result_04 = _mm_madd_epi16 ( result_01,
result_03 );
  result_03 = _mm_unpackhi_epi16 ( aver_hi,
brain_hi );
  result_05 = _mm_madd_epi16 ( result_01,
result_03 );
  result_03 = _mm_mullo_epi16 ( obrain_hi,
sse_local_c );
  result_06 = _mm_mulhi_epi16 ( obrain_hi,
sse_local_c );
  result_04 = _mm_sub_epi32 ( result_04,
_mm_unpacklo_epi16 ( result_03, result_06 )
);
  result_04 = _mm_srli_epi32 ( result_04,
10 );
  result_05 = _mm_sub_epi32 ( result_05,
_mm_unpackhi_epi16 ( result_03, result_06 )
);
  result_05 = _mm_srli_epi32 ( result_05,
10 );
  result_04 = _mm_packs_epi32 ( _mm_
and_si128(result_04, mask), _mm_and_
si128(result_05, mask) );
  result_02 = _mm_packus_epi16 ( result_02,
result_04 );
  return result_02;
}
void brain_vect_cycle( n_byte *local, n_
byte2 *constants ) {
  __m128i local_a = _mm_set1_epi16( con-
stants[0] );
  __m128i local_c = _mm_set1_epi16( con-
stants[2] );
  __m128i local_b = _mm_set1_epi16( con-
stants[1] + constants[2] );
  __m128i *br = (__m128i*)local;
  __m128i *obr = (__m128i*)&local[32 * 32 *
32];
  int i = 0;
  for( i = 0; i < B_SIZE/16; i++ ) {
    int loc = i * 16;
```

```
    __m128i avg_lo, avg_hi;
    brain_avg( &avg_hi, &avg_lo, loc,
(char*)br, (char*)obr );
    __m128i br_tmp = _mm_load_si128( br + i
);
    __m128i obr_tmp = _mm_load_si128( obr +
i );
    _mm_store_si128( obr + i, br_tmp );
    __m128i ret = SSE_ B_FN( avg_hi, avg_lo,
local_a, local_b, local_c, br_tmp, obr_tmp
);
    _mm_store_si128( br + i, ret );
  }
}
```

Both Apple's AltiVec and Intel's SSE implementations hinged on 128-bit processing pipes. It is foreseeable that these concepts will date quickly as many more orders of these processing pipes become the norm. The underlying principles should continue to be useful.

FUTURE DIRECTIONS

The cognitive simulation in Noble Ape, described here, is based on very simple definitions for the interaction between dI/ds and dI/dt. The differential interactions for dI/ds can be expanded further. In fact the dimensionality of the Noble Ape brain, as described, favors no particular direction. It was developed to optimize the propagation of information throughout the brain. We can consider the possibility of changing the cognitive algorithm to something that distinguishes between the spatial dimension. The cognitive equation then could be rewritten as:

$$I_{t+1} = (m * I_t) + (n * dI_t/dx) + (o * dI_t/dy) + (p * dI_t/dz) + (q * dI_t/dt) \tag{9}$$

where m is a normalizing weighting, n, o and p are dimensional skewing desire weightings and q is a fear weighting. Or consider an additional weighting that was applied to the cognitive simulation to one or all of the constant parts:

$$I_{t+1}(x,y,z) = p(x,y,z) * I_t(x,y,z) + q(x,y,z) * dI_t/ds(x,y,z) + r(x,y,z) *dI_t/dt(x,y,z) \tag{10}$$

where p, q and r are location dependent weightings. Transition in the cognitive simulation between the Noble Apes falling asleep and waking up could be linearly interpolated:

$$I_{t+1}(x,y,z) = p(t) * I_t(x,y,z) + q(t) * dI_t/ds(x,y,z) + r(t) * dI_t/dt(x,y,z) \tag{11}$$

where p, q and r are time dependent cognitive simulation weightings that linearly transition between sleep and awake states based on the time. It begs the question if such a transition would yield the kind of stability found in the awake and asleep defined states through the weighted basis of these variables.

To-date the cognitive simulation has been volatile. The brain values are not retained between simulation runs and the cognitive simulation produces the only non-determinate element to the Noble Ape Simulation. Due to the three dimensional spatial representation of the brain model, compression algorithms suited to this data will be required for network transfer of the cognitive simulation to seed additional simulations. It is possible that binary tree spatial models be used to reduce the brain space into smaller compressible cubes and transmit this spatially reduced data over networks faster. With this model either fixed or variable size cubes will be optimized for reduced bit variable length. For example, a group of values in the range of 0 to 31 would be compressed into 5-bit variable space where 5 bytes would contain eight of these 5-bit values.

The discussion of compression also raises the possibility of brain cell sizes larger than bytes being used in the future. It is foreseeable that 16, 32 and 64 bit brain cell sizes be used for more subtle changes in the cognitive simulation. Similarly the size of the Noble Ape brains could increase from

255

32 x 32 x 32 to 128 x 128 x 128 or greater. Other animals in the Noble Ape environment could be cognitively modeled with smaller sub-set brains. Predatory birds and cats could have 4 x 4 x 4 and 16 x 16 x 16 brains respectively.

This document has discussed the Noble Ape cognitive simulation through algorithms and language. Increasingly demonstrations of the Noble Ape Simulation and its cognitive component are given to audiences that require immediate feedback. These demonstrations are exclusively graphical and often given by demonstrators without the mathematical and philosophical grounding discussed in this document (Damer, 2008). The visual demonstration of the cognitive simulation requires descriptive and graphic distinctions between fear and desire to be drawn. These visualization methods to actively identify the different components in the shared algorithms that make up the Noble Ape cognitive simulation may also prove beneficial in teaching these techniques to an audience quickly.

The Noble Ape Simulation contains a single time-cycle scripting language, ApeScript. The Noble Ape file format and ApeScript allows the expert user to both experiment with the existing cognitive simulation, manipulate the cognitive simulation's identity, fear and desire weightings and also devise their own cognitive simulation algorithms (Barbalet, 2005a).

Whilst it has not been the topic of this chapter, some attention to comparing and contrasting the response time and dynamic adaption of the Noble Ape cognitive simulation versus more traditional neural network models is an ongoing area of interest and development. As the Noble Ape Simulation allows for multiple cognitive simulation models, the potential to hybridize elements of PolyWorld and the Noble Ape Simulation is being discussed at the time of writing. This would provide a number of additional metrics to measure the Noble Ape cognitive simulation against the neural network contained in PolyWorld.

It is possible that the cognitive simulation method described here could be implemented next to a neural network to provide distinct modes of information processing for different circumstances. The Noble Ape cognitive simulation has been optimized for immediate reaction with less attention to long-term passive movement. The comparative tests for the cognitive simulation versus neural networks may relate to a number of factors. These include;

- The average life-time of a simulated agent,
- The average energy consumed per day by a simulated agent,
- The survival of a simulated agent through difficult conditions (drought/famine and disease),
- The survival of a simulated agent through predation of a single predator species, and,
- The survival of a simulated agent through predation of multiple predator species.

The Noble Ape cognitive simulation was optimized to respond to the predation and survival concerns in particular. The ability to test the cognitive simulation against and as a hybrid with neural networks such as PolyWorld will further strengthen this aspect of artificial life. This chapter was written as an introduction to the Noble Ape cognitive simulation method. There obviously is a lot more to explore and quantize through the cognitive simulation development.

NEW KINDS OF THINKING

The Noble Ape cognitive simulation represents a new model - understanding information transfer and basic intelligence in a dynamic environment. The basis of the cognitive simulation in simple cellular information transfer is inspired by nature through watching growth patterns in agar. The insight and tuning the method provided has been explored in the chapter.

The Noble Ape development, including the cognitive simulation, is an ongoing work. The theme of the development to-date has been juxtaposing previously unrelated mathematical models as a means of exploring what is possible through conjunction. This is characterized here through a "philosophy first" approach with the view that the mathematics will follow. This allowed the exploration of a variety of novel mathematical methods for simulation. The skills described here in terms of adapting and tuning mathematical methods should provide inspiration for exploration.

The chapter has defined the mathematics and methodology of the Noble Ape cognitive simulation. However it does not eliminate the method being used in other simulations for similar effects. The cognitive simulation shows there are a number of possible uses as a replacement to traditional neural network models.

The advice to instill in new simulators looking to embark on their own simulation development is to ignore tradition. The respect of your peers should come through radical diversity rather than similar acceptance.

REFERENCES

Barbalet, T. S. (1997). Noble Ape Philosophic. *Noble Ape Website*. Retrieved June 20, 2008, from http://www.nobleape.com/man/philosophic.html

Barbalet, T. S. (2004). Noble ape simulation. *IEEE Computer Graphics and Applications, 24*(2), 6–12. doi:10.1109/MCG.2004.1274054

Barbalet, T. S. (2005a). ApeScript Notes. *Noble Ape Website*. Retrieved June 20, 2008, from http://www.nobleape.com/man/apescript_notes.html

Barbalet, T. S. (2005b). Apple's CHUD Tools, Intel and Noble Ape. *Noble Ape Website*. Retrieved June 20, 2008, from http://www.nobleape.com/docs/on_apple.html

Barbalet, T. S. (2005c). *Original Manuals, Noble Ape 1996-1997*. San Mateo, CA: Cafe Press.

Barbalet, T. S. (2008). Noble Ape Source Code. *Noble Ape Website*. Retrieved June 20, 2008, from http://www.nobleape.com/sim/

Barbalet, T. S., & Daigle, J. P. (2006). Interview with John Daigle. *Biota Podcast*. Retrieved June 20, 2008, from http://www.biota.org/podcast/biota_jdaigle_062506.mp3

Barbalet, T. S., & De Jong, G. (2007). Dawkins, Memetics, Commerce and the Future: Part 2 of 3. *Biota Podcast*. Retrieved June 20, 2008, from http://www.biota.org/podcast/biota_080407.mp3

Barbalet, T. S., & Klein, J. (2006). Interview with Jonathan Klein. *Biota Podcast*. Retrieved June 20, 2008, from http://www.biota.org/podcast/biota_jklein_070806.mp3

Barbalet, T. S., & Stauffer, K. (2006). Interview with Ken Stauffer. *Biota Podcast*. Retrieved June 20, 2008, from http://www.biota.org/podcast/biota_kstauffer_080506.mp3

Cranbrook, E. (1987). *Mammals of South-East Asia*. Singapore: Oxford University Press.

Damer, B. (2008). Demonstration of Noble Ape Simulation at GreyThumb Silicon Valley. *YouTube*. Retrieved June 20, 2008, from http://www.youtube.com/watch?v=YBWxFKv3zBk

Dawkins, R. (1976). *The Selfish Gene*. New York, NY: Oxford University Press.

Dawkins, R. (1987). *The Blind Watchmaker*. New York, NY: Norton.

Emmeche, C. (1991). *The Garden in the Machine*. Princeton, NJ: Princeton University Press.

Howarth, L., & Evans, C. (1984). *Write Your Own Fantasy Games for Your Microcomputer*. London: Usborne.

Isaaman, D., & Tyler, J. (1982). *Computer Space-games*. London: Usborne.

Kirsh, D. (1991). Today the earwig, tomorrow man? *Artificial Intelligence, 47*, 161–184. doi:10.1016/0004-3702(91)90054-N

Langton, C. G. (1997). *Artificial Life: An Overview (Complex Adaptive Systems)*. Cambridge, MA: MIT Press.

Levy, S. (1992). *Artificial Life: A Report from the Frontier Where Computers Meet Biology*. New York, NY: Pantheon.

Moore, E. F. (1962). Machine models of self-reproduction. [Providence, RI: The American Mathematical Society.]. *Proceedings of Symposia in Applied Mathematics, 14*, 17–33.

Rushkoff, D. (1999). A technology genius has Silicon Valley drooling - by doing things the natural way. *The Guardian*. Retrieved June 20, 2008, from http://www.guardian.co.uk/technology/1999/oct/07/onlinesupplement17

Russell, B. (1956). The philosophy of logical atomism. In R.C. Marsh (Ed.), *Logic and Knowledge, Essays 1901-50* (pp. 175-281). London: Allen and Unwin.

Sims, K. (1994). Evolving Virtual Creatures. In A. Glassner (Ed.), *ACM SIGGRAPH: Computer Graphics 1994 Proceedings* (pp. 15-22). New York, NY: ACM Press.

Starr, K. (1994). *The Starr Report*. New York, NY: Public Affairs.

Ventrella, J. J. (2005). GenePool: Exploring the Interaction Between Natural Selection and Sexual Selection. In A. Adamatzky (Ed.), *Artificial Life Models in Software* (pp. 81-96). London: Springer-Verlag.

Volterra, V. (1931). Variations and fluctuations of the number of individuals in animal species living together. In R. N. Chapman (Ed.), *Animal Ecology* (pp. 409–448). New York, NY: McGraw-Hill.

von Neumann, J., & Burks, A. W. (1966). *Theory of Self-Reproducing Automata*. Urbana, IL: University of Illinois Press.

Wittgenstein, L. (1953). *Philosophical Investigations*. Oxford: Basil Blackwell.

Yaeger, L. S. (1994). Computational Genetics, Physiology, Metabolism, Neural Systems, Learning, Vision, and Behavior or PolyWorld: Life in a New Context. In C. Langton (Ed.), *Proceedings of the Artificial Life III Conference* (pp. 263-298). Reading, MA: Addison-Wesley.

Chapter 11
Genetic Programming for Robust Text Independent Speaker Verification

Peter Day
d-fine Ltd., UK

Asoke K. Nandi
University of Liverpool, UK

ABSTRACT

Robust Automatic Speaker Verification has become increasingly desirable in recent years with the growing trend toward remote security verification procedures for telephone banking, bio-metric security measures and similar applications. While many approaches have been applied to this problem, Genetic Programming offers inherent feature selection and solutions that can be meaningfully analyzed, making it well suited for this task. This chapter introduces a Genetic Programming system to evolve programs capable of speaker verification and evaluates its performance with the publicly available TIMIT corpora. Also presented are the effects of a simulated telephone network on classification results which highlight the principal advantage, namely robustness to both additive and convolutive noise.

INTRODUCTION

The aim of this chapter is to investigate whether Genetic Programming (GP) can be used as a nature inspired human competitive solution for producing machine. A primary goal of machine learning strategies is to allow the user to state a problem in as high a level as possible and provide a solution without further human intervention. While we are still some way off this goal, GP has proven itself a powerful problem solver in many *hard* domains. We do not go in depth into the background and theory underlying GP, but instead choose to demonstrate its effectiveness at solving a real world problem, namely Automatic Speaker Verification (ASV), and demonstrate human competitive results.

DOI: 10.4018/978-1-60566-705-8.ch011

Figure 1. A typical automatic speaker recognition (ASR) system (Figure originally published in Day and Nandi (2007) © 2007 IEEE)

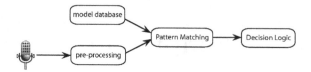

We begin by introducing the problem and giving a brief literature review, and follow this by showing how GP can be used to solve this problem and introduce some recent extensions to GP also inspired by nature that can be used to increase its effectiveness. We conclude the chapter reporting on results obtained using the proposed strategy and analyse these results to show how human innovations are "re-discovered" using GP.

BACKGROUND

The aim of ASV systems is to answer the question, "is the speaker who s/he claims to be". More formally, the challenge of an ASV system is to establish the presence of a speaker within an unknown (open) set of speakers. This problem, together with the related Automatic Speaker Identification (ASI) problem (in which the aim is to establish which speaker is speaking from a closed set of speakers), has enjoyed sustained research interest over recent years.

Most proposed ASV systems share similar strategies. The typical process involves: some form of pre-processing of the data (silence removal) and feature extraction, followed by some form of speaker modelling to estimate class dependent feature distributions (see Figure 1). A comprehensive overview can be found in Campbell (1997). Adopting this strategy the ASV problem can be further divided into the two problem domains:

1. Feature extraction and selection, and
2. Speaker modelling and matching

We discuss each of these in turn below.

Feature Extraction and Selection

The choice of features in any proposed ASV system is of primary concern (Kinnunen, 2003; Gopalan et al., 1999), because if the feature set does not yield sufficient information, then trying to estimate class dependent feature distributions is futile. As with all feature dependent classification problems, the ideal feature set should contain features that have high inter-class variance and low intra-class variability. Ideally the selected features should also be as independent of each other as possible in order to minimize redundancy.

There is a huge amount of information present in a speech signal and speech can be described as having a number of different *levels* of information. From the *top* level down we have:

- *Lexical and Syntactic features*, such as language use and sentence construction. These require a lot of intelligence to understand and interpret, and automating this process is the aim of the speech recognition research.
- *Prosodic Features*, which represent information such as: Intonation, stress and rhythm of speech.
- *Phonetic features* which represent the "sound" of individual syllables.
- *Low-level acoustic features*, which generally give information on the system that creates the sound, such as the speaker's vocal tract.

It is likely that the human brain uses a combination of these levels of information when identifying a speaker. However this does not necessarily imply that a machine needs to understand the syntactic of a sentence in order to correctly identify an individual. Recently, lexical and syntactic features have been used in ASR systems (see Reynolds et al., 2003; Ferrer et al., 2003). These systems tend to be more resilient to noisy transmission paths; however there is a high computational cost as the proposed systems are required to interpret the text at some level, so the systems cannot be considered truly independent of text. If we consider these levels of information as indicators solely of speaker identification, then the purely lexical and syntactic features are largely redundant (it is not usually possible to determine who is speaking from a transcript of something they have said). Similarly, while *Prosodic* and *Phonetic* features may give speaker dependent information, it is also likely to be text or time dependent and thus not obviously suited to this task. Information solely about *how* the sound is produced (from low level acoustic features) on the other hand *should* give enough information to identify accurately a speaker as this is naturally speaker dependent and independent of text.

Most previous work relied on the use of *low-level acoustic features*. Mel-Frequency Cepstral coefficients (MFCCs) have been particularly popular in recent years as they give a highly compact representation of the spectral envelope of a sound. Many proposed systems have relied solely on this data and good results have been reported. Linear Prediction coefficients and the closely related Line Spectrum Pairs have also been popular, as have the related Perceptual Linear Prediction values which have been shown to be more robust in noisy environments. Other work also combines multiple feature sets, such as pitch and MFCCs in the case of Ezzaidi et al. (2001), and this approach has also been shown to give a more robust solution.

It is both conceivable and probable that different features have a different level of *importance* in characterising different voices. For instance, if we meet someone with an unusually high-pitched voice, this is likely to become the primary information that we use when recognising or describing that individual's voice, as it is more obvious than more subtle characteristics such as intonation or accent (and these characteristics are redundant). While in this example the pitch may be enough to characterise the voice, in other cases, where the pitch of an individual voice is, by definition, more *"normal"*, this information is likely to be meaningless and other features (those that do distinguish the individual voice from the *"normal"*) are required. It is easier to remember or describe a voice by deducing how it differs from our experience of what is normal. While successful classification or verification for the majority of voices has been demonstrated using a shared feature set, some voices are harder to classify robustly than others (Doddington et al., 1998). We propose that these more difficult to classify voices are a result of a limited shared feature set. If a system finds it hard to classify a sub-set of the voices it analyses it follows that they are similar, at least as far as the limited feature set is concerned. Following the assumption that the ideal set of features to distinguish an individual voice from all others (i.e. a feature set that *characterises* the voice) will vary between different voices, it can be seen that an ideal strategy would allow some level of feature selection on a *per voice* basis.

Speaker Modelling

The speaker modelling stage of the process varies more in the literature. Speaker modelling takes place when an individual is enrolled into an ASR system with the aim of defining a model (usually feature distribution values) that *characterises* the individual. The two most popular methods in previous work are Vector Quantisation (VQ) and Gaussian Mixture Models (GMM).

In the VQ method (Soong et al., 1987), speaker

models are formed by clustering the speaker's feature vectors in K non-overlapping clusters. Each cluster is represented by its centroid (average vector) and the resulting collection of K centroids is referred to as its codebook and serves as a model for the speaker. The two considerations, when using this method, are: what method to use to perform the clustering and what size codebook to use. There is much literature which discusses these issues and a comprehensive overview can be found in Kinnunen (2003).

The GMM method differs from the VQ method in that it is a parametric method: A GMM consists of K Gaussian distributions parameterised by their *a priori* probabilities, mean vectors and covariance matrices. The parameters are typically estimated by maximum likelihood estimation. A typical implementation of this system for ASR can be found in Reynolds and Rose (1995).

Other techniques such as mono-Gaussian models (Bimbot et al., 1995), decision trees (Navratil et al., 2003), Support Vector Machines (Wan 2003; Wan and Campbell., 2000) and Artificial Neural Networks (Wouhaybi and Al-Alaou, 1999) have also been applied, and a good comparison and overview can be found in Farrell et al. (1994) and Ramachandran et al. (2002). Previous work also includes classifier ensembles Rodriguez-Linares et al. (2003), where multiple modelling techniques are used, chosen according to their suitability to a given feature set. Decisions are made dependent on the values given by several independent classifiers.

While good results have been reported using a variety of different systems, most systems suffer heavily if the bandwidth is limited or the signal is transmitted over a noisy transmission path (such as a telephone network). This is largely blamed on the features used being impaired by noise.

GENETIC PROGRAMMING

Genetic programming (GP) is an *automated programming* technique based on the Darwinian concepts of evolution. While techniques such as ANN have demonstrated good results in the wider field of pattern recognition and classification (and with ASV), GP reflects nature on a larger scale and has been shown to be highly adaptable as well as offers innovative solutions. GP has been applied to other classification tasks with great success (see Guo et al., 2005 for example) and feature selection is inherent in the process of "evolving" a classifier, making it well suited to classification tasks, as feature selection is often done independently of classification - possibly by a pre-cursor to GP, a Genetic Algorithm (GA).

The premise behind GP and all other evolutionary techniques is survival of the fittest. Initially randomly created individuals (candidate solutions) are rated according to their ability to do a given task (in this case, verify a voice), with the fittest being selected for further processing (such as breeding to create new individuals). Each candidate solution in GP is a computer program, and so the GP process can be considered a meta-heuristic search through the *program space* using a population of competing variable length computer programs capable of performing the desired task. In order for the search process to be effective, a fitness function must be used in order to guide the direction of evolution, and typically the fitness function measures how accurately each candidate solution performs a given task.

FOUNDATIONS

The first experiments with GP were reported by Smith (1980) and Cramer (1985), as described in the first book dedicated to GP by Koza (1992). These early experiments were constrained to solving "toy problems", due to computational resources available at the time. Unlike other

Evolutionary Computation (EC) representations, computer programs have both variable structure and variable elements. These two dimensions of search are explored simultaneously, making the potential *search space* much larger and more complex than other implementations of EC. Consequently the computational resources required to carry out a successful search are much higher than other EC methods, due to this GP has only recently, with the continuing increase in computational power available to researchers and advances in the GP methodology, been applied to real world problems and gained interest from the wider research community.

The term *automatic invention machine* has recently been coined to describe GP after recent works have resulted in patented solutions to real world problems (Koza et al., 2003). A current trend among the GP research community is to generate "human-competitive" results, i.e. automatically create solutions to problems that are equal to or better than current human endeavours. This is a bold new direction for a methodology that only a few years ago was constrained to solving trivial "toy problems".

Another key advantage of the GP method is the so called "high A to I ratio" (the ratio of that which is delivered by the automated operation of the *artificial* method to the amount of *intelligence* that is supplied by the human applying the method to a particular problem), inferring that little human effort is required to apply a GP system to a new problem domain. Some claim GP to be the most generalised ML method to date as the solution representation (a computer program) can be applied to many problem domains, and moving between these problem domains does not generally require an adaptation of the method. Later work of Koza (in Koza et al., 1999) introduced a "*general-purpose Genetic Programming Problem Solver*", which could be applied to a wide variety of problems with a trivial amount of human effort.

These claims are an attractive prospect to ML researchers, as combined they imply that GP can be applied to many fields with little effort and outperform human researchers in these fields. There are, however, still issues with GP that hinder its progress in many problem domains (such as sub optimal convergence). While human-competitive results have been demonstrated in *some* problem domains, in other domains, particularly domains with a complex *fitness landscape*, GP has not yet demonstrated the same level of achievement.

When GP is applied to classification problems, the process generally generates a program tree composed of mathematical functions (both linear and non-linear) and input features, so it could be considered a non-linear combination of features. The aim of the evolutionary process is that output of the program should give an indication of the class of the input data.

The use of GP for ASV allows the evolution of programs *tailored* to individuals. This implies that the features used will also be specific to the individuals, which we propose will provide a more robust solution. This also allows solutions to be tailored to different environments as the process does not rely on a single feature set, combinations of features can be inherently selected that perform well for an individual under given circumstances (such as over a telephone line). This system could also be readily extended to include new features if they are required with minimal impact to the evolution and classification process. While the computational cost for evolving a good solution is relatively high, lexical and syntactic features have been excluded so that the evaluation cost is low.

It is beyond the scope of this chapter to describe the GP process comprehensively; readers unfamiliar with this process should refer to Koza (1992) or Banzhaf et al. (1998).

A Fitness Function

The fitness function is the principal concern when establishing a GP process, as this states the problem and thus determines the direction of evolution. In the case of ASV we can simply specify that the ideal program should output a *one* if the speaker is detected and a *zero* otherwise. The simplest way of doing this is to base a fitness measure on the difference between the desired output of the GP program and the measured output for a given set of inputs with an equation as follows:

$$fitness = \sum_{n=1}^{N} (desired_n - given_n)^2 \qquad (1)$$

where, N is the number of training cases, *desired* and *given* are the desired (i.e. expected) result and result produced by the candidate solution for training case n respectively. The ideal fitness will be *zero* (i.e. there is no difference between the given values and the desired values - the program is *ideal*).

While this fitness function may suffice, it has not proved robust for complex classification problems such as ASV in the authors' experience. With this strategy a good fitness value can be achieved by individuals that perform very well with a subset of training cases, but poorly with others. This is clearly not acceptable for classification problems, so measures must be taken to promote convergence to solutions where *all* training cases are correctly classified, i.e. it is better to classify more cases correctly than make fewer cases closer to the desired value.

In order to drive the poorly performing fitness cases (outliers) closer to the desired value we introduce a more complex fitness function: First, we simplify the problem by scaling outputs given by each GP program to the range 0 to 1. Next, each individual is assigned a binary value (p_n) for each of the training cases (n), this value indicates whether the output of the program for the training case is within a given range (k) of the desired value, thus:

$$if\ |\ desired_n - given_n\ | < k,\ \ p_n = 1$$
$$otherwise\ \ p_n = 0 \qquad (2)$$

where k is a dynamic constant that changes during the evolution process. Initially (at generation 0) the value is set to 0.5, so that it determines whether the output of the individual is within the limit of data correctly classified. If an individual succeeds in having all its training data within this range of the expected value (i.e. all p_n values are equal to one) the value of k is reduced to the mean error of that individual for the next generation. This evaluation is carried out in every generation of the evolution process and has the effect of first ensuring that all training cases are classified correctly, thus reducing the intra-class variance.

Considering the p_n values, the resultant raw fitness (f_r) function is then given by:

$$f_r = N + \sum_{n=1}^{N} ((desired_n - given_n)^2 - p_n) \qquad (3)$$

The inclusion of the number of training cases (N) is to ensure that the optimal fitness is *zero*. While this is not essential, it is used to simplify the stopping criteria used.

Finally it is also important to add some parsimony pressure (Soule and Foster, 1998) to prevent code bloat. This process is well documented and established, and the simplest implementation is to penalise individuals according to their size thus:

$$f_p = f_r + cS \qquad (4)$$

where f_p gives the fitness of the individual including parsimony pressure, c is a constant that dictates the penalty associated with size (typically 0.001) and S is the size of the individual (i.e. the total number of nodes).

In our experiments we use this strategy in association with a dynamic tree depth limit (Silva and Almeida, 2003) that sets an initial short maximum depth for individuals when the run is started. Trees are only allowed to exceed this limit if their overall fitness is better than the previous best fitness. If this is the case then the maximum size for allowed trees is increased to the depth of the new best of run individual's depth. There are many other proposed strategies that could also be used to control code bloat (see Zhang and Nandi (2007), for example), but a study of the different methods that could be used is beyond the scope of this chapter.

While this fitness function does steer the direction of evolution towards solutions that classify more solutions correctly, the process still suffers from sub-optimal convergence (i.e. solutions which struggle to classify a subset of training examples). In the following text we introduce some new concepts that further promote convergence at solutions which perform well with *all* training cases.

Comparative Partner Selection

In GP, the reason often cited for sub-optimal convergence is the tendency toward diminishing genetic diversity as the evolutionary process (se-

lection of the fittest) transpires. While arriving at the correct or optimal solution is clearly dependent on individuals that resemble this solution being selected for further processing, this also increases the likelihood of convergence at a sub-optimal solution. The aim of Comparative Partner Selection (CPS) is to promote populations that are capable of performing equally well with all training cases and hence reduce the probability of arriving at a sub-optimal solution (which also leads to smaller population sizes being required) and an increase in the speed of evolution.

CPS is reliant on the method of assigning each individual in a generation a binary string fitness characterisation (BSFC) in addition to the overall fitness value that is required in all evolutionary methods. The BSFC indicates the strengths and weaknesses of the individual and while this appears at first to be a similar concept to the p_n values discussed previously (eq. 2), their applications are quite different. The BSFC is used to give an indication of the behaviour (or *phenotype*) of an individual.

Figure 2. Generation of a binary string fitness measure string for 10 fitness cases. The mean is represented by the dashed line, hence all cases above the line will be represented by a zero (representing a weakness), and all others represented by a one (representing a strength). The resulting fitness string in this case is 1100101100. Figure originally published in Day and Nandi (2007) © 2007 IEEE

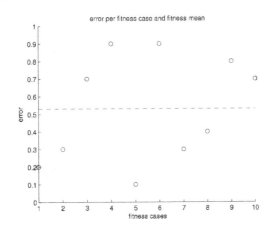

The process for assigning an individual a BSFC is trivial: *one* represents strength, while *zero* represents weakness, i.e. any training case, where the error is less than or equal to the mean error for that individual, results in a *one*, while any training case that performs worse than the mean is indicated by a *zero*. Consequently an individual that gives the "correct" answer will have a fitness string that is solely comprised of ones. An example of this process is shown in Figure 2. The length of the fitness string will be dependent on the number of training cases used. In the case of evolving an ASV program the BSFC will represent how well classified each of the training voices are, i.e. which examples the individual can classify most accurately, and which voices it is not as good at classifying.

It is our contention that it is beneficial to the population as a whole to maintain the *behavioural* diversity of the population, such that the population performs equally well with all training cases. Further, we suggest that strengths and weaknesses (and hence the BSFC described above) can be used as a simple measure of an individuals' behaviour. Following these lines it can be seen that implementing an "opposites attract" strategy when selecting parents for crossover operations will maintain the ability of the population to solve all fitness cases equally, so that a population does not reach a state where it contains no genetic material capable of solving a subset of training cases.

A probability of crossover that increases the chance of crossover if one individual is strong in an area that the other is not, and decreases the chance if they are both weak in the same area can be calculated using simple (and computationally inexpensive) logical operations:

$$p(crossover) = \frac{\sum XOR(f_1, f_2)}{\sum NAND(f_1, f_2)} \qquad (5)$$

where f_n is the binary fitness string of individual n and $\sum$ represents the summation of each bit in the binary string. This process can be seen clearly in Figure 3.

Implementation of this strategy is relatively straightforward:

- An individual is selected according to a standard GP method (such as the roulette system), based solely on the fitness *value*.
- A second individual is selected in the same manner.
- The probability of the two individuals producing offspring is calculated.
- It is decided (by generating a random number) whether the two individuals will reproduce or not.
- If the individuals do reproduce then a new starting individual is selected, otherwise

Figure 3. An example of the CPS process for 2 individuals with 8-bit BSFCs. The lighter squares represent ones, while the darker squares represent zeros. In this case the probability of crossover is 2/3. Figure originally published in Day and Nandi (2007) © 2007 IEEE

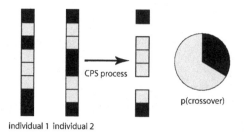

individual 1   individual 2   CPS process   p(crossover)

another secondary individual is selected and the process is repeated.

Clearly it is possible that one individual will not find a suitable individual to reproduce with, if this is the case, after a pre-determined search time (such as meeting 50% of the population) a partner is selected for crossover without considering the fitness strings.

In terms of nature, the fitness values are used to determine the probability of two individuals meeting and the fitness strings are used to determine the probability of two individuals choosing to mate.

Empirical studies carried out by the authors have shown that without CPS, evolving programs capable of performing robust ASV has a poor success rate as the evolutionary process *usually* converges at solutions which perform poorly with a subset of the training cases. Using CPS in conjunction with the fitness function introduced the system is intolerant of convergence to premature solutions and hence provides useful classifiers.

Multiple Populations - The Island Model

It has been shown in previous literature (Folino et al., 2003) that the introduction of the island model to the GP process offers significant advantages in the speed of evolution and avoiding convergence at sub-optimal solutions, and makes the parallelisation of the process simple. In this chapter we use an Asymmetric Island model, similar to the one discussed in Koza (2000). However, using dynamically chosen migration routes we additionally promote migration between genetically different *islands*. This is accomplished by evaluating each *island* in terms of strengths and weaknesses of its current generation. Each population is assigned a fitness string representing how successfully the individuals making up the population solve each of the test cases. The individuals' error values are weighted according to their overall fitness

to stop the worst individuals in the population dominating the overall impression of strengths and weaknesses:

$$popFitnessString_n = \sum_{i=1}^{I} \frac{error_{n,i}}{fitness_{n,i}} \qquad (6)$$

where I is the total number of individuals in the island population, and n represents the fitness case.

A BSFC is then assigned to the island in the same manner as previously described for individuals (see Figure 2). The CPS method (eq 5) is then used to establish "migration" routes, although it is referred to as *Comparative IslandSelection* (CIS) in order to avoid confusion. In our experiments each island has *three* migration routes at the end of every generation, so the process is as follows:

- Create copies of top p individuals
- Stochastically divide copied group into n smaller groups
- Select an Island at random; if it has any "ready to be exported" pools the CIS evaluation is performed (to determine probability of migration).
- Stochastically decide if migration takes place:
  If the migration takes place, individuals from one of the pools of the selected island are imported into the next generation, migration is not symmetrical (each island only selects islands from which to import individuals).
  Otherwise another island is selected and CIS is performed.
- Island selection and evaluation process is repeated until n pools have been imported into the next generation.

If a suitable migration route cannot be found (after performing island selection and CIS evaluation with all potential islands), one of pools of individuals from the "ready to be exported" set

Figure 4. A model of typical voice transmission over a telephone network. Figure originally published in Day and Nandi (2007) © 2007 IEEE

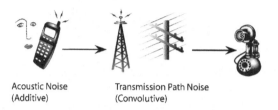

Acoustic Noise
(Additive)

Transmission Path Noise
(Convolutive)

is incorporated back into the next generation. It is possible for one population to set up multiple migration routes with a single island (assuming there are individuals left to import), meaning that more individuals will migrate from that island. The migration rate for all experiments in this chapter is set at 1% per migration route (3% of individuals in total will have migrated). This proportion of migration is consistent with previous works in GP and has proved sufficient to promote diversity.

The effect of multiple populations in solving the ASV problem is not nearly as dramatic as the effect of CPS, in fact the same performance can be achieved by using a single population with around 20% more *total* individuals. However, this strategy does have a dramatic effect on the ability to distribute the process (i.e. run the evolution in parallel over a cluster of computers), making it almost trivial.

TEST DATA

The TIMIT Corpora

The TIMIT corpora (Lamel et al., 1986; Fisher et al., 1986) is used in this chapter due to its high number of speakers and its use in other literature making it useful in comparison with other proposed methods. This corpora contains 630 speakers (438 male and 192 female) each speaking 10 sentences, there are 2 sentences that are spoken by all speakers and the remaining 8 are selected randomly from

a large database. The speech signal is recorded using a high quality microphone with a sampling frequency of 16kHz in a quiet environment.

A Noisy TIMIT

One of the principal applications of ASV systems is remotely confirming the identity of a person for reasons of security such as telephone banking, so we must consider the transmission of the speech over a telephone network when finding a solution, an example of such a system is shown in Figure 4.

In order to create a more realistic training and testing environment, several datasets were derived from the original corpora; these are outlined on Table 1. Firstly a dataset was derived by down-sampling the original corpora to 8 kHz (*TIMIT-8*). Three different simulations of typical phone transmissions were created through the use of three different filters: all three filters include both additive and convolutive noise. *Filter 1* simulates a Plain Old Telephone System (POTS), *Filter 2* simulates a GSM mobile network and *Filter 3* simulates a more complex mobile and POTS system (similar to the model shown in Figure 4). *Filter 3* is reserved purely for testing purposes and is not included in any of the training sets.

Training and Test Sets

Twenty-five speakers were chosen at random (19 male, 6 female) to represent the to-be-verified

Table 1. Description of datasets used

Name	
TIMIT	Standard corpora
F1-TIMIT	Filtered through *filter 1* (see text)
F2-TIMIT	Filtered through *filter 2* (see text)
F3-TIMIT	Filtered through *filter 3* (see text)
TIMIT-8	Corpora down-sampled to 8kHz
F1-TIMIT-8	Down-sampled to 8kHz and filtered through *filter 1*
F2-TIMIT-8	Down-sampled to 8kHz and filtered through *filter 2*
F3-TIMIT-8	Down-sampled to 8kHz and filtered through *filter 3*

(TBV) individuals. A further 45 speakers (32 male, 13 female) were chosen at random to represent the "impostors" in the training process. The remaining speakers were used in the testing procedure.

Each speaker in the TIMIT corpora has around 30 seconds of speech. We divide this into two equal halves for each of the TBV individuals for training and testing respectively. This gives 15 seconds of TBV speech for the training process; this is coupled with 1 second of randomly selected speech from each of the 45 "impostor" individuals (a total of one minute training speech).

In order to increase the initial rate of evolution only a small subset (5 seconds TBV and 10 seconds of "impostor" speech) is introduced at the beginning of the run. This allows individuals to be evaluated more quickly yet there is enough data to give an indication of individuals that are likely to be successful. More training data is added every time the k value from eq 2 is reduced (i.e. when the best individual is correctly classifying all current training examples). Additional training data is not added to all islands simultaneously. If one island has additional training cases when calculating the probability of migration tunnels being formed, then only the first N bits of the populations BSFC are considered (where N is the least number of training cases being used by either island). That is, if Island A has 15 training cases and Island B has 25, the CIS strategy is performed between the population fitness string

of Island A and the first 15 bits of the population fitness string for Island B.

We also experiment using multiple training sets (e.g. TIMIT and F1-TIMIT), with the intention of evolving a classifier that is robust to multiple environments. This strategy also has the benefit of more training data being available.

The test set comprises of the remaining 15 seconds of the TBV individuals data and 100 single second samples randomly chosen from the corpora (not including the training set of "impostor" speakers). Each of the best-of run individuals for each of the TBV individuals is evaluated with all datasets.

SYSTEM IMPLEMENTATION

Application of GP to the ASV problem, to the authors' knowledge, has not been done before. We utilise techniques introduced in previous sections (CPS and CIS) - a full description of the system is given below.

Feature Generation

Audio descriptors are important in many fields (like speech recognition, voice synthesis, and sound classification) and many descriptors have been suggested (see Ellis, 1996; Lu et al., 2001; Zhang and Kuo, 1998 for examples). Using GP has the advantage of allowing the process to select the most important features and discard any unnecessary ones; hence many descriptors are generated, but the initial stages are the same for all.

Firstly the speech signals are sliced into roughly 1 second "portions", each of these portions is treated as a separate input signal. These portions are further divided into windows of 1024 samples (with a 10% overlap) for data sampled at 16kHz and 512 samples for data sampled at 8kHz data (approximately 0.06 seconds), and for each of these windows the following descriptors are generated, and their mean and variance are recorded as the input descriptors.

The range of features included is purposely large, as while some of the features do not relate directly to speaker individuality (such as active sound level), they may be of some use in evolving more complex programs.

Mel-Frequency Cepstral Coefficients

Mel-frequency Cepstral coefficients (Davis and Mermelstein, 1980) have usually been associated with speech analysis and processing, and can be used as a compact representation of the spectral envelope. These coefficients are described as perceptual features as they are chosen to mirror how our brain is understood to comprehend sound. Delta MFCCs (which are believed to indicate the speech rate) are also included as these have shown good results in previous ASR literature. We consider both sets of coefficients up to the 10th order.

Linear Prediction Coefficients (LPC)

Linear prediction, the process of predicting future sample values of a digital signal from a linear system, has been used with success in speech processing and coding; and LPC are believed to give very accurate formant information of acoustic signals. We consider the LPC up to the 14th order (excluding the 0th order coefficient).

Perceptual Linear Prediction Coefficients (PLPs)

PLPs (Hermansky, 1990) are highly related to LPC, but take advantage of psychoacoustic principles and consequently are generally more robust in noisy environments. We consider the first 9 PLPs.

Spectral Descriptors

Further descriptors can be derived that give other information on the spectral envelope.

- Spectral flatness: This is a ratio between the geometric mean and the arithmetic mean of the spectrum. This descriptor gives an idea of the flatness; the higher it is, the closer to white noise the signal is.
- Spectral centroid: the centre of gravity of the spectrum.
- Spectral skewness: the 3rd order central moment gives an indication about the symmetry of the spectra.
- Spectral kurtosis: the 4th order moment gives further indication of the spectra.
- Spectral Crossings: Spectral crossings (at a set threshold) can be used to determine how many strong peaks there are in the spectra.
- Spectral peaks (index and magnitude): the largest five are considered (giving 10 descriptors in total).

Temporal Descriptors

- Zero Crossing Rate: the number of times the signal changes from negative to positive values.
- Active sound level: The amount of acoustic energy present.
- Variances in all the descriptors mentioned between frames (i.e. their variance) can also be considered temporal descriptors.

In total there are 60 descriptors, each with a mean and variance over the 1 second frame, leading to 120 numbers for each individual. Additionally, the possible terminal pool includes integers, fractions, a random number generator and other constants such as π.

The final inclusion is the Perturbable Numerical Value (PNV) (Koza et al., 2003): A value that is initially created at random (within the range -1 to 1), but can be changed, or perturbed, during the evolutionary process. Values are perturbed through a discrete operator, and the '*to be perturbed*' value is considered the mean of a Gaussian distribution (with standard deviation of 0.25), the amount that the value is perturbed is determined by this distribution such that most perturbations will be small in magnitude.

While we concede that many of these inputs are likely to be useless or redundant, the aim of this example is to show how GP can be used to solve problems by providing the system with as much information as plausible and let the evolutionary process perform the feature selection and dimension reduction. Further, it should be noted that the choice of features has been made to cover widely accepted features in the speech analysis community - we have actively tried not to "tailor" the input features to the ASV problem. It could also be argued that we have missed some important features - ideally we would like to include all the features described above and more over a variety of time frames; however, while GP can be said to include in-built feature selection, it is still a search algorithm (albeit one that is searching a "solution program space") and increasing the input or function pools essentially increases the search space and hence makes the process less efficient. So we have compromised by including a large number of input features (by comparison with other published ASV systems), without being exhaustive.

Function Pool

The functions available to GP individuals are shown in Table 2. Both linear and non-linear functions are included in addition to logical operators. The inclusion of logical operators allows the programs to use complex decision logic. Each function also has an *arity*, this is simply the number of input values the function requires.

Using the above descriptors and functions, a candidate solution might look like the tree shown in Figure 5. While successful solutions are generally a lot more complex and consequently hard to analyse meaningfully, this tree gives an impression of the nature of a solution.

Additional Run Parameters

An overview of the run parameters can be seen in Table 3. Due to the nature of GP, most of the parameters are decided by trial and error, or "rule of thumb" approximations. The values used in this chapter are largely based on previous experience and performing a large number of trial and error studies with the ASV problem and have been chosen to give a good chance of convergence at robust solutions. While smaller population sizes may result in equally good solutions (and require considerably less computational cost), the chance of arriving at *good* solutions is low; the population sizes used in this chapter are chosen to provide

Figure 5. A potential candidate solution given the descriptors and functions used

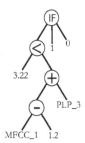

Table 2. The function pool.

Name	arity	function
sin	1	$sin(x)$
log	1	$log(x)$
ln	1	$ln(x)$
logsig	1	$1/(1 + exp(-x))$
tansig	1	$2/(1 + exp(-2x)) - 1$
round	1	round x to nearest integer
ceil	1	round up x to nearest integer
floor	1	round down x to nearest integer
average	2	$mean(x_1, x_2)$
exp	1	$exp(x)$
log10	1	$log_{10}(x)$
lt	2	is x_1 less than x_2
gt	2	is x_1 more than x_2
eq	2	does x_1 equal x_2
neq	2	does x_1 differ from x_2
pow	2	$x_1^{x_2}$
sqrt	1	$\sqrt{x}$
nroot	2	$\sqrt[x_2]{x_1}$
plus	2	$x_1 + x_2$
minus	2	$x_1 - x_2$
multiply	2	$x_1 x_2$
divide	2	x_1 if $x_2 = 0$, else x_1 / x_2
and	2	are x_1 AND $x_2 \geq 1$
Not	1	if $x \geq 1$, 1, else 0
Or	2	are x_1 OR $x_2 \geq 1$
If	3	x_2 if $x_1 \geq 1$ else x_3

a robust solution at the cost computational of power.

In addition to parameters previously discussed, a half-elitist strategy is used. This strategy means that a new generation is made up of half completely new individuals (selected proportionate to fitness) and the remaining half is comprised of the best individuals from the previous generation and the new generation. The majority of these parameters are *typical* values for GP, and have been arrived at empirically.

RESULTS

A summary of results are given in Table 4 as percentage of test cases correctly classified (for all 25 TBV individuals). The classification process simply takes the output of the GP generated program and the range of outputs given by the program for the training data; if the output of the program is closer to the range of the TBV individuals training data it is classified thus, otherwise it is classified as "impostor". A more complicated

Table 3. Run parameters

Parameter	Value(s)	
Generic Operators	**Type**	**Percentage**
	one-offspring Crossover (internal points)	50%
	Terminal Crossover (non PNV)	9%
	PNV Crossover	9%
	Gaussian Mutation of PNV	19%
	Standard Mutation	3%
	Reproduction	10%
Population Size	12 islands of 5000 individuals (60,000 total)	
Population Migration	3% asynchronous Migration (see text)	
Stop Conditions	350 generations or when all $P_n = 1$ and $k < 0.01$ (see eq 2)	
Elitism	Half-Elitist (see text)	
Parent Selection	Roulette Method with CPS	

Table 4. Summary of the classification results for the best of run individuals

Test Set									
Training Set	TIMIT	F1-TIMIT	F2-TIMIT	F3-TIMIT	TIMIT-8	F1-TIMIT-8	F2-TIMIT-8	F3-TIMIT-8	Overall
TIMIT	99.5%	81.2%	77.8%	74.5%	79.0%	78.4%	74.1%	72.0%	79.6%
F1-TIMIT	92.1%	93.5%	89.3%	91.8%	89.1%	83.7%	81.4%	79.8%	87.6%
F2-TIMIT	98.8%	92.4%	97.9%	93.3%	90.4%	89.9%	90.8%	88.5%	92.8%
TIMIT-8	98.6%	88.7%	92.7%	91.1%	97.9%	82.0%	87.8%	90.2%	91.1%
F1-TIMIT-8	98.1%	93.1%	88.9%	90.0%	95.5%	93.7%	90.7%	89.8%	92.5%
F2-TIMIT-8	98.0%	92.8%	96.7%	93.8%	96.2%	91.8%	92.6%	90.3%	94.0%
TIMIT& F1-TIMIT	99.2%	97.3%	93.8%	94.0%	91.6%	91.2%	88.8%	91.6%	93.4%
TIMIT & F2-TIMIT-8	99.8%	96.1%	97.8%	95.7%	98.1%	89.6%	94.6%	93.8%	95.7%
TIMIT & F1-TIMIT & F2-TIMIT-8	99.7%	97.1%	95.8%	96.2%	98.9%	94.7%	90.9%	94.0%	97.0%

decision making process could be adopted, but this simple routine proves sufficient.

When the training and test sets are taken from the standard TIMIT corpora, the correct classification rate is similar to previous published results. Yet, advantages of the process introduced in this chapter become clearer when handling *noisy* data. Indeed, when the training set is comprised of

both clean and noisy data, the resulting program achieves up to 97% correct verification across all testing environments. This is considerably better than other reported results with similar experiments in noisy environments. In van Vuuren (1996) correct classification rate of 92% is reported when the testing environment is the same as the training environment, but this falls to 81.9% when the

Table 5. Results using GMM generated speaker model

Feature Set	Clean environment (TIMIT)	Same noisy environment (F1-TIMIT)	Different noisy environment (F1-TIMIT and F3-TIMIT)
PLP	98.2%	90.2%	78.1%
MFCC	99.6%	86.3%	74.0%
PLP + MFCC	99.1%	93.0%	83.9%

Figure 6. The descriptors used in the solutions generated for the 25 TBV individuals under normal conditions. Note that descriptors marked var indicate the variance of that feature over the 1 second frame. All other values are mean. 5LP represents the 5 Largest Peaks (for other abbreviations see text). Figure originally published in Day and Nandi (2007) © 2007 IEEE

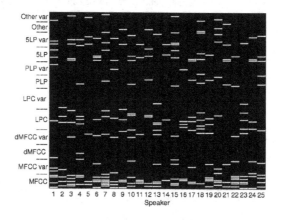

environments are different. While these results are not directly comparable with the results presented in this chapter, as these results are based on 20 seconds of speech and the corpora are different, they do suggest that previous methods struggle in noisy environments.

This is verified in our own experiments with identical training and test sets using a GMM method (based on the method proposed in Reynolds and Rose, 1995). Results are given (in Table 5) for a training set comprising of *TIMIT* for the clean environment and *F1-TIMIT* for the noisy environments. The down-sampled and *F2-TIMIT* datasets are omitted from these experiments. Both the PLP and MFCC features are used (as these have proved effective in previous work), a combination of these features is also used, these features are calculated in the same manner as described for the proposed GP system (only

the mean values are considered). The number of clusters used is 32 (in common with previous work), and 15 iterations Expectation Maximisation are used to train the system. While the Cepstral Mean Subtraction (CMS) method has been used in some previous work, its advantages have not always been consistently observed (van Vuuren, 1996). For example, the above work shows that the average identification error of GMM using either PLP features or those with RASTA compensation in one second segments is not improved with the inclusion of CMS; in any case, CMS is not the issue here. As we aim to provide a baseline that can be computed accurately with the baseline in other work, we have not applied CMS in these investigations.

The results show that the GMM method is not as resilient to noisy transmission paths as the method we have proposed, this can be seen

Figure 7. The descriptors used in the solutions generated for the 25 TBV individuals under noisy conditions. See description of Figure 6 for more details. Figure originally published in Day and Nandi (2007) © 2007 IEEE

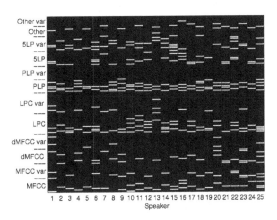

particularly when the training and testing environments are different. For completeness, it is worth noting that in our work GMM has 32 adjustable parameters, while GP has 36 functions and run parameters.

As the solutions generated by the GP process are very large, clear understanding is difficult, although some understanding can be gained by analysing which descriptors each solution uses. Figure 6 shows the use of descriptors in solutions generated using the clean training set (TIMIT) and Figure 7 shows the use of descriptors in solutions generated using the clean and noisy training set (TIMIT, F1-TIMIT & F2-TIMIT-8). It is apparent that the solutions generated using the clean training set use less features (mean of 9.8) when compared to the solutions generated using the hybrid test set (mean of 13.2). It is also apparent that the features used are different for these two environments and that some features are more useful than others in ASV, in fact 21 features are not used by any of the solutions. The vast majority of the unused descriptors are *variance* measurements, indicating that the variance of the descriptors over a one second time frame is of less importance than the mean value over the same time frame. The total number of descriptors used in both environments is 80, and 61 of these are used in both environ-

ments indicating that these 61 descriptors give both an indication of the speakers identity and are somewhat resilient to noise.

Figure 8 shows the percentage of each descriptor type used in each of these training environments. It can be seen that while the solutions generated using the clean training set are highly reliant on the MFCC (accounting for around 40% of all descriptors used) the solutions generated using the hybrid test set are more reliant on PLP (PLPs account for 22% of all descriptors used). This is of particular interest, as previous research has indicated that the use of PLPs gives better performance in noisy environments than MFCCs (see Hermansky, 1990). A more fine grain analysis can be seen in Figure 9. These Figures show that some of the five largest spectral peaks (5LP) give some useful information when performing ASV. While these descriptors alone may not indicate a speaker's identity, they may provide information useful in more complex solutions that consider the spectral peaks when analysing the more conventional spectral descriptors.

Figure 10 shows the descriptor usage frequency for descriptors that are used in both training environments for individual speakers. Interestingly there is not a great deal of overlap in the importance of specific descriptors in identifying

Figure 8. Percentage of descriptors used for clean (TIMIT) and hybrid (TIMIT, F1-TIMIT & F2-TIMIT-8) environments. Figure originally published in Day and Nandi (2007) © 2007 IEEE

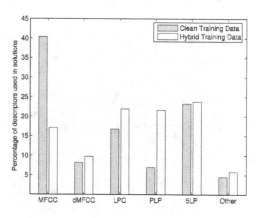

Figure 9. An analysis of the frequency of features used for the clean (TIMIT) and hybrid (TIMIT, F1-TIMIT & F2-TIMIT-8) environments. Figure originally published in Day and Nandi (2007) © 2007 IEEE

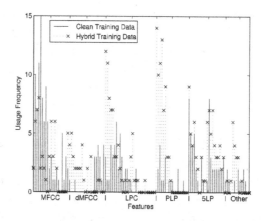

specific speakers independent of environment, except for the descriptors based on the 5 largest spectral peaks (5LP), particularly the *'magnitude'* and *'index variance'* of the largest peak, which appear in 8 and 7 speaker dependent solutions in both training environments respectively.

The lack of significant overlap for other descriptors is most likely due to the redundancy present in these descriptor sets. The information about the 5 largest spectral peaks is independent of other spectral features which generally indicate

the *shape* of the spectrum, and many solutions have found this unique information useful in evolving accurate classifiers. The other spectral descriptors are likely to have a much higher degree of overlap in the information they contain (i.e. they are less independent of one another). Consequently, different descriptors could be used to obtain the same speaker dependent information. The descriptor used is therefore likely to depend on the training environment. The results indicate that in a clean environment the MFCCs generally prove robust

Figure 10. An analysis of the frequency of features used for BOTH the clean (TIMIT) and hybrid (TIMIT, F1-TIMIT & F2-TIMIT-8) environments. Figure originally published in Day and Nandi (2007) © 2007 IEEE

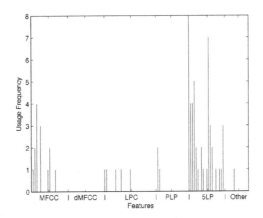

enough, while in the hybrid environment these appear to be replaced with PLPs.

CONCLUSION

This chapter has demonstrated that GP shows great promise in creating robust classifiers for ASV purposes. Through the use of CPS, BSFC, parallel GP (the island model) with dynamic migration paths and a dynamic fitness function, competitive results have been demonstrated. The generated programs can be evolved to be resilient to noisy transmission paths; this is believed to be largely due to the *per-voice* and *environment specific* feature selection inherent in the method. This method does not suffer the limitations associated with a limited feature set as a large number of features can be used and only those useful are included in the final GP generated classification program.

It became apparent during the analysis of results that innovations of other researchers, such as the use of PLP in noisy environments, were naturally incorporated as part of the evolution process. Some of the descriptors were shown to be less important, and further work could exclude these in order to accelerate the evolutionary

process. Equally, a more exhaustive descriptor set, perhaps including some high level features, could be used to increase performance further. Further work could also compare this system to a wider variety of ASV systems, and analyse the effect on performance of using other established techniques (such as CMS).

There is no reason why this classification method cannot be applied to other complex classification tasks with minimal adaptation and future applications are anticipated.

REFERENCES

Banzhaf, W., Nordin, P., Keller, R. E., & Francone, F. D. (1998). *Genetic Programming - An Introduction*. Morgan Kaufmann.

Bimbot, F., Magrin-Chagnolleau, I., & Mathan, L. (1995). Second-order statistical measures for text-independent speaker identification. *Speech Communication, 17*(1-2), 177–192. doi:10.1016/0167-6393(95)00013-E

Campbell, J. (1997). Speaker recognition: A tutorial. *Proceedings of the IEEE, 85*(9), 1437–1462. doi:10.1109/5.628714

Cramer, N. L. (1985). A representation for the adaptive generation of simple sequential programs. In *Proceedings of the First International Conference on Genetic Algorithms and Their Applications* (pp. 183–187).

Davis, S., & Mermelstein, P. (1980). Comparison of parametric representations for monosyllabic word recognition in continuously spoken sentences. *IEEE Transactions on Acoustics, Speech, and Signal Processing, 28*(4), 357–366. doi:10.1109/TASSP.1980.1163420

Day, P., & Nandi, A. K. (2007). Robust text-independent speaker verification using genetic programming. *IEEE Transactions on Audio . Speech and Language Processing, 15*(1), 285–295. doi:10.1109/TASL.2006.876765

Doddington, G., Liggett, W., Martin, A., Przybocki, M., & Reynolds, D. (1998). Sheep, goats, lambs and wolves a statistical analysis of speaker performance in the nist 1998 speaker recognition evaluation. In *Proceedings of the International Conference on Spoken Language Processing,* Paper No. 608.

Ellis, D. (1996). *Prediction-driven Computational Auditory Scene Analysis*. Ph.D. Dissertation, Department of Electrical Engineering and Computer Science, MIT.

Ezzaidi, H., Rouat, J., & O'Shaughnessy, D. (2001). Towards combining pitch and mfcc for speaker identification systems. In *Proceedings of Eurospeech* (pp. 2825–2828).

Farrell, K. R., Mammone, R. J., & Assaleh, K. T. (1994). Speaker recognition using neural networks and conventional classifiers. *IEEE Transactions on Speech and Audio Processing, 2*(1), 194–205. doi:10.1109/89.260362

Ferrer, L., Bratt, H., Gadde, V. R. R., Kajarekar, S., Shriberg, E., Sšonmez, K., et al. (2003). Modeling duration patterns for speaker recognition. In *Proceedings of the Eurospeech* (pp. 2017–2020).

Fisher, W., Doddington, G., & Goudie-Marshall, K. (1986). The darpa speech recognition research database: Specification and status. In *Proceedings of the DARPA Speech Recognition Workshop* (pp. 93–100).

Folino, G., Pizzuti, C., Spezzano, G., Vanneschi, V., & Tomassini, M. (2003). Diversity analysis in cellular and multipopulation genetic programming. In *Proceedings of the IEEE Congress on Evolutionary Computation* (pp. 305–311).

Gopalan, K., Anderson, T., & Cupples, E. (1999). A comparison of speaker identification results using features based on cepstrum and fourier-bessel expansion. *IEEE Transactions on Speech and Audio Processing, 7*(3), 289–294. doi:10.1109/89.759036

Guo, H., Jack, L. B., & Nandi, A. K. (2005). Feature generation using genetic programming with application to fault classification. *IEEE Transactions on Systems, Man, and Cybernetics . Part B, 35*(1), 89–99.

Hermansky, H. (1990). Perceptual linear prediction (plp) analysis for speech. *The Journal of the Acoustical Society of America, 87*, 1738–1752. doi:10.1121/1.399423

Kinnunen, T. (2003). *Spectral Features for Automatic Text-Independent Speaker Recognition*. PhD thesis, University of Joensuu, Finland.

Koza, J. R. (1992). *Genetic Programming: On the Programming of Computers by Means of Natural Selection*. The MIT Press.

Koza, J. R. (2000). *Asynchronous "Island" Approach to Parallelization of Genetic Programming*. http://www.genetic-programming.com/parallel.html

Koza, J. R., Andre, D., Bennett, F. H., III, & Keane, M. (1999). *Genetic Programming 3: Darwinian Invention and Problem Solving*. Morgan Kaufman.

Koza, J. R., Keane, M. A., Streeter, S., Mydlowec, W., Yu, J., & Lanza, L. (2003). *Genetic Programming IV: Routine Human-Competitive Machine Intelligence*. Kluwer Academic Publishers.

Lamel, L., Kassel, R., & Seneff, S. (1986). Speech database development: Design and analysis of the acoustic-phonetic corus. In *Proceedings of the DARPA Speech Recognition Workshop* (pp. 100–110).

Lu, L., Jiang, H., & Zhang, H. (2001). A robust audio classification and segmentation method. In *Proceedings of the 9th ACM International Conference on Multimedia* (pp. 203–211).

Navratil, J., Jin, Q., Andrews, W., & Campbell, J. (2003). Phonetic speaker recognition using maximum-likelihood binary-decision tree models. In *Proceedings of the IEEE International Conference on Acoustics, Speech, and Signal Processing* (pp. 796-799).

Ramachandran, R. P., Farrell, K. R., Ramachandran, R., & Mammone, R. J. (2002). Speaker recognition - general classifier approaches and data fusion methods. *Pattern Recognition, 35,* 2801–2821. doi:10.1016/S0031-3203(01)00235-7

Reynolds, D., Andrews, W., Campbell, J., Navratil, J., Peskin, B., Adam, A., et al. (2003). The supersid project: exploiting highlevel information for high-accuracy speaker recognition. In *Proceedings of the International Conference on Audio, Speech, and Signal Processing* (pp. 784–787).

Reynolds, D. A., & Rose, R. C. (1995). Robust text-independent speaker identification using gaussian mixture speaker models. *IEEE Transactions on Speech and Audio Processing, 3,* 72–83. doi:10.1109/89.365379

Rodriguez-Linares, L., Garcia-Mateo, C., & Alba-Castro, J. (2003). On combining classifiers for speaker authentication. *Pattern Recognition, 36,* 347–359. doi:10.1016/S0031-3203(02)00035-3

Silva, S., & Almeida, J. (2003). Dynamic maximum tree depth. In *Proceedings of the Genetic and Evolutionary Computation Conference* (pp. 1776–1787).

Smith, S. F. (1980). *A Learning System Based on Genetic Adaptive Algorithms*. PhD thesis, Computer Science Department, University of Pittsburgh.

Soong, F. K., Rosenberg, A. E., Rabiner, L. R., & Huang, B. H. (1987). A vector quantization approach to speaker recognition. *AT & T Technical Journal, 66,* 14–26.

Soule, T., & Foster, J. A. (1998). Effects of code growth and parsimony pressure on populations in genetic programming. *Evolutionary Computation, 6*(4), 293–309. doi:10.1162/evco.1998.6.4.293

van Vuuren, S. (1996). Comparison of text-independent speaker recognition methods on telephone speech with acoustic mismatch. In *Proceedings of the Fourth International Conference on Spoken Language* (pp. 1788–1791).

Wan, V. (2003). *Speaker Verification using Support Vector Machines*. Phd thesis, University of Sheffield, UK.

Wan, V., & Campbell, W. M. (2000). Support vector machines for speaker verification and identification. In *Proceedings of Neural Networks for Signal Processing X* (pp. 775–784).

Wouhaybi, R., & Al-Alaou, M. A. (1999). Comparison of neural networks for speaker recognition. In *Proceedings of the Sixth IEEE International Conference on Electronics, Circuits and Systems* (pp. 125–128).

Zhang, L., & Nandi, A. K. (2007). Neutral offspring controlling operators in genetic programming. *Pattern Recognition, 40*(10), 2696–2705. doi:10.1016/j.patcog.2006.10.001

Zhang, T., & Kuo, C. (1998). Content-based classification and retrieval of audio. In *SPIE's 43rd Annual Meeting - Conference on Advanced Signal Processing Algorithms, Architectures, and Implementations VII* (pp. 432–443).

Chapter 12
Combinational Circuit Design with Estimation of Distribution Algorithms

Sergio Ivvan Valdez Peña
Centre for Research in Mathematics, México

Arturo Hernández Aguirre
Centre for Research in Mathematics, México

Salvador Botello Rionda
Centre for Research in Mathematics, México

Cyntia Araiza Delgado
Centre for Research in Mathematics, México

ABSTRACT

The authors introduce new approaches for the combinational circuit design based on Estimation of Distribution Algorithms. In this paradigm, the structure and data dependencies embedded in the data (population of candidate circuits) are modeled by a conditional probability distribution function. The new population is simulated from the probability model thus inheriting the dependencies. The authors explain the procedure to build an approximation of the probability distribution through two approaches: polytrees and Bayesian networks. A set of circuit design experiments is performed and a comparison with evolutionary approaches is reported.

INTRODUCTION

The evolutionary design of combinational circuits is a strategy well known to human designers due to the uncommon characteristics of the solutions. Since evolutionary algorithms search the space and build up solutions from the bottom-up, the delivered circuits can be found through transformations which are correct in the Boolean algebra, but basically unknown to human designers. One

DOI: 10.4018/978-1-60566-705-8.ch012

advantage of the solutions is the circuit size which is frequently smaller than those produced by a human designer. The strategy, however, presents several drawbacks; the most important being the scalability. That is, when the complexity of a circuit is incremented in a linear way, the resources required by an evolutionary algorithm must be exponentially incremented. The main cause of this problem can be explained through the chromosome length. A bigger circuit is represented by a longer chromosome, and unfortunately, a long chromosome translates into convergence troubles for a Genetic Algorithm (and for any other evolutionary algorithms). Since the chromosome length is indeed proportional to the size of the circuit, the approaches to solve the scaling problem can be classified into two groups: 1) special coding to reduce the chromosome length, and 2) divide and conquer algorithms.

- *Use of a Special Coding:* Coding with a binary alphabet favors exploration via the creation of hyperplanes. However, several experimental results on circuit design provide strong evidence that supports the use of alphabets of cardinality greater than 2. For instance, the n-cardinality encoding proposed in Coello et al. (2000) helped to reduce the representation bias, and in fact, produced the best circuits.
- *Divide and Conquer Algorithms:* The goal is to reduce the complexity of the problem by breaking up the whole circuit into subcircuits. Accordingly, the main circuit is automatically split into subcircuits, which are thought to be simpler problems. Once the subcircuits are designed, they are connected to assemble the circuit for the next higher level. Several recent approaches are "divide and conquer" algorithms. Examples of this approach include the Bi-directional Incremental Evolution (Kalganova, 2000), the Generalized Disjunction

Decomposition (Stomeo et al., 2006), the Scalable Approach to Evolvable Hardware (Torresen, 2002; Torresen, 1998), and the Stepwise Dimensional Reduction (Li et al., 2008).

Successful approaches for evolutionary design focus on the design of primitive building blocks which can later be used to construct more complex building blocks. The collected knowledge, encoded as building blocks in a population of chromosomes, has given way to the design of new algorithms whose main goal is *to find and reuse the good partial solutions* available in the population. Note that this approach must not be considered as another instance of the divide and conquer strategy, mainly because the solution is not the summation of n-partial solutions. For Estimation of Distribution Algorithms (EDAs), the goal is to represent promising partial solutions, and afterwards reproduce them in the next generation. Finding promising partial solutions is a big challenge. However, the strategy of EDAs is to learn a conditional probability model of the population, which can represent both the dependencies and the structure of the data.

The goal of this chapter is twofold. The first goal is to introduce two approaches based on EDAs for combinational circuit design. The first approach uses polytrees, while the second uses Bayesian networks. The second goal is to compare design methods based on data dependency models with evolutionary methods (which do not model data dependencies). We should determine whether the knowledge about patterns encoded as correlated variables reduces the number of fitness function evaluations required to design a combinational circuit.

The organization of this chapter is as follows. In Section 2 we introduce the concepts and background of EDAs. Afterwards, we introduce the polytree model in Section 3, and the Bayesian model in Section 4. The description of the problem we are to solve is given in Section 5. A broad set of experiments is described in Section 6, and conclusion is given in Section 7.

ESTIMATION OF DISTRIBUTION ALGORITHMS

The robustness of EDAs can be understood through their ability to model the structure of the data dependencies (data can be continuous or discrete, but we focus on the discrete models). The data dependencies can be observed as data patterns; these patterns may live in the population for a number of generations, or even live throughout all generations. Data dependencies can be tracked by external procedures incorporated on the evolutionary algorithm. An example of such hybrid system for combinational circuit design is presented in Islas et al. (2005). Here, a percentage of the population of a Genetic Algorithm is generated by a Case Based Reasoning System (CBR). The CBR stores interesting design patterns in a database of combinational circuits. The patterns are recalled and reused (injected into the population) when the reasoning system finds similarities between individuals of the population and the database.

We must stress a fundamental idea related to the primitive building blocks: *for any pattern observed in the population, the involved variables are related through conditional dependencies.* The fundamental principle of EDAs is, precisely, the modeling of data dependencies (which encode patterns), via a conditional probability distribution.

The construction of a conditional probability distribution model (CPD) from data is the main goal of EDAs (Larranaga & Lozano, 2002; Lozano et al., 2006). The complexity of a model is directly related to its capacity to represent the relationships among variables. Thus, larger representation capacity translates into increasing complexity, and this fact into computationally expensive, and even difficult, learning algorithms. An example of this increasing model complexity is given in Figure 1.

The Univariate Marginal Distribution Algorithm (UMDA) creates a model with no dependencies (even when dependencies do exist). The Bivariate Marginal Distribution Algorithm (BMDA) creates a forest of trees. In order to build a tree, the pair of variables with strongest dependency, measured by a χ^2 test, are chosen and linked. The Chow-Liu dependency tree is also a bivariate model. However, two variables (X, Y) are linked as $X \rightarrow Y$ only if Y depends conditionally from X. Mutual Information is used to measure the strength of the conditional dependency. Dependency trees always deliver the optimal CPD model, a property not shared by the BMDA. The next model in Figure 1 is the polytree, which is also a conditional model. For polytrees, one variable can depend on more than one parent and no kind of loops is allowed. The Bayesian network can generate the most complex model. For some permutation, a variable n may depend on $n - 1$ parents, and undirected loops are allowed. At the same time, a Bayesian network can generate simpler models. For instance, a polytree is simply a connected Bayesian network; a Chow-Liu tree (Chow & Liu, 1968) would be a polytree whose nodes can have only one parent, therefore, also representable by a Bayesian network. The ability of Bayesian networks to reduce the complexity of its own model is not unique. BMDA, Chow-Liu trees, polytrees, etc can do the same adjustment. However, the learning algorithm of a Bayesian network is considerably more expensive than any other. For this reason, simpler models are chosen whenever possible. Estimating the simplest model that best fits the data is another problem itself, not addressed in this chapter. However, polytrees and Bayesian networks are suitable models for the circuit design problem and we shall describe them later. Interestingly, the simpler models (BMDA, Chou-Liu's dependency tree, etc) could not solve the proposed problem.

All EDAs work with the same basic steps, as shown in Algorithm 1. As noted, the difference would be in the probability model constructed,

Figure 1. Graph-based representation of some probability models used in EDAs

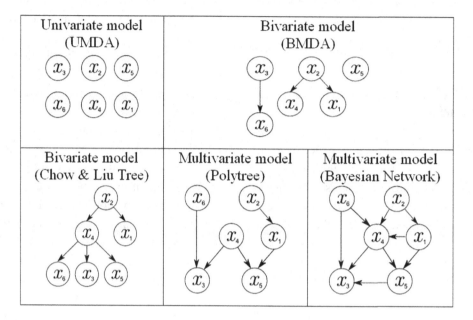

and therefore, in the learning algorithm as well. In step 4, a sample of the best individuals is taken from the population. The conditional probability distribution model is constructed in step 5. In this chapter, we describe how polytrees and Bayesian networks are used to create the probability model. With the model at hand, the new population is simulated to populate the next generation. The two models are introduced next.

Algorithm 1. Pseudocode of a Estimation Distribution Algorithm
1: $P_0 \leftarrow$ Generate initial population with N individuals
2: **repeat**
3: **for** $i = 1, 2, \dots$ **do**
4:     $S_{i-1} \leftarrow$ Select Best M individuals from P_{i-1}
5:     $CPD_i(x) = P(x \mid S_{i-1})$ (find the CPD model that generates the data given the sample)
6:     $P_i \leftarrow$ Generate N new individuals using model $CPD_i(x)$
7: **end for**

8: **until** termination criterion is True

INTRODUCTION TO POLYTREES

EDAs with discrete variables have found strong support in the theory of graphical models for the approximation of probability distributions. A polytree is a directed acyclic graph with only one undirected route between any two nodes (Lauritzen, 1998). They were introduced by Pearl (1988) to enable inference in a belief network. It is another feature that makes polytrees interesting for EDAs. A polytree is the simplest structure that enables the modeling of *conditional dependencies* involving three variables. Simpler models, such as Chow and Liu's dependency trees, are effective tools to model bivariate dependencies (Chow & Liu, 1968). More complex models, such as Bayesian networks, are effective to model conditional dependencies where three or more variables are involved. Although one could consider Bayesian networks as the most powerful tool at hand, their drawback is the high computational complexity of the learning algorithm. Furthermore, if data dependencies are not as complex as the Bayesian network learning algorithm would assume, the learned Bayesian network could be as simple as the UMDA model (see Figure 1), and thus, not including conditional dependencies at all. A polytree learning algorithm can also deliver a model with no dependencies; however, the complexity of the learning algorithm is smaller than that of the Bayesian network. In order to perform a fair comparison between Bayesian networks and polytrees, in this chapter the variables of a Bayesian model are limited to three parents (just one more parent than polytrees).

A polytree is a directed acyclic graph (DAG) where a node with more than one parent and loops (directed or undirected) are not allowed. Its learning algorithm delivers a polytree with the following characteristic: If a third variable C can provide more information about variables A and B, that is, A and B are conditional dependent given C, then a convergent connection is created (shown with number 3 below). Otherwise, A and B are only connected if they are marginally dependent. An arrow from A to B (or vice-versa) would indicate that kind of dependency. Observe that when three variables are involved, three connecting ways are possible: sequential (either to the left or to the right), divergent, and convergent.

1. Sequential: $X_i \rightarrow X_k \rightarrow X_j$
2. Divergent: $X_i \leftarrow X_k \rightarrow X_j$
3. Convergent: $X_i \rightarrow X_k \leftarrow X_j$

It can be easily proved that the sequential and divergent connections cannot represent the conditional dependency involving three variables, but only the convergent, or node to node connection (Lauritzen, 1998) can be represented. This fact reduces the computational complexity of the polytree learning algorithm since there is no need

to search, among the three options, for the proper connecting way. Dep()

Algorithm 2 Polytree learning algorithm

```
 1: G is a graph with no edges
and N nodes
 2: L is an empty list
 3: for every pair of nodes X_i
and X_j do
 4:        Compute Dep(X_i, X_j) =
I(X_i, X_j)
 5:           if Dep(X_i, X_j) > ε_0 then
 6:               Insert edge < X_i,
X_j >in L
 7:        end if
 8: end for
 9: for every edge < X_i, X_j > ∈
Ldo
10:        for every node X_k,
where k ≠ {i, j} do
11:            Compute I(X_i, X_j
|X_k)
12:               if ∃X_k| I(X_i, X_j
|X_k) ≤ ∈_1 then
13:                   Delete edge <
X_i, X_j > from L
14:           end if
15:        end for
16:    Dep_g(X_i, X_j) = min_{X_k} (
Dep_g(X_i, X_j), I(X_i, X_j |X_k))
17: end for
18: Sort list L in descending
order of Dep_g(X_i, X_j)
19: From top of list. Delete
edge < X_i, X_j > from L and in-
sert it in G
20: (do not insert edge if a
loop is created)
21: for each subgraph X_i- X_k-
X_j do
22:        if I(X_i, X_j |X_k) > I(X_i, X_j)
then
```

```
23:         Insert convergent
connection X_i → X_k ← X_j
24:     end if
25: end for
26: Insert remaining edges in a
random way (no loops allowed)
```

Learning a Polytree

The use of polytrees goes back to the work of Pearl (1988). Recently the polytree approximation distribution algorithm was proposed in the framework of EDAs (Soto & Ochoa, 2000). The polytree learning algorithm is shown in Algorithm 2. When this learning algorithm is used at step 5 of the Algorithm 1, the result is called the polytree EDA.

For this learning algorithm, the measure of dependency between variables is estimated by entropy-based methods (Cover & Thomas, 1991). To estimate the dependency between two variables, also called marginal dependency, the learning algorithm uses mutual information $I(X_i, X_j)$.

$$I(X_i, X_j) = \sum_{x_i, x_j} p(x_i, x_j) \log_2 \frac{p(x_i, x_j)}{p(x_i)p(x_j)} \geq 0 \tag{1}$$

Similarly, to investigate whether a third variable X_k provides more information about the pair (X_i, X_j), the conditional mutual information $I(X_i, X_j | X_k)$ is calculated.

$$I(X_i, X_j | X_k) = \sum_{x_i, x_j, x_k} p(x_i, x_j, x_k) \log_2 \frac{p(x_i, x_j, x_k)p(x_k)}{p(x_i, x_k)p(x_j, x_k)} \geq 0 \tag{2}$$

Briefly, if variables A and B become dependent given a third one, C, they are graphically represented by convergent connection. If A and B are independent given C, then they are tested for marginal dependency. If such case is true, A and B are linked by an edge. If they are found independent they are not linked at all. Although the learning algorithm looks somewhat elaborated, the main ideas are the following. It starts with a completely disconnected graph, and therefore, this is a constructive algorithm. When line 8 is reached, the members of list L are the edges whose marginal dependency is greater than a threshold ε_0. Then the edges in L are tested for conditional dependency. Every edge whose conditional dependency is greater than ε_1 will be tested at line 16. Since at this point an edge may have survived both strength tests, the assignment in line 16 chooses the most representative value. The list is sorted by this value and the edges inserted in the graph, avoiding the creation of loops. Whenever the test for a loop returns positive, the edge is not inserted. At this point we only have undirected edges in the graph. All subgraphs of three elements are tested for conditional dependency versus marginal dependency. The convergent connection is created when conditional dependency is stronger than marginal dependency. Some edges which got no direction because they were not tested as part of a subgraph, receive a random direction. The threshold values ε_0 and ε_1 were experimentally calibrated to allow dependencies stronger than the threshold ε_0 is applied to the marginal dependency, whereas ε_1 is applied to the conditional dependency measure. Low threshold values help to create trees with more edges, therefore, high complexity. In the experiments both values are set to 0.05.

INTRODUCTION TO BAYESIAN NETWORKS

Let us recall the polytree case: if X_i has parents X_k and X_j, we need to compute $P(X_i | X_j X_k)$ to estimate the knowledge we have about X_i. However, if another variable, say X_l is also highly correlated with X_i, the polytree would not relate the four variables. The Bayesian network is a directed acyclic graph

(DAG) which can represent the influence (dependencies) of $n - 1$ variables over one variable. A Bayesian network could be represented as a list of parents associated to each variable. As mentioned, learning such a complex model is a hard problem because to find the optimum Bayesian network structure it is necessary to perform the exhaustive enumeration of all the possible structures. The number of possible structures grows exponentially with the number of variables! Therefore, several approaches have been developed to approximate the optimum structure in polynomial time. This could be the best strategy for an EDA based on a Bayesian network (because to solve a difficult combinatorial problem such as automated circuit design presented in this chapter, we must not solve another equally hard problem such as the Bayesian network learning algorithm).

An efficient method which computes Bayesian network structures in polynomial time is the K2 algorithm (Cooper & Herskovits, 1992) which deterministically finds an adequate approximation to the best Bayesian network, given the data D. The complexity of the model returned by the K2 can be bounded by the maximum numbers of parents allowed for each variable. A possible drawback of this algorithm is that it assumes a given ordering to build the Bayesian network. Thus, the possible parents for a given variable are only the predecessors in the ordering. Suppose the variables are ordered, e.g. $\{i, j, k, l\}$. A possible K2-Bayesian network could be $\{i \rightarrow j \rightarrow k \rightarrow l\}$, and one that is not possible is $\{i \leftarrow j \leftarrow k \leftarrow l\}$. Even though this drawback is not as severe as it seems, note that while the arc $\{l \rightarrow j\}$ cannot be added to the structure, there is always the possibility of adding the arc $\{j \rightarrow l\}$, which preserves the notion of dependence between $\{l, j\}$. For the sake of completeness, we must mention that the computational effort for finding the optimum ordering is less than that of finding the optimum structure. The K2 algorithm is a growing, "score and search", method. As the name suggests it, an edge is randomly placed to link

two variables, and a measure of the quality of the model is evaluated. If the recently added link does not improve the model the link is removed and another one is generated. Otherwise, it stays in the model. There is another class of algorithms for constructing Bayesian networks which are based on "dependency measures". The polytree learning algorithm described above is an example of that class. Recall that two dependency measures are evaluated: conditional mutual information, and marginal mutual information. For designing Bayesian networks the PC algorithm (Spirtes et al., 1993) is quite similar to the polytree learning algorithm, although the PC starts with a fully connected graph, and estimates all conditional and unconditional dependencies, removing edges in the process. Since this procedure is computationally expensive, the "score and search" methods, such as the K2 algorithm, are preferred.

Learning a Bayesian Network with the K2 Algorithm

The K2 algorithm introduced in Cooper & Herskovits (1992) is a greedy heuristic search method for maximizing the probability $P(B_s, D)$ of the structure B_s given the data D. The K2 is presented in the Algorithm 3. When this learning algorithm is used at step 5 of the Algorithm 1, the result is called the Bayesian EDA. The Equation 3 is used for maximizing $P(B_s, D)$.

$$g(i, \pi_i) = \prod_{j=1}^{q_i} \frac{(r_i - 1)!}{(N_{ij} + r_i - 1)} \prod_{j=1}^{q_i} N_{ijk}! . \qquad (3)$$

where x_i has r_i possible discrete values. Each variable x_i in B_s has a set of parents, which are represented by a list of variables π_i. N_{ijk} is the number of cases in D in which the variable x_i has the value v_{ik}, and π_i is instantiated as w_{ij}. w_{ij} denote the jth unique instantiation of π_i relative to D, and q_i are the number of such unique instantiations of π_i. $N_{ij} = \sum_{k=1}^{r_i} N_{ijk}$.

The K2 starts assuming an empty set of parents π_i for each node x_i (unconnected graph). The initial g measure is stored in P_{old} as shown in step 3. Then, in lines 5 to 14, the g measure is computed for all the predecessor which are not actually in π_i, and the z parent which returns the maximum $g(i, \pi_i \cup \{z\})$ is chosen (function *Pred(xi)*), then the $g(i, \pi_i \cup \{z\})$ value is stored in P_{new}. If the new z parent improves the structure, say $P_{old} > P_{new}$, it is added to the list π_i, and the loop is repeated considering the new list of parents π_i. Otherwise the loop is terminated and the current list π_i is returned. The algorithm also prevents inserting more than u parents. This fact is very useful considering that the complexity of the algorithm grows exponentially with the number of parents. Note that a *log* version of g could be used to reduce the computational effort.

Algorithm 3 Learning Bayesian networks with the K2Require:

    nvar: number of binary variables.

    nsample: number of binary strings (required to compute g).

    xsample: a set of binary strings (required to compute g).

    u: maximum number of parent nodes for each variable.

    i: Indexes of a given order of the variables.
Ensure:

    For each node x_i, a set of parents π_i.
1: **for** $i = 1$ to *nvar* **do**
2:    $\pi_i \leftarrow \varnothing$
   3:    $P_{old} \leftarrow g(i, \pi_i)$

4:    *OKToProceed* $\leftarrow$ true

5:    **while** *OKToProceed* and $|\pi_i| < u$ **do**
6:      let z be the node in PR $ed(x_i)$ - π_i that maximizes $g(i, \pi_i \cup \{z\})$

7:      $P_{new} \leftarrow g(i, \pi_i \cup \{z\})$
8:       **if** $P_{new} > P_{old}$ **then**
9:        $P_{new} = P_{old}$
10:        $\pi_i = \pi_i \cup z$
11:      **else**
12:        *OKToProceed* = false
13:      **end if**
14:    **end while**
15:    **return** Node: x_i, Parents of this node: π_i
16: **end for**

PROBLEM DESCRIPTION

The problem of interest is to design the combinational circuit with the minimum number of components that fully agrees with its specification given in a truth table. A circuit is evolved inside a matrix, from which it takes its representation. A gate can be connected to the output of any gate in the previous layer. All gates have two inputs. A wire is one possible gate whose first input is simply passed to the output. In Figure 2, the reader can identify the gates inside every cell of the matrix. Every gate is coded with three bits since we are using five of them. The **AND** gate is coded as 000, **NOT** gate as 001, **XOR** gate as 010, wire gate as 011, and **OR** gate as 100. A module 5 operation is applied to numbers 5, 6, and 7 when they appear, thus they are mapped to gates 0, 1 and 2. Every bit needed to code a circuit is considered a random variable by the polytree EDA and the Bayesian EDA.

EXPERIMENTS

Two broad experiments were performed. The first one is in fact a set of 11 combinational circuits found in the specialized literature. The goal is to design the combinational circuit with minimum size (number of gates), that implements a Boolean

Figure 2. Representation of a circuit inside a matrix

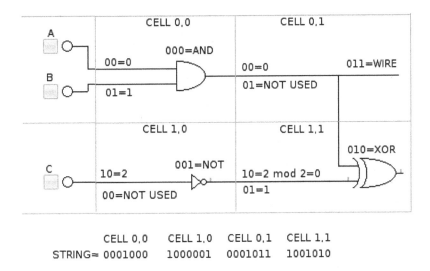

function specified by its truth table. As mentioned, the comparison is made on the number of fitness function evaluations.

The second experiment is the *n*-bit parity check problem. This problem is described as the circuit whose output is equal to (*S* mod 2), and *S* is the summation of the input bits (for example, when the input is "010110", S=3). The goal of this problem is to observe how the Bayesian EDA scales up when the problem complexity increases. The main feature of the parity circuit is that the optimal 2-bit and 3-bit parity circuits are replicated to obtain circuits of larger complexity. The optimal solution uses only XOR gates.

Table 1. Truth tables for circuit 1

Experiment 1				
A	B	C	D	S
0	0	0	0	0
0	0	0	1	1
0	0	1	0	1
0	0	1	1	0
0	1	0	0	1
0	1	0	1	1
0	1	1	0	0
0	1	1	1	1
1	0	0	0	1
1	0	0	1	0
1	0	1	0	1
1	0	1	1	1
1	1	0	0	0
1	1	0	1	1
1	1	1	0	1
1	1	1	1	0

Table 2. Truth tables for circuit 2

Experiment 2				
A	B	C	D	S
0	0	0	0	0
0	0	0	1	0
0	0	1	0	1
0	0	1	1	1
0	1	0	0	0
0	1	0	1	0
0	1	1	0	0
0	1	1	1	0
1	0	0	0	1
1	0	0	1	1
1	0	1	0	0
1	0	1	1	1
1	1	0	0	1
1	1	0	1	1
1	1	1	0	1
1	1	1	1	0

Table 3. Truth tables for circuit 3

Experiment 3					
A	B	C	D	E	S
0	0	0	0	0	0
0	0	0	0	1	0
0	0	0	1	0	0
0	0	0	1	1	1
0	0	1	0	0	0
0	0	1	0	1	1
0	0	1	1	0	0
0	0	1	1	1	0
0	1	0	0	0	0
0	1	0	0	1	0
0	1	0	1	0	0
0	1	0	1	1	0
0	1	1	0	0	0
0	1	1	0	1	0
0	1	1	1	0	0
0	1	1	1	1	0
1	0	0	0	0	0
1	0	0	0	1	0
1	0	0	1	0	0
1	0	0	1	1	0
1	0	1	0	0	0
1	0	1	0	1	0
1	0	1	1	0	0
1	0	1	1	1	0
1	1	0	0	0	0
1	1	0	0	1	0
1	1	0	1	0	0
1	1	0	1	1	0
1	1	1	0	0	0
1	1	1	0	1	0
1	1	1	1	0	0
1	1	1	1	1	0

Table 4. Truth tables for circuit 4

Experiment 4					
A	B	C	D	S_0	S_1
0	0	0	0	1	0
0	0	0	1	1	0
0	0	1	0	1	0
0	0	1	1	0	0
0	1	0	0	1	0
0	1	0	1	1	0
0	1	1	0	0	0
0	1	1	1	0	0
1	0	0	0	1	0
1	0	0	1	0	0
1	0	1	0	0	0
1	0	1	1	0	1
1	1	0	0	0	0
1	1	0	1	0	0
1	1	1	0	0	1
1	1	1	1	0	1

Table 5. Truth tables for circuit 5

Experiment 5						
A	B	C	D	S_0	S_1	S_2
0	0	0	0	0	0	0
0	0	0	1	0	0	1
0	0	1	0	0	1	0
0	0	1	1	0	1	1
0	1	0	0	0	0	1
0	1	0	1	0	1	0
0	1	1	0	0	1	1
0	1	1	1	1	0	0
1	0	0	0	0	1	0
1	0	0	1	0	1	1
1	0	1	0	1	0	0
1	0	1	1	1	0	1
1	1	0	0	0	1	1
1	1	0	1	1	0	0
1	1	1	0	1	0	1
1	1	1	1	1	1	0

Table 6. Truth tables for circuit 6

Experiment 6					
A	B	S_0	S_1	S_2	S_3
0	0	0	0	0	1
0	0	0	0	1	0
0	0	0	1	0	0
0	0	1	0	0	0

Experiment 1: The 11-Circuits Benchmark

A set of experiments was conducted to compare the number of fitness function evaluations required to find the optimum circuit. The Bayesian EDA and the polytree EDA are compared against three paradigms: the Genetic Algorithm, the Particle Swarm Optimization, and the Ant System. All functions were solved with the Bayesian EDA, and the first nine functions with the polytree EDA proposed in this chapter. The number of parents allowed for any variable in the Bayesian EDA is 3 (thus a variable may depend on other three). As explained before, a polytree EDA may find a variable depending on up to two parents.

Table 7. Truth tables for circuit 7

Experiment 7				
A	B	C	D	S_0
0	0	0	0	1
0	0	0	1	0
0	0	1	0	1
0	0	1	1	0
0	1	0	0	1
0	1	0	1	1
0	1	1	0	1
0	1	1	1	1
1	0	0	0	1
1	0	0	1	1
1	0	1	0	0
1	0	1	1	1
1	1	0	0	1
1	1	0	1	0
1	1	1	0	1
1	1	1	1	0

Table 8. Truth tables for circuit 8

Experiment 8				
A	B	C	D	S_0
0	0	0	0	1
0	0	0	1	0
0	0	1	0	0
0	0	1	1	1
0	1	0	0	0
0	1	0	1	1
0	1	1	0	1
0	1	1	1	0
1	0	0	0	0
1	0	0	1	1
1	0	1	0	1
1	0	1	1	0
1	1	0	0	1
1	1	0	1	0
1	1	1	0	0
1	1	1	1	1

Table 9. Truth tables for circuit 9

Experiment 9			
A	B	C	S_0
0	0	0	0
0	0	1	0
0	1	0	0
0	1	1	1
1	0	0	0
1	0	1	1
1	1	0	1
1	1	1	0

Genetic Algorithm. Human designer solutions found through Karnaugh maps complement the comparison (Coello et al., 2000).

The truth tables defining the 11 functions are shown in Tables 1-11. Some properties of the solutions are reviewed next.

Functions 1 to 5. These functions were proposed and solved using a state of the art Particle Swarm Optimization heuristic (Coello et al., 2004).

Functions 6 to 9. These functions were proposed and solved with the Ant Colony Optimization paradigm (Coello et al., 2002).

Functions 10 and 11. These functions were proposed and solved with a binary-coded Genetic Algorithm, and the *n*-cardinality

- The number of gates in the best solutions: Eleven circuit design problems were successfully solved with the Bayesian EDA, and nine with the polytree EDA (the problems not reported for the polytree EDA must not be counted as unsuccessful, but simply the information was not available).

Table 10. Truth tables for circuit 10

Experiment 10				
A	B	C	D	S_0
0	0	0	0	1
0	0	0	1	1
0	0	1	0	0
0	0	1	1	1
0	1	0	0	0
0	1	0	1	0
0	1	1	0	1
0	1	1	1	1
1	0	0	0	1
1	0	0	1	0
1	0	1	0	1
1	0	1	1	0
1	1	0	0	0
1	1	0	1	1
1	1	1	0	0
1	1	1	1	0

Table 11. Truth tables for circuit 11

Experiment 11				
A	B	C	D	S_0
0	0	0	0	1
0	0	0	1	0
0	0	1	0	1
0	0	1	1	0
0	1	0	0	1
0	1	0	1	0
0	1	1	0	1
0	1	1	1	1
1	0	0	0	1
1	0	0	1	1
1	0	1	0	1
1	0	1	1	0
1	1	0	0	0
1	1	0	1	1
1	1	1	0	1
1	1	1	1	1

Table 12. Number of gates of the best solutions obtained by each algorithm. (*=unfeasible, UN = UNavailable, BayNet = Bayesian network, PSO = Particle Swarm Optimization, NGA = n-cardinality Genetic Algorithm, BGA = binary-coded Genetic Algorithm, HD = human designer)

Function	Bayesian	Polytree	PSO	Ant System	NGA	BGA	HD
1	6	6	6	UN	UN	UN	UN
2	5	5	5	UN	UN	UN	UN
3	**10**	12	0*	UN	UN	UN	UN
4	7	7	7	UN	UN	UN	UN
5	8	7	7	UN	UN	UN	UN
6	5	6	UN	5	UN	UN	UN
7	6	6	UN	7	UN	UN	UN
8	4	4	UN	4	UN	UN	UN
9	4	4	UN	4	4	6	6
10	7	UN	UN	UN	8	8	11
11	8	UN	UN	UN	7	8	9

The number of gates that implement the solutions found by either algorithm is shown in Table 12.

- The number of fitness function evaluations: The number of fitness function evaluations required to find the best solution is reported in Table 13.

- The designed circuits: The circuits are interesting for the knowledgeable eye, and

therefore, we present the solutions.

- ° Solutions from polytree EDA: The best circuits found by the polytree EDA are shown in Figure 3.

- ° Solutions from Bayesian EDA: The best circuits found by the Bayesian EDA are shown in Figure 4.

Table 13. Number of evaluations for each algorithm. (* = unfeasible, UN = UNavailable, BayNet = Bayesian network, PSO = Particle Swarm Optimization, NGA = n-cardinality Genetic Algorithm, BGA = binary-coded Genetic Algorithm, HD = human designer)

Function	Bayesian	Polytree	PSO	Ant System	NGA	BGA	HD
1	120000	30000	100000	UN	UN	UN	UN
2	80000	30000	100000	UN	UN	UN	UN
3	400000	75000	500000*	UN	UN	UN	UN
4	160000	90000	200000	UN	UN	UN	UN
5	120000	62500	500000	UN	UN	UN	UN
6	80000	30000	UN	185400	UN	UN	UN
7	80000	40000	UN	185400	UN	UN	UN
8	80000	40000	UN	82400	UN	UN	UN
9	80000	30000	UN	20600	280000	360000	UN
10	160000	UN	UN	UN	400000	800000	UN
11	80000	UN	UN	UN	280000	360000	UN

Figure 3. Best solutions found by the polytree EDA, e.g. 2 to 9. The Function 1 is the same as that shown for the Bayesian EDA

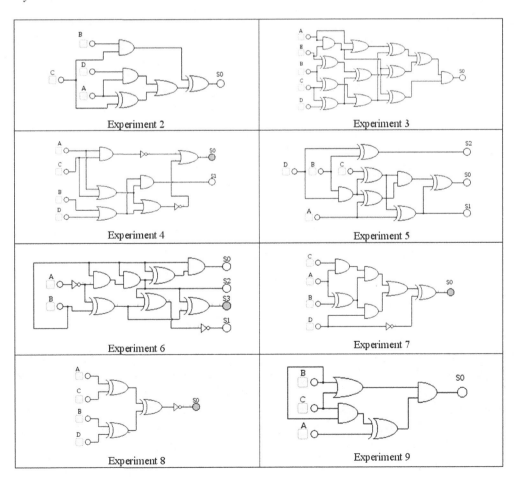

293

Figure 4. Best solutions found by the Bayesian EDA, functions 1 to 11

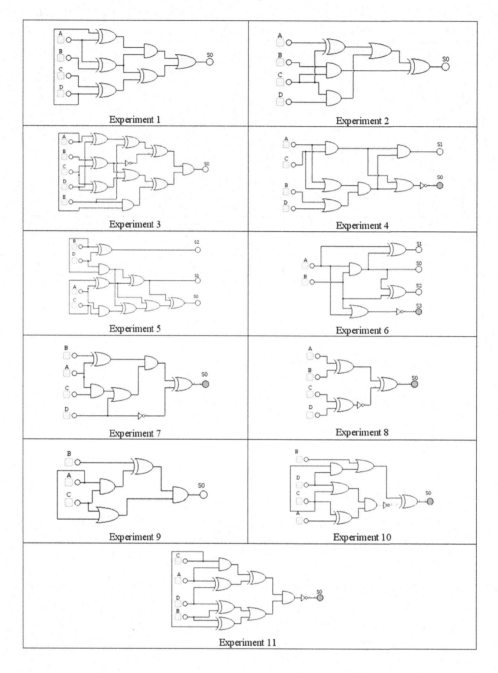

Comments on Solutions from Experiment 1

Number of gates. Taking into account that the best solutions reported in Table 3 are the best known, the number of gates found by Bayesian EDA and polytree EDA are competitive. Notice that for Function 3, the Bayesian EDA found a smaller circuit than the polytree EDA, and the Particle Swarm Optimization did not find the solution. Bayesian EDA is again better than polytree EDA in Function 6, and only in Function 5 the

Table 14. Scalability analysis of the Bayesian network algorithm, by using the parity problem in 30 independent runs

Number of Inputs	Number of Vars	Number of Evals	% of optimum found	% of feasible solutions	Relation *eval/var* x 0.001
3	28	20000	100	100	0.714
4	28	20000	100	100	0.714
5	81	60000	90	97	0.741
6	81	60000	67	67	0.741
7	144	160000	27	47	1.11
8	144	360000	7	10	2.5
9	275	360000	3	27	1.3

polytree EDA is better than the Bayesian EDA (polytree EDA is better in 1 out of 11 problems). The Bayesian EDA is comparable or better than the Ant System in Functions 6, 7, 8 and 9. Ant System is better than polytree EDA in Function 6. For Functions 10 and 11, the Bayesian EDA is comparable with the *n*-cardinality Genetic Algorithm and the binary-coded Genetic Algorithm.

Number of fitness function evaluations. Clearly, the polytree EDA requires less fitness function evaluations than any other tested method

(except for Function 9, where the Ant System excels). The Bayesian EDA needs more fitness function evaluations than polytree EDA, but it is also better than Particle Swarm Optimization, Ant System, and the Genetic Algorithms. The experiments seem to confirm the hypothesis that data dependencies encode circuit structures that are useful for the generation of better circuits.

The polytree EDA and Bayesian EDA required (on average) less number of fitness function evaluations than the other three methods. The Particle

Figure 5. Best solutions found by the Bayesian EDA for 3-bits, 4-bits and 5-bits parity check problem 9 to 11

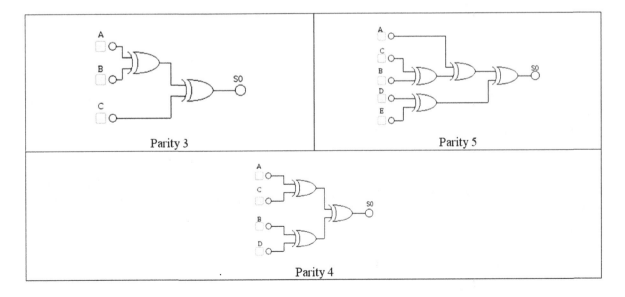

Parity 3

Parity 5

Parity 4

Swarm Optimization and the Genetic Algorithms do not seem to take important advantage of the information encoded in the population.

6.3 Scalability of the Bayesian EDA

In order to analyze the capacity of the Bayesian EDA, the 2, 3, 4, 5, 6, 7, 8, 9-bit parity check problem is solved. All of the solutions reached the optimum solution, known in advance. Table 14 shows the number of fitness function required evaluations to reach the optimum in either problem.

The second column from the left is the number of variables. This number is equal to the number of bits encoding a circuit. The column *Number of Evals* is the number of fitness function evaluations. The column Relation *eval/var* is the number of evaluations divided by the number of variables (or string length). This number is the real effort per bit applied to the string. Consider problems with 3, 6 and 9 bits (two times and three times 3). The relation *evaluations/variables* grows at a slower rate than the number of input bits. So far this is the data available from our experiments. The growth rate of evaluations/variables is expected to be smaller than that of the problem size growth rate. However, we do not yet know the largest parity circuit that can be solved before the computational effort becomes intractable.

Figure 5 shows three basic solutions found by the Bayesian EDA. All circuits are optimally sized.

CONCLUSIONS AND FUTURE WORK

In this chapter, we introduced two new approaches for combinational circuit design based on the polytree EDA and the Bayesian EDA. There is no doubt that the use of data dependencies, hence patterns reduces the number of fitness function evaluations by a really important factor. Other approaches compared in this chapter, with no reuse

of patterns, require larger number of fitness evaluations. It is fair to mention that the computational complexity of the Bayesian model learning algorithm is higher than that of a Genetic Algorithm, Particle Swarm algorithm, and polytree EDA. An important future work is the statistical analysis of the running time. The Bayesian EDA is about 50 times slower than a Genetic Algorithm. A lot of computational effort, via a cluster of computers, was applied to the Bayesian EDA to solve the two experiments. The polytree EDA, as the other reviewed algorithms, needed only one computer. However, the evolutionary approaches are near the limit, as many experiments demonstrate. The potential of the EDA approaches and how they can be improved is part of the future research.

REFERENCES

Chow, C., & Liu, C. (1968). Approximating discrete probability distributions with dependence trees. *IEEE Transactions on Information Theory*, *14*(3), 462–467. doi:10.1109/TIT.1968.1054142

Coello, C. C., Christiansen, A. D., & Aguirre, A. H. (2000). Towards automated evolutionary design of combinational circuits. *Computers & Electrical Engineering*, *27*(1), 1–28. doi:10.1016/S0045-7906(00)00004-5

Coello, C. C., Luna, E. H., & Aguirre, A. H. (2004). A comparative study of encodings to design combinational logic circuits using particle swarm optimization. *Proceedings of the NASA/DoD Conference on Evolvable Hardware* (pp. 71–78). Washington, DC: IEEE Computer Society.

Coello, C. C., Zavala, R., Mendoza, B., & Aguirre, A. H. (2002). Automated design of combinational logic circuits using the ant system. *Engineering Optimization*, *34*(2), 109–127. doi:10.1080/03052150210918

Cooper, G., & Herskovits, E. (1992). A bayesian method for the induction of probabilistic networks from data. *Machine Learning, 9*(4), 309–347.

Cover, T., & Thomas, J. (1991). *Elements of Information Theory*. John Wiley & Sons.

Islas, E., Coello, C. C., & Aguirre, A. H. (2005). Extraction and reuse of design patterns from genetic algorithms using case-based reasoning. *Soft Computing–A Fusion of Foundations. Methodologies and Applications, 9*(1), 44–53.

Kalganova, T. (2000). Bidirectional incremental evolution in extrinsic evolvable hardware. *Proceedings of the 2nd NASA/DoD Workshop on Evolvable Hardware* (pp. 65–74). Washington, DC: IEEE Computer Society.

Larranaga, P., & Lozano, J. (2002). *Estimation of Distribution Algorithms: A New Tool for Evolutionary Computation*. Kluwer Academic Publishers.

Lauritzen, S. (1998). *Graphical Models*. Oxford University Press.

Li, Z., Luo, W., & Wang, X. (2008). A stepwise dimension reduction approach to evolutionary design of relative large combinational logic circuits. *Proceedings of the International Conference on Evolvable Systems* (pp. 11–20). Berlin, Germany: Springer-Verlag.

Lozano, J., Larrañaga, P., Inza, I., & Bengoetxea, E. (2006). *Towards a New Evolutionary Computation*. Springer-Verlag.

Pearl, J. (1988). *Probabilistic Reasoning in Intelligent Systems: Networks of Plausible Inference*. Morgan Kaufmann.

Soto, M., & Ochoa, A. (2000). A factorize distribution algorithm based on polytrees. *Proceedings of the Congress on Evolutionary Computation* (pp. 232–237). Piscataway, NJ: IEEE Press.

Spirtes, P., Glymour, C., & Scheines, R. (1993). *Causation, Prediction, and Search*. Springer-Verlag.

Stomeo, E., Kalganova, T., & Lambert, C. (2006). Generalized disjunction decomposition for evolvable hardware. *IEEE Transactions on Systems, Man, and Cybernetics. Part B, Cybernetics, 36*(5), 1024–1043. doi:10.1109/TSMCB.2006.872259

Torresen, J. (1998). A divide and conquer approach to evolvable hardware. *Proceedings of the 2nd International Conference on Evolvable Systems: From Biology to Hardware* (pp. 57–65). Berlin, Germany: Springer-Verlag.

Torresen, J. (2002). A scalable approach to evolvable hardware. *Genetic Programming and Evolvable Machines, 3*(3), 259–282. doi:10.1023/A:1020163325179

Chapter 13

From the Real Ant to the Artificial Ant:
Applications in Combinatorial Optimization, Data Clustering, Collective Robotics and Image Processing

Moussa Diaf
Université Mouloud Mammeri, Algérie

Kamal Hammouche
Université Mouloud Mammeri, Algérie

Patrick Siarry
Université Paris 12 Val de Marne, France

ABSTRACT

Biological studies highlighting the collective behavior of ants in fulfilling various tasks by using their complex indirect communication process have constituted the starting point for many physical systems and various ant colony algorithms. Each ant colony is considered as a superorganism which operates as a unified entity made up of simple agents. These agents (ants) interact locally with one another and with their environment, particularly in finding the shortest path from the nest to food sources without any centralized control dictating the behavior of individual agents. It is this coordination mechanism that has inspired researchers to develop plenty of metaheuristic algorithms in order to find good solutions for NP-hard combinatorial optimization problems. In this chapter, the authors give a biological description of these fascinating insects and their complex indirect communication process. From this rich source of inspiration for researchers, the authors show how, through the real ant, artificial ant is modeled and applied in combinatorial optimization, data clustering, collective robotics, and image processing.

DOI: 10.4018/978-1-60566-705-8.ch013

INTRODUCTION

In the last 20 years, we have seen a growing number of studies in swarm intelligence. A swarm is made up of a population of simple agents which interact locally with one another and with their environment, without any centralized control dictating the behavior of individual agents (Deneubourg, Aron, Goss & Pasteels, 1990; Moyson & Manderick, 1988). This indirect communication in a self-organizing emergent system, where its individual parts communicate with one another by modifying their local environment, is called *stigmergy* (Abraham, Grosan & Ramos, 2006; Grassé, 1959). The most familiar examples of stigmergy, in natural systems, are observed in ants, bees, wasps, fish school, bird flocks, animal herds, and so on (Brothers, 1999; Gadagkar, 1993). It is this coordination mechanism used by these insects and other social animals that has inspired researchers to develop plenty of metaheuristic computing algorithms. For instance, the observation of the social behavior of some real ant species in finding the shortest paths between the colony and a food source has helped researchers to develop different metaheuristic algorithms used to find good solutions to NP-hard combinatorial optimization problems (Angus, 2006; Ebling, Di Loreto, Presley, Wieland & Jefferson, 1989). This chapter deals with the real ant as well as the artificial one. The biological description of real ants highlighting their life, anatomy and collective behavior in fulfilling various tasks, is given in the following section. This description, absent in most of the known papers related to ant-based algorithms, may be very interesting since the dynamic decision making of real ants constitutes a source of inspiration for the ant-based algorithms. The terms which could be of interest to the engineers are written in bold in the section. Section 3 then shows how, from the study of this fascinating insect, researchers have been induced to develop ant-based algorithms applied in different fields. In section 4, the principles of Ant Colony Optimization (ACO) algorithms, the mathematical foundation and some well-known ACO algorithms are described. In order to illustrate the behavior of some ant-based algorithms and put in evidence its basic components, four examples of applications are given in section 5. The first example of application used, in combinatorial optimization, is the extensively studied Traveling Salesman Problem (TSP). The second example deals with data clustering. The third example is devoted to collective robotics. Following which, in the fourth example, we propose an application of ACO in image segmentation. We conclude this chapter with a discussion of the presented work.

THE REAL ANT

Ant is an insect of the *Formicidae* family, which belongs to the *Hymenoptera* order that includes, among others, bees and wasps (Bolton, Alpert, Ward & Naskrecki, 2007). Ants are millions of billion in number, and their total mass is equivalent to the total mass of the human beings. They have been living on Earth for more than 100 million years and they have colonized all the terrestrial spaces compatible with their lives including the deserts, with the exception of the glacial zones and the marine environments (Hölldobler & Wilson, 1990). They can be divided into 16 subfamilies, 300 kinds and roughly 20,000 species that vary in size, color, and way of life. The largest ant can reach over 25 mm in length, while the smallest is about 2.5 mm. Some ants can lift items 50 times their own weight.

Anatomy of the Ant

Physiologically, an ant consists of a head, a trunk and an abdomen. The head is mainly made up of two **oral antennae** and **mandibles**. The antennae are special organs that help ants to **detect chemicals** (Fanjul-Moles, 2006). They are made up of several segments and covered with **tactile**

Figure 1. Scheme of ant worker anatomy (Villarreal, 2006)

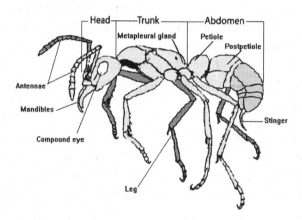

lashes or sensors and serve the functions of **taste**, **touch**, **smell** as well as **communication.** The **hard mandibles** are used for **manipulating or carrying objects**, **handling** and crushing food, constructing nests and defence. Ants, like most insects, generally have **two eyes** constituted of around **hundred facets,** providing a broad 180° vision and very good detection of movements. Most ants have a poor to mediocre eyesight and others are blind altogether. Certain ants see in black and white and others in color. The queens and the males have three small eyes, called *ocelli,* forming a triangle shape on the top of their head. They are **infra-red sensors that detect heat** sources. The thorax, located between the head and the abdomen, is composed of **three rings**, each one carrying a **pair of legs**. The prothorax is the foremost segment, around which the **head is articulated**. The abdomen, composed of 11 or 12 segments, contains digestive cavities like the social stomach and the stomach. For some species of ants, this abdomen is terminated by a stinger for defense against the predators, and a gland which can propel poison at a distance of one meter (Forbes & Kenneth, 2002). (see Figure 1)

Ants and the Environment

The impact of ants on many terrestrial environments is very important due to their activities, such as stirring up the ground to fit up their complex underground nests (Ettershank, 1971). They disperse various species of seeds, which they lose during their way, thus allowing the regeneration of the vegetation. The *Atta* ants collect leaves, which they cut into small pieces, and carry into their nest up to six meters deep, thus contributing to the fertilization of the ground. In South America, certain ants live in the hollow spines of trees of the *Acacia* kind. They are very aggressive and their unceasing patrol protects the trees from herbivores and, moreover, they clean the tree's neighborhood by eliminating all the surrounding vegetation. Thus, they contribute to the survival of these trees. In Europe, the russet-red ants are used for the protection of the forests. In China, another species is employed to protect the orange trees from the devastating insects (Huang & Yang, 1987). In fact, the harmful ants are very few. One such species, found in Argentina, raid houses and attack food stored there; and are very difficult to rid of because of their numerous and small-spaced nests. Other ants, which raise plant lice, are harmful because they destroy many plants.

Social Life of the Ant

Ants are not solitary. An ant colony lives in different types of nests: in underground tunnels, which can be up to 6 meters deep; inside trees; or in certain plants. It is constituted of individuals with different morphological characteristics, each having a specific role. The caste of the workers is constituted of sterile females with physical characteristics adapted to various tasks, namely the breeding of young larvae, construction and maintenance of the nest, and harvesting of food (Moffett & Tobin, 1991). In some ant species, the workers with big head and mandibles are in charge of the nest's defense. Those of intermediate size gather food, and the smallest ones deal with the larvae. However, if needed, any worker can deal with any other activity. The caste of the reproducers includes the queens and the males. The queen, the largest of the ants, spends her life laying eggs and loses her wings after copulation. Its lifespan can be up to 30 years. The males, which are also winged and smaller in size, die a few days after coupling. The reproduction process always occurs during the nuptial flights. Some species hold the flights in the afternoon, while others in the darkness of night. During the nuptial flight, the queen meets the males in the air and receives around 200 millions spermatozoids. After the coupling, it lands, rakes off its wings and digs a hole, where it spits out the packet of fungus it had stored at the bottom of its mouth before the flight and lays eggs together with the fungus. In her lifespan, the queen lays more than 150 millions eggs. If the egg is fertilized, the ant will be a worker, which can live for 1 to 3 years. Otherwise, the ant will be a male, which could fertilize the queen. Ants go through four stages of development: egg, larva, nymph and adult (Heinze & Keller, *2000)*. The small eggs hatch within two to six weeks, and give rise to white larvae. The larvae transform themselves into nymphs, which give birth to the adults. The larvae are fed, cleaned and protected by the workers during their development. Food is given to the larvae by a process called trophallaxis, in which an ant regurgitates food previously held in its crop, for communal storage. Food is distributed amongst the adults in a similar fashion. Larvae and nymphs need to be kept at constant temperature to ensure proper development, and are therefore moved around in the various brood chambers within the colony.

The Communication Process Between Ants

Ants communicate with each other either through pheromones or by touching each other. They smell the pheromones with their mobile antennae, which provide **information** about **direction**, as well as **intensity**. These volatile substances, secreted by different glands, work like **chemical signals**, and constitute of **scented messages** exchanged by the ants. *Dufour's glands* are used to secrete pheromones, which leave scented trails on the soil surface for other ants to follow or gather around. The pheromone produced by the *metapleural* glands are used for recognition, or as a disinfectant substance. The glands situated in the mandibles secrete a special substance, in the event of alarm or to make the foreign workers flee. The glands, *tergales* or *pygidiales*, allow the ants to release a sexual pheromone (Gotwald & Burdette, 1981).

The ants always use the shortest way. Several experiments were carried out to understand how they do this without using visual cues (Harris, Graham & Collett., 2007). In the double-bridge experiment performed by Jean-Louis Deneubourg *et al.*, it was shown that ants find this shortest path to a food source by collectively exploiting pheromones they deposit on the ground while moving (Deneubourg et al. 1990). The higher the accumulation of pheromone, the more attractive the shortest path is for other ants, making the other paths obsolete, where the pheromone disappears by evaporation (see Figure 2). If an obstacle comes to obstruct their path, the ants have the capacity of adaptation to this change by finding the new

Figure 2. Shortest path found by an ant colony (Bonabeau, Dorigo & Theraulaz, 1999)

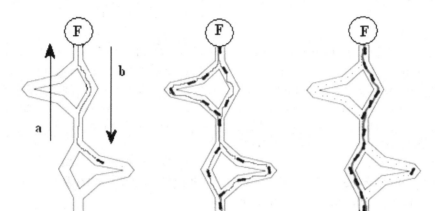

shortest path.

Besides this very sophisticated **communication** process, which includes the sexual communication, the queen-worker communication, the discrimination between eggs, larvae and pupae, warning signals, recruitment for defensive action, etc, ants use the **touch sense**, the **hearing** or **vibration detection**, and **visual communication** too. Very often, ants **send tactile signals** by touching and stroking each others' bodies with their antennae and forelegs. For example, a worker can make another ant regurgitate the liquid food, by spreading a front leg on the labium, therefore causing an emetic reflex of which the other ant can take advantage to feed itself. They also produce high-pitched chirps, known as stridulations, by rubbing together specialized body parts on the abdomen (Roces & Hölldobler, 1996). These stridulations can perform various functions, according to the circumstances, for example, sending **distress signals**. A worker in danger will then emit this signal of distress, which will propagate in the ground, and will express the need for help to the other ants. This type of message is **perceived by the legs** of the ants, which **are real detectors, extremely sensitive to the variations of the ground**. Ants

react little to **the vibrations passed on through the air**. According to the intensity of the emitted vibration, stridulation is also used by a harvester ant, with the aim of attracting sisters and informing them about the quality of the food. The last function of this stridulation is to send a **signal for strengthening**. Indeed, the *Aphenogaster* ants of the desert **scrape**, when they find a large-sized food source, to obtain the help of their sisters.

There are also **sound emissions without stridulatory organs**. When they sense danger, some species strike thier head on a hard substratum, thus sending **a message** which will alert fellow colony members. To transmit warning signals, other species use their abdomen to strike the walls of the ant-hill. As for *Camponotus Ligniperda* ants, they strike the ground alternately with mandibles and the extremity of the abdomen when they are disturbed, and that makes the fellow members to become much more aggressive.

As for **visual communication**, it was one of the forms usually used at the primary stage of evolution, but it has slowly lost its use. This is because of the considerable evolution of the ants, which implies a more effective communication. However, some species still use it for very particular situations. Indeed, if a worker runs into seeds that are too big, it **turns fervently** around them, until the other workers see this ant and come to help. The nest can also be located by the position of the sun, thanks to **specialized cells of ants' eyes** that **detect polarized light** used to determine direction. However, **visual communication** varies according to the species as well as the individuals. For example, for some red ants, the sexual males have a very good sight, contrary to the workers, which are almost blind. The sexual males will, thus, have certain advantage over fellow members of other castes, and they can track down a predator in the forest to warn the ant-hill about it. (see Figure 2)

1) By following path (a), a first ant finds food source (F) and comes back to the nest (N), laying a pheromone trail. 2) Other ants get to (F), through the 4 possible paths. 3) The ants follow the shortest path where pheromone has been accumulated. The pheromone trail of the longest ones has evaporated.

All these various types of communication allow the ant to be a social insect able to **share labor,** by carrying out the tasks of searching for food, **defense, maintenance** and the **construction of the nest**, the **maintenance of larvae** and their **food supply**, etc. All these activities must be simultaneously performed for the survival, development and **good functioning of the colony**. This good functioning is provided by the caste of the workers, who are in charge of the defense or the war, the maintenance of the colony and, therefore, the construction of the nest (Cassill, Tschinkel & Vinson, 2002), the care brought to the queen and to the broods as well as the collection of food.

THE ENGINEER'S POINT OF VIEW

The successful techniques used by ants, particularly, the way in which they **interact** among themselves using various **processes of commu-** nication, **transfer of information**, and by means of special signals, have been widely studied and constitute a field of fascinating inspiration from the engineer's point of view for solving problems in different fields like computer science and robotics. As ants are capable of carrying out difficult tasks **in dynamic and different environments**, the engineer can qualify this type of organization as that of **complex systems** with **elaborated structures** and **distributed organizations**, without **centralized control** or **coordination of a superior level**. They are in the form of **dense heterarchy** and of **horizontal structure,** meaning that the colony forms a highly **connected network**. So, every ant can exchange information with any other by having only **a local knowledge** of its environment, inducing the **robustness** and the **flexibility** of the colony. This robustness allows the system to be capable of continuing to work in case of failure of some ants, and the flexibility provides the **efficiency**, because of its **dynamic character**. Thus, from the observation of the indirect communication and the cooperation between ants by stigmergy, researchers have taken a significant step by designing **the artificial ant**. A high number of ant-based algorithms have been implemented on the basis of real ant activities in theoretical biology. Thus, from **labor division** between real ants, the issue of **task assignmen**t is inferred. From the **cooperative transport** of the real ants, **adaptive** and **distributed robots** and **mobile agents** have been developed. From the **arrangement** of larvae and corpses of the real ants, computer scientists have developed new methods of **data clustering, collective sorting** (Handl, Knowles & Dorigo, 2006) and analyzing **financial transactions** (Sumim, 2004). From the food **foraging** behavior of the real ant, different ACO algorithms have been designed. Since these artificial ant models were adopted, the number of NP-hard combinatorial optimization problems being successfully solved is continuously increasing.

ANT COLONY OPTIMIZATION ALGORITHMS

In this section, some principles of ACO are reminded. More details can be found in some ACO review papers, e.g. Blum (2005). ACO is an algorithmic approach, inspired by the foraging behavior of real ants, which can be applied to solve NP-hard combinatorial optimization problems. The real ant lays down pheromones, directing others to resources while exploring the environment. Similarly, the artificial ant uses artificial pheromone trails for moving, step-by-step, through a discrete search space that represents all the acceptable solutions of the given problem and a probabilistic decision policy, using only local information in space and time without predicting next states (Dorigo & Blum, 2005). The artificial ant builds its own solution so that, in later iterations, solutions of high quality can be reached, thanks to a cooperative behavior between all the artificial ants of the colony. Like the real ant, the artificial pheromone "evaporates" over time, so that artificial ants forget their past history, and direct their searches towards other directions, for finding the shortest way between a starting point and a destination. This artificial pheromone evaporation avoids the convergence to a locally optimal solution. To perform the moves, artificial ants follow a probabilistic decision rule, which is a function of specifications of the problem and of the local changes in their discrete environment. For the real ant, these specifications of the problem are equivalent to structure of the area and the local changes in the discrete environment, to the pheromone trails. The quality and the quantity of the food, in the real case, are equivalent to the objective function to optimize in the case of artificial ants. In addition to this analogy, differences between the areas in which real ants evolve all the feasible solutions of the problem, between trails and artificial trails implemented in an adaptive memory, between the importance of the food and an objective function to optimize

many other operations not existing in the case of real ants, like look-ahead, local optimization and backtracking, hybridization with other metaheuristics, can be introduced in ACO algorithms (Dorigo & Stützle, 2002) in order to increase the efficiency of the system.

Several implementations of the ACO algorithms applied to solve combinatorial optimization problems in different fields have been proposed (Guntsch & Middendorf, 2002; Hu, Zhang & Li, 2008). The problems can be static or dynamic. They are static, when their characteristics are given once and for all, like in the TSP, in which city locations and their relative distances do not change. They are dynamic, if they change at runtime, like in network routing (Di Caro & Dorigo, 1998). In this case, the optimization algorithm must be capable of adapting online to the changing environment. This constitutes an advantage of ACO over some other metaheuristics, when the environment may change dynamically.

Mathematically, a combinatorial optimization problem can be defined as a triplet (S, Ω, f), where S is a discrete search space consisting of a set of feasible solutions, Ω, a set of constraints and f, an objective function to be optimized. If S_Ω is a set of elements of S that satisfy all the constraints, a global optimum is a solution $s^* \in S_\Omega$ if and only if $f(s^*) \leq f(s)$, $\forall s \in S_\Omega$ The goal is to find, at least, one $s^* \in S^*_\Omega$, where $S^*_\Omega \subseteq S_\Omega$ is the set of all globally optimal solutions (Dorigo, Birattari & Stützle, 2006).

In ACO, the representation of a combinatorial optimization problem (S, Ω, f) is often characterized by the given set C of all possible solution components c_{ij}, the set X of all possible sequences of the states of the problem, a pheromone trail value $\tau_{ij} = \tau_{ij}(t)$ which is a function of the iteration of the algorithm associated with each component c_{ij}, the finite set Ω of constraints defining the set of feasible states, a set S^* of feasible states and the objective or cost function $f(s)$.

Ant System (AS) (Dorigo, 1992) is the first ACO developed by Dorigo in 1991. He proposed three variants of its implementation called Ant Cycle, Ant Quantity, and Ant Density. AS algorithm was tested on several TSP. Although it was competitive when sizes are smaller than 75 cities, it was less competitive than some other algorithms designed for the TSP with large instances. Ant Rank (AS_{rank}) (Bullnheimer, Hartl & Strauss, 1999), Ant Colony System (ACS) (Dorigo & Gambardella, 1997b), Elitist strategy (Dorigo, Maniezzo & Colorni, 1996) and Max-Min Ant System (MMAS) (Stützle & Hoos, 2000) are all improvements to Ant System. The major difference between these algorithms resides in the deposition of the pheromone. The other ACO algorithms published in the literature are not introduced in this chapter.

APPLICATIONS OF ANT-BASED ALGORITHMS

Numerous successful implementations of ant-based algorithms mimicking the real ants' behavior are widely applied in different fields such as clustering, image processing, topographic mapping, etc. ACO metaheuristics, particularly, are available in various combinatorial optimization problems, such as TSP, scheduling problems (Colorni, Dorigo, Maniezzo & Trubian, 1994), vehicle routing (Gambardella, Taillard & Agazzi, 1999), connection-oriented network routing (Walkowiak, 2005), graph coloring (Costa & Hertz, 1997), frequency assignment (Maniezzo & Carbonaro, 2000), multiple knapsack (Min, Tian & Kao, 2008), optical networks routing (Katangur, Akkaladevi, Pan & Fraser, 2005), constraint satisfaction (Solnon, 2002), etc. In the industry, ACO are used for optimization applications, such as factory scheduling (Huang, 2001), to solve the complicated, nonconvex, nonlinear economic dispatch problem of power systems (Hou, Wu, Lu & Xiong, 2002), to solve the flowshop scheduling problem with the objective of minimizing the completion-time variance of jobs (Gajpal & Rajendran, 2006), and so forth.

As can be seen, the number of applications is plentiful. In this section, four different applications are given. First, in combinatorial optimization, the most studied TSP is described. The second example deals with data clustering inspired from the way real ants naturally cluster eggs or dead bodies. The third example is devoted to collective robotics, which constitutes the dream for some scientists in transforming the ants into small robots with the same organization and the same social behavior. While the ACO algorithms have been applied successfully to numerous optimization problems, only recently, researchers began to apply them to image processing tasks. As the fourth example, we propose an application of ACO in image segmentation.

Application to the Traveling Salesman Problem (TSP)

The TSP is a classical NP-hard combinatorial problem, which is simple to understand but difficult to solve. It is often used as a benchmark to test new ideas and algorithmic variants. In this problem, a number of cities and the distances which separate them are given. The problem consists of finding a closed tour of minimal length that visits each city once and only once (Dorigo & Gambardella, 1997b). To apply ACO to the TSP, a graph representation is constructed. The set of cities is associated with the set of vertices of the graph. The lengths of the edges between the vertices are proportional to the distances between the cities. Pheromone values and heuristic values are associated with the edges of the graph. Pheromone values are modified at runtime and represent the cumulated experience of the ant colony. Heuristic values are problem dependent values, which are set to be the visibility, *i.e.* the inverse of the lengths of the edges. The optimization problem is transformed into a problem of finding the best path through a weighted graph, which starts and ends at the same vertex, including every other vertex once and minimizing the total cost of edges. By moving on the graph, the artificial ants incrementally construct solutions, as described hereafter.

Each ant starts from a randomly selected vertex of the construction graph and moves along the edges of the graph, at each construction step, while keeping a memory of its path, in order to choose among the edges that do not lead to vertices already visited. The choice of an edge is made on the basis of a probabilistic rule, biased by pheromone values and heuristic information. The higher the pheromone and the heuristic value associated to an edge, the higher the probability that an ant will choose that particular edge. The pheromone on the edges is updated once all the ants have completed their tour. Each of the pheromone values, initially decreased by a certain percentage, receives an amount of additional pheromone, proportional to the quality of the solution to which it belongs. There is one solution per ant. This procedure is repeatedly applied, until a termination criterion is satisfied.

The following algorithm is derived from Dorigo's original proposal for AS. Each ant is a simple agent with the following characteristics. An ant k at city i chooses to visit city j, with a probability $p_{ij}^k(t)$ which is a function of the towns' distance and of the amount of pheromone trail present on the connecting edge.

So, the probability with which ant k, currently at node i, chooses to move to node j at the tth iteration is:

$$p_{ij}^k(t) = \begin{cases} \dfrac{(\tau_{ij}(t))^\alpha (\eta_{ij})^\beta}{\sum_{l \in J_i^k}(\tau_{ij}(t))^\alpha (\eta_{ij})^\beta} & if \ j \in J_j^k \\ 0 & otherwise \end{cases} \quad (1)$$

where:

- $\tau_{ij}(t)$ is the amount of pheromone on each edge of a trail which is updated by the relation in Equation 2.

- $\eta_{ij} = \dfrac{1}{d_{ij}}$ is the *visibility* of arc i,j and is

equal to the reciprocal of the distance d_{ij} between the cities i and j.

- α and β are two parameters controlling the influence of τ_{ij} and the influence of η_{ij} respectively. With $\alpha = 0$, only visibility of the city is taken into consideration. The city nearest is thus selected at each step. On the contrary, with $\beta = 0$, only the trails of pheromone become influential.

The update rule for the trails is given as:

$$\tau_{ij}(t+1)=(1-\rho)\tau_{ij}(t)+\Delta\tau_{ij}(t) \quad (2)$$

where

- ρ is the rate of pheromone evaporation defined by the user. It is employed to avoid unlimited accumulation of the pheromone trails and it enables the algorithm to "forget" previously bad decisions.

- $\Delta\tau_{ij}(t)$ is the amount of pheromone deposited by all ants that used move (ij). It is typically given by $\Delta\tau_{ij}(t)=\sum_{k=1}^m \Delta\tau_{ij}^k(t)$ where:

- $\Delta\tau_{ij}^k(t) = \begin{cases} \dfrac{1}{L^k(t)} & if \ (i,j) \in T^k(t) \ (ant \ k \ travel \ on \ arc(i,j)) \\ 0 & otherwise \end{cases} \quad (3)$

In this expression:

- $T^k(t)$ is the path traversed by the ant k during the iteration t
- L_k is the cost or the length of the kth ant's tour

The initial quantity of pheromone on the edges is a uniform distribution of a small quantity ($\tau(0) \geq 0$).

As was said before, AS is the less competitive algorithm. Some published works with a comparative assessment of ACO algorithms within a TSP environment have shown that ACS performs

Figure 3. Pseudo-code for ant colony system

```
                Ant Colony System

1. Distribute ant agents on different cities
2. i = 0
3. While k < # ants
        ant_k adds new city based on P_{ij} and α q_0
        ant_k updates the trail locally
   End While
4. If i++ < #cities GOTO 3
5. τ_{ij}=ρ.τ_{ij}+Δτ*_{ij(globalbest)}
```

well and, in general, better than almost all other algorithms (Asmar, Elshamli & Areibi, 2005). Figure 3 represents ACS algorithm. Compared to the previous algorithms, ACS performs local update as the solution is being built. Ants deposit pheromone after they have traversed an edge. The trail is multiplied by a constant (less than 1) at edges when ants have just finished crossing. In addition, a probability q_0 is introduced. If q_0 is equal to 1, the ants use a greedy equation to choose the adjacent city to move to. If q_0 is equal to 0, the algorithm uses the AS mechanism.

Application in Data Clustering

Clustering or unsupervised classification is a subject of active research in several fields, including statistics, pattern recognition, machine learning, and data mining. Clustering techniques aim at regrouping a set of multidimensional observations, represented as data points, scattered through an N-dimensional data space, into groups, or clusters, according to their similarities or dissimilarities. Several algorithms have been proposed in the literature to solve clustering problems (Filippone, Camastra, Masulli & Rovetta, 2008; Xu & Wunsch, 2005). Some approaches are based on the way some ant species cluster corpses to form a "cemetery", or sort their larvae into several

piles, to clean the nest (Handl, Knowles & Dorigo, 2003). (see Figure 4)

By taking into account these observations, Deneubourg *et al.* (1991) have developed a model describing the so called corps clustering, where ants collect randomly spread dead ants into clusters. This "basic" model is generalized by Lumer and Faieta (1994) to apply it to exploratory data analysis, by introducing a similarity measure between the data objects. The algorithm of Lumer and Faieta has become very popular and has been improved by several other authors (Boryczka, 2009; Handl & Meyer, 2002; Monmarche, Slimane & Venturini, 1999a; Wu & Shi, 2001). It is described in Figure 5.

Initially, the objects to be classified are randomly projected on a low dimension space, usually a 2D grid. A set of ant agents are placed at a random position on the grid. A cell in the grid may contain one ant, one object, or both an ant and an object, or any object and any ant. The goal of the agents is to move the objects into clusters. The coordinate of a cell is given by the cell-number, along with standard x- and y- directions. At each time step, the agents move randomly to any of the eight neighboring cells. On arriving at a cell, the ant is able to make the decision of dropping or picking up an object. The ant carrying an object drops this object at its current grid position, with

Figure 4. Real ants cluster (Bonabeau et al., 1999)

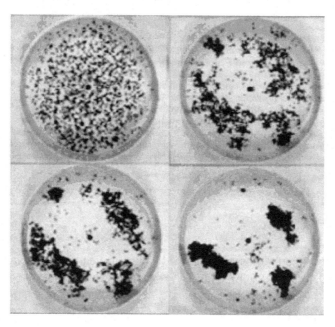

Figure 5. Lumer and Faeita's algorithm

```
/* Initialization phase*/
for every object oᵢ do
   Place randomly the object oᵢ on the grid
end for
for all ants do
   Place randomly ant on the cell of the grid
end for

/* Main loop*/
for all ants do
   for t=1 to tₘₐₓ do
      if (ant is unloaded) and (the cell is occupied by the object oᵢ) then
         Compute f(oᵢ) and pₚ(oᵢ)
         Create a random number R ∈ (0,1)
         if R≤pₚ(oᵢ) then
             Pick up the object oᵢ
         end if
      else
         if (ant carrying object oᵢ then
             Compute f(oᵢ) an pₚ(oᵢ)
             Create random number R ∈ (0,1)
             if R≤p_d(oᵢ) then
                Drop the object oᵢ
             end if
         end if
      end if
      Move randomly to neighboring cell not occupied by other ant
   end for
end for
Print location of objects.
```

a given probability, if this grid cell is not occupied by another object. In case the ant is not carrying any object and is located on a non-empty cell, the ant picks the object with a given probability. By repeating the move of picking or dropping operations, the objects will be gathered into clusters.

The probabilities of picking up $p_p(o_i)$ or dropping $p_d(o_i)$ of an object o_i depend on the distance, in feature space, between that object and other objects in its neighborhood. They are given as follows:

$$p_p(o_i) = \left(\frac{k_1}{k_1 + f(o_i)} \right)^2 \qquad (4)$$

$$p_d(o_i) = \begin{cases} 2f(o_i) & \text{if } f(o_i) \prec k_2 \\ 1 & \text{if } f(o_i) \geq k_2 \end{cases} \qquad (5)$$

where

- k_1, k_2 are two threshold constants,
- $f(o_i)$ is a measure of the average similarity of object o_i with other objects o_j present in the neighborhood of o_i. It is defined as follows:

$$f(o_i) = \begin{cases} \dfrac{1}{s^2} \sum_{o_j \in N_{sxs}} \left[1 - \dfrac{d(o_i, o_j)}{\alpha} \right] & \text{if } f(o_i) \succ 0 \\ 0 & \text{otherwise} \end{cases}$$

$$(6)$$

In this expression:

- N_{SxS} is the set of cell neighboring of size (s x s),
- α is a factor that defines the scale for dissimilarity.

Another ant clustering method, called "Ant-Clust", aims at reproducing the principles inspired by the chemical recognition system of ants (Labroche, Guinot & Venturini, 2004). The main idea of AntClust is to associate an object of the data set to the genome of an artificial ant. It simulates meetings between artificial ants, according to behavioral rules, to allow each ant to find the label that best fits its genome and therefore to place it in the best nest (or best cluster). (see Figure 5)

An ant clustering algorithm proposed in Shelokar, Jayaraman & Kulkarni (2004) mimics the way real ants find the shortest route between a food source and their nest. The ants communicate with one another by means of pheromone trails, and exchange information about which path should be followed. The more the number of ants tracing a given path, the more attractive this path (trail) becomes and is followed by other ants, thus depositing their own pheromone. This autocatalytic and collective behavior is used to solve a clustering problem, by assigning the Q objects in R^N to one of the K clusters, such that the sum of squared Euclidean distances between each object and the center of the cluster where it is located is minimized. The algorithm considers R ants to build solutions. An ant starts with an empty solution string S of length Q, where each element of string corresponds to one of the objects to classify. The value assigned to an element of solution string S represents the cluster number to which the object is assigned. To construct a solution, the ant uses the pheromone trail information to allocate each element of string S to an appropriate cluster label. At the start of the algorithm, the pheromone matrix, τ, is initialized to some small value, τ_0. The trail value τ_{ij}, at location (i,j), represents the pheromone concentration of object o_i associated to the cluster C_j. For the problem of separating N samples into K clusters, the pheromone matrix is of size Q x K. Thus, each object is associated with K pheromone concentrations. At each iteration, the agents develop solutions using the process of pheromone-mediated communication. After generating a population of R solutions, a local search is performed to further improve fitness of

Figure 6. Morphology of the ant which inspired the hexapod robot

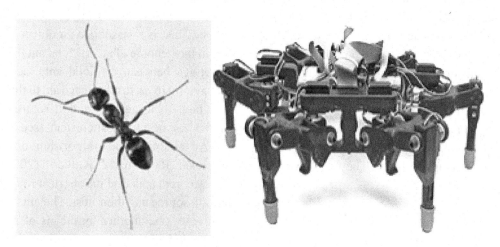

these solutions. The pheromone matrix is then updated, depending on the quality of the solutions produced by the agents, and the above steps are repeated for a certain number of iterations.

Application to Collective Robotics

Collective robotics is an approach to the coordination of a certain number of small and simple robots. When we observe the complex tasks achieved by an ant colony in full activity, we cannot remain without imagining a swarm of small robots which would have the same intelligence, the same organization and the same social behavior. The first stage of this process of transformation is the reconsideration of the mobile robot. At the beginning, for moving, the mobile robot was equipped with wheels. However, the wheels become ineffective when the grounds are broken and present obstacles difficult to cross. In order to overcome this disadvantage, the hexapod robot, capable of moving in all the directions and in any kind of ground, has been created, starting from the study of the morphology of the ant and of some other insects (Wagner & Bruckstein, 2001; Rodney et al., 1989). Figure 6 shows the morphology of the ant which inspired the hexapod robot (Hexapode, 2004).

Thereafter, from the social behavior of the ants and their ability to solve complex problems efficiently and reliably, the idea of a significant number of autonomous robots communicating with each other has started to take form. This concept was already imagined by Rodney Brooks in 1989, in a paper in which he defended the idea that it is largely preferable to conquer space and to discover unknown planets by means of thousands, even millions, of small autonomous robots, rather than by sending only one robot of an imposing size (Arai, Pagello & Parker, 2002). Lately, it was noted that a group of cooperative robots is more successful, in terms of speed and efficiency, than active robots working individually (Caprari, Estier & Siegwart, 2002). Therefore, researchers have developed a great number of algorithms for distributed systems, where a robot is analogous to an ant and a swarm of ant robots to a colony of ants. In addition to the fundamental theories, the practical achievements of swarms of ant robots required several studies, based on technological progress, hardware and software (Wagner, Lindenbaum & Bruckstein, 1998). They are particularly equipped with different actuators and communicate with each other using sensors, including light sensors, infrared receivers, bump sensors, food sensors, and tilt sensors (Trianni & Dorigo, 2006). Similar to real ants, ant robots can follow other ant robots or cover terrain robustly; for directing their moves, they can, for example, use polarized or focused light, as some real ant species do. For this purpose, they can also use chemical odor trace that vanishes with time, as pheromones; tracks of camphor or heat, as environmental information (Tuci et al., 2006). However, ant robots' constitution remains simple and cheap with limited sensing. They have computational capabilities, like the resulting fault tolerance and parallelism and, despite their small size, they are able to carry out complex tasks and, using artificial neural networks, they are capable of controlling their behavior (Groß, Bonani, Mondada & Dorigo, 2006).

The colonies of ant robots are used in a wide range of areas (Dandan, Guangming, Junzhi & Long, 2007). Several projects, using ants as a model and carried out independently in several countries, concern the military industry. Small, inexpensive, behaving as a group, performing a series of physical actions and taking joint decisions; ant robots are, in this case, considered as a robot army. Otherwise, they can also be used to perform the task of cleaning the floor of an unmapped building (Wagner & Bruckstein, 1997), or any task that requires the traversal of an unknown region. Ant robots are also used for mine sweeping, surveillance, surface inspection and guarding terrain, even if this terrain is initially unknown and changes dynamically, or even if they can have very noisy actuators or sensors, or may fail.

Application to Image Processing

Image segmentation refers to the process of partitioning an image into multiple regions. It plays an essential role in the interpretation of various kinds of images. ACO algorithms have recently been applied for image segmentation, where the ants are used to classify the pixels of an image into classes (Ouadfel & Batouche, 2003; Saatchi & Hung, 2007). In Ouadfel and Batouche (2003), each ant works through the image assigning all the pixels in order to optimize a regularity measure. In Saatchi and Hung (2007), the authors combine the ACO method with the *K-means* clustering algorithm as well as the competitive learning algorithm in order to classify the pixels. In both techniques, each ant defines K cluster centers and the part of the ACO is to assign each pixel to a cluster according to a probability which is inversely proportional to the distance between the pixel and cluster centers along with a pheromone level, which is lying to the separability and the compactness of the clusters.

The segmentation of an image can also be considered as a problem of edge detection where the boundary of the regions can be localized at important local changes in the gray level. In Tian, Yu and Xie (2008), a pheromone matrix that represents the edge information presented at each pixel position of the image is constructed according to the movements of a number of ants which are dispatched to move on the image. The movements of these ants are driven by the local variation of the image's intensity values.

Another way to perform image segmentation is image thresholding, which is useful in separating objects from the background, or discriminating objects from objects that have distinct gray levels (Sezgin & Sankur, 2004). Thresholding involves bi-level thresholding and multilevel thresholding. Bi-level thresholding (binarization) classifies the pixels into two groups, one including those pixels with gray levels above a certain threshold, the other including the rest. Multilevel thresholding divides the pixels into several classes. The pixels belonging to the same class have gray levels within a specific range defined by several thresholds. Thresholding leads to an optimization problem, whose solution is computationally expensive and time-consuming, especially when the number of thresholds increases. To our knowledge, there is only one method based on ACO that has been devoted to image thresholding. In this method (Malisia & Tizhoosh, 2006), one ant is assigned to each pixel of an image and then moves to neighbouring pixels until it reaches a certain number of steps. Once the ant completes its path, the pheromone content of the pixels on the ant's path is updated. In this algorithm the pheromone is dropped directly onto pixels, not on the connections between the pixels. Finally, each pixel is classified only in two classes using *K-means* algorithm according to the pheromone contents and the normalized gray values of the pixels. However, this method allows only binarizing the image without computing the threshold value and its computing load can be extensive.

The proposed algorithm in this section is quite different from the approach introduced in Malisia et al. (2006), as it allows us to directly find several values of thresholds (multilevel thresholding) by optimizing any objective function quickly.

Multilevel Thresholding Problem Formulation

The optimal thresholding methods search for the thresholds, such that the segment classes on the histogram satisfy the desired property. This is performed by minimizing or maximizing an objective function, which uses the selected thresholds as parameters.

Let us consider an image I having N pixels, with L gray levels $L=\{0,1,...,L-1\}$. For thresholding purpose, the pixels are classified into K classes $(C_1, C_2,...,C_k,...,C_K)$, using a set of $(K-1)$ thresholds $T=(t_1,t_2,...,t_k,...,t_{K-1})$, such that $t_1<t_2<...<t_{K-1}$. For convenience, we assumed two extreme thresholds $t_0=0$ and $t_K=L$. A pixel with gray level g is assigned to class C_k if $t_{k-1}< g <t_k$, $k=1,2,...,K$.

The thresholding problem consists of selecting the set of thresholds T^* which optimizes an objective function $f(T)$, such that:

$$T^* = \arg\max_{0\leq T\leq L-1} F(T) \tag{7}$$

Several objective functions devoted to thresholding have been proposed in the literature. These functions are generally determined from the histogram of the image, denoted by $h(i)$, $i=0,...,L-1$, where $h(i)$ represents the number of pixels having the gray level i. The normalized probability at level j is defined by the ratio $p_i=h(i)/N$.

Among these functions, the objective function defined by Otsu is the most popular (Otsu, 1979). It defines the weighted sum of within-class variances of the classes:

$$F(T) = \sigma_B^2 = \sum_{k=1}^{K} \omega_k \left(\mu_k - \mu\right)^2 \tag{8}$$

where ω_k, μ_k and μ are the probability, the mean gray level of the class C_k and the total mean gray level of the image, respectively. They are given by:

$$\omega_k = \sum_{i=t_{k-1}}^{t_k-1} p_i \quad \mu_k = \frac{1}{\omega_k} \sum_{j=t_{k-1}}^{t_k-1} ip_i \quad \text{and}$$

$$\omega_k = \sum_{i=t_{k-1}}^{t_k-1} p_i \quad \mu_k = \frac{1}{\omega_k} \sum_{j=t_{k-1}}^{t_k-1} ip_i \quad \mu = \sum_{i=0}^{L-1} ip_i,$$

$$\mu_k = \frac{1}{\omega_k} \sum_{j=t_{k-1}}^{t_k-1} ip_i \quad \mu = \sum_{i=0}^{L-1} ip_i \tag{9}$$

Ant Colony Optimization for Image Thresholding

Similarly, we propose an ACO algorithm for multilevel thresholding, in which a set of concurrent distributed agents collectively discover the optimal threshold values. The summary of the proposed ant algorithm for multilevel thresholding is depicted in Figure 7. In the proposed ACO approach, a colony of N simple agents or artificial ants search for good solutions at every generation. The set of the ants form a population of threshold values. The threshold values produced by the ant j are also denoted by $pop(j)\_t_k$ ($k=1,2,...,K$). Every artificial ant j of a generation builds up a

Figure 7 Pseudo-code for the ant colony optimization thresholding

```
1- Create the pheromone matrix τ
2- Initialize the populations pop and bestpop: bestpop=pop
3- Store the best solution T* of the population bestpop with its fitness in a separate location.
2- For a fixed number of iterations
      Determine the population pop from the pheromone matrix
      For all individuals j in population pop
         If rand >q₀ then
```
$$pop(j)\_t_k = \arg\max \tau_{ik}, i \in \begin{bmatrix} g_{min} & g_{max} \end{bmatrix}$$
```
         Else
```
$$pop(j)\_t_k = rand_{INT}\begin{bmatrix} g_{min} & g_{max} \end{bmatrix}$$
```
      Evaluate population pop (evaluate all candidate solutions)

      Update the population bestpop and the best solution T*
      For all individuals j in population pop
         If pop(j)_fitness is better than bestpop(j)_fitness then
            bestpop(j)_fitness = pop(j)_fitness

      Compare the best individual T of the pop with T*. If T has a fitness value better than T*, then
      replace T* with T. Fmax=f(T*)

      Update the pheromone trails
```
$$\tau_{ik} = \rho \tau_{ik} + (1-\rho)F_{max}$$
```
      endfor //iteration
4- Output best recorded solution T*
```

solution $T=(t_1, t_2, ..., t_k, ..., t_K)$, by using the information provided by the pheromone matrix, denoted by τ, where each element τ_{ik} is trail pheromone that relates the gray level i to the kth threshold, $i=0,1,2;...,L-1$ and $k=1,2,...,K$. Initially, the trail pheromones τ_{ik} are randomly generated in the range $[0,1]$.

To generate a solution T, the agent selects the threshold value for each element of string T, according to the following rule:

- using probability q_0, the gray value having the maximum pheromone concentration is chosen as threshold value: $pop(j)\_t_k=\arg\max \tau_{ik}, i \in [g_{min}g_{max}]$ (10)
- else the kth threshold value is determined, using a stochastic distribution with a probability $(1-q_0)$, such that: $pop(j)\_t_k=rand[g_{min}g_{max}]$ (11)

In these expressions, g_{min} and g_{max} are the minimum and the maximum gray values in the image, respectively.

We note that q_0 is *a priori* defined number, such that $0 < q_0 < 1$. In our simulation, q_0 is fixed to 0.5. Once all ants have their solutions built up, these solutions are evaluated, according to the objective function; then the algorithm records the best one found so far. The value of best solution in memory is updated with the value of the solution obtained as "current iteration's best solution", if it has a better objective function value than that of the best solution in memory. The pheromone trails are then updated. The trail updating process in this algorithm is performed as follows:

$$\tau_{ik}=\rho \tau_{ijk}+(1-\rho)\Delta\tau \qquad (12)$$

where ρ is the persistence of trail that lies within [0, 1] and $(1 - \rho)$ is the evaporation rate. Higher value of ρ suggests that the information gathered in the past iterations is forgotten faster. $\Delta\tau$ denotes the amount of pheromone trail added to τ_{ik} by the best ant corresponding to the best solution found so far: $\Delta\tau = F_{max}$.

Thus, the pheromone matrix is a kind of adaptive memory that contains information provided by the previously found superior solutions, and is updated at the end of the iterations. At any iteration level, the algorithm essentially executes two steps: (1) generation of N new solutions by artificial ants, using the modified pheromone trail information available from previous iteration, and (2) updating pheromone trail matrix. The algorithm repeatedly carries out these two steps for a maximum number of given iterations, and solution having the best function value represents the optimal threshold values.

Experimental Results

In order to compare the quality of the solutions provided by the ACO for the multilevel thresholding, the threshold values T* and the value of the best fitness $F(T^*)$ corresponding to the best threshold solution T* are compared to those provided by the exhaustive research. Of course, the smaller the objective function value, the better the algorithm.

Additional results are presented in order to show the speed of the proposed method.

The proposed multilevel thresholding technique using an ACO has several parameters whose values considerably affect the performance of the algorithms. We have done preliminary testing (which is not presented in this chapter) on this algorithm for the purpose of getting good combinations of parameters. As results, the following parameters are chosen: q_0=0.5, persistence of trail ρ=0.1. The size N of the ants is fixed at 100. The number of iterations depends on the number of thresholds (see Table 1).

Two well-known images, named *Lena* and *Peppers*, of size (256 x 256), with 256 grey levels, are used. These images are shown in Figure 8 and Figure 9 with their respective histograms.

The optimal threshold values and the optimal objective function values, found by an exhaustive research and the ACO, with a threshold number varying from 1 to 4, are given in Table 1. The processing times are also given in this table. Figure 10 shows the threshold images. Experimental results show that the optimal threshold values given by the ACO are similar to those obtained by the exhaustive search, with a great gain in processing time when the number of thresholds increases.

Table 1. Comparative results of the thresholding between the exhaustive search and the ACO

	K	Exhaustive Search			ACO			
		Threshold values	Objective function	Time (ms)	Threshold values	Objective function	Time (ms)	Number of iterations
Lena	2 3 4 5	102 78-145 57-106-159 47-84-119-164	0.31280 0.14381 0.07103 0.04285	5 470 37000 ≈2^{10^6}	102 78-145 57-105-160 46-79-118-163	0.31280 0.14381 0.07115 0.04362		10 100 10000 10000
Peppers	2 3 4 5	117 67-132 62-116-160 44-83-121-162	0.30282 0.13551 0.07544 0.04930	10 590 50240 ≈2^{10^6}	117 67-132 61-115-159 45-83-118-158	0.30282 0.13551 0.07550 0.05017		10 100 10000 10000

CONCLUSION

The algorithms inspired by ant colonies have begun to be better described and formalized. The main properties describing them are known: the probabilistic construction of a solution, a heuristic on the instance of the problem, the use of an indirect memory ant and a structure comparable to those of an auto-organized system. The ACO metaheuristic could be described as a distributed system where interactions between components, by means of a stigmergic process, enable it to bring to the foreground a global coherent behavior, allowing the system to resolve difficult optimization problems.

ACO algorithms possess interesting characteristics, such as high intrinsic parallelism, flexibility (the colony adapts itself to environment changes), robustness (a colony is capable of maintaining its activity even if some individuals are failing), in addition to decentralization and self-organization. Therefore, this approach is useful for difficult problems, such as the non-supervised classification, the collective robotics and the search for the overall optimum, in combinatorial optimization problems. The use of ACO metaheuristics for the solution of dynamic, multiobjective (Garcia-Martinez, Cordon & Herrera, 2007), stochastic, continuous and mixed-variable optimization problems, as well as the creation of parallel implementations (Talbi,

Figure 8. Test images. (a) Lena, (b) Peppers

a   b

Figure 9. Grey-level histograms of test images. (a) Lena, (b) Peppers

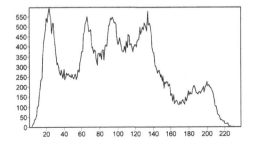
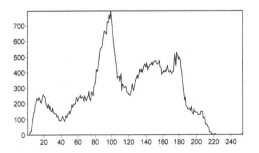

Figure10. Thresholded images with various numbers of thresholds: (a-a'):1, (b-b'):2, (c-c'):3 and (d-d'):4

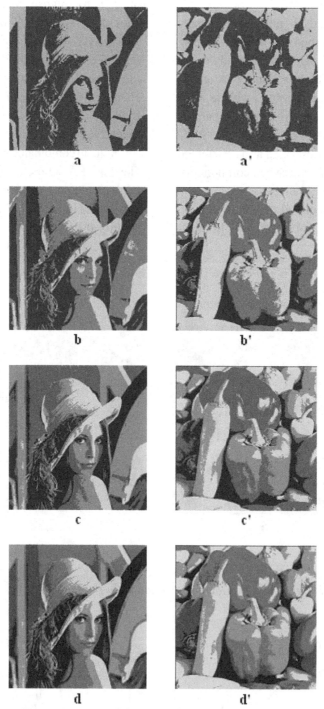

Roux & Fonlupt, 2001; Zhao, Zhaoheng & Dao, 2007) capable of taking advantage of the new available parallel hardware constitute currently attractive topics. For more efficiency, they are also often hybridized with other metaheuristics (Bullnheimer, Kotsis & Strauss, 1998); Dréo & Siarry, 2007; Monmarché, Slimane & Venturini, 1999b; Xia, Xuehui & Jihong, 2003). ACO was successfully applied to numerous combinatorial optimization problems in different fields of the industrial world. Several results have proven the efficiency of these new algorithms, which can compete with other stochastic optimization methods, like simulated annealing and genetic algorithms, in terms of solution quality. ACO has also been used in several other fields. The way ants sort and cluster their brood and their dead individuals has inspired researchers to work on a way of analyzing financial transactions. The use of ACO in medicine where antlike agents could mimic the interactions of simple chemicals in the body and in drugs, has been predicted by some ACO specialists, even though much research and development remains to be done (Evkli & Sevilgen, 2008). However, these studies are more and more extended to the social behaviors of other animals and other insects, leading to various new algorithms inspired by these models (Poli, Kennedy & Blackwell, 2007; Pham et al., 2006; Ressom, Vincent & Anyakoha, 2008; Yang, 2008; Govil, Govil & Nandra, 2008).

REFERENCES

Abraham, A., Grosan, C., & Ramos, V. (2006). (Eds.). *Stigmergic Optimization*. Studies in Computational Intelligence, Berlin, Germany: Springer Verlag.

Angus, D. (2006). *Ant Colony Optimisation: From Biological Inspiration to an Algorithmic Framework*, (Technical Report n. TR013). Melbourne, Australia: Centre for Intelligent Systems & Complex Processes, Faculty of Information & Communication Technologies, Swinburne University of Technology.

Arai, T., Pagello, E., & Parker, L. (2002). Advances in multi-robot systems. *IEEE Transactions on Robotics and Automation, 18*, 655–661.

Asmar, D. C., Elshamli, A., & Areibi, S. (2005 July). A Comparative Assessment of ACO Algorithms within a TSP Environment. *Proceedings of the DCDIS 4th International Conference on Engineering Applications and Computational Algorithms* (pp. 27-29), Guelph, Ontario, Canada.

Banks, A., Vincent, J., & Anyakoha, C. (2008). A review of particle swarm optimization. Part II: hybridisation, combinatorial, multicriteria and constrained optimization, and indicative applications. *Natural Computing, 6*, 467–484.

Blum, C. (2005). Ant colony optimization: Introduction and recent trends. *Physics of Life Reviews, 2*, 353–373.

Bolton, B., Alpert, G., Ward, P. S., & Naskrecki, P. (2007). *Bolton's Catalogue of Ants of the World*. Cambridge, Massachusetts: Harvard University Press.

Bonabeau, E., Dorigo, M., & Theraulaz, G. (1999). *Swarm Intelligence: From Natural to Artificial Systems*. New York, NY: Oxford University Press, Santa Fe Institute Studies in the Sciences of Complexity.

Boryczka, U. (2009). Finding groups in data: Cluster analysis with ants. *Applied Soft Computing, 9*(1), 61–70.

Brothers, D. J. (1999). Phylogeny and evolution of wasps, ants and bees (Hymenoptera, Chrysisoidea, Vespoidea, and Apoidea). *Zoologica Scripta, 28*, 233–249.

Bullnheimer, B., Hartl, R. F., & Strauss, C. (1999). A new rank-based version of the ant system: a computational study. *Central European Journal for Operations Research and Economics, 7*(1), 25–38.

Bullnheimer, B., Kotsis, G., & Strauss, C. (1998). Parallelization strategies for the Ant System. In R. De Leone, A. Murli, P. Pardalos, & G. Toraldo (Eds.), *High Performance Algorithms and Software in Nonlinear Optimization, 24*, 87-100. Dordrecht, NL: Kluwer Academic Publishers.

Caprari, G., Estier, T., & Siegwart, R. (2002). Fascination of down scaling – Alice the sugar cube robot. *Journal of Micromechatronics, 1*, 177–189.

Cassill, D. L., Tschinkel, W. R., & Vinson, S. B. (2002). Nest complexity, group size and brood rearing in the fire ant, Solenopsis invicta. *Insectes Sociaux, 49*, 158–163.

Colorni, A., Dorigo, M., Maniezzo, V., & Trubian, M. (1994). Ant System for jobshop scheduling. *Belgian Journal of Operations Research. Statistics and Computer Science, 34*, 39–53.

Costa, D., & Hertz, A. (1997). Ants can colour graphs. *The Journal of the Operational Research Society, 48*, 295–305.

Dandan, Z., Guangming, X., Junzhi, Y., & Long, W. (2007). Adaptive task assignment for multiple mobile robots via swarm intelligence approach. *Robotics and Autonomous Systems, 55*(7), 572–588.

Deneubourg, J.-L., Aron, S., Goss, S., & Pasteels, J. M. (1990). The self-organizing exploratory pattern of the Argentine ant. *Journal of Insect Behavior, 3*, 159–168.

Deneubourg, J.-L., Goss, S., Franks, N., Sendova-Franks, A., Detrain, C., & et al. (1991). The dynamics of collective sorting: robot-like ant and ant-like robot. *Proceedings of the First International Conference on Simulation of Adaptive Behavior: From Animals to Animats* (pp. 356-363), Paris, France.

Di Caro, G., & Dorigo, M. (1998). AntNet: Distributed stigmergetic control for communications networks. *Journal of Artificial Intelligence Research, 9*, 317–365.

Dorigo, M. (1992). *Optimization, Learning and Natural Algorithms*. Ph.D. Thesis. Italy: Politecnico di Milano.

Dorigo, M., Birattari, M., & Stützle, T. (2006). Ant Colony Optimization -Artificial ants as a computational intelligence technique. *IEEE Computational intelligence Magazine, 1*(4), 28-29.

Dorigo, M., & Blum, C. (2005). Ant colony optimization theory: A survey. *Theoretical Computer Science, 344*(2-3), 243–278.

Dorigo, M., & Gambardella, L. M. (1997a). Ant colonies for the traveling salesman problem. *Bio Systems, 43*, 73–81.

Dorigo, M., & Gambardella, L. M. (1997b). Ant Colony System: A cooperative learning approach to the traveling salesman problem. *IEEE Transactions on Evolutionary Computation, 1*, 53–66.

Dorigo, M., Maniezzo, V., & Colorni, A. (1991). *Ant System: An Autocatalytic Optimizing Process*. (Technical Report 91-016). Italy, Milano: Dipartimento di Elettronica e Informazione, Politecnico di Milano.

Dorigo, M., Maniezzo, V., & Colorni, A. (1996). The Ant System: Optimization by a Colony of Cooperating Agents. *IEEE Transactions on Systems, Man, and Cybernetics–Part B, 26*(1), 29–41.

Dorigo, M., & Stützle, T. (2002). The Ant Colony Optimization metaheuristic: Algorithms, Applications and Advances. Kluwer Academic Publishers. Glover, F. & Kochenberger, G. (Eds.). *Handbook of Metaheuristics* (pp. 250-285). New York: Springer.

Dréo, J., & Siarry, P. (2007). Hybrid Continuous Interacting Ant Colony aimed at enhanced global optimization. *Algorithmic Operations Research*, *2*, 52–64.

Ebling, M., Di Loreto, M., Presley, M., Wieland, F., & Jefferson, D. (1989). An Ant Foraging Model Implemented On the Time Warp Operating System. In Unger, B. & Fujimoto, R. (Eds.), *Proceedings of the SCS Multiconference on Distributed Simulation* (pp. 21-26). San Diego, CA: Society For Computer Simulation.

Ettershank, G. (1971). Some aspects of the ecology and nest microclimatology of the meat ant, Iridomyrmex purpureus (Sm). *Royal Society of Victoria Proceedings*, *84*, 137–151.

Evkli, Z., & Sevilgen, E. E. (2008). A Hybrid Particle Swarm Optimization Algorithm for Function Optimization. *Applications of Evolutionary Computing*, *4974*, 585–595.

Fanjul-Moles, M. L. (2006). Antennal olfactory sensitivity in response to task-related odours of three castes of the ant Atta mexicana (hymenoptera: formicidae). *Physiological Entomology*, *31*, 353–360.

Filippone, M., Camastra, F., Masulli, F., & Rovetta, S. (2008). A survey of kernel and spectral methods for clustering. *Pattern Recognition*, *41*, 176–190.

Forbes, M. G., & Kenneth, D. W. (2002). Ant sting mortality in Australia. *Toxicon*, *40*, 1095–1100.

Gadagkar, R. (1993). And now: eusocial thrips! *Current Science*, *64*, 215–216.

Gajpal, Y., & Rajendran, C. (2006). An ant-colony optimization algorithm for minimizing the completion-time variance of jobs in flowshops. *International Journal of Production Economics*, *101*, 259–272.

Gambardella, L. M., Taillard, E. D., & Agazzi, G. (1999). A multiple ant colony system for vehicle routing problems with time windows. In D. Corne & M. Dorigo & F. Glover (Eds.), *New Ideas in Optimization* (pp.63-76). London: McGraw Hill.

Garcia-Martinez, C., Cordon, O., & Herrera, F. (2007). A Taxonomy and an Empirical Analysis of Multiple Objective Ant Colony Optimization Algorithms for Bi-criteria TSP. *European Journal of Operational Research*, *180*(1), 116–148.

Gotwald, W. H., & Burdette, A. W. (1981). Morphology of the male internal reproductive system in army ants: phylogenetic implications (Hymenoptera: Formicidae). *Proceedings of the Entomological Society of Washington*, *83*, 72–92.

Govil, J., Govil, J., & Nandra, A. (2008). An Insight into Swarm Intelligence for adapting to Business and Technology. *Proceedings of the IEEE Region 5 Conference* (pp. 1-5). India, Delhi: Maharshi Dayanand University.

Grassé, P. P. (1959). La reconstruction du nid et les coordinations interindividuelles chez Belicositermes natalensis et Cubitermes sp. La théorie de la Stigmergie: Essai d'interprétation du comportement des termites constructeurs. *Insectes Sociaux*, *6*, 41–80.

Groß, R., Bonani, M., Mondada, F., & Dorigo, M. (2006). Autonomous Self-Assembly in Swarm-Bots. *IEEE Transactions on Robotics*, *22*(6), 1115–1130.

Guntsch, M., & Middendorf, M. (2002). Applying Population Based ACO to Dynamic Optimization Problems. Springer Verlag. In Dorigo, M. and Di Caro, G. & Sampels, M. (Eds.), *Proceedings of the Third International Workshop on Ant Algorithms* (pp. 111-122), Brussels, Belgium.

Handl, J., Knowles, J., & Dorigo, M. (2003). *Ant-based clustering: a comparative study of its relative performance with respect to k-means, average link and 1d-som.* (Technical Report TR/IRIDIA/2003-24. IRIDIA), Belgium: Université Libre de Bruxelles.

Handl, J., Knowles, J., & Dorigo, M. (2006). Ant-based clustering and topographic mapping. *Artificial Life, 12,* 35–61.

Handl, J., & Meyer, B. (2002). Improved ant-based clustering and sorting in document retrieval interface. *Proceedings of the Seventh International Conference on Parallel Problem Solving from Nature* (pp. 913-923). LNCS 2439, Berlin: Springer.

Harris, R. A., Graham, P., & Collett, T. S. (2007). Visual cues for the retrieval of landmark memories by navigating wood ants. *Current Biology, 17,* 93–102.

Heinze, J., & Keller, L. (2000). Alternative reproductive strategies: a queen perspective in ants. *Trends in Ecology & Evolution, 15*(12), 508–512.

Hexapode, 2004. Université Laval, Faculté des Sciences et de Génie, Département de Génie mécanique, Laboratoire de robotique. Extracted in June 2008 from *http:/*www.robot.gmc.ulaval.ca.).

Hölldobler, B., & Wilson, E. O. (1990). *The ants.* Cambridge, Massachussets: Harvard University Press.

Hou, Y.-H., Wu, Y.-W., Lu, L.-J., & Xiong, X.-Y. (2002). Generalized ant colony optimization for economic dispatch of power systems. *Power System Technology, 1,* 225–229.

Hu, X. M., Zhang, J., & Li, Y. (2008). Protein Folding in Hydrophobic-Polar Lattice Model: A Flexible Ant-Colony Optimization Approach. *Protein and Peptide Letters, 15*(5), 469–477.

Huang, H. T., & Yang, P. (1987). The Ancient Cultured Citrus Ant. *Bioscience, 37,* 665–671.

Huang, S.-J. (2001). Enhancement of hydroelectric generation scheduling using ant colony system based optimization approaches. *IEEE Transactions on Energy Conversion, 16,* 296–301.

Katangur, A. K., Akkaladevi, S., Pan, Y., & Fraser, M. D. (2005). Routing in optical multistage interconnection networks with limited crosstalk using Ant Colony Optimization. *International Journal of Foundations of Computer Science, 16*(2), 301–320.

Labroche, N., Guinot, C., & Venturini, G. (2004). Fast Unsupervised Clustering with Artificial Ants. *Proceedings of the Parallel Problem Solving from Nature* (pp. 1143-1152). LNCS 3242, Berlin: Springer.

Lumer, E. D., & Faieta, B. (1994). Diversity and adaptation in populations of clustering ants. *Proceedings of the Third international Conference on Simulation of Adaptive Behavior: From Animals to Animats* (pp. 501-508), Brighton, UK.

Malisia, A. R., & Tizhoosh, H. R. (2006). Image thresholding using ant colony optimization. *In Proceedings of the Third Canadian Conference on Computer and Robotic Vision* (pp.26-26), Québec City, Canada.

Maniezzo, V., & Carbonaro, A. (2000). An ANTS heuristic for the frequency assignment problem. *Future Generation Computer Systems, 16,* 927–935.

Min, J., Tian, P., & Kao, Y. (2008). A new ant colony optimization algorithm for the multidimensional knapsack problem. *Computers & Operations Research, 35*(8), 2672–2683.

Moffett, M. W., & Tobin, J. E. (1991). Physical castes in ant workers: a problem for *Daceton armigerum* and other ants. *Psyche, 98*, 283–292.

Monmarché, N., Slimane, M., & Venturini, G. (1999a). On improving clustering in numerical databases with artificial ants. *Advances in Artificial Life* (pp. 626-635). LNCS 1674, Berlin: Springer.

Monmarché, N., Slimane, M., & Venturini, G. (1999b). AntClass, Découverte de classes dans des données numériques grâce à l'hybridation d'une colonie de fourmis et l'algorithme des centres mobiles. *Conférence d'Apprentissage* (pp.169-176). France, Paleseau: Ecole Polytechnique.

Moyson, F., & Manderick, B. (1988). The collective behaviour of Ants: an Example of Self-Organization in Massive Parallelism. *Proceedings of the AAAI Spring Symposium on Parallel Models of Intelligence*. Stanford, California.

Otsu, N. (1979). A threshold selection method for grey level histograms. *IEEE Transactions on Systems, Man, and Cybernetics, SMC-9*, 62–66.

Ouadfel, S., & Batouche, M. (2003). MRF-based image segmentation using Ant Colony System. *Electronic Letters on Computer Vision and Image Analysis, 2*(2), 12–24.

Pham, D. T., Ghanbarzadeh, A., Koç, E., Otri, S., Rahim, S., et al. (2006). The Bees Algorithm – A Novel Tool for Complex Optimization Problems. *Proceedings of IPROMS 2006, Innovative Production Machines and Systems Virtual Conference* (pp.454-461), Cardiff, UK.

Poli, R., Kennedy, J., & Blackwell, T. (2007). Particle swarm optimization. *Swarm Intelligence, 1*, 33–57.

Ressom, H. W., Varghese, R. S., Drake, S. K., Hortin, G. L., & Abdel-Hamid, M. (2007). Peak selection from MALDI-TOF mass spectra using ant colony optimization. *Bioinformatics (Oxford, England), 23*, 619–626.

Roces, F., & Hölldobler, B. (1996). Use of stridulation in foraging leaf-cutting ants: Mechanical support during cutting or short-range recruitment signal? *Behavioral Ecology and Sociobiology, 39*(5), 293–299.

Rodney, A. (1989). Fast, Cheap and out of Control: a Robot Invasion of the Solar System. *Journal of the British Interplanetary Society, 42*, 478–485.

Saatchi, S., & Hung, C.-C. (2007). Swarm intelligence and image segmentation. In F. T. S. Chan & M. K. Tiwari (Eds.), *Swarm Intelligence, Focus on Ant and Particle Swarm Optimization* (pp. 163-178). Vienna, Austria: I-Tech Education and Publishing.

Sezgin, M., & Sankur, B. (2004). Survey over image thresholding techniques and quantitative performance evaluation. *Journal of Electronic Imaging, 13*, 146–156.

Shelokar, P.S., Jayaraman, V.K., & Kulkarni, B.D. (2004). An ant colony approach for clustering. *Analytica Chimica Acta, 509*, 187–195.

Solnon, C. (2002). Ants can solve constraint satisfaction problems. *IEEE Transactions on Evolutionary Computation, 6*, 347–357.

Stützle, T., & Hoos, H. H. (2000). MAX-MIN Ant System. *Future Generation Computer Systems, 16*, 889–914.

Sum-im, T. (2004). Economic dispatch by ant colony search algorithm. *Proceedings of the IEEE Conference on Cybernetics and Intelligent Systems, 1*, 416–421.

Talbi, E. G., Roux, O., & Fonlupt, C. (2001). Parallel ant colonies for the quadratic assignment problem. *Future Generation Computer Systems*, *17*, 441–449.

Tian, J., Yu, W., & Xie, S. (2008). An ant colony optimization algorithm for image edge detection. *Proceedings of the IEEE Congress on Evolutionary Computation* (pp. 751-756), Hong Kong.

Trianni, V., & Dorigo, M. (2006). Self-Organisation and Communication in Groups of Simulated and Physical Robots. *Biological Cybernetics*, *95*(3), 213–231.

Tuci, E., Ampatzis, C., Vicentini, F., & Dorigo, M. (2006). Evolved homogeneous neuro-controllers for robots with different sensory capabilities: Coordinated motion and cooperation. *Proceedings of the 9th International Conference on Simulation of Adaptive Behavior: From Animals to Animate 9* (pp. 679-690). Berlin: Springer.

Villarreal, M. R. (2006). Image: Scheme ant worker anatomy. Retrieved in September 2008 from http://en.wikipedia.org/wiki/Image:Scheme_ant_worker_anatomy-en.svg.

Wagner, I. A., & Bruckstein, A. M. (1997). Cooperative Cleaners - a Study in Ant Robotics. In A. Paulraj, V. Roychowdhury & C. D. Schaper (Eds), *Communications, Computation, Control, and Signal Processing: A Tribute to Thomas Kailath* (pp. 289-308). Kluwer Academic Publishers.

Wagner, I. A., & Bruckstein, A. M. (2001). From Ants to A(ge)nts: A Special Issue on Ant-Robotics. *Annals of Mathematics and Artificial Intelligence*, *31*(1-4), 1–5.

Wagner, I. A., Lindenbaum, M., & Bruckstein, A. M. (1998). Efficiently Searching a Graph by a Smell-Oriented Vertex Process. *Annals of Mathematics and Artificial Intelligence*, *24*, 211–223.

Walkowiak, K. (2005). Ant algorithm for flow assignment in connection-oriented networks. *International Journal of Applied Mathematics & Computer Science*, *15*, 205–220.

Wu, B., & Shi, Z. (2001). A clustering based on swarm intelligence. *Proceedings of the IEEE International Conferences on Info-Tech and Info-net* (pp.58-66), Bejing, China.

Xia, L., Xuehui, L., & Jihong, Z. (2003, Dec.). Codebook design by a hybridization of ant colony with improved LBG algorithm. *Proceedings of the International Conference on Neural Networks and Signal Processing* (pp. 469-472). China: Shenzhen University.

Xu, R., & Wunsch, D. (2005). Survey of clustering algorithms. *IEEE Transactions on Neural Networks*, *16*, 645–678.

Yang, X.-S. (2008). *Nature-Inspired Metaheuristic Algorithms*. Luniver Press, UK.

Zhao, J.-H., Zhaoheng, L., & Dao, M.-T. (2007). Reliability optimization using multiobjective ant colony system approaches. *Reliability Engineering & System Safety*, *92*, 109–120.

Chapter 14
Nature–Inspired Informatics for Telecommunication Network Design

Sergio Nesmachnow
Universidad de la República, Uruguay

Héctor Cancela
Universidad de la República, Uruguay

Enrique Alba
Universidad de Málaga, Spain

ABSTRACT

The speedy pace of change in telecommunications and its ubiquitous presence have drastically altered the way people interact, impacting production, government, and social life. The infrastructure for providing telecommunication services must be continuously renewed, as innovative technologies emerge and drive changes by offering to bring new services to the end users. In this context, the problem of efficiently designing the underlying networks in order to satisfy different requirements while at the same time keeping the capital and operative expenditures bounded is of ever growing importance and actuality. Network design problems have many variations, depending on the characteristics of the technologies to be employed, as well as on the simplifying hypothesis that can be applied on each particular context, and on the planning horizon. Nevertheless, in most cases they are extremely complex problems, for which exact solutions cannot be found in practice. Nature-inspired optimization techniques (belonging to the metaheuristic computational methods) are important tools in these cases, as they are able to achieve good quality solutions in reasonable computational times. The objective of this chapter is to present a systematic review of nature-inspired techniques employed to solve optimization problems related to telecommunication network design. The review is aimed at providing an insight of different approaches in the area, in particular covering four main classes of applications: minimum spanning trees, reli-

DOI: 10.4018/978-1-60566-705-8.ch014

able networks, local access network design and backbone location, and cellular and wireless network design. A large proportion of the papers deal with single objective models, but there is also a growing number of works that study multi-objective problems, which search for solutions that perform well in a number of different criteria. While genetic algorithms and other evolutionary algorithms appear most frequently, there is also significant research on other methods, such as ant colony optimization, particle swarm optimization, and other nature-inspired techniques.

INTRODUCTION

In the last twenty years, our society has witnessed the fast development of the telecommunication technologies for communication of data, voice, video, and resources all around the globe. It has also observed the rapid evolution of network infrastructures, the great expansion of the Internet, cellular, satellite, Wi-Fi networks, and numerous networking applications that are at the very heart of the functioning and success of our modern society. As a consequence, there has been a renewed interest in structural network design problems, due to the critical need to properly design a telecommunication infrastructure to satisfy customer requirements. In a general formulation, network design problems challenge problem techniques to find a connection topology that guarantees an optimized utilization of network resources under specified constraints, ensuring reliability, Quality of Service (QoS), and other important features for source-to-destination communication.

Since the size of the existing communication networks is continuously enlarging, the underlying instances of related optimization problems frequently pose a challenge to classical algorithms. The research community is nowadays searching for new techniques that are able to replace and improve over to the traditional exact ones, whose low efficiency often makes them useless for solving complex real-life problems of large complexity in reasonable times. Heuristic algorithms have been successfully applied to solve network design problems, exploiting their ability to obtaining ac-

curate solutions in a reasonable time. Although heuristics and metaheuristics could sometimes fail in computing an optimum for the problem, they get appropriate quasi-optimal solutions that satisfy network designers. Among a whole new set of heuristics and modern optimization techniques, newly nature-inspired computational methods have emerged as flexible and robust tools for solving the underlying complex optimization problems found in telecommunication network design, exhibiting high level of problem solving effectiveness also shown in many other areas of application (Blum & Roli, 2003; Glover & Kochenberger, 2003).

Nowadays, telecommunication networks are increasingly complex, dynamic, and often composed of heterogeneous devices. These characteristics imply several challenging issues to the network topology design, essentially concerning performance, robustness, and security in data transmission. The emergent computational heuristics inspired from nature are an appealing option for network topology design, as they have provided accurate results for tackling many problems with this kind of distinctive characteristics. Natural and biological systems have key properties, such as self-organization, adaptation, robustness, scalability, and distribution, which are highly desirable for dealing with the high complexity of designing current and future telecommunication networks that are able to properly handle highly increasing amount of data. Therefore, in recent years, an increasing number of accurate and efficient techniques for solving optimization problems related to network design have been proposed taking inspiration from the observation of natural systems and processes such as biological evolution, insect colonies, immune systems, cultural systems, and collective behaviors of groups of animals, among others (Zomaya, 2006).

This chapter provides a survey of the current state-of-the-art on using nature-inspired techniques to solve structural telecommunication network design problems. The survey focuses mainly on application areas, regarding only to those problems inherently related to topology design. The analysis explicitly excludes other applications, such as network routing and problems concerning commodities transportation or resource assignment, unless the network topology design was also considered in the optimization process.

A plethora of papers can be found in the related literature stating that the exploration pattern of nature-inspired models is beneficial for the search in large solution spaces. To the authors' knowledge, this is the first effort to report the application of nature-inspired methods to solve optimization problems related to telecommunication network design. Two previous works have collected bibliography of published papers in evolutionary telecommunications: *The Evolutionary Telecommunications Bibliography* (Sinclair, 1999) and the (unpublished) commented bibliography by Kampstra, van der Mei and Eiben (2006). Both works mainly focus on enumerating the applications of evolutionary algorithms (EAs) to telecommunication problems, and so they only provided short comments (if any) on the proposals in each article. Other surveys have included brief discussions on nature-inspired methods for solving different problems in the telecommunication domain. For example, Nesmachnow, Cancela, Alba and Chicano (2005) presented a survey of parallel metaheuristics applied to telecommunication problems. Ren and Meng (2006) presented a review of diverse biologically inspired methods applied to solve problems arising in wireless sensor networks, but mainly focusing in network operation instead on the actual design. More recently, Ribeiro, Martins and Rossetti (2007) reviewed the general strategies for the parallelization of metaheuristics and included examples of their successful application to solve optimization problems in telecommunications, but the work was not mainly focused on nature-inspired methods.

This chapter includes a systematic review of works that have applied nature-inspired methods to solve optimization problems related to telecommunication network design. The methods reviewed include genetic algorithms (GA) and other EAs, ant colony optimization (ACO), particle swarm optimization (PSO), and other nature-inspired agent-based techniques. The review is aimed at providing an insight of different nature-inspired approaches in the area, and it should be helpful to the research community to reveal the useful potential of nature-inspired techniques to tackle the complex underlying optimization problems when designing large telecommunication networks.

The survey classifies the applications in four categories: *minimum spanning trees, reliable networks, local access network (LAN) design and backbone location*, and *cellular and wireless network design*. Figure 1 presents the problem taxonomy employed. All those applications related to finding minimum cost tree-like network topologies are commented in the *minimum spanning trees* section. The *reliable networks* category includes those problems related to designing a network topology with features for providing source-to-destination communication when network components fail. The *LAN design and backbone location* group includes problems concerning the location of multiplexers and other primary high-speed hardware, especially in Asynchronous Transfer Mode (ATM) networks. The *cellular and wireless network design* collection involves those problems related to the topological design of cellular mobile communication networks, and wireless ad-hoc networks. The number of reviewed publications per year (journal and conference

Figure 1. Network design problems classification

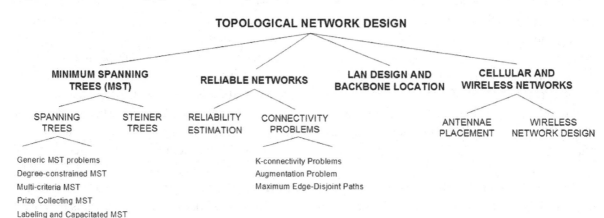

papers) is presented in Figure 2 (as this work has been done during 2008, this year information is not included).

MINIMUM SPANNING TREES

A minimum spanning tree (MST) defines the cheapest subset of edges that keeps a graph in one connected component. Finding the MST is one of the major problems in wired telecommunications, as it provides the minimum cost infrastructure to connect a set of communicating sites. Although a tree-like network topology does not tolerate even a single component failure, MST is a practical

model to provide a simple and easy-to-calculate connection pattern, useful to reflect some global properties of the network.

When applied on realistic scenarios, the class of network design problems modeled by the MST often has a significant number of constraints and this has been taken into account in more recent works which tackle different variants of the main problem. Table 1 lists in chronological order relevant works that have proposed to face several flavors of MST in order to address different network design problems with diverse characteristics and constraints. Those proposals are commented in this section, classifying them into two groups: traditional spanning tree applications and Steiner

Figure 2. Number of reviewed publications per publication year

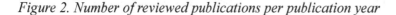

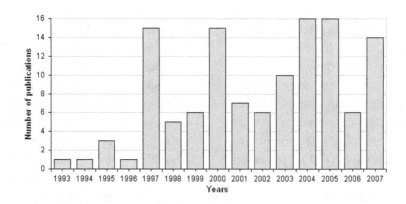

Table 1. Nature-inspired methods applied to minimum spanning tree problems

Author	Year	Problem	Method
Palmer & Kershenbaum	1995	Optimal Communication Spanning Tree	GA & meta-GA
Soper and McKenzie	1997	Constrained MST	CHC
Zhou & Gen	1997	Degree-constrained MST	GA
Cheng & Gen, Gen et al.	1997	Bicriteria Shortest Path	Compromise GA
Gen et al.	1998	Multiobjective Local Area Network design	MOEA
Chu & Premkumar	1997, 2001	Degree-constrained MST	GA
Zhou & Gen	1999	Multi-criteria MST	EA
Knowles & Corne	2000	Degree-constrained MST	Hybrid ssGA
Xianwei et al.	2000	Steiner Tree Problem	Hybrid GA
Dror et al.	2000	Generalized Minimum Spanning Tree	Hybrid GA
Raidl	2000, 2003	Degree-constrained MST	EA
Zhou & Gen	2003	Leaf-constrained MST	GA
Shyu et al.	2003	Generalized Minimum Spanning Tree	ACO
Lo Re et al.	2003, 2004	Prize Collected Steiner Tree Problem	PGA
Gamvros et al.	2003, 2005	Multi Level Capacitated MST	GA
Gen & Lin	2004	Bicriteria Network Design	Fuzzy MOEA
Klau et al.	2004	Prize Collected Generalized MST	MA
Duin & Voss	2004	Generalized Minimum Spanning Tree	-
Delbem et al.	2004	Degree-constrained MST	EA
Gen et al.	2004, 2005	Bicriteria Network Design	Hybrid MOEA
Hang & Wang	2005	Degree-constrained MST	GA
Soak et al.	2005	Optimal Communication Spanning Tree	Lamarckian EA
Xiong et al.	2005, 2006	Minimum Labeling Spanning Tree	GA
Bui and Zrncic	2006	Degree-constrained MST	ACO
Cheena et al.	2007	Multi-criteria MST	EA
Zhou et al.	2007	Centralized network design	EA
Luyet et al.	2007	Steiner Tree Problem	ACO
Consoli et al.	2007	Minimum Labeling Steiner Tree Problem	PSO
Tsuji et al.	2007	Minimum Spanning Tree	GA
Golden et al.	2008	Prize Collected Generalized MST	GA

problem applications.

Spanning Trees

This section reviews those papers that have tackled MST variants using nature-inspired techniques. The works have been classified according to the problem variant in generic MST problems, degree-

constrained MST, multi-criteria MST, labeling and capacitated MST, and prize-collecting MST.

Generic MST Problems

A pioneering work on applying GA to tree-like network design was presented by Palmer and Kershenbaum (1995). The authors faced the Optimal

Communication Spanning Tree (OCST) problem, which proposes to find a minimum cost network topology able to handle a set of predefined traffic constraints. The *node-link biased* encoding was proposed, where the chromosome contains an integer bias value for each node in the network to represent the convenience of being an interior node or a leaf in a solution. It also uses bias values for links, to provide a general useful tree representation, and a meta-GA is employed to tune the bias values. Several networks connecting US cities, with 6 to 98 nodes, varied traffic constraints, and link costs from a tariff database were used in the experimental evaluation. The results provided a comparison of the node-link biased coded GA, a random search, the star search, and the local exchange heuristic. The analyses mainly aim to explore the ability of GA to face dynamic scenarios, where heuristics fail. Even without employing a bias correction schema, the GA found accurate results. The authors also studied the node-link biased coded GA for solving the minimum delay MST. The results showed the GA adaptation to diverse goals and meaning of the solutions. However, the empirical evaluation was not focused on finding accurate solutions but rather to investigate the consistency and versatility of the GA approach.

Soper and McKenzie (1997) tackled a constrained MST with a maximum link capacity and a fixed cost link that does not depend on traffic flow, using the CHC (Cross generational elitist selection, Heterogeneous recombination, and Cataclysmic mutation) algorithm by Eshelman (1991). The authors employed an indirect encoding of weights that modify the link cost matrix, and the corresponding network is constructed using Prim's algorithm. The work focused on comparing the results of the proposed method vs. several deterministic heuristics on small and medium sized networks (also comparing against the optimal value when available), showing that it is possible to improve the heuristic results with limited computational effort. The results are said

to improve on a previous work that tried to solve the problem with a GA employing a direct representation of the solution.

The *compromise approach* was proposed by Cheng and Gen (1997) to solve the bicriteria shortest path problem (finding efficient paths with respect to both cost and performance criteria). The approach identifies those solutions close to the ideal one, and it can be regarded as a goal attainment method using an aggregation function. Gen, Cheng, and Wang (1997) introduced a priority-based encoding to deal with two difficulties: (1) the variable number of nodes in each path, and (2) that not any random sequence of edges defines a path. Each gene position represents a node, and the gene value codifies the priority of the node for building a path among candidates. The GA is evaluated using a randomly generated problem with 100 nodes and 473 edges (each edge is associated with time and cost values). The obtained Pareto solutions are depicted, and the ideal solution (computed by the Floyd-Warshall algorithm for each objective) and compromise solutions for different weights are presented. The authors concluded that the compromise GA is able to find accurate solutions, and it can be applied to other multiple objective optimization problems, using the priority based encoding method.

Gen, Ida, and Kim (1998) used a multiobjective EA (MOEA) for tackling the local network (LN) design problem. A common infrastructure consists of several LN segments connected together via bridges, which requires loop-free paths between segments, thus only spanning tree topologies can be used as active LN configurations. The authors considered the objectives of minimizing cost and average message delay using a spanning tree-based EA, facing two main issues: clustering (finding how many segments should the LN be divided into, and performing the workstations-to-segment allocation) and routing (finding the interconnecting spanning tree). The MOEA uses the Prüfer encoding to represent the spanning tree, a Pareto-based fitness evaluation, and a repairing strategy to deal with unfeasible solutions. A single test scenario with 30 users and 6 service centers was used in the experimental evaluation. The Pareto front suggested a good MOEA behavior when considering the best compromise solution, calculated using an order preference by similarity to ideal solution.

Zhou and Gen (2003) introduced the leaf-constrained MST (1c-MST) problem, to model network design problems with constraints related with the performance and the availability of some classes of devices. This MST flavor is useful in practice, since typically the software and hardware associated with a "degree-1" node (leaf) is cheaper than those used in other nodes. 1c-MST requires that the tree solution contains at least k leafs. The proposed GA employs a tree-based representation, using a 2D integer matrix for encoding the nodes of a spanning tree and the degree value of each node. The encoding preserves the tree structure, it guarantees the solutions feasibility when modifying the number of leafs, and it also possesses good locality properties, since small changes in the coding result in small changes in the tree. The GA uses order crossover, and exchange and insertion mutation operators. Five 1c-MST instances with 10 to 50 nodes and 3 to 15 leafs were used in the experimental analysis. The reported results show the effectiveness of the proposed GA, when compared with a specific heuristic and lower bounds calculated using Prim's algorithm for the unconstrained MST.

The quadratic MST (q-MST) arises when there are costs related to the interface between two links, thus the cost of the network is a quadratic function of the edges' variables. Soak, Corne and Ahn (2005) studied the performance of a Lamarckian-based EA to solve both the OCST and the q-MST. The EA uses an encoding that assigns weights to the links, builds a spanning tree from a chromosome including links ordered by their weights, and modifies these weights after evaluating the quality of the solution. The EA objective is to "learn" the weights leading to the optimal solution. The

results over a benchmark OCST instances and over random q-MST instances were comparable and in many cases superior to those obtained by EAs based in ideas from the previous literature: edge-sets encoding (Raidl & Julstrom, 2003), node-link biased encoding (Palmer & Kershenbaum, 1995), and Prüfer encoding (Zhou & Gen, 1997).

Several works by Gen and others have faced the Bicriteria Network Design Problem (BNDP), with the two conflicting objectives of minimizing cost and maximizing network flow. Gen and Lin (2004) studied the hybridization of a MOEA with fuzzy logic control and local search techniques, showing that the main positive effect of the hybridization is the improvement in the convergence speed to the Pareto front. Gen, Lin and Cheng (2004) applied the priority-based GA (pbGA) to solve the BNDP, considering both the maximum flow and the minimum cost models. The work incorporates the adaptive weight approach, including useful information from the current population to readjust weights for guiding the search toward a positive ideal point. Gen and Lin (2005) merged ideas from the two previous works, by combining the pbGA with adaptive weight approach and the hybridization with fuzzy logic control and local search techniques. The MOEA uses a new *weight-mapping* crossover, and a migration operator that increase exploration while maintaining the exploitation level. The insertion mutation is used as local search method, and fuzzy logic is employed to regulate the crossover and mutation probabilities during the evolution, depending on the variation of mean fitness values. The evaluation experiments consider two test problems with 25 nodes and 49 and 56 edges, reporting the number of obtained solutions, the ratio of nondominated solutions and the distance from a reference solution set. The MOEA got shorter values of distance and better ratios of nondominated solutions than the pbGA for the two instances studied, showing the positive effect of the hybrid technique to achieve the convergence to the Pareto front.

Tsuji, Munetomo, and Akama (2007) studied

two methods aimed at identifying and combining useful building blocks within a GA to find the lower cost tree network topology with link capacities depending on the communication demands. The authors studied D5, a linkage identification method that tries to identify building blocks, and Context Dependent Crossover (CDC), designed for exchanging overlapping building blocks with minimum disruption. The problem was chosen because in network design it is difficult to find the relevant building blocks and their linkage properties. The experimental analysis included two instances of less than 250 nodes, also used in a previous work (Tsuji, Munetomo & Akama, 2003). The results show that the GA employing D5 and CDC outperforms both the "vanilla" GA variant and the GA using only D5 in terms of solution quality and of convergence speed.

Degree-Constrained MST

The degree-constrained MST (dc-MST) problem is a special case of the MST problem that imposes additional degree constraints on each network node, trying to overcome the vulnerability of simple tree-like topologies. Therefore, the dc-MST is a more realistic representation of the practical network design problem than the classical MST version.

One of the first evolutionary approaches to solve the dc-MST was proposed by Zhou and Gen (1997). Their GA uses the Prüfer encoding, which allows to explicitly include the information of each vertex degree, and a $(\mu+\lambda)$ selection strategy. The evaluation experiments consider a nine-nodes complete graph with known optimal solution and five randomly generated graphs with 10 to 50 nodes, and edge costs uniformly distributed over [10, 100]. The experiments show that the GA is able to achieve accurate results, when compared with lower bounds found by the MST algorithm without constraints. To further verify the effectiveness of the proposed GA, the authors also applied it to other MST problems (stochastic

MST, probabilistic MST, and quadratic MST), finding that the GA was able to get accurate results in most cases.

Chu and Premkumar have also studied GAs for solving network design problems modeled by the dc-MST problem. In a first proposal (Chu, Premkumar, Chou & Sun, 1999), they presented the basic GA approach. Later (Chou, Premkumar & Chu, 2001), they analyzed the impact of encoding, crossover, and mutation on the results quality. The authors studied two encoding methods (Prüfer and determinant encoding), three crossover methods (SPX, 2PX, and UX) and two mutation methods (insert and exchange) for solving an experimental test instance with 48 cells, 10 data points, and variable number of nodes (20, 40, 60, and 80). The results suggest that encoding plays a major role on the GA search mechanism, being the main factor on solution quality. The combination of determinant encoding, exchange mutation and uniform crossover achieves better results than other combinations, getting a significant cost reduction for the problem instances studied, while demanding reasonable computation time.

The dc-MST problem was also tackled by Knowles and Corne (2000), who introduced a novel tree construction algorithm: the Randomized Primal Method (RPM). RPM builds degree-constrained trees of low cost, and it was applied in three stochastic methods: SA, multistart hillclimbing, and a steady state GA (with only one crossover and one mutation per generation). Trying to prevent premature convergence, the authors incorporated a restrictive local mating selection, considering the mapping of individuals a 2-D grid. The experimental evaluation used 20 graphs with 50 to 250 nodes and degree from 9 to 13, created using two random graph generators, specially designed to produce challenging problem instances. The results are given in terms of the ratio of the best d-MST weight found to the known weight of the (unconstrained) MST of the graph (found by using Prim's algorithm). The authors found that the GA using RPM outperforms both Simulated Annealing (SA) and multistart hillclimbing. They also demonstrated that the GA employing RPM is superior to the GA by Zhou and Gen (1997), by comparing the results obtained for the same test instances. The results suggest that the RPM encoding, which uses edge cost information to reduce the search space, helps the GA to find better solutions than the GA using a Prüfer number encoding.

Raidl (2000) presented edge-sets, a new encoding schema for solving MST problems. Edge-sets was designed concerning several aspects: to be a biunique coding for all spanning trees, to maintain feasibility, to allow efficient implementations of decoding, crossover and mutation operators, to provide high level of locality after applying the evolutionary operators, and to be suitable to easy incorporation of problem specific heuristics or local improvement operators. Since edge-sets encoding requires special evolutionary operators, both an edge-crossover and an edge-insertion mutation was provided to solve the dc-MST. Empirical results presented for 24 problem instances with up to 500 nodes show that edge-sets provides high locality, and that problem dependent information can be included without significantly downgrading the computational efficiency. Raidl presented an exhaustive analysis comparing the edge-sets EA and several methods: d-Prim, two Prüfer-coded EAs, the weight-coded EA, problem space search, SA, and branch-and-bound, for the small instances; and also compares with the dual simplex heuristic, the EA by Knowles and Corne (2000) and the weight-coded EA for hard problem instances. The results indicate the superiority of edge-sets EA over the other approaches, regarding both solution quality and execution times. Later, Raidl and Julstrom (2003) extended the edge-sets proposal, giving a detailed combinatorial analysis, an empirical comparison of spanning trees generated using randomized Prim and Kruskal methods, and showed their applicability to solve the One-Max-Tree problem.

Delbem et al. (2004) proposed a general encoding to represent spanning forests applied in an EA to solve the dc-MST. The encoding is based on the concept of node depth in a graph tree, using a list containing a vector of pairs of tree nodes and their depths. The work presents two operators to produce new spanning forests from an undirected graph. Both operators produce only one new individual, so they should be considered as mutation operators. In the generic formulation, the node-depth based EA (ndEA) does not apply recombination. The authors present an evaluation of the ndEA to solve the 11 complete dc-MST instances from Knowles and Corne (2000), with number of nodes from 15 to 1000, and constraint degree varies from 3 to 5. The ndEA outperforms the edge sets EA (Raidl & Julstrom, 2003) in the tests instances studied, and it is also able to deal with large dc-MSTP instances.

The GA by Han and Wang (2005) used a direct set-of-edges encoding scheme when solving the dc-MST problem. The GA uses an initialization method based on a Dijkstra's algorithm, selecting random edges without violating the degree constraint. A new flavor of the uniform crossover operator is applied, trying to preserve only "good" genes from common edges of parents and building offspring using ideas from Kruskal's algorithm. In addition, a mutation operator that favors adding low-cost edges and deleting high-cost edges is used. The evolutionary operators are efficient, and they always generate feasible spanning trees. One of the main contributions of the work is that the convergence of the GA to globally optimal solution with probability one is proved based on theoretical results from Bäck (1998). Due to the lack of standard dc-MST benchmark problems available, the GA was evaluated to solve 7 benchmark TSP problems of medium size. The results show that the GA is able to obtain the optimum solutions (calculated with Dijkstra's MST algorithm) for all problem instances.

Bui and Zrncic (2006) tackle the dc-MST using an ant-based approach with the special feature that each individual ant does not build a whole solution, but just a part of the graph. After all the ants have completed the exploration, a construction stage follows, where the most usually employed edges are selected, and a greedy algorithm is used to construct a dc-MST solution. This information is then used to update the pheromone trails, and to start a new cycle. A large set of experiments was performed using test sets from previous works, as Knowles and Corne (2000), Raidl and Julstrom (2003) and Delbem et al. (2004). The ant-based approach obtained accurate results, often improving upon the previous published GA ones; but in some specially misleading instances, the ant algorithm was unable to achieve the best-known results.

Multi-Criteria MST

Zhou and Gen (1999) presented the multi-criteria MST (mc-MST), to supply a realistic model of real-life network design problems where each communication link has many attributes (i.e., cost, performance, and reliability). The authors proposed an EA for solving the mc-MST using the Prüfer encoding, and applying both the multiple criteria decision making (linear aggregation of objectives) and the nondominated sorting technique used in NSGA (Srinivas & Deb, 1994) to effectively approximate the Pareto optimal solutions (either focused on the region near the ideal point or distributed all along the Pareto front). The experimental analysis on five problem instances with 10 to 50 nodes shows the effectiveness of the EA approach on the mc-MST problem, compared with the enumeration method of Pareto optimal solutions.

The mc-MST was tackled with a steady-state GA using Prüfer encoding in the recent work of Chena, Chenc, Guob and Chen (2007). The authors were mainly concerned in maintaining population diversity, so they designed a new *dislocation crossover* operator and built a niche evolution procedure to replace the worst individuals of the population. Besides these qualities, the proposed GA follows a simple schema. The multi-criteria GA was evaluated on two test instances of 10 and 15 nodes. Results show that GA is able to find accurate solutions when compared with solution sets obtained with an improved version of the enumeration method of Zhou and Gen (1999) for enumerating all Pareto optimal spanning trees.

Labeling and Capacitated MST

Given a network with labeled edges as input, the Minimum Labeling Spanning Tree (MLST) problem proposes to find a spanning tree with the minimum number of labels. This problem has direct application in communications network design, i.e. when nodes need to communicate with each other by means of different types of communications media.

Xiong, Golden and Wasil (2005) presented the *one-parameter GA* to solve the MLST. The GA encodes feasible solutions using a set of labels that induces a connected subgraph, uses a special ordering in the crossover, and employs an add-delete mutation operator. The "one parameter" that names the GA is the population size, since unitary probabilities for crossover and mutation are used. The approach tries to design a simple GA, which is less sensitive to the parameter values. The experimental analysis uses 78 randomly generated MLST problem instances from 20 to 200 nodes. The results show that the GA beats MVCA, the most popular MLST heuristic in the literature, in 58 cases. In addition, the GA obtains accurate solutions for the hardest family of graphs, while MVCA gets poor results. Later, Xiong et al. (2006) presented an improved GA, blending the MCVA as local optimizer in the crossover. Although the computational time required increases, the hybrid GA is able to improve the previous results, becoming the best alternative when considering both accuracy and running time.

Gamvros, Golden, Raghavan and Stanojevic

(2005) faced the Multi-Level Capacitated MST, a MLST generalization regarding multiple types of facilities with diverse capacities, available to the network planner. Two separate subproblems were tackled: a clustering problem aimed at finding groups of nodes subject to capacity constraints, solved with a GA; and building the MST for connecting nodes in each group with a central node, solved with a saving heuristic (Gamvros, Golden & Raghavan, 2003). The GA uses a dual encoding to represent nodes and groups, and the population is initialized using a capacitated MST heuristic. Special crossover and shuffling mutation were designed to maintain feasibility, and the fitness evaluation uses a heuristic to find a MST within each group. The experimental analysis uses three sets of 50 problems with 51 nodes, and one set of 50 problems with 100 nodes, and compares the GA results with lower bounds found by solving the linear programming relaxation using CPLEX. The GA solutions quality relies heavily on the construction heuristic for the MST subproblem, so the authors devised an improved capacitated MST heuristic. When combining this efficient heuristic with the GA powerful exploration pattern, the method is able to achieve accurate results for all instances, with gap values lower than 10% even for the larger instances studied.

Zhou, Cao, Cao and Meng (2007) applied a GA to designing centralized networks, where all communication is to and from a single site, another problem modeled by the capacitated MST problem. The GA adopted the tree-based permutation encoding, allowing keeping the tree structure and the locality properties, and used exchange, inversion and insertion mutation to maintain solution feasibility. The insert mutation is also used to repair those individuals that violate the capacity constraint. The GA uses a special $(\mu+\lambda)$ selection strategy incorporating random new individuals when similarity is detected, trying to avoid premature convergence. The GA was tested on a unique scenario: a problem with 16 nodes, unitary traffic between each node and

the central site, and a capacity restriction. The GA was able to find the optimal solution for the test case studied (solved using an augmented Lagrangean based method), but no further details are provided about the GA applicability to solve more complex scenarios.

Prize Collecting MST

The prize collecting MST (pc-MST) is a version of the MST problem that models the design of backbone networks with a tree structure spanning exactly one candidate gateway in each LAN, but compensation is collected if some candidate gateway sites are selected. The solutions of this problem describe a natural trade-off between minimizing the implementation costs and maximizing the sum of profits over all selected customers.

Klau et al. (2004) faced the pc-MST using a Memetic Algorithm (MA) that combines a steady-state EA and an exact local improvement subroutine for finding trees efficiently. The MA uses the edge-set encoding and employs specific problem-dependent evolutionary operators together with a clustering procedure aimed at improving the results. A post-processing optimization technique is applied on the solutions found, solving a relaxation of an integer linear programming model. The method was exhaustively tested on 114 well-known benchmark problem instances, and the results show that the MA favorably compares with previously published results, regarding both solution quality and computational efficiency.

Recently, Golden, Raghavan and Stanojevic (2008) evaluated several methods for solving the pc-MST. They included a GA that follows the previous approach of Gamvros et al. (2005), with minor differences in the initialization and genetic operators (some starting solutions and offspring are enhanced using a cost improving local search method). The GA uses an integer vector to encode the nodes selected for the spanning tree, and a combination of elitism and rank-based selection is employed. The experimental analysis considered a set of 296 TSPLIB-based problem instances where the optimal solution is known, and 100 randomly generated test problems up to 200 nodes. The GA approach achieved successful results, rapidly finding the optimum in all TSPLIB instances and near-optimal solutions for all of the test instances.

Steiner Trees

While the MST problem deals with connecting the whole set of nodes in the network, the Steiner tree problem (STP) allows using additional nodes to reduce the network design cost. The STP consists of finding a minimum-cost network spanning a set of distinguished *terminal nodes*, optionally using some intermediate *Steiner nodes*. The STP provides a basic low-cost connection topology and also is the topological structure behind multi-cast communications.

Xianwei, Changjia and Gang (2000) proposed a hybrid GA for finding a connection topology that guarantees the "best use" of network resources, under specified constraints. Using a binary representation to encode actual Steiner nodes, the GA combines a heuristic to decode the genotype and build the associated Steiner tree. The encoding scheme assures working with feasible solutions, avoiding penalty terms in the fitness measure. Also, standard network reduction techniques and an evolution strategy are used to reduce the total cost. Although they did not offer numerical results, the authors claimed to reach better quality solutions than those obtained with deterministic heuristics, even within moderate execution times.

Based on MPH, the classic minimum path greedy method from Takahashi and Matsuyama (1980), Luyet et al. (2007) developed ANT-STP, an ACO method for solving the STP. In ANT-STP, each ant builds an independent solution using MPH to connect terminal nodes to the partial solution. The visibility used in the probabilistic action choice rule is equal to the inverse cost of the minimum path used to connect each terminal node. The pheromone trail values are associated to the Steiner nodes, and for each terminal node a local pheromone trail update computes the average of pheromone values of Steiner nodes in the shortest path used. After each ant of the population has built a solution, the trails are globally updated using a classic evaporation and reinforcement rule. The analysis used 42 standard test instances of classes B, C and D from the OR-Library, to compare ANT-STP with both a multi-start MPH method and an efficient Tabu Search (TS) algorithm from Gendreau, Larochelle and Sansó (1999). The reported results show that ANT-STP obtains better solutions than the multi-start MPH. However, ANT-STP needs more computation time to achieve similar solutions quality than those obtained with the TS algorithm.

The generalized minimum spanning tree (GMST) problem models the design of telecommunications network where a clusters of nodes needs to be connected using a tree topology using exactly one node per cluster. GMST is strongly related to STP, and several works have addressed both problems simultaneously.

Dror, Haouari and Chaouachi (2000) solved the GMST with a simple binary-encoded GA, using a linear model to penalize infeasible solutions and incorporating the insertion heuristic by Takahashi and Matsuyama (1980). The experimental evaluation showed that the GA performed significantly better than four other heuristics on a randomly generated set of 20 GMST instances with 25 to 500 nodes. Later, Shyu, Yin, Lin and Haouari (2003) developed Ant-tree, extending the classic ACO approach by incorporating a tree construction heuristic, a reinforcement pheromone updating rule, and a stopping criterion to get quality solutions in a reasonable time. Ant-tree provided comparable results to the previous GA (Dror et al., 2000) for the same set of problem instances, while taking less CPU time. Duin and Voss (2004), however, pointed out that certain GMST problems can be transformed to the STP, and found that an exact STP solver outperformed the GA developed by

Dror et al. (2000), both in terms of the solution quality and computational effort. In the set of 20 problems, the GA provided solutions that were on average 6.53% from optimality, while the exact STP procedure achieved optimal solutions for all test instances, without spending excessive CPU times.

Lo Re and Lo Presti studied the prize-collecting STP, which has important applications in LAN design. In a first article (Di Fatta, Lo Presti, & Lo Re, 2003), they developed a master-slave parallel GA (PGA) obtaining promising speedup values when solving Beasley's OR Library standard test problems. An extension of the previous proposal (Lo Re, Lo Presti, Storniolo, & Urso, 2004) presented a parallel hybrid method that combines a distributed GA and a local search strategy using a specific STP heuristic. The computational efficiency analysis shows that the distributed model achieves higher speedup values than the master-slave approach, since it employs few synchronization points, and thus it can be executed over a wide-area grid-computing environment. These results encouraged the authors to face high dimension problems, with sizes ranging from 1000 to 2000 nodes: 400 problems randomly created and 50 subnetworks with real Internet data extracted from the Mercator project. The grid PGA is able to obtain the best-known solutions on about 70% of the instances.

In the same line of work, Consoli, Moreno-Pérez, Darby-Dowman and Mladenovic (2007) proposed using the novel method Jumping Particle Swarm Optimization (JPSO) to solve the minimum labeling STP. JPSO is a variant of standard PSO that, while taking inspiration in the social behavior of individuals inside swarms in nature, tries to adapt the movements to discrete spaces. The method takes into account the separation between neighbor solutions to define a group of agents that cross the space in discrete jumps, resembling the behavior of jumping frogs in a swamp. The JPSO works with feasible STP solutions and considers three attractors for particle movement: its own best position to date, the best position of its social neighborhood, and the best position to date obtained by all particles. A local search method is applied trying to delete some labels while maintaining feasibility. The evaluation experiments were performed on 48 test instances with 100 to 500 nodes and compares JPSO with an exact method and the basic Multi-Start method (with and without an embedded local search). The results show that JPSO achieves the best results when using a maximum allowed CPU time as the stopping criterion. The authors conclude that JPSO is the most effective algorithm for the minimum labeling STP with respect to both solution quality and computational running time.

Remarks and Conclusions

This section is devoted to telecommunication network design models based on MST and STP variants. The classical MST and STP problems (defined over graphs) have been long studied by the computer science, mathematical graph theory and operational research communities, so there is an important understanding of their properties and a wealth of exact and approximate algorithms, as well as efficient data structures, that can be useful as building blocks for heuristic methods.

When applied to telecommunication network design, the classical MST and STP formulations need to be modified to take into account different network features in order to provide more realistic models of real-life situations. As a consequence, the papers included in this section tackle many different variants, and their results are not easily comparable with each other. One exception is the case of degree-constrained MST discussed in Subsection 2.1.2, where there has been a sequence of papers, starting from Zhou and Gen (1997), which have tackled the same problem by GA and have even used in many cases the same problem instances for experimental results. This has resulted in a wealth of alternative encodings developed specifically for this context: Prüfer encoding, determinant encoding, edge-sets, node-depth, etc. These encodings are complemented with suitable crossover and mutation operators. A number of the papers compared part or all of these variants, showing their efficiency even for large instances. The same encodings and other alternative ones have been also used for other tree construction problem variants. One active area that has recently been the prize-collecting variants of MST and STP, which can better represent some economic tradeoffs in real-life problems. Papers like the one by Golden, Raghavan and Stanojevic (2008) have been able to successfully transpose techniques from standard versions to the pricing setting, obtaining high-quality results for large instances. Their review also presented a few papers employing ACO and PSO to solve tree problems. The ant-based algorithms generally have some hybrid features, as the most classical scheme for constructing an ant-based solution is not always easy to implement directly in the case of tree topologies. Nevertheless, the results obtained show that the methods have been able to find competitive results in terms of solution quality, even if the computational times are very large in some cases.

RELIABLE NETWORKS

Besides cost and performance, reliability is another important issue in telecommunication network design. Reliability metrics evaluates the probability that the network works properly, given that some components (nodes or links) can fail. Survivability is a concept strongly related to reliability, which refers to the aptitude of the network to continue operation even after the failure of a single component. Given that the exact evaluation of reliability metrics is a very difficult problem itself, the research often uses alternative approaches considering several options: using reliability estimations calculated via Monte Carlo simulation, imposing connectivity constraints on the network topology, employing related vulnerability parameters (such as the number of disjoint paths between terminals), etc. This section summarizes the works that have proposed using nature-inspired techniques to the design of reliable and survivable networks. Table 2 resumes the articles included in this section, which have been grouped in two classes: those that use reliability estimation metrics and those related with connectivity constraints.

Topology Design Based on Reliability Estimation

The exact evaluation of network reliability is an NP-hard problem (Ball, 1979), so alternative metrics are often employed in reliable network design problems. Two common approaches consist of using related metrics to approximate reliability, and employing stochastic estimation using Monte Carlo simulation.

In 1993, Kumar, Pathak and Gupta (1993) made one of the first proposals on applying GA to reliable network design problems. The approach considered several network properties related with both performance and reliability, such as network diameter, average distance, number of ports at each node, and number of links in a network. Three network design problems were faced, taking into account three different approaches: to maximize reliability under diameter constraint, to maximize diameter under degree constraint, and to minimize average distance under degree constraint. The GA uses a binary encoding to represent the links between nodes in the full network, and the random node field swap crossover and a repair mechanism are employed. The experimental analysis considers only tiny problem instances (up to 9 nodes) and is mainly concerned to demonstrate the ability of GA to achieve the optimum solutions (computed using an exhaustive search) for each problem. Whereas the GA succeeded in this task, the authors concluded that evolutionary approaches were a competitive alternative to solve reliable network

Table 2. Nature-inspired methods applied to reliable network design problems

Author	Year	Problem	Method
Kumar et al.	1993	Reliable Network Design	GA
Ma et al.	1997	3-connectivity	GA
Ko et al.	1997	Mesh design	GA
Deeter & Smith	1997, 1998	Reliable Network Design	GA
Dengiz et al.	1997a, 1997b	All-terminal reliability	GA
Cheng	1998	1 Fault Tolerant network design	GA
Konak & Smith	1999	Reliable Network Design	Hybrid GA
Barán & Laufer	1999	Reliable Network Design	A-Team
Huang et al.	1999	3-connectivity	PGA
Ombuki et al.	1999	3-connectivity	GA
Kulturel-Konak et al.	2000	2-connectivity	GA
Ljubic et al.	2000	Augmentation Problem	GA
Lo & Chang	2000	Capacitated Multipoint Network Design	Hybrid MOEA
Kumar et al.	2000, 2002	Multiobjective Network Design	PCGA
Duarte & Barán	2001, 2003	Multiobjective Network Design	MOEA
Elhaggaz	2002	Augmentation Problem	GA
Konak & Smith	2002, 2004	Multiobjective Network Design	MOEA
Ljubic & Raidl	2003	Augmentation Problem	MA
Rappos & Hadjiconstantinou	2004	2-connectivity	ACO
Nowe et al.	2004, 2006	Edge Disjoint Paths	ACO
Blum & Blesa	2004, 2006, 2007	Edge Disjoint Paths	ACO
Marseguerra	2005	Reliability Uncertain	MOEA
Premprayoon & Wardkein	2005	Reliable Network Design	ACO
Konak & Smith	2005	Reliable Network Design	Hybrid GA
Tamasi et al.	2005	Reliable VoIP network design	EA
Lin & Gen	2006	All-terminal Reliability	Fuzzy ssGA
Nesmachnow et al.	2007	Generalized Steiner Problem	EAs

design problem.

The works of Dengiz, Altiparmak and Smith (1997a, 1997b) proposed a hybrid EA to face the problem of network design considering the all-terminal network reliability (defined as the probability that every pair of nodes can communicate with each other). Although the problem is intrinsically multiobjective, the authors tackled single objective versions, formulated to either maximize reliability given a cost constraint or to minimize cost given a minimum network reliability constraint. The communication network is modeled by a probabilistic graph with bidirectional links, and a variable-length integer string representation is used. The fitness function evaluates the total cost of the network links, and incorporates a quadratic penalty function for networks that fail to meet the minimum reliability constraint (reliability is estimated using a specific heuristic, well-known upper bounds, and Monte Carlo simulation) A explicit procedure generates the initial population with highly reliable networks, trying to improve the search. The algorithm employs a uniform crossover operator with a repairing mechanism to ensure obtaining 2-connected offspring, while the mutation operator implements a randomized greedy local search. The authors evaluate their algorithm using 79 randomly generated small test problems (with 6 to 20 nodes), showing that GA is able to find the optimal solutions at a fraction of the computational cost of branch and bound.

Deeter and Smith (1997, 1998) faced the network design considering all-terminal reliability. Instead of using the usual problem formulation to maximize reliability given an upper bound on cost, the authors consider minimizing the network cost given a reliability constraint. This approach is more reflective of real-life network design scenarios, and also provides flexibility, allowing tackling many others related problems. The authors used a GA to identify the best network topology to jointly meet cost and network reliability demands, using an integer vector encoding to represent the type or level of each possible link in the network. The GA results were promising, while exerting a small fraction of the computational effort required for enumerative methods to solve the problem. A very small network of 5 nodes was used in the experimental analysis, thus a backtracking algorithm allows to exactly calculate the network reliability. However, the authors mentioned the GA extension including Monte Carlo simulation for reliability estimation and report similar results for networks up to 18 nodes.

Regarding a network model that assigns a reliability value to each link, Barán and Laufer (1999) applied a parallel Asynchronous Team (A-Team) to reliable network design. A-Team is a hybrid method combining different methods interacting to solve the same global problem. The proposed A-Team merges a parallel GA with reliability estimation and topological optimization methods subject to reliability constraints. The parallel GA follows an island model with broadcast migration,

employs a binary encoding, and special initialization, crossover, and mutation. A repair mechanism is included to keep the solutions under the 2-connectivity constraint. Two approaches are used to estimate network reliability: an upper bound of all solutions in the population is efficiently calculated, and after that, a Monte Carlo simulation is used to get good estimations of the all-terminal reliability. The empirical results show good values for medium-size networks, while achieving a sublinear speedup.

Duarte and Barán (2001) also faced a multiobjective version of the previous problem, using a parallel asynchronous version of SPEA (Zitzler & Thiele, 1999) to find optimal network topologies. The parallel algorithm is made up of several SPEA processes, which perform the real optimization work, and one organizer process, which creates the workers, collects the results, and applies the Pareto dominance test. The parallel results outperform the sequential ones, considering standard metrics in the multiobjective domain. In addition, the parallel version is fully scalable, showing almost linear speedup values and the ability of obtaining better solutions when the number of processors increases. Later, Duarte, Barán, and Benítez (2003) published a comparison of several parallel MOEAs for solving the same reliable network design problem. The authors present experimental results for asynchronous parallel versions of SPEA and NSGA using external populations. The analyses confirm the previous findings, showing that the quality of the results improves when using more processors. They also illustrate that SPEA is able to obtain better results than NSGA using shorter execution times.

Marseguerra, Zio, Podofillini and Coit (2005) used a stochastic model for network reliability, using a function of imperfectly known reliability parameters of network components. The authors posit that most decision makers would not be content with just maximizing the (mean) estimate network reliability, but would also be interested in the variance of this estimation, which gives a measure of the uncertainty. The work focuses on searching the Pareto solutions maximizing the expectation and minimizing the variance of the network reliability measure. The problem is posed as finding the type and redundancy level of components to be allocated within a fixed topology, where each component has an associated reliability probability distribution. The proposed MOEA solve the problem using a rank-based fitness assignment and an external archive for maintaining the Pareto front. A Monte Carlo method is used to incorporate the uncertainty in the reliability values; the repeated evaluations of the good individuals are accumulated, to enhance the significance of the estimations. The numerical examples consider only very small networks (with 7 and 8 links), and allow to examine the Pareto optimal solutions obtained and to easily identify the differences in the configurations.

Premprayoon and Wardkein (2005) tackle a variant of the reliable network design problem that look for the topological structure and also the cost and reliability characteristics of each link, which can be chosen from a given set. The objective is to minimize network cost subject to a requirement of attaining at least a given reliability level. The authors employ an ACO method, using penalties for unfeasible solutions; the network reliability evaluation is done by backtracking (as only very small network topologies are studied). The computational results are given over two very small cases (4 and 5 nodes respectively), the results are compared with the ones obtained by a Local Search and a TS approaches, giving better results for ACO.

To ensure the integrity of network services when component failures happen, Konak and Smith (2005) proposed a hybrid GA that employs network resilience as a design criterion. Resilience has been practically ignored as a network design objective in optimization because it is very hard to evaluate due to its computational complexity, and often requires estimation by simulation. The hybrid GA uses uniform crossover with a 2-node

connectivity repair algorithm and two kind of local search operators (heuristic perturbations and add-remove-exchange mutation). Monte Carlo simulation is used to estimate network resilience, and the authors proposed an original way to deal with stochastic noise in the fitness evaluation due to simulation, while minimizing the computational effort. The GA uses a dynamic population size, employs a diversity preservation technique, and includes an adaptive penalty model for infeasible solutions. Two small test problems of 10 and 20 nodes were used in the numerical evaluation. The results show that the hybrid GA is useful for this class of network design problems, and they also suggest that the noise in the objective function has a significant effect on the solution quality. Although the number of simulation replications required is small, the computational efficiency tends to reduce as networks get denser. This work illustrates that network resilience measures represent a viable alternative approach to reliability measures, and that these problems can be solved using GA and Monte Carlo simulation.

Lin and Gen (2006) proposed the self-controlled GA (scGA), adopting fuzzy logic control to tune the probabilities of the GA operators depending on the average fitness variation. scGA was applied to the all-terminal network reliability problem, using an two-part edge-based encoding to represent both a spanning tree for a network and the edges that are not included in the spanning tree. The encoding allows avoiding feasibility checking after applying operators, thus improving the efficiency of the search. Two special operators are proposed: a Kruskal-based crossover and the highest degree-lowest cost mutation, a strategy that tries to exploit the best solution for improvement while ignoring the exploration of the search space. A test set of nine problems with 8 to 10 nodes and 28 to 45 edges is used to evaluate the scGA, and a fitness plot shows that scGA has better convergence speed than other simple GAs. The scGA has slightly best numerical results than both the GA by Dengiz, et al. (1997a) and the GA by Altiparmak, Gen, Dengiz and Smith (2004), when solving the same problem instances.

Connectivity Problems

Problems in this area are classified into k-connectivity problems, augmentation problems, and maximum edge-disjoint paths problems; all are related but still provide different ways of using connectivity constraints or employing vulnerability parameters to avoid the computational effort of computing the exact network reliability.

K-Connectivity Problems

One usual methodology to provide a certain reliability level is to ensure that in the presence of node or link failures, the data flows may be re-routed to reach the destination. In order to do it, at least two disjoint paths between any pair of nodes are necessary, and often a fixed number k of paths are required (the so-called *k-connectivity* constraint approach). For many real-life networks the probability failure is rather small, so a level of redundancy that provides connectivity in case of a single or double component failure is useful. Therefore, researchers have mainly focused on cases of the problem where $k = 2$ or $k = 3$ disjoints paths are needed.

Ma, Huang, and Tsuboi (1997) presented a GA for solving the 3-connectivity network design problem, adopting an iterative method based on finding the minimum cost paths between each pair of terminal nodes. The algorithm uses a node-based encoding including three paths between each source-target pair and information related to connectivity constraints. A specific crossover operator was designed to maintain feasible solutions, thus not requiring additional computational effort to apply a repair mechanism. The experimental analysis compares the GA with a previous EA and several other heuristics, using two problem instances with 30 and 58 nodes and different capacity requirements. The obtained

results show that the GA improves the effectiveness and the computational efficiency over the other studied methods.

Later, the same authors presented two parallel versions of the previous algorithm, applying a domain decomposition partitioning the connectivity requirements, and a fully distributed GA (Huang, Tsuboi & Ma, 1997). The authors analyze the influence of several virtual topologies for both strategies and conclude that the double-ring topology obtains the best performance for the distributed GA when partitioning the requirements, and the torus topology is the most suitable when dividing the population. Over this last model, they also verified that the best results are obtained with the most frequent exchange of solutions with neighbors, but the communication overhead increases significantly. Setting the most frequent communication interval value (one generation) and limiting the interactions to only one neighbor produces an appropriate balance between the quality of the results and the computational effort required.

Ko, Tang, Chan, Man, and Kwong (1997) presented an EA applied to the design of mesh communication networks, a complex problem with a solution that targets optimal topological connections, routing, and link capacity assignments. The problem model assumes known predicted traffic requirements; a distance cost function, and also accounted for different line rates (6, 45, and 150 Mbps). The network must be 2-connected and has a maximum allowable packet delay of 0.1 second. The approach divides the problem of network design into three optimization stages -for topology, routing, and capacity-, and a GA is applied to each subproblem, to minimize the total connection cost. A binary adjacency matrix representation is used in the network topology optimization stage. For a given topology, the capacity assignment and routing problems require the simultaneous optimization of both the flow and link capacities. The second GA uses a path list representing routes between nodes, and yields a vector that specifies the link flow. The last optimization problem is to choose capacity for each link, while minimizes network cost. In general, a smaller maximum average delay value requires higher link capacities, so a multiobjective optimization problem arises, for which a Pareto-based EA is proposed using an integer array encoding. The three-stage EA was tested for designing a small packet-switched mesh communication network among 10 major Chinese cities. The authors claim that the method can also be used for networks of reasonable size with realistic topology and traffic requirements, but no further details are presented.

Cheng (1998) considered the problem of backbone network design under minimal total link cost and fault-tolerant to 1 link-failure (1-FT) constraints. Cheng designed C/TO, a GA approach to network topological optimization that uses a deterministic model for link costs. The GA encodes a backbone layout using a list of ordered links. The evolutionary operators attempt to generate a more cost-effective or reliable layout, while maintaining the solution feasibility. C/TO uses a discrete method that combines the multipoint and a knowledge-based crossover, which has the closure property: after its application, the resultant graphs are always 1-FT. The mutation operator attempts to remove links to reduce the total cost, or to explore a new, possibly better, search region. To remove links while maintaining the 1-FT requirement, the C/TO mutation uses the concept of tangency of rings. C/TO is evaluated using several randomly generated network backbone layout instances, up to 20 nodes and 190 links. The results show that the GA is able to find accurate results, outperforming Branch & Bound (this deterministic technique allows solving instances up to 12 nodes) and SA.

Ombuki, Nakamura, Nakao, and Onaga (1999) faced the 3-connected networks design problem, trying to find a low cost topology such that every source-destination pair can successfully communicate via at least one of three different paths. The objective is to minimize the total link connection

costs while maintaining the 3-connectivity constraint. The authors developed a greedy heuristic with a repair mechanism, and a GA using a fixed length integer coding and a fitness with a linear penalty function to deal with non-feasible solutions. An arc assignment scheme converts each GA chromosome into a network topology. The experimental evaluation was performed using a randomly generated set of 10 problem instances with 10 to 20 nodes, 45 to 190 links, and links costs between 0 and 100. The GA consistently outperforms the greedy algorithm for the problem instances considered.

In the same line of work, Kulturel-Konak, Konak, and Smith (2000) used an EA to find the 2-edge-connected minimal Steiner graph spanning points in the rectilinear plane. A coding scheme was developed regarding theoretical properties of optimal solutions. Although the encoding increases the probability of having terminal nodes with at least two edges, it cannot guarantee that every solution is a 2-edge-connected graph, so a repair mechanism is required. The GA uses random and local search mutations, and both $(\mu+\lambda)$ and (μ, λ) strategies were tested. A single small 15-point test problem is used in the EA evaluation, and the results are compared with the optimal TSP tour of the given points, so the results are not definite at all.

Konak and Smith (1999) tackled the topological design of backbone networks considering reliability and survivability, using a hybrid approach combining a GA and local search methods. Given the node locations, the traffic requirements, and the capacity of links, the problem proposes to minimize the network design and operation costs, subject to QoS and reliability constraints. The hybrid GA uses a binary encoding and uniform crossover with a k-node connectivity repair algorithm. The mutation operator incorporates logic from the Cut-Saturation Algorithm (CSA): add-only, delete-only, perturbations, and chain collapsing. CSA is an expensive method; therefore the mutation is only applied to good candidates, which are most likely to improve upon the best feasible solution. Due to the hard constraints, the GA uses a special selection scheme, allowing "good" infeasible solutions to survive just one generation, which might improve them further. A problem-specific fitness function is used, evaluating the cost of the network, the average traffic flow and also testing the k-node-connectivity. The hybrid approach aims to efficiently improve the solutions by using specific information in the local search, while the GA explores different regions of the solution space. The evaluation results on a set of networks with 10 to 23 nodes show that the hybrid GA improves upon previous approaches (TS and SA), but the improvements are less significant when the network is densely connected (due to limitations of the CSA search pattern).

Later, Konak and Smith (2002, 2004) proposed a multiobjective version of the previous problem, to simultaneously minimize the network cost and the packet delay. The classic Survivable Network Design Problem (SNDP) proposes to design a reliable, minimum cost network, ignoring the objective of maximizing performance. Konak and Smith modeled a more realistic situation, merging the Capacitated Network Design Problem (CNDP), and the SNDP into one problem, considering the network topology, the link capacities, and the traffic routes. In this approach, the network performance and survivability are not independent, and a MOEA is used to find topologies with diverse cost and performance tradeoffs. Combining both survivability and performance optimization makes the problem extremely difficult, thus heuristic are required to find accurate solutions. Trying to keep a simple representation, the MOEA only encodes capacitated networks topologies, while routes are found by solving the routing problem. The previously described uniform crossover with repair is used to handle the 2-node connectivity constraint. Several mutation operators (add, delete, and exchange) perturb the solutions while preserving feasibility. The MOEA keeps Pareto optimal solutions found during the search, and uses niche methods to maintain diversity. The experimental analysis was performed using the same instances than the previously single objective GA. The results show that the MOEA is able to significantly improve upon the single objective methods, and also provides the user with a set of diverse near-optimum Pareto network designs.

The Capacitated Multipoint Network Design Problem (CMNDP) proposes to find the network topology that minimize both the weighted sum of the shortest paths between pairs of nodes and the sum of average packet delays, while satisfying capacity and reliability constraints. Lo and Chang (2000) designed MOHGA, a hybrid MOEA for solving the CMNDP. MOHGA uses four subpopulations, generated according to the elitism reservation strategy, the shifting Prüfer vector (a new technique proposed to deal with the loss of locality when using Prüfer encoding), the stochastic universal sampling, and the complete random method, respectively. The selection mixes these four subpopulations, in such a scheme that resembles the process used in VEGA (Schaffer, 1985). To evaluate MOHGA, the authors generate a set of randomly CMNDP instances with up to 56 nodes and one deterministic instance with 56 nodes. The number of non-dominated solutions is counted and compared with those obtained using VEGA and the single-objective SOGA. The results suggest that MOHGA can effectively search the feasible solution space due to population diversity, finding more non-dominated solutions than VEGA and SOGA, and also showing better computational efficiency behavior.

The works of Kumar (Kumar, Krishnan, & Santhanakrishnan, 2000; Kumar, Parida, & Gupta, 2002) faced the multiobjective network design problem of minimizing cost and traffic delay, considering reliability constraints. The approach considers the number of articulation points (a node whose removal disconnects the network) as a network unreliability indicator. The authors used the Pareto Converging Genetic Algorithm (PCGA) from Kumar and Rockett (1997), which uses tied Pareto ranking for fitness assignment. Each chromosome encodes a possible topology, including the link capacities and the routing vector that defines the path between every pair of nodes. A single case scenario is presented, and the discussion mainly focuses on analyzing how the set of non-dominated solutions moves towards the Pareto front, but no further details are offered. The work of Kumar (2003) presents a parallel PCGA able to achieve similar results than an exhaustive search for a small 10-nodes network. When solving a 36-nodes instance with both the PCGA and the Branch Exchange Heuristic (BEH), the results show that PCGA obtains higher solutions diversity than BEH. Banerjee and Kumar (2007) used the PCGA to tackle the previous problem using realistic traffic models. The work proposed the Pareto Branch Exchange (PBE), a multiobjective heuristic search that tries to simultaneously minimize the average cost and the network delay. However, PBE needs to evaluate and rank all possible networks to obtain the Pareto-optimal set. The complexity of the exhaustive search turns out to be exponential, so PBE is applicable for small-size networks only. The experimental evaluation uses real traffic data from communication networks in China (10 cities), U.S. (21 cities) and Europe (36 cities). The results show that PGCA is able to achieve better solutions than deterministic heuristics, and that the topologies generated for self similar traffic have much higher delays than those of Poisson traffic.

Tamasi, Orincsay, Jozsa and Magyar (2005) faced the problem of designing a Voice over Internet Protocol (VoIP) network, addressing survivability concerns. Two separate problems were tackled: assigning two gateways for each VoIP end node, and finding two disjoint paths between each pair of gateways. The last problem matches to finding a 2-connected network, but it is not directly solved. Instead, the authors focus on the gateway assignment problem, but they embed in this problem some considerations about the second steps, so that the network can have a smaller overall cost. They define some utility functions for the feasible assignments of gateways to the VoIP nodes, and evaluate different heuristics for finding two disjoint paths between each pair of gateways. The utility function is used within the objective functions for an EA and a SA algorithm. The reported results for networks with 500 VoIP nodes show that better overall costs can be found when incorporating a measure of the total cost of the network assignments The EA was also faster and gave better results than the SA.

Nesmachnow, Cancela, and Alba (2007) tackled the Generalized Steiner Problem, which proposes to find a minimum cost topology such that for each pair of nodes (i,j) there exists at least r_{ij} edge-disjoint paths, in order to provide a fault-tolerant design. A GSP solution have a preset number of independent paths linking each pair of terminal nodes using intermediate Steiner nodes to ensure path redundancy, while trying to minimize the overall cost. The work present a comparative study of sequential and parallel versions of different metaheuristics applied to medium-sized test cases. The methods comprise a standard GA, a SA, two GA+SA hybrid algorithms, and the CHC evolutionary method, all of them using the same binary codification. Standard mutation and recombination operators were applied; the resulting individuals were accepted only when they correspond to feasible solutions. For the parallel versions of the EAs, the population was split into 8 demes, applying a migration operator working on a unidirectional ring topology. The results for the sequential methods showed that CHC is the best alternative in terms of solution quality. For the parallel methods, the experiments over an 8-machine cluster showed that both the standard GA and one of the GA+SA hybrids obtained the best performances in solution quality and speedup.

Augmentation Problem

The Augmentation Problem (AP) is another model often related to telecommunication networks reliability and survivability. The AP problem proposes to find the minimum cost set of connections (or nodes) that, when added to an existing network topology, makes it survivable against failures of any single edge (or node).

The work of Ljubic, Raidl, and Kratica (2000) presents a hybrid GA applied to the edge-biconnectivity AP, combining a reduction technique and a GA using binary representation for candidate edges to be added to the original graph. Two strategies are presented to deal with infeasible solutions during the evolution: a simple detect-and-discard method, and a repairing mechanism adding low cost edges until the network becomes edge-biconnected. The GA itself is adapted from the work of Ljubic and Kratica (2000) to solve the node-biconnectivity AP. Later, Ljubic and Raidl (2003) presented a memetic approach for the minimum-cost node-biconnectivity AP, combining an EA with several local-improvement strategies and heuristic search methods. The MA incorporates a deterministic preprocessing algorithm that reduces the search space, and uses a local improvement technique that removes redundant edges until a locally optimal solution is found. The MA is evaluated to solve a set of well-known randomly generated problem instances and several other TSP-based instances. The empirical results show that the MA is able to obtain better solutions than heuristic methods previously published, and also it scales well to instances of large size.

A more ambitious variant of the AP was studied by Elhaggaz, Ghassempoory and Brown (2002) to model the network expansion design problem. The time horizon is divided in a number of phases, and the network topology expands at each phase. At every expansion step, the network must be able to survive n link failures, and it must also satisfy node degree and link optimization constraints. The solution method is a relatively straightforward

GA, where a chromosome encodes the network adjacency matrices for each of the design phases and the assigned link capacities, and where ad-hoc crossover and mutation rules have been defined over this structure. The experiments correspond to a 12-node problem with 2-connectivity restriction (with data obtained from a telecom carrier in Spain), expanding over a five years period. The results mainly concentrate on the improvement obtained by using a heuristic to populate the initial generation, instead of using a random method, but do not include other parameters for evaluating the effectiveness of the GA method on this quite difficult problem.

Another variant of the problem consists in finding a 2-edge connected minimum cost network, where the terminal pairs have known demands, and the edges have fixed and (linear) variable costs depending on the flows. Rappos and Hadjiconstantinou (2004) proposed an ACO to solve this problem using two kinds of ants (flow ants and reliability ants), and two pheromone trails, which are combined to guide the different kinds of ants. The ants are grouped for exploring the search space, and an ant group can be converted into a solution of the original problem following a simple algorithm. The proposed ACO is benchmarked against known solutions (optimal in some cases, feasible ones in the rest) over a set of small and medium-sized (up to 50 nodes) randomly generated problems. In some instances, the ACO heuristic performed extremely well (less than 4% far away from the optimum), but for instances with large fixed costs, the results were less good (up to 22% far away from the best known results).

Maximum Edge-Disjoint Paths

An alternative approach to get reliability in a telecommunication network involves finding redundant connection paths between nodes, in such a way that a path do not interfere with each other. Given a network of terminal nodes and switches and a list of connection requests (i.e., pairs of nodes representing endpoints demanding to be connected by a path), the maximum edge-disjoint paths (EDP) proposes to find the maximum number of node pairs that can be connected by mutually edge (or node) disjoint paths.

In their proposal of a cooperative ACO, Nowé, Verbeeck, and Vrancx (2004) studied the EDP problem. The work was aimed at presenting the new ACO, and EDP was used as a problem example, without mentioning its application to network design. Blesa and Blum (2004) proposed the first ACO that attempted to solve realistic EDP instances with application to network design. They followed a decomposition approach, assigning one ant to solve the subproblem of finding a path for each connection request. Since the subproblems are not independent, the model includes a secondary evaluation criterion to count the shared edges of ant solutions. Each ant uses its own pheromone model and dynamic updating rule, and a deterministic construction method that leads to promising areas in early stages of the search. An experimental evaluation benchmark was designed, regarding three medium size networks with up to 500 nodes and 1020 links. For each network, 20 different instances with up to 75 randomly selected connection requirements were generated, and so 240 instances were studied to compare the ACO with a multi-start greedy method. The results showed that ACO achieves better solutions than the multi-start greedy approach, both in terms of solution quality and computation time. A new version of the ACO was presented two years later by the authors (Blesa & Blum, 2006), and new test instances with Internet like-topologies were included. At the same time, Vrancx and Nowe (2006) improved their previous proposal and presented an application to solve realistic EDP instances. In their multi-type ACO, a group of ants of the same type work together for solving each subproblem, but compete with ants of a different type for the use of resources (edges). Each ant type has its own pheromone, which attracts ants of their own type, but repulses ants of other

types. The using probability of each edge follows an adapted version of the Ant System formula. The results on 12 EDP instances from Blesa and Blum (2007) show that the multi-type ACO outperforms the previous best results on the largest instances. In 2007, Blesa and Blum developed additional features to their ACO algorithm, such as the parallel construction of paths, the use of a candidate list for the exploitation of the promising choices at each construction step, an explicit two phase search pattern, and a method to avoid local optima. The new ACO algorithm showed an improved performance, without downgrading the computational efficiency (Blesa & Blum, 2007).

Remarks and Conclusions

A large part of the papers discussed in this section present methods to design the topology of a network, using a network reliability function either as an objective function (in some cases as one of the functions to maximize within a multi-objective setting) or to set a constraint. The decision variables of the problem range from selecting which links to include, as in Kumar, Pathak and Gupta (1993), to deciding the type and redundancy level of components to be allocated within a fixed network topology, as in Marseguerra, Zio, Podofillini and Coit (2005).

Most of the papers employ some EA method, except for one case where ACO is used (and applied to very small test cases). The classical representations (binary encodings or integer list encodings) have often been used, but the work of Lin and Gen (2006), which uses an edge-based encoding with two parts to represent a spanning tree, plus some additional edges, has shown that more sophisticated encodings can improve the computational efficiency of the search, as well as allow to apply at low cost some special operators taking advantage of the structure of the solution.

Since computing the exact reliability is an

NP-hard problem, in many cases Monte Carlo simulation is employed, meaning that the algorithms used must cope with the presence of errors in the objective function. In the work of Konak and Smith (2005) there is a report on the (negative) impact of these errors in the solution quality; this is an important aspect, which is not always studied in detail in other works, even if there are some proposals trying to cope with it; for instance, Barán and Laufer (1999) first use a bound on reliability and then employ simulation to refine this first evaluation, and Marseguerra, Zio, Podofillini and Coit (2005) improve the estimation quality of high quality solutions by accumulating repeated Monte Carlo evaluations during the successive generations of their GA.

Taking all these points into account, the main conclusions point out to the need to further develop more sophisticated encodings and to improve in the understanding the effect of reliability estimation errors in the methods, as well as to find out ways to diminish its impact. One particularity of this problem is that no good local search strategies are available, and that in many cases the encodings lead to the use of repair procedures to maintain feasibility. These aspects greatly impair the performance of EA techniques. The computational examples are restricted to small networks, and further progress may be needed before tackling successfully larger, more realistic cases.

The second part of this section is devoted to connectivity problems, where instead of computing a reliability function, the survivability of the network is attained by ensuring some topological properties such as k-connectivity or other related ones.

Many of the remarks mentioned for reliability problems are valid also in this context. The majority of the works employ some EA variant, but there are more cases of application of ACO, sometimes with very good results. Like in the previous case, the classical encodings also are binary encodings and integer list encodings; nevertheless, a larger variety of other problem-specific encodings have

been proposed, trying to take advantage of the structure of the problems under hand, and in some cases obtained very good results. This kind of problems do not have the problem of computing an NP-hard objective function, although maintaining the feasibility of the solutions after crossover and mutation is not always easy or even possible, and strategies such as penalizing unfeasible solutions or employing repair strategies are very common. The computational experiments vary widely in the size and complexity of the problems tackled; in some cases there are topologies with hundreds of nodes, but in other cases there are also many works that study small topologies with only up to ten nodes.

Parallel implementations have been successfully applied in order to deal with the search in complex spaces, for both classes of reliability problems presented. Several proposals of parallel nature-inspired methods have been reviewed in this section (such as those by Huang, Tsuboi and Ma (1997), Barán and Laufer (1999), Duarte and Barán (2001), Kumar (2003), and Nesmachnow, Cancela, and Alba (2007)). All these proposals were conceived to improve the search efficiency and also to reduce the computational effort of solving the reliability network design problems by splitting the work and using several processing elements. Most of parallel nature-inspired methods reviewed follow the distributed subpopulation model, since it provides a simple and efficient pattern for distributing both the estimation of network reliability and the topology optimization.

LOCAL AREA NETWORKS AND BACKBONE NETWORKS

A typical problem in the design of ATM networks consists of finding a cost-effective topology that, while assuring low end-to-end delay, also optimize the link capacities and utilization in order to carry out the expected traffic, and to keep minimal cell loss due to buffer overflow. A standard approach to achieve cost-effectiveness in communication networks proposes designing a multilevel hierarchical structure of LANs and a backbone network. LAN is the lower level of this hierarchy, in which the users in a defined proximity are connected with each other directly or via a communication center. In the higher level, the backbone network connects LANs to each other. LAN design and backbone location are crucial problems for achieving the desired objectives in network design. The backbone location problem was especially important to allow digital transmission of voice and data over telephone wires, such as Integrated Services Digital Network (ISDN), and also to provide high-speed multimedia services. Table 3 resumes the work related to nature-inspired approaches to LAN design and backbone location, which are commented in this section.

LAN Design and Backbone Location

In a pioneering work, Routen (1994) faced the problem of LAN design using GA. The author

follows the classical approach from Tanenbaum, considering three optimization problems to determine the concentrator assignment (CAP), the terminal layout (TLP), and the concentrator location (CLP). Given the sites and concentrators locations, the CAP proposes to find the assignment that minimizes the cost of connecting each site to a concentrator. A simple GA is applied to solve an example CAP instance already tackled by Tagliarini and Page (1988) using a Hopfield network approach. The GA uses a string representation that ensures feasibility and a fitness function that considers both the minimization of the connections cost and the maximization of each concentrator capacity. Routen reported to achieve significant better results than Tagliarini and Page, and pointed out that the GA does not suffer the scalability problem of the Hopfield network method, but their claims were based on a single, small-sized CAP instance resolution. TLP concerns the design of paths for the connection of terminal nodes to a central site, considering limits to the number of terminals that can be connected by a single path.

Table 3. Nature-inspired methods applied to LAN design and backbone location problems

Author	Year	Problem	Method
Routen	1994	LAN Design	GA
Celli et al.	1995	B-ISDN Location	GA
Qin et al.	1997	B-ISDN Design	GA
Webb et al.	1997, 1998	Backbone Location	GA
Ko et al.	1997	ATM Design	GA
Sinclair	1998, 1998b, 1999b, 2000	WDM Network Design	Hybrid GA
Thompson & Bilbro	2000	ATM Design	GA
Sleem et al.	2000	ATM Design	Parallel GA
Sayoud et al.	2001	Network Design & Assignment	Hybrid GA
Gen et al.	2001, 2003	Various	EAs
Krommenacker	2002	Ethernet Network Design	GA
Jeyakumar, et al.	2003	WDM Network Design	GA
Teo et al.	2004	WDM Network Design	PSO
Runggeratigul	2004	WDM Network Design	GA
Din	2005	Backbone Location	GA
Routray et al.	2007	ATM Design	GA

Routen applied a GA using a string representation and a fitness function that incorporates the costs of the connections and penalties for the violation of soft constraints concerning the path capacities. The GA showed a robust behavior, and was able to find accurate results when using the simple strategy of discarding non-feasible solutions. CLP is strongly related to CAP and TLP, proposing to find the optimal number of concentrators, their locations and connections that minimize the network design cost. While CLP could be solved in a similar way than TLP, the string representation does not facilitate identifying the number of concentrators employed, thus requiring an explicit representation to guide the search. Routen proposed two alternative representations: the double search representation, using a binary-coded GA to find partial solutions and a second GA to evaluate their fitness (solving the CAP defined by the concentrators given by the binary string); and the tagged-string representation, coupling the TLP coding with a variable-length configuration string which describes how the former should be interpreted as a tree. Even though Routen did not provide significant numerical results, his work showed the first suggestions that three capital problems that model the LAN design were suited to a GA solution approach.

Celli, Costamagna, and Fanni (1995) tackled the problem of locating multiplexers on a Broadband ISDN (B-ISDN), in order to design a network based on a single exchange facility connected through multiplexed links to many users. Three types of nodes are involved: the users, the multiplexers, and the exchangers (users are connected to a multiplexer or directly to the exchange by the links of the distribution network). The optimization problem proposes to minimize the overall network cost, finding the site of the exchange, the number and location of the active multiplexers, the topology and size of the transport network (i.e. the links connecting the exchange and the multiplexers, and their capacities), and also the topology and size of the distribution network.

The authors proposes a binary-coded GA, using a fitness function that relates the network cost with the cost of a pure star tree structure, with no active multiplexers and users directly connected to the exchange. To deal with the computational needs to evaluate the fitness function, a master-slave PGA was developed: the master process performs the evolution, while the slaves evaluate the fitness function. The experimental evaluation faced 12 instances of the problem ranging from 45 to 153 nodes, classified in two groups: random scenarios, and a set of more realistic scenarios with an inherent structure and clustering. The design of a real world network (from Oristano, in Italy), whose data were supplied by the Italian public telephone company, is also presented. The GA was able to obtain accurate solutions, outperforming previous results obtained with a heuristic algorithm specifically designed for the problem. The parallel implementation effectively helped to reduce the computation times, and also showed a good speedup and scalability behavior, allowing tackling large problems that would be intractable with the sequential GA.

Qin, Wu, and Law (1997) addressed the topology design of B-ISDN networks using a GA. They faced the typical ATM network planning problem of selecting links connecting a given set of nodes, trying to minimize the total cost subject to traffic and reliability constraints. The GA incorporates a constructive initialization to obtain a k-degree network topology by adding links, and a shortest path routing method to assign capacities. To assure feasibility, a repair method to guarantee 2-connectivity is used. The article presents results for a single 20-node test problem, but lacks of both discussion and comparison with other techniques.

Webb, Turton, and Brown (1997, 1998) proposed a GA to determine the optimal location of backbones, with the purpose of illustrating how tariffing can affect the optimal component placement. Unlike most papers, this work studies a cost model that is derived from the true economic cost (connection and rental charges extracted from the Tarifica manual), rather than indirect related measures. Two cost models are used to illustrate how geography has small influence on the optimal topology when designing enterprise networks using international tariffs. Since ring topologies are considered to be cost-effective and provide performance and survivability, the objective network structure is a self-healing ring that comprises a number of backbone nodes, while the access nodes occupy the remaining locations. The GA uses a binary encoding to represent the presence of an access node or a backbone node, and a fitness function proportional to the overall network cost, including the total switch costs and link tariffs. A special repair heuristic is used to assure feasibility after applying the evolutionary operators. The GA was tested using a small network of 20 candidate node locations (main European cities) and with backbone sizes ranging from 3 to 7 nodes. The authors conclude that the GA is an effective search tool, particularly useful to search the space of the true economic cost, but their claim is not well justified, since they only present a unique test case of small dimension, and the GA is compared with a random search method. The main contribution of the article is the experimental verification that the cost structure significantly changes the resultant network design, leading towards non-intuitive topologies.

The path-list based GA proposed in the work of Ko et al. (1997) was adapted by Tang, Ko, Man, and Kwong (1998) to solve the problem of designing an ATM network embedded in a digital cross connect system (DCS) network. Given the underlying DCS network topology, the trunk and switch capacities of the backbone network, and the traffic flow requirements, the purpose is to find the topology, routing and capacity assignment of the embedded ATM network. The fitness of a specific routing scheme is evaluated using the optimal solution obtained from GENOCOP, the GA-based program for constrained and unconstrained optimization by Michalewicz (1992).

The method is able to achieve better results, both in network performance and computation speed, than an existing heuristic approach, but the only numerical results are reported for a very small problem instance of five nodes.

Thompson and Bilbro (2000) proposed applying a GA to the optimization of the topological ATM network design, considering the placement of links and the number and placement of concentrators. The problem intends to find a low-cost network topology that satisfies traffic QoS constraints, characterized as acceptable buffer overflow probability. The initialization of the GA population uses low-cost solutions obtained from a greedy-drop heuristic that places the largest capacity concentrator at every candidate location. A small population size is employed to speed convergence, and a multipoint crossover operator is used to maintain diversity in the population. The mutation operator implements a neighborhood search, aimed at refining the local minima. The proposed GA was compared with a Simulated Annealing algorithm, which starts with an initial feasible low-cost solution and explores using a movement operator that randomly adds, delete or exchanges concentrator locations. The authors evaluate both algorithms to solve a realistic problem instance, showing that GA is able to find solutions with a lower average cost that those obtained with SA, and significantly improving the cost of the least-cost greedy-drop heuristic solution.

Sleem, Ahmed, Kumar, and Kamel (2000) studied two parallel GAs for finding cost-effective ATM network with low end-to-end delay, and optimized link capacities and utilization. Based on a previous two-tier GA (Madhuram, 1995), the work compares two different PGA models: a distributed memory GA and a shared-memory GA. Both GAs follow the subpopulation model, but an additional level of functional decomposition is used: each subpopulation executes a GA to solve the network delay optimization subproblem, and after that a panmictic GA solves the network cost optimization problem. To compare the parallel versions, Sleem et al. faced the design of a single server ATM network, considering small instances with different problem sizes (up to 10 nodes) and different processor loading. The results show that GA performance does not always increase by just adding computational resources, due to the increasing communication overhead. The distributed version showed an improved performance over the serial version, while in the shared-memory GA the enhancement was not as high as expected. The best performance for the distributed GA is achieved when keeping the number of processes close to the number of physical processors available.

A hybrid GA with a local search hill-climbing was applied to solve the network design and capacity assignment (TDCA) problem by Sayoud, Takahashi, and Vaillant (2001). Given the network node locations, the traffic requirements, and link and node cost functions, the TDCA proposes to optimize the total cost of the network by optimally selecting links and capacities. The hybrid algorithm combines a steady-state GA and a simplex downhill method (SDM) applied to selected solutions from a set of nondominated solutions. The authors presented a single case experimental analysis, using the 20-nodes TDCA problem instance from Qin et al (1997). The hybrid method was compared vs. four simple GAs: the Generational Replacement GA, SSGA, the Struggle GA, and the GA from Qin et al (1997). The results showed that the hybrid GA-SDM was able to achieve better results than the other methods.

Two state-of-the art surveys (Gen, Cheng, & Oren, 2001) (Gen and Cheng, 2003) summarize Gen et al.'s research on applying hybrid EAs to solve topological network design and other related problems. They provide simple EA formulations to solve a large list of example applications that includes the centralized network design, the LAN design, the multicritera shortest path problem, and also the dc-MST. All these problems are illustrated from the point of genetic encoding skill and evolutionary operators with hybrid strategies. The degree-based permutation, an integer-based two-dimension coding structure proposed by Zhou and Gen (1997), is often employed to represent spanning trees, using one dimension for node permutations and the other for degree constraints. Since this encoding is essentially a permutation type, traditional operators such as order crossover, swap and insertion mutations were adopted. The exhaustive numerical experiments provided show the effectiveness and efficiency of such kind of EA-based approach to solve network topology design problems.

Krommenacker, Rondeau, and Divoux (2002) tackled the problem of physical layer topology optimization for industrial Ethernet network design. They proposed a two-level hierarchical topology (a tree where the leaves are the devices and the internal nodes are Ethernet switches) and linear connection between the middle tiers. As the networks have a part of (high priority) static traffic, the problem looks for a topology that maximizes intra-switches communications and minimizes inter-switches communications, to provide load balancing. The authors presented a standard GA to solve the underlying graph partitioning problem, aiming at dividing the nodes into disjoint subsets such that the sum of the vertex weights of each subset is close to the average sum, while minimizing the total cost of the edges connecting nodes in different subsets. The GA was compared against a recursive spectral bisection method to solve a 40 devices-5 switches instance. The results showed that the GA is able to obtain better results in terms of some network performance metrics (link load, switch load, delay time).

In fiber-optic communications, the Wavelength-Division Multiplexing (WDM) technology allows multiplexing multiple optical carrier signals on a single optical fiber, by using different wavelengths of laser light. This feature enables both increasing the communication capacity, and providing bidirectional communications over one fiber strand. The PhD thesis work by Sinclair, also published in various papers (Sinclair 1998, 1998b, 1999b, 2000), proposed the development of GA/heuristic hybrids, employing problem-specific encoding and operators, and combining the best existing heuristics for the problem within an overall GA framework. These algorithms were employed to solve mesh network topology design and wavelength-path routing, fiber choice and wavelength allocation. Jeyakumar, Baskaran, and Sumathy (2003) looked at the design of WDM network topologies that guarantee, with high degree of confidence, to deliver multicast traffic in user specified limits on time. The problem consists in finding a virtual topology between the nodes of the network, and a routing of the multicast patterns in this virtual topology. The authors employ a standard GA, where the fitness measure is a linear combination of cost, a measure of reliability and traffic. When a solution is found, it is mapped using shortest path heuristics into the physical network. Heuristics methods are applied to further reduce the number of involved wavelengths (as wavelength converters are costly equipment, they usually are only installed in a few nodes in the network). The experimental results, obtained for 2 to 6 multicast patterns over on a 14-node WAN test case, show that the GA is able to obtain feasible solutions in all cases (although the solution quality is not compared with the ones obtained by other methods).

Teo et al. (2004) applied a PSO to WDM network design. In this setting, the network topology, the link capacity, and the communication demand matrix is supposed to be known; the problem consists in choosing a number of network nodes to be equipped with wavelength converters, in order to minimize the blocking probability (i.e., the probability that a given communication cannot be established, due to the impossibility of establishing a source-to-terminal light path on the same wavelength, even if the individual links have available capacity). The PSO results are explored, looking at the convergence patterns depending on the number of particles used in the algorithm. Also,

the results are employed to compare the relative merits of adding more wavelength converting equipment vs. adding more wavelengths on the links of the network, showing that the last option is preferable.

Runggeratigul, Thongsri, and Sumsiripong (2004) looked at a more general variant of the previous problem. Instead of having a predetermined number of wavelength converters to install, they tried to determine both the number and the location of these equipments, so that a bound on blocking call probability can be ensured. To solve this problem, the authors employed a standard GA, with a binary codification for representing which nodes will be hosting converters. The proposed algorithm is compared with methods iterating upon the number of converters and solving for each fixed number, like the solution by Siregar, Takagi, and Zhang (2002), which supposed a fixed number of converters was given. The computational times are (unsurprisingly) much better for the GA.

The backbone location problem also has applications to wireless network design. Din (2005) studied the wireless ATM backbone network design problem, which proposes to find the minimum cost backbone link topology under service constraints, and proposed a GA to solve it. The approach separates the backbone network in two parts: the spanning tree and a set of augmented edges, and the GA uses a Prüfer encoding with two parts to represent feasible solutions. Several crossover and mutation operators are studied using a set of randomly generated problem instances with up to 100 switches. The GA efficacy is compared with results obtained with a Dijkstra-based heuristic and lower bounds computed using CPLEX. The results show that GA outperforms the heuristic specifically designed for the problem, and it also achieves reduced gaps when comparing with the lower bounds computed.

Routray, Sherry, and Reddy (2007) presented a GA to tackle the ATM network design using optical fiber, a cost-effective solution to provide high-demand services. The optimal backbone

ATM network design tries to minimize the cost of fiber ducts while satisfying customer demands. A two-level topology is proposed: a set of primary nodes connected in a ring, and a group of secondary nodes between primary nodes and end users. The GA uses a two-type encoding: a list to represent allocation and a bit string to represent the signal split level and node positions. Standard crossover and mutation operators were used to perform an analysis on two problems instances with 30 and 50 nodes. The authors claimed that GA is a "powerful tool" for facing the network design task. However, the instances faced are quite simple, and the authors do not provide additional empirical results, or comparisons with other techniques.

Remarks and Conclusions

The papers presented in this section deal with variants of real-life or real-life inspired network design problems, very near to the actual implementation (while the previous ones dealt with more abstract problems). As such, there are wide differences between the diverse models, which must take into account many details dependent on the actual technologies to be employed in the networks. GA methods are predominant, even if the utilization of a PSO method (Teo et al., 2004) can be noted. In many cases, the problems to be solved have common characteristics or can be seen as variants, incorporating additional information, of some of the topological design problems we have seen in Section 2 and Section 3. This has allowed some authors to take advantage of sophisticated encodings developed for those other, simpler problems; in the cases where this has been possible, the quality of the results has usually been very satisfying.

Other authors developed problem-specific encodings, or in some cases a simple binary encoding (although this sometimes leads to the use of repair heuristics for maintaining feasibility). As problems are very complex, in some cases they are split into different stages, each one of them being solved by a different algorithm. This introduces an additional error, which is the price to pay for reducing the complexity of finding solutions to the original problem. Also, in some cases the solution found by the optimization techniques must be mapped by some algorithm or heuristic back to the real life network, adding an additional step. The methods proposed cover a very wide variety of situations and problems, and have been applied in many cases to real-life data, showing that the lessons learned in the more abstract design problems can be employed to develop good quality methods in the more complex real-life settings.

CELLULAR AND WIRELESS NETWORKS DESIGN

With the popularization of both cellular phones and wireless technology, the interest in cellular networks has been emphasized. While several aspects related to this kind of network are not new in the telecommunications domain, some other aspects appear only in this context, such as antennae placement and cell planning. This section presents those works that have focused on cellular and wireless networks design using nature-inspired methods. Table 4 summarizes those works, which have been organized into two groups: antennae placement and wireless network design.

Antennae Placement

In radio networks, the localization and placement of antennae have an important influence on the quality and cost of the service. This problem is especially important in cellular networks where, in addition to cost and quality requirements, coverage and handover constraints are found. In this context, the Radio Network Design (RND) problem consists of determining the optimal locations for Base Stations (BS) transmitters in a geographical

Table 4. Nature-inspired methods applied to cellular and wireless network design problems

Author	Year	Problem	Method
Shahbaz	1995	Fixed Network Design	GA
Tang et al.	1997, 2001	WLAN Design	Hierarchical GA
Calégari et al.	1997a, 1997b, 2001	Radio Network Design	GA, PGA
Meunier et al.	2000	Radio Network Design	Parallel GA
Li et al.	2000	CDMA Planning	Hierarchical GA
Krishnamachari & Wicker	2000	Radio Network Design	several
Zimmermann et al.	2000, 2003	Radio Network Design	ES
Watanabe et al.	2001	Radio Network Design	Parallel MOEA
Chan et al.	2002	CDMA Handoff	GA
Tongheng & Chundi	2002	Radio Network Design	Parallel GAs
Cahon et al.	2004	Radio Network Design	Parallel MOEA
Wade et al.	2004	BFWA Design	Agent-based
Raisanen & Whitaker	2004, 2005	Radio Network Design	Hybrid MOEA
Alba et al.	2004, 2005	Radio Network Design	Parallel EAs
Zhang et al.	2005	Radio Network Design	PSO
Liu et al.	2005	Radio Network Design	Parallel EDA
Créput et al.	2005	Cellular Network Dimensioning	Parallel EA
Quintao et al.	2005	Wireless Sensor Network Design	GA
Talbi et al.	2006, 2007	Radio Network Design	MOEA
Nebro et al.	2007	Radio Network Design	MOCHC
Prim et al.	2007	Radio Network Design	DE
Danoy et al.	2007	Ad-hoc Network Design	Coevolutionary GA
Vega et al.	2007a	Radio Network Design	several
Vega et al.	2007b	Radio Network Design	DE
Aydin et al	2007	Radio Network Design	several

area in order to get a maximum coverage using a minimum number of BS.

Calégari, Guidec, and Kuonen have proposed several EAs applied to find the optimal placement of antennae. A distributed GA prototype was presented in their earlier proposals (Calégari, Guidec, Kuonen, & Wagner, 1997; Calégari, Guidec, Kuonen, & Kobler, 1997). Later, the authors compared a greedy technique, a Darwinian algorithm, and a PGA (Calégari, Guidec, Kuonen, & Nielsen, 2001). The EAs use a bit string encoding for the whole set of possible antenna locations and a parametric fitness function (to evaluate the covered area as a function of a parameter that can be tuned

in order to obtain acceptable service ratio values). The evaluation experiments were performed on two real-life cases: Vosges (a rural scenario, in France) and Geneva (an urban scenario, in Italy). On average, the PGA and the greedy technique show the same solution quality. However, when an optimal solution is known, it can be found using the PGA whereas the greedy approach usually falls in bad attractive local optima.

Zimmermann, Höns, and Mühlenbein (2000, 2003) studied the antennae location problem in the context of EU project ARNO (Algorithms for Radio Network Optimization). The fitness function combines site cost, interference and cell shape, and takes into account traffic and coverage hard constraints. A three-phase Evolutionary Strategy (ES) algorithm is proposed: the initialization phase tries to exploit the local structure around a site, computing an initial placement probability; the repair phase corrects non-feasible initial solutions using a set of heuristic procedures; and the optimization phase is guided by several heuristic methods, to find accurate solutions. A stagnation stop criterion is used for the purposes of ARNO project. Eight real world problem instances with data provided by France Telecom are considered in the experimental evaluation, but the authors only reported the results for three instances (with 250, 568, and 747 possible sites, respectively). The results show that the ES is a promising method, able to deal with RND problem complexity.

Watanabe, Hiroyasu, and Mikiand (2001) worked out two parallel MOEAs for deciding the antennae placement and configuration in cellular networks: the Master-Slave with Local Cultivation Genetic Algorithm (MSLC) and the Divided Range Multi-Objective Genetic Algorithm (DRMOGA). MSLC is a standard master-slave PGA, but the evolutionary operators are carried out on the slaves using a two-individual population and the evolution follows the minimal generation gap model. DRMOGA is a standard distributed island model that uses domain decomposition. The empirical analysis compares the two models proposed against MOGA (Fonseca & Fleming, 1993 and a standard distributed GA. They show that MSLC gets the best results of Pareto front covering and non-dominated individuals, while establishing that DRMOGA results are affected by the number of subpopulations: the number of non-dominated individuals decreases when the number of subpopulations grows.

Meunier, Talbi, and Reininger (2000) presented a parallel MOEA with multilevel encoding deciding the activation of sites, the number and type of antennae, and the parameters of each BS. Two modified versions of the classical genetic operators, named geographical crossover and multilevel

mutation, are introduced. The fitness evaluation utilizes a MOGA-based ranking function, and a sharing technique is employed to preserve genetic diversity. In addition, a linear penalization model is used to handle the covering constraint. A master-slave MOEA is presented for solving high dimension problems in reasonable times, with each slave processing a part of the geographical working area. The algorithm is evaluated with a realistic large highway area generated by France Telecom. The authors analyze the convenience of using the sharing strategy proposed instead of concentrating on a small part of the Pareto front, showing that a better Pareto front sampling is obtained in the first case. Later, Cahon, Melab and Talbi (2004) faced the problem using three parallel/distributed GA models implemented in the ParadisEO (PARAllel and DIStributed Evolving Objects) framework: the *island (a)synchronous cooperative* model, the *parallel evaluation* model, and the *distributed evaluation* model. Working on a cluster of 40 Pentium III PCs, the Pareto fronts obtained for the test instances studied confirmed the robustness and efficiency of the island model for solving the problem. The computational efficiency analysis showed that the parallel evaluation model follows almost-linear speedup behavior. The distributed evaluation model scales superlinearly up to 10 processors, and then it follows a logarithmic decay.

Tongheng and Chundi (2002) study the same antennae placement problem, solving it with coarse-grained PGAs which also include the application of a specialized local search operator. The paper compares the performances of using different neighbor topologies: ring, bi-directional ring and torus, finding that the last one gives the best optimization quality and speed. There is also a comparison showing better results than the EA by Calégari et al. (1997a), possibly due to the use of the local search method already mentioned.

Raisanen and Whitaker (2004) introduced a new hybrid approach for solving a Global System for Mobile communications (GSM) network planning problem, concerning both the BS positioning and the transmission power levels configuration. Inspired by the idea of nest bird building, the method works in two phases. A nest builder agent follows a given movement pattern, visiting candidate BS sites and deciding where to leave nesting material, aimed at controlling cell density and overlap for constructing efficient sub-optimal network topologies that provide 100% area coverage. The nest builder is not capable of improving the topologies, so the NSGA-II (Deb, Agrawal, Pratap & Meyarivan, 2000) is used to search for new move orderings trying to optimize both objectives. The work investigated the efficiency of the new hybrid approach for solving two real-life instances containing 244 and 568 candidate BS sites, 56792 and 50225 reception test points, and 17393 and 48512 service test points with a specific assigned QoS threshold, respectively. Two site visiting patterns were compared: MCP (power awareness visitation) and MCS (by-site visitation), and the results showed that MCS weakly dominated MCP both in terms of traffic and overlap, the main pair of objectives considered. However, MCP weakly dominated MCS in terms of both cover and cost, and cover and overlap, suggesting that MCS achieves better results due to very high traffic coverage. The authors pointed out the strength of the hybrid method, and proposed to develop advanced strategies based on the nest builder approach. Later, Raisanen and Whitaker (2005) presented a detailed comparison on the performance of several MOEAs (PESA, SPEA-II, NSGA-II, and SEAMO) for the antennae placement problem. The empirical study evaluates several metrics such as convergence to the Pareto front, distribution and also computational efficiency. The results show that all MOEAs were able to find acceptable solutions, but both NGSA-II and SPEA2 achieves the best relation between solutions quality and execution time.

Alba (2004) analyzed several binary-coded sequential and parallel GAs to tackle the problem of finding the optimal placement of antennae. The article studied two fitness functions: a standard model already used in Calégari et al (1997) and an original penalization model that tries to account for the features that an optimal solution should exhibit. The results show that the distributed steady state GA is an efficient and accurate tool for solving RND, which even outperforms existing parallel solutions. In a later work, Alba and Chicano (2005) performed a deep study on the parallel approach, evaluating the influence of the number of locations, the number of processors, and the migration rates. They found a sublinear speedup and concluded that subpopulations isolation is beneficial for the search. In a recent work with Nebro et al. (2007), the authors presented a multiobjective version of the CHC algorithm (MOCHC) applied to the problem. MOCHC is compared against both a binary-coded NSGA-II and provided results in the literature. The results indicate that MOCHC outperforms NSGA-II and it is also more efficient finding the optimal solutions than single-objectives techniques.

Zhang, Ji, Yuan, Li, Wang and Wang (2004) considered a bi-objective version of the antennae placement problem, separating area coverage and total cost as different objective functions. They do not discretize the location of the BS, and employ a PSO method for finding non-dominated solutions. A distributed computing version of the method is implemented, where each subpopulation explores a part of the solution space, by concentrating on one of the objective functions for a given number of iterations. An external archive is used to join all the solutions obtained. The results were compared against those obtained by a MOEA, the computational times are much smaller for the PSO method, and the quality of results seems comparable, but the quality of the Pareto fronts obtained is not formally contrasted.

Liu, Zeng, Zou, Liu and Zhou (2005) faced the antennae placement problem, but using a more general profit function that takes into account heterogeneous weights for different covered areas, as well as loss weights for uncovered areas. The authors employ a parallel Estimation of Distribution Algorithm (EDA), which uses the same encoding as the GA by Calégari et al. (1997, 2001) and Tongheng and Chundi (2002). The parallel version follows an island-based paradigm, with ring, bidirectional ring and mesh topologies for migration. The parallel EDA is compared vs. a serial EDA and a serial standard GA, giving better results independent of the migration topologies; nevertheless, the mesh topologies give the best overall results.

A multiobjective model for the RND problem regarding cost, held traffic, QoS objectives, as well as coverage and handover constraints was formalized by Talbi, Cahon, and Melab (2007) when presenting DEMARNO, a platform for radio network optimization that extends the ParadisEO framework for nature-inspired metaheuristics. DEMARNO combines MOEAs, local search methods and hybridization mechanisms for solving optimization problems using the power of large-scale metacomputing grids to speed-up the search. DEMARNO includes a specific coding scheme, extends the three parallel models in ParadisEO, and implements the hybridization with specific local searches that embeds RND problem-specific knowledge. Talbi et al. evaluates DEMARNO using three realistic instances from France Telecom (a highway area and two urban zones), using a dedicated cluster of 53 CPUs (80 days of CPU time) and a grid of 100 heterogeneous, non-dedicated processors (15 days). The results suggest that DEMARNO algorithms are able to handle multiple objectives and constraints, and to create and maintain a set of diversified solutions on the Pareto front, helping the network designer to find a suitable topology. The parallel model allows an efficient resolution of large scenarios, and also provides a better understanding of the problem structure.

Aydin, Yang and Zhang (2007) look at Wideband Code Division Multiple Access (WCDMA) networks using power control and soft handover mechanisms. They model the network planning problem (selecting the antennae placement) as a *p*-median problem, by dividing the whole area into *p* regions, and then selecting within each region the location for the BS among a finite number of candidate sites. To evaluate the performance of the algorithms, the authors develop a WCDMA network simulator, working on a very detailed scenario of a 18 km. x 16 km. area with 19 BS and 3-sector antennas. A GA, a TS and a hybrid evolutionary SA algorithm are implemented. The results show that the TS obtains very accurate solutions, and that the evolutionary SA algorithm has also good performances; the GA instead does not attain the same levels, even if it is clearly superior to a greedy heuristic.

The works of Vega-Rodríguez, et al. (2007b) and Priem-Mendes, et al. (2007) present a Differential Evolution (DE) algorithm to solve the RND problem. The DE method follows the traditional floating-point encoded, panmictic, steady-state EA schema. Two variation operator classes are presented: the Genetic Variation (GV), using traditional evolutionary operators, and the Differential Mutation Variation (DM), using operators derived from the original DE approach. GV includes two crossover operators and a mutation specifically designed to avoid stagnation due to genetic drift. DM includes to operators: Nearest Point Differential Mutation (NPDM) and α-Neighbourhood Differential Mutation (α-DM). A novel initialization heuristic was designed, trying to reduce the space and guide the search, to provide diversity, and to evaluate the ability of the variation operators to overcome stagnation. The experimental evaluation shows that all the operators converge, suggesting that DE suits for the operators presented. NPDM achieved the best result in all experiments, with a 99% cover rate, providing evidence to be the best operator in the comparison set. The same authors (Vega-Rodríguez, et al., 2007a) evaluated several bio-inspired metaheuristics to solve the RND problem. The study includes Population-Based Incremental Learning (PBIL), a hybrid of GA and the competitive learning strategy (often used in neural networks), DE, SA, and CHC. A large set of experiments was performed considering a single test instance, aimed at efficiently solving the problem. PBIL, SA and CHC obtained the optimal solution, while DE is the method requiring lower computation time to achieve good quality results. Both PBIL and CHC obtain the best normalized execution times and the best number of evaluations, but in average PBIL needs slightly less evaluations to reach the optimal fitness value.

Wireless Network Design

Besides RND and cell planning, several other optimization problems related to cellular and wireless network design have been addressed using nature-inspired techniques. A miscellaneous collection of relevant applications is summarized below.

In 1995, Shahbaz presented GOTND (Genetic Optimizer for Topological Network Design), a pioneer optimization tool for the topological GSM network design (Shahbaz, 1995). GOTND is a multi-purpose tool, aimed at optimizing the topology of local networks between cellular networks components: Base Transceiver Stations (BTS), Base Station Controllers (BSC), and Mobile services Switching Centers (MSC). The problem formulation uses fixed node prices and linear cost link functions (following the German Telecom approach), while considering that line types depends on the link length, the amount of traffic transmitted and the blocking probability. The work focuses on the fixed network optimization, and assumes that the radio planning has been performed (i.e., BTS are already positioned). Pairs of source-destination communication requirements describe the traffic, and the number of BTSs, BSCs and the amount of traffic that they can handle is restricted. A original set of seven chromosomes is used to encode the coordinates of BSCs and MSCs, and the paths between them, and the fitness function evaluates the total cost of network components.

GOTND uses problem-related evolutionary operators, specifically developed according to the chromosome set structure. A set of 17 local search operators was studied (based on moving, disconnecting, changing, assigning, and reconnecting network elements), assigning a higher probability of application to those operators that achieve the maximal improvements. The author presented an experimental evaluation of GOTND for solving a single scenario of 100 BTSs, four BSCs and one MSC. The results were not conclusive, as they show a cost reduction of 19% when comparing with randomly generated network topologies, but no further analysis was made.

Krishnamachari and Wicker (2000) pointed out that the problem of finding the BSC locations and the assignment of BS heavily impacts on the overall cost of a cellular system. The authors used several heuristic methods to select where to locate a number of BSC, such that every BS is connected to a BSC (which can only attend up to a maximum number of connections), while minimizing the overall costs. They present a comparison between TS, GA, SA and Random Walk over a particular test case. TS has the best overall results, and the GA is very near, while the other two strategies perform rather worse.

Before the arriving of the 3G cellular systems, both GSM and CDMA were continuously promoted as the leader technologies in 2G cellular networks. Li, Guan and Soong (2000) presented a two-layer network planning model to solve the BS positioning and parameter optimization problems in CDMA networks. The authors propose a hierarchical two-layer GA to solve both problems simultaneously, using a mixed matrix and binary encoding to represent BS locations and BS and user equipment parameters, respectively. In the BS positioning optimization, the GA uses new crossover and mutation operators, able to work with the matrix-coded solutions. The parameter optimization is carried out using a simple GA. A single test case is presented, so results cannot be considered as conclusive. In the same line of work, Chan, Kwong, Man, and Tang (2002) used a GA to minimize the hard handoff in CDMA networks. The authors present single and multiobjective formulations for the problem, and propose both a penalty function and a chromosome repair mechanism to deal with infeasible solutions. The GA uses an integer encoding to represent BS Controller locations, but no further details on the operators employed are provided. The experimental evaluations consider a single test problem, and the authors found that GA is able to find better results than those obtained with a previous SA approach.

Tang, Man, and Kwong (2001) applied a hierarchical genetic algorithm (HGA) for designing a wireless local area network (WLAN) for a factory in Hong Kong. The problem consists in finding the number of BS locations and their places over a specified area, in order to provide adequate radio coverage for a specified power level. An accurate problem model is provided, including a realistic path loss model and considering the density of the obstacles. Three objectives are taken into account to minimize: the required number of BS (to minimize the total cost), the sum of the path loss predictions with respect to the BS location, and the maximum of the path loss predictions over the design space (the worst case QoS scenario). HGA is a Pareto-ranking based MOEA capable of handling discrete constraints, which uses a hierarchical multilevel chromosome structure already employed for WLAN design (Tang, Man, & Ko, 1997). The binary coded *control genes* decide the activation or deactivation of the corresponding problem element (in this case, each BS) and the *parameter genes* define the variables of the problem (in this case, the BS coordinates). Inactive genes always exist within the chromosome, as they are in the DNA, and so the encoding contains more information than usual. In this way, HGA does not assume a prefixed chromosome or phenotype structure, allowing a more powerful search pattern. Two niche techniques are employed to provide diversity: a

mating restriction based on the distance between individuals, and a fitness sharing technique. Conventional operators are used for the binary-coded control genes, while specialized genetic operations were adopted for the real-number-coded parameter genes. The experimental evaluation involved installing the WLAN in the indoor scenario, and the results demonstrated that HGA is capable of identifying the required number of BS as well as their corresponding locations simultaneously, for different power loss thresholds.

Wade, Hurley, Allen, Taplin, and Craig (2004) presented an agent-based self organized system to address the design of Broadband Fixed Wireless Access (BFWA) networks. In order to offer low-cost high-speed telephony and data services, BFWA networks requires an effective design and planning. In the proposal of Wade et al. a population of agents represents potential users and BS sites that disseminate and react to local information to optimize global design objectives such as coverage and QoS criteria. The iterative optimization procedure has three phases: the user phase (to select the BS sites), the site phase (to choose and configure the network infrastructure) and finally the control phase (to store the best network found so far). Each user-agent communicates with its neighbors to perform a survey of service information, and uses the local knowledge to decide on several actions, such as the migration of users between cells of the network. The site-agents receive petitions from user-agents and use their information to build a local area map that allows deciding when to take structural changes in the network, such as creating a new sector or reconfiguring an existing one. The algorithm extends an existing network optimization tool, and the preliminary results for a data set covering the city of Malvern (U.K.) show the potential of the new method when compared with the more expensive SA algorithm used in the optimization tool.

Créput, Koukam, Lissajoux, and Caminada (2005) faced the adaptive meshing (AM) process for dimensioning a cellular network to cover a city, subject to QoS and traffic requirements. In the AM process, a pattern of regular hexagonal cells is transformed according to traffic density, geometrical constraints, and other parameters. For solving the problem with moderate computational effort, the authors propose the Hybrid Islands Evolutionary Strategy (HIES), combining a hill-climbing local search with a subpopulation distributed ES. Each island contains only one individual, so HIES resembles to memetic algorithms, incorporating a geographical isolation distribution for individuals, like in a cellular PGA. All three HIES operators (local search, crossover and macromutation) are stochastic procedures, specifically designed for the problem. Créput et al. used a linear aggregative fitness function considering the minimization of the total number of BS and constraints related to the resource distribution, the regularity of cells geometry, the number of visible cells, and the overloaded cells. The experimental evaluation includes a real-life scenario (Lyon, France) and three problems built for representing typical application cases. The results showed satisfactory meshing patterns, while eliminating overloaded cells. HIES achieves highly adapted solutions using a moderate number of generations, and the results improve as population size increases. The parallel version obtains better results than sequential versions with similar number of function evaluations. There is room to improve the HIES efficiency by executing on a cluster, since the simulations required from 5 to 20 hours of execution time for the test scenarios studied.

Quintao, Nakamura, and Mateus (2005) studied a dynamic coverage problem arising in wireless sensor networks design. Given a number of sensor nodes present in a given area, the problem consists in deciding which sensor nodes to turn on or off at each period within a given time window, so that the area is covered, and at the same time the energy consumption and the transmissions interference between the nodes is minimized. The problem is studied using both an integer linear programming model and a GA. The GA codifies

in each chromosome the network configuration at each of the periods considered, using binary representation. The crossover is done by giving to a child half of the periods of each of the parents, while several mutation operators (including a greedy strategy) are implemented. A local search operator is applied to restore feasibility if lost after mutation. The results over a relatively small test case (4 periods, 16 nodes over a 60 m. × 60 m. area) show that some of GA variants can obtain results quite competitive with the results obtained by commercial solvers (CPLEX) over the integer linear programming formulation. On the other hand, the greedy mutation strategy gives bad results, and should not be used.

Recently, Danoy, Bouvry and Hogie (2007) presented two coevolutionary GAs applied to ad-hoc wireless network design, aiming to improve the network connectivity by defining a set of long distance connections ("bypass links") among geographical neighborhoods of nodes. The GAs uses the concept of coevolution, considering several species that evolve cooperatively. The authors use the Cooperative Coevolutionary GA (CCGA) and the Loosely Coupled GA (LCGA). CCGA follows a symbiotic approach, where the fitness of an individual depends on its ability to collaborate with individuals from other species. While an independent EA controls the evolution of each species, CCGA allows the recombination of parents from different species, creating accurate solutions by putting together the best individuals from each subpopulation. LCGA implements the paradigm of competitive coevolution, based in non-cooperative models of game theory, by splitting the problem into several components and using agents to reach its local optima (Nash equilibrium). The local fitness function for each subpopulation is related with the payoff of each agent in the competition, and the evolutionary operators are applied locally to the subpopulations of actions. Danoy et al. use Dafo, an agent-oriented problem-solving environment dedicated to evolutionary optimization. Both GAs uses a binary encoding to represent possible bypass links and a linear aggregation fitness function that includes the cluster coefficient, the characteristic path length (related to the number of hops needed to cross the network), and the number of required bypass links. The authors evaluate LCGA and CCGA using an ad-hoc network with 42 nodes, 3 clusters and 745 possible links, using the Madhoc simulator for managing the scenario communications. The results state that coevolutionary algorithms outperform a classical GA and a steady state GA. CCGA achieves better results than LCGA, both in terms of best solution found and convergence speed, but requiring large average execution times.

Remarks and Conclusions

Most of the papers reviewed in this section deal with antenna and base station placement and configuration, as well as other problems related to cellular and wireless network design. These problems are directly related to geometrical and geographical aspects, and have characteristics quite different from the ones treated in previous sections. Even if EAs are still the most used, it comes as no surprise that there is a wider variety of methods being applied, such as hierarchical GA, DE, and other EA variants. An important consideration is whether locations are considered among a discrete set of possibilities or can be fixed given real coordinates in a plane. This last option is the one taken by Zhang, Ji, Yuan, Li, Wang and Wang (2004), but most of the other papers either choose from a previously defined discrete set of locations, or discretize the area of study in possible locations (usually using hexagonal or square cells). Binary encoding is frequently used, but other more sophisticated encodings also appear. As much information about technological aspects of the networks must be used in order to evaluate the quality of the solution as well as its feasibility, usually specific local search operators are applied in order to improve the quality of the solutions taking into account the particular characteristics

of the problems. Many of the papers employ real-life data case studies, as the problems under study are motivated by the rapid development and deployment of wireless networks and the successive technological changes.

CONCLUSION

This chapter presents a survey of the current state-of-the-art on using nature-inspired techniques to solve telecommunication structural network design problems. The long list of existing works and also the diversity of the proposals reflect the growing attention paid to this domain. Researchers have intensively used these methods, trying to take advantage of their high versatility and powerful search patterns to tackle the hard optimization problems underlying network design.

In order to organize the many works reviewed according to a standard protocol, they have been divided into four main problem classes: minimum spanning tree, reliable networks, local access network and backbone location, and cellular and wireless network design. The proposed taxonomy is just one of the many potential proposals, and readers are expected to find in it just a guide to better understand and classify the contributions made in network design.

Among the long list of interesting operators, algorithms and design approaches, there is a remarkably growing importance of multiobjective models of design problems versus the more classical single objective problem formulations. The application of multiobjective models allows a better representation of real-life situations, taking into account conflicting objectives regarding different desired features of the network infrastructure, which can hardly be condensed into a single measure by linear combination of the target goals. It is important to notice that the key point here is to use Pareto dominance in the algorithms, in order to offer a set of solutions to the network designer (decision maker) for a higher flexibility.

Regarding the application of EAs, an important number of papers employ binary encodings for representing the candidate solutions. This is probably due to their easy implementation and utilization, and not to any scientific reason. Other more sophisticated encodings allow EAs to face larger instances. In some cases, the encoding developed for a given problem can also be applied to other similar ones, a nice effort in the sense of knowledge reutilization, which is a salient feature of EAs. What is also clear in the literature is that operators having complexities larger than linear or logarithmic are of little use in this domain since they will not scale to larger real-life problem instances.

The analysis of the kind of nature-inspired methods applied shows that, while EAs are the most popular ones, there is also a significant research interest in the application of other new methods, such as ACO, PSO, etc plus a very evident global preference for local search procedures. ACO provides a "natural way" for finding paths in graphs (e.g. in spanning trees), but the constructive technique is not directly extended for efficiently solving other kinds of network design problems. Hybrid and memetic methods provide a powerful manner of combining heuristics, problem-specific operators and sophisticated problem representations, regularly reporting real improvements over traditional heuristics.

Almost a third of the papers regarding cellular and wireless network design problems apply parallelism, using clusters with many tens of processors, and reporting very efficient/accurate results. This represents an appealing complementary view of several domains, in which parallelism helps to design complex networks that in turn could be used to run parallel programs.

All these considerations reveal the high impact of using nature-inspired techniques for solving network design problems. This is a hot topic in research, in which metaheuristics in general have a main role to play. It is also interesting to see how long-standing problems for traditional networks are of renewed interest due to the introduction in scene of novel challenges in metropolitan, ad-hoc and mobile vehicle networks; this means that a good deal of information on existing studies can be rethought for fast utilization, which clearly justifies our survey in this chapter.

ACKNOWLEDGMENT

This work has been partially funded by several institutions: the Sectorial Committee for Research (CSIC), Universidad de la República (Uruguay), the Brazilian National Council for Research - CNPq, under contract PROSUL Proc. 490333/2004-4 (Discrete Optimization and Graphs: Theory, Algorithms and Applications network), the Spanish Ministry of Industry under contracts FIT-330210-2006-49 and FIT-330225-2007-1 (CARLINK), the Spanish Ministry of Education and Science under contract TIN2005-08818-C04-01 (OPLINK), and the Regional Government of Andalusia under contract P07-TIC-03044 (DIRICOM).

REFERENCES

Alba, E. (2004). Evolutionary algorithms for optimal placement of antennae in radio network design. In *Proceedings of the 18th International Parallel and Distributed Processing Symposium* (p. 168).

Alba, E., & Chicano, F. (2005). On the behavior of parallel genetic algorithms for optimal placement of antennae in telecommunications. *International Journal of Foundations of Computer Science, 16*(2), 343–359. doi:10.1142/S0129054105003029

Altiparmak, F., Gen, M., Dengiz, B., & Smith, A. (2004). A network-based genetic algorithm for design of communication networks. *Journal of Society of Plant Engineers Japan, 15*(4), 184–190.

Aydin, M., Yang, J., & Zhang, J. (2007). Comparative investigation on heuristic optimization of WCDMA radio networks. In *EvoWorkshops 2007*. *Lecture Notes in Computer Science, 4448*, 111–120. doi:10.1007/978-3-540-71805-5_12

Bäck, T. (1998). *Evolutionary Algorithms in Theory and Practice*. New York: Oxford University Press.

Ball, M. (1979). Computing network reliability. *Operations Research, 27*(4), 832–836. doi:10.1287/opre.27.4.823

Banerjee, N., & Kumar, R. (2007). Multiobjective network design for realistic traffic models. In *Proceedings of the 9th Annual Conference on Genetic and Evolutionary Computation* (pp. 1904-1911).

Barán, B., & Laufer, F. (1999) Topological optimization of reliable networks using A-Teams. In *Proceedings of World Multiconference on Systemics, Cybernetics and Informatics*.

Blesa, M., & Blum, C. (2004). Ant colony optimization for the maximum edge-disjoint paths problem. In G. R. Raidl (Ed.), *Proceedings of EvoWorkshops 2004*. Lecture Notes in Computer Science 3005, 160-169.

Blesa, M., & Blum, C. (2006). A nature-inspired algorithm for the disjoint paths problem. In *20th International Parallel and Distributed Processing Symposium* (pp. 25-29).

Blesa, M., & Blum, C. (2007). Finding edge-disjoint paths in networks by means of artificial ant colonies. *Journal of Mathematical Modelling and Algorithms, 6*(3), 361–391. doi:10.1007/s10852-007-9060-y

Blum, C., & Roli, A. (2003). Metaheuristics in combinatorial optimization: Overview and conceptual comparison. *ACM Computing Surveys, 35*(3), 268–308. doi:10.1145/937503.937505

Bui, T., & Zrncic, C. (2006). An ant-based algorithm for finding degree-constrained minimum spanning tree. In *Genetic and Evolutionary Computation Conference* (pp. 11-18).

Cahon, S., Melab, N., & Talbi, E. (2004). ParadisEO: A framework for the reusable design of parallel and distributed metaheuristics. *Journal of Heuristics, 10*(3), 357–380. doi:10.1023/B:HEUR.0000026900.92269.ec

Calégari, P., Guidec, F., Kuonen, P., & Kobler, D. (1997). Parallel island-based genetic algorithm for radio network design. *Journal of Parallel and Distributed Computing, 47*(1), 86–90. doi:10.1006/jpdc.1997.1397

Calégari, P., Guidec, F., Kuonen, P., & Nielsen, F. (2001). Combinatorial optimization algorithms for radio network planning. *Theoretical Computer Science, 263*(1-2), 235–265. doi:10.1016/S0304-3975(00)00245-0

Calégari, P., Guidec, F., Kuonen, P., & Wagner, D. (1997). Genetic approach to radio network optimization for mobile systems. In *IEEE 47th Vehicular Technology Conference, 2*, 755-759.

Celli, G., Costamagna, E., & Fanni, A. (1995). Genetic algorithms for telecommunication network optimization. In *IEEE International Conference on Systems, Man and Cybernetics, 2*, 1227-1232.

Chan, T., Kwong, S., Man, K., & Tang, K. (2002). Hard handoff minimization using genetic algorithms. *Signal Processing, 82*(8), 1047–1058. doi:10.1016/S0165-1684(02)00213-X

Chena, G., Chenc, S., Guob, W., & Chen, H. (2007). The multi-criteria minimum spanning tree problem based genetic algorithm. *Information Sciences, 177*(22), 5050–5063. doi:10.1016/j.ins.2007.06.005

Cheng, R., & Gen, M. (1997). *Compromise approach-based genetic algorithms for bicriterion shortest path problems*. Technical Report, Ashikaga Institute of Technology.

Cheng, S. (1998). Topological optimization of a reliable communication network. *IEEE Transactions on Reliability, 47*(3), 225–233. doi:10.1109/24.740489

Chou, H., Premkumar, G., & Chu, C.-H. (2001). Genetic algorithms for communications network design - an empirical study of the factors that influence performance. *IEEE Transactions on Evolutionary Computation, 5*(3), 236–249. doi:10.1109/4235.930313

Chu, C., Premkumar, G., Chou, C., & Sun, J. (1999). Dynamic Degree Constrained Network Design: A Genetic Algorithm Approach. In *Genetic and Evolutionary Computation Conference* (pp. 141-148).

Consoli, S., Moreno-Pérez, J.A., Darby-Dowman, K., & Mladenovic, N. (2007). Discrete Particle Swarm Optimization for the minimum labeling Steiner tree problem. In *II workshop on Nature Inspired Cooperative Strategies for Optimization* (pp. 11-14).

Créput, J.-C., Koukam, A., Lissajoux, T., & Caminada, A. (2005). Automatic mesh generation for mobile network dimensioning using evolutionary approach. *IEEE Transactions on Evolutionary Computation, 9*(1), 18–30. doi:10.1109/TEVC.2004.837923

Danoy, G., Bouvry, P., & Hogie, L. (2007). Coevolutionary genetic algorithms for Ad hoc injection networks design optimization. In *IEEE Congress on Evolutionary Computation* (pp. 4273-4280).

Deb, K., Agrawal, S., Pratap, A., & Meyarivan, T. (2000). A Fast Elitist Non-dominated Sorting Genetic Algorithm for Multi-objective Optimisation: NSGA-II. In *Proceedings of the 6th international Conference on Parallel Problem Solving from Nature. Lecture Notes in Computer Science, 1917*, 849–858. doi:10.1007/3-540-45356-3_83

Deeter, D., & Smith, A. (1997) Heuristic optimization of network design considering all-terminal reliability. In *Proceedings Annual Reliability and Maintainability Symposium* (pp. 194-199).

Deeter, D., & Smith, A. (1998). Economic design of reliable networks . *IIE Transactions, 30*(12), 1161–1174.

Delbem, C., de Carvalho, A., Policastro, C., Pinto, A., Honda, K., & García, A. (2004). Node-depth encoding for evolutionary algorithms applied to network design. In *Genetic and Evolutionary Computation Conference . Lecture Notes in Computer Science, 3102*, 678–687.

Dengiz, B., Altiparmak, F., & Smith, A. E. (1997a). Efficient optimization of all-terminal reliable networks, using an evolutionary approach. *IEEE Transactions on Reliability, 46*(1), 18–26. doi:10.1109/24.589921

Dengiz, B., Altiparmak, F., & Smith, A. E. (1997b). Local search genetic algorithm for optimal design of reliable networks. *IEEE Transactions on Evolutionary Computation, 1*(3), 179–188. doi:10.1109/4235.661548

Di Fatta, G., Lo Presti, G., & Lo Re, G. (2003). A Parallel Genetic Algorithm for the Steiner Problem in Networks. In *Proceedings of the 15th International Conference on Parallel and Distributed Computing and Systems* (pp. 569-573).

Din, D. (2005). Wireless ATM Backbone Network Design Problem. *Transactions on Fundamentals of Electronics, Communications and Computer Sciences . E (Norwalk, Conn.), 88-A*(7), 1777–1785.

Dror, M., Haouari, M., & Chaouachi, J. (2000). Generalized spanning trees. *European Journal of Operational Research, 120*(3), 583–592. doi:10.1016/S0377-2217(99)00006-5

Duarte, S., & Barán, B. (2001). Multiobjective network design optimisation using parallel evolutionary algorithms. In *XXVII Conferencia Latinoamericana de Informática* (text in Spanish).

Duarte, S., Barán, B., & Benítez, D. (2003). Telecommunication network design with parallel multiobjective evolutionary algorithms. In *Proceedings of IFIP/ACM Latin America Networking Conference* (pp. 1-11).

Duin, C., & Voß, S. (2004). Solving group Steiner problems as Steiner problems. *European Journal of Operational Research, 154*(1), 323–329. doi:10.1016/S0377-2217(02)00707-5

Elhaggaz, S., Ghassempoory, M., & Brown, J. (2002). A reliable phased network topology design using evolutionary algorithm. In *Student Conference on Research and Development* (pp. 253-256).

Eshelman, L. (1991). The CHC adaptive search algorithm: how to have safe search when engaging in non-traditional genetic recombination. In *Foundations of Genetic Algorithms* (pp. 265-283).

Fonseca, C., & Fleming, P. (1993). Genetic algorithms for multiobjective optimization: Formulation, discussion and generalization. In *Proceedings of the 5th International Genetic Algorithms Conference* (pp. 416–423).

Gamvros, I., Golden, B., & Raghavan, S. (2003). An Evolutionary Approach to the Multi-Level Capacitated Minimum Spanning Tree problem. In G. Anandalingam & S. Raghavan (Ed.), *Telecommunications Network Design and Management*. Boston, USA: Kluwer Academic Press.

Gamvros, I., Golden, B., Raghavan, S., & Stanojevic, D. (2005). Heuristic Search for Network Design. In H. Greenberg (Ed.), *Tutorials on Emerging Methodologies and Applications in Operations Research*. New York: Springer.

Gen, M., & Cheng, R. (2003). Evolutionary network design: Hybrid genetic algorithms approach. *International Journal of Computational Intelligence and Applications, 3*(4), 357–380. doi:10.1142/S1469026803001075

Gen, M., Cheng, R., & Oren, S. (2001). Network Design Techniques using Adapted Genetic Algorithms. *Advances in Engineering Software, 32*(9), 731–744. doi:10.1016/S0965-9978(01)00007-2

Gen, M., Cheng, W., & Wang, D. (1997). Genetic algorithms for solving shortest path problems. In *Proceedings of IEEE International Conference on Evolutionary Computation* (pp. 401–406).

Gen, M., Ida, K., & Kim, J. (1998). A spanning tree-based genetic algorithm for bicriteria topological network design. In *Proceedings of IEEE International Conference on Evolutionary Computation*, (pp.15-20).

Gen, M., & Lin, L. (2004). Multiobjective hybrid genetic algorithm for bicriteria network design problem. In *The 8th Asia Pacific Symposium on Intelligent and Evolutionary Systems*.

Gen, M., & Lin, L. (2005). Multi-objective hybrid genetic algorithm for bicriteria network design problem. *Complexity International, 11*, 73–83.

Gen, M., Lin, L., & Cheng, R. (2004). Bicriteria Network Optimization Problem using Priority-based Genetic Algorithm. *IEEJ Transactions on Electronics . Information Systems, 124-C*(10), 1972–1978.

Gendreau, M., Larochelle, J., & Sansó, B. (1999). A tabu search heuristic for the Steiner tree problem. *Networks*, *34*(2), 162–172. doi:10.1002/(SICI)1097-0037(199909)34:2<162::AID-NET9>3.0.CO;2-9

Glover, F., & Kochenberger, G. (2003). *Handbook of Metaheuristics*. Boston: Kluwer.

Golden, B., Raghavan, S., & Stanojevic, D. (2008). The prize-collecting generalized minimum spanning tree problem. *Journal of Heuristics*, *14*(1), 69–93. doi:10.1007/s10732-007-9027-1

Han, L., & Wang, Y. (2005). A New Genetic Algorithm for the Degree-Constrained Minimum Spanning Tree Problem. In *Proceedings of 2005 IEEE International Workshop on VLSI Design and Video Technology* (pp. 125-128).

Huang, R., Tsuboi, E., & Ma, J. (1997). A Parallel Distributed Genetic Algorithm for Designing 3-connectivity Communication Networks. In *Proceedings of the International Conference on Parallel and Distributed Computing and Systems* (pp. 501-506).

Jeyakumar, A., Baskaran, K., & Sumathy, V. (2003). Genetic algorithm for optimal design of delay bounded WDM multicast networks. In *Conference on Convergent Technologies for Asia-Pacific Region* (pp. 1224-1228).

Kampstra, P., van der Mei, R. D., & Eiben, A. (2006). *Evolutionary Computing in Telecommunication Network Design: A Survey*. Unpublished paper, Vrije Universiteit Amsterdam. Retrieved May 21, 2008 from www.cs.vu.nl/~mei/articles/2006/kampstra/art.pdf.

Klau, G., Ljubic, I., Moser, A., Mutzel, P., Neuner, P., Raidl, G., & Weiskircher, R. (2004). Combining a memetic algorithm with integer programming to solve the prize-collecting Steiner tree problem. In *Genetic and Evolutionary Computation Conference . Lecture Notes in Computer Science*, *3102*, 1304–1315.

Knowles, J., & Corne, D. (2000). A New Evolutionary Approach to the Degree-Constrained Minimum Spanning Tree Problem. *IEEE Transactions on Evolutionary Computation*, *4*(2), 125–134. doi:10.1109/4235.850653

Ko, K., & Tang, K. Chan, C., & Man, K. (1997). Packet switched communication network designs using GA. In *2nd International Conference On Genetic Algorithms in Engineering Systems: Innovations and Applications* (pp. 398-403).

Ko, K., Tang, K., Chan, C., Man, K., & Kwong, S. (1997). Using genetic algorithms to design mesh networks. *Computer*, *30*(8), 56–61. doi:10.1109/2.607086

Konak, A., & Smith, A. (1999). A Hybrid Genetic Algorithm Approach for Backbone Design of Communication Networks. In *Proceedings of the Congress on Evolutionary Computation* (pp. 1817-1823).

Konak, A., & Smith, A. (2002). Multiobjective Optimization of Survivable Networks Considering Reliability. In *Proceedings of the 10th International Conference on Telecommunication Systems*, Naval Postgraduate School, Monterey, CA.

Konak, A., & Smith, A. (2004). Capacitated Network Design Considering Survivability: An Evolutionary Approach. *Engineering Optimization*, *36*(2), 189–205. doi:10.1080/03052150310001633223

Konak, A., & Smith, A. (2005). Designing Resilient Networks Using a Hybrid Genetic Algorithm Approach. In *Proceedings of Genetic and Evolutionary Computation Conference* (pp. 1279-1285).

Krishnamachari, B., & Wicker, S. (2000). Optimization of fixed network design in cellular systems using local search algorithms. In *IEEE Vehicular Technology Conference* (pp.1632-1638).

Krommenacker, N., Rondeau, E., & Divoux, T. (2002). Genetic algorithms for industrial Ethernet network design. In *4th IEEE International Workshop on Factory Communication Systems* (pp. 149-156).

Kulturel-Konak, S., Konak, A., & Smith, A. (2000). Minimum cost 2-edge-connected Steiner graphs in rectilinear space: an evolutionary approach. In *Proceedings of the Congress on Evolutionary Computation* (pp. 97-103).

Kumar, A., Pathak, R., & Gupta, M. (1993). Genetic algorithm based approach for designing computer network topology. In *Proceedings of the ACM Conference on Computer Science* (pp. 358-365).

Kumar, R. (2003). Multicriteria network design using distributed evolutionary algorithm. In T. Pinkston & V. Prasanna (Eds.), *Proceedings of the High Performance Computing*, Lecture Notes in Computer Science, 2913, 343-352.

Kumar, R., Krishnan, V., & Santhanakrishnan, K. (2000). Design of an optimal communication network using multiobjective genetic optimization. In *. Proceedings of IEEE International Conference on Industrial Technology*, *1*, 515–520.

Kumar, R., Parida, P., & Gupta, M. (2002). Topological design of communication networks using multiobjective genetic optimization. In *Proceedings of the Congress on Evolutionary Computation* (pp. 425-430).

Kumar, R., & Rockett, P. (1997). Assessing the convergence of rank-based multiobjective genetic algorithms. In *2nd International Conference on Genetic Algorithms in Engineering Systems: Innovations and Applications* (pp.19-23).

Lee, C., & Kang, H. (2000). Cell planning with capacity expansion in mobile communications: A tabu search approach. *IEEE Transactions on Vehicular Technology*, *49*(5), 1678–1690. doi:10.1109/25.892573

Li, J., Guan, Y., & Soong, B. (2000). Effect of genetic algorithm parameters on PCS network planning. In *25th Annual IEEE Conference on Local Computer Networks* (pp. 400-404).

Lin, L., & Gen, M. (2006). A Self-controlled Genetic Algorithm for Reliable Communication Network Design. In *IEEE Congress on Evolutionary Computation* (pp. 640-647).

Liu, F., Zeng, Y., Zou, Y., Liu, J., & Zhou, H. (2005). Parallel island-based estimation of distribution algorithms for wireless network planning. In *International Conference on Wireless Communications, Networking and Mobile Computing* (pp. 1056-1059).

Ljubic, I., & Kratica, J. (2000). A genetic algorithm for biconnectivity augmentation problem, in *Proceedings of the IEEE congress on Evolutionary Computation* (pp. 89–96).

Ljubic, I., & Raidl, G. (2003). A memetic algorithm for minimum-cost vertex-biconnectivity augmentation of graphs. *Journal of Heuristics*, *9*(5), 401–428. doi:10.1023/B:HEUR.0000004810.27436.30

Ljubic, I., Raidl, G., & Kratica, J. (2000). A hybrid GA for the edge-biconnectivity augmentation problem, in *Proceedings of the 6th Parallel Problem Solving from Nature VI Conference. Lecture Notes in Computer Science*, *1917*, 641–650. doi:10.1007/3-540-45356-3_63

Lo, C., & Chang, W. (2000). A multiobjective hybrid genetic algorithm for the capacitated multipoint network design problem. *IEEE Transactions on Systems, Man, and Cybernetics . Part B*, *30*(3), 461–470.

Lo Re, G., Lo Presti, G., Storniolo, P., & Urso, A. (2004). A grid enabled parallel hybrid genetic algorithm for SPN. In *Proceedings of International Conference on Computational Science. Lecture Notes in Computer Science*, *3039*, 156–163.

Luyet, L., Zufferey, N., & Varone, S. (2007). An ant algorithm for the Steiner tree problem in graphs. In *EVOCOMNET. Lecture Notes in Computer Science, 4448*, 42–51. doi:10.1007/978-3-540-71805-5_5

Ma, J., Huang, R., & Tsuboi, E. (1997). A Genetic Algorithm for Optimal 3-connected Telecommunication Network Designs. *Lecture Notes in Computer Science, 1336*, 159–170. doi:10.1007/BFb0024213

Madhuram, S. (1995). *The Design of ATM Networks Using Genetic Algorithms*. Unpublished Master Thesis, University of Louisville, Kentucky.

Maple, C., Guo, L., & Zhang, J. (2004). Parallel genetic algorithms for third generation mobile network planning. In *Proceedings of the International Conference on Parallel Computing in Electrical Engineering* (pp. 229-236).

Marseguerra, M., Zio, E., Podofillini, L., & Coit, D. (2005). Optimal design of reliable network systems in presence of uncertainty. *IEEE Transactions on Reliability, 54*(2), 243–253. doi:10.1109/TR.2005.847279

Meunier, H., Talbi, E.-G., & Reininger, P. (2000). A multiobjective genetic algorithm for radio network optimization. In *Proceedings of the 2000 Congress on Evolutionary Computation* (pp. 317–324).

Michalewicz, Z. (1992). *Genetic Algorithms + Data Structures = Evolution Programs*. Springer-Verlag.

Nebro, A., Alba, E., & Molina, G. Chicano, F., Luna, F., & Durillo, J. (2007). Optimal antenna placement using a new multi-objective CHC algorithm. In *Proceedings of the 9th Annual Conference on Genetic and Evolutionary Computation* (pp. 876-883).

Nesmachnow, S., Cancela, H., & Alba, E. (2007). Evolutionary algorithms applied to reliable communication network design. *Engineering Optimization, 39*(7), 831–855. doi:10.1080/03052150701503553

Nesmachnow, S., Cancela, H., Alba, E., & Chicano, F. (2005). Parallel metaheuristics in telecommunications. In E. Alba (Ed.), *Parallel metaheuristics: a new class of algorithms* (pp. 495-515). John Wiley & Sons: Hoboken, N.J.

Nowé, A., Verbeeck, K., & Vrancx, P. (2004) Multi-type ant colony: the edge disjoint paths problem. In *4th International Workshop on Ant Colony Optimization and Swarm Intelligence. Lecture Notes in Computer Science, 3172*, 202-213.

Ombuki, B., Nakamura, M., Nakao, Z., & Onaga, K. (1999). Evolutionary computation for topological optimization of 3-connected computer networks. In *Proceedings of IEEE International Conference on Systems, Man, and Cybernetics* (pp. 659-664).

Palmer, C., & Kershenbaum, A. (1995). An approach to a problem in network design using genetic algorithms. *Networks, 26*, 151–163. doi:10.1002/net.3230260305

Premprayoon, P., & Wardkein, P. (2005). Topological communication network design using ant colony optimization. In *Proceedings of the 7th International Conference on Advanced Communication Technology* (pp. 1147-1151).

Priem-Mendes, S., Gomez-Pulido, J., Vega-Rodriguez, M., Pereira, A., Perez, J., & Sanchez, J. (2007). Fast Wide Area Network Design Optimisation Using Differential Evolution. In *Proceedings of the International Conference on Advanced Engineering Computing and Applications in Sciences* (pp. 3-10).

Qin, Z., Wu, F., & Law, N. (1997). Designing B-ISDN network topologies using the genetic algorithm. In *Proceedings of the 5th International Workshop on Modeling, Analysis, and Simulation of Computer and Telecommunication Systems* (pp.140-145).

Quintao, F., Nakamura, F., & Mateus, G. (2005). Evolutionary algorithm for the dynamic coverage problem applied to wireless sensor networks design. In *Proceedings of the IEEE Congress on Evolutionary Computation* (pp. 1589-1596).

Raidl, G. R. (2000). An efficient evolutionary algorithm for the degree-constrained minimum spanning tree problem. In C. Fonseca, J.-H. Kim, & A. Smith (Eds.), *Proceedings of the IEEE Congress on Evolutionary Computation* (pp. 104-111).

Raidl, G. R., & Julstrom, B. A. (2003). Edge sets: an effective evolutionary coding of spanning trees. *IEEE Transactions on Evolutionary Computation, 7*(3), 225–239. doi:10.1109/TEVC.2002.807275

Raisanen, L., & Whitaker, R. (2004). The Application of Nature-Inspired Nest Building to Wireless Site Selection. In *Proceedings of Parallel Problem Solving from Nature* VIII. *Lecture Notes in Computer Science, 3242.*

Raisanen, L., & Whitaker, R. (2005). Comparison and evaluation of multiple objective genetic algorithms for the antenna placement problem. *Mobile Networks and Applications, 10*, 79–88. doi:10.1023/B:MONE.0000048547.84327.95

Rappos, E., & Hadjiconstantinou, E. (2004). An Ant Colony Heuristic for the Design of Two-edge Connected Flow Networks. In *Proceedings of 4th International Workshop on Ant Colony Optimization and Swarm Intelligence. Lecture Notes in Computer Science, 3172*, 270-277.

Ren, H., & Meng, M. (2006). Biologically Inspired Approaches for Wireless Sensor Networks. In *Proceedings of the IEEE International Conference on Mechatronics and Automation* (pp.762-768).

Ribeiro, C., Martins, L., & Rossetti, I. (2007). Metaheuristics for optimization problems in computer communications. *Computer Communications, 30*(4), 656–669. doi:10.1016/j.comcom.2006.08.027

Routen, T. (1994). Genetic algorithm and neural network approaches to local access network design. In *Proceedings of the 2nd International Workshop on Modeling, Analysis, and Simulation of Computer and Telecommunication Systems* (pp. 239-243).

Routray, S., Sherry, A., & Reddy, B. (2007). ATM network planning: a genetic algorithm approach. *Journal of Theoretical and Applied Information Technology*, (pp. 74-79).

Runggeratigul, S., Thongsri, P., & Sumsiripong, P. (2004). Optimal number of wavelength converters for WDM network design. In *Proceedings of the Conference on Convergent Technologies for Asia-Pacific Region* (pp. 93-96).

Sayoud, H., Takahashi, K., & Vaillant, B. (2001). A genetic local tuning algorithm for a class of combinatorial networks design problems. *IEEE Communications Letters, 5*(7), 322–324. doi:10.1109/4234.935756

Schaffer, J. (1985). Multiple Objective Optimization with Vector Evaluated Genetic Algorithms. In J. Grefenstette (Ed.) *Proceedings of the 1st international Conference on Genetic Algorithm* (pp. 93-100).

Shahbaz, M. (1995). Fixed network design of cellular mobile communication networks using genetic algorithms. In *Proceedings of the IEEE International Conference on Universal Personal Communications* (pp. 163-167).

Shyu, S., Yin, P., Lin, B., & Haouari, M. (2003). Ant-tree: an ant colony optimization approach to the generalized minimum spanning tree problem. *Journal of Experimental & Theoretical Artificial Intelligence*, *15*(1), 103–112. doi:10.1080/0952813021000032699

Sinclair, M. C. (1998). Minimum Network Wavelength Requirement Design Using a Genetic-algorithm/Heuristic Hybrid. *Electronics Letters*, *34*(4), 388–389. doi:10.1049/el:19980282

Sinclair, M. C. (1998b). Minimum Cost Routing and Wavelength Allocation Using a Genetic-algorithm/Heuristic Hybrid Approach. In *Proceedings of 6th IEE Conference on Telecommunications*, (pp. 67-71).

Sinclair, M. C. (1999). Evolutionary Telecommunications: A Summary. In *Genetic and Evolutionary Computation Conference* (pp. 209-212).

Sinclair, M. C. (1999b). Optical Mesh Topology Design using Node-Pair Encoding Genetic Programming. In *Genetic and Evolutionary Computation Conference* (pp. 1192-1197).

Sinclair, M. C. (2000). Node-Pair Encoding Genetic Programming for Optical Mesh Network Topology Design. In D.Corne, M. Oates, & G. Smith (Eds.), *Telecommunications Optimization: Heuristic and Adaptive Techniques* (pp. 99-114). Wiley.

Siregar, J., Takagi, H., & Zhang, Y. (2002). Optimal wavelength converter placement in optical networks by genetic algorithms. *IEICE Transactions on Communications . E (Norwalk, Conn.)*, *85-B*(6), 1075–1081.

Sleem, A., Ahmed, M., Kumar, A., & Kamel, K. (2000). Comparative Study of Parallel vs. Distributed Genetic Algorithm Implementation for ATM Networking Environment. In *Proceedings of the Fifth IEEE Symposium on Computers and Communications* (pp. 152-157).

Soak, S.-M., Corne, D., & Ahn, B.-H. (2005). A new evolutionary algorithm for spanning-tree based communication network design. *IEICE Transactions on Communications*, *E88*(10), 4090–4094. doi:10.1093/ietcom/e88-b.10.4090

Soper, A., & McKenzie, S. (1997). The use of a biased heuristic by a genetic algorithm applied to the design of multipoint connections in a local access network. In *Proceedings of the 2nd International Conference On Genetic Algorithms in Engineering Systems: Innovations and Application* (pp. 113-116).

Srinivas, N., & Deb, K. (1994). Multi-objective optimization using non-dominated sorting in genetic algorithms. *Evolutionary Computation*, *2*(3), 221–248. doi:10.1162/evco.1994.2.3.221

Tagliarini, G., & Page, E. (1988) A neural-network solution to the concentrator assignment problem. In *IEEE Conference on Neural Information Processing Systems-Natural and Synthetic* (pp. 775-782).

Takahashi, H., & Matsuyama, A. (1980). An approximate solution for the Steiner problem in graphs. *Mathematica Japonica*, *24*, 573–577.

Talbi, E.-G., Cahon, S., & Melab, N. (2007). Designing cellular networks using a parallel hybrid metaheuristic on the computational grid. *Computer Communications*, *30*(4), 698–713. doi:10.1016/j.comcom.2006.08.017

Tamasi, L., Orincsay, D., Jozsa, B., & Magyar, G. (2005). Design of survivable VPN based VoIP networks. In *Proceedings of the 5th International Workshop on Design of Reliable Communication Networks* (pp. 473-480).

Tang, K., Ko, K., Man, K., & Kwong, S. (1998). Topology design and bandwidth allocation of embedded ATM networks using genetic algorithm. *IEEE Communications Letters*, *2*(6), 171–173. doi:10.1109/4234.681362

Tang, K., Man, K., & Ko, T. (1997). Wireless LAN design using hierarchical genetic algorithm. In *Proceeding of 7th International Conference on Genetic Algorithms* (pp. 629-635).

Tang, K., Man, K., & Kwong, S. (2001). Wireless Communication Network Design in IC Factory. *IEEE Transactions on Industrial Electronics, 48*(2), 452–459. doi:10.1109/41.915425

Teo, C., Foo, Y., Chien, S., Low, A., Venkatesh, B., & You, A. (2004). Optimal placement of wavelength converters in wdm networks using particle swarm optimizer. In *Proceedings of the IEEE International Conference on Communications* (pp. 1669-1673).

Thompson, D., & Bilbro, G. (2000). Comparison of a Genetic Algorithm with a Simulated Annealing Algorithm for the Design of an ATM Network. *IEEE Communications Letters, 4*(8), 267–269. doi:10.1109/4234.864190

Tongheng, G., & Chundi, M. (2002), Radio network design using coarse-grained parallel genetic algorithms with different neighbor topology. In *Proceedings of the 4th World Congress on Intelligent Control and Automation* (pp. 1840-1843).

Tsuji, M., Munetomo, M., & Akama, K. (2003). Metropolitan area network design using GA based on hierachical linkage identification. In *Proceedings of the Genetic and Evolutionary Computation Conference. Lecture Notes in Computer Science, 2724*, 1616–1617. doi:10.1007/3-540-45110-2_52

Tsuji, M., Munetomo, M., & Akama, K. (2007). A network design problem by a GA with linkage identification and recombination for overlapping building blocks. In *Proceedings of the IEEE Congress on Evolutionary Computation* (pp. 349-356).

Vega-Rodríguez, M., Gómez Pulido, J., Alba, E., Vega-Pérez, D., Priem-Mendes, S., & Molina, G. (2007a). Evaluation of Different Metaheuristics Solving the RND Problem. In *EvoWorkshops 2007* (pp. 101-110).

Vega-Rodríguez, M., Gómez Pulido, J., Alba, E., Vega-Pérez, D., Priem-Mendes, S., & Molina, G. (2007b). Using Omnidirectional BTS and Different Evolutionary Approaches to Solve the RND Problem. In *EUROCAST 2007* (pp. 853-860).

Vrancx, P., & Nowe, A. (2006). Using Pheromone Repulsion to Find Disjoint Paths. In *Proceedings of the 5th International Workshop Ant Colony Optimization and Swarm Intelligence. Lecture Notes in Computer Science, 4150*, 522–523. doi:10.1007/11839088_62

Wade, A., Hurley, S., Allen, S., Taplin, R., & Craig, K. (2004). Optimisation of BFWA Networks using Emergent Intelligence. In *3rd IASTED International Conference on Communications, Internet and Information Technology*, ACTA Press.

Watanabe, S., Hiroyasu, T., & Mikiand, M. (2001). Parallel evolutionary multi-criterion optimization for mobile telecommunication networks optimization. In *Proceedings of the EUROGEN2001 Conference* (pp. 167–172).

Webb, A., Turton, B., & Brown, J. (1997). Application of a genetic algorithm to the design and optimisation of a self-healing ring network. In *Proceedings of 4th Communication Networks Symposium* (pp. 2-5).

Webb, A., Turton, B., & Brown, J. (1998). Application of genetic algorithm to a network optimisation problem. In *Proceedings of 6th IEEE Conference on Telecommunications* (pp. 62-66).

Xianwei, Z., Changjia, C., & Gang, Z. (2000). A genetic algorithm for multicasting routing problem. In *Proceedings of International Conference on Communication Technology* (pp. 1248-1253).

Xiong, Y., Golden, B., & Wasil, E. (2005). A one-parameter genetic algorithm for the minimum labeling spanning tree problem. *IEEE Transactions on Evolutionary Computation, 9*(1), 55–60. doi:10.1109/TEVC.2004.840145

Xiong, Y., Golden, B., & Wasil, E. (2006). Improved Heuristics for the Minimum Label Spanning Tree Problem. *IEEE Transactions on Evolutionary Computation, 10*(6), 700–703. doi:10.1109/TEVC.2006.877147

Zhang, Y., Ji, C., Yuan, P., Li, M., Wang, C., & Wang, G. (2004). Particle swarm optimization for base station placement in mobile communication. In *Proceedings of the IEEE International Conference on Networking, Sensing and Control* (pp. 428-432).

Zhou, G., Cao, Z., Cao, J., & Meng, Z. (2007). A Centralized Network Design Problem with Genetic Algorithm Approach. In Y. Wang, Y. Cheung, H. Liu (Eds.), *International Conference on Computational Intelligence and Security. Lecture Notes in Computer Science, 4456*, 123-132.

Zhou, G., & Gen, M. (1997). A note on genetic algorithms for degree constrained spanning tree problems. *Networks, 30*, 91–95. doi:10.1002/(SICI)1097-0037(199709)30:2<91::AID-NET3>3.0.CO;2-F

Zhou, G., & Gen, M. (1999). Genetic Algorithm Approach on Multi-criteria Minimum Spanning Tree Problem. *European Journal of Operational Research, 114*, 141–151. doi:10.1016/S0377-2217(98)00016-2

Zhou, G., & Gen, M. (2003). A genetic algorithm approach on tree-like telecommunication network design problem. *The Journal of the Operational Research Society, 54*(3), 248–254. doi:10.1057/palgrave.jors.2601510

Zimmermann, J., Höns, R., & Mühlenbein, H. (2000). The Antenna Placement Problem: An Evolutionary Approach, In *Proceedings of the 8th International Conference on Telecommunication Systems* (pp. 358-366).

Zimmermann, J., Höns, R., & Mühlenbein, H. (2003). ENCON: an evolutionary algorithm for the antenna placement problem. *Computers & Industrial Engineering, 44*, 209–226. doi:10.1016/S0360-8352(02)00176-6

Zitzler, E., & Thiele, L. (1999). Multiobjective evolutionary algorithms: A comparative case study and the strength Pareto approach. *IEEE Transactions on Evolutionary Computation, 3*(4), 257–271. doi:10.1109/4235.797969

Zomaya, A. (2006). *Handbook of Nature-Inspired and Innovative Computing: Integrating Classical Models with Emerging Technologies*. Springer-Verlag, New York.

Compilation of References

Aarts, E. H. L. (2004). Ambient intelligence: A multimedia perspective. *IEEE MultiMedia, 11*(1), 12–19. doi:10.1109/MMUL.2004.1261101

Abraham, A., Grosan, C., & Ramos, V. (2006). (Eds.). *Stigmergic Optimization.* Studies in Computational Intelligence, Berlin, Germany: Springer Verlag.

Abrahamson, W. G. E. (1989). *Plant-Animal Interaction.* McGraw-Hill Inc.

Adamatzky, A. (2001). *Computing in nonlinear media and automata collectives.* IoP Publishing, Bristol.

Adamatzky, A., & De Lacy Costello, B. (2002). Experimental logical gates in a reaction-diffusion medium: The XOR gate and beyond. *Physical Review E, 66*(2), 046112.1–046112.6.

Adleman, L. M. (1994). Molecular computation of solutions to combinatorial problems. *Science, 266,* 1021–1024. doi:10.1126/science.7973651

Ahmed, F. E. (2005). Artificial neural networks for diagnosis and survival prediction in colon cancer. *Molecular Cancer, 4,* 29. http://www.molecular-cancer.com/content/4/1/29. doi:10.1186/1476-4598-4-29

Aickelin, U., & Greensmith, J. (2007). Sensing danger: Innate immunology for intrusion detection. *Elsevier Information Security Technical Report,* (pp. 218–227).

Al-Amad, S., McCullough, M., Graham, J., Clement, J., & Hill, A. (2006). Craniofacial identification by computer-mediated superimposition. *The Journal of Forensic Odonto-Stomatology, 24,* 47–52.

Alba, E. (2004). Evolutionary algorithms for optimal placement of antennae in radio network design. In *Proceedings of the 18th International Parallel and Distributed Processing Symposium* (p. 168).

Alba, E., & Chicano, F. (2005). On the behavior of parallel genetic algorithms for optimal placement of antennae in telecommunications. *International Journal of Foundations of Computer Science, 16*(2), 343–359. doi:10.1142/S0129054105003029

Alba, E., & Tomassini, M. (2002). Parallelism and evolutionary algorithms. *IEEE Transactions on Evolutionary Computation, 6*(5), 443–461. doi:10.1109/TEVC.2002.800880

Allaby, M. (1998). *Oxford Dictionary of Ecology.* New York, NY: Oxford University Press.

Altiparmak, F., Gen, M., Dengiz, B., & Smith, A. (2004). A network-based genetic algorithm for design of communication networks. *Journal of Society of Plant Engineers Japan, 15*(4), 184–190.

Álvarez-Díaz, M., & Álvarez, A. (2005). Genetic multi-model composite forecast for non-linear prediction of exchange rates. *Empirical Economics, 30*(3), 643–663. doi:10.1007/s00181-005-0249-5

Andreou, A. S., Georgopoulos, E. F., & Likothanassis, S. D. (2002). Exchange-rates forecasting: a hybrid algorithm based on genetically optimized adaptive neural networks. *Computational Economics, 20*(3), 191–210. doi:10.1023/A:1020989601082

Angus, D. (2006). *Ant Colony Optimisation: From Biological Inspiration to an Algorithmic Framework,* (Technical Report n. TR013). Melbourne, Australia: Centre for Intelligent Systems & Complex Processes, Faculty of Information & Communication Technologies, Swinburne University of Technology.

Angus, D., & Woodward, C. (2009). Multiple objective ant colony optimisation. *Swarm Intelligence, 3*(1), 69–85. doi:10.1007/s11721-008-0022-4

Anthony, S. (1989). *Foreign Exchange in Practice*. The Law Book Company Limited.

Aono, M., & Kunii, T. L. (1984). Botanical Tree Image Generation. *IEEE Computer Graphics and Applications, 4*(5), 10–34. doi:10.1109/MCG.1984.276141

Arai, T., Pagello, E., & Parker, L. (2002). Advances in multi-robot systems. *IEEE Transactions on Robotics and Automation, 18*, 655–661.

Areibi, S., & Yang, Z. (2004). Effective memetic algorithms for VLSI design = genetic algorithms + local search + multi-level clustering. *Evolutionary Computation . Special Issue on Memetic Algorithms, 12*(3), 327–353.

Arvind, D. K., & Wong, K. J. (2004). Speckled computing: Disruptive technology for networked information appliances. In *Proceedings of the IEEE International Symposium on Consumer Electronics* (pp. 219-223), UK.

Arvo, J., & Kirk, D. (1988). *Modeling Plants with Environment Sensitive Automata.* Paper presented at the Proceedings of AustGraph '88.

Asmar, D. C., Elshamli, A., & Areibi, S. (2005 July). A Comparative Assessment of ACO Algorithms within a TSP Environment. *Proceedings of the DCDIS 4th International Conference on Engineering Applications and Computational Algorithms* (pp. 27-29), Guelph, Ontario, Canada.

Attrill, M. J., & Rundle, S. D. (2002). Ecotone or ecocline: ecological boundaries in estuaries. *Estuarine, Coastal and Shelf Science, 55*, 929–936. doi:10.1006/ecss.2002.1036

Aulsebrook, W.A., Iscan, M.Y., Slabbert, J.H., & Becker, P. (1995). Superimposition and reconstruction in forensic facial identification: a survey. *Forensic Science International, 75*(2-3), 101–120. doi:10.1016/0379-0738(95)01770-4

Avizienis, A. (1985). The N-version approach to fault-tolerant software. *IEEE Transactions on Software Engineering*, SE-111491–SE-111501.

Aydin, M., Yang, J., & Zhang, J. (2007). Comparative investigation on heuristic optimization of WCDMA radio networks. In *EvoWorkshops 2007 . Lecture Notes in Computer Science, 4448*, 111–120. doi:10.1007/978-3-540-71805-5_12

Bäck, T. (1996). *Evolutionary algorithms in theory and practice*. Oxford University Press.

Bäck, T. (2002). Adaptive business intelligence based on evolution strategies: Some application examples of self-adaptive software. *Information Sciences— Applications . International Journal (Toronto, Ont.), 148*(1-4), 113–121.

Bäck, T., Fogel, D. B., & Michalewicz, Z. (1997). (Eds.) *Handbook of evolutionary computation*. IOP Publishing Ltd and Oxford University Press.

Bäck, T., Fogel, D. B., & Michalewicz, Z. (2000a). *Basic algorithms and operators*. Institute of Physics Publishing. *Evolutionary Computation*, 1.

Bäck, T., Fogel, D. B., & Michalewicz, Z. (2000b). *Advanced algorithms and operators*. Institute of Physics Publishing. *Evolutionary Computation*, 2.

Back, T., Hammel, U., & Schwefel, H.-P. (1997). Evolutionary computation: Comments on the history and current state. *IEEE Transactions on Evolutionary Computation, 1*(1), 3–17. doi:10.1109/4235.585888

Badran, K. M. S., & Rockett, P. I. (2007). The roles of diversity preservation and mutation in preventing population collapse in multiobjective genetic programming. *GECCO '07: Proceedings of the 9th Annual Conference on Genetic and Evolutionary Computation*, (pp. 1551-1558).

Bak, P. (1996). *How Nature Works: The Science of Self-Organized Criticality*. New York, NY: Springer-Verlag.

Ball, M. (1979). Computing network reliability. *Operations Research, 27*(4), 832–836. doi:10.1287/opre.27.4.823

Ballerini, L., Cordón, O., Damas, S., & Santamaría, J. (2008). *Craniofacial superimposition in Forensic identification using genetic algorithms*. Technical Report ECSC AFE 2008-03, European Center for Soft Computing.

Ballerini, L., Cordón, O., Damas, S., Santamaría, J., Alemán, I., & Botella, M. (2007). *Identification by computer aided photographic supra-projection: a survey*. Technical Report AFE 2007-04, European Centre for Soft Computing.

Banerjee, N., & Kumar, R. (2007). Multiobjective network design for realistic traffic models. In *Proceedings of the 9th Annual Conference on Genetic and Evolutionary Computation* (pp. 1904-1911).

Banks, A., Vincent, J., & Anyakoha, C. (2008). A review of particle swarm optimization. Part II: hybridisation, combinatorial, multicriteria and constrained optimization, and indicative applications. *Natural Computing, 6*, 467–484.

Banzhaf, W., Beslon, G., Christensen, S., Foster, J. A., Kepes, F., & Lefort, V. (2006). From artificial evolution to computational evolution: a research agenda. *Nature Reviews. Genetics, 7*, 729–735. doi:10.1038/nrg1921

Banzhaf, W., Nordin, P., Keller, R. E., & Francone, F. D. (1998). *Genetic programming – An introduction on the automatic evolution of computer programs and its application.* Morgan Kaufmann.

Barán, B., & Laufer, F. (1999) Topological optimization of reliable networks using A-Teams. In *Proceedings of World Multiconference on Systemics, Cybernetics and Informatics.*

Barbalet, T. S. (1997). Noble Ape Philosophic. *Noble Ape Website.* Retrieved June 20, 2008, from http://www.nobleape.com/man/philosophic.html

Barbalet, T. S. (2004). Noble ape simulation. *IEEE Computer Graphics and Applications, 24*(2), 6–12. doi:10.1109/MCG.2004.1274054

Barbalet, T. S. (2005a). ApeScript Notes. *Noble Ape Website.* Retrieved June 20, 2008, from http://www.nobleape.com/man/apescript_notes.html

Barbalet, T. S. (2005b). Apple's CHUD Tools, Intel and Noble Ape. *Noble Ape Website.* Retrieved June 20, 2008, from http://www.nobleape.com/docs/on_apple.html

Barbalet, T. S. (2005c). *Original Manuals, Noble Ape 1996-1997.* San Mateo, CA: Cafe Press.

Barbalet, T. S. (2008). Noble Ape Source Code. *Noble Ape Website.* Retrieved June 20, 2008, from http://www.nobleape.com/sim/

Barbalet, T. S., & Daigle, J. P. (2006). Interview with John Daigle. *Biota Podcast.* Retrieved June 20, 2008, from http://www.biota.org/podcast/biota_jdaigle_062506.mp3

Barbalet, T. S., & De Jong, G. (2007). Dawkins, Memetics, Commerce and the Future: Part 2 of 3. *Biota Podcast.* Retrieved June 20, 2008, from http://www.biota.org/podcast/biota_080407.mp3

Barbalet, T. S., & Klein, J. (2006). Interview with Jonathan Klein. *Biota Podcast.* Retrieved June 20, 2008, from http://www.biota.org/podcast/biota_jklein_070806.mp3

Barbalet, T. S., & Stauffer, K. (2006). Interview with Ken Stauffer. *Biota Podcast.* Retrieved June 20, 2008, from http://www.biota.org/podcast/biota_kstauffer_080506.mp3

Barnum, H., Bernstein, H. J., & Spector, L. (2000). Quantum circuits for OR and AND of ORs. *Journal of Physics. A, Mathematical and General, 33*(45), 8047–8057. doi:10.1088/0305-4470/33/45/304

Basiri, M. E., Ghasem-Aghaee, N., & Aghdam, M. H. (2008). Using ant colony optimization-based selected features for predicting post-synaptic activity in proteins. In E. Marchiori & J. H. Moore (Eds.), *Evolutionary Computation, Machine Learning and Data Mining in Bioinformatics* (LNCS 4973, pp. 12-23). Berlin: Springer Verlag.

Batada, N. N., & Hurst, L. D. (2007). Evolution of chromosome organization driven by selection for reduced gene expression noise. *Nature Genetics, 39*, 945–949. doi:10.1038/ng2071

Beaumont, L. J., Hughes, L., & Poulsen, M. (2005). Predicting species distributions: use of climatic parameters in BIOCLIM and its impact on predictions of species' current and future distributions. *Ecological Modelling, 186*(2), 251–270. doi:10.1016/j.ecolmodel.2005.01.030

Bender, A. (2007, October). A Primer on Molecular Similarity in QSAR and Virtual Screening. Part III – Connecting descriptors and experimental measurements – model generation. *QSARWorld Strand Life Sciences,* (pp. 1-4).

Benes, B., & Cordoba, J. A. (2003). *Modeling virtual gardens by autonomous procedural agents.* Paper presented at the Proceedings of the Theory and Practice of Computer Graphics (TPCG'03).

Benes, B., & Millan, E. U. (2002). *Virtual Climbing Plants Competing for Space.* Paper presented at the Proceedings of Computer Animation.

Bentley, P. J. (2005). Investigations into graceful degradation of evolutionary developmental software. *Journal of Natural Computing, 4*, 417–437. doi:10.1007/s11047-005-3666-7

Bentley, P. J. (2007a). Climbing Through Complexity Ceilings. In A. Burke & T. Tierney (Eds.), *Network Practices: New strategies in architecture and design* (pp. 178-197). NJ: Princeton Architectural Press.

Bentley, P. J. (2007b). Systemic computation: A model of interacting systems with natural characteristics. *International Journal of Parallel. Emergent and Distributed Systems, 22*(2), 103–121. doi:10.1080/17445760601042803

Bentley, P. J. (2008). Designing biological computers: Systemic computation and sensor networks. In P. Liò et al (Eds.), *Bio-inspired computing and communication* (LNCS 5151, pp. 352-363). Springer-Verlag.

Bentley, P. J., Greensmith, J., & Ujjin, S. (2005). Two ways to grow tissue for artificial immune systems. In *Proceedings of the Fourth International Conference on Artificial Immune Systems* (LNCS 3627, pp. 139–152). Springer-Verlag.

Besl, P. J., & McKay, N. D. (1992). Iterative point matching for registration of free-form curves and surfaces. *IEEE Transactions on Pattern Analysis and Machine Intelligence, 14*, 239–256. doi:10.1109/34.121791

Biles, J. A. (2001). GenJam: Evolution of a jazz improviser. In P. J. Bentley & D. W. Corne (Eds.), *Creative evolutionary systems* (pp. 165-187). San Francisco: Morgan Kaufmann.

Bilge, Y., Kedici, P., Alakoc, Y. U. K., & Ilkyaz, Y. (2003). The identification of a dismembered human body: a multidisciplinary approach. *Forensic Science International, 137*, 141–146. doi:10.1016/S0379-0738(03)00334-7

Bimbot, F., Magrin-Chagnolleau, I., & Mathan, L. (1995). Second-order statistical measures for text-independent speaker identification. *Speech Communication, 17*(1-2), 177–192. doi:10.1016/0167-6393(95)00013-E

Bjorkman, O. (1968). Further studies on differentiation of photosynthetic properties in sun and shade ecotypes of Solidago virgaurea. *Physiologia Plantarum, 21*, 84–99. doi:10.1111/j.1399-3054.1968.tb07233.x

Blesa, M., & Blum, C. (2004). Ant colony optimization for the maximum edge-disjoint paths problem. In G. R. Raidl (Ed.), *Proceedings of EvoWorkshops 2004.* Lecture Notes in Computer Science 3005, 160-169.

Blesa, M., & Blum, C. (2006). A nature-inspired algorithm for the disjoint paths problem. In *20th International Parallel and Distributed Processing Symposium* (pp. 25-29).

Blesa, M., & Blum, C. (2007). Finding edge-disjoint paths in networks by means of artificial ant colonies. *Journal of Mathematical Modelling and Algorithms, 6*(3), 361–391. doi:10.1007/s10852-007-9060-y

Blickle, T. (1997). *Tournament selection.* In T. Bäck, D. B. Fogel, & Z. Michalewicz (Eds.), *Handbook of Evolutionary Computation*, IOP Publishing Ltd and Oxford University Press, C2.3.

Blickle, T., & Thiele, L. (1996). A comparison of selection schemes used in evolutionary algorithms. *Evolutionary Computation, 4*(4), 361–394. doi:10.1162/evco.1996.4.4.361

Blum, C. (2005). Ant colony optimization: Introduction and recent trends. *Physics of Life Reviews, 2*, 343–373. doi:10.1016/j.plrev.2005.10.001

Blum, C., & Roli, A. (2003). Metaheuristics in combinatorial optimization: Overview and conceptual comparison. *ACM Computing Surveys, 35*(3), 268–308. doi:10.1145/937503.937505

Bolton, B., Alpert, G., Ward, P. S., & Naskrecki, P. (2007). *Bolton's Catalogue of Ants of the World.* Cambridge, Massachusetts: Harvard University Press.

Bonabeau, E., & Theraulaz, G. (2000). Swarm Smarts. *Scientific American, 282*, 72–79.

Bonabeau, E., Dorigo, M., & Theraulaz, G. (1999). *Swarm Intelligence: From Natural to Artificial Systems.* New York, NY: Oxford University Press, Santa Fe Institute Studies in the Sciences of Complexity.

Boryczka, U. (2009). Finding groups in data: Cluster analysis with ants. *Applied Soft Computing, 9*(1), 61–70.

Bowyer, K. W., Chang, K., & Flynn, P. (2006). A survey of approaches and challenges in 3D and multi-modal 3D + 2D face recognition. *Computer Vision and Image Understanding, 101*, 1–15. doi:10.1016/j.cviu.2005.05.005

Brabazon, A., & O'Neill, M. (2004). Evolving trading rules for spot foreign-exchange markets using grammatical evolution. *Computational Management Science, 1*(3-4), 311–327. doi:10.1007/s10287-004-0018-5

Bratton, D., & Kennedy, J. (2007). Defining a standard for particle swarm optimization. *Proceedings of the IEEE Swarm Intelligence Symposium* (pp. 120-127). Honolulu, HI, USA.

Brooks, A. C. (1994, December). Prostate cancer: diagnosis by computer - neural network trained to identify men with prostate cancer and to predict recurrence. *Brief ArticleScience News*. Retrieved February 21 2008, from http://findarticles.com/p/articles/mi_m1200/ is_n23_v146/ai_15972193.

Brothers, D. J. (1999). Phylogeny and evolution of wasps, ants and bees (Hymenoptera, Chrysisoidea, Vespoidea, and Apoidea). *Zoologica Scripta, 28*, 233–249.

Bry, F., Hattori, T., Hiramatsu, K., Okadome, T., Wieser, C., & Yamada, T. (2005). Context modeling in owl for smart building services. In S. Brass & C. Goldberg (Eds.), *Tagungsband zum 17. GI-Workshop über Grundlagen von Datenbanken (17th GI-Workshop on the Foundations of Databases)* (pp. 38–42).

Bui, T., & Zrncic, C. (2006). An ant-based algorithm for finding degree-constrained minimum spanning tree. In *Genetic and Evolutionary Computation Conference* (pp. 11-18).

Bullnheimer, B., Hartl, R. F., & Strauss, C. (1999). A new rank-based version of the ant system: a computational study. *Central European Journal for Operations Research and Economics, 7*(1), 25–38.

Bullnheimer, B., Kotsis, G., & Strauss, C. (1998). Parallelization strategies for the Ant System. In R. De Leone, A. Murli, P. Pardalos, & G. Toraldo (Eds.), *High Performance Algorithms and Software in Nonlinear Optimization, 24*, 87-100. Dordrecht, NL: Kluwer Academic Publishers.

Burke, E. K., & Smith, A. J. (2000). Hybrid evolutionary techniques for the maintenance scheduling problem. *IEEE Transactions on Power Systems, 15*(1), 122–128. doi:10.1109/59.852110

Busby, J. R. (1991). BIOCLIM - A Bioclimatic Analysis and Prediction System. In C. R. Margules & M. P. Austin (Eds.), *Nature Conservation: Cost Effective Biological Surveys and Data Analysis* (pp. 64-68). Canberra: CSIRO.

Bussmann, S., & Schild, K. (2000). Self-organizing manufacturing control: An industrial application of agent technology. *Proceedings of the 4th International Conference on Multi-Agent Systems* (pp. 87-94). Boston, MA, USA.

Cahon, S., Melab, N., & Talbi, E. (2004). ParadisEO: A framework for the reusable design of parallel and distributed metaheuristics. *Journal of Heuristics, 10*(3), 357–380. doi:10.1023/B:HEUR.0000026900.92269.ec

Cahon, S., Melab, N., & Talbi, E.-G. (2004). Building with paradiseo reusable parallel and distributed evolutionary algorithms. *Parallel Computing, 30*(5-6), 677–697. doi:10.1016/j.parco.2003.12.010

Cairns, D. M. (2001). A Comparison of Methods for Predicting Vegetation. *Plant Ecology, 156*, 3–18. doi:10.1023/A:1011975321668

Calégari, P., Guidec, F., Kuonen, P., & Kobler, D. (1997). Parallel island-based genetic algorithm for radio network design. *Journal of Parallel and Distributed Computing, 47*(1), 86–90. doi:10.1006/jpdc.1997.1397

Calégari, P., Guidec, F., Kuonen, P., & Nielsen, F. (2001). Combinatorial optimization algorithms for radio network planning. *Theoretical Computer Science, 263*(1-2), 235–265. doi:10.1016/S0304-3975(00)00245-0

Calégari, P., Guidec, F., Kuonen, P., & Wagner, D. (1997). Genetic approach to radio network optimization for mobile systems. In *IEEE 47th Vehicular Technology Conference, 2*, 755-759.

Camazine, S., Deneubourg, J. L., Franks, N. R., Sneyd, J., Theraulaz, G., & Bonabeau, E. (2001). *Self-Organization in Biological Systems*. Princeton, NJ.: Princeton University Press.

Campbell, J. (1997). Speaker recognition: A tutorial. *Proceedings of the IEEE, 85*(9), 1437–1462. doi:10.1109/5.628714

Canhos, V., Souza, S., Giovanni, R., & Canhos, D. (2004). Global Biodiversity Informatics: setting the scene for a "new world" of ecological forecasting. *Biodiversity Informatics, 1,* 1–13.

Cantu-Paz, E. (2000). *Efficient and Accurate Parallel Genetic Algorithms.* Kluwer.

Caponio, A., Cascella, G. L., Neri, F., Salvatore, N., & Sumner, M. (2007). A fast adaptive memetic algorithm for online and off-line control design of PMSM drives. *IEEE Transactions on System, Man and Cybernetics, Part B . Special Issue on Memetic Algorithms, 37*(1), 28–41.

Caponio, A., Neri, F., & Tirronen, V. (2008). (to appear). Super-fit control adaptation in memetic differential evolution frameworks. *Soft Computing – A Fusion of Foundations . Methodologies and Applications.*

Caprari, G., Estier, T., & Siegwart, R. (2002). Fascination of down scaling – Alice the sugar cube robot. *Journal of Micromechatronics, 1,* 177–189.

Cassill, D. L., Tschinkel, W. R., & Vinson, S. B. (2002). Nest complexity, group size and brood rearing in the fire ant, Solenopsis invicta. *Insectes Sociaux, 49,* 158–163.

Celli, G., Costamagna, E., & Fanni, A. (1995). Genetic algorithms for telecommunication network optimization. In *IEEE International Conference on Systems, Man and Cybernetics, 2,* 1227-1232.

Ch'ng, E. (2007a). Modelling the Adaptability of Biological Systems. *The Open Cybernetics and Systemics Journal, 1,* 13–20.

Ch'ng, E. (2007b). Using Games Engines for Archaeological Visualisation: Recreating Lost Worlds. *11th International Conference on Computer Games: AI, Animation, Mobile, Educational & Serious Games, CGames '07,* (pp. 26-30).

Ch'ng, E., & Stone, R. J. (2006a). *3D Archaeological Reconstruction and Visualization: An Artificial Life Model for Determining Vegetation Dispersal Patterns in Ancient Landscapes.* Paper presented at the Computer Graphics, Imaging and Visualization (CGiV), Sydney, Australia.

Ch'ng, E., & Stone, R. J. (2006b). Enhancing Virtual Reality with Artificial Life: Reconstructing a Flooded European Mesolithic Landscape. *Presence (Cambridge, Mass.), 15*(3). doi:10.1162/pres.15.3.341

Ch'ng, E., Stone, R. J., & Arvanitis, T. N. (2004, 7-10 December 2004). *The Shotton River and Mesolithic Dwellings: Recreating the Past from Geo-Seismic Data Sources.* Paper presented at the The 5th International Symposium on Virtual Reality, Archaeology and Cultural Heritage, VAST04: Interdisciplinarity or "The Best of Both Worlds": The Grand Challenge for Cultural Heritage Informatics in the 21st Century, Brussels, Belgium.

Chan, T., Kwong, S., Man, K., & Tang, K. (2002). Hard handoff minimization using genetic algorithms. *Signal Processing, 82*(8), 1047–1058. doi:10.1016/S0165-1684(02)00213-X

Chang, T. T., & Chang, H. C. (2000). An efficient approach for feducing harmonic voltage distortion in distribution systems with active power line conditioners. *IEEE Transactions on Power Delivery, 15*(3), 990–995. doi:10.1109/61.871364

Chapin, F. S. (1980). The mineral nutrition of wild plants. *Annual Review of Ecology and Systematics, 11,* 233–260. doi:10.1146/annurev.es.11.110180.001313

Chari, R. S., Lowe, R. C., Afdhal, N. H., & Anderson, C. (2008). Clinical manifestations and diagnosis of cholangiocarcinoma. *UpToDate.* Retrieved May 24 2008, from http://www.uptodate.com/patients/content/topic.do?topicKey=gicancer/23806.

Chatterjee, A., Pulasinghe, K., Watanabe, K., & Izumi, K. (2005). A particle-swarm-optimized fuzzy-neural network for voice-controlled robot systems. *IEEE Transactions on Industrial Electronics, 52*(6), 1478–1489. doi:10.1109/TIE.2005.858737

Chellapilla, K., & Fogel, D. (1999). Evolving neural networks to play checkers without relying on Expert Knowledge. *IEEE Transactions on Neural Networks, 10*(6), 1382–1391. doi:10.1109/72.809083

Chellapilla, K., & Fogel, D. (2001). Evolving expert checkers playing program without using human expertise. *IEEE Transactions on Evolutionary Computation, 5*(4), 422–428. doi:10.1109/4235.942536

Chen, H., Perich, F., Finin, T., & Joshi, A. (2004). Soupa: Standard ontology for ubiquitous and pervasive applications. In *Proceedings of the International Conference on Mobile and Ubiquitous Systems: Networking and Services* (pp. 258–267).

Chen, S. H., & Yeh, C. H. (1996). Genetic programming in the coordination game with a chaotic best-response function. In L. J. Fogel, P. J. Angeline & T. Bäck (Eds.), *Evolutionary programming V: Proceedings of the 5th Annual Conference on Evolutionary Programming* (pp. 277-286). Cambridge, MA: The MIT Press.

Chen, W., Zhang, R. T., Cai, Y. M., & Xu, F. S. (2006). Particle swarm optimization for constrained portfolio selection problems. In *Proceedings of the International Conference on Machine Learning and Cybernetics* (pp. 2425-2429). Piscataway, NJ: IEEE Press.

Chena, G., Chenc, S., Guob, W., & Chen, H. (2007). The multi-criteria minimum spanning tree problem based genetic algorithm. *Information Sciences, 177*(22), 5050–5063. doi:10.1016/j.ins.2007.06.005

Cheng, R., & Gen, M. (1997). *Compromise approach-based genetic algorithms for bicriterion shortest path problems.* Technical Report, Ashikaga Institute of Technology.

Cheng, S. (1998). Topological optimization of a reliable communication network. *IEEE Transactions on Reliability, 47*(3), 225–233. doi:10.1109/24.740489

Chidambaran, N. K. (2003). New simulation methodology for risk analysis: genetic programming with monte carlo simulation for option pricing. *WSC '03: Proceedings of the 35th Conference on Winter Simulation,* (pp. 285-292).

Chien, B., Lin, J. Y., & Yang, W. (2004). Learning effective classifiers with z-value measure based on genetic programming. *Pattern Recognition, 37*(10), 1957–1972. doi:10.1016/j.patcog.2004.03.016

Chipcon (2004). *Cc1010 data sheet revision 1.3.* Available at www-mtl.mit.edu/Courses/6.111/labkit/datasheets/CC1010.pdf.

Chou, H., Premkumar, G., & Chu, C.-H. (2001). Genetic algorithms for communications network design - an empirical study of the factors that influence performance. *IEEE Transactions on Evolutionary Computation, 5*(3), 236–249. doi:10.1109/4235.930313

Chow, C., & Liu, C. (1968). Approximating discrete probability distributions with dependence trees. *IEEE Transactions on Information Theory, 14*(3), 462–467. doi:10.1109/TIT.1968.1054142

Chu, C., Premkumar, G., Chou, C., & Sun, J. (1999). Dynamic Degree Constrained Network Design: A Genetic Algorithm Approach. In *Genetic and Evolutionary Computation Conference* (pp. 141-148).

Clarida, R. H., & Taylor, M. P. (1997). The term structure of forward exchange premiums and the forecastability of spot exchange rates: correcting the errors. *The Review of Economics and Statistics, 79*(3), 353–361. doi:10.1162/003465397556827

Clarida, R. H., Sarno, L., Taylor, M. P., & Valente, G. (2003). The out-of-sample success of term structure models as exchange rate predictors: a step beyond. *Journal of International Economics, 60*(1), 61–83. doi:10.1016/S0022-1996(02)00059-4

Clark, J. R., & Benforado, J. (1981). *Wetlands of Bottomland Hardwood Forests.* New York: Elsevier.

Clarkson, D. T., & Hanson, J. B. (1980). The mineral nutrient of higher plants. *Annual Review of Plant Physiology, 31*, 239–298. doi:10.1146/annurev.pp.31.060180.001323

Clarkson, M. J., Rueckert, D., Hill, D. L. G., & Hawkes, D. J. (2001). Using photo-consistency to register 2D optical images of the, human face to a 3D surface model. *IEEE Transactions on Pattern Analysis and Machine Intelligence, 23*(11), 1266–1280. doi:10.1109/34.969117

Cobzas, D. Birkbeck, N., Schmidt, M., Jagersand, M., & Murtha, A. (2007). 3D Variational Brain Tumor Segmentation using a High Dimensional Feature Set. *Workshop on Mathematical Methods in Biomedical Image Analysis,* (pp. 1-8).

Coello Coello, C. A., Luna, E. H., & Aguirre, A. H. (2003). Use of Particle Swarm Optimization to Design Combinational Logic Circuits. In A. M. Tyrrell, P. C. Haddow & J. Torresen (Eds.), *Evolvable Systems: From biology to hardware* (LNCS 2606, pp. 123-130). Berlin: Springer Verlag.

Coello, C. C., Christiansen, A. D., & Aguirre, A. H. (2000). Towards automated evolutionary design of combinational circuits. *Computers & Electrical Engineering, 27*(1), 1–28. doi:10.1016/S0045-7906(00)00004-5

Coello, C. C., Luna, E. H., & Aguirre, A. H. (2004). A comparative study of encodings to design combinational logic circuits using particle swarm optimization. *Proceedings of the NASA/DoD Conference on Evolvable Hardware* (pp. 71–78). Washington, DC: IEEE Computer Society.

Coello, C. C., Zavala, R., Mendoza, B., & Aguirre, A. H. (2002). Automated design of combinational logic circuits using the ant system. *Engineering Optimization, 34*(2), 109–127. doi:10.1080/03052150210918

Colorni, A., Dorigo, M., Maniezzo, V., & Trubian, M. (1994). Ant System for jobshop scheduling. *Belgian Journal of Operations Research. Statistics and Computer Science, 34*, 39–53.

Connell, J. H. (1961). The influence of interspecific competition and other factors on the distribution of the barnacle Chthamalus stellatus. *Ecology, 42*, 710–723. doi:10.2307/1933500

Consoli, S., Moreno-Pérez, J. A., Darby-Dowman, K., & Mladenovic, N. (2007). Discrete Particle Swarm Optimization for the minimum labeling Steiner tree problem. In *II workshop on Nature Inspired Cooperative Strategies for Optimization* (pp. 11-14).

Cooper, G., & Herskovits, E. (1992). A bayesian method for the induction of probabilistic networks from data. *Machine Learning, 9*(4), 309–347.

Cordón, O., Damas, S., & Santamaría, J. (2006a). A fast and accurate approach for 3D image registration using the scatter search evolutionary algorithm. *Pattern Recognition Letters, 27*(11), 1191–1200. doi:10.1016/j.patrec.2005.07.017

Cordón, O., Damas, S., & Santamaría, J. (2006b). Feature-based image registration by means of the CHC evolutionary algorithm. *Image and Vision Computing, 24*(5), 525–533. doi:10.1016/j.imavis.2006.02.002

Cordón, O., Damas, S., & Santamaría, J. (2007). A practical review on the applicability of different EAs to 3D feature-based registration. In S. Cagnoni, E. Lutton, & G. Olague (Eds.), *Genetic and Evolutionary Computation in Image Processing and Computer Vision*, EURASIP Book Series on SP&C (pp. 241–263).

Costa, D., & Hertz, A. (1997). Ants can colour graphs. *The Journal of the Operational Research Society, 48*, 295–305.

Cover, T., & Thomas, J. (1991). *Elements of Information Theory*. John Wiley & Sons.

Cramer, N. L. (1985). A representation for the adaptive generation of simple sequential programs. In *Proceedings of the First International Conference on Genetic Algorithms and Their Applications* (pp. 183–187).

Cranbrook, E. (1987). *Mammals of South-East Asia*. Singapore: Oxford University Press.

Crawley, M. J. (1992). Seed Predators and Plant Population Dynamics. In M. Fenner (Ed.), *Seeds: The Ecology of Regeneration* (2nd ed.): Cabi Publishing.

Crawley, M. J. E. (1986). *Plant Ecology*. Oxford: Blackwell Scientific Publications.

Créput, J.-C., Koukam, A., Lissajoux, T., & Caminada, A. (2005). Automatic mesh generation for mobile network dimensioning using evolutionary approach. *IEEE Transactions on Evolutionary Computation, 9*(1), 18–30. doi:10.1109/TEVC.2004.837923

Crick, F. H., & Orgel, L. E. (1973). Directed Panspermia. *Icarus, 19*, 341–346. doi:10.1016/0019-1035(73)90110-3

Cross, J. W. (2003). *Wearable Computing for Field Archaeology*. The University of Birmingham, UK.

Damer, B. (2008). Demonstration of Noble Ape Simulation at GreyThumb Silicon Valley. *YouTube*. Retrieved June 20, 2008, from http://www.youtube.com/watch?v=YBWxFKv3zBk

Damer, B., Marcelo, K., & Revi, F. (1998). *Nerve Garden: A public terrarium in cyberspace*. Paper presented at the Proceedings of Virtual Worlds and Simulation Conference (VWSIM '99).

Dandan, Z., Guangming, X., Junzhi, Y., & Long, W. (2007). Adaptive task assignment for multiple mobile robots via swarm intelligence approach. *Robotics and Autonomous Systems, 55*(7), 572–588.

Danoy, G., Bouvry, P., & Hogie, L. (2007). Coevolutionary genetic algorithms for Ad hoc injection networks design optimization. In *IEEE Congress on Evolutionary Computation* (pp. 4273-4280).

Darnell, J. E., Lodish, H. F., & Baltimore, D. (1990). *Molecular cell biology.* New York: Scientific American Books.

Darwin, C. (1858). On the tendency of species to form varieties; and on the perpetuation of varieties and species by natural means of selection. I. Extract from an unpublished work on species, II. Abstract of a letter from C. Darwin, Esq., to Prof. Asa Gray. J. *Proc Linn. Soc. London, 3,* 45–53.

Darwin, C. (1859). *The oigin of species by means of natural selection.* London: John Murray.

Das, S., Franguiadakis, T., Papka, M. E., Defanti, T. A., & Sandin, D. J. (1994). A genetic programming application in virtual reality. In *Proceedings of the 1st IEEE Conference on Evolutionary Computation* (pp. 480-484). Piscataway, NJ: IEEE Press.

Davis, A. J., Jenkinson, L. S., Lawton, J. H., Shorrocks, B., & Wood, S. (1998). Making mistakes when predicting shifts in species range in response to global warming. *Nature, 391,* 783–786. doi:10.1038/35842

Davis, M. B., & Shaw, R. G. (2001). Range Shifts and Adaptive Responses to Quaternary Climate Change. *Science, 292,* 673–679. doi:10.1126/science.292.5517.673

Davis, S., & Mermelstein, P. (1980). Comparison of parametric representations for monosyllabic word recognition in continuously spoken sentences. *IEEE Transactions on Acoustics, Speech, and Signal Processing, 28*(4), 357–366. doi:10.1109/TASSP.1980.1163420

Dawid, H. (1999). *Adaptive learning by genetic algorithms: Analytical results and applications to economic models.* Springer Verlag.

Dawkins, R. (1976). *The selfish game.* Oxford University Press.

Dawkins, R. (1987). *The Blind Watchmaker.* New York, NY: Norton.

Day, P., & Nandi, A. K. (2007). Robust text-independent speaker verification using genetic programming. *IEEE Transactions on Audio. Speech and Language Processing, 15*(1), 285–295. doi:10.1109/TASL.2006.876765

de Castro, L. N. (2007). Fundamentals of natural computing: An overview. *Physics of Life Reviews, 4*(1), 1–36. doi:10.1016/j.plrev.2006.10.002

de Vega, F. F., Roa, L. M., Tomassini, M., & Sanchez, J. M. (2000). Medical knowledge representation by means of multipopulation genetic programming: An application to burn diagnosing. In *Proceedings of the 22nd Annual International Conference of the IEEE Engineering in Medicine and Biology Society* (pp. 619-622), Chicago, IL, USA.

Deb, K., Agrawal, S., Pratap, A., & Meyarivan, T. (2000). A Fast Elitist Non-dominated Sorting Genetic Algorithm for Multi-objective Optimisation: NSGA-II. In *Proceedings of the 6th international Conference on Parallel Problem Solving from Nature. Lecture Notes in Computer Science, 1917,* 849–858. doi:10.1007/3-540-45356-3_83

Deeter, D., & Smith, A. (1997) Heuristic optimization of network design considering all-terminal reliability. In *Proceedings Annual Reliability and Maintainability Symposium* (pp. 194-199).

Deeter, D., & Smith, A. (1998). Economic design of reliable networks . *IIE Transactions, 30*(12), 1161–1174.

Degenhard, A., Tanner, C., Hayes, C., Hawkes, D. J., Leach, M. O., & Study, T. U. M. B. S. (2002). Comparison between radiological and artificial neural network diagnosis in clinical screening. *Physiological Measurement, 23*(4), 727–739. doi:10.1088/0967-3334/23/4/311

Delbem, C., de Carvalho, A., Policastro, C., Pinto, A., Honda, K., & García, A. (2004). Node-depth encoding for evolutionary algorithms applied to network design. In *Genetic and Evolutionary Computation Conference . Lecture Notes in Computer Science, 3102,* 678–687.

Deneubourg, J.-L., Aron, S., Goss, S., & Pasteels, J. M. (1990). The self-organizing exploratory pattern of the Argentine ant. *Journal of Insect Behavior, 3,* 159–168.

Dengiz, B., Altiparmak, F., & Smith, A. E. (1997a). Efficient optimization of all-terminal reliable networks, using an evolutionary approach. *IEEE Transactions on Reliability, 46*(1), 18–26. doi:10.1109/24.589921

Dengiz, B., Altiparmak, F., & Smith, A. E. (1997b). Local search genetic algorithm for optimal design of reliable networks. *IEEE Transactions on Evolutionary Computation, 1*(3), 179–188. doi:10.1109/4235.661548

Deussen, O., Hanrahan, P., Lintermann, B., Mech, R., Pharr, M., & Prusinkiewicz, P. (1998). *Realistic modeling and rendering of plant ecosystems.* Paper presented at the Proceedings of SIGGRAPH '98 Annual Conference Series 1998.

Dewdney, A. K. (1984). Computer recreations: In the game called core war hostile programs engage in a battle of bits. *Scientific American, 250*(5), 14–22.

Di Caro, G., & Dorigo, M. (1998). AntNet: Distributed stigmergetic control for communications networks. *Journal of Artificial Intelligence Research, 9*, 317–365.

Di Fatta, G., Lo Presti, G., & Lo Re, G. (2003). A Parallel Genetic Algorithm for the Steiner Problem in Networks. In *Proceedings of the 15th International Conference on Parallel and Distributed Computing and Systems* (pp. 569-573).

Din, D. (2005). Wireless ATM Backbone Network Design Problem. *Transactions on Fundamentals of Electronics, Communications and Computer Sciences . E (Norwalk, Conn.), 88-A*(7), 1777–1785.

Doddington, G., Liggett, W., Martin, A., Przybocki, M., & Reynolds, D. (1998). Sheep, goats, lambs and wolves a statistical analysis of speaker performance in the nist 1998 speaker recognition evaluation. In *Proceedings of the International Conference on Spoken Language Processing*, Paper No. 608.

Doran, B., & Olsen, P. (2001, 24-26 September 2001). *Customizing BIOCLIM to investigate spatial and temporal variations in highly mobile species.* Paper presented at the Proceedings of the 6th International Conference on GeoComputation, University of Queensland, Brisbane, Australia.

Dorigo, M. (1992). *Optimization, learning and natural algorithms.* Doctoral thesis, Politecnico di Milano, Italy.

Dorigo, M., & Blum, C. (2005). Ant colony optimization theory: A survey. *Theoretical Computer Science, 344*(2-3), 243–278.

Dorigo, M., & Gambardella, L. M. (1997). A cooperative learning approach to the traveling salesman problem. *IEEE Transactions on Evolutionary Computation, 1*(1), 53–66. doi:10.1109/4235.585892

Dorigo, M., & Gambardella, L. M. (1997a). Ant colonies for the traveling salesman problem. *Bio Systems, 43*, 73–81.

Dorigo, M., & Gambardella, L. M. (1997b). Ant Colony System: A cooperative learning approach to the traveling salesman problem. *IEEE Transactions on Evolutionary Computation, 1*, 53–66.

Dorigo, M., & Stützle, T. (2002). The Ant Colony Optimization metaheuristic: Algorithms, Applications and Advances. Kluwer Academic Publishers. Glover, F. & Kochenberger, G. (Eds.). *Handbook of Metaheuristics* (pp. 250-285). New York: Springer.

Dorigo, M., Birattari, M., & Stützle, T. (2006). Ant Colony Optimization -Artificial ants as a computational intelligence technique. *IEEE Computational intelligence Magazine, 1*(4), 28-29.

Dorigo, M., Maniezzo, V., & Colorni, A. (1991). *Ant System: An Autocatalytic Optimizing Process.* (Technical Report 91-016). Italy, Milano: Dipartimento di Elettronica e Informazione, Politecnico di Milano.

Dorigo, M., Maniezzo, V., & Colorni, A. (1991). Positive feedback as a search strategy. *Technical report 91-016, Dipartimento di Elettronica e Informatica, Politecnico di Milano.*

Dorigo, M., Maniezzo, V., & Colorni, A. (1996). The Ant System: Optimization by a Colony of Cooperating Agents. *IEEE Transactions on Systems, Man, and Cybernetics–Part B, 26*(1), 29–41.

Dréo, J., & Siarry, P. (2007). Hybrid Continuous Interacting Ant Colony aimed at enhanced global optimization. *Algorithmic Operations Research, 2*, 52–64.

Dror, M., Haouari, M., & Chaouachi, J. (2000). Generalized spanning trees. *European Journal of Operational Research, 120*(3), 583–592. doi:10.1016/S0377-2217(99)00006-5

Duarte, S., & Barán, B. (2001). Multiobjective network design optimisation using parallel evolutionary algorithms. In *XXVII Conferencia Latinoamericana de Informática* (text in Spanish).

Duarte, S., Barán, B., & Benítez, D. (2003). Telecommunication network design with parallel multiobjective evolutionary algorithms. In *Proceedings of IFIP/ACM Latin America Networking Conference* (pp. 1-11).

Dubowsky, S., Lagnemma, K., Liberatore, S., Lambeth, D. M., Plante, J. S., & Boston, P. J. (2005). *A Concept*

Mission: Microbots for Large-Scale Planetary Surface and Subsurface Exploration. Paper presented at the Space Technology and Applications International Forum.

Duin, C., & Voß, S. (2004). Solving group Steiner problems as Steiner problems. *European Journal of Operational Research, 154*(1), 323–329. doi:10.1016/S0377-2217(02)00707-5

Duncan, B. S., & Olson, A. J. (1996). Applications of evolutionary programming for the prediction of protein-protein iInteractions. In L. J. Fogel, P. J. Angeline & T. Bäck (Eds.), *Evolutionary programming V: Proceedings of the 5th Annual Conference on Evolutionary Programming* (pp. 411-417). Cambridge, MA: The MIT Press.

Dzeroski, S., de Raedt, L., & Driessens, K. (2001). Relational reinforcement learning. *Machine Learning, 43,* 7–52. doi:10.1023/A:1007694015589

Ebert, D., & Singer, M. (2004). GIS, Predictive Modelling, Erosion, Site Monitoring. *Assemblage,* 8.

Ebling, M., Di Loreto, M., Presley, M., Wieland, F., & Jefferson, D. (1989). An Ant Foraging Model Implemented On the Time Warp Operating System. In Unger, B. & Fujimoto, R. (Eds.), *Proceedings of the SCS Multiconference on Distributed Simulation* (pp. 21-26). San Diego, CA: Society For Computer Simulation.

Edmonds, B. (1998). Meta-genetic programming: *Co-evolving the operators of variation (CPM Report 98-32).* Aytoun St., Manchester, M1 3GH. UK: Centre for Policy Modelling, Manchester Metropolitan University, UK.

Eiben, A. E., & Smith, J. E. (2003). *Introduction to evolutionary computation.* Springer Verlag.

Eichardt, R., Haueisen, J., Knosche, T. R., & Schukat-Talamazzini, E. G. (2008). Reconstruction of multiple neuromagnetic sources using augmented evolution strategies – A comparative study. *IEEE Transactions on Bio-Medical Engineering, 55*(2), 703–712. doi:10.1109/TBME.2007.912656

Elhaggaz, S., Ghassempoory, M., & Brown, J. (2002). A reliable phased network topology design using evolutionary algorithm. In *Student Conference on Research and Development* (pp. 253-256).

Ellis, D. (1996). *Prediction-driven Computational Auditory Scene Analysis.* Ph.D. Dissertation, Department of Electrical Engineering and Computer Science, MIT.

Emmeche, C. (1991). *The Garden in the Machine.* Princeton, NJ: Princeton University Press.

Encarnacao, J. L., & Kirste, T. (2005). Ambient intelligence: Towards smart appliances ensembles. In *From Integrated Publication and Information Systems to Information and Knowledge Environments*, volume 3379 of *Lecture Notes in Computer Science* (pp. 261–270). Springer-Verlag.

Engelbrecht, A. (2006). *Fundamentals of Computationial Swarm Intelligence.* John Wiley.

Ercal, F., Chawla, A., Stoecker, W. V., Lee, H.-C., & Moss, R. H. (1994). Neural network diagnosis of malignant melanoma from color images. *IEEE Transactions on Bio-Medical Engineering, 41*(9), 837–845. doi:10.1109/10.312091

Eriksson, D. (1997). A principal exposition of Jean-Louis Le Moigne's systemic theory. *Review Cybernetics and Human Knowing, 4*(2-3), 35–77.

Eshelman, L. (1991). The CHC adaptive search algorithm: how to have safe search when engaging in non-traditional genetic recombination. In *Foundations of Genetic Algorithms* (pp. 265-283).

Eshelman, L. J. (1993). Real-coded genetic algorithms and interval schemata. In L. D. Whitley (Ed.), *Foundations of Genetic Algorithms 2*, (pp. 187–202) Morgan Kaufmann, San Mateo.

Etemadi, H., Rostamy, A. A. A., & Dehkordi, H. F. (2009). A genetic programming model for bankruptcy prediction: Empirical evidence from Iran. *Expert Systems with Applications, 36*(2), 3199–3207. doi:10.1016/j.eswa.2008.01.012

Ettershank, G. (1971). Some aspects of the ecology and nest microclimatology of the meat ant, Iridomyrmex purpureus (Sm). *Royal Society of Victoria Proceedings, 84,* 137–151.

Etterson, J. R., & Shaw, R. G. (2001). Constraint to adaptive evolution in response to global warming. *Science, 294,* 151–154. doi:10.1126/science.1063656

Evkli, Z., & Sevilgen, E. E. (2008). A Hybrid Particle Swarm Optimization Algorithm for Function Optimization. *Applications of Evolutionary Computing, 4974,* 585–595.

Ezzaidi, H., Rouat, J., & O'Shaughnessy, D. (2001). Towards combining pitch and mfcc for speaker identification systems. In *Proceedings of Eurospeech* (pp. 2825–2828).

Fanjul-Moles, M. L. (2006). Antennal olfactory sensitivity in response to task-related odours of three castes of the ant Atta mexicana (hymenoptera: formicidae). *Physiological Entomology, 31*, 353–360.

Farmer, D., & Packard, N. (1986). Evolution, Games, and Learning: Models for Adaptations in Machines and Nature. *Physica D. Nonlinear Phenomena, 22D*(1).

Farrell, K. R., Mammone, R. J., & Assaleh, K. T. (1994). Speaker recognition using neural networks and conventional classifiers. *IEEE Transactions on Speech and Audio Processing, 2*(1), 194–205. doi:10.1109/89.260362

Ferrer, G. J., & Martin, W. N. (1995). Using genetic programming to evolve board evaluation functions. In *Proceedings of the IEEE International Conference on Evolutionary Computation* (pp. 747-752). Piscataway, NJ: IEEE Press.

Ferrer, L., Bratt, H., Gadde, V. R. R., Kajarekar, S., Shriberg, E., Sšonmez, K., et al. (2003). Modeling duration patterns for speaker recognition. In *Proceedings of the Eurospeech* (pp. 2017–2020).

Fieldsend, J. E., & Singh, S. (2002). A multi-objective algorithm based upon particle swarm optimisation, an efficient data structure and turbulence. *Proceedings of the Workshop on Computational Intelligence* (pp. 34-44). Birmingham, UK.

Filippone, M., Camastra, F., Masulli, F., & Rovetta, S. (2008). A survey of kernel and spectral methods for clustering. *Pattern Recognition, 41*, 176–190.

Firbank, F. G., & Watkinson, A. R. (1985). A model of interference within plant monocultures. *Journal of Theoretical Biology, 116*, 291–311. doi:10.1016/S0022-5193(85)80269-1

Firpi, H., Goodman, E., & Echauz, J. (2005). On prediction of epileptic seizures by computing multiple genetic programming artificial features. In M. Keijzer *et al.* (Eds.), *Proceedings of the 8th European Conference on Genetic Programming* (LNCS 3447, pp. 321-330). Berlin: Springer Verlag.

Fisher, J. B. (1977). How predictive are computer simulations of tree architecture. *International Journal of Plant Sciences, 153 (suppl.)*(1992), 137-146.

Fisher, R. A., & Marshall, M. (1988). *Iris plants database*. UCI Machine Learning Repository [http://www.ics.uci.edu/mlearn/MLRepository.html]

Fisher, W., Doddington, G., & Goudie-Marshall, K. (1986). The darpa speech recognition research database: Specification and status. In *Proceedings of the DARPA Speech Recognition Workshop* (pp. 93–100).

Fitter, A. H., & Haw, R. K. M. (1981). *Environmental Physiology of Plants*. London: Academic Press.

Flood, I. (2001). Neural networks in civil engineering: A review. In B. H. V. Topping (Ed.), *Civil and structural engineering computing: 2001* (pp. 185-209). Saxe-Coburg Publications.

Fogel, D. B. (1995). *Evolutionary Computation: Toward A New Philosophy of Machine Intelligence*. IEEE Press, Piscataway, NJ, USA.

Fogel, D. B., Wasson, E. C., Boughton, E. M., & Porto, V. W. (1998). Evolving artificial neural networks for screening features from mammograms. *Artificial Intelligence in Medicine, 14*(3), 317–326. doi:10.1016/S0933-3657(98)00040-2

Fogel, G., & Corne, D. (2003). *Evolutionary computation in bioinformatics*. Morgan Kaufmann Publishers.

Fogel, L. J., Owens, A. J., & Walsh, M. J. (1965). Artificial intelligence through a smulation of the evolution. In A. M. Maxfield & L. J. Fogel (Eds.), *Biophysics and cybernetics systems* (pp. 131-156). Washington, DC: Spartan Book Co.

Fogel, L. J., Owens, A. J., & Walsh, M. J. (1996). *Artificial intelligence through simulated evolution*. John Wiley & Sons, Inc.

Folino, G., Pizzuti, C., Spezzano, G., Vanneschi, V., & Tomassini, M. (2003). Diversity analysis in cellular and multipopulation genetic programming. In *Proceedings of the IEEE Congress on Evolutionary Computation* (pp. 305–311).

Fonseca, C., & Fleming, P. (1993). Genetic algorithms for multiobjective optimization: Formulation, discussion and generalization. In *Proceedings of the 5ᵗʰ International Genetic Algorithms Conference* (pp. 416–423).

Forbes, M. G., & Kenneth, D. W. (2002). Ant sting mortality in Australia. *Toxicon, 40*, 1095–1100.

Freeland, S. J., Wu, T., & Keulmann, N. (2003). The case for an error minimizing genetic code. *Origins of Life and Evolution of the Biosphere, 33*(4/5), 457–477. doi:10.1023/A:1025771327614

Freitas, A. A. (2001). Understanding the crucial role of attribute interaction in data mining. *Artificial Intelligence Review, 16*(3), 177–199. doi:10.1023/A:1011996210207

Freitas, A. A. (2002). *Data mining and knowledge discovery with evolutionary algorithms.* Secaucus, NJ, USA: Springer-Verlag New York, Inc.

Fujita, H., Katafuchi, T., Uehara, T., & Nishimura, T. (1992). Application of Artificial Neural Network to Computer-Aided Diagnosis of Coronary Artery Disease in Myocardial SPECT Bull's-eye Images. *Journal of Nuclear Medicine, 33*(2), 272–276.

Furlong, J., Dupuy, M., & Heinsimer, J. (1991). Neural Network Analysis of Serial Cardiac Enzyme Data. *American Journal of Clinical Pathology, 96*(1), 134–141.

Fyfe, R. (2005). GIS and the application of a model of pollen deposition and dispersal: a new approach to testing landscape hypotheses using the POLLANDCAL models. *Journal of Archaeological Science, XXXIII*(4), 1–11.

Gadagkar, R. (1993). And now: eusocial thrips! *Current Science, 64*, 215–216.

Gajpal, Y., & Rajendran, C. (2006). An ant-colony optimization algorithm for minimizing the completion-time variance of jobs in flowshops. *International Journal of Production Economics, 101*, 259–272.

Gambardella, L. M., Taillard, E. D., & Agazzi, G. (1999). A multiple ant colony system for vehicle routing problems with time windows. In D. Corne & M. Dorigo & F. Glover (Eds.), *New Ideas in Optimization* (pp.63-76). London: McGraw Hill.

Gamvros, I., Golden, B., & Raghavan, S. (2003). An Evolutionary Approach to the Multi-Level Capacitated Minimum Spanning Tree problem. In G. Anandalingam & S. Raghavan (Ed.), *Telecommunications Network Design and Management.* Boston, USA: Kluwer Academic Press.

Gamvros, I., Golden, B., Raghavan, S., & Stanojevic, D. (2005). Heuristic Search for Network Design. In H. Greenberg (Ed.), *Tutorials on Emerging Methodologies and Applications in Operations Research.* New York: Springer.

Garcia-Martinez, C., Cordon, O., & Herrera, F. (2007). A Taxonomy and an Empirical Analysis of Multiple Objective Ant Colony Optimization Algorithms for Bicriteria TSP. *European Journal of Operational Research, 180*(1), 116–148.

Garrett, J. H., Case, M. P., Hall, J. W., Yerramareddy, S., Herman, A., & Sun, R. F. (1993). Engineering applications of neural networks. *Journal of Intelligent Manufacturing, 4*(1), 1–21. doi:10.1007/BF00124977

Gen, M., & Cheng, R. (2003). Evolutionary network design: Hybrid genetic algorithms approach. *International Journal of Computational Intelligence and Applications, 3*(4), 357–380. doi:10.1142/S1469026803001075

Gen, M., & Lin, L. (2004). Multiobjective hybrid genetic algorithm for bicriteria network design problem. In *The 8ᵗʰ Asia Pacific Symposium on Intelligent and Evolutionary Systems.*

Gen, M., & Lin, L. (2005). Multi-objective hybrid genetic algorithm for bicriteria network design problem. *Complexity International, 11*, 73–83.

Gen, M., Cheng, R., & Oren, S. (2001). Network Design Techniques using Adapted Genetic Algorithms. *Advances in Engineering Software, 32*(9), 731–744. doi:10.1016/S0965-9978(01)00007-2

Gen, M., Cheng, W., & Wang, D. (1997). Genetic algorithms for solving shortest path problems. In *Proceedings of IEEE International Conference on Evolutionary Computation* (pp. 401–406).

Gen, M., Ida, K., & Kim, J. (1998). A spanning tree-based genetic algorithm for bicriteria topological network design. In *Proceedings of IEEE International Conference on Evolutionary Computation,* (pp.15-20).

Gen, M., Lin, L., & Cheng, R. (2004). Bicriteria Network Optimization Problem using Priority-based Genetic Algorithm. *IEEJ Transactions on Electronics . Information Systems, 124-C*(10), 1972–1978.

Gendreau, M., Larochelle, J., & Sansó, B. (1999). A tabu search heuristic for the Steiner tree problem. *Networks, 34*(2), 162–172. doi:10.1002/(SICI)1097-0037(199909)34:2<162::AID-NET9>3.0.CO;2-9

Ghosh, A.K., & Sinha, P. (2001). An economised craniofacial identification system. *Forensic Science International, 117*(1-2), 109–119. doi:10.1016/S0379-0738(00)00454-0

Glover, F., & Kochenberger, G. (2003). *Handbook of Metaheuristics*. Boston: Kluwer.

Goldberg, D. E. (1989). *Genetic Algorithms in Search, Optimization and Machine Learning*. Addison-Wesley Longman Publishing Co., Inc., Boston, MA, USA.

Goldberg, D. E. (2002). *The design of innovation: lessons from and for competent genetic algorithms*. Boston: Kluwer Academic.

Golden, B., Raghavan, S., & Stanojevic, D. (2008). The prize-collecting generalized minimum spanning tree problem. *Journal of Heuristics, 14*(1), 69–93. doi:10.1007/s10732-007-9027-1

Goldstein, J. (1999). Emergence as a Construct . *History and Issues, 1*(1), 49–72.

Gonzalez, R., & Woods, R. (2002). *Digital image processing* (2nd Edition)., Upper Saddle River, NJ: Prentice Hall.

Goos, M. I., Alberink, I. B., & Ruifrok, A. C. (2006). 2D/3D image (facial) comparison using camera matching. *Forensic Science International, 163*, 10–17. doi:10.1016/j.forsciint.2005.11.004

Gopalan, K., Anderson, T., & Cupples, E. (1999). A comparison of speaker identification results using features based on cepstrum and fourier-bessel expansion. *IEEE Transactions on Speech and Audio Processing, 7*(3), 289–294. doi:10.1109/89.759036

Gordon, R. (1999). *Ants at Work: How an Insect Society is Organized*. New York: Free Press.

Gotwald, W. H., & Burdette, A. W. (1981). Morphology of the male internal reproductive system in army ants: phylogenetic implications (Hymenoptera: Formicidae).

Proceedings of the Entomological Society of Washington, 83, 72–92.

Govil, J., Govil, J., & Nandra, A. (2008). An Insight into Swarm Intelligence for adapting to Business and Technology. *Proceedings of the IEEE Region 5 Conference* (pp. 1-5). India, Delhi: Maharshi Dayanand University.

Grassé, P. P. (1959). La reconstruction du nid et les coordinations interindividuelles chez Belicositermes natalensis et Cubitermes sp. La théorie de la Stigmergie: Essai d'interprétation du comportement des termites constructeurs. *Insectes Sociaux, 6*, 41–80.

Greene, C. S., White, B. C., & Moore, J. H. (2007). An expert knowledge-guided mutation operator for genome-wide genetic analysis using genetic programming. *Lecture Notes in Bioinformatics, 4774*, 30–40.

Greene, C. S., White, B. C., & Moore, J. H. (2008a). Ant colony optimization for genome-wide genetic analysis. *Lecture Notes in Computer Science, 5217*, 37–47. doi:10.1007/978-3-540-87527-7_4

Greene, C. S., White, B. C., & Moore, J. H. (2008b). Using expert knowledge in initialization for genome-wide analysis of epistasis using genetic programming. *Gecco '08: Proceedings of the 10th annual conference on genetic and evolutionary computation* (pp. 351–352). New York, NY, USA: ACM.

Greene, N. (1989). *Voxel Space Automata: Modelling with Stochastic Growth Processes in Voxel Space.* Paper presented at the Proceedings of SIGGRAPH '89 Annual Conference Series.

Greene, N. (1991). *Detailing tree skeletons with voxel automata.* Paper presented at the SIGGRAPH '91, Course Notes on Photorealistic Volume Modeling and Rendering Techniques.

Grime, J. P., Hodgson, J. G., & Hunt, R. (1988). *Comparative Plant Ecology: A functional approach to common British species*. London: Unwin Hyman Ltd.

Groß, R., Bonani, M., Mondada, F., & Dorigo, M. (2006). Autonomous Self-Assembly in Swarm-Bots. *IEEE Transactions on Robotics, 22*(6), 1115–1130.

Guisan, A., & Zimmermann, N. E. (2000). Predictive habitat distribution models in ecology. *Ecological Modelling, 135*, 147–186. doi:10.1016/S0304-3800(00)00354-9

Guntsch, M., & Middendorf, M. (2002). Applying Population Based ACO to Dynamic Optimization Problems. Springer Verlag. In Dorigo, M. and Di Caro, G. & Sampels, M. (Eds.), *Proceedings of the Third International Workshop on Ant Algorithms* (pp. 111-122), Brussels, Belgium.

Guo, H., Jack, L. B., & Nandi, A. K. (2005). Feature generation using genetic programming with application to fault classification. *IEEE Transactions on Systems, Man, and Cybernetics . Part B, 35*(1), 89–99.

Gutowitz, H. (1991). Cellular automata: Theory and experiment. *Physica D. Nonlinear Phenomena, 45*, 1–3.

Hamilton, W. D., Axelrod, R., & Tanese, R. (1990). Sexual reproduction as an adaptation to resist parasites (A review). *Proceedings of the National Academy of Sciences of the United States of America, 87*(9), 3566–3573. doi:10.1073/pnas.87.9.3566

Han, L., & Wang, Y. (2005). A New Genetic Algorithm for the Degree-Constrained Minimum Spanning Tree Problem. In *Proceedings of 2005 IEEE International Workshop on VLSI Design and Video Technology* (pp. 125-128).

Hanan, J., Prusinkiewicz, P., Zalucki, M., & Skirvin, D. (2002). Simulation of insect movement with respect to plant architecture and morphogenesis. *Computers and Electronics in Agriculture, 35*(2-3), 255–269. doi:10.1016/S0168-1699(02)00022-4

Handl, J., & Meyer, B. (2002). Improved ant-based clustering and sorting in document retrieval interface. *Proceedings of the Seventh International Conference on Parallel Problem Solving from Nature* (pp. 913-923). LNCS 2439, Berlin: Springer.

Handl, J., Knowles, J., & Dorigo, M. (2003). *Ant-based clustering: a comparative study of its relative performance with respect to k-means, average link and 1d-som.* (Technical Report TR/IRIDIA/2003-24. IRIDIA), Belgium: Université Libre de Bruxelles.

Handl, J., Knowles, J., & Dorigo, M. (2006). Ant-based clustering and topographic mapping. *Artificial Life, 12*, 35–61.

Hansen, N., & Ostermeier, A. (2001). Completely derandomized self-adaptation in evolution strate-gies. *Evolutionary Computation, 9*(2), 159–195. doi:10.1162/106365601750190398

Harris, R. A., Graham, P., & Collett, T. S. (2007). Visual cues for the retrieval of landmark memories by navigating wood ants. *Current Biology, 17*, 93–102.

Heinze, J., & Keller, L. (2000). Alternative reproductive strategies: a queen perspective in ants. *Trends in Ecology & Evolution, 15*(12), 508–512.

Helwig, S., & Wanka, R. (2007). Particle swarm optimization in high-dimensional bounded search spaces. *Proceedings of the IEEE Swarm Intelligence Symposium* (pp. 198-205). Honolulu, HI, USA.

Hermansky, H. (1990). Perceptual linear prediction (plp) analysis for speech. *The Journal of the Acoustical Society of America, 87*, 1738–1752. doi:10.1121/1.399423

Herrera, F., Lozano, M., & Verdegay, J. L. (1998). Tackling real-coded genetic algorithms: operators and tools for the behavioral analysis. *Artificial Intelligence Review, 12*(4), 265–319. doi:10.1023/A:1006504901164

Herrero, J. G., Portas, J. A. B., de Jesús, A. B., López, J. M. M., de Miguel Vela, G., & Corredera, J. R. C. (2003). Application of evolution strategies to the design of tracking filters with a large number of specifications. *EURASIP Journal on Applied Signal Processing*, (8), 766–779. doi:10.1155/S1110865703302057

Hexapode, 2004. Université Laval, Faculté des Sciences et de Génie, Département de Génie mécanique, Laboratoire de robotique. Extracted in June 2008 from *http:/*www.robot.gmc.ulaval.ca.).

Hibbert, E. G., & Dalby, P. A. (2005). Directed evolution strategies for improved enzymatic performance. *Microbial Cell Factories, 4*, 29. doi:10.1186/1475-2859-4-29

Hinton, G. E. (1989). Deterministic Boltzmann learning performs steepest descent in weight-space. *Neural Computation, 1*, 143–150. doi:10.1162/neco.1989.1.1.143

Holland, J. H. (1973). Genetic algorithms and the optimal allocation of the trials. *SIAM Journal on Computing, 2*, 88–105. doi:10.1137/0202009

Holland, J. H. (1975). *Adaptation in natural and artificial systems.* Ann Arbor, MI: University of Michigan Press.

Holland, J. H. (1992a). *Adaptation in natural and artificial systems: An introductory analysis with applications to biology, control, and artificial intelligence.* The MIT Press. Holland, J. H. (1992b). Genetic algorithms. *Scientific American, 278,* 66–72.

Holland, J. H. (1995). *Hidden Order: How adaptation builds complexity.* Reading, MA: Helix Books, Addison-Wesley Publishing.

Holland, J. H. (1998). *Emergence from Chaos to order.* Oxford: Oxford University Press.

Hölldobler, B., & Wilson, E. O. (1990). *The ants.* Cambridge, Massachussets: Harvard University Press.

Holton, M. (1994). Strands, Gravity and Botanical Tree Imagery. *Computer Graphics Forum, 13*(I), 57–67. doi:10.1111/1467-8659.1310057

Honda, H. (1971). Description of the form of trees by the parameters of the tree-like body: Effects of the branching angle and the branch length on the shape of the tree-like body. *Journal of Theoretical Biology, 31,* 331–338. doi:10.1016/0022-5193(71)90191-3

Honda, H., Tomlinson, P. B., & Fisher, J. B. (1981). Computer simulation of branch interaction and regulation by unequal flow rates in botanical trees. *American Journal of Botany, 68,* 569–585. doi:10.2307/2443033

Hopfield, J. J. (1982). Neural networks and physical systems with emergent collective computational abilities. *Proceedings of the National Academy of Sciences of the United States of America, 79*(8), 2554–2558. doi:10.1073/pnas.79.8.2554

Horning, J. J., Lauer, H. C., Melliar-Smith, P. M., & Randell, B. (1974). A program atructure for error detection and recovery. In *Proceedings of an International Symposium on Operating Systems* (LNCS 16, pp. 171-187). Springer-Verlag.

Hou, Y.-H., Wu, Y.-W., Lu, L.-J., & Xiong, X.-Y. (2002). Generalized ant colony optimization for economic dispatch of power systems. *Power System Technology, 1,* 225–229.

Howarth, L., & Evans, C. (1984). *Write Your Own Fantasy Games for Your Microcomputer.* London: Usborne.

Howe, H. F. (1990). Seed dispersal by birds and mammals: Implications for seedling demography. In K. S. Bawa & M. Hadley (Eds.), *Reproductive Ecology of Tropical Forest Plants* (Vol. 7, pp. 191-218): Taylor & Francis Ltd.

Hu, X. M., Zhang, J., & Li, Y. (2008). Protein Folding in Hydrophobic-Polar Lattice Model: A Flexible Ant-Colony Optimization Approach. *Protein and Peptide Letters, 15*(5), 469–477.

Hu, X., Eberhart, R. C., & Shi, Y. (2003). Engineering optimization with particle swarm. In *Proceedings of the IEEE Swarm Intelligence Symposium* (pp. 53-57). Piscataway, NJ: IEEE Press.

Huang, F. Y., Li, R. J., Liu, H. X., & Li, R. (2006). A modified particle swarm algorithm combined with fuzzy neural network with application to financial risk early warning. In *Proceedings of the IEEE Asia-Pacific Conference on Services Computing* (pp. 168-173). Washington, DC: IEEE Computer Society.

Huang, H. T., & Yang, P. (1987). The Ancient Cultured Citrus Ant. *Bioscience, 37,* 665–671.

Huang, R., Tsuboi, E., & Ma, J. (1997). A Parallel Distributed Genetic Algorithm for Designing 3-connectivity Communication Networks. In *Proceedings of the International Conference on Parallel and Distributed Computing and Systems* (pp. 501-506).

Huang, S.-J. (2001). Enhancement of hydroelectric generation scheduling using ant colony system based optimization approaches. *IEEE Transactions on Energy Conversion, 16,* 296–301.

Hughes, E. J. (2003). Multi-objective binary search optimisation. In C. M. Fonseca (Eds.), *Evolutionary Multi-Criterion Optimization* (pp. 72-87). LNCS 2632, Berlin, Germany: Springer-Verlag.

Hutchison, W. R., & Stephens, K. R. (1987). The airline marketing tactician (AMT): A commercial application of adaptive networking. In *Proceedings of the 1ˢᵗ IEEE International Conference on Neural Networks* (pp. 753-756). Piscataway, NJ: IEEE Press.

Huth, A., & Wissel, C. (1992). The simulation of the movement of fish schools. *Journal of Theoretical Biology, 156,* 365–385. doi:10.1016/S0022-5193(05)80681-2

Ibáñez, O., Cordón, O., Damas, S., & Santamaría, J. (2008). Craniofacial superimposition by means of genetic algorithms and fuzzy location of cephalometric landmarks. *Hybrid Artificial Intelligence Systems, LNAI, 5271*, 599–607. doi:10.1007/978-3-540-87656-4_74

Ippolito, A. M., Laurentiis, M. D., Rosa, G. L. L., Eleuteri, A., Tagliaferri, R., & Placido, S. D. (2004). Immunostaining for Met/HGF Receptor May be Useful to Identify Malignancies in Thyroid Lesions Classified Suspicious at Fine-Needle Aspiration Biopsy. *Thyroid, 14*(12), 1065–1071. doi:10.1089/thy.2004.14.1065

Isaaman, D., & Tyler, J. (1982). *Computer Spacegames.* London: Usborne.

Iscan, M. Y. (1993). Introduction to techniques for photographic comparison. In M. Y. Iscan, & R. Helmer (Eds.), *Forensic Analysis of the Skull* (pp. 57-90). Wiley. Laguna, M., & Martí, R. (2003). *Scatter search: methodology and implementations in C.* Kluwer Academic Publishers.

Ishibuchi, H., Yoshida, T., & Murata, T. (2003). Balance between genetic search and local search in memetic algorithms for multi-objective permutation flow shop scheduling. *IEEE Transactions on Evolutionary Computation, 7*(2), 204–223. doi:10.1109/TEVC.2003.810752

Islas, E., Coello, C. C., & Aguirre, A. H. (2005). Extraction and reuse of design patterns from genetic algorithms using case-based reasoning. *Soft Computing–A Fusion of Foundations . Methodologies and Applications, 9*(1), 44–53.

Itoh, H., & Nakamura, K. (2004). Towards Learning to learn and plan by relational reinforcement learning. *Proceedings of the Workshop on Relational Reinforcement Learning* (pp. 34-39). Banff, Alberta, Canada.

Jan, B., & Dirk, O. (1999). *SEMIFAR Forecasts, with Applications to Foreign Exchange Rates.* Center of Finance and Econometrics, University of Konstanz.

Jeyakumar, A., Baskaran, K., & Sumathy, V. (2003). Genetic algorithm for optimal design of delay bounded WDM multicast networks. In *Conference on Convergent Technologies for Asia-Pacific Region* (pp. 1224-1228).

Johnson, M. A., & Kendall, G. Cote, P.J., & Meisel, L.V. (1995). Neural Networks in Seizure Diagnosis. *Report no. A926592 (Army Armament Research Development and*

Engineering Center Watervliet NY Benet Labs). Retrieved February 21 2008, from http://www.stormingmedia. us/92/9265/A926592.html.

Johnson, S. (2002). *Emergence: The Connected Lives of Ants, Brains, Cities, and Software.* Sribner.

Jones, D., Schonlau, M., & Welch, W. (1998). Efficient global optimization of expensive black-box functions. *Journal of Global Optimization, 13*, 455–492. doi:10.1023/A:1008306431147

Joshi, R., & Sanderson, A. C. (1999). Minimal representation multisensor fusion using differential evolution. *IEEE Transactions on Systems, Man and Cybernetics . Part A, 29*(1), 63–76.

Kadrovach, B. A., & Lamont, G. (2002). A particle swarm model for swarm-based networked sensor systems. In *Proceedings of the ACM Symposium on Applied Computing* (pp. 918-924). New York: ACM Press.

Kajitani, I., Murakawa, M., Nishikawa, D., Yokoi, H., Kajihara, N., Iwata, M., et al. (1999). An evolvable hardware chip for prosthetic hand controller. In *Proceedings of the 7th International Conference on Microelectronics for Neural, Fuzzy and Bio-inspired Systems* (pp. 179-186). Washington, DC: IEEE Computer Society.

Kalganova, T. (2000). Bidirectional incremental evolution in extrinsic evolvable hardware. *Proceedings of the 2nd NASA/DoD Workshop on Evolvable Hardware* (pp. 65–74). Washington, DC: IEEE Computer Society.

Kampstra, P., van der Mei, R. D., & Eiben, A. (2006). *Evolutionary Computing in Telecommunication Network Design: A Survey.* Unpublished paper, Vrije Universiteit Amsterdam. Retrieved May 21, 2008 from www.cs.vu. nl/~mei/articles/2006/kampstra/art.pdf.

Kandel, E. R., Schwartz, J. H., & Jessel, T. M. (1991). (Eds.). *Principles of neural science* (3rd Edition).New York: Elsevier.

Kari, L., & Rozenberg, G. (2008). The many facets of natural computing. *Communications of the ACM, 51*(10), 72–83. doi:10.1145/1400181.1400200

Karr, C. L., & Freeman, L. M. (1998). *Industrial applications of genetic algorithms.* CRC Press.

Katangur, A. K., Akkaladevi, S., Pan, Y., & Fraser, M. D. (2005). Routing in optical multistage interconnection networks with limited crosstalk using Ant Colony Optimization. *International Journal of Foundations of Computer Science, 16*(2), 301–320.

Kauffman, S. A. (1993). *The Origins of Order: Self-Organization and Selection in Evolution.* Oxford: Oxford University Press.

Kauffman, S. A. (1996). *At Home in the Universe: The search for laws of complexity.* Harmondsworth: Penguin.

Kaye, P., Laflamme, R., & Mosca, M. (2007). *An introduction to quantum computing.* Oxford University Press.

Keller, E. F., & Segel, L. A. (1970). Initiation of Slime Mold Aggregation Viewed as an Instability. *Journal of Theoretical Biology, 26*, 399–415. doi:10.1016/0022-5193(70)90092-5

Kennedy, J., & Eberhart, R. C. (1995). Particle swarm optimization. *Proceedings of the IEEE International Conference on Neural Networks* (pp. 1942-1948). Perth, Australia.

Kennedy, J., & Eberhart, R. C. (1995). Particle swarm optimization. In *Proceedings of IEEE International Conference on Neural Networks* (pp. 1942-1948). Piscataway, NJ: IEEE Press.

Kennedy, J., & Eberhart, R. C. (2001). *Swarm Intelligence.* Morgan Kaufmann.

KHosraviani. B., Levitt, R. E., & Koza, J. R. (2004). *Organization design optimization using genetic programming.* Late Breaking Papers at the 2004 Genetic and Evolutionary Computation, Seattle, Washington, USA.

Kim, K. C. (1993). Biodiversity, conservation and inventory: why insects matter. *Biodiversity and Conservation, 2*, 191–214. doi:10.1007/BF00056668

Kim, K. C., & Byrne, L. B. (2006). Biodiversity loss and the taxonomic bottleneck: emerging biodiversity science. *Ecological Research, 21*, 794–810. doi:10.1007/s11284-006-0035-7

Kinnunen, T. (2003). *Spectral Features for Automatic Text-Independent Speaker Recognition.* PhD thesis, University of Joensuu, Finland.

Kira, K., & Rendell, L. A. (1992). A practical approach to feature selection. *Proceedings of the 9th International Workshop on Machine Learning* (pp. 249-256). Morgan Kaufmann Publishers.

Kirsh, D. (1991). Today the earwig, tomorrow man? *Artificial Intelligence, 47*, 161–184. doi:10.1016/0004-3702(91)90054-N

Klau, G., Ljubic, I., Moser, A., Mutzel, P., Neuner, P., Raidl, G., & Weiskircher, R. (2004). Combining a memetic algorithm with integer programming to solve the prize-collecting Steiner tree problem. In *Genetic and Evolutionary Computation Conference . Lecture Notes in Computer Science, 3102*, 1304–1315.

Klockgether, J., & Schwefel, H. P. (1970). Two-phase nozzle and hollow core jet experiments. In D. G. Elliott (Ed.), *Proceedings of the 11th Symposium on Engineering Aspects of Magnetohydrodynamics* (pp. 141-148). Pasadena, CA: California Institute of Technology.

Knowles, J., & Corne, D. (2000). A New Evolutionary Approach to the Degree-Constrained Minimum Spanning Tree Problem. *IEEE Transactions on Evolutionary Computation, 4*(2), 125–134. doi:10.1109/4235.850653

Ko, K., & Tang, K. Chan, C., & Man, K. (1997). Packet switched communication network designs using GA. In *2nd International Conference On Genetic Algorithms in Engineering Systems: Innovations and Applications* (pp. 398-403).

Ko, K., Tang, K., Chan, C., Man, K., & Kwong, S. (1997). Using genetic algorithms to design mesh networks. *Computer, 30*(8), 56–61. doi:10.1109/2.607086

Koestler, A. (1989). *The ghost in the machine.* London: Arkana Books.

Konak, A., & Smith, A. (1999). A Hybrid Genetic Algorithm Approach for Backbone Design of Communication Networks. In *Proceedings of the Congress on Evolutionary Computation* (pp. 1817-1823).

Konak, A., & Smith, A. (2002). Multiobjective Optimization of Survivable Networks Considering Reliability. In *Proceedings of the 10th International Conference on Telecommunication Systems,* Naval Postgraduate School, Monterey, CA.

Konak, A., & Smith, A. (2004). Capacitated Network Design Considering Survivability: An Evolutionary Approach. *Engineering Optimization, 36*(2), 189–205. doi:10.1080/03052150310001633223

Konak, A., & Smith, A. (2005). Designing Resilient Networks Using a Hybrid Genetic Algorithm Approach. In *Proceedings of Genetic and Evolutionary Computation Conference* (pp. 1279-1285).

Kononenko, I. (1994). Estimating attributes: Analysis and extension of relief. *Proceedings of European Conference on Machine Learning* (pp. 171-182).

Koza, J. R. (1992). *Genetic programming: On the programming of computers by means of natural selection.* The MIT Press.

Koza, J. R. (1994). *Genetic programming II: automatic discovery of reusable programs.* Cambridge, MA, USA: MIT Press.

Koza, J. R. (2000). *Asynchronous "Island" Approach to Parallelization of Genetic Programming.* http://www.genetic-programming.com/parallel.html

Koza, J. R. (2003). *Genetic programming IV: Routine human-competitive machine intelligence.* Norwell, MA, USA: Kluwer Academic Publishers.

Koza, J. R., Andre, D., Bennett, F. H., & Keane, M. A. (1999). *Genetic programming III: Darwinian invention & problem solving.* San Francisco, CA, USA: Morgan Kaufmann Publishers Inc.

Koza, J. R., Keane, M. A., Streeter, S., Mydlowec, W., Yu, J., & Lanza, L. (2003). *Genetic Programming IV: Routine Human-Competitive Machine Intelligence.* Kluwer Academic Publishers.

Krasnogor, N. (2002). *Studies in the theory and design space of memetic algorithms.* Doctoral thesis, University of West England, UK.

Krasnogor, N. (2004). Towards robust memetic algorithms. In W. E. Hart, N. Krasnogor & J. E. Smith (Eds.), *Recent advances in memetic algorithms* (pp. 185-207). Studies in Fuzziness and Soft Computing 166, Berlin: Springer Verlag.

Krasnogor, N., Blackburne, B., Burke, E., & Hirst, J. (2002). Multimeme algorithms for protein structure prediction. In J. J. M. Guervós *et al.* (Eds.), *Parallel problem solving from nature – PPSN VII LNCS 2439* (pp. 769-778). Berlin: Springer Verlag.

Kress, M., & Seese, D. (2007a). Executable product models - the intelligent way. *Proceedings of the IEEE International Conference on Systems, Man, and Cybernetics* (pp. 1987-1992). Montreal, Quebec, Canada.

Kress, M., & Seese, D. (2007b). Flexibility enhancements in BPM by applying executable product models and intelligent agents. *Proceedings of the 1st International Working Conference on Business Process and Services Computing* (pp. 93-104). Leipzig, Germany.

Kress, M., Melcher, J., & Seese, D. (2007). Introducing executable product models for the service industry. *Proceedings of the 40th Annual Hawaii International Conference on System Sciences* (p. 46). Waikoloa, HI, USA.

Krishna, A., Narayanan, A., & Keedwell, E. C. (2005). Neural networks and temporal gene expression data. In F. Rothlauf et al. (Eds.), *Applications on evolutionary computing,* (LNCS 3449, pp. 64-73). Berlin: Springer Verlag.

Krishnamachari, B., & Wicker, S. (2000). Optimization of fixed network design in cellular systems using local search algorithms. In *IEEE Vehicular Technology Conference* (pp.1632-1638).

Krivenko, S., & Burtsev, M. (2007). Simulation of the evolution of aging: Effects of aggression and kin-recognition. In F. A. e Costa et al. (Eds.), *Advances in artificial life.* (LNCS 4648, pp. 84-92) Berlin: Springer Verlag.

Krohling, R. A., Knidel, H., & Shi, Y. (2002). Solving numerical equations of hydraulic problems using particle swarm optimization. In *Proceedings of the IEEE Congress on Evolutionary Computation* (pp. 1688-1690). Washington, DC: IEEE Computer Society.

Krommenacker, N., Rondeau, E., & Divoux, T. (2002). Genetic algorithms for industrial Ethernet network design. In *4th IEEE International Workshop on Factory Communication Systems* (pp. 149-156).

Kube, C. R., & Zhang, H. (1993). Collective robotics: From social insects to robots. *Adaptive Behavior, 2*(2), 189–219. doi:10.1177/105971239300200204

Kulturel-Konak, S., Konak, A., & Smith, A. (2000). Minimum cost 2-edge-connected Steiner graphs in rectilinear space: an evolutionary approach. In *Proceedings of the Congress on Evolutionary Computation* (pp. 97-103).

Kumar, A., Pathak, R., & Gupta, M. (1993). Genetic algorithm based approach for designing computer network topology. In *Proceedings of the ACM Conference on Computer Science* (pp. 358-365).

Kumar, R. (2003). Multicriteria network design using distributed evolutionary algorithm. In T. Pinkston & V. Prasanna (Eds.), *Proceedings of the High Performance Computing*, Lecture Notes in Computer Science, 2913, 343-352.

Kumar, R., & Rockett, P. (1997). Assessing the convergence of rank-based multiobjective genetic algorithms. In *2nd International Conference on Genetic Algorithms in Engineering Systems: Innovations and Applications* (pp.19-23).

Kumar, R., Krishnan, V., & Santhanakrishnan, K. (2000). Design of an optimal communication network using multiobjective genetic optimization. In . *Proceedings of IEEE International Conference on Industrial Technology, 1*, 515–520.

Kumar, R., Parida, P., & Gupta, M. (2002). Topological design of communication networks using multiobjective genetic optimization. In *Proceedings of the Congress on Evolutionary Computation* (pp. 425-430).

Küster, J., Ryndina, K., & Gall, H. (2007). Generation of business process models for object life cycle compliance. In G. Alonso, P. Dadam & M. Rosemann (Eds.), *Business Process Management* (pp. 165-181). LNCS 4714, Berlin, Germany: Springer-Verlag.

Labroche, N., Guinot, C., & Venturini, G. (2004). Fast Unsupervised Clustering with Artificial Ants. *Proceedings of the Parallel Problem Solving from Nature* (pp. 1143-1152). LNCS 3242, Berlin: Springer.

Lai, L. L., & Ma, J. T. (1997). Application of evolutionary programming to reactive power planning – Comparison with nonlinear programming approach. *IEEE Transactions on Power Systems, 12*(1), 198–206. doi:10.1109/59.574940

Lamel, L., Kassel, R., & Seneff, S. (1986). Speech database development: Design and analysis of the acoustic-phonetic corus. In *Proceedings of the DARPA Speech Recognition Workshop* (pp. 100–110).

Lan, N., Feng, H. Q., & Crago, P. E. (1994). Neural network generation of muscle stimulation patterns for control of arm movements. *IEEE Transactions on Rehabilitation Engineering, 2*(4), 213–224. doi:10.1109/86.340877

Lane, B., & Prusinkiewicz, P. (2002). *Generating Spatial Distribution for Multilevel Models of Plant Communities.* Paper presented at the Proceedings of Graphics Interface '02.

Langdon, W. B., & Buxton, B. F. (2003). *The application of genetic programming for drug discovery in the pharmaceutical industry.* (Final Report of EPSRC project GR/S03546/01 with GlaxoSmithKline). UK: University College London.

Langdon, W. B., & Koza, J. R. (1998). *Genetic programming and data structures: Genetic programming + data structures = automatic programming!* Norwell, MA, USA: Kluwer Academic Publishers.

Langdon, W. B., & Poli, R. (2001). *Foundations of genetic programming.* Springer Verlag.

Lange, H., Thies, B., Kastner-Maresch, A., Dorwald, W., Kim, J. T., & Hauhs, M. (1998). *Investigating Forest Growth Model Results on Evolutionary Time Scales.* Paper presented at the Artificial Life VI: Proceedings of the Sixth International Conference on Artificial Life.

Langton, C. G. (1986, 20th-24th May 1985). *"Studying Artificial Life with Cellular Automata.* Paper presented at the Evolution, Games and Learning: Models of Adaptation in Machines and Nature, Proceedings of the Fifth Annual Conference of the Centre for Nonlinear Studies, Los Alamos.

Langton, C. G. (1990). *Artificial Life.* Boston, MA: Addison-Wesley Longman Publishing Co., Inc.

Langton, C. G. (Ed.). (1989). *Artificial Life, Proceedings of an Interdisciplinary Workshop on the Synthesis and Simulation of Living Systems.* Redwood City: Addison-Wesley Publishing.

Larranaga, P., & Lozano, J. (2002). *Estimation of Distribution Algorithms: A New Tool for Evolutionary Computation.* Kluwer Academic Publishers.

Lauritzen, S. (1998). *Graphical Models.* Oxford University Press.

Le Martelot, E., Bentley, P. J., & Lotto, R. B. (2007a). A systemic computation platform for the modelling and analysis of processes with natural characteristics. In *Proceedings of the 9th Genetic and Evolutionary Computation Conference (GECCO 2007) Workshop: Evolution of Natural and Artificial Systems - Metaphors and Analogies in Single and Multi-Objective Problems* (pp. 2809-2819), London, UK.

Le Martelot, E., Bentley, P. J., & Lotto, R. B. (2007b). Exploiting natural asynchrony and local knowledge within systemic computation to enable generic neural structures. In *Proceedings of the 2nd International Workshop on Natural Computing (IWNC 2007)* (pp. 122-133), Nagoya University, Nagoya, Japan.

Le Martelot, E., Bentley, P. J., & Lotto, R. B. (2008a). Crash-proof systemic computing: A demonstration of native fault-tolerance and self-maintenance. In *Proceedings of the 4th IASTED International Conference on Advances in Computer Science and Technology* (pp. 49-55), Langkawi, Malaysia.

Le Martelot, E., Bentley, P. J., & Lotto, R. B. (2008b). Eating data is good for your immune system: An artificial metabolism for data clustering using systemic computation. In *Proceedings of the 7th International Conference on Artificial Immune Systems* (LNCS 5132, pp. 412-423). Springer-Verlag.

Lee, C., & Kang, H. (2000). Cell planning with capacity expansion in mobile communications: A tabu search approach. *IEEE Transactions on Vehicular Technology, 49*(5), 1678–1690. doi:10.1109/25.892573

Lee, C.-Y., & Antonsson, E. K. (2000). Variable length genomes for evolutionary algorithms. In *Proceedings of the Genetic and Evolutionary Computation Conference (GECCO '00),* (p. 806).

Levy, S. (1992). *Artificial Life: A Report from the Frontier Where Computers Meet Biology.* New York, NY: Pantheon.

Lewes, G. H. (1875). *Problems of Life and Mind* (Vol. 2). London: Kegan Paul, Trench, Turbner, & Co.

Lewin, R. (1993). *Complexity: Life on the Edge of Chaos.* London: Phoenix.

Li, J., Guan, Y., & Soong, B. (2000). Effect of genetic algorithm parameters on PCS network planning. In *25th Annual IEEE Conference on Local Computer Networks* (pp. 400-404).

Li, Z., Luo, W., & Wang, X. (2008). A stepwise dimension reduction approach to evolutionary design of relative large combinational logic circuits. *Proceedings of the International Conference on Evolvable Systems* (pp. 11–20). Berlin, Germany: Springer-Verlag.

Liao, C. J., Tseng, C. T., & Luarn, P. (2007). A discrete version of particle swarm optimization for flowshop scheduling problems. *Computers & Operations Research, 34*(10), 3099–3111. doi:10.1016/j.cor.2005.11.017

Lim, M. H., Wuncsh, D., & Ho, K. W. (2000). An evolutionary programming methodology for portfolio selection. In *Proceedings of the IEEE/IAFE/INFORMS Conference on Computational Intelligence for Financial Engineering* (pp. 42-46), New York, USA.

Limonadi, F. M., McCartney, S., & Burchiel, K. J. (2006). Design of an Artificial Neural Network for Diagnosis of Facial Pain Syndromes. *Stereotactic and Functional Neurosurgery, 84*(5-6), 212–220. doi:10.1159/000095167

Lin, L., & Gen, M. (2006). A Self-controlled Genetic Algorithm for Reliable Communication Network Design. In *IEEE Congress on Evolutionary Computation* (pp. 640-647).

Lindenmayer, A. (1971a). Developmental systems without cellular interaction, their languages and grammar. *Journal of Theoretical Biology, 30,* 455–484. doi:10.1016/0022-5193(71)90002-6

Lindenmayer, A. (1971b). Mathematical models for cellular interaction in development, Parts I and II. *Journal of Theoretical Biology, 18*(1968), 280-315.

Liu, B., Wang, L., & Jin, J. H. (2007). An effective PSO-based memetic algorithm for flow shop scheduling. *IEEE Transactions on Systems, Man and Cybernetics . Part B, 37*(1), 18–27.

Liu, F., Zeng, Y., Zou, Y., Liu, J., & Zhou, H. (2005). Parallel island-based estimation of distribution algorithms for wireless network planning. In *International Conference on Wireless Communications, Networking and Mobile Computing* (pp. 1056-1059).

Liu, J., & Lampinen, J. (2005). A fuzzy adaptive differential evolution algorithm. *Soft Computing – A Fusion of Foundations . Methodologies and Applications, 9,* 448–462.

Livingstone, D. J., & Salt, D. W. (2005). Judging the significance of multiple linear regression models. *Journal of Medicinal Chemistry, 48*(3), 661–663. doi:10.1021/jm049111p

Ljubic, I., & Kratica, J. (2000). A genetic algorithm for biconnectivity augmentation problem, in *Proceedings of the IEEE congress on Evolutionary Computation* (pp. 89–96).

Ljubic, I., & Raidl, G. (2003). A memetic algorithm for minimum-cost vertex-biconnectivity augmentation of graphs. *Journal of Heuristics, 9*(5), 401–428. doi:10.1023/B:HEUR.0000004810.27436.30

Ljubic, I., Raidl, G., & Kratica, J. (2000). A hybrid GA for the edge-biconnectivity augmentation problem, in *Proceedings of the 6ᵗʰ Parallel Problem Solving from Nature VI Conference. Lecture Notes in Computer Science, 1917,* 641–650. doi:10.1007/3-540-45356-3_63

Lo Re, G., Lo Presti, G., Storniolo, P., & Urso, A. (2004). A grid enabled parallel hybrid genetic algorithm for SPN. In *Proceedings of International Conference on Computational Science. Lecture Notes in Computer Science, 3039,* 156–163.

Lo, C., & Chang, W. (2000). A multiobjective hybrid genetic algorithm for the capacitated multipoint network design problem. *IEEE Transactions on Systems, Man, and Cybernetics . Part B, 30*(3), 461–470.

Logeswaran, R. (2005). Scale-space Segment Growing For Hierarchical Detection of Biliary Tree Structure. *International Journal of Wavelets, Multresolution, and Information Processing, 3*(1), 125–140. doi:10.1142/S0219691305000750

Logeswaran, R. (2006). Neural Networks Aided Stone Detection in Thick Slab MRCP Images. *Medical & Biological Engineering & Computing, 44*(8), 711–719. doi:10.1007/s11517-006-0083-8

Logeswaran, R., & Eswaran, C. (2006). Discontinuous Region Growing Scheme for Preliminary Detection of Tumor in MRCP Images. *Journal of Medical Systems, 30*(4), 317–324. doi:10.1007/s10916-006-9020-5

Lohn, J. D., Hornby, G. S., & Linden, D. S. (2005). Evolution, re-evolution, and prototype of an X-band antenna for NASA's space technology 5 mission. In J. M. Moreno, J. Madrenas & J. Cosp (Eds.), *Evolvable systems: From biology to hardware.* (LNCS 3637, pp. 205-214). Berlin: Springer Verlag.

Lopes, H. S., & Perretto, M. (2008). An ant colony system for large-scale phylogenetic tree reconstruction. *Journal of Intelligent and Fuzzy Systems, 18*(6), 575–583.

Lovberg, M., & Krink, T. (2002). Extending particle swarm optimisers with self-organized criticality. *Proceedings of the IEEE Congress on Evolutionary Computation* (pp. 1588-1593). Honolulu, HI, USA.

Lozano, J., Larrañaga, P., Inza, I., & Bengoetxea, E. (2006). *Towards a New Evolutionary Computation.* Springer-Verlag.

Lozano, M., Herrera, F., Krasnogor, N., & Molina, D. (2004). Real-coded memetic algorithms with crossover hill Climbing. *Evolutionary Computation . Special Issue on Memetic Algorithms, 12*(3), 273–302.

Lu, L., Jiang, H., & Zhang, H. (2001). A robust audio classification and segmentation method. In *Proceedings of the 9th ACM International Conference on Multimedia* (pp. 203–211).

Luck, M., & Aylett, R. (2000). Applying Artificial Intelligence to Virtual Reality: Intelligent Virtual Environments. *Applied Artificial Intelligence, 14,* 3–32. doi:10.1080/088395100117142

Luke, S., & Spector, L. (1997). A comparison of crossover and mutation in genetic programming. In J. R. Koza et al. (Eds.), *Genetic programming 1997: Proceedings of the 2ⁿᵈ Annual Conference* (pp. 240-248). San Francisco: Morgan Kaufmann.

Lumer, E. D., & Faieta, B. (1994). Diversity and adaptation in populations of clustering ants. *Proceedings of the Third international Conference on Simulation of Adaptive Behavior: From Animals to Animats* (pp. 501-508), Brighton, UK.

Luyet, L., Zufferey, N., & Varone, S. (2007). An ant algorithm for the Steiner tree problem in graphs. In *EVOCOMNET. Lecture Notes in Computer Science, 4448,* 42–51. doi:10.1007/978-3-540-71805-5_5

Ma, J., Huang, R., & Tsuboi, E. (1997). A Genetic Algorithm for Optimal 3-connected Telecommunication Network Designs. *Lecture Notes in Computer Science, 1336*, 159–170. doi:10.1007/BFb0024213

Maass, W. (1997). Networks of spiking neurons: The third generation of neural network models. *Neural Networks, 10*, 1659–1671. doi:10.1016/S0893-6080(97)00011-7

Madhuram, S. (1995). *The Design of ATM Networks Using Genetic Algorithms.* Unpublished Master Thesis, University of Louisville, Kentucky.

Maeda, N., Klyce, S. D., & Smolek, M. K. (1995). Neural Network Classification of Corneal Topography Preliminary Demonstration. *Investigative Ophthalmology & Visual Science, 36*, 1327–1335.

Mahfoud, S. W. (1995). *Niching methods for genetic algorithms.* Doctoral dissertation. University of Illinois at Urbana-Champaign.

Majeed, H., & Ryan, C. (2006a). A less destructive, context-aware crossover operator for GP. *Lecture Notes in Computer Science, 3905*, 36–48. doi:10.1007/11729976_4

Majeed, H., & Ryan, C. (2006b). Using context-aware crossover to improve the performance of GP. *GECCO '06: Proceedings of the 8th annual conference on Genetic and evolutionary computation* (pp. 847-854). New York, NY, USA: ACM.

Majeed, H., & Ryan, C. (2007a). Context-aware mutation: a modular, context aware mutation operator for genetic programming. *GECCO '07: Proceedings of the 9th annual conference on Genetic and evolutionary computation* (pp. 1651-1658). New York, NY, USA: ACM.

Majeed, H., & Ryan, C. (2007b). On the constructiveness of context-aware crossover. *GECCO '07: Proceedings of the 9th annual conference on Genetic and evolutionary computation* (pp. 1659–1666). New York, NY, USA: ACM.

Malisia, A. R., & Tizhoosh, H. R. (2006). Image thresholding using ant colony optimization. *In Proceedings of the Third Canadian Conference on Computer and Robotic Vision* (pp.26-26), Québec City, Canada.

Mandelbrot, B. (1982). *The Fractal Geometry of Nature.* San Francisco: W.H. Freeman and Co.

Mango, L. J., & Valente, P. T. (1998). Comparison of neural network assisted analysis and microscopic rescreening in presumed negative Pap smears. *Acta Cytologica, 42*, 227–232.

Maniezzo, V., & Carbonaro, A. (2000). An ANTS heuristic for the frequency assignment problem. *Future Generation Computer Systems, 16*, 927–935.

Manos, S., Large, M. C. J., & Poladian, L. (2007). Evolutionary design of single-mode microstructured polymer optical fibres using an artificial embryogeny representation. In *Proceedings of the Genetic and Evolutionary Computation Conference* (pp. 2549-2556). New York: ACM Press.

Maple, C., Guo, L., & Zhang, J. (2004). Parallel genetic algorithms for third generation mobile network planning. In *Proceedings of the International Conference on Parallel Computing in Electrical Engineering* (pp. 229-236).

Marchevsky, A. M., Tsou, J. A., & Laird-Offringa, I. A. (2004). Classification of Individual Lung Cancer Cell Lines Based on DNA Methylation Markers Use of Linear Discriminant Analysis and Artificial Neural Networks. *The Journal of Molecular Diagnostics, 6*(1), 28–36.

Marinakis, Y., & Dounias, G. (2008). Nature inspired intelligence in medicine: Ant colony optimization for Pap-smear diagnosis. *International Journal of Artificial Intelligence Tools, 17*(2), 279–301. doi:10.1142/S0218213008003893

Marinakis, Y., Marinaki, M., & Zopounidis, C. (2008). Application of ant colony optimization to credit risk assessment. *New Mathematics and Natural Computation, 4*(1), 107–122. doi:10.1142/S1793005708000957

Marseguerra, M., Zio, E., Podofillini, L., & Coit, D. (2005). Optimal design of reliable network systems in presence of uncertainty. *IEEE Transactions on Reliability, 54*(2), 243–253. doi:10.1109/TR.2005.847279

Matzinger, P. (1994). Tolerance, danger and the extended family. *Annual Review of Immunology, 12*, 991–1045.

Mayo Clinic. (2008). Bile Duct Cancer. Retrieved May 24 2008, from http://www.mayoclinic.org/bile-duct-cancer/.

McCallum, B. T. (1994). A reconsideration of the uncovered interest parity relationship. *Journal of Monetary Economics, 33*(1), 105–132. doi:10.1016/0304-3932(94)90016-7

McCulloch, W., & Pitts, W. (1943). A logical calculus of the ideas immanent in nervous activity. *Bulletin of Mathematical Biology, 5*(4), 115–133.

McLaughlin, B. P. (1992). *The Rise and Fall of British Emergentism. Emergence or Reduction?: Essays on the Prospects of Nonreductive Physicalism.* Berlin: Walter de Gruyter.

Mech, R., & Prusinkiewicz, P. (1996). Visual models of plants interacting with their environment. *SIGGRAPH, Proceedings of the 23rd annual conference on Computer graphics and interactive techniques* (pp. 397-410).

Merkle, D., Middendorf, M., & Schmeck, H. (2002). Ant colony optimization for resource-constrained project scheduling. *IEEE Transactions on Evolutionary Computation, 6*(4), 333–346. doi:10.1109/TEVC.2002.802450

Merz, P. (2003). Analysis of gene expression profiles: An application of memetic algorithms to the minimum sum-of-squares clustering problem. *BioSystems, 72*(1-2), 99–109. doi:10.1016/S0303-2647(03)00137-0

Meunier, H., Talbi, E.-G., & Reininger, P. (2000). A multiobjective genetic algorithm for radio network optimization. In *Proceedings of the 2000 Congress on Evolutionary Computation* (pp. 317–324).

Meyer, C. R., Park, H., Balter, J. M., & Bland, P. H. (2003). Method for quantifying volumetric lesion change in interval liver CT examinations . *Medical Imaging, 22*(6), 776–781. doi:10.1109/TMI.2003.814787

Michalewicz, Z. (1992). *Genetic Algorithms + Data Structures = Evolution Programs.* Springer- Verlag.

Michalewicz, Z., & Fogel, D. B. (2004). *How to Solve It: Modern Heuristics.* Springer.

Michalewicz, Z., & Schmidt, M. (2007). Parameter control in practice. In F. G. Lobo, C. F. Lima & Z. Michalewicz (Eds.), Parameter setting in evolutionary algorithms). *Studies in Computational Intelligence 54,* 277-294. Berlin: Springer Verlag.

Mihata, K. (1997). The Persistence of 'Emergence'. In A. E. Raymond, Horsfall, S., Lee., M.E. (Eds.), *Chaos, Complexity & Sociology: Myths, Models & Theories* (pp. 30-38). California: Sage: Thousand Oaks.

Mill, J. S. (1843). *System of Logic* (8th ed.). London: Longmans, Green, Reader, and Dyer.

Miller, J., & Franklin, J. (2002). Modeling the distribution of four vegetation alliances using generalized linear models and classification trees with spatial dependence. *Ecological Modelling, 157,* 227–247. doi:10.1016/S0304-3800(02)00196-5

Min, J., Tian, P., & Kao, Y. (2008). A new ant colony optimization algorithm for the multidimensional knapsack problem. *Computers & Operations Research, 35*(8), 2672–2683.

Mingers, J. (1995). *Self-Producing Systems: Implications and Applications of Autopoiesis.* New York and London: Plenum Press.

Moallemi, C. (1991). Classifying Cells for Cancer Diagnosis Using Neural Networks . *Intelligent Systems and Their Applications, 6*(6), 8–12.

Moffett, M. W., & Tobin, J. E. (1991). Physical castes in ant workers: a problem for *Daceton armigerum* and other ants. *Psyche, 98,* 283–292.

Moisen, G. G., & Frescino, T. S. (2002). Comparing five modelling techniques for predicting forest characteristics. *Ecological Modelling, 157,* 209–225. doi:10.1016/S0304-3800(02)00197-7

Monmarché, N., Slimane, M., & Venturini, G. (1999a). On improving clustering in numerical databases with artificial ants. *Advances in Artificial Life* (pp. 626-635). LNCS 1674, Berlin: Springer.

Monmarché, N., Slimane, M., & Venturini, G. (1999b). AntClass, Découverte de classes dans des données numériques grâce à l'hybridation d'une colonie de fourmis et l'algorithme des centres mobiles. *Conférence d Apprentissage* (pp.169-176). France, Paleseau: Ecole Polytechnique.

Moore, E. F. (1962). Machine models of self-reproduction. [Providence, RI: The American Mathematical Society.]. *Proceedings of Symposia in Applied Mathematics, 14,* 17–33.

Moore, J. H. (2003). The ubiquitous nature of epistasis in determining susceptibility to common human diseases. *Human Heredity, 56*, 73–82. doi:10.1159/000073735

Moore, J. H. (2004). Computational analysis of gene-gene interactions using multifactor dimensionality reduction. *Expert Review of Molecular Diagnostics, 4*(6), 795–803. doi:10.1586/14737159.4.6.795

Moore, J. H. (2007). Genome-wide analysis of epistasis using multifactor dimensionality reduction: feature selection and construction in the domain of human genetics. In D. Zhu (Ed.), *Knowledge Discovery and Data Mining: Challenges and Realities with Real World Data*, IGI Global, in press.

Moore, J. H., & White, B. C. (2006). Exploiting expert knowledge in genetic programming for genome-wide genetic analysis. *Lecture Notes in Computer Science, 4193*, 969–977. doi:10.1007/11844297_98

Moore, J. H., & White, B. C. (2007a). Genome-wide genetic analysis using genetic programming: The critical need for expert knowledge. In R. Riolo, T. Soule, & B. Worzel (Eds.), *Genetic programming theory and practice IV* (pp. 11-28). Springer.

Moore, J. H., & White, B. C. (2007b). Tuning ReliefF for genome-wide genetic analysis. *Lecture Notes in Computer Science, 4447*, 166–175. doi:10.1007/978-3-540-71783-6_16

Moore, J. H., Andrews, P. C., Barney, N., & White, B. C. (2008). Development and evaluation of an open-ended computational evolution system for the genetic analysis of susceptibility to common human diseases. *Lecture Notes in Computer Science, 4973*, 129–140. doi:10.1007/978-3-540-78757-0_12

Moore, J. H., Barney, N., Tsai, C. T., Chiang, F. T., Gui, J., & White, B. C. (2007). Symbolic modeling of epistasis. *Human Heredity, 63*(2), 120–133. doi:10.1159/000099184

Moore, J. H., Gilbert, J. C., Tsai, C. T., Chiang, F. T., Holden, T., Barney, N., & White, B. C. (2006). A flexible computational framework for detecting, characterizing, and interpreting statistical patterns of epistasis in genetic studies of human disease susceptibility. *Journal of Theoretical Biology, 241*(2), 252–261. doi:10.1016/j.jtbi.2005.11.036

Moore, J. H., Greene, C. S., Andrews, P. C., & White, B. C. (2009). Does complexity matter? Artificial evolution, computational evolution and the genetic analysis of epistasis in common human diseases. In R. Riolo, T. Soule & B. Worzel (Eds.), *Genetic programming theory and practice VI* (pp. 125-144). Springer.

Moore, J. H., Parker, J. S., Olsen, N. J., & Aune, T. (2002). Symbolic discriminant analysis of microarray data in autoimmune disease. *Genetic Epidemiology, 23*, 57–69. doi:10.1002/gepi.1117

Morse, M. (1949). Equilibria in Nature. *Proceedings of the American Philosophical Society, 93*, 222–225.

Moscato, P., & Norman, M. (1989). *A competitive-cooperative approach to complex combinatorial search.* (Technical Report C3P-790). Pasadena, CA: California Institute of Technology.

Mostaghim, S., Halter, W., & Wille, A. (2006). Linear multi-objective particle swarm optimization. In A. Abraham, C. Grosan & V. Ramos (Eds.), *Stigmergy optimization* (pp. 209-237). SCI 31, Berlin, Germany: Springer-Verlag.

Moyson, F., & Manderick, B. (1988). The collective behaviour of Ants: an Example of Self-Organization in Massive Parallelism. *Proceedings of the AAAI Spring Symposium on Parallel Models of Intelligence.* Stanford, California.

Müller, D., Reichert, M., & Herbst, J. (2007). Data-driven modeling and coordination of large process structures. In R. Meersman & Z. Tari (Eds.), *On the Move to Meaningful Internet Systems 2007: CoopIS, DOA, ODBASE, GADA, and IS* (pp. 131-149). LNCS 4803, Berlin, Germany: Springer-Verlag.

Muñoz, J., & Felicísimo, Á. M. B. (2004). Comparison of statistical methods commonly used in predictive modelling. *Journal of Vegetation Science, 15*, 285–292.

Murdoch, A. J., & Ellis, R. H. (1992). Dormancy, Viability and Longevity. In M. Fenner (Ed.), *Seeds: The Ecology of Regeneration*: Cabi Publishing.

Nagel, E. (1961). *The Structure of Science.* New York: Harcourt, Brace and Wilson.

Naguib, R. N. G. (Ed.) & Sherbet, G.V. (Ed.) (2001). *Artificial Neural Networks in Cancer Diagnosis, Prog-*

nosis, and Patient Management (Biomedical Engineering Series). CRC.

Nakagaki, T. (2000). Maze-solving by an amoeboid organism. *Nature, 407*, 470. doi:10.1038/35035159

Navratil, J., Jin, Q., Andrews, W., & Campbell, J. (2003). Phonetic speaker recognition using maximum-likelihood binary-decision tree models. In *Proceedings of the IEEE International Conference on Acoustics, Speech, and Signal Processing* (pp. 796-799).

Nebro, A., Alba, E., & Molina, G. Chicano, F., Luna, F., & Durillo, J. (2007). Optimal antenna placement using a new multi-objective CHC algorithm. In *Proceedings of the 9th Annual Conference on Genetic and Evolutionary Computation* (pp. 876-883).

Neely, C. J., & Weller, P. A. (2003). Intraday technical trading in the foreign exchange market. *Journal of International Money and Finance, 22*(2), 223–237. doi:10.1016/S0261-5606(02)00101-8

Nenortaite, J., & Simutis, R. (2005). Adapting particle swarm optimization to stock markets. In *Proceedings of the 5ᵗʰ International Conference on Intelligent Systems Design and Applications* (pp. 520-525). Washington, DC: IEEE Computer Society.

Neri, F., Toivanen, J., & Mäkinen, R. A. E. (2007). An adaptive evolutionary algorithm with intelligent mutation local searchers for designing multidrug therapies for HIV. *Applied Intelligence, 27*(3), 219–235. doi:10.1007/s10489-007-0069-8

Neri, F., Toivanen, J., Cascella, G. L., & Ong, Y. S. (2007). An adaptive multimeme algorithm for designing HIV multidrug therapies. *IEEE/ACM Transactions on Computational Biology and Bioinformatics, 4*(2), 264–278. doi:10.1109/TCBB.2007.070202

Nesmachnow, S., Cancela, H., & Alba, E. (2007). Evolutionary algorithms applied to reliable communication network design. *Engineering Optimization, 39*(7), 831–855. doi:10.1080/03052150701503553

Nesmachnow, S., Cancela, H., Alba, E., & Chicano, F. (2005). Parallel metaheuristics in telecommunications. In E. Alba (Ed.), *Parallel metaheuristics: a new class of algorithms* (pp. 495-515). John Wiley & Sons: Hoboken, N.J.

Neuro, X. L. (2003). Neural networks for medical and psychiatric diagnosis. Retrieved February 21 2008, from http://www.neuroxl.com/neural_networks_psychiatry.htm.

Ng, W. K., Leng, G. S. B., & Low, Y. L. (2004). *Coordinated movement of multiple robots for searching a cluttered environment.* Paper presented at the IEEE/RSJ International Conference on Intelligent Robots and Systems (IROS 2004).

Nickerson, B. A., Fitzhorn, P. A., Koch, S. K., & Charney, M. (1991). A methodology for near-optimal computational superimposition of two-dimensional digital facial photographs and three-dimensional cranial surface meshes. *Journal of Forensic Sciences, 36*(2), 480–500.

NIDDK – National Institute of Diabetes and Digestive and Kidney Diseases. (2008). Digestive diseases dictionary A-D: biliary track. *National Digestive Diseases Information Clearinghouse (NDDIC)*. Retrieved February 21 2008, from http://digestive.niddk.nih.gov/ddiseases/pubs/dictionary/pages/a-d.htm.

Niwa, H. S. (1994). Self-organizing dynamic model of fish schooling. *Journal of Theoretical Biology, 171*, 123–136. doi:10.1006/jtbi.1994.1218

Nix, H. A. (1986). Biogeographic analysis of Australian elapid snakes. In R. Longmore (Ed.), *Atlas of Elapid Snakes, Australian Flora and Fauna Series, 7*, 4-15. Canberra: Australian Government Publishing Service.

Nowé, A., Verbeeck, K., & Vrancx, P. (2004) Multi-type ant colony: the edge disjoint paths problem. In *4th International Workshop on Ant Colony Optimization and Swarm Intelligence. Lecture Notes in Computer Science, 3172*, 202-213.

Nwana, H. S., & Ndumu, D. T. (1998). *A Brief Introduction to Software Agent Technology*. New York: Springer-Verlag.

O'Neill, M., & Ryan, C. (2003). *Grammatical evolution: Evolutionary automatic programming in an arbitrary language*. Norwell, MA, USA: Kluwer Academic Publishers.

O'Reilly, R. C. (1996). Biologically plausible error-driven learning using local activation differences: The generalized recirculation algorithm. *Neural Computation, 8*, 895–938. doi:10.1162/neco.1996.8.5.895

Oczkowski, W. J., & Barreca, S. (1997). Neural network modeling accurately predicts the functional outcome of stroke survivors with moderate disabilities. *Archives of Physical Medicine and Rehabilitation*, *78*(4), 340–345. doi:10.1016/S0003-9993(97)90222-7

Ofria, C., & Wilke, C. O. (2004). Avida: A software platform for research in computational evolutionary. *Biology*, *10*, 191–229.

Ombuki, B., Nakamura, M., Nakao, Z., & Onaga, K. (1999). Evolutionary computation for topological optimization of 3-connected computer networks. In *Proceedings of IEEE International Conference on Systems, Man, and Cybernetics* (pp. 659-664).

Omran, M., Salman, A., & Engelbrecht, A. (2002). Image classification using particle swarm optimization. In *Proceedings of the 4th Asia-Pacific Conference on Simulated Evolution and Learning* (pp. 370-374). Singapore: Nanyang Technical University Press.

Ong, Y. S., & Keane, A. J. (2004). Meta-Lamarkian learning in memetic algorithms. *IEEE Transactions on Evolutionary Computation*, *8*(2), 99–110. doi:10.1109/TEVC.2003.819944

Ong, Y. S., Lim, M. H., Zhu, N., & Wong, K. W. (2006). Classification of adaptive memetic algorithms: A comparative study. *IEEE Transactions on Systems, Man and Cybernetics . Part B*, *36*(1), 141–152.

Oppenheimer, P. (1986). *Real Time Design and Animation of Fractal Plants and Trees*. Paper presented at the Proceedings of SIGGRAPH '86 Annual Conference Series.

Otsu, N. (1979). A threshold selection method for grey level histograms. *IEEE Transactions on Systems, Man, and Cybernetics*, SMC-9, 62–66.

Ouadfel, S., & Batouche, M. (2003). MRF-based image segmentation using Ant Colony System. *Electronic Letters on Computer Vision and Image Analysis*, *2*(2), 12–24.

Palmer, C., & Kershenbaum, A. (1995). An approach to a problem in network design using genetic algorithms. *Networks*, *26*, 151–163. doi:10.1002/net.3230260305

Pan, Q. K., Tasgetiren, M. F., & Liang, Y. C. (2008). A discrete particle swarm optimization algorithm for the no-wait flowshop scheduling problem. *Computers & Operations Research*, *35*(9), 2807–2839. doi:10.1016/j.cor.2006.12.030

Parpinelli, R., Lopes, H., & Freitas, A. (2001). An Ant Colony Based System for Data Mining: Applications to Medical Data. *Proceedings of the Genetic and Evolutionary Computation Conference* (pp. 791-797).

Parsopoulos, K., & Vrahatis, M. (2002). Recent approaches to global optimization problems through particle swarm optimization. *Natural Computing*, *1*(2/3), 235–306. doi:10.1023/A:1016568309421

Patel, T. (2002). Worldwide trends in mortality from biliary tract malignancies. [PMID 11991810.]. *BMC Cancer*, *2*, 10. doi:10.1186/1471-2407-2-10

Pattin, K., & Moore, J. (2008). Exploiting the proteome to improve the genome-wide genetic analysis of epistasis in common human diseases. *Human Genetics*, *124*(1), 19–29. doi:10.1007/s00439-008-0522-8

Pearl, J. (1988). *Probabilistic Reasoning in Intelligent Systems: Networks of Plausible Inference.* Morgan Kaufmann.

Pearson, R. G., & Dawson, T. P. (2003). Predicting the impacts of climate change on the distribution of species: are bioclimate envelope models useful? *Global Ecology and Biogeography*, *12*, 361–371. doi:10.1046/j.1466-822X.2003.00042.x

Peterson, A. T., Sánchez-Corderob, V., Soberónc, J., Bartleyd, J., Buddemeierd, R. W., & Navarro-Sigüenza, A. G. (2001). Effects of global climate change on geographic distributions of Mexican Cracidae. *Ecological Modelling*, *144*(1), 21–30. doi:10.1016/S0304-3800(01)00345-3

Peterson, C., & Anderson, J. R. (1987). A mean field theory learning algorithm for neural networks. *Complex Systems*, *1*, 995–1019.

Pétrowski, A. (1996). A clearing procedure as a niching method for genetic algorithms. *Proceedings of IEEE International Conference on Evolutionary Computation* (pp. 798–803).

Pham, D. T., Ghanbarzadeh, A., Koç, E., Otri, S., Rahim, S., et al. (2006). The Bees Algorithm – A Novel Tool for Complex Optimization Problems. *Proceedings of IPROMS 2006, Innovative Production Machines and Sys-*

tems Virtual Conference (pp.454-461), Cardiff, UK.

Phillips, A., & Cardelli, L. (2004). A correct abstract machine for the stochastic PI-calculus. In *Proceedings of the Workshop on Concurrent Models in Molecular Biology (BioConcur 2004)*, London, UK.

Piszcz, A., & Soule, T. (2006). A survey of mutation techniques in genetic programming. *GECCO '06: Proceedings of the 8th Annual Conference on Genetic and Evolutionary Computation*, (pp. 951-952).

Poli, R., Kennedy, J., & Blackwell, T. (2007). Particle swarm optimization: An overview. *Swarm Intelligence*, *1*(1), 33–57. doi:10.1007/s11721-007-0002-0

Poli, R., Kennedy, J., & Blackwell, T. (2007). Particle swarm optimization. *Swarm Intelligence*, *1*, 33–57.

Premprayoon, P., & Wardkein, P. (2005). Topological communication network design using ant colony optimization. In *Proceedings of the 7th International Conference on Advanced Communication Technology* (pp. 1147-1151).

Price, K. V., Storn, R., & Lampinen, J. (2005). *Differential evolution: A practical approach to global optimization.* Springer Verlag.

Priem-Mendes, S., Gomez-Pulido, J., Vega-Rodriguez, M., Pereira, A., Perez, J., & Sanchez, J. (2007). Fast Wide Area Network Design Optimisation Using Differential Evolution. In *Proceedings of the International Conference on Advanced Engineering Computing and Applications in Sciences* (pp. 3-10).

Prince, M. R. (2000). MRCP Protocol. Retrieved 2008 May 25, from http://www.mrprotocols.com/MRI/Abdomen/MRCP_Dr.P_Protocol.htm.

Prusinkiewicz, P., & Lindenmayer, A. (1990). *The algorithmic beauty of plants.* New York: Springer-Verlag.

Prusinkiewicz, P., & Remphrey, W. R. (2005). Characterization of architectural tree models using L-systems and Petri nets. In M. Labrecque (Ed.), *L'arbre -- The Tree* (pp. 177-186).

Prusinkiewicz, P., Hammel, M., Hanan, J., & Mech, R. (1996). Visual models of plant development. In G. Rozenberg, & A. Salomaa (Eds.), *Handbook of Formal Languages*: Springer-Verlag.

Prusinkiewicz, P., Hammel, M., Mech, R., & Hanan, J. (1995). *The Artificial Life of Plants.* Paper presented at the Artificial life for Graphics, Animation, and Virtual Reality Siggraph '95 Course Notes.

Prusinkiewicz, P., Hanan, J., & Mech, R. (1999). *An L-system-based plant modeling language.* Paper presented at the Proceedings of AGTIVE 1999, Lecture Notes in Computer Science 1779.

Qin, A. K., & Suganathan, P. N. (2005). Self-adaptive differential evolution algorithm for numerical optimization. In *Proceedings of the IEEE Congress on Evolutionary Computation* (pp. 1785-1791). Piscataway, NJ: IEEE Press.

Qin, Z., Wu, F., & Law, N. (1997). Designing B-ISDN network topologies using the genetic algorithm. In *Proceedings of the 5th International Workshop on Modeling, Analysis, and Simulation of Computer and Telecommunication Systems* (pp.140-145).

Quintao, F., Nakamura, F., & Mateus, G. (2005). Evolutionary algorithm for the dynamic coverage problem applied to wireless sensor networks design. In *Proceedings of the IEEE Congress on Evolutionary Computation* (pp. 1589-1596).

Raidl, G. R. (2000). An efficient evolutionary algorithm for the degree-constrained minimum spanning tree problem. In C. Fonseca, J.-H. Kim, & A. Smith (Eds.), *Proceedings of the IEEE Congress on Evolutionary Computation* (pp. 104-111).

Raidl, G. R., & Julstrom, B. A. (2003). Edge sets: an effective evolutionary coding of spanning trees. *IEEE Transactions on Evolutionary Computation*, *7*(3), 225–239. doi:10.1109/TEVC.2002.807275

Raisanen, L., & Whitaker, R. (2004). The Application of Nature-Inspired Nest Building to Wireless Site Selection. In *Proceedings of Parallel Problem Solving from Nature VIII. Lecture Notes in Computer Science, 3242.*

Raisanen, L., & Whitaker, R. (2005). Comparison and evaluation of multiple objective genetic algorithms for the antenna placement problem. *Mobile Networks and Applications*, *10*, 79–88. doi:10.1023/B:MONE.0000048547.84327.95

Raja, A., Meister, A., Tuulik, V., & Lossmann, E. (1995). A neural network approach to EEG classification in brain chemical injuries diagnosis. *MEDICON '95: VII Mediterranean Conference on Medical & Biological Engineering (IFMBE)* (pp. 133–133), Jerusalem, Israel.

Ramachandran, R. P., Farrell, K. R., Ramachandran, R., & Mammone, R. J. (2002). Speaker recognition - general classifier approaches and data fusion methods. *Pattern Recognition, 35*, 2801–2821. doi:10.1016/S0031-3203(01)00235-7

Ramsey, C. L., Jong, K. A. D., Grefenstette, J. J., Wu, A. S., & Burke, D. S. (1998). Genome length as an evolutionary self-adaptation. In *PPSN V: Proceedings of the 5th International Conference on Parallel Problem Solving from Nature* (pp. 345–356), London, UK: Springer-Verlag.

Rappos, E., & Hadjiconstantinou, E. (2004). An Ant Colony Heuristic for the Design of Two-edge Connected Flow Networks. In *Proceedings of 4th International Workshop on Ant Colony Optimization and Swarm Intelligence. Lecture Notes in Computer Science, 3172*, 270-277.

Ray T. S. (1990). http://life.ou.edu/tierra

Rechenberg, I. (1973). *Evolutionstrategie: Optimierung Technisher Systeme nach prinzipien des Biologischen Evolution*. Fromman-Hozlboog Verlag.

Rechenberg, I. (1994). *Evolutionsstrategie*. Frommann-Holzboog Verlag, Stuttgart, Germany.

Reeves, W., & Blau, R. (1985). *Approximate and Probabilistic Algorithms for Shading and Rendering Structured Particle Systems*. Paper presented at the Proceedings of SIGGRAPH '85 Annual Conference Series.

Ren, H., & Meng, M. (2006). Biologically Inspired Approaches for Wireless Sensor Networks. In *Proceedings of the IEEE International Conference on Mechatronics and Automation* (pp.762-768).

Resnick, M. (1994). *Turtles, Termites, and Traffic Jams: Explorations in Massively Parallel Microworlds*. Cambridge, Massachusetts: MIT Press.

Resnick, M., & Silverman, B. (1996). *The Facts of Life*. Retrieved 3 January 2006, 2006, from http://llk.media.mit.edu/projects/emergence/life-intro.html

Ressom, H. W., Varghese, R. S., Drake, S. K., Hortin, G. L., & Abdel-Hamid, M. (2007). Peak selection from MALDI-TOF mass spectra using ant colony optimization. *Bioinformatics (Oxford, England), 23*, 619–626.

Reynolds, C. W. (1987). Flocks, Herds, and Schools: A Distributed Behavioral Model. *Computer Graphics, Siggraph '87 Conference Proceedings, 21*, 25-34.

Reynolds, D. A., & Rose, R. C. (1995). Robust text-independent speaker identification using gaussian mixture speaker models. *IEEE Transactions on Speech and Audio Processing, 3*, 72–83. doi:10.1109/89.365379

Reynolds, D., Andrews, W., Campbell, J., Navratil, J., Peskin, B., Adam, A., et al. (2003). The supersid project: exploiting highlevel information for high-accuracy speaker recognition. In *Proceedings of the International Conference on Audio, Speech, and Signal Processing* (pp. 784–787).

Ribeiro, C., Martins, L., & Rossetti, I. (2007). Metaheuristics for optimization problems in computer communications. *Computer Communications, 30*(4), 656–669. doi:10.1016/j.comcom.2006.08.027

Ricci, A., Marella, G. L., & Apostol, M. A. (2006). A new experimental approach to computer-aided face/skull identification in forensic anthropology. *The American Journal of Forensic Medicine and Pathology, 27*(1), 46–49. doi:10.1097/01.paf.0000202809.96283.88

Ricklefs, R. E. (1990). *Ecology*. New York: W.H. Freeman, (page 332).

Ripley, B. D. (1995). Statistical ideas for selecting network architectures. *Neural Networks: Artificial Intelligence and Industrial Application* (pp. 183-190). Springer.

Ritchie, M. D., Hahn, L. W., Roodi, N., Bailey, L. R., Dupont, W. D., & Parl, F. F. (2001). Multifactor dimensionality reduction reveals high-order interactions among estrogen metabolism genes in sporadic breast cancer. *American Journal of Human Genetics, 69*, 138–147. doi:10.1086/321276

Robbins, K. R., Zhang, W., Bertrand, J. K., & Rekaya, R. (2007). The ant colony algorithm for feature selection in high-dimension gene expression data for disease classification. *Mathematical Medicine and Biology: A Journal of the IMA, 24*(4), 413-426.

Robinson, J., & Rahmat-Samii, Y. (2004). Particle swarm optimization in electromagnetics. *IEEE Transactions on Antennas and Propagation, 52*(2), 397–407. doi:10.1109/TAP.2004.823969

Robinson, K. (2005). Efficient pre-segmentation. *PhD thesis, Dublin,* from http://www.eeng.dcu.ie/~robinsok/pdfs/Robinson PhDThesis2005.pdf

Robnik-Sikonja, M., & Kononenko, I. (2003). Theoretical and empirical analysis of relieff and rrelieff. *Machine Learning, 53*(1/2), 23–69. doi:10.1023/A:1025667309714

Roces, F., & Hölldobler, B. (1996). Use of stridulation in foraging leaf-cutting ants: Mechanical support during cutting or short-range recruitment signal? *Behavioral Ecology and Sociobiology, 39*(5), 293–299.

Rodney, A. (1989). Fast, Cheap and out of Control: a Robot Invasion of the Solar System. *Journal of the British Interplanetary Society, 42,* 478–485.

Rodriguez-Linares, L., Garcia-Mateo, C., & Alba-Castro, J. (2003). On combining classifiers for speaker authentication. *Pattern Recognition, 36,* 347–359. doi:10.1016/S0031-3203(02)00035-3

Romero, J., & Machado, P. (Eds.). (2008). *The art of artificial evolution: A handbook on evolutionary art and music.* Natural Computing Series, Springer Verlag. Salerno, J. (1997). Using the particle swarm optimization technique to train a recurrent neural model. In *Proceedings of the 9th IEEE International Conference on Tools with Artificial Intelligence* (pp. 45-49). Washington, DC: IEEE Computer Society.

Room, P. M., Maillette, L., & Hanan, J. (1994). Module and metamer dynamics and virtual plants. *Advances in Ecological Research, 25,* 105–157. doi:10.1016/S0065-2504(08)60214-7

Ross, A. H. (2004). Use of digital imaging in the identification of fragmentary human skeletal remains: A case from the Republic of Panama. *Forensic Science Communications, 6*(4), [online].

Rouet, J. M., Jacq, J. J., & Roux, C. (2000). Genetic algorithms for a robust 3-D MR-CT registration. *IEEE Transactions on Information Technology in Biomedicine, 4*(2), 126–136. doi:10.1109/4233.845205

Routen, T. (1994). Genetic algorithm and neural network approaches to local access network design. In *Proceedings of the 2nd International Workshop on Modeling, Analysis, and Simulation of Computer and Telecommunication Systems* (pp. 239-243).

Routray, S., Sherry, A., & Reddy, B. (2007). ATM network planning: a genetic algorithm approach. *Journal of Theoretical and Applied Information Technology,* (pp. 74-79).

Roy, A. (2000). Artificial neural networks – a science in trouble. *Special Interest Group on Knowledge Discovery and Data Mining, 1,* 33–38.

Runggeratigul, S., Thongsri, P., & Sumsiripong, P. (2004). Optimal number of wavelength converters for WDM network design. In *Proceedings of the Conference on Convergent Technologies for Asia-Pacific Region* (pp. 93-96).

Runions, A., Fuhrer, M., Lane, B., Federl, P., Rolland-Lagan, A. G., & Prusinkiewicz, P. (2005). Modeling and visualization of leaf venation patterns. *ACM Transactions on Graphics, 24*(3), 702–711. doi:10.1145/1073204.1073251

Rushkoff, D. (1999). A technology genius has Silicon Valley drooling - by doing things the natural way. *The Guardian.* Retrieved June 20, 2008, from http://www.guardian.co.uk/technology/1999/oct/07/onlinesupplement17

Russell, B. (1956). The philosophy of logical atomism. In R.C. Marsh (Ed.), *Logic and Knowledge, Essays 1901-50* (pp. 175-281). London: Allen and Unwin.

Saatchi, S., & Hung, C.-C. (2007). Swarm intelligence and image segmentation. In F. T. S. Chan & M. K. Tiwari (Eds.), *Swarm Intelligence, Focus on Ant and Particle Swarm Optimization* (pp. 163-178). Vienna, Austria: I-Tech Education and Publishing.

Saha, D., & Mukherjee, A. (2003). Pervasive computing: A paradigm for the 21st century. *Computer, 36*(3), 25–31. doi:10.1109/MC.2003.1185214

Sakaguchi, T., & Ohya, J. (1999). *Modeling and animation of botanical trees for interactive virtual environments.* Paper presented at the VRST 99, London, UK.

Santamaría, J., Cordón, O., & Damas, S. (2007). Evolutionary approaches for automatic 3D modeling of skulls in forensic identification. *Applications of Evolutionary Computing, LNCS, 4448,* 415–422.

Santamaría, J., Cordón, O., Damas, S., Alemán, I., & Botella, M. (2007). A scatter search-based technique for pair-wise 3D range image registration in forensic anthropology. *Soft Computing, 11*(9), 819–828. doi:10.1007/s00500-006-0132-0

Sarkar, I. N. (2007). Biodiversity informatics: organizing and linking information across the spectrum of life. *Briefings in Bioinformatics, 8*(5), 347–357. doi:10.1093/bib/bbm037

Sayoud, H., Takahashi, K., & Vaillant, B. (2001). A genetic local tuning algorithm for a class of combinatorial networks design problems. *IEEE Communications Letters, 5*(7), 322–324. doi:10.1109/4234.935756

Schaefer, L. A., Mackulak, G. T., Cochran, J. K., & Cherilla, J. L. (1998). *Application of a general particle system model to movement of pedestrians and vehicles.* Paper presented at the 1998 Winter Simulation Conference (WSC'98).

Schaffer, J. (1985). Multiple Objective Optimization with Vector Evaluated Genetic Algorithms. In J. Grefenstette (Ed.) *Proceedings of the 1ˢᵗ international Conference on Genetic Algorithm* (pp. 93-100).

Schiffmann, W., Joost, M., & Werner, R. (1993). Application of genetic algorithms to the construction of topologies for multilayer perceptrons. In *Proceedings of the International Conference on Artificial Neural Nets and Genetic Algorithms* (pp. 676–682).

Schmidhuber, J. (2002). The speed prior: A new simplicity measure yielding near-optimal computable predictions. In J. Kivinen & R. H. Sloan (Eds.), *Proceedings of the 15ᵗʰ Annual Conference on Computational Learning Theory* (LNAI 2375, pp. 123-127). Berlin: Springer Verlag.

Schopf, J. W., Kudryavtsev, A. B., Agresti, D. G., Wdowiak, T. J., & Czaja, A. D. (2002). Laser-Raman imagery of Earth's earliest fossils. *Nature, 416,* 73–76. doi:10.1038/416073a

Schraudolph, N. N., & Grefenstette, J. J. (1992). *A user's guide to GAucsd 1.4.* Technical Report CS92-249, Computer Science and Engineering Department, University of California, San Diego, La Jolla, CA.

Schütze, O., Mostaghim, S., Dellnitz, M., & Teich, J. (2003). Covering pareto sets by multilevel evolutionary subdivision techniques. In C. M. Fonseca (Ed.), *Evolutionary Multi-Criterion Optimization* (pp. 118-132). LNCS 2632, Berlin, Germany: Springer-Verlag.

Schwaerzel, R., & Bylander, T. (2006). Predicting currency exchange rates by genetic programming with trigonometric functions and high-order statistics. *GECCO '06: Proceedings of the 8th Annual Conference on Genetic and Evolutionary Computation,* (pp. 955-956).

Schwarzer, G., Vach, W., & Schumacher, M. (2000). On the misuses of artificial neural networks for prognostic and diagnostic classification in oncology. *Statistics in Medicine, 19,* 541–561. doi:10.1002/(SICI)1097-0258(20000229)19:4<541::AID-SIM355>3.0.CO;2-V

Schwefel, H. (1981). *Numerical optimization of computer models.* John Wiley & Sons, Inc.

Schwefel, H.-P. P. (1995). *Evolution and Optimum Seeking: The Sixth Generation.* John Wiley & Sons, Inc., New York, NY, USA.

Segel, L. A. (2001). Computing an Organism. *Proceedings of the National Academy of Sciences of the United States of America, 98*(7), 3639–3640. doi:10.1073/pnas.081081998

Sezgin, M., & Sankur, B. (2004). Survey over image thresholding techniques and quantitative performance evaluation. *Journal of Electronic Imaging, 13,* 146–156.

Shahbaz, M. (1995). Fixed network design of cellular mobile communication networks using genetic algorithms. In *Proceedings of the IEEE International Conference on Universal Personal Communications* (pp. 163-167).

Shelokar, P.S., Jayaraman, V.K., & Kulkarni, B.D. (2004). An ant colony approach for clustering. *Analytica Chimica Acta, 509,* 187–195.

Shi, L., & Xu, G. (2001). Self-adaptive evolutionary programming and its application to multi-objective optimal operation of power systems. *Electric Power Systems Research, 57*(3), 181–187. doi:10.1016/S0378-7796(01)00086-4

Shyu, S. J., & Tsai, C. Y. (2009). Finding the longest common subsequence for multiple biological sequences by ant colony optimization. *Computers & Operations Research*, *36*(1), 73–91. doi:10.1016/j.cor.2007.07.006

Shyu, S., Yin, P., Lin, B., & Haouari, M. (2003). Ant-tree: an ant colony optimization approach to the generalized minimum spanning tree problem. *Journal of Experimental & Theoretical Artificial Intelligence*, *15*(1), 103–112. doi:10.1080/0952813021000032699

Silander, J. A., & Antonovics, J. (1982). Analysis of interspecific interactions in a coastal plant community - a perturbation approach. *Nature*, *298*, 557–560. doi:10.1038/298557a0

Silva, S., & Almeida, J. (2003). Dynamic maximum tree depth. In *Proceedings of the Genetic and Evolutionary Computation Conference* (pp. 1776–1787).

Sima, J., & Orponen, P. (2003). General purpose computation with neural networks: A Survey of Complexity Theoretic Results. *Neural Computation*, *15*, 2727–2778. doi:10.1162/089976603322518731

Sims, K. (1994). Evolving Virtual Creatures. In A. Glassner (Ed.), *ACM SIGGRAPH: Computer Graphics 1994 Proceedings* (pp. 15-22). New York, NY: ACM Press.

Sinclair, M. C. (1998). Minimum Network Wavelength Requirement Design Using a Genetic-algorithm/Heuristic Hybrid. *Electronics Letters*, *34*(4), 388–389. doi:10.1049/el:19980282

Sinclair, M. C. (1998b). Minimum Cost Routing and Wavelength Allocation Using a Genetic-algorithm/Heuristic Hybrid Approach. In *Proceedings of 6th IEE Conference on Telecommunications*, (pp. 67-71).

Sinclair, M. C. (1999). Evolutionary Telecommunications: A Summary. In *Genetic and Evolutionary Computation Conference* (pp. 209-212).

Sinclair, M. C. (1999b). Optical Mesh Topology Design using Node-Pair Encoding Genetic Programming. In *Genetic and Evolutionary Computation Conference* (pp. 1192-1197).

Sinclair, M. C. (2000). Node-Pair Encoding Genetic Programming for Optical Mesh Network Topology Design. In D.Corne, M. Oates, & G. Smith (Eds.), *Tele-communications Optimization: Heuristic and Adaptive Techniques* (pp. 99-114). Wiley.

Sinha, P. (1998). A symmetry perceiving adaptive neural network and facial image recognition. *Forensic Science International*, *98*(1-2), 67–89. doi:10.1016/S0379-0738(98)00137-6

Sipper, M. (1998). Fifty years of research on self-replication: an overview. *Artificial Life*, *4*, 237–257. doi:10.1162/106454698568576

Sipper, M., & Reggia, J. A. (2001). Go forth and replicate. *Scientific American*, *285*, 34–43.

Siregar, J., Takagi, H., & Zhang, Y. (2002). Optimal wavelength converter placement in optical networks by genetic algorithms. *IEICE Transactions on Communications . E (Norwalk, Conn.)*, *85-B*(6), 1075–1081.

Slatyer, R. O. (1967). *Plant-Water Relationships*. London: Academic Press.

Sleem, A., Ahmed, M., Kumar, A., & Kamel, K. (2000). Comparative Study of Parallel vs. Distributed Genetic Algorithm Implementation for ATM Networking Environment. In *Proceedings of the Fifth IEEE Symposium on Computers and Communications* (pp. 152-157).

Smith, A. (1984). Plants, Fractals and Formal Languages. *Proceedings of SIGGRAPH '84 Annual Conference Series*, *18*(3), 1-10.

Smith, J. (2004). The co-evolution of memetic algorithms for protein structure prediction. In W. E. Hart, N. Krasnogor & J. Smith (Eds.), *Recent advances in memetic algorithms* (pp. 105-128). Studies in Fuzziness and Soft Computing 166, Berlin: Springer-Verlag.

Smith, S. F. (1980). *A Learning System Based on Genetic Adaptive Algorithms*. PhD thesis, Computer Science Department, University of Pittsburgh.

Soak, S.-M., Corne, D., & Ahn, B.-H. (2005). A new evolutionary algorithm for spanning-tree based communication network design. *IEICE Transactions on Communications*, *E88*(10), 4090–4094. doi:10.1093/ietcom/e88-b.10.4090

Solbrig, O. T. (1981). Studies on the population biology of the genus Viola. II. The effect of plant size on fitness in Viola sororia. *Evolution; International Journal of Organic Evolution*, *35*, 1080–1093. doi:10.2307/2408122

Soler, C., Sillion, F. X., Blaise, F., & Dereffye, P. (2003). An Efficient Instantiation Algorithm for Simulating Radiant Energy Transfer in Plant Models. *ACM Transactions on Graphics, 22*(2), 204–233. doi:10.1145/636886.636890

Solnon, C. (2002). Ants can solve constraint satisfaction problems. *IEEE Transactions on Evolutionary Computation, 6*, 347–357.

Soong, F. K., Rosenberg, A. E., Rabiner, L. R., & Huang, B. H. (1987). A vector quantization approach to speaker recognition. *AT & T Technical Journal, 66*, 14–26.

Soper, A., & McKenzie, S. (1997). The use of a biased heuristic by a genetic algorithm applied to the design of multipoint connections in a local access network. In *Proceedings of the 2nd International Conference On Genetic Algorithms in Engineering Systems: Innovations and Application* (pp. 113-116).

Soto, M., & Ochoa, A. (2000). A factorize distribution algorithm based on polytrees. *Proceedings of the Congress on Evolutionary Computation* (pp. 232–237). Piscataway, NJ: IEEE Press.

Soule, T., & Foster, J. A. (1998). Effects of code growth and parsimony pressure on populations in genetic programming. *Evolutionary Computation, 6*(4), 293–309. doi:10.1162/evco.1998.6.4.293

Soulié, F. F., & Gallinari, P. (Eds.). (1998). *Industrial applications of neural networks*. World Scientific.

Spector, L. (2001). Autoconstructive evolution: Push, PushGP, and Pushpop. In *Proceedings of the Genetic and Evolutionary Computation Conference* (pp. 137-146). San Francisco: Morgan Kaufmann.

Spector, L. (2003). An essay concerning human understanding of genetic programming. In R. L. Riolo & B. Worzel (Eds.), *Genetic programming theory and practice* (pp. 11-24). Kluwer.

Spector, L., & Robinson, A. (2002). Genetic programming and autoconstructive evolution with the push programming language. *Genetic Programming and Evolvable Machines, 3*(1), 7–40. doi:10.1023/A:1014538503543

Spikins, P. (1999). *Mesolithic Northern England: Environment, Population and Settlement* (Vol. 283). England: Basingstoke Press.

Spikins, P. (2000). GIS Models of Past Vegetation: An Example from Northern England, 10,000-5000 BP. *Journal of Archaeological Science, 27*, 219–234. doi:10.1006/jasc.1999.0449

Spinney, L. (2008). The Lost World. *Nature, 454*, 151–153. doi:10.1038/454151a

Spirtes, P., Glymour, C., & Scheines, R. (1993). *Causation, Prediction, and Search*. Springer-Verlag.

Srinivas, N., & Deb, K. (1994). Multi-objective optimization using non-dominated sorting in genetic algorithms. *Evolutionary Computation, 2*(3), 221–248. doi:10.1162/evco.1994.2.3.221

Stacey, R. (1996). *Complexity and Creativity in Organizations*. San Francisco: Berrett-Koehler.

Starr, K. (1994). *The Starr Report*. New York, NY: Public Affairs.

Stockwell, D. R. B., & Peters, D. P. (1999). The GARP modelling system: Problems and solutions to automated spatial prediction. *International Journal of Geographic Information Systems, 13*(2), 143–158. doi:10.1080/136588199241391

Stomeo, E., Kalganova, T., & Lambert, C. (2006). Generalized disjunction decomposition for evolvable hardware. *IEEE Transactions on Systems, Man, and Cybernetics. Part B, Cybernetics, 36*(5), 1024–1043. doi:10.1109/TSMCB.2006.872259

Storn, R. (2005). Designing nonstandard filters with differential evolution. *IEEE Signal Processing Magazine, 22*(1), 103–106. doi:10.1109/MSP.2005.1407721

Storn, R., & Price, K. (1995). *Differential evolution – A simple and efficient adaptive scheme for global optimization over continuous spaces*. (Technical Report TR-095-012). Berkeley, CA: International Computer Science Institute.

Storn, R., & Price, K. (1997). Differential evolution of simple and efficient heuristic for global optimization over continuous spaces. *Journal of Global Optimization, 11*, 341–359. doi:10.1023/A:1008202821328

Stützle, T., & Hoos, H. H. (1997). MAX-MIN Ant System and local search for the traveling salesman problem. *Proceedings of the IEEE International Conference on Evolutionary Computation* (pp. 309–314).

Stützle, T., & Hoos, H. H. (2000). MAX – MIN ant system. *Future Generation Computer Systems, 16*(8), 889–914. doi:10.1016/S0167-739X(00)00043-1

Sum-im, T. (2004). Economic dispatch by ant colony search algorithm. *Proceedings of the IEEE Conference on Cybernetics and Intelligent Systems, 1*, 416–421.

Tagliarini, G., & Page, E. (1988) A neural-network solution to the concentrator assignment problem. In *IEEE Conference on Neural Information Processing Systems-Natural and Synthetic* (pp. 775-782).

Takahashi, H., & Matsuyama, A. (1980). An approximate solution for the Steiner problem in graphs. *Mathematica Japonica, 24*, 573–577.

Talbi, E. G., Roux, O., & Fonlupt, C. (2001). Parallel ant colonies for the quadratic assignment problem. *Future Generation Computer Systems, 17*, 441–449.

Talbi, E.-G., Cahon, S., & Melab, N. (2007). Designing cellular networks using a parallel hybrid metaheuristic on the computational grid. *Computer Communications, 30*(4), 698–713. doi:10.1016/j.comcom.2006.08.017

Tamasi, L., Orincsay, D., Jozsa, B., & Magyar, G. (2005). Design of survivable VPN based VoIP networks. In *Proceedings of the 5th International Workshop on Design of Reliable Communication Networks* (pp. 473-480).

Tan, T. Z., Quek, C., & Ng, G. S. (2005). Ovarian cancer diagnosis by hippocampus and neocortex-inspired learning memory structures. *Neural Networks, 18*(5-6), 818–825. doi:10.1016/j.neunet.2005.06.027

Tang, H., Tan, K. C., & Yi, Z. (2007). *Neural networks: Computational models and* applications. Berlin: Springer-Verlag.

Tang, K., Ko, K., Man, K., & Kwong, S. (1998). Topology design and bandwidth allocation of embedded ATM networks using genetic algorithm. *IEEE Communications Letters, 2*(6), 171–173. doi:10.1109/4234.681362

Tang, K., Man, K., & Ko, T. (1997). Wireless LAN design using hierarchical genetic algorithm. In *Proceeding of 7th International Conference on Genetic Algorithms* (pp. 629-635).

Tang, K., Man, K., & Kwong, S. (2001). Wireless Communication Network Design in IC Factory. *IEEE Transactions on Industrial Electronics, 48*(2), 452–459. doi:10.1109/41.915425

Tang, M., & Yao, X. (2007). A memetic algorithm for VLSI floor planning. *IEEE Transactions on Systems, Man and Cybernetics . Part B, 37*(1), 62–69.

Taverna, K., Urban, D. L., & McDonald, R. I. (2005). Modeling landscape vegetation pattern in response to historic land-use: a hypothesis-driven approach for the North Carolina Piedmont, USA. *Landscape Ecology, 20*, 689–702. doi:10.1007/s10980-004-5652-3

Tempesti, G., Mange, D., Mudry, P.-A., Rossier, J., & Stauffer, A. (2007). Self-replicating hardware for reliability: The embryonics project. *ACM Journal on Emerging Technologies in Computing Systems, 3*(2), 9. doi:10.1145/1265949.1265955

Tempesti, G., Roggen, D., Sanchez, E., & Thoma, Y. (2002). A POEtic Architecture for Bio-Inspired Hardware. In *Artificial Life VIII: Proceedings of the 8th International Conference on the Simulation and Synthesis of Living Systems* (pp. 111-115). MIT Press, Cambridge, MA.

Tenneti, B., & Allada, V. (2008). Robust supplier set selection for changing product architectures. *International Journal of Computer Applications in Technology, 31*(3/4), 197–214. doi:10.1504/IJCAT.2008.018157

Teo, C., Foo, Y., Chien, S., Low, A., Venkatesh, B., & You, A. (2004). Optimal placement of wavelength converters in wdm networks using particle swarm optimizer. In *Proceedings of the IEEE International Conference on Communications* (pp. 1669-1673).

The International HapMap Consortium. (2005, October 27). A haplotype map of the human genome. *Nature, 437*(7063), 1299–1320. doi:10.1038/nature04226

Thierauf, G., & Cai, J. (2000). Evolution strategies - Parallelisation and application in engineering optimization. In B. H. V. Topping (Ed.), *Parallel and distributed processing for computational mechanics: Systems and tools* (pp. 329-349). Edinburgh, UK: Civil-Comp Press.

Thoma, Y., Tempesti, G., Sanchez, E., & Moreno Arostegui, J.-M. (2004). POEtic: An electronic tissue for bio-inspired cellular applications. *Bio Systems, 76*, 191–200. doi:10.1016/j.biosystems.2004.05.023

Thomas, C. D., Bodsworth, E. J., Wilson, R. J., Simmons, A. D., Davies, Z. G., & Musche, M. (2001). Ecological and evolutionary processes at expanding range margins. *Nature, 411*, 577–581. doi:10.1038/35079066

Thompson & Morgan (2004). *Successful Seed Raising Guide*: Thompson & Morgan Inc.

Thompson, D., & Bilbro, G. (2000). Comparison of a Genetic Algorithm with a Simulated Annealing Algorithm for the Design of an ATM Network. *IEEE Communications Letters, 4*(8), 267–269. doi:10.1109/4234.864190

Thomson (Lord Kelvin), W. (1871). Inaugural address to the British Association Edinburgh. *Nature, 4*, 262.

Thornton, C. (1994). The worrying statistics of connectionist representation. *Technical Report CSRP 362, Cognitive and computing sciences.* University of Sussex. United Kingdom.

Tian, J., Yu, W., & Xie, S. (2008). An ant colony optimization algorithm for image edge detection. *Proceedings of the IEEE Congress on Evolutionary Computation* (pp. 751-756), Hong Kong.

Tirronen, V., Neri, F., Kärkkäinen, T., Majava, K., & Rossi, T. (2008). An enhanced memetic differential evolution in filter design for defect detection in paper production. *Evolutionary Computation, 16*(4), 529–555. doi:10.1162/evco.2008.16.4.529

Toffoli, T., & Margolus, N. (1987). *Cellular automata machines: A new environment for modelling.* Cambridge: MIT Press.

Tongheng, G., & Chundi, M. (2002), Radio network design using coarse-grained parallel genetic algorithms with different neighbor topology. In *Proceedings of the 4th World Congress on Intelligent Control and Automation* (pp. 1840-1843).

Topliss, J. G., & Edwards, R. P. (1979). Chance factors in studies of quantitative structure-activity relationships. *Journal of Medicinal Chemistry, 22*(10), 1238–1244. doi:10.1021/jm00196a017

Torresen, J. (1998). A divide and conquer approach to evolvable hardware. *Proceedings of the 2nd International Conference on Evolvable Systems: From Biology to Hardware* (pp. 57–65). Berlin, Germany: Springer-Verlag.

Torresen, J. (2002). A scalable approach to evolvable hardware. *Genetic Programming and Evolvable Machines, 3*(3), 259–282. doi:10.1023/A:1020163325179

Trianni, V., & Dorigo, M. (2006). Self-Organisation and Communication in Groups of Simulated and Physical Robots. *Biological Cybernetics, 95*(3), 213–231.

Tse, S.-M., Liang, Y., Leung, K.-S., Lee, K.-H., & Mok, T.-K. (2007). A memetic algorithm for multiple-drug cancer chemotherapy schedule optimization. *IEEE Transactions on Systems, Man, and Cybernetics . Part B, 37*(1), 84–91.

Tsuji, M., Munetomo, M., & Akama, K. (2003). Metropolitan area network design using GA based on hierachical linkage identification. In *Proceedings of the Genetic and Evolutionary Computation Conference. Lecture Notes in Computer Science, 2724*, 1616–1617. doi:10.1007/3-540-45110-2_52

Tsuji, M., Munetomo, M., & Akama, K. (2007). A network design problem by a GA with linkage identification and recombination for overlapping building blocks. In *Proceedings of the IEEE Congress on Evolutionary Computation* (pp. 349-356).

Tuci, E., Ampatzis, C., Vicentini, F., & Dorigo, M. (2006). Evolved homogeneous neuro-controllers for robots with different sensory capabilities: Coordinated motion and cooperation. *Proceedings of the 9th International Conference on Simulation of Adaptive Behavior: From Animals to Animate 9* (pp. 679-690). Berlin: Springer.

Turing, A. (1936). On computable numbers, with an application to the Entscheidungsproblem. *Proceedings of the London Mathematical Society, 2*(42), 230–265.

Turner, C. J., Tiwari, A., & Mehnen, J. (2008). A genetic programming approach to business process mining. In *Proceedings of the Genetic and Evolutionary Computation Conference* (pp. 1307-1314). New York: ACM Press.

Ubelaker, D. H. (2000). A history of Smithsonian-FBI collaboration in forensic anthropology, especially in regard to facial imagery. *Forensic Science Communications, 2*(4), [online].

Ubelaker, D. H., Bubniak, E., & O'Donnel, G. (1992). Computer-assisted photographic superimposition. *Journal of Forensic Sciences, 37*(3), 750–762.

UCSF Medical Center. (2008). *Cholangiocarcinoma.* Retrieved May 24 2008, from http://www.ucsfhealth.org/adult/medical_services/gastro/cholangiocarcinoma/conditions/cholang/signs.html.

Upegui, A., Thoma, Y., Sanchez, E., Perez-Uribe, A., Moreno, J.-M., & Madrenas, J. (2007). The perplexus bio-inspired reconfigurable circuit. In *Proceedings of the Second NASA/ESA Conference on Adaptive Hardware and Systems* (pp. 600-605). IEEE Computer Society Press, Washington, DC.

v Smagt, P. d., & Hirzinger, G. (1998). Why feed-forward networks are in bad shape. *Proceedings 8th International Conference on Artificial Neural Networks* (pp. 159-164).

van der Aalst, W. M. P., Reijers, H. A., & Limam, S. (2001). Product-driven workflow design. *Proceedings of the 6th International Conference on Computer Supported Cooperative Work in Design* (pp. 397-402). London, Ontario, Canada.

van Vuuren, S. (1996). Comparison of text-independent speaker recognition methods on telephone speech with acoustic mismatch. In *Proceedings of the Fourth International Conference on Spoken Language* (pp. 1788–1791).

Vega-Rodríguez, M., Gómez Pulido, J., Alba, E., Vega-Pérez, D., Priem-Mendes, S., & Molina, G. (2007a). Evaluation of Different Metaheuristics Solving the RND Problem. In *EvoWorkshops 2007* (pp. 101-110).

Vega-Rodríguez, M., Gómez Pulido, J., Alba, E., Vega-Pérez, D., Priem-Mendes, S., & Molina, G. (2007b). Using Omnidirectional BTS and Different Evolutionary Approaches to Solve the RND Problem. In *EUROCAST 2007* (pp. 853-860).

Veldhuizen, D. A. V., & Lamont, G. B. (1998). Evolutionary computation and convergence to a pareto front. In *Stanford University, California* (pp. 221–228). Morgan Kaufmann.

Venkatesan, P., & Anitha, S. (2006). Application of a radial basis function neural network for diagnosis of diabetes mellitus. *Current Science, 91*(9), 1195–1198.

Venter, G., & Sobieszczanski-Sobieski, J. (2003). Particle swarm optimization. *AIAA Journal, 41*(8), 1583–1589. doi:10.2514/2.2111

Ventrella, J. J. (2005). GenePool: Exploring the Interaction Between Natural Selection and Sexual Selection. In A. Adamatzky (Ed.), *Artificial Life Models in Software* (pp. 81-96). London: Springer-Verlag.

Villarreal, M. R. (2006). Image: Scheme ant worker anatomy. Retrieved in September 2008 from http://en.wikipedia.org/wiki/Image:Scheme_ant_worker_anatomy-en.svg.

Vincent, L., & Soille, P. (1991). Watersheds in digital spaces: an efficient algorithm based on immersion simulations. *Transactions on Pattern Analysis and Machine Intelligence, 13*, 583–598. doi:10.1109/34.87344

Vitousek, P. M. (1982). Nutrient cycling and nutrient use efficiency. *American Naturalist, 119*, 553–572. doi:10.1086/283931

Volterra, V. (1931). Variations and fluctuations of the number of individuals in animal species living together. In R. N. Chapman (Ed.), *Animal Ecology* (pp. 409–448). New York, NY: McGraw-Hill.

von Neumann, J. (1966). *The theory of self-reproducing automata.* A. Burks (ed.), Urbana: University of Illinois Press.

von Neumann, J., & Burks, A. W. (1966). *Theory of Self-Reproducing Automata.* Urbana IL: University of Illinois Press.

Vrancx, P., & Nowe, A. (2006). Using Pheromone Repulsion to Find Disjoint Paths. In *Proceedings of the 5th International Workshop Ant Colony Optimization and Swarm Intelligence. Lecture Notes in Computer Science, 4150*, 522–523. doi:10.1007/11839088_62

Wade, A., Hurley, S., Allen, S., Taplin, R., & Craig, K. (2004). Optimisation of BFWA Networks using Emergent Intelligence. In *3rd IASTED International Conference on Communications, Internet and Information Technology*, ACTA Press.

Wagner, A. (2005). *Robustness and evolvability in living systems (Princeton studies in complexity).* Princeton, NJ: Princeton University Press.

Wagner, I. A., & Bruckstein, A. M. (1997). Cooperative Cleaners - a Study in Ant Robotics. In A. Paulraj, V. Roychowdhury & C. D. Schaper (Eds), *Communications, Computation, Control, and Signal Processing:*

A Tribute to Thomas Kailath (pp. 289-308). Kluwer Academic Publishers.

Wagner, I. A., & Bruckstein, A. M. (2001). From Ants to A(ge)nts: A Special Issue on Ant-Robotics. *Annals of Mathematics and Artificial Intelligence, 31*(1-4), 1–5.

Wagner, I. A., Lindenbaum, M., & Bruckstein, A. M. (1998). Efficiently Searching a Graph by a Smell-Oriented Vertex Process. *Annals of Mathematics and Artificial Intelligence, 24*, 211–223.

Wagner, N., Michalewicz, Z., Khouja, M., & McGregor, R. R. (2007). Time series forecasting for dynamic environments: the DyFor genetic program model. *IEEE Transactions on Evolutionary Computation, 11*(4), 433–452. doi:10.1109/TEVC.2006.882430

Waldrop, M. M. (1993). *Complexity: The Emerging Science at the Edge of Order and Chaos*. London: Viking.

Walker, S., Barstow, W. J., Steel, J. B., Rapson, G. L., Smith, B., & King, W. M. (2003). Properties of ecotones: evidence from five ecotones objectively determined from a coastal vegetation gradient. *Journal of Vegetation Science, 14*, 579–590.

Walkowiak, K. (2005). Ant algorithm for flow assignment in connection-oriented networks. *International Journal of Applied Mathematics & Computer Science, 15*, 205–220.

Wallace, A. R. (1858). On the tendency of species to form varieties; and on the perpetuation of varieties and species by natural means of selection. III. On the tendency of varieties to depart indefinitely from the original type. *J. Proc Linn. Soc. London, 3*, 53–62.

Wallenta, C., Kim, J., Bentley, P. J., & Hailes, S. (2008). (to appear). Detecting interest cache poisoning in sensor networks using an artificial immune algorithm. *Applied Intelligence*.

Wan, V. (2003). *Speaker Verification using Support Vector Machines*. Phd thesis, University of Sheffield, UK.

Wan, V., & Campbell, W. M. (2000). Support vector machines for speaker verification and identification. In *Proceedings of Neural Networks for Signal Processing X* (pp. 775–784).

Wang, J. (2000). Trading and hedging in S&P 500 spot and futures markets using genetic programming. *Journal of Futures Markets, 20*(10), 911–942. doi:10.1002/1096-9934(200011)20:10<911::AID-FUT3>3.0.CO;2-K

Watanabe, S., Hiroyasu, T., & Mikiand, M. (2001). Parallel evolutionary multi-criterion optimization for mobile telecommunication networks optimization. In *Proceedings of the EUROGEN2001 Conference* (pp. 167–172).

Webb, A., Turton, B., & Brown, J. (1997). Application of a genetic algorithm to the design and optimisation of a self-healing ring network. In *Proceedings of 4th Communication Networks Symposium* (pp. 2-5).

Webb, A., Turton, B., & Brown, J. (1998). Application of genetic algorithm to a network optimisation problem. In *Proceedings of 6th IEEE Conference on Telecommunications* (pp. 62-66).

Weber, J., & Penn, J. (1995, August 6-11, 1995). *Creation and rendering of realistic trees*. Paper presented at the Proceedings of SIGGRAPH '95, Los Angeles, California.

Weiser, M. (1993). Some computer science issues in ubiquitous computing. *Communications of the ACM, 36*(7), 75–84. doi:10.1145/159544.159617

Welcker, H. (1867). Der schädel Dantes. In K. Witte, & G. Boehmer (Eds.), *Jahrbuch der deutschen Dantegesellschaft*, 1, 35–56, Brockhaus, Liepzig.

Weyns, D., & Hovoet, T. (2007) An architectural strategy for self-adapting systems. *Proceedings of the International Workshop on Software Engineering for Adaptive and Self-Managing Systems* (p. 3). Minneapolis, MN, USA.

Wheeler, M., & Clark, A. (1999). Genic representation: Reconciling content and causal complexity. *The British Journal for the Philosophy of Science, 50*, 103–135. doi:10.1093/bjps/50.1.103

White, B. C., Gilbert, J. C., Reif, D. M., & Moore, J. H. (2005). A statistical comparison of grammatical evolution strategies in the domain of human genetics. *Proceedings of the IEEE Congress on Evolutionary Computing* (pp. 676–682).

Whitley, D., Richards, M., Beveridge, R., & da Motta Salles Barreto, A. (2006). Alternative evolutionary algorithms for evolving programs: evolution strategies and steady state GP. *GECCO '06: Proceedings of the 8th Annual Conference on Genetic and Evolutionary Computation*, (pp. 919-926).

Wikipedia (2008). *Artificial neural network*. Retrieved September 17 2008, updated September 14 2008, from http://en.wikipedia.org/wiki/Artificial_neural_network.

Wilson, G., & Heywood, M. I. (2007). Foundations for an intelligent business logic engine using genetic programming and ruleML-based services. *International Journal of Business Process Integration and Management, 2*(4), 282–291. doi:10.1504/IJBPIM.2007.017753

Wittgenstein, L. (1953). *Philosophical Investigations*. Oxford: Basil Blackwell.

Wolberg, W. H., Street, W. N., & Mangasarian, O. L. (1992). *Breast Cancer Wisconsin (Diagnostic) Data Set*. UCI Machine Learning Repository [http://archive.ics.uci.edu/ml/]

Wolfram, S. (2002). *A new kind of science*. Wolfram Media, Inc.

Wolpert, D., & Macready, W. (1997). No free lunch theorems for optimization. *IEEE Transactions on Evolutionary Computation, 1*(1), 67–82. doi:10.1109/4235.585893

Wong, P., & Zhang, M. (2006). Algebraic simplification of GP programs during evolution. *GECCO '06: Proceedings of the 8th Annual Conference on Genetic and Evolutionary Computation*, (pp. 927-934).

Woodcock, S. (2000). Flocking: A Simple Technique for Simulating Group Behaviour. In M. A. DeLoura (Ed.), *Game Programming Gems*. Rockland, Massachusetts: Charles River Media, Inc.

Woodward, F. I. (1990). The impact of low temperatures in controlling the geographical distribution of plants. *Philosophical Transactions of the Royal Society of London. Series B, Biological Sciences, 326*(1237), 585–593. doi:10.1098/rstb.1990.0033

Worzel, W. P., Yu, J., Almal, A. A., & Chinnaiyan, A. M. (2009). Applications of genetic programming in cancer research. *The International Journal of Biochemistry & Cell Biology, 41*(2), 405–413. doi:10.1016/j.biocel.2008.09.025

Wouhaybi, R., & Al-Alaou, M. A. (1999). Comparison of neural networks for speaker recognition. In *Proceedings of the Sixth IEEE International Conference on Electronics, Circuits and Systems* (pp. 125–128).

Wu, B., & Shi, Z. (2001). A clustering based on swarm intelligence. *Proceedings of the IEEE International Conferences on Info-Tech and Info-net* (pp.58-66), Bejing, China.

Wu, Y., Giger, M. L., Doi, K., Vyborny, C. J., Schmidt, R. A., & Metz, C. E. (1993). Artificial neural networks in mammography: Application to decision making in the diagnosis of breast cancer. *Radiology, 187*, 81–87.

Xi, B., Liu, Z., Raghavachari, M., Xia, C. H., & Zhang, L. (2004). A smart hill-climbing algorithm for application server configuration. In S. I. Feldman, M. Uretsky, M. Najork & C. E. Wills (Eds.), *Proceedings of the 13th international conference on World Wide Web, (WWW 2004)* (pp. 287–296). ACM Press.

Xia, L., Xuehui, L., & Jihong, Z. (2003, Dec.). Codebook design by a hybridization of ant colony with improved LBG algorithm. *Proceedings of the International Conference on Neural Networks and Signal Processing* (pp. 469-472). China: Shenzhen University.

Xianwei, Z., Changjia, C., & Gang, Z. (2000). A genetic algorithm for multicasting routing problem. In *Proceedings of International Conference on Communication Technology* (pp. 1248-1253).

Xie, X. F., Zhang, W. J., & Yang, Z. L. (2002). Adaptive particle swarm optimization on individual level. *Proceedings of the 6th International Conference on Signal Processing* (pp. 1215-1218). Beijing, China.

Xiong, Y., Golden, B., & Wasil, E. (2005). A one-parameter genetic algorithm for the minimum labeling spanning tree problem. *IEEE Transactions on Evolutionary Computation, 9*(1), 55–60. doi:10.1109/TEVC.2004.840145

Xiong, Y., Golden, B., & Wasil, E. (2006). Improved Heuristics for the Minimum Label Spanning Tree Problem. *IEEE Transactions on Evolutionary Computation, 10*(6), 700–703. doi:10.1109/TEVC.2006.877147

Xu, F. S., & Chen, W. (2006). Stochastic portfolio selection based on velocity limited particle swarm optimization. In *Proceedings of the 6th World Congress on Intelligent Control and Automation* (pp. 3599-3603), Dalian, China.

Xu, R., & Wunsch, D. (2005). Survey of clustering algorithms. *IEEE Transactions on Neural Networks, 16*, 645–678.

Yaeger, L. S. (1994). Computational Genetics, Physiology, Metabolism, Neural Systems, Learning, Vision, and Behavior or PolyWorld: Life in a New Context. In C. Langton (Ed.), *Proceedings of the Artificial Life III Conference* (pp. 263-298). Reading, MA: Addison-Wesley.

Yamany, S. M., Ahmed, M. N., & Farag, A. A. (1999). A new genetic-based technique for matching 3D curves and surfaces. *Pattern Recognition, 32*, 1817–1820. doi:10.1016/S0031-3203(99)00060-6

Yang, X.-S. (2008). *Nature-Inspired Metaheuristic Algorithms*. Luniver Press, UK.

Yoon, J.-H., & Gores, G. J. (2003). Diagnosis, staging, and treatment of cholangiocarcinoma. *Current Treatment Options in Gastroenterology, 6*, 105–112. doi:10.1007/s11938-003-0011-z

Yoshida, H., Kawata, K., Fukuyama, Y., Takayama, S., & Nakanishi, Y. (2000). A particle swarm optimization for reactive power and voltage control considering voltage security assessment. *IEEE Transactions on Power Systems, 15*(4), 1232–1239. doi:10.1109/59.898095

Yoshino, M., Matsuda, H., Kubota, S., Imaizumi, K., Miyasaka, S., & Seta, S. (1997). Computer-assisted skull identification system using video superimposition. *Forensic Science International, 90*, 231–244. doi:10.1016/S0379-0738(97)00168-0

Yu, L., Lai, K. K., & Wang, S. Y. (2008). An evolutionary programming based knowledge ensemble model for business risk identification. In Bhanu Prasad (Ed.), *Soft computing applications in business* (pp. 57-72). Studies in Fuzziness and Soft Computing 230, Berlin: Springer Verlag.

Yu, T., Riolo, R., & Worzel, B. (2006). *Genetic programming: Theory and practice*. Springer.

Yuan, X. H., Yuan, Y. B., Wang, C., & Zhang, X. P. (2005). An improved PSO approach for profit-based unit commitment in electricity market. In *Proceedings of the IEEE/PES Transmission and Distribution Conference and*

Exhibition: Asia and Pacific (pp. 1-4), Dalian, China.

Yuan, X. J., Situ, N., & Zouridakis, G. (2008). Automatic segmentation of skin lesion images using evolution strategies. *Biomedical Signal Processing and Control, 3*(3), 220–228. doi:10.1016/j.bspc.2008.02.003

Zhang, L., & Nandi, A. K. (2007). Neutral offspring controlling operators in genetic programming. *Pattern Recognition, 40*(10), 2696–2705. doi:10.1016/j.patcog.2006.10.001

Zhang, T., & Kuo, C. (1998). Content-based classification and retrieval of audio. In *SPIE's 43rd Annual Meeting - Conference on Advanced Signal Processing Algorithms, Architectures, and Implementations VII* (pp. 432–443).

Zhang, Y., Ji, C., Yuan, P., Li, M., Wang, C., & Wang, G. (2004). Particle swarm optimization for base station placement in mobile communication. In *Proceedings of the IEEE International Conference on Networking, Sensing and Control* (pp. 428-432).

Zhang, Z. (1994). Iterative point matching for registration of free-form curves and surfaces. *International Journal of Computer Vision, 13*(2), 119–152. doi:10.1007/BF01427149

Zhao, J.-H., Zhaoheng, L., & Dao, M.-T. (2007). Reliability optimization using multiobjective ant colony system approaches. *Reliability Engineering & System Safety, 92*, 109–120.

Zhou, G., & Gen, M. (1997). A note on genetic algorithms for degree constrained spanning tree problems. *Networks, 30*, 91–95. doi:10.1002/(SICI)1097-0037(199709)30:2<91::AID-NET3>3.0.CO;2-F

Zhou, G., & Gen, M. (1999). Genetic Algorithm Approach on Multi-criteria Minimum Spanning Tree Problem. *European Journal of Operational Research, 114*, 141–151. doi:10.1016/S0377-2217(98)00016-2

Zhou, G., & Gen, M. (2003). A genetic algorithm approach on tree-like telecommunication network design problem. *The Journal of the Operational Research Society, 54*(3), 248–254. doi:10.1057/palgrave.jors.2601510

Zhou, G., Cao, Z., Cao, J., & Meng, Z. (2007). A Centralized Network Design Problem with Genetic Algorithm Approach. In Y. Wang, Y. Cheung, H. Liu (Eds.), *International Conference on Computational Intelligence and Security. Lecture Notes in Computer Science, 4456*, 123-132.

Zimmermann, J., Höns, R., & Mühlenbein, H. (2000). The Antenna Placement Problem: An Evolutionary Approach, In *Proceedings of the 8th International Conference on Telecommunication Systems* (pp. 358-366).

Zimmermann, J., Höns, R., & Mühlenbein, H. (2003). ENCON: an evolutionary algorithm for the antenna placement problem. *Computers & Industrial Engineering, 44*, 209–226. doi:10.1016/S0360-8352(02)00176-6

Zitova, B., & Flusser, J. (2003). Image registration methods: a survey. *Image and Vision Computing, 21*, 977–1000. doi:10.1016/S0262-8856(03)00137-9

Zitzler, E., & Thiele, L. (1999). Multiobjective evolutionary algorithms: A comparative case study and the strength Pareto approach. *IEEE Transactions on Evolutionary Computation, 3*(4), 257–271. doi:10.1109/4235.797969

Zomaya, A. (2006). *Handbook of Nature-Inspired and Innovative Computing: Integrating Classical Models with Emerging Technologies*. Springer-Verlag, New York.

About the Contributors

Raymond Chiong is a tenured academic at the School of Computing & Design, Swinburne University of Technology (Sarawak Campus), Malaysia. He is leading the Intelligent Informatics Research Group under the Information & Security Research Lab (iSECURES Lab). He serves as an Associate Editor for the Interdisciplinary Journal of Information, Knowledge, and Management (IJIKM), and reviews for IEEE Transaction on Evolutionary Computation and Springer's Memetic Computing. He also serves in the IEEE Computer Society Technical Committee on Intelligent Informatics (TCII), IASTED Technical Committee on Artificial Intelligence, as well as IASTED Technical Committee on Modelling and Simulation. His main research interests include nature-inspired computing and its application to complex systems. He has numerous publications in books, international journals and conference proceedings, and is currently involved with four edited books.

* * *

Arturo Hernández Aguirre received a BSc in Electronics from the Universidad Autónoma Metropolitana, Mexico, and MSc and PhD in Computer Science from Tulane University in New Orleans, LA, USA. Dr. Hernández joined the Centro de Investigación en Matemáticas (CIMAT) in Guanajuato, México, where he works as a researcher at the Computer Science Department. He has authored over 14 journal papers, 100 conference papers and 7 book chapters. His areas of interest are evolutionary computation and bio-inspired algorithms for global and constrained optimization.

Enrique Alba obtained his Engineering degree (1992) and PhD in Computer Science (1999) from the University of Málaga, Spain. He works as a Professor in this university with different teaching duties at graduate and master programs. Dr. Alba leads a team of 7 doctors and 8 engineers (PhD candidates) in the field of complex optimization. In addition to the organization of international events (IEEE IPDPS-NIDISC, IEEE MSWiM 06, IEEE DS-RT 06), Dr. Alba has offered dozens of doctorate courses and seminars in more than 20 international institutions and has directed several research projects. Also, Dr. Alba has directed 5 contracts for innovation and transference to the industry and at present he also works as invited Professor at INRIA and the University of Luxembourg. He is editor in 13 international journals and one book series of Springer-Verlag, and he often reviews articles for more than 30 impact journals. He has published 7 books, 24 book chapters, 26 articles in journals indexed by Thomson ISI, 16 articles in national journals, 31 papers in LNCS, and more than 70 refereed conferences. Dr. Alba has merited 6 awards to his professional activities, and his H index is 13, with more than 500 cites to his works (excluding self-cites).

Tom Barbalet created the Noble Ape Simulation in 1996 and continues its development to this day. Noble Ape is used by Apple and Intel as well as a number of universities to teach biodiversity, multimedia education, vector processing, real-time graphical interfaces and a number of other technologies. Since 2005, he has been the editor of Biota.org, a leading community resource for artificial life developers. He is the host of the weekly Biota Live Internet radio show, where he discusses a variety of topics relating to artificial life, artificial intelligence and simulation philosophy with a variety of guests. He is also the co-chair of the International Game Developers' Association's Intellectual Property Rights Special Interest Group.

Peter Bentley is an Honorary Senior Research Fellow at the Department of Computer Science, University College London (UCL), Collaborating Professor at the Korean Advanced Institute for Science and Technology (KAIST), a consultant and a freelance writer. He runs the Digital Biology Interest Group at UCL. His research investigates evolutionary algorithms, computational development, artificial immune systems, swarming systems and other complex systems, applied to diverse applications including design, control, novel robotics, nanotechnology, fraud detection, security, art, and music composition. He regularly gives plenary speeches at international scientific conferences and is a consultant, convenor, chair and reviewer for workshops, conferences, journals and books in the field of evolutionary computation and complex systems. He has published over 160 scientific papers and is editor of the books "Evolutionary Design by Computers", "Creative Evolutionary Systems" and "On Growth, Form and Computers", and author of "The PhD Application Handbook" and the popular science books "Digital Biology", "The Book of Numbers" and "The Undercover Scientist: Investigating the Mishaps of Everyday Life".

Muneer Buckley is a PhD candidate at the University of Adelaide in the fields of Commerce and Computer Science. His research involves investigating the strengths and weaknesses of modern heuristic methods when compared against alternative financial models in many fields of Finance. Of particular interest are evolutionary algorithms and foreign exchange markets.

Héctor Cancela is currently a Full Professor at the Engineering School of the Universidad de la República in Uruguay. He is also a researcher at the National Program for the Development of Basic Sciences (PEDECIBA), Uruguay. Prof. Cancela holds a PhD. degree in Computer Science (1996) from the University of Rennes 1, INRIA Rennes, France, and a Computer Systems Engineer degree (1990) from the Universidad de la República, Uruguay. His research interests are in Operational Research techniques, especially in stochastic process models as well as graph and network models, along with their application jointly with combinatorial optimization metaheuristics to solve different practical problems. He has published more than 40 papers in international journals and proceedings of refereed conferences, and has acted as thesis advisor of MSc. and PhD. students. He has led different research projects and participated in contracts with the industry and government.

Eugene Ch'ng is currently a Senior Lecturer at the School of Computing and Information Technology, the University of Wolverhampton, UK. He holds a PhD in Electronic, Electrical and Computer Engineering from the University of Birmingham, UK. He has in the past worked on a number of virtual environments and interactive 3D projects related to defence training and simulators, archaeological visualisation, and scientific modelling and simulation of biological systems. His research interests include artificial life, biodiversity informatics, autonomous and multi-agent systems, and enhanced virtual environments. His research merges these interdisciplinary fields for the modelling and visualisation of climate-change and biodiversity research for marine and terrestrial environments. Eugene's work has been featured in over 30 international media, websites, broadcast and printed media, including Nature.

Oscar Cordón received his M.S. degree (1994) and his Ph.D. (1997) both in Computer Science from the University of Granada, Spain, where he was a Professor at the Department of Computer Science and Artificial Intelligence from 1995 till 2007, and an Associate Professor since January, 2001. He was also the creator and head of its Virtual Learning Center (CEVUG) between 2001 and 2005, and was awarded with the Young Researcher Career Award in 2004. Since April 2006, he is the Principal Researcher of the "Applications of Fuzzy Logic and Evolutionary Algorithms" research unit at the European Centre for Soft Computing. He has published more than 200 peer-reviewed scientific publications. He is also a co-author of the book "Genetic Fuzzy Systems: Evolutionary Tuning and Learning of Fuzzy Knowledge Bases" by World Scientific, 2001. He has participated in 20 national/international research projects. Besides that, he is the Area Editor of the International Journal of Approximate Reasoning since 2005, Associate Editor of the IEEE Transactions on Fuzzy Systems since 2008, and was treasurer of the EUS-FLAT Society between 2005 and 2007. He was also co-chairman of the First International Workshop on Genetic Fuzzy Systems (GFS 2005), held in Granada, in March 2005. He will be the publicity co-chair of the IEEE Symposium Series on Computational Intelligence 2009 (SCCI 2009) and the finance co-chair of the IFSA-EUSFLAT 2009 World Congress. He also created in 2004 the Genetic Fuzzy Systems Task Force (currently Evolutionary Fuzzy Systems Task Force), Fuzzy Systems Technical Committee, IEEE Computational Intelligence Society, and was the chair till 2007.

Sergio Damas received his M.Sc. degree and PhD in Computer Science at the University of Granada, Spain, where he has been an Assistant Professor since 1995. Dr. Damas has been involved in several projects funded by the Spanish Ministry of Science and Technology, on topics related to the application of soft computing techniques to pattern recognition. He is co-author of more than 20 peer-reviewed scientific publications. He regularly serves as a reviewer for major journals and conferences. Dr. Damas is also a member of the European Society for Fuzzy Logic and Technology (EUSFLAT), the Soft Computing in Image Processing (SCIP) working group and the Soft Computing and Intelligent Information Systems research group.

Peter Day completed his Ph.D. in 2005 at the University of Liverpool with a thesis titled "Advances in Genetic Programming with application is Speech and Audio". Since leaving the University he has moved into Finance and is now a senior consultant with d-fine, a leading European consulting firm specialising in quantitative finance and risk management. His particular areas of specialization include portfolio optimization, stock market prediction, dynamic hedging strategies and novel risk measures. He has enjoyed success working with some of the world's leading investment banks and hedge funds, and is currently developing his own algorithmic trading strategies.

Cyntia Araiza Delgado received a BSc in Computational Systems Engineering from the Instituto Tecnológico de Delicias, México, and an MSc in Computer Science from the Centro de Investigación en Matemáticas (CIMAT) in Guanajuato, Mexico. She has authored several papers about Combinational Circuit Design with estimation of distribution algorithms (EDAs). Her research interests are genetic Algorithms, differential evolution, numerical optimization, evolvable hardware and estimation of distribution algorithms. Currently, she is a researcher and professor at the Instituto Tecnológico de Delicias of the Computer Science Department.

Moussa Diaf received the Engineering degree from the « Ecole Nationale Polytechnique », Algeria, in 1978, the Ph.D degree in Automatic Control from the University of Science and Technology of Lille, France, and the "Docteur es Sciences" degree in Automatic Control from the University Mouloud Mammeri, Tizi-Ouzou, Algeria. He is a Professor at the same university since 1988. He is currently the Vice-Dean of the Post Graduation, Scientific Research and External Relations in the Electronic Engineering and Computer Science Faculty, University Mouloud Mammeri, Tizi-Ouzou. He is the head of the "Robotics and Vision" research laboratory in the same university. His research interests include image processing, pattern recognition and metaheuristics.

Stefan Goldmann studied Computer Science at the University of Rostock in Germany, with the focus on networking and computer graphics. He received his MS in 2006. Since 2007, he is a Ph.D. student at the Institute of Applied Microelectronics and Computer Engineering, University of Rostock, Germany. His research interest is in evolutionary algorithms, in particular the distributed evolutionary systems. His personal interests are devoted to his family and to his singing in a rockpop acapella-band.

Casey Greene received his B.S. in Chemistry from Berry College in 2005. He is currently a Ph.D. candidate in the Department of Genetics at Dartmouth College. Casey's work focuses on developing machine learning and evolutionary computing methods to detect and characterize genetic and environmental predictors of common human disease in the absence of single-factor effects. His research is supported by the Superfund Basic Research Program from the National Institute of Environmental Health Sciences.

Kamal Hammouche was born in 1965 in Tizi-Ouzou, Algeria. He received the Engineering degree in Electronics in 1989, the Master of Philosophy degree in Industrial Automatic Control in 1996 and the "Docteur es Sciences" degree in Automatic Control in 2007, all from the University Mouloud Mammeri, Tizi-Ouzou, Algeria. He is a permanent teacher in the Automatic Control Department of the Electrical Engineering and Computer Science Faculty, University Mouloud Mammeri, Tizi-Ouzou, Algeria. His research interests are in the area of image processing and pattern recognition.

Óscar Ibáñez received his Technical Engineering degree in Computer Science at the Pontificia University of Salamanca in 2002 and the M.Sc. degree in Computer Science at the University of La Coruña in 2006. He was a member of the RNASA/IMEDIR research group at University of La Coruña between 2006 and 2008. He was working in the project PROLIT, founded by the European Union, and was given a research grant by the Xunta of Galicia. He has published more than 10 papers in international journals, peer-review conferences and international books. Since March 2008, he is a Research Assistant in the Applications of Fuzzy Logic and Evolutionary Algorithms Unit at the European Centre for Soft-Computing.

Markus Kress studied Business Administration and Industrial Engineering at the University of Karlsruhe in Germany, with courses focusing on Operations Research and Computer Science. Currently, he is a PhD student at the Institute of Applied Informatics and Formal Description Methods, University of Karlsruhe. He works on machine learning algorithms with focus on their applications in the area of business process management. Besides his PhD study, he works part time as a Solution Architect for a consultancy.

Rajasvaran Logeswaran graduated from Imperial College (University of London) in the United Kingdom, and received his postgraduate Masters and Ph.D. qualifications from Multimedia University, Malaysia. An active researcher in medical image processing, neural networks and data compression, he has published many articles in peer-reviewed journals, conferences and books. His academic achievements include several scholarships and awards, such as the Brain Gain Malaysia and Brain Korea 21 programs, and from Telekom Malaysia and the Jaffnese Cooperative Society of Malaysia. This senior member of the IEEE is an academic with Multimedia University, where he has led several medical image analysis and neural network projects, and contributed in numerous administrative positions. Currently, Logeswaran is serving as a Malaysia-sponsored scientist undertaking research in Seoul, Korea.

Erwan Le Martelot is currently finishing his doctorate at University College London, where he is investigating systemic computation, a novel form of computation grounded in analogies from biology. He is member of the Digital Biology Interest Group at University College London. Over the past years he took part in various research projects involving computation, biology, software engineering, artificial intelligence, graphics and sci-art. His research interests include natural and bio-inspired computation, evolutionary computation and artificial life. He also takes a particular interest in graphics generation, from random fractal algorithms to the on-line mapping of dynamic systems.

Bob McKay received his BSc in Pure Mathematics from the Australian National University in 1971, and his PhD in the Theory of Computation from the University of Bristol, UK, in 1976. He was a Research Scientist in computer typesetting at the (Australian) Commonwealth Scientific and Industrial Research Organisation from 1976 to 1985, before joining the University of New South Wales at the Australian Defence Force Academy as a Lecturer and subsequently Senior Lecturer, with research interests in artificial intelligence, evolutionary computation and ecological modelling. In 2005, he took up an Associate Professorship at Seoul National University, Korea, where he is continuing these interests. In recent years, he has authored around 100 refereed research papers in these subjects. Bob was General Chair of the Computational Intelligence Society's 2003 Congress on Evolutionary Computation, and currently serves as a member of its Evolutionary Computation Technical Committee. He has chaired a number of national and regional conferences in Evolutionary Computation and Artificial Intelligence. He is an Associate Editor of the IEEE Transactions on Evolutionary Computation, an editorial board member of Genetic Programming and Evolvable Machines and of Ecological Informatics, and an advisory board member of the International Journal of Knowledge-Based and Intelligent Engineering Systems.

Zbigniew Michalewicz is a Professor at the School of Computer Science, University of Adelaide. He completed his MSc degree at Technical University of Warsaw in 1974 and received his PhD degree from Institute of Computer Science, Polish Academy of Sciences, in 1981. His current research interests are in the field of evolutionary computation. He has published several books, and over 200 technical papers in journals and conference proceedings. He was one of the Editors-in-Chiefs of the "Handbook of Evolutionary Computation". He was the general chairman of the First IEEE International Conference on Evolutionary Computation held in Orlando, June 1994. He currently spends his time evenly between his evolutionary computation research, his company, SolveIT Software, which uses leading computational intelligence methods to address complex business problems for large corporations and government agencies, and work on his brainchild: puzzle based learning, a new learning methodology that is being adopted at many universities internationally.

Jason Moore received his B.S. in Biological Sciences from Florida State University. He then received an M.S. in Human Genetics, an M.A. in Statistics and a Ph.D. in Human Genetics from the University of Michigan. He served as Assistant Professor of Molecular Physiology and Biophysics (1999-2003) and Associate Professor of Molecular Physiology and Biophysics with tenure (2003-2004) at Vanderbilt University. While at Vanderbilt, he held an endowed position as an Ingram Associate Professor of Cancer Research. He also served as Director of the Bioinformatics Core and Co-Founder and Co-Director of the Vanderbilt Advanced Computing Center for Research and Education (ACCRE). In 2004, he accepted a position as the Frank Lane Research Scholar in Computational Genetics, Associate Professor of Genetics, Associate Professor of Community and Family Medicine, and Director of Bioinformatics at Dartmouth Medical School. He was promoted to Full Professor with tenure in 2008. He also holds adjunct positions in the Department of Computer Science at the University of New Hampshire, the Department of Computer Science at the University of Vermont and as an Adjunct Investigator at the Translational Genomics Research Institute (TGen) in Phoenix. He serves as Director of the Computational Genetics Laboratory and the Bioinformatics Shared Resource for the Norris-Cotton Cancer Center, Director of the Integrative Biology Core for the Center for Environmental Health Sciences and Founder and Director of The DISCOVERY Resource, a 500-processor parallel computer cooperatively operated for the Dartmouth community. His research has been communicated in more than 175 scientific publications and is supported by three NIH R01 grants in his name. He has previously served as Program Chair for the Bioinformatics and Computational Biology track at GECCO and as Chair of the European Conference on Evolutionary Computation, Machine Learning and Data Mining in Bioinformatics (EvoBIO).

Sanaz Mostaghim is currently working as a Research Assistant and Lecturer at the University of Karlsruhe in Germany. She received her PhD degree in Electrical Engineering from the University of Paderborn, Germany, in 2004. After her PhD, she worked as a Post Doctoral Fellow at the Swiss Federal Institute of Technology (ETH) in Zurich, Switzerland. She has worked on multi-objective optimization algorithms using evolutionary algorithms and particle swarm optimization, and has successfully applied them to several different applications from Geology to Computational Chemistry. Parallel optimization, multi-objective optimization, particle swarm optimization, grid computing, and organic computing are her research interests.

Asoke Nandi received the degree of Ph.D. in High Energy Physics from the University of Cambridge (Trinity College), UK, in 1979. In March 1999, he took up the David Jardine Chair of Signal Processing in the Department of Electrical Engineering and Electronics at the University of Liverpool, UK. He has been carrying out research in blind source separation, development and applications of machine learning, machine condition monitoring, communication signal processing, and biomedical signal processing. He has authored or co-authored over 350 technical publications; these include two books, entitled "Automatic Modulation Recognition of Communications Signals" and "Blind Estimation Using Higher-Order Statistics", and over 150 journal papers. In 1983 he was a member of the UA1 team at CERN that discovered the three fundamental particles known as W^+, W^- and Z° providing the evidence for the unification of the electromagnetic and weak forces, which was recognized by the Nobel Committee for Physics in 1984. Professor Nandi was awarded the Mounbatten Premium, Division Award of the Electronics and Communications Division, of the Institution of Electrical Engineers of the UK in 1998 and the Water Arbitration Prize of the Institution of Mechanical Engineers of the UK in 1999. He is a Fellow of the Cambridge Philosophical Society, the Institution of Engineering and Technology, the Institute of Mathematics and its applications, the Institute of Physics, the Royal Society for Arts, the Institution of Mechanical Engineers, and the British Computer Society.

Ferrante Neri received his MSc and PhD in Electrical Engineering from the Technical University of Bari, Italy, in 2002 and 2007, respectively. He received the PhD in Computer Science (Scientific Computing and Optimization) in 2007 from the University of Jyväskylä, Finland. He is currently an Assistant Professor in Simulation and Optimization with the Department of Mathematical Information Technology, University of Jyväskylä, Finland. He is a member of the IEEE Task Force on Memetic Computing, the Task Force on Evolutionary Computation in Dynamic and Uncertain Environments, and the Computational Intelligence Society. He is also a member of the editorial board of Memetic Computing Journal, Springer, the International Journal of Organizational and Collective Intelligence, IGI Global, and the Journal of Engineering, Design and Technology, Emerald. His research interests include computational intelligence algorithms in optimization, and in particular memetic algorithms, differential evolution, evolutionary optimization in the presence of uncertainties and optimization algorithms for computationally expensive problems.

Sergio Nesmachnow is currently an Adjoint Professor at the Engineering School of the Universidad de la República in Uruguay, teaching several courses at graduate and postgraduate levels. He holds an MSc. degree in Computer Science (2004) and a Computer Systems Engineer degree (2000) from the Universidad de la República. His current PhD studies are related to parallel metaheuristics for solving combinatorial optimization problems. His research interests include numerical analysis, parallel processing techniques and evolutionary algorithms, applied to solve telecommunication network design problems, scheduling problems and numerical models of physical phenomena. Nesmachnow has participated in several research projects and also worked in joint works with the industry and Uruguayan government. He has published more than 20 papers in international journals and refereed conference proceedings.

Sergio Ivvan Valdez Peña received a BSc in Mechanical Engineering from the Instituto Tecnológico de Celaya, Mexico, and an MSc in Computer Science from the Centro de Investigación en Matemáticas (CIMAT) in Guanajuato, Mexico. He is currently a graduate student pursuing a PhD in Computer Science in the Department of Computer Science at CIMAT. He has authored several papers on optimization and evolutionary computation. His research interests are evolutionary computation, multi-objective optimization, the finite element method, estimation of distribution algorithms and parallel computing.

Salvador Botello Rionda received a BSc degree in Civil Engineering from the Universidad de Guanajuato, Mexico, an MSc in Structures Engineering from the Instituto Tecnológico de Monterrey, Mexico, and his PhD in Ingeniero de Caminos Canales y Puertos from the Universitat Politècnica de Catalunya, Barcelona, Spain. He is a Research Professor in the Department of Computer Science at the Centro de Investigación en Matemáticas (CIMAT) in Guanajuato, Mexico. His research interests are image processing and computational vision, optimization, the finite element method, evolutionary computation, multi-objective optimization and the development of finite element software for solid mechanics applications.

Ralf Salomon is a Professor at the University of Rostock, Germany, since 2002. His major research interests include the application and analysis of evolutionary algorithms, evolvable hardware, and the design of self-adaptive control architectures for autonomous mobile robots. He is currently contributing to the development of an evolutionary platform that allows for the self-organization of smart-appliance ensembles. Ralf is also very active in the following areas: (1) evolutionary design of low-power consuming circuits; (2) self-organized routing in sensor networks; and (3) usability aspects of graphical user interfaces.

José Santamaría received the M.Sc. and the Ph.D. degrees in Computer Science at the University of Granada, Spain. He has been an Assistant Professor in Computer Science at the E.T.S. de Ingenierías Informática y de Telecomunicación of the University of Granada, and also at the E.S. de Ingeniería of the University of Cádiz, Spain. Currently, he is an Assistant Professor at the E.P.S. de Linares of the University of Jaén. He is actively involved in several projects funded by the Spanish Ministry of Science and Technology, and he is co-author of several peer-reviewed scientific publications.

Detlef Seese (Diploma in Mathematics, 1973, Humboldt-University Berlin; Dr. rer.nat., 1976, Humboldt-University Berlin; Dr. sc. nat., 1980, Akademy of Sciences Berlin) was head of the Division of Discrete Mathematics, Algebra, Logic and Mathematical Foundations of Informatics at the Karl-Weierstrass-Institut for Mathematics (1990-1992) and Professor for Applied Informatics at the University of Duisburg (1990-1992). Since 1992, he is a Professor for Applied Informatics at the University of Karlsruhe. Since 1999, he is head of the group Complexity Management and one of the directors of the Institute for Applied Informatics and Formal Description Methods (AIFB) at the University of Karlsruhe. Since 2000, he is member of the board of directors of the Institute for Applications of Informatics at the University Karlsruhe, and since 2002 he is foundation member of the Center for Risk Management and Disaster Reduction Technology. He was Guest Professor at the University of Toronto and worked for three years at different universities abroad. Since 1999, he is a member of the editorial board of the Journal of Universal Computer Science (J. UCS).

Patrick Siarry was born in France in 1952. He received the PhD degree from the University Paris 6 in 1986 and the Doctorate of Sciences (Habilitation) from the University Paris 11, in 1994. He was first involved in the development of analog and digital models of nuclear power plants at Electricité de France (E.D.F.). Since 1995, he is a Professor in Automatics and Informatics. His main research interests are computer-aided design of electronic circuits, and the applications of new stochastic global optimization heuristics to various engineering fields. He is also interested in the fitting of process models to experimental data, the learning of fuzzy rule bases, and of neural networks.

Ralf Zurbruegg is a Professor of Finance at the University of Adelaide Business School. He publishes widely on topics relating to risk management and investment practise, as well as being actively engaged in consulting to the Finance industry. He serves on a number of editorial boards as well as being the joint editor of the International Journal of Managerial Finance.

420

Index

Symbols